GLOBALL.
RESPONSIBLᴇ
LEADERSHIP

GLOBALLY RESPONSIBLE LEADERSHIP

Managing According to the UN Global Compact

Editors

JOANNE T. LAWRENCE
Hult International Business School

PAUL W. BEAMISH
Richard Ivey School of Business
Western University

Los Angeles | London | New Delhi
Singapore | Washington DC

Los Angeles | London | New Delhi
Singapore | Washington DC

FOR INFORMATION:

SAGE Publications, Inc.
2455 Teller Road
Thousand Oaks, California 91320
E-mail: order@sagepub.com

SAGE Publications Ltd.
1 Oliver's Yard
55 City Road
London EC1Y 1SP
United Kingdom

SAGE Publications India Pvt. Ltd.
B 1/I 1 Mohan Cooperative Industrial Area
Mathura Road, New Delhi 110 044
India

SAGE Publications Asia-Pacific Pte. Ltd.
3 Church Street
#10-04 Samsung Hub
Singapore 049483

Acquisitions Editor: Patricia Quinlin
Assistant Editor: MaryAnn Vail
Editorial Assistant: Katie Guarino
Production Editor: Laureen Gleason
Copy Editor: Lana Todorovic-Arndt
Typesetter: C&M Digitals (P) Ltd.
Proofreader: Scott Oney
Cover Designer: Anupama Krishnan
Marketing Manager: Liz Thornton
Permissions Editor: Karen Ehrmann

Printed in the United States of America

Library of Congress Cataloging-in-Publication Data

Globally responsible leadership : managing according to the UN Global Compact / editors, Joanne T. Lawrence, Paul W. Beamish.

p. cm.
Includes bibliographical references and index.

ISBN 978-1-4129-3875-4 (pbk. : acid-free paper)

1. Leadership—Moral and ethical aspects. 2. Social responsibility of business. 3. Global Compact. 4. Sustainability. I. Lawrence, Joanne. II. Beamish, Paul W., 1953-

HD57.7.G596 2013
658.4′092—dc23   2011042894

This book is printed on acid-free paper.

12 13 14 15 16 10 9 8 7 6 5 4 3 2 1

Contents

PART II. THE TEN PRINCIPLES OF THE UN GLOBAL COMPACT

PART III. CASE STUDIES: THE TEN PRINCIPLES IN PRACTICE

PART IV. APPENDIXES: EXCERPTS FROM
THE UN GLOBAL COMPACT WEBSITE

Foreword

Georg Kell

Executive Director, UN Global Compact Office

Through the United Nations Global Compact, close to 7,000 business leaders in nearly 140 countries have made a commitment to corporate sustainability in the spirit of universal values. These companies represent nearly every industry sector and size, hailing equally from developed and developing countries. In addition, approximately 3,000 civil society stakeholders—nongovernmental organizations, academia, labour, and foundations—are engaged in the Global Compact, working to advance responsible business practices as a partner in common causes, as provider of information and support, or as a watchdog to hold companies accountable.

Today, sustainability ranks highly on the corporate agenda as executives everywhere recognize the growing relevance and urgency of global environmental, social, and economic challenges. Regardless of size, location, or sector, businesses are looking beyond the traditional drivers of financial performance, seeing how sustainability issues can affect their bottom line. Market disturbances, civil unrest, or natural resource constraints can indeed have wide-ranging and material impacts. But sustainability issues are not only viewed from a risk management perspective. Increasingly, business leaders are discovering the tangible benefits and opportunities of greater sustainability—particularly associated with green growth and base-of-the-pyramid approaches.

Yet, the Global Compact's almost 7,000 business participants represent only a sliver of the world's estimated 70,000 multinationals and millions of smaller enterprises. And of those companies that are engaged, only a minority have taken the agenda seriously enough. Just one quarter of Global Compact participants consider their sustainability efforts to be at an advanced level, suggesting that a very small percentage of the broader business community is at the leading edge of sustainability practice. Too many companies are still using corporate social responsibility or sustainability as a public relations vehicle, with little intent to make meaningful changes to their practices.

A new level of corporate performance will be needed to deliver on the sustainability promise. This will involve increasing the scale and intensity of current efforts—reaching companies that have yet to embrace corporate responsibility, motivating less-advanced companies to deepen their commitment, and spurring front-runners to lead the way to the next generation of sustainability performance.

This book is a welcome contribution to these efforts, as it gives students valuable guidance on how to manage corporations based on the Global Compact principles. Through practice cases spanning a wide range of issue areas, the reader learns firsthand how companies tackle challenges and seize opportunities in their day-to-day operations.

It is also a critical resource for educators who are engaged in the Principles for Responsible Management Education (PRME), an initiative launched by the Global Compact and key academic partners to provide a framework for integrating the Global Compact's principles into the curriculum and research of management education.

Introduction

Why Globally Responsible Leadership?

Joanne T. Lawrence and Paul W. Beamish

Today's multinational corporations have grown in size and influence in large part due to the trust, consent, and support of the constituents they serve. As businesses have grown more global, the challenge becomes how to retain this trust and balance the diverse needs and motivations of their various stakeholder constituents: higher profits for shareholders; lower prices for consumers; better jobs and higher wages for employees; less pollution and waste for communities; and healthier, safer products for families. Furthermore, there is the growing call, often from those very same constituents, to heed a moral imperative about how to behave, especially in emerging markets. As business has expanded its reach and influence and communication technology has made many actions transparent, to what standards should it adhere, and should those standards be voluntary or mandatory?

In business schools, we teach international marketing, finance, and operations using fundamental principles that cross regions and national borders, yet when it comes to universal standards to guide how we make decisions and behave toward those very same stakeholders, we often fall short. We justify actions based solely on local laws and cultural norms, yet globalization has made "but that's how it's done here" or "when in Rome do as the Romans do" increasingly unacceptable responses. Communication technology has given us a real-time window into the world that most of us can't ignore, making cultural relativism one of management's greatest challenges.

This book grew out of our separate efforts to come up with a way to teach corporate responsibility to international students aspiring to be global managers. It seemed that there was no consistent way to identify and approach the topics that would be needed to be successful in, and common to, every student's native culture yet cross all of them. It became clear that there was a need for some framework that would place the big, globally relevant issues in context—the ones that large corporations operating globally would need to address strategically and embed organizationally in order to be effective, respected, and successful.

As we each sought a solution, we came across a common idea: organize the multifaceted topic of corporate responsibility into an overarching framework that captures its core substance and provides a base of knowledge applicable worldwide. What does a truly global manager today need to know to lead responsibly? How does he or she develop the necessary core management competencies?

As the world's largest voluntary corporate citizenship initiative, with close to 10,000 business and civil society participants from nearly 140 countries, the UN Global Compact and its ten principles emerged as the global guideline we were seeking.

How This Book Is Organized

Globally Responsible Leadership uses the UN Global Compact and its ten principles as a framework for understanding the issues facing global business managers today. Drawing on the knowledge of contributors from different parts of the world, the book strives to show readers the intersection between business and the major global issues of our time—human rights, labour, the environment, anti-corruption—and, most critically, how to address these issues in the day-to-day running of their operations.

Globally Responsible Leadership views corporate responsibility as both a core managerial competence (how do you identify, nurture, and meaningfully engage stakeholders, for example?) and a core corporate competence (how might an organizational culture of corporate responsibility lead to greater innovation and be a source of operational and strategic advantage?).

Ideally, the book helps readers to appreciate that by adhering to these principles, business can be part of the solution, especially in helping to progress and transform the livelihoods and lives of those billions of people in emerging markets that fall within a company's sphere of influence. It presents corporate responsibility as integral to a just and civil workplace and to a thriving and prosperous global society.

There are four parts to the book:

Part I provides an overview of the UN Global Compact, its history, its intended role, and how it fits into the larger infrastructure for corporate responsibility that continues to emerge. It presents the pros, the cons, and the ethical foundation on which they are based.

Part II gives perspectives on each of the four areas of the Compact, written by academics from around the world who have focused their passion and research in each.

These four areas comprise the content of corporate responsibility and the knowledge areas that every manager operating globally should be aware of.

Part III contains case studies, organized within the four areas, enabling readers to consider these areas in actual contextual situations. These case studies provide an opportunity for thinking through the issues and seeing how managers facing the same conundrums actually addressed them.

Part IV includes exhibits from the UN Global Compact website to give readers a sense of how organizations express their commitment to these principles, how they measure and report on their progress against them, and a blueprint for how to integrate them into their operations.

At the end of Parts I and II, there are study questions intended to provoke thoughts about what these issues mean in a global context as well as from the perspective of the lives they touch. Within the references, there are lists of articles, books, and websites that we encourage you to consider in order to learn more. Finally, there are appendixes that contain links to the working documents used by UN Global Compact signatories as they seek to embed these principles into the very fabric of their businesses.

At the end of a course using *Globally Responsible Leadership,* students should better understand

- The major issues affecting multinational enterprises and the need to address the complex dynamics between business, society, and the environment successfully
- That stakeholders are all interconnected and need to be respectfully and meaningfully engaged by managers as they make their business decisions and seek global solutions
- The need to create a responsible organizational culture around a core set of universally accepted values
- That responsible resource management can be integrated into strategy and be a source of innovation and competitive advantage
- That corporate responsibility is fundamental to good corporate governance, the long-term credibility and viability of a business, and creating enduring value for all stakeholders

Finally, to understand at the deepest level that corporate responsibility must begin and end with business managers—you!—actually being responsible and accountable, and that it must be led from the top.

We welcome you on our shared journey.

The Ten Principles of the UN Global Compact

The UN Global Compact asks its participating companies to embrace, support, and enact, within their sphere of influence, a set of core values in the areas of human rights, labour standards, the environment, and anti-corruption, and to support the broader UN goals, such as the Millennium Development Goals (MDGs).

Human Rights

Principle 1: Businesses should support and respect the protection of internationally proclaimed human rights; and

Principle 2: make sure that they are not complicit in human rights abuses.

Labour

Principle 3: Businesses should uphold the freedom of association and the effective recognition of the right to collective bargaining;

Principle 4: the elimination of all forms of forced and compulsory labour;

Principle 5: the effective abolition of child labour; and

Principle 6: the elimination of discrimination in respect of employment and occupation.

Environment

Principle 7: Businesses should support a precautionary approach to environmental challenges;

Principle 8: undertake initiatives to promote greater environmental responsibility; and

Principle 9: encourage the development and diffusion of environmentally friendly technologies.

Anti-corruption

Principle 10: Businesses should work against corruption in all its forms, including extortion and bribery.

Note: For more information, visit www.unglobalcompact.org.

The Eight Millennium Development Goals

The Millennium Development Goals (MDGs) are a universally agreed-on set of goals developed to fight global poverty. They were introduced in 2000 and signed by 191 member countries of the UN:

> We recognize that, in addition to our separate responsibilities to our individual societies, we have a collective responsibility to uphold the principles of human dignity, equality and equity at the global level. As leaders we have a duty therefore to the entire world's people, especially the most vulnerable and, in particular, the children of the world, to whom the future belongs. . . .
>
> We consider certain fundamental values to be essential to international relations in the twenty-first century. These include
>
> - **Shared responsibility.** Responsibility for managing worldwide economic and social development, as well as threats to international peace and security, must be shared among the nations of the world and should be exercised multilaterally. As the most universal and most representative organization in the world, the United Nations must play the central role. (UN Millennium Goals Declaration, September 8, 2000)

The signatories set themselves an ambitious target: to eradicate poverty by 2015. To gauge their progress, the eight MDGs break down into 21 quantifiable targets that are measured by 60 indicators.

The goals to which they agreed are:

Goal 1: Eradicate extreme poverty and hunger

Goal 2: Achieve universal primary education

Goal 3: Promote gender equality and empower women

Goal 4: Reduce child mortality

Goal 5: Improve maternal health

Goal 6: Combat HIV/AIDS, malaria, and other diseases

Goal 7: Ensure environmental sustainability

Goal 8: Develop a global partnership for development

Business is considered an essential player in this effort, especially with regard to Goal 8, which seeks to help developing countries gain greater access to markets, finance, essential medicines at affordable prices, and new technologies, especially information and communication.

For more information, visit www.un.org/millenniumgoals.

Acknowledgments

This book represents the collective wisdom and experiences of many, some of whom have expressed their views within in its pages, others whose beliefs and actions informed those views, and still others whose stories are told in the cases. We would like to take this opportunity to acknowledge a few people in particular.

We must begin by thanking Manuel Escudero, the former Head of the PRME Secretariat, UN Global Compact Office, now the Director General of Deusto Business School in Spain and a Special Advisor to the PRME Secretariat. It was Manuel who first suggested that we join forces to create this book. His encouragement and enthusiasm were pivotal as we prepared our proposal for consideration.

We owe an equal debt of gratitude to his successor, Jonas Haertle, the current Head of the PRME Secretariat. Jonas patiently answered all questions, provided access to UN Global Compact staff, introduced us to numerous potential chapter authors, and helped us to pilot potential study projects that would actively engage students. Jonas saw the book's potential as a means of aligning the next generation of business leaders with globally accepted behavioral standards. He brought the book to the attention of Georg Kell, Executive Director of the UN Global Compact, whom we also thank for taking the time to support our efforts by graciously agreeing to write the Foreword.

We would like to acknowledge our insightful and knowledgeable contributors— David Cooperrider, Daniel Malan, Andreas Rasche, Michael J. D. Roberts, Peter Rodriguez, Sandra Waddock, Florian Wettstein, and Nadya Zhexembayeva—all of whom, without exception, were cooperative and supportive throughout this entire process. Their commitment to the principles of the UN Global Compact and faith in the ability of business to be a positive force is without question. Andreas Rasche, in particular, played a pivotal role early on as we sought contributors. He continued to be a steady source of encouragement throughout the project.

We would also like to thank the many academics around the world whom we contacted, and while unable to participate directly, offered helpful advice and their support.

We extend our personal gratitude to Adrian Payne, a former adjunct professor in corporate responsibility at Hult's London campus and a senior associate at MHC International, who carefully reviewed our manuscript, and to Ivey professors Mike Valente and Oana Branzei, who helped in the case selection process. We thank the authors of the many cases and the organizations that cooperated in their preparation, the staff of Ivey Publishing, and Ivey itself for funding much of the case writing. We would also like to acknowledge the Hult MBA students (Alexandre Lemille, Aditya Nag, Wendy Tan, and Donna Tsui) who participated in the pilot studies involving the Compact's Communication on Progress reports, and all our students, whose multicultural backgrounds and perspectives constantly challenged us to seek a universal standard of acceptable business behavior. Indeed, they were the inspiration behind this book.

A special thanks must go to Lisa Cuevas Shaw, Senior Executive Editor at SAGE, who saw the potential of the book in filling a particular global niche in this area of leadership, and to our team at SAGE: Mayan White, Laureen Gleason, Helen Salmon, and in particular, our copy editor, Lana Todorovic-Arndt, whose attention to detail was without equal. We also appreciate the insights of our reviewers: Lucille Pilling, Robert M. McManus, James Toth, Thomas Creely, and Thomas J. Howard.

Finally, we would be remiss not to thank those whose ongoing support makes all things possible: Richard and Juno, ever by Joanne's side, and for Paul, his wife Maureen.

—Joanne Lawrence (Boston, MA) and
Paul Beamish (London, Ontario), February 28, 2012

SAGE and the editors gratefully acknowledge the contributions of the following reviewers:

Thomas Creely, *Georgia State University*

Thomas J. Howard, *St. Edwards University*

Robert M. McManus, *Marietta College*

Lucille Pilling, *New York University*

James Toth, *Northeastern University*

About the Editors

Joanne T. Lawrence is global professor of corporate responsibility and social innovation at Hult International Business School (Boston-Dubai-London-San Francisco-Shanghai). Prior to Hult, she was an adjunct professor of strategy and management at INSEAD (1993–2007), where she addressed the critical role of strategic communication, stakeholder relationships, and aligned organizational cultures in realizing strategy and was involved in Project RESPONSE, a pathfinding study of global corporate responsibility.

With extensive hands-on international corporate, consulting, and academic experience, she brings a pragmatic, informed approach to management education. A firm believer in the transformative potential of business to meet the global challenges of our time, her focus is developing ethical, trustworthy leaders and holistic, strategic thinkers who can effectively and innovatively leverage resources to achieve social, environmental, and business objectives.

She has worked across multiple industries with multinational companies and global organizations such as BP and the World Bank, as well as with smaller, socially focused enterprises such as Tom's of Maine and Economic Development Imports. As a vice president of corporate communications and investor relations, she received numerous awards and recognition in both the United States and the United Kingdom for her work. While vice president at UK-based healthcare company SmithKline Beecham (today part of GlaxoSmithKline), she coordinated Simply Better, a groundbreaking, global organizational change initiative that was the subject of *From Promise to Performance: The Journey of Transformation at SmithKline Beecham* (Harvard Business School Press, 1997) and an award-winning INSEAD case study. Contact: joanne.lawrence@faculty.hult.edu

Paul W. Beamish holds the Canada Research Chair in International Business at the Richard Ivey School of Business, Western University, London, Canada. He is the author or coauthor of over 50 books and 100 refereed articles and is the recipient of numerous best research awards. He served as Editor-in-Chief of *Journal of International Business Studies* from 1993 to 1997 and is a Fellow of the Royal Society of Canada, Academy of International Business, and Asia Pacific Foundation.

At Ivey, he has taught on a variety of school programs, including the Executive MBA offered at its campus in Hong Kong and the MSc program, with its major in international business. From 1999 to 2004, he served as Associate Dean Research. He worked for Procter & Gamble and Wilfrid Laurier University before joining Ivey's faculty in 1987. Beamish also has responsibility for Ivey Publishing, the distributor of Ivey's case collection.

Beamish has authored over 100 case studies, primarily in the international management area. These have appeared in case journals and in over 125 books. Over 2.5 million copies of his cases have been studied worldwide.

Ivey was the first Canadian business school to join the Global Compact. Professor Beamish's coauthored publications relating to the Global Compact include the monograph *Moving Upwards: The Involvement of Boards of Directors in the UN Global Compact*, the *Globe and Mail* article "When It Comes to Doing Good, We Can Do Better," and a book chapter, "The Future of the Transnational: An Evolving Global Role." Contact: pbeamish@ivey.uwo.ca

About the Contributors

David Cooperrider is the Fairmount Minerals professor of social entrepreneurship and is the chair of the Fowler Center for Sustainable Value at the Weatherhead School of Management, Case Western Reserve University. David is past president of the Academy of Management's Organization Development Division, and he has lectured at Harvard, Stanford, the Massachusetts Institute of Technology, and Cambridge, among other places. He advises senior executives in business and societal leadership roles, including five presidents and Nobel laureates such as Kofi Annan and His Holiness the Dalai Lama. David's founding theoretical work on Appreciative Inquiry has created a positive revolution in the field of change.

David has received distinguished awards: the Top 10 Visionaries by Training Magazine (2000), the ASTD Award for distinguished contribution in the organizational learning field (2004), the Porter Award for best writing in Organization Development (2004), and the Aspen Faculty Pioneer Award for impact in the sustainability field (2007). In 2010, he was honored as a Peter F. Drucker Distinguished Fellow.

David has published 15 books and authored over 50 articles including *Appreciative Inquiry: A Positive Revolution in Change* (with Diana Whitney); *The Organization Dimensions of Global Change* (with Jane Dutton); and the four-volume series *Advances in Appreciative Inquiry* (with Michel Avital). Contact: david.cooperrider@case.edu

Daniel Malan is a senior lecturer in ethics and governance at the University of Stellenbosch Business School (USB) and director of the Centre for Corporate Governance in Africa at the USB. His focus areas are corporate governance, business ethics, and corporate responsibility. Previously he was an associate director with KPMG Sustainability Services and the regional coordinator for Ethics and

Editors' Note: In seeking to establish a universal, globally acceptable standard for responsible leadership, this book has deliberately drawn on the expertise of faculty from all over the world.

Integrity Services in KPMG's Europe, Middle East, and Africa region. He is a member of the World Economic Forum's Global Agenda Council on Values in Decision Making, the International Corporate Governance Network's Integrated Business Reporting Committee, and the Anti-Corruption Working Group of the United Nations PRME. His educational qualifications include a master's degree in philosophy as well as a master's degree in business administration, both from the University of Stellenbosch in South Africa. Contact: daniel.malan@usb.ac.za

Andreas Rasche is associate professor of business in society at the International Centre for Governance and Public Management at Warwick Business School. Since 2007, he has collaborated on various projects with the United Nations Global Compact Office in New York. He holds a PhD (Dr. rer. pol.) from European Business School, Germany and a habilitation (Dr. habil.) from Helmut Schmidt University, Hamburg. He regularly contributes to leading international journals on questions related to corporate responsibility. He has lectured widely on corporate social and environmental responsibility at different institutions throughout Europe. Recently, he coedited *The United Nations Global Compact: Achievements, Trends and Challenges* (Cambridge University Press). More information is available at http://www.arasche.com.

Michael J. D. Roberts is a PhD candidate in international business and management at the Richard Ivey School of Business, Western University. Prior to his PhD studies, he taught at the KAIST Graduate School of Business in Seoul, South Korea. He has over 10 years of international teaching and curriculum development experience. His areas of research are organizational and institutional change, the global talent pool, foreign knowledge transfer, and emerging market multinational enterprises. Michael is committed to research and teaching that promotes an environment where business leaders are intellectually creative and morally grounded. He believes that business education must be based on the principles of social justice and intellectual diversity. Contact: miroberts@ivey.uwo.ca

Peter Rodriguez is senior associate dean for degree programs and chief diversity officer at the Darden School of Business, University of Virginia. He teaches classes on global macroeconomics and international business. Dr. Rodriguez is an economist and specializes in the study of international business and economic development.

Peter is an active researcher whose interests include the interaction of globalization, economic development, and social institutions; the consequences of corruption for multinationals; and seed-stage finance in emerging markets. Previously, Dr. Rodriguez was a lecturer at Princeton University and a professor at Texas A&M University. Peter served on the faculty of Semester at Sea and has taught in universities around the world. Peter has published research on international trade policies and the measurement and effects of corruption and practice-based studies of issues in international business. Peter holds an MA and PhD in economics from Princeton University. Contact: rodriguezp@darden.virginia.edu

Sandra Waddock is the Galligan Chair of Strategy and professor of management at Boston College's Carroll School of Management. Her recent books include *SEE Change* (with Malcolm McIntosh), *The Difference Makers, Leading Corporate Citizens,* and *Total Responsibility Management* (with Charles Bodwell). Author of over 100 papers on corporate responsibility, system change, and collaboration, among other topics, Dr. Waddock was a cofounder of the Boston College Leadership for Change Program, the Institute for Responsible Investing, and the Business Ethics' 100 Best Corporate Citizens ranking, and she also edited the *Journal of Corporate Citizenship* from 2003 to 2004. The Social Issues in Management Division of the Academy of Management presented her with their 2004 Sumner Marcus Award for Distinguished Service and the Best Book Award of 2011 for *The Difference Makers.* She received the 2005 Faculty Pioneer Award for External Impact by Aspen Institute's Business in Society Program and the World Resources Institute and was a visiting scholar at the University of Virginia's Darden Graduate School of Business (2000) and Harvard's Kennedy School of Government (2006–2007). Contact: waddock@bc.edu

Florian Wettstein is assistant professor of business ethics and director of the Institute for Business Ethics at the University of St. Gallen in Switzerland. Between 2007 and 2011, he was an assistant professor in the Department of Ethics and Business Law at Opus College of Business, University of St. Thomas in Minneapolis/ St. Paul. Previous appointments include sessional assistant professor in the Business and Society Program in the Division of Social Science at York University in Toronto and visiting scholar at Carroll School of Management at Boston College. Also, in 2005–2006, he was awarded a fellowship in the Program on Human Rights and Justice at the Massachusetts Institute of Technology. Florian's work has appeared in journals such as *Business Ethics Quarterly, Journal of Business Ethics, Business and Society Review, Journal of Corporate Citizenship,* and *Zeitschrift für Wirtschafts- und Unternehmensethik.* He is the author of *Multinational Corporations and Global Justice: Human Rights Obligations of a Quasi-Governmental Institution,* published by Stanford University Press in 2009. Contact: florian.wettstein@unisg.ch

Nadya Zhexembayeva, PhD, is the Coca-Cola Chair of Sustainable Development at IEDC-Bled School of Management, Slovenia, where she teaches, researches, and consults on leadership, change management, design thinking, and sustainability. Nadya's first book, *Embedded Sustainability: The Next Big Competitive Advantage*, was coauthored with Chris Laszlo and published by Stanford University Press and Greenleaf Publishing in 2011.

In 2007, Dr. Zhexembayeva joined U.S.-based Sustainable Value Partners, one of the oldest sustainability consultancies in the world. In 2008, Nadya was elected vice president of the United Nations Global Compact Slovenia. She has also served as vice president of Challenge:Future, a global student think tank, since 2009.

Nadya earned her PhD in organizational behavior at the Weatherhead School of Management, Case Western Reserve University, where she had also served as an associate director at the Center for Business as an Agent of World Benefit, now Fowler Center for Sustainable Value, until 2008. Contact: nadya.zhexembayeva@iedc.si

Part I

Background

1

Responsible Business

A Brief Perspective

Joanne T. Lawrence
Hult International Business School

"Successful companies are those that focus on responsibility rather than power, on long-term success and societal reputation rather than piling short-term results one on top of the other."

—Peter Drucker (1909–2005)

What is the purpose of business? Are companies discrete economic entities whose primary role is to produce goods, generate profits, and pay taxes, or are they corporate citizens with the same responsibilities overall to society that individuals have? To whom are they responsible and why?

The Evolution of Business as Socially Responsible

While debates over corporate responsibility and globalization may be front and center today, they have been evolving over centuries. From the days of trading goods between villages to ships traveling the world in search of exotic goods and adventurers seeking new trading routes, individuals and governments have been seeking international commerce as a means of bettering themselves and their societies. As world trade grew and societies prospered, so did the opportunity for the exploitation of human and natural resources and the potential for conflict over rights and claims. Treaties, laws, boycotts, even wars, became part of the ongoing attempt to protect and govern burgeoning international commerce and growing nation-states.

With the advent of the industrial age in the late 19th and early 20th centuries, even as businesses entered foreign lands and prosperity spread, so did concern over corruption, pollution, and poor working conditions. While new inventions were being celebrated for their ingenuity and hailed for their labour-saving attributes, writers from Charles Dickens to Upton Sinclair were also telling tales of underpaid, overworked workers struggling in unsafe factories and unhealthy cities.

The onset of two world wars, as well as the Great Depression in the first half of the 20th century, revealed further the world's growing economic and political interdependence. In their aftermath, the desire for a universal body to help avoid such devastation led to the creation of the League of Nations (1919) and then to the formation of the United Nations (1946). In the years in between, a number of securities regulations were passed to help regulate what many felt had been the under-regulation of U.S. financial markets that had been responsible for the Great Depression (1929).

The role of international business as a critical political, social, and economic force was being increasingly recognized, eventually leading to the creation of two important entities to help govern its growing global influence and guide the invisible hand of free markets.

The first was the creation of the International Labour Organization (ILO) following World War I. "The ILO was founded in 1919, in the wake of a destructive war, to pursue a vision based on the premise that universal, lasting peace can be established only if it is based on social justice" (International Labour Organization, n.d.).

And social justice, it was believed, could only be achieved through ensuring fair and safe working conditions. The ILO became the first specialized agency of the United Nations in 1946.

The second was the founding of the United Nations and the determination to prevent the atrocities of World War II from ever being repeated. One of the United Nations' earliest acts was to "guarantee the rights of every individual everywhere" (United Nations, 2011). The joint efforts of the international working party would eventually become the Universal Declaration of Human Rights, which was taken up at the first session of the UN General Assembly in 1946 and approved in December 1948. Within those articles were several relating to the fair and equitable treatment of workers.

As the world put itself back together, companies that had focused inward during the turbulent, war-torn years once again looked outside their borders in search of raw materials, low cost production, new markets, and innovative technologies.

As these seeds of globalization were being sown, so too were the controversies. Were multinationals an economic engine for growth, raising standards, and lifting those in both developed and developing countries or an exploitative machine that used up human and natural resources and only widened the gap between rich and poor nations? Were free markets fair and truly self-regulating, or was more government intervention and regulation needed?

The Environment as Protagonist

Fast forward to 1962, and the publication of *Silent Spring* by Rachel Carson that related the use of one of the wonder chemicals of the time, the pesticide DDT, to the indiscriminate killing of birds and contamination of the food chain. Carson's book is often cited as the wake-up call that started the modern environmental movement. Indeed, the following decade saw the first Earth Day and founding of the U.S. Environmental Protection Agency (1970), the establishment of Greenpeace in Canada (1971), the creation of the United Nations Environment Programme (1972), and the launch of green political parties in the United Kingdom (1973) and Europe. DDT itself was banned in 1977.

But even as developed countries established tougher environmental laws, there were few to no laws governing the same actions in emerging markets. Air pollution, water contamination, and uncontrolled waste seemed to go unchecked, with the poor bearing an inordinate amount of their harmful effects in the form of disease and hunger.

After four years of study, the World Commission on Environment and Development, also known as the Brundtland Commission, reported its findings and addressed the link between accelerating environmental degradation and its disproportionately negative impact on the poor. Entitled "Our Common Future," the 1987 report contained what is today the most widely accepted definition of *sustainability* in the context of preserving the Earth's ecosystems:

> Sustainable development is development that meets the needs of the present without compromising the ability of future generations to meet their own needs. It contains within it two key concepts:
>
> - the concept of "needs," in particular the essential needs of the world's poor, to which overriding priority should be given; and
> - the idea of limitations imposed by the state of technology and social organization on the environment's ability to meet present and future needs. (World Commission on Environment and Development, 1987)

In its Resolution of December 11, 1987, the UN General Assembly agreed that

> Sustainable development . . . should become a central guiding principle of the United
> Nations, Governments and private institutions, organizations and enterprises . . . in view
> of the global character of major environmental problems, recognizing the common inter-
> est of all countries to pursue policies aimed at sustainable and environmentally sound
> development.

The last decade of the 20th century saw concerns over greenhouse gas emissions,
waste, and climate change enter the mainstream along with growing awareness of
sweatshops, unfair wages, and poor working conditions. The United Nations—as
the world's only globally accepted convening body—accelerated its efforts to help
instill a sense of global responsibility toward the environment and society in businesses and nations. The UN Conference on Environment and Development held in
Rio de Janeiro in 1992 called for further cooperation between nations and commitment to the effort "to protect the integrity of the global environmental and developmental system, recognizing the integral and interdependent nature of Earth, our
home" (United Nations Environment Programme, 1992). The growing problem of
bribery and corruption was also capturing the United Nations' attention, and it
adopted a declaration against both in 1996 (United Nations, 1996).

The 20th century ended with unprecedented riots against the gathering of the
influential World Trade Organization (WTO) in Seattle, Washington. People from
diverse groups came together as they condemned what they felt to be the negative
effects of globalization on the poor. The riots marked a milestone in the WTO's
history and a rise in the visibility and worldwide backlash against globalization.

What had been a widely accepted view—that unfettered, free-market capitalism
was for the most part always beneficial—was increasingly being challenged.

Shareholders Versus Stakeholders

The same year that *Silent Spring* garnered world attention, *Capitalism and Freedom*
was published wherein famed economist Milton Friedman put forward his view
about the role of business in society. The book sparked today's more contemporary
debate, captured in this well-known quote:

> There is one and only one social responsibility of business—to use its resources and engage
> in activities designed to increase its profits so long as it stays within the rules of the game,
> which is to say, engages in open and free competition without deception or fraud. (As cited
> in Friedman, 1970)

For Friedman, the free-market model meant the shareholder assumed primacy: by serving the shareholder best and focusing on ever-increasing profits, business served society—consumers, employees, communities—best. But was this always the case? The public seemed to be growing disillusioned with big business. When companies were perceived to be more focused on sales and profits than on the consequences of their actions, they found society's response to be swift and damaging.

Nestle, for example, after promoting its infant formula over breast-feeding in emerging markets, found consumers horrified when they learned of the negative health impact on children and called for a worldwide boycott of all Nestle products. Investors concerned about apartheid in South Africa demanded major corporations withdraw from the country or risk a sell-off of their shares, and when news about bribery and corruption among major corporations and foreign government officials hit the headlines ("Lockheed's Defiance," 1975), a scandalized United States passed the stringent Foreign Corrupt Practices Act (1977).

At the same time, small, socially conscious companies, like Ben and Jerry's Ice Cream (1978) with its founders' mantra of "linked prosperity," started to thrive, raising the consciousness of a new generation that business needed to serve multiple constituents equally well.

In seeking to identify these constituents, the term *stakeholder*—defined as "any group or individual who can affect or be affected by the achievement of an organization's objectives" (Freeman, 1984)—emerged. With this expanded view of the firm came more questions about the consequences of business's actions—intended or not—on each constituency.

Business was increasingly being viewed not simply as a profit-generating machine for investors but as an institution that pervades every part of society—from the products it makes to the jobs it creates and to the standard of living it provides. As such, it is responsible to multiple constituents, including employees, customers, communities, suppliers, and investors. Stakeholders were not discrete, but interconnected, with each often playing multiple roles.

The debate over whether companies were accountable to shareholders versus stakeholders began in earnest. Legal compliance, which often set minimum standards for corporate behavior, was no longer enough. Despite Friedman's comments to position corporate responsibility as subversive, as a concept, it was gaining momentum.

Defining Corporate Responsibility

What is corporate responsibility? Is it a management function that is centrally located, like finance and accounting; a business process related to operations, like the supply chain or quality manufacturing; or is it a corporate resource, like research and development?

Or is it none of these, but more a behavior, a state of mind to be instilled and a body of knowledge to be disseminated and integrated into an organizational culture rather than a discrete function or process to be managed?

Known at various times as *corporate citizenship*, *corporate social responsibility*, *corporate responsibility*, *social responsibility*, and *sustainability*, the definitions from around the world sound very similar, captured in the following examples. According to the World Council on Sustainable Business Development (1999),

> Corporate social responsibility is the continuing commitment by business to behave ethically and contribute to economic development while improving the quality of life of the workforce and their families as well as of the local community and society at large. (p. 3)

The European Commission (2011) defines it as

> The responsibility of enterprises for their impacts on society . . . To fully meet their corporate social responsibility, enterprises should have in place a process to integrate social, environmental, ethical and human rights concerns into their business operations and core strategy in close collaboration with their stakeholders. (p. 6)

In addition, ISO 26000 (2010) defines sustainable development as

> Responsibility of an organization for the impacts of its decisions and activities on society and the environment through transparent and ethical behavior that
>
> - contributes to sustainable development, including health and the welfare of society
> - takes into account the expectations of stakeholders
> - is in compliance with applicable law and consistent with international norms of behavior
> - is integrated throughout the organization and practiced in its relationships (as cited in Lowellyne, 2011)

In summary, corporate responsibility is an attitude, a value system, a holistic approach to managing a company that recognizes the integration of business, society, and the environment and takes into account the needs and motivations of an ever-widening array of stakeholders. It is a culture that advocates that we share a collective responsibility as managers, investors, consumers, employees, and members of a worldwide community.

This question of what a business should be and to whom it is responsible continues to be redefined: from Bill Gates calling for a new definition of capitalism to

CEO-supported movements such as Conscious Capitalism (Sacks, 2009) and Long-Term Capitalism (Barton, 2011) and to still others seeking a fundamental redesign of the corporation (e.g., B Corporations, with B representing *benefit*) to reflect a fiduciary responsibility to multiple stakeholders (Steiman, 2007).

It seems it is no longer enough to create jobs and generate profits; it is becoming more about creating "shared value" (Porter & Kramer, 2011), or what this author prefers to think of as "enduring value"—value that meets the needs of multiple constituents for the long term and doing it in a way that respects all resources: human, natural, and financial. (Note: This concept is consistent with the concept of sustainable value as defined in Chapter 7.) Business is viewed as a force that can do enormous good or enormous harm.

Corporate Responsibility in the 21st Century

In this new century, not only are the global issues growing more intense; they are being joined by what some feel has been business's egregious behavior of pursuing greed at the expense of basic values such as integrity, honesty, and fairness. No industry or country seems exempt: from Enron to Parmalat, from Barings to Lehman Brothers, the list of companies that have imploded and disappeared, along with the economic value they once created, has grown exponentially. Simmering anger against big business and the growing gap between the haves and have-nots some feel it has helped to create erupted further in September 2011. Frustrated by a stubborn global recession, continuing high unemployment, and unstable financial markets, what started as "Occupy Wall Street" in a single park in New York City soon led to protests in cities around the world. But aside from the crisis of confidence created recently by the errant behavior of the few, history shows that this movement toward asking multinational corporations to accept more responsibility has been ongoing for some time. It has accelerated due to some fundamental defining trends:

Increasing globalization has fueled the responsibility debate as more and more companies cross borders, often with incentives provided by local governments. As the more traditional government and philanthropic approaches to providing aid to developing nations have been seen to fail, many nations are seeking market-based approaches to development, feeling that business's expertise will be more effective at generating sustainable revenues and creating jobs for the billions of the world's poor who earn less than $2 a day. Many companies are picking up the challenge but finding that managing both large and small enterprises in environments characterized by poor infrastructure and cultural differences in labour practices and business customs is extremely complex.

Those in favor of globalization argue that it results in more efficient use of resources, provides greater consumer access and choice, and can be a rapid means to economic growth for those in developing countries. Those who are against say that globalization accelerates environmental degradation, increases unemployment, lowers wages, and adds to the vulnerability and inability of poor countries to adapt (Effland, Normile, Roberts, & Wainio, 2008). According to this view, free trade isn't really free, nor is it always fair.

In the words of Ehrenfeld (2005), "Globalization can be a great boon. It is not globalization per se, but the unfairness and damaging results from the way it is developing that is the moral and humanitarian problem."

What does all this mean for managers? Suddenly, they are faced with challenges posed by differing cultures, traditions, and laws in places many of them could hardly identify on a map a decade ago. Many have limited experience or training in these emerging markets yet are expected to deliver against financial targets often based on their expertise in, and the business practices of, an established and well-understood home market.

Examples of management miscues abound: Nike trying to distance itself from suppliers' sweatshops in Southeast Asia, Google seeking ways to address censorship in China, the tragic consequences of Shell's extracting oil in the Niger Delta, and Coca-Cola's unintended impact on water supplies in India.

Communication technology/social media has increased awareness among multiple stakeholders of events unfolding around the world in real time. When Nike was accused of supporting sweatshop conditions in Southeast Asia, the story was bigger than the company realized. It was one of the first examples where the power of the Internet was used to gain the attention of Nike's target customers—young people—and call them to action. From its initial response implying that how suppliers ran their factories was not their problem and being a "poster child for irresponsibility" (Zadek, 2004), Nike has gone on to become a leader in responsible business practices.

When their companies become the subject of these viral campaigns, the dilemma for managers is that the stories quickly become the reality and are hard to refute or clarify. Issues are often not placed in any particular cultural or national context (e.g., wages in Southeast Asia being compared with those of a U.S. factory worker, rather than with a fair wage appropriate in that market). Actions are often judged based on an observer's own experiences in his or her home market and can be harsh and quick, resulting in lost trust and value seemingly overnight. It can take companies years to regain their often hard-earned reputation, if they ever can. What is the replacement cost of lost trust?

Societal expectations and empowerment are rising, in part enabled by the same communication technology. As people see more, they expect and want more. One only needs to look to the 2011 popular revolts in the Middle East to see how powerful the growth of social media has become in leveling the effectiveness of the players. Where corporations and governments once wielded unquestionable might and dominated channels of communication, the power now lies more and more in the hands of the people—consumers, employees, investors, and communities. Nongovernmental organizations (NGOs) have especially raised their profile and effectiveness, with many demanding and getting the changes they seek. Consider the number of unethical or ineffective CEOs brought down by shareholder activists, the increase in emission standards sought by environmentalists, or the food labeling requirements now being demanded by concerned health advocates. The practices of entire industries (e.g., tobacco) have been affected as a result of avid stakeholder movements, many of which draw their power from the trust the public places in them as opposed to corporations.

For managers, the choice becomes one of reacting to empowered stakeholders after the fact or trying to anticipate and manage the risk beforehand through collaboration and engagement of their constituents as part of a strategic and organizational decision-making process. Stakeholder management—being able to accurately identify and understand the motivations of various stakeholders, assess the gaps and vulnerabilities of the corporation, and then constructively engage and align the disparate groups around a common purpose—is rapidly becoming one of the required core competencies for managers of the 21st century (Post, Preston, & Sachs, 2002).

Add to this list the growing concern over diminishing natural resources and the increasing need for skilled and talented workers in an aging society and throughout emerging markets, and a very challenging picture is painted for today's managers.

What follows then is a dilemma: given a stakeholder view of the firm, what factors should managers consider when deciding what is economically, socially, and environmentally responsible?

Global Challenges Need Global Solutions

With their expansive geographical reach and immense resources, there are multinational companies today that generate more revenues than some countries and are able to accomplish more than some governments. As their influence has grown exponentially and communication technology linked us globally, it is no wonder that societal expectations as to what role business should play have also grown. This is becoming especially so where governments are seen to be unable to provide the basic needs of their electorate, such as food, water, or sanitation.

Whether the financial crisis, climate change, or poverty, the challenges today are extremely complex and global. And just as the problems cross boundaries, so must the solutions. To overcome these challenges will require more coordinated efforts than a less interconnected world permitted in the past, demand greater accountability and more collective responsibility, and require enlightened, ethical leaders who are capable of building and retaining both value *and* trust. Business managers will need to think more deeply and broadly before they act, mindful of the consequences that may fall both within and well beyond their particular spheres of influence, as well as be cognizant of the potential opportunities that behaving responsibly may present.

It is for all these reasons that corporate responsibility as a business imperative has risen within today's business agenda. At one time, companies focused exclusively on creating shareholder value, considering corporate responsibility a "nice to do" and simply about giving back to society or making a philanthropic donation. Today, for many companies, it has become a "need to do" and more about their day-to-day behavior, actions and performance against a triple bottom line (social, environmental, and financial). Yet what constitutes socially acceptable business practices and desired value often differs from continent to continent and from country to country within a continent, making the interpretation and consistent implementation of corporate responsibility on a global basis an elusive goal.

With varying legal frameworks, different traditions, and multiple social norms, even the most well-intentioned global managers often find themselves perplexed: What practices are appropriate? Whose standards or regulations do they adhere to? What may be totally acceptable in one culture may be completely intolerable in another. Yet what happens in Kansas or Kazakhstan no longer stays there. With 24/7, 'round the clock news coverage, there is simply no place to hide what may be perceived (rightly or wrongly) as bad business practice. Cultural relativism may indeed be the "single most important ethical issue for businesses operating in a global environment" today (Freeman & Gilbert, 1987).

Leadership in today's interconnected, multicultural, and multicentric business environment is a demanding task, requiring greater collaboration and cooperation than ever before to balance what are often conflicting interests. As a global community, there needs to be a shared sense of purpose and a set of universal principles to which all agree and around which lasting solutions can be fashioned that ideally generate enduring value for multiple constituents. International business managers require a common, globally accepted, value-driven framework that helps to guide day-to-day operational actions and long-term strategic business decisions.

The Case for Globally Responsible Leadership and Transformative Innovation

In the end, the foundation and currency of an effective and functioning economy is trust. Consumers need to trust the products they buy. Employees need to trust that their employers will pay them fairly and provide safe working conditions. Investors need to be able to trust the integrity of the information they receive. Trust becomes even more crucial as companies expand into emerging markets where collaboration with nontraditional partners and skeptical local communities—some of whom feel they have been exploited by corporations before—are fundamental to success.

In recent years, trust has eroded as business has been seen to have used human, natural, and financial resources recklessly in pursuit of ever higher profits and share prices—appeasing one stakeholder often at the expense of the many.

But the game is changing and with it the definition of winning. It is no longer about how much profit a company makes: today, it is also about *where* and *how* they make it. The means is becoming as important as the outcome.

As news headlines illustrate, business leadership today—more than ever—is about leading with purpose and a vision that extends beyond next quarter's financial results, seeking the solutions that are right for the business and the society within which it operates over the longer term. It is about acting with courage and integrity at multiple levels: as an individual manager, a multinational corporation, and a global society, acting consciously and with conscience to integrate responsible business practices throughout an organization and across all business disciplines, from strategic planning to finance, to sales and marketing, and to operations and human resources.

The arguments for corporate responsibility are moral (it is the right thing to do) but also rational (treating stakeholders well is good business). As Alan Greenspan (1966), former chairman of the U.S. Federal Reserve (1987–2006), once wrote, "It is in the self-interest of every businessman to have a reputation for honest dealings and a quality product. . . . Reputation or 'good will' is as much an asset as physical plant and equipment. . . . Reputation, in an unregulated economy, is thus a major competitive tool."

The more advanced, enlightened leaders go even further, embracing responsible management of resources not only as a moral imperative, but as extremely strategic, operational, and a source of true competitive advantage.

Bartlett and Beamish (2008), in their article on the future of the transnational corporation, noted that companies do seem to be gradually evolving, moving away from the more primitive stages of exploiting workers and resources in search of ever lower costs to, at a minimum, being compliant and seeking to "do no harm." Many now realize that obeying local laws in letter and in spirit makes more economic sense than ignoring or trying to work around them.

These actions may fall short for some NGOs, however, that argue that sometimes local laws (e.g., child labour) are not sufficient, and therefore, they hold companies to higher standards. Just because one *can* do it according to the law doesn't mean one *should* do it. These NGOs are challenging companies to use their enormous resources and skills to take a more proactive, transformational role, to look more widely at their constituent base, expanding it to be more inclusive and respectful of emerging markets and the environment. There are a growing number of companies who are taking up the challenge, seeing it as the next innovation frontier, such as Unilever empowering women as entrepreneurs in emerging markets, IKEA addressing the root cause of child labour in India, HP applying its technology to global health and education, Philips integrating the environment into its innovation strategy, Pepsi developing low impact, plant-based packaging, and Nestle and Starbucks seeking to help coffee farmers in Africa create sustainable livelihoods for themselves and their families. While these initiatives alone may not eradicate the many social inequalities that exist in the world, they are certainly steps in the right direction as they seek to improve lives and livelihoods, transforming society for the better.

Bartlett and Beamish (2008) have neatly summarized these evolving postures of the transnational corporation and their perceived levels of responsibility toward society as

Exploitative: Seek ever lower costs, regardless of the consequences

Transactional: Respect local laws and are nonoppressive; "do no harm"

Responsive: Incorporate a broader view of constituents and contribute to the communities wherein the company operates

Transformative: See their responsibility to use corporate resources to fundamentally improve society (pp. 730–740)

In the final analysis, the truly enlightened leaders, recognizing the enormity of their company's resources and ability to bring divergent groups together, have moved away from exploitative practices and doing the bare minimum toward being more transformational, in many cases working alongside their former antagonists to truly help change societies for the better.

It also seems that more and more, doing the right thing for society is also the right thing for the business. According to Post, Preston, and Sachs (2002), as "a network of interrelated stakeholders that create, sustain, and enhance its value-creating capacity. . . . the capacity of the firm to generate sustainable wealth over time is determined by its relationship with critical stakeholders" (pp. 7–9).

Companies with strong values, clear practices, and committed, purposeful managers are finding themselves attracting the best talent, the most loyal customers, and the more astute investor who recognizes corporate responsibility as fundamental to building value over the long term. The growing number of indexes, such as the FTSE4Good and the Dow Jones Sustainability Index, and the increasing amounts being invested in socially responsible investment funds underscores this change in attitude about corporate responsibility from fringe to mainstream—from being outside the context of business to being integral to its very definition of success.

There is a growing body of evidence that shows companies can do well financially and do it responsibly. In an AT Kearney study, for example, share prices of companies truly committed to sustainable business practices significantly outperformed their competitors during the 2008 financial slowdown. One of the reasons cited by participants was that managers at these companies were perceived to be leading edge, winning investor confidence with their ability to withstand the market turbulence (Mahler, Barker, Besland, & Schulz, 2009).

"Doing" Corporate Responsibility

Corporate responsibility involves the ability to understand the often conflicting values and needs of an organization's multiple constituents, to weigh seemingly disparate options and sometimes make tough choices, and to somehow create a win-win goal that from the outset seems elusive. To be able to effectively manage human, natural, and financial resources in ways that are effective, responsible, and respectful of multiple constituents is today's global leadership challenge.

As more and more managers come to understand the breadth, depth, and complexity of this challenge, the questions that arise continuously are both "What?" and "How?"

- What do managers need to know to act responsibly? What are the knowledge areas of corporate responsibility?

- How does a company act responsibly? What are the roles, processes, and practices it needs to have in place? How do I, as a manager, gain support for these and implement them?

This is where the UN Global Compact and its ten principles come in.

A Framework for Responsible Leadership: The UN Global Compact

In the end, the subject of what constitutes truly global responsible leadership must begin with a globally accepted value system and common framework—a set of philosophical underpinnings and operational guideposts for making decisions.

In 2000, the United Nations established the UN Global Compact that sets forth ten principles to help guide business behavior and to advance the United Nations' goal of reducing poverty. The premise is that these principles establish a fundamental set of values and behaviors for companies operating globally. They cross countries, continents, and cultures and establish a level playing field. While not legally binding, they are perhaps similar to what the Golden Rule or Ten Commandments are to a just and civil society: they set minimum yet absolute standards for creating a just and civil global workplace.

With these principles in place and the challenge out to every corporation to abide by them, it seems right that those studying business today understand what these universal principles are and recognize the complexity of implementing them in businesses that are increasingly located in both developed and developing countries. (For an illustration of this integration, see the Blueprint for Corporate Sustainability Leadership in Appendix C.)

The pages that follow strive to do exactly that. Parts I and II seek to provide the *what*—the *core content* of corporate responsibility by explaining the UN Global Compact and its four major areas: human rights, labour, environment, and anti-corruption, using it as a guiding framework that crosses all countries and all cultures as universally accepted behaviors. Parts III and IV explore the *how*—*the core competencies* needed to lead businesses with purpose and principles by placing those subject areas within some context through case studies and appendixes drawn from the UN Global Compact website. The cases have also been selected for the diversity of their locations, illustrating the different challenges posed by *where*.

Through understanding and embracing these ten principles as integral to leadership and fundamental to organizational behavior, the promise of business as a positive force for creating enduring value for all stakeholders can be realized, moving the global community that we have become ever forward.

Study/Discussion Questions

1. What do you think is the role of business in society? Do you agree with Milton Friedman? Why or why not?

2. What are the arguments for and against globalization?

3. What do you think: is free trade always free or fair? Why? Is more government intervention needed?

4. How would you define corporate responsibility? Why do you think it has become *the* defining issue for businesses today?

5. What is a stakeholder? What are some examples? How might you identify and prioritize them?

6. How might companies move from a posture of exploitation to transformation?

7. If you were going to redefine capitalism, how would you?

8. What might be the pros and cons of businesses operating according to a universal framework of values?

9. As a global manager, what are some of the challenges you face in order to lead responsibly?

10. What might be some core competencies you need to be an effective global leader?

References

Bartlett, C. A., & Beamish, P. W. (2008). The future of the transnational: An evolving global role. In C. A. Bartlett, S. Ghoshal, & P. W. Beamish (Eds.), *Transnational management: Text, cases, and readings in cross-border management* (5th ed., pp. 727–741). Burr Ridge, IL: McGraw-Hill/Irwin.

Barton, D. (2011, March). Capitalism for the long term. *Harvard Business Review.*

Effland, A., Normile, M., Roberts, D., & Wainio, J. (2008, June). World Trade Organization and globalization help facilitate growth in agricultural trade. *Amber Waves Newsletter.* Retrieved from http://www.ers.usda.gov/AmberWaves/June08/Features/WTO.htm

Ehrenfeld, S. (2005). Ethical dilemmas of globalization [Speech to Ethical Society of Boston]. Retrieved from www.ethicalfocus.org/platform/46-world-affairs/125-ethical-dilemmas-of-globalization

European Commission. (2011). Communication from the Commission to European Parliament, the Council, the European Economic and Social Committee: A renewed EU strategy 2011–14 for corporate social responsibility. Retrieved from http://ec.europa.eu/enterprise/policies/sustainable-business/files/csr/new-csr/act_en.pdf

Freeman, R. E. (1984). *Strategic management: A stakeholder approach.* Cambridge, UK: Cambridge University Press.

Freeman, R. E., & Gilbert, D. (1987). *Corporate strategy and the search for ethics.* Englewood Cliffs, NJ: Prentice Hall.

Friedman, M. (1970, September 3). The social responsibility of business is to increase its profits. *The New York Times Magazine.*

Greenspan, A. (1966). The assault on integrity. In A. Rand (Ed.), *Capitalism: The unknown ideal* (pp. 112–116). New York, NY: New American Library.

International Labour Organization. (n.d.). Origins and history. Retrieved from http://www.ilo.org/global/about-the-ilo/history/lang--en/index.htm

Lockheed's defiance: A right to bribe? (1975, September). Retrieved from www.time.com/time/magazine/article/0,9171,917751,00.html

Lowellynne, J. (2011, March 5). ISO 26000 standard—defining good corporate governance [Web log post]. Retrieved from http://lowellynejames.blogspot.com/2011/03/iso-26000-standard-defining-good.html

Mahler, D., Barker, J., Besland, L., & Schulz, O. (2009). Green winners: The performance of sustainability-focused companies during the financial crisis. Chicago, IL: AT Kearney.

Porter, M. E., & Kramer, M. R. (2011, January/February).Creating shared value. *Harvard Business Review.*

Post, J. E., Preston, L., & Sachs, S. (2002, Fall). Managing the extended enterprise: The new stakeholder view. *California Management Review, 45*(1), 1–24.

Sacks, D. (2009, December 1). John Mackey's Whole Foods vision to reshape capitalism. *Fast Company Magazine.* Retrieved from http://www.fastcompany.com/magazine/141/the-miracle-worker.html

Steiman, H. C. (2007, July). A new kind of company: The B corporation. *Inc. Magazine.*

United Nations. (1987). Report of the world commission on environment and development. Retrieved from http://www.un.org/documents/ga/res/42/ares42-187.htm

United Nations. (1996, December 16). Declaration against corruption and bribery in international commercial transactions [A/RES/51/191]. Retrieved from http://www.un.org/documents/ga/res/51/a51r191.htm

United Nations. (2011). Universal declaration on human rights: History of the document. Retrieved from www.un.org/en/documents/udhr/history.shtml

United Nations Environment Programme. (1992, June 14). Rio declaration on environment and development. Retrieved from http://www.unep.org/Documents.Multilingual/Default.asp?documentid=78&articleid=1163

World Commission on Environment and Development. (1987). Report of the world commission on environment and development: Our common future. Retrieved from http://www.un-documents.net/ocf-02.htm

World Council on Sustainable Business Development. (1999). Social corporate responsibility: Meeting changing expectations. Retrieved from http://www.wbcsd.org/Pages/EDocument/EDocumentDetails.aspx?ID=82&NoSearchContextKey=true

Zadek, S. (2004, December). The path to corporate responsibility. *Harvard Business Review*.

2

The Business of Business Is (Responsible) Business

Daniel Malan

University of Stellenbosch Business School

Hardly any corporation would currently support the views expressed by Milton Friedman in his famous article, "The Social Responsibility of Business Is to Increase Its Profits," that was originally published in the *New York Times Magazine* in 1970 (Friedman, 2002). In this article, Friedman accuses those businessmen who argue that business has responsibilities to provide employment, eliminate discrimination, and avoid pollution as "preaching pure and unadulterated socialism" (p. 33).

Friedman's view was that corporations could engage in some of the activities mentioned above, as long as they do it because they believe that it will increase their profits and not because of a moral obligation. For example, he approves of a company that would spend money to provide amenities to a local community, but his approval is based on the belief that this will result in the attraction of more desirable employees, reduce the likelihood of sabotage, and possibly provide tax benefits (Friedman, 2002, p. 36).

This type of argument resonates quite strongly with current risk-based approaches to corporate responsibility.[1] In terms of this approach corporations

---

[1]The terms *corporate responsibility* and *corporate social responsibility* are used interchangeably, although the former seems to be the preferred one at the moment.

should take their social responsibilities seriously because it will assist them to manage risks and exploit opportunities. It is therefore highly likely that Friedman would applaud many of the current corporate social responsibility (CSR) programs that emphasize the business case above everything else.

For example, following a fairly scathing review of CSR by *The Economist* (Crook, 2005), a new report was published in 2008 by *The Economist*, where it refers to the fact that the 2005 report "acknowledge[d], with regret, that the CSR movement had won the battle of ideas" ("Just Good Business," 2008, p. 4). Whether this regret had anything to do with Friedman's views of CSR as unadulterated socialism is not clear, but the 2008 report—as indicated by the title "Just Good Business"—acknowledges, with no regret this time, that "clearly CSR has arrived" (p. 4). It then proceeds to explain how companies should view this development:

> One way of looking at CSR is that it is part of what businesses need to do to keep up with (or, if possible, stay slightly ahead of) society's fast-changing expectations. It is an aspect of taking care of a company's reputation, managing its risks and gaining a competitive edge. This is what good managers ought to do anyway. ("Just Good Business," 2008, p. 14)

But there is a twist in the tale. Those who support the concept of CSR from a *moral* point of view increasingly support the "just good business" approach from an *operational* point of view. In other words, by integrating corporate responsibility into the strategic elements of the corporation instead of having a marginalized CSR department with a separate budget, the moral obligation can be fulfilled most effectively. The unintended consequence of this approach is that an outsider will not easily be able to distinguish between a deeply committed moral approach and a deeply cynical business approach or anything in between. This raises the question of intentionality: does it count from a moral point of view if you do not take action from a sense of moral duty? Kant would say that it does not count, but many beneficiaries of corporate responsibility, for example the recipients of health care or appropriate technology in developing countries, will simply not care.

Taking the nonmoral approach to its logical conclusion, one can move beyond doing something for enlightened self-interest to doing it because it is required by law! However, the debate about whether corporate responsibility should become mandatory from a legal point of view falls outside the scope of this chapter.

The *enlightened self-interest* approach is a problematic one because it only works up to a point. There is always the realization that from time to time a corporation has to make a decision that will conflict with either its own self-interests or those of its stakeholders. It works well to justify why bribery is wrong (even if you win the contract, you might go to jail) or why it is good to invest huge amounts of money in environmental technology not required by law (it will improve reputation, and ultimately, you will save money). It does not work so well if you have to decide whether to retrench employees, close plants, or pay wages that do not conform to trade union demands.

In terms of the broader debate about the purpose of the corporation, the view supported in this chapter is that corporations have moral responsibilities and that their purpose should therefore be far broader than making profits, that is, that they should act as responsible corporate citizens. One of the most concise and convincing arguments in favor of this position is provided by Kaptein and Wempe (2002): "Corporations are moral entities because they consist of independent practices that can be subjected to moral evaluation" (p. 125). Based on these assumptions, one of the most influential contributions in the field of international business ethics is provided by Tom Donaldson and Thomas Dunfee. Donaldson and Dunfee provide a practical framework for decision making that is based on sound theory, without getting stuck in the metadebate about whether there can be one, all-encompassing approach to ethics.

In his earlier work, Donaldson (1989) argues that morality *should* be applied to international affairs and—more specifically—international business. According to him, this is the case whether morality is simply defined as enlightened self-interest or something more fundamental. He provides a detailed discussion of both cultural relativism and traditional Hobbesianism and illustrates how both these approaches fail to argue convincingly against the application of morality. Elsewhere, he discusses how morality can be applied to international business in a way that avoids both relativism and absolutism (Donaldson, 2001). In this article from 1996 the basic outline of Integrative Social Contracts Theory (discussed below) is already present, and Donaldson (2001) proposes that companies must be guided by three principles: respect for core human values, which determine the absolute moral threshold for all business activities, respect for local traditions, and the belief that context matters when deciding between right and wrong (p. 478).

The core human values (also referred to as hypernorms) that Donaldson (2001) refers to are defined as respect for human dignity, respect for basic rights, and good citizenship (p. 479). Because these values are too vague to provide specific guidance, there is a requirement for companies to develop more specific codes. The development and implementation of effective internal codes are not addressed in any detail here. Rather, the focus is on the development of global codes, of which the United Nations Global Compact (the Global Compact) is one of the most important examples.

The Global Compact is the world's largest voluntary corporate citizenship initiative and describes itself as a leadership platform that "seeks to align business operations and strategies everywhere with ten universally accepted principles in the areas of human rights, labour, environment and anti-corruption" (UN Global Compact Office, 2011).

The ten principles were derived from the Universal Declaration of Human Rights, the International Labour Organization's Declaration on Fundamental Principles and Rights at Work, the Rio Declaration on Environment and Development, and the United Nations Convention Against Corruption. In terms of human rights, businesses should support and respect the protection of internationally proclaimed human rights (1) and make sure that they are not complicit in human rights abuses (2). In terms of labour standards, businesses should uphold the freedom of association and the effective recognition of the right to collective bargaining (3), the elimination of all forms of forced and compulsory labour (4), the effective abolition of child labour (5), and the elimination of discrimination in respect of employment and occupation (6). In terms of the environment, businesses should support a precautionary approach to environmental challenges (7), undertake initiatives to promote greater environmental responsibility (8), and encourage the development and diffusion of environmentally friendly technologies (9). In terms of anti-corruption, businesses should work against corruption in all its forms, including extortion and bribery (10).

Integrative Social Contracts Theory

Integrative Social Contracts Theory (ISCT) was developed by Tom Donaldson and Thomas Dunfee to provide guidance on ethical issues in international business. The basic message of ISCT[2] is that "implicit agreements constitute part of the basic software of business ethics" (Donaldson & Dunfee, 2000, p. 437). As opposed to traditional social contract theory that investigates the contracts between citizens and governments, ISCT focuses on how economic participants will define business ethics. The veil of ignorance[3] in ISCT is more revealing than the one suggested by

---

[2]This summary of ISCT is based on the original publication (Donaldson & Dunfee, 1999) as well as a précis provided by the authors for a special publication of *Business and Society Review* (Donaldson & Dunfee, 2000a).

[3]The original veil of ignorance is described as follows by Rawls (2001): "Somehow we must nullify the effects of specific contingencies which put men at odds and tempt them to exploit social and natural circumstances to their own advantage. Now in order to do this I assume that the parties are situated behind a veil of ignorance. They do not know how the various alternatives will affect their own particular case and they are obliged to evaluate principles solely on the basis of general considerations" (p. 55).

Rawls. The basic assumption is made that participants do not know their economic standing, e.g., which company they work for or what their personal wealth is. However, they are granted knowledge about their economic and political preferences, as well as a basic sense of right and wrong. Under these circumstances, participants are then hypothetically gathered for "a global congress to construct an agreement that would provide a fundamental framework for ethical behaviour in economic activities" (Donaldson & Dunfee, 2000a, p. 438). The use of "integrative" emphasizes that

> ISCT is based upon a hypothetical social contract whose terms allow for the generation of binding ethical obligations through the recognition of actual norms created in real social and economic communities. A hypothetical social contract is thereby integrated with real or extant social contracts. (Dunfee, 2006, p. 304)

Donaldson and Dunfee argue that their hypothetical global congress for business ethics will not be able to agree on a detailed set of ethical rules and guidelines but rather will agree on a process or broad framework. According to Donaldson and Dunfee (1999), this framework of business ethics as social contracts is what they call the Global ISCT Macrosocial Contract for Economic Ethics and includes, among others, the following characteristics:

1. Local economic communities have moral free space in which they may generate ethical norms for their members through microsocial contracts.

2. Norm-generating microsocial contracts must be grounded in consent, buttressed by the rights of individual members to exercise voice[4] and exit.

3. In order to become obligatory (legitimate), a microsocial contract norm must be compatible with hypernorms. (p. 46)

Moral free space is defined as "[t]he freedom of individuals to form or join communities and to act jointly to establish moral rules applicable to the members of the community" (Donaldson & Dunfee, 1999, p. 38). If a norm or a moral rule is generated within moral free space and has the support of the majority of the community, it is said to be "authentic." A community is defined as "a self-defined, self-circumscribed group of people who interact in the context of shared tasks, values, or goals and who are capable of establishing norms of ethical behavior for themselves" (Donaldson & Dunfee, 1999, p. 39). Even though Donaldson and

---

[4]The right of voice is defined as "the right of members of a community to speak out for or against existing and developing norms" (Donaldson & Dunfee, 1999, p. 43).

Dunfee make a distinction between their definition of community and the concept of stakeholders, I would argue that the concepts are sufficiently similar for ISCT to be interpreted as entirely compatible with stakeholder theory.

Members of a particular community have an ethical obligation to abide by the existing authentic norms, as long as these norms do not violate hypernorms. Hypernorms are defined as "principles so fundamental that they constitute norms by which all others are to be judged" and are "discernible in a convergence of religious, political and philosophical thought" (Donaldson & Dunfee, 2000a, p. 441). According to Donaldson and Dunfee (1999), there are three distinct hypernorm categories:

1. Procedural hypernorms—these stipulate the rights of voice and exit, and are defined as the conditions "essential to support consent in microsocial contracts";

2. Structural hypernorms—principles "that establish and support essential background institutions in society"; these are necessary for political and social organisation; and

3. Substantive hypernorms—these are the fundamental "concepts of the right and the good." (p. 53)

Whether hypernorms have their origin in natural law or elsewhere does not concern Donaldson and Dunfee (1999) that much:

> Whatever the final answer to the question of whether hypernorms have sources in nature as immutable verities, or instead reflect the common humanity of global citizens as similar solutions are found to shared problems across the world, that answer is not critical to their value within ISCT. (p. 52)

Donaldson and Dunfee (1999) include the following types of evidence in support of hypernorms—two or more of these would be sufficient for a "rebuttable presumption that it constitutes a hypernorm":

- Widespread consensus that a principle is universal;
- Inclusion in well-known global industry standards;
- Supported by prominent nongovernmental organizations, regional government organizations, global business organizations or an international community of professionals;
- Consistently referred to as a global ethical standard by the international media;

- Consistent with precepts of major religions and philosophies, as well as findings concerning universal human values; and
- Supported by the laws of many different countries. (p. 60)

If an authentic norm violates a hypernorm, it is not a legitimate norm. A member of a community would be within his or her rights to deny the legitimacy of an authentic norm in such a case. Donaldson and Dunfee are not specific about whether there would be a moral obligation on the member(s) to oppose the norm, but they do acknowledge the right to civil disobedience. Even if a norm is both authentic and legitimate, this does not mean that each member of the community has to agree with it (although they have to abide by it). Members have the right of voice (to speak up) or exit (to leave). Both of these, especially the right to exit, can come at a high price, and this is acknowledged by Donaldson and Dunfee (1999, p. 42).

ISCT and the Global Compact

It is argued here that ISCT can assist a better understanding of the Global Compact, and enable signatories to the initiative to respond to the formal *and* moral requirements of the Compact in such a way that it will strengthen their corporate responsibility programs and ultimately have a fundamental impact on how corporations deal with responsibility.

Donaldson (2010) states the following in support of his own view that self-interest is linked to the health of society:

> When UN Secretary-General Kofi Annan in an address to The World Economic Forum on January 31, 1999, called upon global corporations to unite in affirming the principles of the UN Global Compact, he appealed not only to their moral idealism. He appealed also to their enlightened egoism. (p. 3)

This is in line with a previous position taken by him that companies must take three steps to satisfy all conditions of the Global Compact: egoism, cooperative egoism, and corporate citizenship (Donaldson, 2003). Corporate egoism provides the empirical no-brainer, where there is a direct short-term benefit to the company, e.g., switch off the lights to save on your electricity bill. Cooperative egoism alludes to the efficiency hypernorm, where companies cooperate because it is in their collective self-interest to do so, e.g., even though an individual bribe might result in an immediate short-term advantage for a particular company, if all companies agree not to undermine the political and judicial systems through acts of bribery, the system will be more efficient and will be to everyone's advantage. Corporate citizenship is the third, and most difficult, rung of the ladder, because it expects companies to do something simply because it is the right thing to do, e.g., to provide basic housing and health services in locations where these are not available.

Donaldson has not written extensively about the application of ISCT to the Global Compact, and that is what I would like to focus on in the remainder of this chapter. My basic argument is as follows.

The ten principles of the Global Compact can be regarded as substantive hypernorms. To qualify as hypernorms, there are certain conditions that must be met—as discussed above, they relate to general consensus, alignment with existing standards, support by major stakeholder groups, consistency with major religions and philosophies, and incorporation into existing legal frameworks. It is clear that all ten Global Compact principles are supported by the majority of these types of evidence.[5]

The way in which hypernorms limit moral free space can provide practical guidance to companies that have subscribed to the Global Compact, not only in how they need to adhere to the ten principles, but how they can structure and implement their broader corporate responsibility programs. In my view, the following statement by Donaldson and Dunfee (1999) supports this position: "Since such principles [hypernorms] are designed to impose limiting conditions on *all* micro contracts, they cannot be derived from a single micro contract, but must emanate from a source that speaks with univocal authority for all micro contracts" (p. 50).

One potential difference in the application of ISCT is that Donaldson and Dunfee developed the theory as a guide for practical decision making. In their very detailed examples of the application of ISCT, they always start with the need to recognize an ethical problem. In other words, when faced with the need to make an ethical decision in practice, the decision maker proceeds to identify the appropriate hypernorms. Within the context of ISCT and the Global Compact, my argument suggests—to some extent—a reversal of the process. In the words of one of the South African wine pioneers when he defended the practice to place wooden chips inside a barrel of wine to obtain a more wooded nose: "If you can put the wine in the wood (the barrel), you can put the wood in the wine." Viewing the Global Compact as a (nonexhaustive) set of substantive hypernorms, I suggest that

---

[5]It is important to point to a potential circular argument. One of the types of evidence presented by ISCT is the inclusion in well-known global industry standards, but clearly the inclusion of the ten principles in the Global Compact cannot be used as a part of this particular argument on why they should be regarded as hypernorms!

decision makers can determine appropriate actions and programs from these norms, and explore appropriate moral free space within them. This interpretation gives the Global Compact a certain dynamic power that is not present if it is merely seen as a voluntary code that conforms to a set of static principles. For many large corporations, the Global Compact serves merely as a way to reframe what is happening in any event. However, through an application of ISCT the Global Compact could become a driving force for the design and implementation of effective corporate responsibility programs. Although Dunfee is circumspect in acknowledging that hypernorms alone may provide guidance to solve ethical dilemmas, I think it should be acknowledged that this could happen if the hypernorm is merely seen as a point of departure to explore moral free space. Out of this activity, a practical guideline or solution could then be developed, which will apply at the level of the local community.

There are dangers attached to this process, as highlighted by Dunfee (2006): "the search for hypernorms occurs in the context of decision making, they are not to be fully 'discovered' *ex ante*" (p. 308). However, if the ten principles are seen as a framework that can coordinate expectations,[6] this potential objection can be accommodated. Just as Donaldson and Dunfee (1999) refuse to suggest a finite list of hypernorms, because that would constitute moral absolutism, the Global Compact should also not be regarded as a finite list that will provide an all-inclusive framework (p. 54). The fact that the initial nine principles were later supplemented by the tenth (on anti-corruption) and the increasing convergence with the ideals of the Millennium Development Goals illustrate this point clearly.

Let's look at a hypothetical example. Company A has decided to become a signatory to the Global Compact. It has a good reputation for corporate responsibility and wants to be part of the growing community of Global Compact signatories. Its initial thinking was probably something along these lines:

- The Global Compact is the largest voluntary corporate citizenship initiative in the world; we want to be a part of this growing movement, and association with the UN will be good for our reputation.
- Since we are already a responsible citizen and implicitly support all the principles, the impact on our company would be minimal; we can continue what we are doing in any case and must simply ensure that we fulfill the technical requirements.
- The most onerous of these requirements (and the only one that is actively monitored and could lead to delisting) is the need to submit an annual

---

[6]For a detailed discussion on the coordination of expectation, see Hsieh (2006).

Communication on Progress. We are already preparing a sustainability report according to the Global Reporting Initiative guidelines, and we can therefore submit our existing report as our Communication on Progress.

I believe the above approach is indicative of how many companies approach their participation in the Global Compact. There is nothing inherently questionable from a moral point of view and, for 99% of the time, this approach will probably not lead to any serious problems. It is in line with the first two rungs in Donaldson's "ladder of justification": corporate egoism and cooperative egoism (supported by the efficiency hypernorm). But it does not lead to the third rung of citizenship: "The Compact is asking companies to do many things simply because *they are the right thing to do*" (Donaldson, 2003, p. 71).

Let us assume that company A becomes a convert to ISCT and accordingly reexamines its participation in the Global Compact. I believe it is likely that they will come up with the following approach:

- We support the Global Compact because it provides a *moral* framework for responsible corporate citizenship. We believe that the ten principles are in line with our own values as a company, and we regard them as nonnegotiable, even if this means that in some cases this support might not be in our own perceived self-interest;
- To prevent the Global Compact from becoming a list of empty and vague principles, we will actively investigate moral free space in all the communities and geographical locations where we operate around the globe. We will demonstrate fundamental respect for the ten principles, but also for local cultures and traditions, and we will implement the principles in such a way that it makes a real and positive difference at the local level;
- We understand that the activities that we will engage in have to be both authentic (i.e., supported by all our material stakeholders) and legitimate (i.e., in line with the substantive hypernorms of the Global Compact and other relevant hypernorms that we might identify).

Conclusion

The application of ISCT to the Global Compact, and specifically the reversal of the process of decision making advocated here, can provide a dynamic framework for companies to develop and implement effective corporate responsibility programs. This holds true for both signatories and nonsignatories of the Global

Compact. Another reversal that is suggested is that the third rung of Donaldson's "ladder of justification" should become the first rung. Once a company takes the most difficult step of making the moral commitment to citizenship and acknowledging that this might lead to difficult decisions, the other rungs of the ladder become attractive as well. But making the self-imposed entry level more difficult will probably lead to less, rather than more, active participants. This has implications for the Global Compact's target of 20,000 signatories by 2020. Such ambitious targets can only be achieved by emphasizing corporate egoism above citizenship, but it comes at a cost. It presents an attractive and strong business case, but is ultimately more closely aligned with the thoughts of Friedman than what might be appropriate.

Study/Discussion Questions

1. Does intentionality matter, i.e., does it matter whether a company approaches CSR from a moral or operational point of view as long as its behavior is appropriate?

2. What does it mean when CSR is promoted as enlightened self-interest? How does the view fall apart?

3. What view of the corporation does the author support? Why?

4. What are the three fundamental principles proposed by Donaldson that must guide companies?

5. What does *moral absolutism* mean? What about *cultural relativism*? How would you interpret the statement that "cultural relativism is the single most ethical issue for businesses operating in a global environment" (Freeman & Gilbert, 2008)?

6. What are the core human values? Why are codes of conduct needed?

7. What is Integrative Social Contracts Theory? How does it differ from traditional social contracts theory?

8. What are three types of hypernorms? Can you give examples?

9. What is *moral free space*?

10. What are three steps suggested by Donaldson that are needed to fulfill the conditions of the Compact?

References

Crook, C. (2005, January 22). The good company: A survey of corporate social responsibility. *The Economist.*

Donaldson, T. (1989). *The ethics of international business.* New York, NY: Oxford University Press.

Donaldson, T. (2001). Values in tension: Ethics away from home. In M. Hoffman, R. Frederick, & M. Schwartz (Eds.), *Business ethics: Readings and cases in corporate morality* (4th ed., pp. 475–483). New York, NY: McGraw-Hill.

Donaldson, T. (2003). De-compacting the Global Compact. *Journal of Corporate Citizenship, 11,* 69–72.

Donaldson, T. (2010). Steps for global transformation: The 2008–2009 economic crisis. Retrieved from http://www.griffith.edu.au/business-commerce/sustainable-enterprise/resources/the-un-global-compact-looking-forward-ten-years-after

Donaldson, T., & Dunfee, T. W. (1999). *Ties that bind: A social contracts approach to business ethics.* Boston, MA: Harvard University Press.

Donaldson, T., & Dunfee, T. (2000a). Précis for "Ties that bind." *Business and Society Review, 105*(4), 436–443.

Donaldson, T., & Dunfee, T. (2000b). Securing the ties that bind: A response to commentators. *Business and Society Review, 105*(4), 480–492.

Dunfee, T. (2006). A critical perspective of intregrative social contracts theory: Recurring criticisms and next generation research topics. *Journal of Business Ethics, 68,* 303–328.

Freeman, R. E. (2002). Stakeholder theory of the modern corporation. In T. Donaldson, P. Werhane, & M. Cording (Eds.), *Ethical issues in business: A philosophical approach* (7th ed., pp. 38–49). Englewood Cliffs, NJ: Prentice Hall.

Freeman, R. E., & Gilbert, D. (2008). *Corporate strategy and the search for ethics* (Rev. ed.). Englewood Cliffs, NJ: Prentice Hall.

Friedman, M. (2002). The social responsibility of business is to increase its profits. In T. Donaldson, P. Werhane, & M. Cording (Eds.), *Ethical issues in business: A philosophical approach* (7th ed., pp. 33–38). Englewood Cliffs, NJ: Prentice Hall.

Hsieh, N. (2006). Voluntary codes of conduct for multinational corporations: Coordinating duties of rescue and justice. *Business Ethics Quarterly, 16*(2), 119–135.

Just good business: A special report on corporate social responsibility. (2008). *The Economist.*

Kaptein, M., & Wempe, J. (2002). *The balanced company: A theory of corporate integrity.* Oxford, UK: Oxford University Press.

Rawls, J. (2001). Justice as fairness. In M. Hoffman, R. Frederick, & M. Schwartz (Eds.), *Business ethics: Readings and cases in corporate morality* (4th ed., pp. 53–59). New York, NY: McGraw-Hill.

UN Global Compact Office. (2011, February). *UN Global Compact: Corporate sustainability in the world economy.* New York, NY: Author.

3

The United Nations and Transnational Corporations

How the UN Global Compact Has Changed the Debate

Andreas Rasche

Warwick Business School, University of Warwick

> *"I propose that you, the business leaders gathered in Davos, and we, the United Nations, initiate a global compact of shared values and principles, which will give a human face to the global market."*
>
> —Kofi Annan at the *World Economic Forum* in Davos (United Nations, 1999, p. 1)

When former secretary-general Kofi Annan addressed business leaders at the World Economic Forum in Davos in 1999, he not only started to initiate the Global Compact, but also, at the same time, fundamentally redefined the relationship between the private sector and the United Nations (UN) system. After its operational launch in 2000, the Global Compact swiftly emerged as the world's leading corporate responsibility initiative with currently close to 7,000 business and more than 3,000 nonbusiness participants in nearly 140 countries. The Global Compact can be described as a multistakeholder (yet business-led) initiative that enlists corporations in support of ten universal principles as well as

33

broader UN goals (e.g., the Millennium Development Goals). Participation in the initiative is voluntary and open to large transnational corporations (TNCs)[1] as well as small and medium-sized enterprises (SMEs) from all sectors and regions (Rasche & Kell, 2010).

This chapter explains what the Global Compact is (and what it is not). The first section introduces the basic pillars of the initiative and explores the related historical shift of UN-business relations from confrontation to collaboration. The following section discusses why there is a need for something like a global compact between business and other stakeholders. The discussion highlights the existence of global governance gaps, which are currently not sufficiently addressed through intergovernmental action and hence require the creation of more inclusive policy-making arenas. The next section sets out to revisit the debate around the Global Compact by introducing critics' arguments and relevant counterarguments. The last section looks at the Compact's achievements and also identifies future challenges.

The UN Global Compact: What It Is (and What It Is Not)

From Code to Compact: A Short History of UN-Business Relations

The Global Compact is not the first attempt of the United Nations to deal with TNCs. As the reach of TNCs gained momentum throughout the late 1960s and early 1970s, the UN started to look into their social and economic impact on nations, particularly the developing world (Coleman, 2003). At this time, the UN saw the existence of TNCs largely as a reason for concern, mostly because cross-border economic activities were believed to disadvantage host countries (in many cases developing nations). As a result, the United Nations Economic and Social Council (ECOSOC) formed a commission, which was tasked with developing a code of conduct to regulate and police the behavior of TNCs. However, conflicting political interests slowed down the overall progress on the code. While the United States adopted a pro-business stance arguing against the binding nature of the code, developing nations insisted on the legal enforceability by host and home countries (Feld, 1980; Tesner, 2000). In addition, there was significant disagreement

---

[1]Corporations with cross-border operations were initially termed *multinational corporations* within the UN system. The United Nations Economic and Social Council (ECOSOC), however, adopted the term *transnational corporation* in 1974. See also the discussion by Coleman (2003).

about whether authority to implement the code should be delegated to the United Nations. In the end, no agreement could be reached, and the code vanished from the UN agenda by 1994.

There are two important points to notice about the failed attempt to initiate a binding code of conduct: first, the process of code development was driven by intergovernmental negotiations. Other actors relevant to the governance of economic activity (e.g., civil society organizations or unions) did not participate. Second, the code was developed as a regulatory instrument to tame the increasing power of TNCs and hence was seen as an expression of the largely confrontational and openly hostile attitude of the UN toward business. The launch of the Global Compact in 2000 fundamentally shifted UN-business relations. Although the Global Compact is legitimized by a series of intergovernmental resolutions (the latest in 2010: A/RES/64/223), it also includes a variety of other stakeholders and thus reflects a "beyond-state" model of engagement (Coleman, 2003; Thérien & Pouliot, 2006). Moreover, the Global Compact reaches beyond the formerly confrontational attitude and instead emphasizes that a partnership-based approach between the UN and the global business community is more fruitful and promising. It is critical to understand this historical shift of UN-business relations when evaluating the achievements and challenges of the Global Compact. Unlike other corporate responsibility initiatives, the Compact remains embedded in the political and institutional context of the UN system (Rasche, 2009b).

How Does the Global Compact Work?

One way to understand how the Global Compact works is to compare it with other corporate responsibility initiatives. In recent years, an entire new institutional infrastructure for corporate responsibility emerged, containing a variety of (partly competing) voluntary initiatives (Gilbert, Rasche, & Waddock, 2011; Waddock, 2008). (See Waddock on page 51 of this text.) Some of these initiatives aim at monitoring single production facilities (e.g., Social Accountability 8000 or the Fair Labor Association), while yet others provide a framework for disclosing social and environmental information to stakeholders (e.g., the Global Reporting Initiative). The Global Compact does not monitor factories, nor does it define a comprehensive reporting framework (Rasche & Esser, 2006). Instead, it offers businesses the opportunity to voluntarily align their operations and strategies with ten universal principles (see Figure 3.1). Participants are expected to use a variety of engagement mechanisms (e.g., working groups and Local Networks) to initiate dialogue with other stakeholders and to learn from their experiences. Once a business joins the

Figure 3.1   The Ten Principles of the UN Global Compact

Human Rights	Business should support and respect the protection of international human rights; and make sure they are not complicit in human rights abuses.
Labour Rights	Business should uphold the freedom of association and the effective recognition of the right to collective bargaining; the elimination of all forms of forced and compulsory labour; the effective abolition of child labour; and the elimination of discrimination in respect of employment and occupation.
Environment	Business should support a precautionary approach to environmental challenges; undertake initiatives to promote greater environmental responsibility; and encourage the development and diffusion of environmentally friendly technologies.
Anti-corruption	Business should work against all forms of corruption, including extortion and bribery.

Source: http://www.unglobalcompact.org/AboutTheGC/TheTenPrinciples/index.html

Global Compact, it enters into a continuous improvement process regarding its social and environmental performance.

As the Global Compact does not contain any monitoring mechanisms, participants joining the initiative need to be held accountable for their actions and omissions. Over the years, the Global Compact has taken a variety of actions to establish an accountability framework to protect the integrity of the initiative (Wynhoven & Stausberg, 2010). First, there is a clear logo policy limiting the possibility to use the UN and Global Compact logos in any commercial way. It is also important to understand that the United Nations does not publicly endorse the corporate responsibility practices of Global Compact participants. Hence, the Global Compact is no seal of approval and should not be used in this way. Second, the Global Compact Office has established a complaint procedure allowing stakeholders to report systematic abuse of the initiative's underlying aims. Although the Global Compact will not involve itself in any legal action related to a complaint, it will assist in the resolution of the matter whenever possible and appropriate. Last but not least, all business participants are required to submit an annual Communication on Progress report that outlines their implementation progress. Even though the Compact does not define a reporting framework, it encourages companies to use the well-established Global

Reporting Initiative's GRI G3 Guidelines while compiling their reports. All reports are publicly available on the Global Compact's website (www.unglobalcompact.org), and interested stakeholders are invited to comment on report content. If a company fails to submit a report, it is labeled *noncommunicating*. Business participants that have been noncommunicating for more than one year are permanently delisted from the Global Compact database (Hamid & Johner, 2010). (See Appendix B for details on the Communication on Progress reports.)

While the Global Compact is based on universally valid and hence global principles, implementation of these principles is always embedded in local contexts. Needless to say, these contexts differ significantly in terms of their regulatory environment and socioeconomic conditions. To support the contextualization of the ten principles and to create local spaces for discourse and learning, the Global Compact has launched a variety of so-called Local Networks. Such networks reflect "clusters of participants who come together voluntarily to advance the Global Compact and its Principles at the local level . . . by providing on-the-ground support and capacity-building tied to distinct cultural, economic and linguistic needs" (Whelan, 2010, p. 318). So far, Local Networks have been established in more than 90 countries. These networks are important in two interrelated ways: On the one hand, they take global solutions and best practices downstream for replication, which always requires a certain degree of adaptation (Rasche, 2010). On the other hand, Local Networks can also be used to push innovative local solutions upstream for further dissemination.

How Is the Global Compact Governed?

The governance of the Global Compact *itself* is an important, yet often neglected, topic. Governance in this context refers to how the initiative itself is organized, who is involved in major decisions and strategic direction setting, and how, in general, decision-making powers are allocated (Crane, 2010). There are three guiding principles underlying Global Compact governance. First, the authority to govern is not centralized in a single entity. Rather, governance is decentralized and emerges through the interplay of five entities (i.e., Board, Global Compact Office, Local Networks, Inter-Agency Team, and Donor Group) as well as two convening platforms (i.e., the annual Local Networks Forum and the triennial Leaders Summit; for a detailed discussion, see Wynhoven & Stausberg, 2010). This decentralized way of governance provides the necessary flexibility to adapt the initiative to changes in the socioeconomic and political environment.

Second, governance is based on multistakeholder collaboration. Although the Global Compact is a business-led initiative (as businesses have the primary responsibility for implementation), governance entities such as the Board and

Local Networks include a variety of other stakeholders such as nongovernmental organizations (NGOs), organized labour, and UN representatives. Multistakeholder governance is an important characteristic of many recently emerging corporate responsibility initiatives, as it can be considered a key condition of a *legitimate* involvement of non-state actors into regulatory processes (Rasche & Esser, 2006). In addition, multistakeholder governance can also help to avoid "capture" by any particular group of actors. However, research has also shown that multistakeholder governance processes depend on consensus, which is often hard to reach in practice (Scherer & Palazzo, 2007).

Third, and last, Global Compact governance also considers the initiative's voluntary nature. Contrary to a traditional command-and-control type of governance, the Compact requires participants themselves to endorse any changes to the way the initiative works. Participants are not just on the receiving end of governance, but are empowered to actively shape the design and future functioning of the Compact. Bottom-up communication through Local Networks, as well as the above-mentioned two convening platforms, plays an important role in this context. Empowering participants is essential, since sustained support and participant buy-in are unlikely to occur in an environment where decisions are dictated.

Why Do We Need a Global Compact?

Redrawing the Line Between the State, the Market, and Civil Society

The rise of the global economy and the increasing power and spread of TNCs has created enormous governance challenges. For instance, many companies operate global production networks where they can split their operations and move them to those countries where wages, taxes, and regulations are lowest (Scherer & Palazzo, 2008). As a result, a variety of countries have entered into a "race to the bottom" competing for corporate investments by lowering their regulations. Since the sovereignty of government authorities remains limited to the nation-state context, governance problems resulting from cross-border economic operations cannot be addressed easily. TNCs have been involved (either directly or indirectly) in many of these problems—the cases of sweatshop labour conditions in supply factories (Locke, Amengual, & Mangla, 2009), human rights violations while operating abroad (Clapham, 2006), and cooperation with repressive regimes (Taylor, 2004) are just a few prominent examples.

The Global Compact addresses these global governance gaps, as it is based on the idea that a web of joint universal values (i.e., the ten principles) offers a "moral compass" to companies (Kell, 2005). Although the initiative does not regulate corporate behavior, it provides firms with a basic idea about what the international community of nation-states regards as universally valid values. The ten principles translate existing UN core conventions, which are aimed at nation-states, into relevant business principles. Because nation-states are often unwilling or unable to enforce these conventions, the Global Compact sidesteps missing enforcement actions by nation-states by dealing with corporations directly. This direct involvement of corporations into governance solutions is even more important if we remind ourselves that the fundamental imbalance in global rule making still prevails. While rules supporting global economic liberalization have become stronger (e.g., the trade regime) and have extended the rights of corporations, rules covering social and environmental problems lag behind (Kell & Ruggie, 1999). All of this is *not* to downplay the importance of governments as the primary implementers of universal values. Voluntary initiatives like the Global Compact can only supplement (but not substitute for) the effective exercise of state authority (Rasche, 2009a).

The Global Compact also reflects changes in the way global governance itself is understood and exercised. Traditionally, global governance arrangements were based exclusively on intergovernmental action, because states reflected the *global public domain*. However, in recent years this global public domain has moved beyond the sphere of the nation-state. On the one hand, NGOs grew significantly in terms of numbers as well as size and increasingly entered the international political sphere. The number of NGOs with consultative status at the UN grew significantly, from 1,041 in 1996 to 3,050 in 2007 (United Nations, 2008). NGOs are increasingly involved in addressing some of the governance gaps mentioned above, often through partnerships with governments, international organizations, and corporations. On the other hand, there has also been a notable increase in *private regulation* through multistakeholder initiatives (Bremer, 2008; Vogel, 2010). Private regulation operates in the domain of soft law, because of the absence of legally binding regulations and a delegation of implementation authority to non-state actors (Abbott & Snidal, 2000). The Global Compact reflects these two developments, as it understands itself as a partnership between multiple stakeholders and hence recognizes the increasing public role of private actors.

The Importance of Voluntary Action

The question of why the Global Compact is needed can also be approached from a different, albeit complementary, angle. For this, we should understand that the main argument *against* the Global Compact is its voluntary and nonbinding nature (see the discussion below). Yet, the distinction between legally enforceable regulation and voluntary approaches to corporate responsibility introduces an unnecessary dichotomy. Voluntary approaches can produce a variety of positive effects that complement regulation by nation-states. Legal regulation often lags behind the problems it is trying to regulate (e.g., because of rigid administrative processes). Corporate responsibility, however, addresses problems (e.g., climate change) that cannot and should not be postponed until nation-states "get it right." Understood in this way, the Global Compact is needed because it reflects a flexible and pragmatic way to address those omnipresent governance gaps that the rise of the global economy has created.

Another critical point to consider is the role of innovation. Legal regulation not only is reactive, but also prescribes what is *not* to be done. Learning and innovation, both of which are critical in the context of addressing novel governance problems, can hardly be achieved in such an environment. From its inception, the Global Compact has highlighted the pivotal role of learning and innovation while improving corporate responsibility practices (Ruggie, 2002, 2004). The initiative provides an institutionalized space for creating and disseminating innovative responsible business practices, for instance through participants' engagement in issue-specific learning platforms (e.g., on climate change and water sustainability). Learning and dialogue enable consensus-based solutions, which help to secure stakeholder acceptance. Participating in the Global Compact allows for finding practical ways for advancing human rights, labour rights, environmental protection, and anti-corruption in the specific industry and regional contexts that firms face on a day-to-day basis.

Although the Global Compact is a voluntary initiative, firms face a variety of pressures "forcing" (or at least encouraging) them to participate. Perez-Batres, Miller, and Pisani (2011), for instance, find that institutional pressure plays an important role. Their study shows that publicly listed firms show mimetic adoption behavior. Such behavior is based on the belief that *not* copying the actions of peers might compromise a firm's own perceived legitimacy. The role of investors and financial markets is also important. Janney, Dess, and Forlani (2009) find that the decision by publicly listed firms to join the Global Compact leads to cumulative abnormal positive returns in financial markets. In other words, signing up to the Global Compact creates a first positive impression in the eyes of investors. These results are consistent with Amer-Maistriau's (2009) study finding that the Compact's delisting of participants leads to abnormal negative returns in financial markets. It is also widely known that corporations are constantly subject to NGO pressure and hence can use the Global Compact as one way to legitimize their behavior (Centindamar & Husoy, 2007).

The Global Compact and Its Critics: Exploring the Debate

Ever since its operational launch in 2000, the Global Compact has been criticized from various angles. The following paragraphs revisit the three most frequently raised assertions and offer a counterperspective in defense of the Global Compact. This is not to say that all critique is irrelevant or wrong (as various changes to the Global Compact were initiated by critical concerns) but that critics often want the Compact to be something it never intended or pretended to be.

"The Compact Is Not Accountable Due to a Lack of Monitoring"

The first allegation, that the Compact is not accountable because it does not independently monitor and verify compliance with its principles, is probably the most well-known critique (Bigge, 2004; Deva, 2006; Nolan, 2005; Rizvi, 2004). Nolan (2005), for instance, argues that "accountability, or rather the lack of it, is the crucial issue that faces the Global Compact" (p. 462). Critics argue that a lack of monitoring, sanctions, enforceable rules, and independent verification fosters the misuse of the Compact as a marketing tool. In the eyes of these critics, the Compact is a public relations smokescreen without substance that allows powerful TNCs to *bluewash* their damaged image. In other words, they seek to associate their operations with the blue UN flag in order to gain legitimacy. Ultimately, the fear is that such a lack of accountability can lead to adverse selection in that those companies most eager to join are the ones in need of a good public image (Williams, 2004, p. 762).

One cannot and should not criticize the Compact for something it has never pretended or intended to be—a compliance-based mechanism that verifies and measures corporate behavior. From its inception, the initiative was never designed as a seal of approval for participating companies, as certification would require far more resources than are currently available. The Compact instead expects proactive behavior from its participants. Its learning approach is advantageous insofar as a code of conduct (that would be needed for monitoring) is always static and thus does not allow participants to react flexibly to varying environmental circumstances (Ruggie, 2002). Without a doubt, it should be in the enlightened self-interest of the Compact

---

Author's Note: Parts of this section are adopted and modified from the following publication: Rasche, A. (2009a): "'A Necessary Supplement': What the United Nations Global Compact Is (Not)." This paper was published in *Business & Society,* 48/4, December/2009 by SAGE Publications, Inc. All rights reserved. © SAGE Publications, Inc. The article can be accessed at http://bas.sagepub.com.

to prevent free riders from misusing the initiative. The above-mentioned integrity measures were created for exactly this purpose.

Even if desired, monitoring of participants would be nearly impossible, as it requires performance indicators relevant to *all* companies in *all* countries and *all* sectors. Without such measures, a meaningful comparison of monitoring results, and thus the creation of sanctions, is not only impossible but would also weaken the Compact's accountability, because any imposed sanctions would be perceived as arbitrary. Moreover, the Global Compact currently has no political mandate to monitor or verify compliance with its principles. Since the initiative is embedded within the UN system, the establishment of legally binding regulations would require the support of the UN General Assembly, which is unlikely given the current political climate and the history of UN-business relations. In addition, the logistical and financial resources to effectively and efficiently monitor TNCs and their supply chains (let alone SMEs around the world) are simply not available. Given that there are currently over 6,200 business participants, annual (or even biannual) monitoring of corporate behavior would require personal, logistical, and financial resources that are way beyond the Compact's current capacity. It is precisely for this reason that certification initiatives such as SA 8000 award certificates for just *one* production facility but never for an entire corporation and/or supply chain (Gilbert & Rasche, 2007). The addressees of the Compact, however, are entire corporations and not single production facilities.

"The Global Compact Allows Businesses to 'Capture' the UN"

Another allegation is that the Compact opens a window of opportunity for business to "capture" the UN. Zammit (2003), for example, argues that there is a basic inconsistency between the policy interests of developing countries and those promoted by the UN's corporate partners. The fear is that big business will pursue its policy interests within the UN more directly by signing up to initiatives like the Global Compact. Critics are concerned about a break in the UN's traditional, non-business position on economic issues and fear that the institution is adopting a pro-market spin that could, in time, lead to its silent privatization.

Despite widely shared beliefs, the Global Compact is by no means the first, nor the only, attempt to establish partnerships between the UN and business. Almost from its inception, the UN has had partnerships with businesses and business associations. Businesses and NGOs even joined the 51 nations that gathered in San Francisco, California, in 1945 to sign the UN Charter and were *expected* to be part of the solution to foster peace and development. As indicated above, what has changed is the attitude of the UN system toward the inclusion of non-state actors.

UN-business partnerships are neither a new nor exclusive feature of the Global Compact; however, they have increased in number over the last decade. This increase may be due to the fact that many UN agencies have undergone an ideological shift from confrontation to cooperation.

It is also important to understand that it is not the Global Compact that allows corporations to be closer to the agenda of policymakers, but that corporations *are already* political players, quite independently of the Compact. Businesses design and implement social and environmental standards (McIntosh, Thomas, Leipziger, & Coleman, 2003), are involved in peacekeeping (Fort & Schipani, 2002), provide education and healthcare (Williams, 2004), and fight corruption (Cavanagh, 2004). All of these issues are also on the UN agenda. This engagement has not been imposed on TNCs but is necessary since (a) national governments, especially in developing countries, often fail to set a regulative framework under which such issues can be resolved and (b) many of today's problems cannot be solved on a national level at all but need to be addressed globally, for example by *transnational* companies (Scherer, Palazzo, & Baumann, 2006). Under these conditions, collaboration between the UN and business is not only desirable but also needed, since the UN's goals can no longer be achieved in isolation. In a world of growing interdependencies, neglecting and devaluing UN-business partnerships can only come at the price of sticking to existing ideologies.

Collaboration between the UN and the business community is, of course, not without problems. It is not the direct capture of the UN by businesses, but instead the ability of the latter to use the Compact as a means to position a specific idea of what corporate responsibility is about (i.e., learning, *not* regulation) that needs to be watched carefully. As discussed above, learning is a supplement, but not a substitute, for more compliance-based corporate responsibility initiatives as well as national law. For corporations, the UN is particularly attractive in this context as influencing the public understanding of what good corporate responsibility is about requires discursive legitimacy which the UN clearly offers (Levy, 2008; Levy & Prakash, 2003).

"The Global Compact Promotes Vague Principles"

Another criticism pertains to the Compact's lack of clarity with regard to its principles. Deva (2006), for instance, argues that "the language of these principles is so general that insincere corporations can easily circumvent or comply with them without doing anything" (p. 129). Similarly, Bigge (2004) claims that the Compact is surrounded by a lack of precision in content that does not even attempt to clarify its principles for its participants. Murphy (2005) thus concludes that the Compact is at best a minimalist code of corporate conduct.

These critics want the Compact to be a clearly structured code of conduct against which compliance can be measured. However, as already mentioned, the very idea of the Compact is the creation of a long-term learning network that is used by business and nonbusiness participants to share innovative ideas and best practices as to how the ten principles can be implemented. These principles provide a yardstick for the exchange of ideas and are not meant to be a benchmark against which to assess compliance. Overspecified principles could even turn out to be counterproductive, as they would limit the scope of possible solutions right from the beginning. Although regional in its impact, the Global Compact is designed as a global initiative with no restrictions on the size, sector, or region of its participants. The wide variety in corporate size, sector, region, and available resources of participating companies does not allow for the introduction of clear-cut principles. For instance, a "precautionary approach to environmental challenges" has a different meaning for a large TNC operating in the chemical sector, compared with an Indian SME doing business in the IT industry.

Each participant needs to fill the ten principles with contextualized meaning during the process of implementation. The goal must be to reflect the meaning and significance of each principle against the geographic, socioeconomic, and cultural environment that a participant operates in. It is the very idea of the Compact to act as a moral compass for participants: a compass that addresses corporate diversity through a learning-based approach, which allows firms to contextualize the general principles within their respective business environment. The bottom line is that there are a variety of ways to implement the principles. The Compact's values need to be *translated* into action, a task (like any other management task) that can be approached from different angles.

Retrospect and Prospect—Achievements and Challenges

The Global Compact has grown from 50 participants in 2000 to over 8,900 participants in 2011. While this growth rate is an impressive achievement, it has also created the challenge to balance quantitative *and* qualitative growth. The Compact's own annual impact studies reveal that implementation gaps still exist in a variety of contexts (United Nations Global Compact Office, 2010). For instance, corporate responsibility practices often remain limited to headquarters and are not pushed down to subsidiaries and suppliers. The recently announced differentiation of participants in terms of their implementation quality is an important and timely concept in this regard, as it motivates laggards to catch up while publicly rewarding leading companies. In the future, the Global Compact will need to reconcile two developments: on the one hand, the initiative should not stop growing in terms of participants (as this would impede its reach and impact). On the other hand, the initiative also needs to ensure that more participants do more in support of the ten principles (as this secures sustained legitimacy in the eyes of the wider public).

The Global Compact has also achieved what some other corporate responsibility initiatives miss: a good presence on the local level. The number and reach of Local Networks has grown significantly throughout the last twelve years. It is particularly noteworthy that Local Networks exist in some of the key emerging economies, such as China and India, as well as in the developing world (Whelan, 2010). The network-based character of the initiative created two advantages over time: First, network-based governance generated the necessary flexibility to reconcile abstract global principles with local realities. Second, network-based governance also allowed for adopting a risk-minimization strategy. Since networks are only loosely coupled, weak performing networks do not negatively influence leading networks. The key challenge for the future will be to maintain the loosely coupled nature of networks, while increasing inter-network collaboration and coordination. More coordination and collaboration among networks would increase the Compact's ability to address governance challenges transcending the borders of sovereign nation-states.

Another, and often neglected, achievement of the Global Compact is its contribution to a silent reform of the UN system (Kell, Slaughter, & Hale, 2007). Shortly after its launch, the Compact was lauded for reflecting "the most creative reinvention" of the UN system to date (Christian Science Monitor, 2000). It is widely known and accepted that the UN reflects a rather hierarchical system following a bureaucratic way of organization. Flexibility and innovation, which are needed in today's swiftly moving political and economic context, are hard to sustain in such an environment. The decentralized network-based governance structure, involving UN agencies, businesses, and other non-state actors, has already created a space for innovation and experimentation. The Compact's underlying idea of creating change by empowering actors and creating shared incentives (rather than mandating change through hierarchical control) could be an important building block of UN reform. Given that UN core agencies are increasingly cooperating with businesses and civil society organizations, such a reform would be both necessary and timely.

Looking beyond the Global Compact, the biggest challenge will be to start rethinking management itself. Renowned management thinker Peter Drucker (1909–2005) once said that "management is doing things right; leadership is doing the right things." There is no doubt that to change present business practices we need both management *and* leadership. We need inspiring leaders who fundamentally rethink existing business models and align them with the changing economic realities. And we need managers who turn this vision into reality by developing and implementing new business practices. This, however, requires a different way of thinking and, as a consequence, a new set of leadership skills. Most importantly, managers need to look at the global economy and their business practices from a systems perspective. The global economy affects and is affected by many systems—for instance, but not limited to, the natural environment, financial markets, political leadership, civil society, and business practices on the ground. These systems interact, often in unpredictable ways. The Global Compact is one very practical way to open up an organization for systems thinking. If taken seriously, participation can help firms to better understand and manage how systems work and interrelate. In this sense, we should look at the Compact not only as one among many other corporate responsibility initiatives, but also, and maybe most of all, as a way of learning how to see business differently.

If we look up the word *compact* in *Webster's Third New International Dictionary,* we are told that it reflects "an agreement, understanding, or covenant between two or more parties" echoing "a degree of strength." The Global Compact's underlying agreement between the UN system, the global business community, and civil society has emerged significantly ever since its operational launch. The main challenge will be to sustain the created dynamics by further strengthening and deepening links among existing and new participants.

Study/Discussion Questions

1. Why did earlier attempts by the UN to create a more binding code of conduct for business fail?

2. According to the author, what exactly is the UN Global Compact?

3. How does the Compact fit the adage "Think global, act local"?

4. How does the Compact address global governance gaps?

5. What are the three guiding principles underlying the governance of the UN Global Compact?

6. What is *bluewashing*?

7. What are the three major criticisms of the Global Compact? Do you agree or disagree?

8. What is the meaning for the author behind the quote by famed management guru Peter Drucker (1909–2005) who said that "management is doing things right; leadership is doing the right things"?

9. What challenges does the UN Global Compact face? How do you think the UN might address them?

10. What might be examples of translating the principles into action?

References

Abbott, K. W., & Snidal, D. (2000). Hard and soft law in international governance. *International Organization, 54,* 421–456.

Amer-Maistriau, E. (2009). *Communicating progress to the Global Compact as a mechanism of regulation of the business activity.* Paper presented at the annual meeting of the SASE Annual Conference, Sciences Po, Paris, France.

Bigge, D. M. (2004). Bring on the bluewash—A social constructivist argument against using Nike v. Kasky to attack the UN Global Compact. *International Legal Perspectives, 14,* 6–21.

Bremer, J. A. (2008). How global is the Global Compact? *Business Ethics: A European Review, 17,* 227–244.

Cavanagh, G. F. (2004). Global business ethics—regulation, code, or self-restraint. *Business Ethics Quarterly, 14,* 625–642.

Centindamar, D., & Husoy, K. (2007). Corporate social responsibility practices and environmentally responsible behavior: The case of the United Nations Global Compact. *Journal of Business Ethics, 76,* 163–176.

Christian Science Monitor. (2000). *A new global compact.* Retrieved from http://www.csmonitor.com/2000/0908/p10s1.html

Clapham, A. (2006). *Human rights obligations of non-state actors.* Oxford, UK: Oxford University Press.

Coleman, D. (2003). The United Nations and transnational corporations: From an internation to a "beyond state" model of engagement. *Global Society, 17,* 339–357.

Crane, A. (2010). From governance to governance: On blurring boundaries. *Journal of Business Ethics, 94,* 17–19.

Deva, S. (2006). Global Compact: A critique of the UN's "public-private" partnership for promoting corporate citizenship. *Syracuse Journal of International Law and Communication, 34,* 107–151.

Feld, W. J. (1980). *Multinational corporations and UN politics: The quest for codes of conduct.* Frankfurt, Germany: Pergamon Press.

Fort, T. L., & Schipani, C. A. (2002). The role of the corporation in fostering sustainable peace. *Vanderbilt Journal of Transnational Law, 35,* 389–435.

Gilbert, D. U., & Rasche, A. (2007). Discourse ethics and social accountability: The ethics of SA 8000. *Business Ethics Quarterly, 17,* 187–216.

Gilbert, D. U., Rasche, A., & Waddock, S. (2011). Accountability in a global economy: The emergence of international accountability standards. *Business Ethics Quarterly, 21,* 23–44.

Hamid, U., & Johner, O. (2010). The United Nations Global Compact communication on progress policy: Origins, trends and challenges. In A. Rasche & G. Kell (Eds.), *The United Nations Global Compact: Achievements, trends and challenges* (pp. 265–280). Cambridge, UK: Cambridge University Press.

Janney, J. J., Dess, G., & Forlani, V. (2009). Glass houses? Market reactions to firms joining the UN Global Compact. *Journal of Business Ethics, 90,* 407–423.

Kell, G. (2005). The Global Compact: Selected experiences and reflections. *Journal of Business Ethics, 59*(1/2), 69–79.

Kell, G., & Ruggie, J. G. (1999). Global markets and social legitimacy: The case for the "Global Compact." *Transnational Corporations, 8,* 101–120.

Kell, G., Slaughter, A.-M., & Hale, T. (2007). Silent reform through the Global Compact. *UN Chronicle, 44,* 26–30.

Levy, D. L. (2008). Political contestation in global production networks. *Academy of Management Review, 33,* 943–963.

Levy, D. L., & Prakash, A. (2003). Bargains old and new: Multinational corporations in global governance. *Business and Politics, 5,* 131–150.

Locke, R. M., Amengual, M., & Mangla, S. (2009). Virtue out of necessity? Compliance, commitment, and the improvement of labor conditions in global supply chains. *Politics and Society, 37,* 319–351.

McIntosh, M., Thomas, R., Leipziger, D., & Coleman, G. (2003). *Living corporate citizenship: Strategic routes to socially responsible business.* London, England: FT Prentice Hall.

Murphy, S. D. (2005). Taking multinational corporate codes of conduct to the next level. *Columbia Journal of Transnational Law, 43,* 388–433.

Nolan, J. (2005). The United Nations Global Compact with business: Hindering or helping the protection of human rights? *The University of Queensland Law Journal, 24,* 445–466.

Perez-Batres, L. A., Miller, V. V., & Pisani, M. J. (2011). Institutionalizing sustainability: An empirical study of corporate registration and commitment to the United Nations Global Compact guidelines. *Journal of Cleaner Production, 19,* 843–851.

Rasche, A. (2009a). "A necessary supplement": What the United Nations Global Compact is (not). *Business & Society, 48,* 511–537.

Rasche, A. (2009b). Toward a model to compare and analyze accountability standards: The case of the UN Global Compact. *Corporate Social Responsibility and Environmental Management, 16,* 192–205.

Rasche, A. (2010). The limits of corporate responsibility standards. *Business Ethics: A European Review, 19,* 280–291.

Rasche, A., & Esser, D. (2006). From stakeholder management to stakeholder accountability: Applying Habermasian discourse ethics to accountability research. *Journal of Business Ethics, 65,* 251–267.

Rasche, A., & Kell, G. (2010). *The United Nations Global Compact: Achievements, trends and challenges.* Cambridge, UK: Cambridge University Press.

Rizvi, H. (2004). UN pact with business lacks accountability. *Global Policy Forum.* Retrieved from http://www.globalpolicy.org

Ruggie, J. G. (2002). Trade, sustainability and global governance. *Columbia Journal of Environmental Law, 27*, 297–307.

Ruggie, J. G. (2004). Reconstituting the global public domain: Issues, actors, and practices. *European Journal of International Relations, 10*, 499–531.

Scherer, A. G., & Palazzo, G. (2007). Toward a political conception of corporate responsbility: Business and society viewed from a Habermasian perspective. *Academy of Management Review, 32*, 1096–1120.

Scherer, A. G., & Palazzo, G. (2008). Globalization and corporate social responsibility. In A. McWilliams, D. Matten, J. Moon, & D. Siegel (Eds.), *The Oxford handbook of corporate social responsibility* (pp. 413–431). Oxford, UK: Oxford University Press.

Scherer, A. G., Palazzo, G., & Baumann, D. (2006). Global rules and private actors: Toward a new role of the transnational corporation in global governance. *Business Ethics Quarterly, 16*, 505–532.

Taylor, K. M. (2004). Thicker than blood: Holding Exxon Mobile liable for human rights violations committed abroad. *Syracuse Journal of International Law and Commerce, 31*, 274–297.

Tesner, S. (2000). *The United Nations and business: A partnership recovered.* New York, NY: St. Martin's Press.

Thérien, J. P., & Pouliot, V. (2006). The Global Compact: Shifting the politics of international development. *Global Governance, 12*, 55–75.

United Nations. (1999, February 1). Secretary-general address to the World Economic Forum in Davos [Press Release SG/SM/6881]. New York, NY: Author.

United Nations. (2008). Number of NGOs in consultative status with the council. Retrieved from http://esa.un.org/coordination/ngo/new/index.asp

United Nations Global Compact Office. (2010). *United Nations Global Compact annual review 2010.* New York, NY: Author.

Vogel, D. (2010). The private regulation of global corporate conduct: Achievements and limitations. *Business and Society, 49*, 69–87.

Waddock, S. (2008). Building a new institutional infrastructure for corporate responsibility. *Academy of Management Perspectives, 22*, 87–108.

Whelan, N. (2010). Building the United Nations Global Compact local network model: History and highlights. In A. Rasche & G. Kell (Eds.), *The United Nations Global Compact: Achievement, trends and challennges* (pp. 317–339). Cambridge, UK: Cambridge University Press.

Williams, O. F. (2004). The UN Global Compact: The challenge and the promise. *Business Ethics Quarterly, 14*, 755–774.

Wynhoven, U., & Stausberg, M. (2010). The United Nations Global Compact's governance framework and integrity measures. In A. Rasche & G. Kell (Eds.), *The United Nations Global Compact: Achievements, trends and challenges* (pp. 251–264). Cambridge, UK: Cambridge University Press.

Zammit, A. (2003). *Development at risk: Rethinking UN-business partnerships.* New York, NY: The South Centre and United Nations Research Institute for Social Development.

4

Context and Dynamics
of the UN Global Compact

An Idea Whose Time Has Come

Sandra Waddock

Boston College, Carroll School of Management

T he UN Global Compact arose in a context of turmoil and questioning about
  the proper role of large corporations in society and particularly in developing
nations around the world. In efforts to reduce costs, many companies had long
been outsourcing production to developing nations around the world, moving their
production operations global and also doing business globally. Outsourced work is
typically located in nations where wages are considerably less than in developed
nations and where working and environmental standards are necessarily not held
to the higher prevailing norms and legislation of many corporations' home countries. While developing nations benefited from the jobs created by these processes
of globalization, domestic workers, trade and labour unions, environmentalists,
and anti-sweatshop activists, among others, were appalled at the conditions in
which many workers found themselves.

Author's Note: Portions of this paper and the ideas presented were published in my article "Building
a New Institutional Infrastructure for Corporate Responsibility," *Academy of Management
Perspectives*, August 2008, 22(3), 87–108. Used with permission.

In the face of numerous controversies around globalization, Dr. Klaus Leisinger (2002), president of the Novartis Foundation, reported that multinational corporations (MNCs) actually paid higher than average local wages and offered better working conditions than domestic companies. Issues around globalization and its impact spread into the public consciousness and created a complex and problematic situation for many companies, who believed that they were doing the right thing by providing jobs in the first place. Although Leisinger (2002) pointed out that many claims about the impacts of globalization were biased by the point of view of the observer, it is clear that by 1999, when then secretary-general Kofi Annan made his speech to the World Economic Forum in Davos and called for a new social compact between business and society, the time was ripe for change. As Annan noted,

> Globalization is a fact of life. But I believe we have underestimated its fragility. The problem is this. The spread of markets outpaces the ability of societies and their political systems to adjust to them, let alone to guide the course they take. History teaches us that such an imbalance between the economic, social and political realms can never be sustained for very long. . . . Our challenge today is to devise a . . . compact on the global scale, to underpin the new global economy . . . to embrace, support and enact a set of core values in the areas of human rights, labour standards, and environmental practices. . . .
>
> We have to choose between a global market driven only by calculations of short-term profit, and one which has a human face. Between a world which condemns a quarter of the human race to starvation and squalor, and one which offers everyone at least a chance of prosperity, in a healthy environment. Between a selfish free-for-all in which we ignore the fate of the losers, and a future in which the strong and successful accept their responsibilities, showing global vision and leadership. (United Nations, 1999)

Annan's speech made an immediate impact on the executives in attendance in part because they were already well attuned to the criticisms of globalization that their companies faced and were open to doing something constructive about those criticisms. Annan's call for what became the UN Global Compact very visibly put into place a globally acknowledged and morally persuasive piece of an emerging global corporate responsibility infrastructure that aims at pressuring companies for greater responsibility and sustainability. The responsibility infrastructure consists of numerous elements of an emerging and still voluntary system of responsibility assurance for corporations (Waddock, 2008) including (1) internal company responsibility management systems and approaches; (2) external (and internal) codes of conduct, standards, and principles; (3) credible verification, monitoring, and certification services; and (4) generally accepted reporting systems.

The emergence of responsibility assurance, however, is not the only important development that has taken place in recent years as counterpoint to the short-termism and shareholder wealth maximization emphasis that has beset the business world. Other types of institutions have responded to perceived needs or opportunities or been created to tap into the latter. For example, one major set of initiatives and incentives has developed in the form of the social investment movement, which works alongside the nascent responsibility assurance system to focus fiduciary responsibility on material risks emerging from social and ecological sources, as well as financial ones. Ratings and rankings have evolved to evaluate businesses along multiple dimensions. Businesses and other institutions have formed numerous associations that focus on greater corporate responsibility and sustainability, and educational programs that address issues such as responsibility, accountability, and sustainability have also emerged in recent years. Finally, social entrepreneurship has begun to be an important element of the context and landscape in which the UN Global Compact is situated. Below, I will discuss the emergence of notions of corporate citizenship and responsibility, along with highlighting each of these elements of the landscape of corporate responsibility that now exists.

A Changing Landscape of Pressures and Institutions

Since the early 1990s, we have seen a shift in the understanding of corporate social responsibility (CSR) from simply being the philanthropic/charitable, volunteer, and community relations efforts of companies to being far more integrated with companies' business models—what I call *corporate responsibility* or *corporate citizenship* to differentiate it from CSR, the "do good" stuff. Corporate responsibility initiatives, like the UN Global Compact, arose in conjunction with the increasing visibility and transparency provided by the Internet, which make it increasingly difficult for companies to hide their activities from stakeholders. They also developed in part as a consequence of several highly visible corporate incidents that called company, particularly MNC, behaviors and practices into question (e.g., Union Carbide's 1984 massive gas leak in Bhopal, India, which killed thousands; the 1989 Exxon Valdez oil spill in Alaska; Royal Dutch Shell's thwarted efforts to dispose of its Brent Spar oil rig in 1996 and its perceived involvement in executions of activists in Nigeria in 1997; and then CEO Phil Knight's disclaimer that Nike's suppliers problems with sweatshops were not Nike's problem in 1997).

Of course, the early 2000s saw their share of corporate problems with the fraudulent practices of Enron, the collapse of its accountant Arthur Anderson, and related implosions of firms. Then, of course, the world was faced with the massive economic meltdown associated with the financial services and mortgages industries in 2008. The growing global consensus on human-induced climate change and other issues related to sustainability—and companies' roles in these crises—also continue to bring escalating attention to issues of corporate responsibility.

In part because of globalization and in part because of the visibility of these and other issues, there has been enormous growth in interest in corporate citizenship (CC), corporate responsibility (CR), and corporate social responsibility (CSR)—the three most popular terms—since the 1970s. As Figure 4.1 suggests, this interest has grown explosively since the popularization of the Internet and some of the notable scandals around 1995. To assess this growth, I did a count of citations to the terms *corporate responsibility*, *corporate citizenship*, and *corporate social responsibility* in *Business Source Complete* (titles and abstracts) from 1970 to 2010. As the chart indicates, there is decided growth in usage of all three of the terms starting around 1995 and almost exponential growth in usage since then, particularly for the term CSR, which is and remains the most popular term. Note that usage skyrockets after about 2000, around the time when the UN Global Compact and other important initiatives related to the corporate responsibility infrastructure, such as the Global Reporting Initiative, the SA 8000 labour standards, and the AA 1000 stakeholder engagement and accountability standards, began to gain momentum.

Mentions of corporate responsibility, whatever name it goes by, in published articles are certainly one indicator of interest in this field, but in the rest of this chapter, we will explore the infrastructure that arguably created the conditions or context in which all this interest has been generated. There are a number of what can be called pressure points that place greater attention on and pressure for corporate responsibility, particularly for large MNCs. One important pressure point is that new concerns and issues about business practices keep arising—the scope and content of responsibilities to which companies are expected to attend keeps growing and changing with the times. Simultaneously, public expectations about what companies are supposed to do are constantly rising in spite of all the scandals and problems that seem to keep occurring. Rising public expectations are basically a moving target that any company hoping to avoid the risks associated with being caught by an issue needs to keep in mind, partly because of the increasing transparency that the Internet has brought. No longer can companies operate as if they were separate from society, if indeed they ever could. Too many bloggers, Twitter users, Facebook aficionados, and others adept with web 2.0 based social media are paying attention and publicizing what happens inside and outside of companies as well as in company relationships with a wide variety of stakeholders.

Furthermore, thanks in part to the growing pressures on companies by the rapid evolution and growing numbers of activist organizations, public interest groups,

Figure 4.1 Mentions of Corporate Social Responsibility (CSR), Corporate
Responsibility (CR), and Corporate Citizenship (CC) in *Business
Source Complete,* 1970–2010

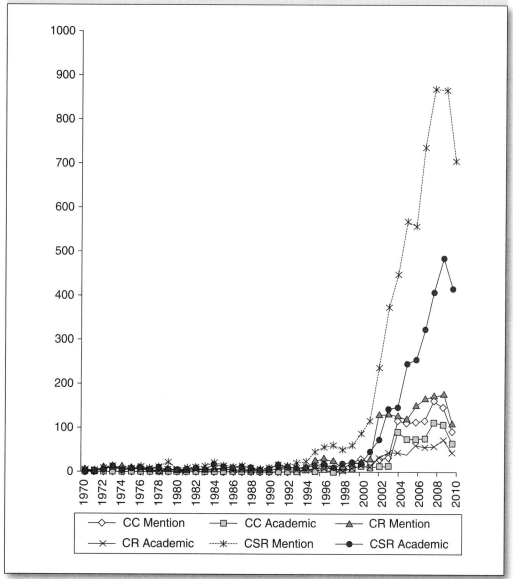

and nongovernmental organizations (NGOs), new issues keep arising so that,
simultaneously with scandals that draw attention to company actions, higher
expectations are put in place (see Rivoli & Waddock, 2011). Arguably, the ability

to organize is fueled in part by the Internet, so it's not entirely coincidental that business interest in CR/CSR has paralleled the advances in electronic communication (starting about 1995 when the World Wide Web became easily accessible).

Consider the following issues now facing businesses, most of which were not even on the radar screen but a few years ago:

- Security of information, persons, and corporate resources
- Responses to terrorism or threats of terrorism
- Implications of participation in zones of conflict or abusive regimes and the need to generate peace
- Obesity, particularly for food and beverage companies
- Climate change, global warming, and other ecological considerations
- Regionalization, "slow food," and local living economies versus globalization (with sub-issues of how far food travels to get to the table, what type of food we are serving, the way food is produced, and food's nutritional value)
- Excessive CEO/executive compensation
- Increasing concerns about overconsumption and materialism tied to the material economy
- The role of stress and ever-increasing pace of life in business and society generally
- Hedge funds and private equity, derivatives, and other sophisticated financial instruments—understanding them, disclosure, and dealing with their power
- The reality that some activist shareholder resolutions are now generating more than 50% of the vote

The list could go on virtually endlessly, but the picture is clear—the demands on companies to pay attention to their impact on stakeholders, including communities and nature (one definition of corporate responsibility), are ever changing and ever growing. And it isn't just issues that have created a context in which corporate (social) responsibility has become important to companies and to others, such as pressure groups. There has been tremendous growth in the corporate responsibility infrastructure, supporting moves toward greater corporate responsibility and even pressuring companies, especially big ones, to participate in this infrastructure (Waddock, 2008).

The Emerging Corporate Responsibility Infrastructure

In this section, we will explore the broad outlines of the emerging responsibility infrastructure. Generally, it involves dynamics and forces coming from the three sectors of society: market-based or private sector entities, civil society entities, and governmental initiatives and entities. Below we will briefly explore the corporate responsibility developments in each of these sectors.

Market-Based Dynamics

In the market for responsibility, or what author David Vogel (2006) has called the *market for virtue*, companies have begun developing numerous internal codes of conduct and responsibility management approaches that help them think more explicitly about how to manage their stakeholder relationships and impacts. In other writing, Charles Bodwell and I have called these approaches *total responsibility management* approaches or TRM, with a distinct analogy to total quality management (TQM) approaches to quality (Waddock & Bodwell, 2007). Broader in scope than TQM approaches, TRM focuses on all of a company's stakeholder relationships and impact and argues that, just as companies began to manage quality (e.g., Cole, 1998; Crosby, 1992; Deming, 1982; Rao et al., 1996) and their environmental impact (e.g., Buchholz, 1998; Curkovic, Melnyk, Handfield, & Calantone, 2000; Hart & Milstein, 2003) as part of their quest for competitive advantage, so today, they do need to manage their various (stakeholder and natural environment) responsibilities if they hope to remain competitive.

Responsibility Assurance

In part, these internal responsibility management approaches have come into existence because companies are responding to external pressures. One set of market-based pressures that they are facing can be called a *responsibility assurance system*, which has three core elements: (1) standards, codes, and principles; (2) credible monitoring, verification, and certification approaches for various aspects of stakeholder and environmental relations; and (3) a generally accepted accounting and reporting mechanism reporting on the company's activities within the environmental, social, and governance (ESG) domains, as current terminology frames these issues.

Standards, Codes, and Principles. Although there has been an enormous proliferation of standards, codes, and principles (including many internally developed codes of conduct), perhaps the best known and certainly the most visible of these initiatives is the UN Global Compact. As must be clear from other chapters in this book, because the UN Global Compact's ten principles are based on internationally agreed treaties, and because they carry the moral authority of the United Nations, they have both moral standing and near-universal legitimacy among the variety of stakeholders interested in corporate citizenship and responsibility. Other standards of importance also exist, however, including the United Nations' Organization for Economic Cooperation and Development (OECD) Guidelines for Multinational Corporations, the Caux Roundtable Principles, the CERES environmental principles, and numerous others. In addition, the Global Compact has spawned a number of important related principles, such as the Principles for Responsible Investment (at this writing with more than 900 signatories globally) and the Principles for Responsible Management Education aimed at business schools.

Credible Monitoring, Verification, and Certification Approaches. The second aspect of responsibility assurance, beyond codes and principles, is having systems available through which a company's activities and practices can be monitored, verified, and certified. Because many external stakeholders of companies, such as NGOs, activist groups, pressure groups, social investors, and the media, are aware of phenomena like *greenwashing*, in which companies try to make themselves look sustainable without really changing their practices, or *bluewashing*, in which they wrap themselves in the United Nations' blue flag, and because there is little public trust in companies after all the scandals of the early 2000s, there is an increasing need for global companies to provide evidence that they are living up to their claims about responsibility. External monitoring, certification, and verification activities are undertaken by both NGOs (e.g., SAI International and Verité) and for-profit enterprises (e.g., some of the big accounting firms). Although they are typically paid for by the firms being monitored, they are considered more credible than monitoring that is done solely by the company itself. Among the leaders in this arena are SAI International, which has developed the SA 8000 labour standards for global supply chain management, and AccountAbility, which has developed the AA 1000 stakeholder engagement and ESG standards.

A development that falls between a set of standards or principles and a framework for monitoring is ISO 26000, a voluntary set of guidance standards for corporate social responsibility. ISO 26000 was issued by the International Organization for Standardization (ISO) that also produces quality and environmental standards, among many others. Developed not as a monitoring tool, but rather a guidance document, ISO 26000 attempts to help companies and other types of organizations benefit from operating responsibly. ISO 26000 emphasizes seven core areas including community involvement and development, human rights, consumer issues, labour practices, fair operating practices, and the natural environment, which it views as interdependent in creating the potential for holistic guidance for enterprises interested in operating responsibly.[1] This guidance document is potentially important because ISO is the world's most important standards-setting body, with an international reputation and reach, so its attention to corporate responsibility represents, in a sense, the institutionalization of responsibility at an international level.

Generally Accepted Reporting for ESG. In accounting, generally accepted accounting principles, often known as GAAP, help guide companies in producing financial reports in ways that enable comparison of companies in different industries and even different countries on the basis of their financial performance. While GAAP is far from perfect (consider all the recent business problems, some of which are associated with misreporting), they provide a necessary common standard and language. When companies began issuing ESG, triple/multiple bottom line, environmental, sustainability, and related reports in the mid-1990s, there was no clear common reporting framework analogous to GAAP. At the time, however, there were no clear reporting guidelines, so companies were able to (and still can to some extent) issue their ESG reports in whatever format and with whatever content they wanted.

Then, in 1997, the Global Reporting Initiative (GRI) was established to do just that: to provide generally accepted reporting principles for ESG issues. Today, GRI is the global standard for such reporting, and numerous companies are issuing reports using this framework. Indeed, at the Global Leaders Summit of the UN Global Compact in 2010, the UN Global Compact issued a recommendation that future Communications on Progress, which signatory companies must produce annually, use the GRI framework as their guide, and also report on all ten of the Global Compact principles.

At this writing, there is considerable international conversation about creating what are called integrated reports—that is, financial and ESG reports produced in a common and fully integrated format. An International Integrated Reporting Committee has been established to bring together standard setters and regulatory bodies responsible for individual elements of reporting and attempt to create a common standard for integrated reporting. The goal of this committee, which was established in 2010, is

> to create a globally accepted integrated reporting framework which brings together financial, environmental, social and governance information in a clear, concise, consistent, and comparable format. The aim is to help with the development of more comprehensive and comprehensible information about organizations, prospective as well as retrospective, to meet the needs of a more sustainable, global economy. (International Integrated Reporting Committee, n.d.)

---

[1]More information about ISO 26000 can be found at http://www.iso.org/iso/social_responsibility.

The work of this group is rather new, but with all of the big accounting firms and other accrediting and standards-setting bodies involved in its development and with some progressive firms already beginning to issue integrated reports, integrated reporting is likely to be the way that reporting is done in the future.

Business Associations and Consultancies

To supplement the emerging responsibility assurance infrastructure, a number of other types of business-oriented entities have evolved. Among these is an array of both for- and not-for-profit consultancies that support ESG work, reporting, and monitoring. In addition, there are numerous business membership organizations that now focus on ESG issues.[2] Perhaps the most notable of these are the World Economic Forum and the World Business Council for Sustainable Development.

Global Action Networks

Other developments include what are called Global Action Networks (GANs) (Waddell, 2003, 2011), in which industry actors come together with other interested parties to set standards and do their own monitoring of corporate practice. Examples include the Forest Stewardship Council, the Marine Stewardship Council, the Fair Trade Association, Rugmark, and numerous others. Such groups frequently fall between business associations and multistakeholder coalitions, as they often involve numerous actors outside the industry, who serve as watchdogs and activists with respect to industry issues.

GANs are innovative networks that address important global issues, including climate change, poverty, education, and human security, among others. According to Waddell (2011), GANs have specific characteristics that differentiate them from other types of networks: they are global and multilevel. GANs are entrepreneurial and action oriented and produce public (vs. simply private) goods, that is, goods that benefit the general public, and they embrace diversity, crossing north-south and other boundaries. They are formed as interorganizational networks, not individually oriented, but they are not necessarily structured by markets or the principles of hierarchy, as they tend to be flat and democratically structured. They work toward systems changes, often voluntarily creating new norms and standards that others then have to live by. Both the UN Global Compact and the GRI are examples of GANs in their structure and change orientations.

---

[2]Listings of many of these entities can be found in the tables in my 2008 paper, "Building a New Institutional Infrastructure for Corporate Responsibility," cited in the reference list.

(Socially) Responsible Investing

One arena that taps the market system as it currently exists is responsible (aka social or ethical) investment. The responsible investment movement, with roots in the investment practices of religious orders in the 1950s, began to take shape in earnest in the late 1970s and early 1980s and to mature in the 1990s. The elements of the responsible investment infrastructure include responsible investment funds and firms, including institutional investors such as Calvert, Trillium, PaxWorld, and Domini Social Funds.

There are now multiple indices that track the ESG and stakeholder performance of firms, designating some as suited for responsible investors, omitting others; e.g., the Dow Jones Sustainability Index, the FTSE4Good in England, and the MSCI KLD 400 Index. Supporting social investors today are also numerous country-based ESG research firms operating in many countries around the world. These firms, of which what is now MSCI ESG (launched as KLD in 1990) is the pioneer, gather stakeholder, social, governance, and sustainability data about companies and sell it to the investment community.

The responsible investment movement has also evolved a number of professional organizations, including Social Investment Forums in the United States, United Kingdom, and Europe, and Social Investment Research Analysts Network (SIRAN), and multiple conferences, of which the SRI in the Rockies Conference in the United States is among the most notable. In addition, the social investment world includes multiple professional organizations like the Social Investment Forum and the European Social Investment Forum (EuroSIF).

There are a number of other entities, particularly associations geared to the professional development of the industry or activism around corporate issues that can be raised through investor mechanisms like shareholder resolutions. One well-known entity is the Interfaith Center on Corporate Responsibility (ICCR), which annually submits more than 200 shareholder resolutions encouraging positive corporate change. In addition, there are other groups and associations, such as Coop America, an information resource for social investors, GoodMoney, a nonprofit and publishing company educating investors on social responsibility, and Harvard Kennedy School's Initiative for Responsible Investing (IRI), which provides information, convenings, and other services to socially responsible investors and thought leaders.

Civil Society Forces and Dynamics

Numerous entities in civil society serve as activists and pressure points for companies wanting to be responsible. The UN Global Compact, of course, brings together companies with actors in civil society (NGOs in particular) and governments through the United Nations itself, as well as inviting academic participation and research in Global Compact activities. NGOs, activists, and pressure groups play important roles in civil society in raising issues related to company performance and practices; in putting pressures on companies for positive changes; and in publicizing problems through the Internet, social media, and traditional print and broadcast means. Many of these activist organizations are critical of corporate behaviors and find that the new media allow them ways of getting out the word about company practices quickly and effectively. What these capabilities mean for companies is that they no longer have the option of keeping things private or avoiding public scrutiny, becoming what Tapscott and Ticoll (2003) termed *naked*, or in less colorful language, *transparent*.

This transparency has other consequences for companies, who now find that they actually need to engage with key stakeholders, such as NGOs or pressure groups, who may be critical of their behaviors and strategies. These engagements with civil society stakeholders such as NGOs can occur at the company level, particularly if companies have stakeholder engagement policies and can help companies figure out where future problems and issues might arise before they become problematic. Increasingly, such engagements are also occurring in larger settings in what are called multistakeholder coalitions that come together around particular issues and problems for interaction and sometimes for problem solving.

Transparency is also evident in the numerous ratings and rankings with which companies must now contend—whether they want to or not. Not only have social investors begun evaluating company performance along ESG dimensions that are far broader than just financial performance, but ratings and rankings now regularly appear on a wide range of stakeholder related topics. For example, companies are ranked on their overall corporate citizenship, the way they treat minorities and women, and their reputations, just to mention a few of the many ratings and rankings that now exist.

In addition to engaging with NGOs and other critics, many companies and particularly entities that companies join, like the UN Global Compact, engage with academics and researchers so that they can continue to learn about how to better deal with issues of business in society.

Government Initiatives—Mandate

Governments, too, are frequently interested in corporate practices with respect to ESG issues and since the late 1990s have in many places begun putting into place a range of laws about ESG disclosure. For instance, all companies listed on the French stock exchange must issue triple or multiple bottom line reports, and analysts in the United Kingdom have to disclose how they take ESG issues into consideration in their investment decisions. In China, for example, the state-owned Assets Supervision and Administration Commission, which has a lot of influence in the business community, issued a nonbinding directive strongly encouraging state-owned enterprises to follow sound CSR practices. The governments of Nordic countries, Denmark, Sweden, and Norway, have expressed strong support for companies publishing ESG information. Even in the United States, which tends to lag in legislation on ESG issues, the Securities and Exchange Commission now requires disclosure on the material impact associated with compliance with environmental laws as well as other ESG-related issues that are likely to be material (Lydenberg & Grace, 2009).

Alternative Business Models

In what my collaborator Malcolm McIntosh and I have called SEE Change—change to a sustainable enterprise economy (SEE) (Waddock & McIntosh, 2011), numerous new and emerging business models are also part of the context in which corporate responsibility takes place today. Not only do companies face competitors with dramatically new business models, often based on either social media or the Internet (one only need think of Google, eBay, and Amazon.com to understand how important such models are now), but new types of enterprises are popping up with very different understandings of their role in society than traditional companies have.

Rather than emphasizing solely the maximization of shareholder wealth that has been a corporate mantra since the early 1980s, companies that sign on as *B corporations* begin their lives with a multiple-bottom-line orientation, trying to "do well and do good" at the same time. Some organizations form as social enterprises right from the start—either as businesses with a social goal, but also a desire for profits, or as socially oriented organizations that use business models and practices to achieve their social goals. *Social entrepreneurship* has become an important buzzword—and practice—since Ashoka's founder Bill Drayton began popularizing the term some years ago and particularly since 2006 when the late C. K. Prahalad published his pathbreaking book *The Fortune at the Bottom of the Pyramid*, which argued that companies were passing up business opportunities by not producing relevant products for the nearly four billion people on the planet who are still in either abject or relative poverty compared with the industrialized world.

One example of a business model with a social goal that has been widely adopted (albeit not without criticism or worries about its effectiveness) is that of microfinance. Many large financial institutions have been unable or unwilling to deal effectively with the poor or with small, entrepreneurial businesses. As a result, alternative mechanisms for financing have arisen and spread globally. Microlending, the lending of very small amounts of money to the very poor, using community-based resources to ensure repayment, was pioneered by Dr. Mohammed Yunas in 1976 when he founded the Grameen Bank in Bangladesh, focused predominantly on poor women. Grameen has since expanded its reach to encompass 8.36 million borrowers (97% women), 2,565 branches with services in more than 81,000 villages, and numerous offspring organizations that attempt to help the poor in other ways, like providing phone service or healthy food products (Grameen Bank, 2011). Based on the model provided by Grameen, microfinance organizations can now be found all around the world in both not-for-profit and for-profit forms.

Progress and the Future

As must be clear from this very brief overview and the rest of the chapters in this book, despite all the scandals that businesses have faced and even fostered, the landscape in which they operate today is very different from the laissez-faire atmosphere of the latter part of the 20th century. In the past several decades, the explosion of communication abilities associated with digital technologies has forced transparency on companies, whether they wished to be transparent or not, and numerous other institutions and entities have developed in all sectors that attempt to place constructive pressures on companies for better responsibility performance. Companies have responded by joining initiatives like the UN Global Compact and the many others that now exist, which does not mean that their problems have fully gone away. But it does place companies under significantly more scrutiny from a wide array of stakeholders than was even possible a few decades ago. Combined with the implosion created by the financial meltdown of 2008, the advent of new laws and regulations around corporate responsibility and disclosure, and a looming crisis (which some believe is already here) with respect to climate change and sustainability, it is clear that the economic system in which companies could simply do what they wanted to do without anyone noticing has changed. Indeed, the system in which business exists is itself changing, as the rapid development of the UN Global Compact over its relatively short lifespan attests. Businesses need to coexist with increased public expectations on them and a system that is in crisis itself, even if that crisis is not yet widely recognized within the business community.

The issues associated with the current system, which emphasizes free trade, based on neoliberalism (Cavanagh et al., 2002), have focused some people's attention on developing alternative ways of measuring quality of life and programs. It has long been known that the most used indicator of wealth, gross national product (GNP), is a flawed measure that does not account for many important aspects of life and takes many things, like tragedies and problems, as economic pluses when repairs are done for damages incurred. Thus, strip mining and deforestation for logging are counted as economic benefits—when their environmental and sometimes social consequences are not taken into account at all.

Among the notable new measurement tools are the UN Millennium Goals, which focus on improving life for those people most disadvantaged by the current system. Further, the group Redefining Progress has developed a *genuine progress indicator*, which attempts to measure progress in terms that go well beyond traditional measures of gross domestic product, focusing on real benefits to humanity and the natural environment as pluses and subtracting problematic practices, illness, and the like. The social fund Calvert has worked with futurist Hazel Henderson to develop the Calvert-Henderson Quality of Life Indicators. Other indicators that are broader than GNP include the United Nations' Human Development Index, the Happy Planet Index, and the Gross Happiness Indicator, all of which attempt to get at a definition of welfare or well-being that goes beyond mere financial wealth.

Hopefully, the other chapters in this book and this chapter have made clear that in the future, businesses will need new measures of their own progress to cope with those that are emerging in other parts of societies in which they operate. They will need, as companies that have already signed the Global Compact know, to take into account fundamental principles related to human and natural environmental well-being, and these principles increasingly will need to be incorporated into their business models as part of their social contract—the ability to operate legitimately in societies. They will need to act on those principles authentically, in ways that are integrated into their strategies and business models—not just as add-ons or "do good" activities. Business in the future, in short, needs to understand that it is integrated into society, as an important—but not *the* only important—element of society.

Study/Discussion Questions

1. What does the responsibility infrastructure consist of? How does the author support her contention that there is now an emerging infrastructure for CSR?

2. How does Waddock distinguish between CR and CSR?

3. What are the core elements of the responsibility assurance system and what purpose do they serve?

4. What are SA 8000, AA1000, and ISO 26000, and how do they differ?

5. What is the GRI, and how does it relate to the UN Global Compact?

6. What are the World Economic Forum and the World Business Council for Sustainable Development?

7. What are examples of GANs and what purpose do they serve?

8. What do you think the rise in socially responsible investment funds does to legitimize CSR?

9. Transparency is thought to build trust. Do you agree? Why or why not?

10. What are some examples of the new business models that are emerging to meet growing stakeholder demands that companies "do well and do good"?

References

Buchholz, R. A. (1998). *Principles of environmental management: The greening of business* (2nd ed.). Englewood Cliffs, NJ: Prentice Hall.

Cavanagh, J., Mander, J., Anderson, S., Barker, D., Barlow, M., Bellow, W., . . . Wallach, L. (2002). *Alternatives to economic globalization*. San Francisco, CA: Berrett-Koehler.

Cole, R. E. (1998, Fall). Learning from the quality movement: What did and didn't happen and why? *California Management Review, 41*(1), 43–62.

Crosby, P. B. (1992). *Quality is free: The art of making quality certain*. New York, NY: Mentor Books.

Curkovic, S., Melnyk, S. A., Handfield, R. B., & Calantone, R. (2000, November). Investigating the linkage between total quality management and environmentally responsible manufacturing. *IEEE Transactions on Engineering Management, 47*(4), 444–464.

Deming, W. E. (1982). *Out of the crisis*. Cambridge: Massachusetts Institute of Technology Center for Advanced Engineering Study.

Grameen Bank. (2011). Introduction. Retrieved from http://www.grameen-info.org/index .php?option=com_content&task=view&id=16&Itemid=112

Hart, S. L., & Milstein, M. B. (2003). Creating sustainable value. *Academy of Management Executive, 17*(2), 56–69.

International Integrated Reporting Committee. (n.d.). Mission statement. Retrieved from http://www.theiirc.org/the-iirc/

Leisinger, K. (2002). *Globalization, "minima moralia" and the responsibilities of multinational companies*. Retrieved from http://www.unglobalcompact.org/docs/news_events/9.5/ leisinger.pdf

Lydenberg, S., & Grace, K. (2008). *Innovations in social disclosure outside the United States*. New York, NY: Domini Social Investments and Social Investment Forum.

Rao, A., Carr, L. P., Dambolena, I., Kopp, R. J., Martin J., Rafii, F., & Schlesinger, P. F. (1996). *Total quality management: A cross functional perspective*. New York, NY: Wiley.

Rivoli, P., & Waddock, S. (2011, Winter). "First they ignore you . . .": The time-context dynamic and corporate responsibility. *California Management Review, 53*(2), 87–104.

Tapscott, D., & Ticoll, D. (2003). *The naked corporation: How the age of transparency will revolutionize business*. New York, NY: Free Press.

United Nations. (1999, February 1). Secretary-general proposes global compact on human rights, labour, environment, in address to World Economic Forum in Davos [Press Release SG/SM/6881]. Retrieved from http://www.un.org/News/Press/docs/1999/19990201 .sgsm6881.html

Vogel, D. (2006). *The market for virtue: The potential and limits of corporate social responsibility*. Washington, DC: Brookings Institution Press.

Waddell, S. (2003, Winter). Global action networks: A global invention helping business make globalization work for all. *Journal of Corporate Citizenship, 12*, 27–42.

Waddell, S. (2011). *Global action networks: Creating our future together*. Basingstoke, England: Palgrave Macmillan.

Waddock, S. (2008, August). Building a new institutional infrastructure for corporate responsibility. *Academy of Management Perspectives, 22*(3), 87–108.

Waddock, S., & Bodwell, C. (2007). *Total responsibility management: The manual*. Sheffield, UK: Greenleaf.

Waddock, S., & McIntosh, M. (2011). *SEE Change: Making the transition to a sustainable enterprise economy*. Sheffield, UK: Greenleaf.

Part II

The Ten Principles of the UN Global Compact

"The United Nations Global Compact is a strategic policy initiative for businesses that are committed to aligning their operations and strategies with ten universally accepted principles in the areas of human rights, labour, environment and anti-corruption."

—www.unglobalcompact.org

Human Rights

Principle 1: Businesses should support and respect the protection of internationally proclaimed human rights; and

Principle 2: make sure that they are not complicit in human rights abuses.

Labour

Principle 3: Businesses should uphold the freedom of association and the effective recognition of the right to collective bargaining;

Principle 4: the elimination of all forms of forced and compulsory labour;

Principle 5: the effective abolition of child labour; and

Principle 6: the elimination of discrimination in respect of employment and occupation.

Environment

Principle 7: Businesses should support a precautionary approach to environmental challenges;

Principle 8: undertake initiatives to promote greater environmental responsibility; and

Principle 9: encourage the development and diffusion of environmentally friendly technologies.

Anti-corruption

Principle 10: Businesses should work against corruption in all its forms, including extortion and bribery.

Human Rights

Principles 1 and 2

The first two principles of the UN Global Compact are related to human rights:

Principle 1: Businesses should support and respect the protection of internationally proclaimed human rights; and

Principle 2: make sure that they are not complicit in human rights abuses.

5

Human Rights as
Ethical Imperatives for Business

The UN Global Compact's Human Rights Principles

Florian Wettstein

University of St. Gallen, Switzerland

The subject of business and human rights is one of the fast developing areas in the broader discussion on business ethics and corporate responsibility both in practice and in academia. Today, an ever-growing number of companies are adopting formal human rights policies and, partly as a consequence and partly as an underlying cause, a rather diverse and dynamic discourse has developed on the subject. Needless to say, it has not always been this way. Until recently, human rights have arguably played a rather negligible role in the decision-making processes and strategic outlooks, let alone business plans, of corporations. Some would say that overall, corporations have been much more creative in finding ways to suppress and violate human rights for their own benefit than in finding innovative solutions for their protection and realization. Thus, approaching questions of corporate responsibility specifically through the lens of human rights is a fairly recent occurrence, and it was not until the mid-1990s that a systematic debate on business and human rights started to evolve. The title of Peter Muchlinski's (2001) influential article "Multinational Corporations and Human Rights: Is There a

Problem?" reflects the state of the debate at that time: even only a decade ago, we were still debating whether or not there actually was something to discuss in the intersection of business and human rights.

Once the question is asked, however, the conclusion that there is indeed a problem seems inevitable. Concordantly, the difficulty and subsequent core concern at the heart of what we now call the "business and human rights debate" (Chandler, 2003; Ruggie, 2007, p. 839) is not so much to identify the problems that occur in the intersection of business and human rights, but to make a case for why these problems should actually matter to business. After all, even in cases in which corporate abuse is evident, the conventional view has been that this is not primarily the corporation's own problem, but rather that of the respective government. In other words, responsibility for corporate human rights violations is not primarily to be assigned to the corporation itself, but to the government that has the obligation to protect its citizens from such corporate abuse. Thus, corporate human rights violations have commonly been seen primarily as a failure not of corporate, but of governmental responsibility.

The view that the responsibility for the protection and promotion of human rights rests with governments alone has dominated human rights thinking in the past. As a consequence, all other, that is nongovernmental, institutions have been perceived to have merely indirect human rights obligations, insofar and to the extent as they are assigned to them by the domestic laws of the countries in which they operate (Cragg, 2010, p. 267; United Nations, 2007, p. 12). However, this focus has come under increasing scrutiny in recent years. The globalization of markets in particular has greatly constrained the reach and effectiveness of state action, and the regulation especially of transnational companies in human rights matters has become increasingly difficult. These developments have raised doubts about the effectiveness of the state as the sole protector of people's most basic rights. As a result, the call for extending human rights responsibility to non-state actors in general and into the private sphere in particular has become louder (e.g., Alston, 2005; Clapham, 1993, 2006).

In light of these profound global transformations we are witnessing today, human rights expert David Weissbrodt (2005) calls the persistence of the state centrism that still informs much of conventional human rights thinking "remarkable." Granted that there has been a shift in attention to individual responsibility in matters of war crimes, genocides, and crimes against humanity in general, as Weissbrodt points out, but "there is one category of very powerful non-state actors that has not received sufficient attention," and those are "transnational corporations and, indeed, all businesses" (pp. 282–283). It is in this context that the human rights principles of the UN Global Compact must be interpreted and in which they aim at filling a crucial void. Before having a closer look at these principles, however, it is worth adding a few brief remarks on the nature of human rights in general.

Why Human Rights?

In 1948, the General Assembly of the United Nations adopted the Universal Declaration of Human Rights in the hopes of preventing a repetition of the horrors of the Holocaust and World War II. Consisting of 30 articles, the Universal Declaration spells out the most fundamental rights to be enjoyed by all human beings irrespective of their nationality, race and color, gender, or sexual orientation and establishes them as a foundational part of international law. Since its inception, the Universal Declaration has been complemented by the two Covenants on social, economic, and cultural rights and on civil and political rights, respectively. Together, these documents are known as the International Bill of Human Rights.

While such documents define the legal or political dimension of human rights, they are not, in essence, constitutive for human rights as such. The existence and validity of human rights is independent of their legal or political codification; their foundation is a distinctly moral one. In fact, only the moral foundation of human rights can lend such political or legal interpretations and manifestations justification in the first place. Thus, human rights are, in essence, to be understood as prepolitical and prelegal, that is, as moral rights. They are, in Amartya Sen's (2004) words, "quintessentially ethical articulations, and they are not, in particular, putative legal claims" (p. 321).

Human rights are those rights that we are said to have simply by virtue of being human. Thus, they apply to all human beings in equal fashion. They are based on and protect the inherent and distinct human dignity of all human beings, which undeniably derives from their status as moral persons, that is, as persons endowed with the capacity to respect themselves and their surroundings. It is this capacity that defines human beings as autonomous subjects, and it is the autonomy of human beings that human rights aim at protecting. Human rights, in other words, protect our most fundamental freedoms, that is, the freedoms necessary to live a truly human and thus dignified life. The moral imperative deriving from human rights, as a result, is of the most fundamental kind; it trumps all other moral considerations, which are not themselves based on human rights. In particular, and perhaps especially relevant when discussing human rights in the business context, this includes considerations based on mere utility.

In essence, there is nothing we must do or be other than being human in order to deserve and insist on our human rights, and there is nothing that we or anyone else can do to justifiably lose them. This is not to say that human rights cannot be infringed on, sometimes justifiably, but this does not negate the *existence* of those rights as such; if anything, it presupposes it. Human rights, in sum, are universal (they apply to all human beings); equal (they apply to all human beings equally); and inalienable (they cannot be revoked from or given up by any human being) rights. As such, they represent the normative floor, that is, the moral minimum in regard to the decent treatment of human beings anywhere and irrespective of legal or cultural contexts. This alone makes them a powerful platform and reference point for the formulation of cross-cultural ethics and thus an almost natural starting point for our reflections on corporate responsibility in an increasingly global marketplace.

Principle 1: Direct Human Rights Responsibilities for Corporations

According to the UN Global Compact's first principle, "businesses should support and respect the protection of internationally proclaimed human rights." While this formulation does not challenge governments or states as the primary responsibility bearers for human rights, it does assume a direct, rather than merely an indirect, obligation for business to "respect" or "not infringe"[1] on human rights alongside governments. As such, Principle 1 stands in direct contrast to the state-centrism that characterizes conventional human rights thinking as outlined above. By assigning human rights responsibility directly to transnational institutions such as multinational corporations, it aims at filling the gap or incongruence between the nonterritorial nature of human rights and their violation on the one hand and the territorial limitation of governmental human rights protection on the other. Hence, corporations signing up to the Global Compact pledge to respect human rights on a voluntary basis even if or precisely when domestic laws fail to hold them accountable for it.

Despite the dominant view that only governments can have international legal personalities and be subject to international legislation, there is a good case to be made that the foundations of such corporate human rights responsibilities can, in fact, be found in international human rights law as well. For example, the Universal Declaration of Human Rights, even though principally focusing on nation-states, does not per se exclude other institutions as addressees, but explicitly states in its

---

[1]http://www.unglobalcompact.org/AboutTheGC/TheTenPrinciples/principle1.html

preamble that it applies to "every individual and every organ of society" (Weissbrodt, 2005, p. 283; Pegg, 2003, p. 16). Furthermore, at least in regard to a most basic responsibility to respect human rights, articles 29 and 30 of the Universal Declaration state that not only states, but *any person or group* must resist performing any action that might pose a threat to human rights (Frey, 1997, p. 163). Similarly, articles 5 of both Covenants state that

> Nothing in the present Covenant may be interpreted as implying for *any State, group or person* [italics added] any right to engage in any activity or to perform any act aimed at the destruction of any of the rights or freedoms recognized herein, or at their limitation to a greater extent than is provided for in the present Covenant.

As such, the principal and conceptual basis for extending the scope of international human rights legislation into the private sphere and thus into the corporate realm, it seems, would be given.

However, one does not need to and perhaps should not rely primarily on international legislation to justify a corporate responsibility to respect human rights as stipulated in the Global Compact's first principle. As elaborated in-depth above, the imperative deriving from human rights is first and foremost a moral one. In other words, human rights responsibilities of corporations are primarily moral responsibilities; corporations have them irrespective of what the law says. In fact, only a complete disregard of the moral status and foundation of human rights can lead one to conclude that governments should be the only parties directly obligated by human rights. If we hold that human rights represent inherent and equal moral entitlements of all human beings irrespective of their heritage and background, we cannot deny that they logically obligate not just governments, but everyone. Thus, taking the moral nature of human rights seriously means to engage in a much broader dialogue on potential duties and duty-bearers at the outset, rather than limiting them to governments, whose capabilities to cope with human rights problems on their own might already be severely compromised. By stipulating direct human rights responsibility for corporations, Principle 1 of the UN Global Compact provides the institutional foundation that is necessary for doing so.

Principle 2: Corporate Complicity in Human Rights Abuses

While direct and often overt and blatant human rights abuse by corporations occurs frequently, an even more pervasive and perhaps a more challenging problem to deal with involve indirect human rights violations. Indirect human rights violations are violations that are not committed by the corporation itself, but to which it has contributed in some significant way nevertheless.[2] Because of the special nature of such cases of corporate complicity, the UN Global Compact addresses them in a separate human rights principle, i.e., in Principle 2.

In general terms, corporate complicity can be defined as "aiding and abetting" a violation of human rights committed by a third party (e.g., Clapham & Jerbi, 2001, p. 340; Kobrin, 2009, p. 351; Ramasastry, 2002, p. 95). Three specifications are of particular importance when deciding whether or not a corporation meets the condition of aiding and abetting in the context of human rights violations:

- First, it is unimportant whether or not the corporation actually wanted or intended to contribute to a wrongdoing; no malicious intent is needed for a corporation to become complicit in human rights violations. In fact, one of the challenges of dealing with such cases of complicity is precisely that they do not readily fit in our conventional paradigm of individual, intentional wrongdoing (Kutz, 2000, p. 1). They are rarely based on a corporation's deliberate assault on the rights of people, but instead often derive from a corporation's regular business conduct, which would be unconcerning outside of the given context.
- Second, while malicious intent is not a requirement for complicity, what is needed is knowledge. In other words, it is necessary that the corporation knows or should know, or to be precise, could reasonably be expected to know that its actions may, in one way or the other, contribute to the violation of human rights. Only a corporation that knowingly contributes to the violation of human rights can justifiably be accused of complicity (Clapham & Jerbi, 2001, p. 342).
- Third, for a corporation to become complicit in a human rights violation, its contribution needs to have a substantial effect on it. However, it does not need to be indispensible. Substantiality must be interpreted widely; it does not only include individual actions of great magnitude and scope, but also ongoing supporting activities with small individual impacts over a significant time period (Ramasastry, 2002, p. 150). Hence, even corporations that merely

---

[2]Note the different use of the terms *direct* and *indirect* here: while in the previous section I referred to direct or indirect human rights obligations, I am now speaking of direct and indirect violations of human rights. Having direct human rights obligations means that corporations are held directly responsible for their human rights conduct. On the other hand, a direct human rights violation is one that occurs as a direct result of the corporation's conduct, i.e., corporations can be held directly responsible for both direct (Principle 1) and indirect (Principle 2) human rights violations.

facilitate human rights violations rather than directly contribute to them can justifiably be accused of complicity (Clapham, 2004, p. 68).[3]

Commonly, the literature distinguishes between three types of complicity that are based on the kind of contribution the company is making toward the human rights violation: direct complicity, beneficial complicity, and silent complicity (e.g., Clapham & Jerbi, 2001, pp. 342–350). These three categories of complicity are the basis also for the second principle of the UN Global Compact.

Direct complicity occurs if a corporation directly and actively contributes to or assists in the violation of human rights committed by a third party. It does not require involvement in a sense that the corporation is actually carrying out a part of the rights violation, but it presupposes a direct, tangible contribution to it. A corporation that knowingly makes available its facilities or offers equipment to authorities for the interrogation and torture of protesters, unionists, or other groups of people, for example, can be accused of direct complicity. In the year 1997, police forces in India used helicopters provided by Enron Corporation to survey and violently suppress demonstrations and protests by activists (Human Rights Watch, 1999). Also, Yahoo's history of handing over confidential information about user accounts of Chinese dissidents to the Chinese government can be interpreted as a case of direct complicity. In some instances, even the mere payment of taxes in oppressive regimes can be problematic, since it can be seen as a contribution to the financing of structures that bolster the regime and perpetuate systematic violations of human rights (e.g., Howen, 2005, p. 14).

In contrast to direct complicity, beneficial complicity does not require an active contribution on the part of the company, but "merely" that it benefits from the human rights violations committed by a third party. Thus, a corporation does not even have to provide equipment for a violent crackdown of demonstrations to run the risk of being accused of complicity; it may be enough for the corporation to derive a substantial benefit from it over an extended period of time. For example, the suppression of protests that are targeting oil companies such as Shell or BP for the environmental destruction they are causing may benefit the companies insofar as it protects them from disruptions in their production processes. If the companies accept such benefits over an extended period of time, they may rightfully be accused of beneficial complicity. Note that the distinction between a legal and a moral perspective on human rights is of particular importance in such cases; while

---

[3]Note that, from a deontological point of view, any knowing contribution to human rights violations by corporations would per se have to be considered ethically problematic; substantiality would then not be needed as a necessary condition.

it seems difficult to make a legal case for beneficial complicity in the absence of an actual contribution to the human rights violation by the corporation, it certainly does provide a sufficient basis to attach moral blame.

There is growing agreement that even without benefit the mere silence or inactivity of a corporation in the face of human rights abuses can denote a form of complicity. A bystander who has the ability to act but chooses to remain silent when the rights of people are trampled underfoot risks being perceived as condoning the human rights violation and as lending its moral support to the perpetrator (Wettstein, 2010). Its silence, in other words, may have a legitimizing, encouraging, or emboldening effect on the party that violates human rights. The notion of silent complicity, as Clapham and Jerbi (2001) comment, "reflects the growing acceptance within companies that there is something culpable about failing to exercise influence in such circumstances" (p. 348). And as Margaret Jungk (1999) from the Danish Center for Human Rights concludes: "even where a company's operations do not directly impact upon human rights issues, the company may nonetheless be called upon to speak out or act when an oppressive government violates its citizens' rights" (p. 171).

In a recent article, Brenkert (2009) added a fourth category of corporate complicity, which he calls "obedient complicity" (p. 459). Obedient complicity, according to Brenkert, occurs "when a business follows laws or regulations of a government to act in ways that support its activities that intentionally and significantly violate people's human rights." In other words, corporate activities that may be entirely unconcerning outside of the context of oppressive laws may turn into complicity if they are undertaken in compliance with laws that are designed to violate human rights (Brenkert, 2009, p. 459). The case of Google's compliance with Chinese censorship laws is a prominent and instructive example to illustrate this. As an institution of the private sector, as Brenkert points out, Google is free to choose and decide what information to make available to its users. Google, in other words, "is not obligated to provide any particular piece of information to its users" (Brenkert, 2009, p. 459). However, if the blocking of information is carried out to comply with laws that are designed by a government to prevent people from accessing information, it must be considered a form of complicity. The reason for this is that in contrast to Google, the government that is enforcing such laws does have an obligation not to arbitrarily block and censor the information that its citizens seek to access. By complying with such laws, Google is assisting the Chinese government in the violation of the human right to free expression stipulated in article 19 of the Universal Declaration of Human Rights.

Brenkert's point is well taken; understanding such more subtle forms of complicity is of key importance for the assessment of corporate wrongdoing in today's global age. However, it seems that if we extend direct human rights responsibility into the corporate realm, as is done in the first principle of the UN Global Compact, then it is at least questionable whether Google really has no obligation outside of the context of oppressive laws in regard to what and how much information it makes available to its users. If human rights are to protect human beings from abuse of power in general rather than merely from the power of governments, then Google too must have a responsibility to uphold the right to free access to information quite independently from any government action or policy.

Irrespective of whether in the case of Google in China we are dealing with direct or obedient complicity or even with a direct violation of human rights, the company's announcement in 2009 that it would no longer comply with Chinese censorship laws even if it meant to withdraw from the vast Chinese market was widely commended within the human rights community because it was a rare showing of a company actually taking a stance for the protection of human rights even at a potentially substantial economic cost to itself. However, the fact that the respect and protection of human rights may not always pay for companies and that it often comes at an actual cost raises the uncomfortable question of whether the UN Global Compact really can be sufficient in ensuring the protection of human rights in the economic realm. I will briefly address this question in the concluding section of this chapter.

Business and Human Rights: What's Next?

The fundamental nature of human rights and of the moral imperative deriving from them does not sit well with a merely voluntary commitment of corporations to respect them. While nearly 9,000 subscribers to the UN Global Compact certainly make for a success story without precedent in regard to such voluntary codes and standards, it cannot be denied that they still represent only a marginal share of businesses operating worldwide. Granted that the Global Compact includes many of the largest and most visible companies operating in global markets today, a vast number of less exposed companies are still flying entirely under the public radar when it comes to their human rights conduct. This raises two central questions in regard to the effectiveness of voluntary human rights principles: first, can the impact of voluntary standards be more than a drop in the bucket relative to the global human rights situation? Second and connected to it, can a voluntary code sufficiently level the playing field so that those companies who are serious in their commitment will not be put at a competitive disadvantage relative to the laggards in the market? It seems that the first question crucially depends on how we answer the second one, and I am afraid that the answer to the second question is negative.

In order to truly level the playing field and to prevent irresponsible players in the field from undercutting and outperforming their more responsible peers, the establishment of a mandatory standard would be key. While Google sent an important message by putting human rights responsibilities over future profits, we can safely assume and in fact know that not all corporations would act the same way. For any corporation forgoing profits in the name of integrity there are others that will gladly jump in the void. As long as this unfortunate truth prevails, only a mandate for corporations to respect human rights can solicit the kind of commitment needed to have a profound and lasting impact on the global human rights situation.

In 1998, a working group of the Sub-Commission on the Promotion and Protection of Human Rights launched an attempt to establish such a binding and thus enforceable human rights code in the form of the "Norms on the Responsibilities of Transnational Corporations and Other Business Enterprises with Regard to Human Rights" (UN Draft Norms). In large part, the UN Draft Norms reflected and were based on existing international human rights norms such as, for example, the Universal Declaration of Human Rights or the two Covenants. In 2003, the working group submitted its draft to the Sub-Commission, which subsequently handed it on to the UN Commission on Human Rights for formal approval. However, the UN Draft Norms faced harsh opposition from prominent exponents of the business community that perceived them as a "legal error" (International Chamber of Commerce & International Organization of Employers [ICC/IOE], 2004, p. 3) and "an extreme case of privatization of human rights" (ICC/IOE, 2004, p. 2). Human rights obligations, as they argued, apply to corporations on a strictly voluntary basis since only states can directly be held responsible under international human rights law. They called the UN Draft Norms a danger to the progress achieved by the UN Global Compact and a threat to the very institution of human rights as such (ICC/IOE, 2004, p. 1). Faced with such criticism, the Commission rejected the UN Draft Norms, which meant that the project had effectively failed.[4]

Despite the ultimate failure of the UN Draft Norms, the need for a more institutionalized discourse on business and human rights became apparent during the heated discussion that accompanied their drafting process. The subsequent creation of the position of the UN secretary-general's special representative on business and human rights (SRSG) in 2005 can be interpreted as a direct result of this insight. Harvard professor John Ruggie became the first SRSG and was tasked, among

---

[4]For more information on the UN Draft Norms see Weissbrodt (2005), Weissbrodt and Kruger (2005), and Arnold (2010, pp. 373–376).

other things, with identifying and clarifying standards for corporate human rights responsibility as well as contrasting them with the role of states as regulators and primary responsibility bearers. Special emphasis was put on researching and clarifying the concept of complicity in regard to corporate human rights abuse. It is hardly a coincidence that Professor Ruggie's mandate was very much aimed at the further specification of the broad areas of relevance identified already by the UN Global Compact.

In 2008, Ruggie published two much anticipated and widely shared reports on these questions that concluded his first tenure as SRSG (United Nations, 2008a, 2008b). The reports outline a tripartite framework consisting of a corporate responsibility to *respect* all human rights, the state duty to *protect* human rights, and the need for more effective access to *remedy* in cases of human rights abuse. Thus, according to the SRSG's framework, corporations are expected and obligated to respect all human rights in their interactions with their stakeholders, while states are obligated to protect their citizens from corporate human rights abuse. Both the state and the corporations share a responsibility to put adequate grievance mechanisms in place for the victims of human rights violations. Granted that Ruggie's framework is neither binding nor enforceable in a way that the UN Draft Norms were supposed to be, but it is based on the premise that all corporations have direct human rights responsibilities irrespective of any prior voluntary commitment. As such, it takes a crucial step beyond the UN Global Compact and makes a big contribution toward establishing direct corporate human rights obligations as a constitutive part of contemporary human rights thinking.

Nonetheless, in its current state, the framework merely establishes a platform or reference point to assign blame to corporations that fail to respect human rights, but not, however, mechanisms and instruments to enforce such a responsibility and hold them accountable for it. In order to make this possible, the establishment of a mandatory human rights code similar to the UN Draft Norms will be inevitable in the long run. The UN Global Compact will be of crucial importance not only for filling the void in the meantime, but also for the facilitation of the discussion and debates we must necessarily have to eventually get there.

Study/Discussion Questions

1. What is a human right? Generally, whose role is it to protect human rights?

2. Do you agree or disagree that there is a place in business for a discussion of human rights? Why or why not? Why should human rights matter to business?

3. What are three attributes of human rights? What does the author mean when he says they are the starting point for any corporate responsibility discussion?

4. What constitutes complicity? What are the three types a company needs to be aware of?

5. Why did one author see the need for the fourth category? What is a recent example that exemplifies this type of complicity?

6. Should mere silence be considered a form of complicity? Should a corporation use its influence to press foreign governments to improve their human rights record?

7. Does a corporation's human rights responsibility stop with a duty to respect human rights, or should corporations take proactive measures to promote and realize human rights?

8. Do you agree that only governments can be responsible for human rights? Why or why not?

9. What business processes might be affected by human rights considerations? What might be a process for integrating human rights considerations into a company?

10. In your opinion, what contribution can a voluntary approach like the UN Global Compact make? Do we need mandated human rights rules for corporations? If so, who should develop them, and how should they be enforced?

For Cases Relevant to Human Rights Principles, See Pages 149 to 234

Killer Coke: The Campaign Against Coca-Cola
Henry W. Lane, David T. A. Wesley

Google in China
Deborah Compeau, Prahar Shah

Ethics of Offshoring: Novo Nordisk and Clinical Trials in Emerging Economies
Klaus Meyer

Talisman Energy Inc.
Lawrence G. Tapp, Gail Robertson

References

Alston, P. (Ed.). (2005). *Non-state actors and human rights*. New York, NY: Oxford University Press.

Arnold, D. (2010). Transnational corporations and the duty to respect basic human rights. *Business Ethics Quarterly*, 20(3), 371–399.

Brenkert, G. G. (2009). Google, human rights, and moral compromise. *Journal of Business Ethics*, 85(4), 453–478.

Chandler, G. (2003). The evolution of the business and human rights debate. In R. Sullivan (Ed.), *Business and human rights: Dilemmas and solutions* (pp. 22–32). Sheffield, UK: Greenleaf.

Clapham, A. (1993). *Human rights in the private sphere*. Oxford, UK: Clarendon Press.

Clapham, A. (2004). State responsibility, corporate responsibility, and complicity in human rights violations. In L. Bomann-Larsen & O. Wiggen (Eds.), *Responsibility in world business: Managing harmful side-effects of corporate activity* (pp. 50–81). New York, NY: United Nations University Press.

Clapham, A. (2006). *Human rights obligations of non-state actors*. Oxford, UK: Oxford University Press.

Clapham, A., & Jerbi, S. (2001). Categories of corporate complicity in human rights abuses. *Hastings International and Comparative Law Review*, 24, 339–350.

Cragg, W. (2010). Business and human rights: A principle and value-based analysis. In G. G. Brenkert & T. L. Beauchamp (Eds.), *The Oxford handbook of business ethics* (pp. 267–304). Oxford, UK: Oxford University Press.

Frey, B. A. (1997). The legal and ethical responsibilities of transnational corporations in the protection of international human rights. *Minnesota Journal of Global Trade*, 6, 153–188.

Howen, N. (2005). Responsibility and complicity from the perspective of international human rights law. In M. Shinn (Ed.), *The 2005 business & human rights seminar report: Exploring responsibility and complicity* (pp. 12–15). London, England: Business & Human Rights Seminar.

Human Rights Watch. (1999). *The Enron corporation: Corporate complicity in human rights violations*. Retrieved from http://www.hrw.org/reports/1999/enron/

International Chamber of Commerce & International Organization of Employers. (2004). Joint views of the IOE and ICC on the draft "Norms on the responsibilities of transnational corporations and other business enterprises with regards to human rights." Retrieved from http://www.reports-and-materials.org/IOE-ICC-views-UN-norms-March-2004.doc

Jungk, M. (1999). A practical guide to addressing human rights concerns for companies operating abroad. In M. K. Addo (Ed.), *Human rights standards and the responsibility of transnational corporations* (pp. 171–183). The Hague, The Netherlands: Kluwer Law International.

Kobrin, S. J. (2009). Private political authority and public responsibility: Transnational politics, transnational firms and human rights. *Business Ethics Quarterly*, 19(3), 349–374.

Kutz, C. (2000). *Complicity: Ethics and law for a collective age.* Cambridge, UK: Cambridge University Press.

Muchlinski, P. (2001). Human rights and multinationals: Is there a problem? *International Affairs*, 77(1), 31–47.

Pegg, S. (2003). An emerging market for the new millennium: Transnational corporations and human rights. In J. G. Frynas & S. Pegg (Eds.), *Transnational corporations and human rights*. Basingstoke, England: Palgrave Macmillan.

Ramasastry, A. (2002). Corporate complicity: From Nuremberg to Rangoon. An examination of forced labor cases and their impact on the liability of multinational corporations. *Berkeley Journal of International Law*, 20(1), 91–159.

Ruggie, J. G. (2007). Business and human rights: The evolving international agenda. *American Journal of International Law*, 101, 819–840.

Sen, A. (2004). Elements of a theory of human rights. *Philosophy and Public Affairs*, 32(4), 315–356.

United Nations. (2007). Business and human rights: Mapping international standards of responsibility and accountability for corporate acts [Report by John Ruggie, A/HRC/4/35]. Retrieved from http://www.business-humanrights.org/Documents/RuggieHRC2007

United Nations. (2008a). Clarifying the concepts of "sphere of influence" and "complicity" [Report by John Ruggie, A/HRC/8/16]. Retrieved from http://www.reports-and-materials.org/Ruggie-companion-report-15-May-2008.pdf

United Nations. (2008b). Protect, respect and remedy: A framework for business and human rights [Report by John Ruggie, A/HRC/8/5]. Retrieved from http://www.reports-and-materials.org/Ruggie-report-7-Apr-2008.pdf

Weissbrodt, D. (2005). Corporate human rights responsibilities. *Zeitschrift für Wirtschafts- und Unternehmensethik*, 6(3), 279–297.

Weissbrodt, D., & Kruger, M. (2003). Norms on the responsibilities of transnational corporations and other business enterprises with regard to human rights. *American Journal of International Law*, 97, 901–922.

Wettstein, F. (2010). The duty to protect: Corporate complicity, political responsibility, and human rights advocacy. *Journal of Business Ethics*, 96(1), 33–47.

Labour

Principles 3, 4, 5, and 6

The four principles of the UN Global Compact related to labour are

Principle 3: Businesses should uphold the freedom of association and the effective recognition of the right to collective bargaining;

Principle 4: the elimination of all forms of forced and compulsory labour;

Principle 5: the effective abolition of child labour; and

Principle 6: the elimination of discrimination in respect of employment and occupation.

6

Our Role as Managers in Understanding and Fulfilling the Labour Principles of the UN Global Compact

Michael J. D. Roberts

Richard Ivey School of Business, Western University

There are few things in our modern industrial societies that divide us as much as our attitudes toward organized labour and labour laws. In fact, at the core of many of our political parties is a professed alignment with organized labour or with business interests. Stories that highlight the successes and failures of firms to generate wealth and distribute it in an equitable manner and stories that demonstrate the value and detriment of organized labour to our free-market system are the straw that politicians and pundits use to make hay. In fact, your stance toward the organized labour movement is a major determinant of whether you are seen as being on the so called "left" or "right" of the political spectrum.

The goal of this chapter then is for us to temporarily suspend our biases for or against the organized labour movement as we have experienced it and to consider at a more fundamental level the value of supporting principles that promote the rights of people in their roles as labourers. This is not an easy task as we all have our own experiences that have deeply shaped our opinions. Perhaps some of us have been raised in families that were able to feed, clothe, and educate us because our parents were represented by large and powerful unions. Perhaps others are from cities that seem to be imploding due to the high cost of labour and perceived inflexibility of union bosses that represent workers. We may view the rights of labour as an issue only affecting developing countries and that those in the developed world have moved beyond the need for a labour movement. The newspapers we read, the TV channels we watch, and even the academic departments in which we study all influence our political opinion of this topic.

As students of business administration, there are guiding principles that we need not suspend when discussing this topic. The first is the superiority of the free-market economy[1] over a command economy[2] to organize our economic activity. The second is a commitment to democracy.[3] The labour principles of the UN Global Compact are built on the principles of the free-market economy and democracy. A market cannot be free, however, when the power differential between a buyer and seller is too great. Ideally, the free market is based on a system of many buyers and many sellers. When the number of buyers and sellers is sufficiently large and equal, no party will have the power to extract a large economic rent. Thus, a free and fair market for labour requires that labourers and the firms that employ them enjoy a reasonably equitable amount of power in negotiating a wage.

However, the labour market in industrial society often has a large number of potential sellers of labour (individual labourers) and a relatively smaller number of buyers (firms). Thus, in the absence of collective bargaining rights, the power differential between labour and firms is strongly on the side of firms. In addition, a

---

[1]A free-market economy is an "economic system . . . in which most of the means of production are privately owned, and production is guided and income distributed largely through the operation of markets" ("Capitalism," 2011). The markets are controlled by free buyers and sellers.

[2]A command economy is an "economic system in which the means of production are publicly owned and economic activity is controlled by a central authority" ("Command Economy," 2011). Central planners determine the assortment of goods to be produced, allocate raw materials, fix quotas for each enterprise, and set prices. Most communist countries have had command economies.

[3]Democracy is "a philosophy that insists on the right and the capacity of a people, acting either directly or through representatives, to control their institutions for their own purposes. Such a philosophy places a high value on the equality of individuals and would free people as far as possible from restraints not self-imposed. It insists that necessary restraints be imposed only by the consent of the majority and that they conform to the principle of equality" ("Democracy," 2011).

market cannot be free when coercive measures are used to force compliance. A free market requires that the seller has a reasonable opportunity to refuse to sell. If the refusal to sell would result in the seller suffering death or great injury, the market cannot be said to be free. Thus, in a free market, workers must be able to refuse work agreements without that refusal having grave consequences for them or their families, and they must have an equitable amount of power to negotiate a fair price for their labour.

The UN Global Compact labour principles flow from these fundamental principles of power and freedom—fundamental principles that also underpin our free-market economy. The large numbers of businesses that embrace these principles recognize that their long-term success and the sustainability of our economic system are linked to the development of freedom and democracy in society. To this end, the UN Global Compact has four labour principles:

Principle 3: Businesses should uphold the freedom of association and the effective recognition of the right to collective bargaining;

Principle 4: the elimination of forced or compulsory labour;

Principle 5: the effective abolition of child labour; and

Principle 6: the elimination of discrimination in respect of employment and occupation.

History

According to the International Labour Office (2008), the UN International Labour Organization (ILO) is responsible for establishing international labour standards. The membership of the ILO is drawn from businesses, governments, and employee groups. With the expansion of Multinational Corporations (MNCs) to newly developing parts of the world, the ILO codified four categories of basic labour principles and rights that can help guide employers. These principles and rights are especially important in countries where governments are not actively protecting the basic labour rights of their citizens. In 1995, through eight core conventions (see Exhibit 6.1), the ILO codified these four basic labour rights into conventions that led to the creation of the ILO Declaration on Fundamental Principles and Rights at Work in 1998. The Declaration asserts that all states belonging to the ILO have an obligation to respect, promote, and ensure employer compliance to the principles concerning the fundamental rights of workers as laid out in the declaration.

Exhibit 6.1   Core Labour Conventions

Freedom of association and the right to collective bargaining
- Freedom of Association and Protection of the Right to Organize Convention (No. 87), 1948
- Right to Organize and Collective Bargaining Convention (No. 98), 1949

Forced Labour
- Forced Labour Convention (No. 29), 1930
- Abolition of Forced Labour Convention (No. 105), 1957

Child Labour
- Minimum Age Convention (No. 138), 1973
- Worst Forms of Child Labour Convention (No. 182), 1999

Discrimination in Respect of Employment and Occupation
- Equal Remuneration Convention (No. 100), 1951
- Discrimination (Employment and Occupation) Convention (No. 111), 1958

Source: International Labour Office (2008).

While other documents lay out more specific policies and standards, these four principles are considered fundamental rights.

Principle 3: Freedom of Association and Right to Collective Bargaining

The first core labour principle essentially states that workers have the right to form unions. While unions may have an expanded role in developed countries, their fundamental purpose is to engage in collective bargaining on behalf of their members. The International Labour Office (2008) states that "collective bargaining is a voluntary process through which employers and workers discuss and negotiate their relations, in particular terms and conditions of work. Participants include employers and employees" (p. 15). In general, the employees are represented by a trade union that they have freely elected. Collective bargaining not only gives workers more equitable power in the process of selling their labour, but it also helps create a stable and reliable labour source for firms. Upon the successful conclusion of a labour agreement, a firm will enjoy an extended period of labour stability at a fixed price.

In order to make collective bargaining a viable option, nations need to enact a legal framework that allows this to be a constructive process. Because management/labour relations involve the forming of complex organizations to negotiate detailed contracts that need to be enforced over long periods of time, stable regulations by governments are needed to ensure that the process is not corrupted and that parties live up to their agreements. As the stakes are most often very high for both parties in a labour relationship, the potential for societal instability and even violence are high when the process is poorly managed and viewed as corrupt.

In order to form a labour union that truly represents the workers, individuals must have freedom of association for the purpose of forming a labour group:

> Freedom of association implies a respect for the right of all employers and workers to freely and voluntarily establish and join groups for the promotion and defence of their occupational interests. Workers and employers have the right to set up, join and run their own organizations without interference from the State or any other entity. Employers should not interfere in workers' decision to associate, try to influence their decision in any way, or discriminate against either those workers who choose to associate or those who act as their representatives. (International Labour Office, 2008, p. 15)

The United Nations adopted the Freedom of Association and Protection of the Right to Organise Convention in 1948 (No. 87). This convention sets out the rights and guarantees of workers and employers. Some of the key elements of this convention are that labourers and managers have the right to form their own organizations or associations and allow members to join those associations without inference from any governmental or private agent. Membership criteria are subject only to the rules of the organizations. Second, the rules and constitutions of those organizations and the people elected to govern them must be democratically established and elected by the members. The associations must have full freedom to organize their administration and activities without interference from outside parties. Third, these organizations shall not be arbitrarily dissolved or otherwise influenced by agents of the state. Fourth, these organizations shall have the right to associate and form alliances with other like-minded domestic and international organizations.

The Roles of Responsible Managers

In order to promote the freedom of association of their employees, managers should work to remove barriers in the workplace, at the bargaining table, and in society at large. In the workplace, management should, in keeping with national laws, respect employees' rights to join or form a union and not threaten them with reprisal or engage in intimidation. Firms should not discriminate against unionized workers in the areas of advancement, dismissal, or transfer. In addition, managers need to provide union representatives with sufficient facilities and support to assist in the process of negotiating and ratifying a collective agreement.

At the bargaining table, it is important that managers not attempt to undermine the negotiation power of the trade union by attempting to negotiate with individual workers. The managers must respect that the trade union, which must have been elected from a majority of the employees for which it is bargaining, has the right to bargain for a collective agreement. Second, firms must send representatives who are able to make decisions and enter into agreements on behalf of the firm. Third, the managers must disclose a reasonable amount of financial and other information to the trade union to ensure that there is not knowledge asymmetry. The trade union must know what the management knows about the financial situation of the firm in order to negotiate a fair and equitable wage. Also, the management must attempt to "address any problem-solving or other needs of interest to workers and management, including restructuring and training, redundancy procedures, safety and health issues, grievance and dispute settlement procedures, and disciplinary rules" (International Labour Office, 2008, p. 19).

Above all, at the bargaining table, all parties must adhere to an honest policy of bargaining in good faith. This means that both parties must be honestly attempting to reach an agreement that can be mutually accepted. Collective bargaining can only function effectively if it is conducted freely and in good faith by all parties. This implies that all parties should make an "effort to reach an agreement; carry out genuine and constructive negotiations; avoid unjustified delays; respect the agreements concluded and apply them in good faith; and give sufficient time for the parties to discuss and settle collective disputes" (International Labour Office, 2008, p. 16).

In society at large, firms should take an active role to promote free association and collective bargaining with national employers' organizations. Managers should also seek to enhance the overall climate of "labour-management relations, especially in those countries without an adequate institutional and legal framework for recognizing trade unions and for collective bargaining," and responsible firms should "inform their local community, media and public authorities of company endorsement of the UN Global Compact and the company's intention to respect the provisions, including those on fundamental workers' rights" (International Labour Office, 2008, p. 19).

Principle 4: Elimination of Forced and Compulsory Labour

While many of us would like to believe that a discussion of forced labour and slavery belongs in our history books, the increased mobility of migrant labourers, who often have extremely limited protection under the law, has made modern slavery and indentured servitude a real problem not only in developing but also in developed countries. As an anecdote, a recent article in the *Globe and Mail* reported on a 21-year-old African woman who was lured to Canada under the false pretense of a job in a hair salon, only to be enslaved in a house and made to work 18 hours a day without pay ("RCMP Charge West Vancouver Woman," 2011). Police investigating the crime admit that while human trafficking for the purpose of slavery is not common in Canada, it does exist. According to the International Labour Office (2008),

> Forced or compulsory labour is any work or service that is exacted from any person under the menace of any penalty, and for which that person has not offered himself or herself voluntarily. Providing wages or other compensation to a worker does not necessarily indicate that the labour is not forced or compulsory. By right, labour should be freely given and employees should be free to leave, subject to previous notice of reasonable length. (p. 21)

Kidnapping or luring workers into jobs with little or no pay and with no opportunity, or no reasonable opportunity, to leave constitutes forced labour, and it is a real problem throughout the world. While the largest percentage of victims of forced labour are poor women and children in developing countries, men—especially migrant workers—also suffer from this injustice of forced labour even while working in more developed countries. According to the International Labour Office (2008), children represent at least 40% of all victims (p. 21).

Forced labour occurs throughout the world. While it is most prevalent in less developed countries, it occurs in the developed world where it affects mainly trafficked migrant workers who have little opportunity or are too intimidated to seek help from authorities. Forced labour is a violation of fundamental human rights. The ILO estimates the number of victims of forced labour at 12.3 million people and that over 80% of forced labour occurs at the hands of private agents. Most victims are forced to live in extremely unhealthy and unsafe conditions and receive little or no pay. Often what little pay they receive is extorted back from them in fees and other illegitimate expenses (International Labour Office, 2008).

Forced labour differs from other forms of labour exploitation in that it involves the employer, whether a state or private firm, having almost total control over the labourer. Forced labour occurs when the employer is able to threaten the labourers with severe deprivation, including withholding food, perpetrating physical violence or sexual abuse, and restricting movement by locking them up.

Most multinational enterprises (MNEs) and legitimate local firms do not engage in forced labour. However, companies can participate in these practices through association with their suppliers and outsourcers. The International Labour Office (2008) further points out that managers must be sensitive and aware of the forms and causes of forced labour to ensure that they can recognize when it occurs in associated firms (p. 21). The way in which forced labour is carried out changes from industry to industry and country to country.

The principle against forced labour is an absolute standard and cannot be waived for "less desirable" people or for "good cause." For example, governments that impose compulsory participation in certain public projects or force people to work for political causes can be guilty of forced labour. It is often debated if the principle of forced labour applies to prisoners who are forced for their subsistence to participate in commercial activities without their free consent.

Private agents often use slavery, bonded labour, or debt-bondage to exploit workers and create a system of forced labour. In these cases, human traffickers will often charge their victims enormous sums of money with extortionary interest rates that must be paid before the victim is free. However, payments and interest rates are often structured so that workers are never able to pay off their debts (International Labour Office, 2008, pp. 21–22). Exhibit 6.2 can help managers identify forced labour practices.

Exhibit 6.2   Identifying Forced Labour in Practice

Lack of consent to work (the "route into" forced labour)	Menace of a penalty (the means of keeping someone in forced labour)
• Birth/descent into "slave" or bonded status • Physical abduction or kidnapping • Sale of person into the ownership of another • Physical confinement in the work location—in prison or in private detention • Psychological compulsion, i.e., an order to work, backed up by a credible threat of a penalty for noncompliance • Induced indebtedness (by falsification of accounts, inflated prices, reduced value of goods or services produced, excessive interest charges, etc.) • Deception or false promises about types and terms of work • Withholding and non-payment of wages • Retention of identity documents or other valuable personal possessions	• Physical violence against worker or family or close associates • Sexual violence • Imprisonment or other physical confinement • Financial penalties • Denunciation to authorities (police, immigration, etc.) and deportation • Exclusion from future employment • Exclusion from community and social life • Removal of rights or privileges • Deprivation of food, shelter or other necessities • Shift to worst working conditions • Loss of social status

Source: International Labour Office (2008).

The Roles of Responsible Managers

Managers need to be proactive to root out forced labour. Forced labourers most often have no voice to fight for their rights. In fact, forced labour can exist and only be perpetrated on a group that has been marginalized to such an extreme point that they have no freedom to express themselves or stand up against their oppressors. Thus, unlike Principle 3, which demands a spirit of cooperation from managers with labour, Principle 4 requires managers to seek out solutions for victims of forced labour.

In the workplace, managers must adhere to provisions of national laws and regulations concerning forced labour, and where national law is insufficient, take account of international labour standards. When they deal with other businesses, managers need to ensure that employment contracts have been provided to all employees. These contracts should state the terms and conditions of service, the voluntary nature of employment, the freedom to leave, and any penalties that may be associated with a departure or cessation of work. Managers should refrain from any practice that requires workers to lodge financial deposits with the company. If forced labour is found within the company's sphere of influence, managers should provide for the removal of such workers from the workplace with adequate services (International Labour Office, 2008, p. 24).

In society at large, firms should contribute, where possible, to broader community efforts to eliminate forced labour and help workers freed from forced labour to find freely chosen work. Firms can also work in partnership with other companies, sectorial associations, employers' organizations, and national agencies to develop an industry-wide approach to address the issue, and build bridges with trade unions, law enforcement authorities, labour inspectorates, and others (International Labour Office, 2008, p. 24).

Principle 5: Elimination of Child Labour

Many of our largest and most successful MNEs have faced the embarrassing truth that their subcontractors in the developing world are exploiting the labour of very young children. Images of malnourished children fashioning the shoes that children in the developed world will use for play and sport bring to light a real problem. Since the industrial revolution in Britain in the 18th century, controlling and eliminating child labour has been crucial for the development of modern society. The abolition of child labour rests on the principle that childhood is a period that must be spent in the development of the mind, body, and spirit. Engaging in labour from a young age will stymie this important growth period. A society will not develop if its children are not nurtured.

ILO conventions (Minimum Age Convention, No. 138 and the Worst Forms of Child Labour Convention, No. 182) define child labour by using minimum age standards for entering the workforce (International Labour Office, 2001). For regular work, the ideal minimum standard is 15 years old. Children 13 years and older may engage in light work, and hazardous work should only be done by adults over the age of 18. However, in countries where economic and educational facilities are less developed, these minimum standards have been lowered—for regular work, children should be 14 years old, and for light work, at least 12 years old. In addition, there should be no circumstances where children are asked to do hazardous work (see Exhibit 6.3).

Exhibit 6.3   Minimum Age for Admission to Employment or Work

	Developed Countries	Developing Countries
Regular Work	15 years	14 years
Hazardous Work	18 years	18 years
Light work	13 years	12 years

Source: International Labour Office (2008).

According to UN Recommendation No. 190, hazardous work includes

work which exposes children to physical, psychological or sexual abuse; work underground, under water, at dangerous heights or in confined spaces; work with dangerous machinery, equipment and tools, or which involves the manual handling or transport of heavy loads; work in an unhealthy environment which may, for example, expose children to hazardous substances, agents or processes, or to temperatures, noise levels, or vibrations damaging to their health; work under particularly difficult conditions such as work for long hours or during the night or work where the child is unreasonably confined to the premises of the employer. (International Labour Office, 2001, p. 184)

According to the International Labour Office (2008), "child labour damages a child's physical, social, mental, psychological and spiritual development. Child labour deprives children of their childhood and their dignity. They are deprived of an education and may be separated from their families" (p. 28). Children who are involved in child labour have neither the time, opportunity, nor energy needed to learn basic literacy skills needed to become competent as adults for most jobs in the modern economy. Thus, a child who is forced to work before he or she has achieved literacy is destined to work in low-paid unskilled work for life. This deprives society of a better future workforce. Those who do not have basic literacy skills are also less able to provide an environment in which their own children can learn and develop. Thus, the cycle of low-skilled, low-paid employment cannot be broken until child labour is eliminated.

Children have all the same rights and dignities afforded to adults. In addition, they are a special class of people that require distinct rights. Because children are young, they must be protected and nurtured. All children have the right to receive a basic amount of education to allow them to develop into literate and healthy adults. Thus, they have the right to be excluded from the workforce.

Since their bodies and minds are growing and they lack knowledge and experience, they have the right to be protected from economic exploitation and work that may be dangerous to their health, safety, and morals. Children are not in a position to decide for themselves which types of activities are dangerous to their health and safety or what may corrupt their morals, so they have the right to be protected by law and society.

Thus, the goal of Principle 5 is to eliminate all forms of child labour. That said, the ILO asked managers to address this issue of child labour with a degree of sensitivity. A child should not be removed from a workplace until the management can ensure that the child is entering into a reasonably safe environment. Turning children out of a workplace can result in them becoming victims of more exploitive forms of work (International Labour Office, 2008, p. 29).

Beyond employment of children to do work that should otherwise be done by adults, the principle of abolition of child labour also applies to the elimination of "the worst forms of child labour." These include all forms of slavery or practices similar to slavery, prostitution, the production of pornography or pornographic performances, and illicit activities. Beyond being criminal behavior, such activities corrupt the psychological, spiritual, and mental development of children.

The Roles of Responsible Managers

For the most part, if managers act with due diligence in their own firms and with their subcontractors, they can prevent underage children engaging in inappropriate work in their firms. Managers should adhere to minimum age provisions of national labour laws and regulations, and where national law is insufficient, take account of international labour standards. Care should be taken to use adequate and verifiable mechanisms for age verification and to remove children below the legal working age from the workplace. However, the UN convention on "the worst forms of child labour" cautions managers to be sensitive and ensure that, when children are removed from the workplace, they are not forced into a situation which may force working children into more exploitative forms of work. When possible, children removed from the workplace should be provided with adequate support.

In society at large, managers should contribute, where possible, to broader community efforts to eliminate child labour and to help children removed from work access quality education and social protection. Managers should also support and build bridges with law enforcement authorities, labour inspectorates, and other agencies and trade unions. Within the company's sphere of influence, managers should provide support for reintegration programs for former child labourers by providing skills development and job training opportunities (International Labour Office, 2008).

Principle 6: Elimination of Discrimination in Employment and Occupation

Fighting discrimination in the workplace is an ongoing concern in the most developed countries. In newly developed countries and developing countries, ending job discrimination against minorities and women may still be a low priority among managers. Thus, this is a principle which still requires all managers to be sensitive and actively engaged.

People should be considered for employment based on relevant qualifications, experience, or characteristics for the position for which they have applied. Employment and occupation discrimination occurs when characteristics that are not related to the candidate's merit or are not required to do the job successfully are used to favor or eliminate a candidate. Normally, candidates should not be discriminated against based on race, color, sex, religion, political opinion, nationality, or social origin. More recently, some countries have extended discrimination protection to include sexual orientation, age, and HIV/AIDS. Employment discrimination occurs in all walks of life from rural to urban workplaces and from the factory floor to the boardroom.

Discrimination harms both the individual being discriminated against and the general community by limiting the pool of people who can contribute to society. As indicated by the International Labour Office (2008),

> Discrimination can arise in a variety of work-related activities. These include access to employment, particular occupations, training and vocational guidance and social security.

Moreover, it can occur with respect to the terms and conditions of employment, such as:

- recruitment
- remuneration
- hours of work and rest, paid holidays
- maternity protection
- security of tenure
- job assignments
- performance assessment and advancement
- training opportunities
- promotion prospects
- occupational safety and health
- termination of employment (p. 31)

In some cases, discrimination is explicit. Laws and rules may make it difficult or impossible for some groups to access certain types of employment. For example, in some countries women or ethnic minority groups may not be allowed access to the education needed to gain certain types of employment. In other cases, people may have to belong to a certain political party to be considered for some types of employment. However, for the most part, discrimination occurs informally through socially embedded attitudes and beliefs (International Labour Organization, 2008, p. 32).

A policy of nondiscrimination means that employers will consider potential employees based solely on their ability to carry out the duties stated in the job requirements. Beyond what is reasonably required to do the job correctly, no other distinction, exclusion, or preference should be considered. Being denied a work opportunity because of discrimination is an infringement on a worker's fundamental human rights.

Eliminating discrimination in the workplace can serve as an important step toward freeing society from discrimination. Because organizations can impose antidiscrimination policies by fiat, they can work toward eliminating stereotypes and attitudes that allow people to rationalize discrimination. When people of different sex, age, and race work together, they can form relationships based on equality as they strive toward a common goal. Also, eliminating discrimination in the workplace helps expand possibilities for the next generations of workers by providing role models. For example, employing women in traditionally male dominated jobs opens up possibilities and may inspire young girls to consider those careers.

Eliminating discrimination often involves changing fundamental societal beliefs and values. This can be difficult to do without strong legal incentives.

The ILO principles are meant to set minimum standards to drive these changes. Organizations should embrace these and other national laws in order to push individuals and groups to change their attitudes and create an environment that does not accept discrimination (International Labour Organization, 2008, p. 32).

The Roles of Responsible Managers

Eliminating discrimination in the workplace takes a sustained commitment from managers over a long period of time. Many of the criteria used to discriminate against people are rooted in deep cultural beliefs and biases. Unlike child labour, for example, that can at least be objectively identified, many forms of discrimination are subtle and not even well appreciated by many managers and employees.

Managers should institute company policies and procedures that make qualifications, skills, and experience the basis for the recruitment, placement, training, and advancement of staff at all levels. Senior managers should take an active role in developing company-wide policies and procedures to guide equal employment practices and link advancement to desired performance in this area. This sends a message that ending discrimination is a priority for the firm. Employees should be provided training on nondiscrimination policies and practices, including disability awareness. Appropriate procedures and record keeping will help ensure that the principles are being put in place and progress can be tracked. Finally, the firms should eliminate formal and informal barriers to employees raising concerns and grievances.

In society at large, managers should encourage and support efforts to build a climate of tolerance and equal access to opportunities for occupational development such as adult education programs and health and childcare services (International Labour Office, 2008, p. 33).

The Roles of Responsible Managers in MNEs

Managers in MNEs have a special responsibility to ensure that the labour principles of the UN Global Compact are being fulfilled in their firms. MNEs often use their global sourcing abilities to take advantage of cheap low-skilled labour in developing countries. Many of these countries do not have the legal frameworks in place to protect workers' rights. MNEs have a responsibility to proactively respect the UN labour principles and to take reasonable steps to ensure that their subcontractors abide by these principles as a condition of doing business with the MNE.

Study/Discussion Questions

1. What is *collective bargaining*?

2. What does *freedom of association* mean?

3. How large is the issue of forced labour? Who is affected? How might an MNE become entangled in forced labour issues?

4. What are some causes of forced labour? What can managers do to solve forced labour issues?

5. What might be the longer term impact of child labour on a society?

6. What are ways business can help to abolish child labour and support children?

7. What are examples of how discrimination occurs?

8. How can fighting discrimination in the workplace lead to a freer society?

9. What makes discrimination particularly hard to distinguish and eliminate?

10. What can managers do to eliminate discrimination?

For Cases Relevant to Labour Principles, See Pages 235 to 374

Netcare's International Expansion
Saul Klein, Albert Wöcke

Nestle's Nescafe Partners' Blend: The Fairtrade Decision (A)
Niraj Dawar, Jordan Mitchell

Jinjian Garment Factory: Motivating Go-Slow Workers
Tieying Huang, Junping Liang, Paul W. Beamish

Textron Ltd.
Lawrence A. Beer

Bayer CropScience in India (A): Against Child Labor
Charles Dhanaraj, Oana Branzei, Satyajeet Subramanian

L'Oréal S.A.: Rolling Out the Global Diversity Strategy
Cara C. Maurer, Ken Mark

Huxley Maquiladora
Paul W. Beamish, Jaechul Jung, Joyce Miller

Staffing Wal-Mart Stores, Inc. (A)
Alison Konrad, Ken Mark

References

Capitalism. (2011). In *Encyclopædia Britannica*. Retrieved from http://www.britannica.com/EBchecked/topic/93927/capitalism

Command economy. (2011). In *Encyclopædia Britannica*. Retrieved from http://www.britannica.com/EBchecked/topic/127708/command-economy

Democracy. (2011). In *Columbia Encyclopedia Online*. Retrieved from http://education.yahoo.com/reference/encyclopedia/entry/democrac

International Labour Office. (2001). *International labour standards: A global approach*. Geneva, Switzerland: International Labour Organization.

International Labour Office. (2008). *The labour principles of the United Nations Global Compact: A guide for business*. Geneva, Switzerland: International Labour Organization.

RCMP charge West Vancouver woman with human trafficking over migrant's plight. (2011, May 16). The Canadian Press. Retrieved from http://www.news1130.com/news/national/article/227343--rcmp-charge-west-vancouver-woman-with-human-trafficking-over-migrant-s-plight

Environment

Principles 7, 8, and 9

The UN Global Compact principles relating to the environment are

Principle 7: Businesses should support a precautionary approach to environmental challenges;

Principle 8: undertake initiatives to promote greater environmental responsibility; and

Principle 9: encourage the development and diffusion of environmentally friendly technologies.

7

Embedded Sustainability and the Innovation-Producing Potential of the UN Global Compact's Environmental Principles

David Cooperrider

*Case Western Reserve University,
The Fowler Center for Sustainable Value*

Nadya Zhexembayeva

IEDC-Bled School of Management

"Chief executives believe overwhelmingly that sustainability has become critical to their success and could be fully embedded into core business within ten years."

—The 2010 Accenture-UN Global Compact Survey

"There can be few people in business today that could doubt that social and environmental sustainability will be the defining business driver for multinational corporations in the first part of this century."

—Patrick Cescau, Group CEO, Unilever

As the quote from Patrick Cescau, CEO of Unilever, indicates, sustainability may be the defining business driver of the 21st century. And yet, few are as prepared as they would like to be. Year after year, CEOs talk about the complexities of execution, as the most recent 2010 annual survey of the UN Global Compact organizations concludes. Georg Kell, executive director of the Global Compact, summed up the following in the 2010 annual report:

> Finally, chief executives cite the complexity of integrating sustainability throughout their companies and into their supply chain as a key barrier. Business is challenged to move from strategy to execution, from policy to action—a key finding of our annual survey for three consecutive years. (United Nations Global Compact Office, 2010, p. 6)

In this chapter, we bring a special focus to the increasingly critical question of "how?" and look to the state of the art of embedding the principles of environmental sustainability across the enterprise in a way where sustainability is not a "bolted on" program but becomes embedded into the heart of strategy, operations, and innovation. Indeed this chapter has a bias that sustainability is in fact an innovation engine and is emerging as the most important business opportunity, not barrier or problem, of the 21st century.

This chapter begins with the remarkable story of the UN Global Compact and with a special focus on the three principles on environmental sustainability. Here we share insights from recent surveys and numerous published reports but also draw significantly from our own participant observation of at least three global summits, several best practice sharing "leading company retreats," and direct work with UN Global Compact signatories seeking to embed and act upon the environmental principles. With the stage set, we move into the heart of the chapter where we examine three leading edge methods—(1) the seven levels of sustainable value strategy framework; (2) "the sustainable design factory"—a whole-system-in-the-room large group design thinking methodology based on the strengths-based approach of Appreciative Inquiry; and (3) the transorganizational partnership methods revolving around issue-specific action platforms, often uniting corporations with the larger UN agenda. In each instance of *how*, we will draw on firsthand experience and case stories of Global Compact participants with vignettes interspersed with conceptual insights and business results. In all of this, one concept is threaded throughout. It's the concept of sustainable value as the new North Star not just for UN Global Compact organizations but the whole of management. *Sustainable value* (Laszlo & Zhexembayeva, 2011) is defined as a dynamic state that occurs when a company creates ongoing value for shareholders and stakeholders, and it becomes embedded instead of bolted on when the environmental, health, and social value is incorporated into a company's core business with no tradeoff in price or quality.

Let Us Choose

During and following the ethical meltdown of Enron, World Com, and Arthur Anderson, the debate about business in society rose to a fever pitch. Activists were arising—almost all of them citing the statistic that, out of the world's top 100 economies, 49% were not nation-states but global corporations such as Exxon—and they were positioned at every major global economic meeting, mostly in protest. It was not long before CEOs were also publicly raising their own self-reflective, honest critique. Claus Schwab, founder of the World Economic Forum for CEOs, came out strong on the subject, albeit a few years later. In a *Newsweek* article, he said, "In today's trust-starved climate, our market-driven system is under attack. . . . Large parts of the population feel that business has become detached from society—that business interests are no longer aligned with societal interests" (Schwab, 2003, p. 6).

So this, a vocal critique, was one side of the debate. On the other side, there were major thinkers, such as Stanford engineer and world modeler Willis Harman, who were beginning to see signs of another side of business. In his forecasting work, examining trends from climate change, population growth, declining fisheries, and loss of forests to state of the world statistics on child mortality, conflict and terror, peak oil, and more, Harman and his colleagues developed three distinct scenarios for the future. Two of the scenarios were about collapse, one slow and the other a sudden and out-of-control downward spiral. The only scenario that positioned a positive or optimistic future was one where business emerged as one of the most powerful forces for good. As an engineer, not a business scholar, Harman saw his own presumptions changed when he explored the new equations. The world modeling exercise led him to a new conclusion—that business might well emerge in the 21st century as the new creative force on the planet. Here was his logic, in brief:

> Business, the motor of our society, has the opportunity to be the new creative force on the planet, a force which could contribute to the well-being of many . . . the modern corporation is as adaptable an organizational form as has ever been invented, so that in a time of fundamental change it may be expected to be on the cutting edge. (Harman, 1991, p. 31)

Harman's logic and intuition were institutional. He was comparing past institutional forms, for example, the medieval church as an institutional form, and the organizational characteristics of bureaucratic governments. And for him, it was clear that the modern corporation had a myriad of organizational strengths in comparative terms—huge communications and technological reach; the pragmatism of markets and management tools; major investment capacities; the ability to rapidly change shape and adapt; the ability to get things done; and the entrepreneurial mind-set for finding solutions and innovations for the creation and mutual exchange of value. From this vantage point, the assets of business were significant and perhaps decisive as an observable variable affecting and touching everything.

So the debate stretched along two opposite poles: one stating that business was detrimental and detached from societal interests and the other proposing that business could become the most positive force for building a better world.

But rather than making predictions about the future, as if trajectories were inevitable such as laws of nature, or instead of joining in the polarizing critiques, Kofi Annan, then secretary-general of the UN, presented a third way. The occasion was the 1999 World Economic Forum. And the secretary-general was about to give a speech to hundreds of CEOs. Everyone was wondering what he might say. Again the backdrop included the 1999 protests that would soon rock Seattle, and the Enron scandal of corporate greed and corruption was about to break. Many expected a voice of critique. But Kofi Annan had something else in store. Perhaps he knew, in the back of his mind, that we will never be able to eradicate extreme poverty in the world or realize any of the other Millennium Development goals for healing the environment or creating cultures of peace without the strengths, innovation capacity, and effectiveness of new business models and better markets. So Kofi Annan reached out his hand in partnership. He spoke about choice. And his words touched a chord. He said to the business leaders, "Let us choose to unite the strengths of markets with the power of universal ideals. Let us choose to reconcile the creative forces of private entrepreneurship with the needs of the disadvantaged and the requirements of future generations" (Cooperrider, 2007, p. 425).

The CEOs responded. An active working group was created. A set of principles for business and society for the 21st century was jointly developed (see Chapter 3 in this book for full detail), and the UN Global Compact was officially launched at the UN headquarters in New York on July 26, 2000.

The three principles focusing on the environment included a precautionary principle, a product or sustainable technologies innovation principle, and a responsibility principle:

Principle 7: Businesses should support a precautionary approach to environmental challenges;

Principle 8: undertake initiatives to promote greater environmental responsibility; and

Principle 9: encourage the development and diffusion of environmentally friendly technologies.

Each of these foundations, meant as a starting point, was derived from years of universal consensus building in the form of major UN meetings held earlier including the historic Brundtland (1987) commission report calling for sustainable development "that is development that meets the needs of the present without compromising the ability of future generations to meet their own needs" (p. 8). The principles were also derived from the Rio Declaration, which was, at the time, the largest effort in human history to look at the state of the world. In the spirit of Kofi Annan's speech focusing on partnership and "Let us choose," the principles would be voluntary and the UN Global Compact would serve as the first truly universal convening body for business and society actors across the world's kaleidoscopic landscape of cultures and societies. So important was this development that it attracted hundreds and soon thousands of the world's top corporations, civil society leaders, and governmental organizations to a shared initiative. By 2011, with nearly 10,000 corporate participants and other stakeholders from nearly 140 countries, the UN Global Compact had become the largest voluntary corporate responsibility initiative in the world. The goals were the following:

1. Mainstream the ten principles into business activities around the world

2. Catalyze actions in support of broader UN goals, including the Millennium Development Goals (MDGs)

Today, there is scarcely a corporation that is not going green in some way. The most recent and the largest CEO survey ever conducted on the topic of sustainability recently headlined its finding: "Chief executives believe overwhelmingly that sustainability has become critical to their success and could be fully embedded into core business within ten years" (Lacy, Cooper, Hayward, & Nueberger, 2010, p. 2). But how?

Studies now also show, especially among leading companies, that two things are true. First, the universal framework of the UN Global Compact principles, along with the positive and rapid transfer of learning across organizations that is made possible because of the convening power of the UN, helps to accelerate the effectiveness of sustainable enterprise. Second, that as the principles become embedded into the strategy and operations of a business, a shift happens. What may have started out as a moral imperative becomes a source of business success and sometimes truly disruptive innovation—a source of new markets, new industries, and changing the rules of the business landscape. Sustainability, once embedded, begins to create surprise and opportunity. New products are discovered. Risks are better managed. Employees want to be engaged and express a sense of meaning. So-called "firms of endearment"—the sustainability high performers—begin to win the hearts and minds of customers (Sisodia, Sheth, & Wolfe, 2007). New partnerships across greening supply chains and like-minded companies are forged. Investor rankings are significantly and positively affected and so is access to capital.

In other words, a shift happens from sustainable development to the strategic creation of sustainable value (to be defined in the next section). And from our first engagement with the UN Global Compact in 2004, we have partnered with authors such as Chris Laszlo (see Cooperrider & Lazslo, 2010; Laszlo & Zhexembayeva, 2011) to detail and model the strategic pathways and have begun to sort through a vast array of *how to* tools for moving from the instillation of principles to the capturing of new sources of value. We now turn to three key pathways that resonate with Kofi Annan's call to "Let us choose." For in many ways, we can choose to design a factory that generates and gives back cleaner, renewable energy to its local community than it uses; it's being done. We can choose to create a fair trade coffee brand that stabilizes prices in poor communities and at the same time advances the consumer's quality product; it's being done. We can choose to create a system that turns waste to profit and profitably eliminates the very concept of waste; it's being done. And we can choose to design greener supply chains that send ripple effects throughout a wider sphere of influence than ever thought possible. Give a design team the simple assignment to design a new sneaker that wins on price, wins on human rights practices, is produced in net zero ways, and creates no landfill waste and, in addition, can be planted in the ground after its use and will enrich the soil and turn into a flower. Do you know what the product designers will say? They will say, "it's already been done—someone has already chosen to design such a shoe using those exact design requirements." Companies are becoming more intentional, choosing to design for the environment in ways that are not simply "less bad" but are actually capable of producing *positive good* (Cooperrider & Fry, 2010). Just as the quality movement destroyed the myth that low price and high quality could not coexist, sustainable value tools, with their call to innovation, are showing that embedded sustainability is an exciting frontier with a high performance trajectory. And it is moving quickly, shifting into high gear.

From Global Compact Principles to Embedded Sustainability

A decade after the original Global Compact principles were developed, new market pressures are transforming environmental sustainability from annoying obligations into a thriving business opportunity. Among those pressures, three particular sustainability trends—declining resources, radical transparency, and increasing expectations—have redefined the way we do business.

You might have noticed that sushi restaurants now regularly post *toro*, the fatty cut from the belly of the prized bluefin tuna, at market price. Traveling in airports around the world, you will also find it marked "unavailable" on the menu. In all but the Antarctic waters, the bluefin has been so heavily overfished that stocks are now at less than 10% of what they once were. It has become so rare that a single, healthy-sized tuna recently fetched US$396,000 in Tokyo's largest fish market ("Fish Story," 2011).

Bluefin tuna is just one visible example of the decline of natural resources from clean water and topsoil to food crops, fossil fuels, and biodiversity. During the 2007–2009 downturn, the World Wildlife Fund (2008), a leading environmental conservation organization, warned that "the possibility of financial recession pales in comparison to the looming ecological credit crunch." The signs of a crisis in natural resources are starkly evident: the commodity price index, a measure of price movements for 22 basic commodities, has more than tripled since 2002 and in 2010 alone rose 27% with commodities such as cotton rising almost 100% (Commodity Research Bureau, 2011). Combined with higher-than-average price volatility, these upward price trends and growing scarcities pose a serious challenge to the security of supply chains.

To declining natural resources, we add two more trends: radical transparency and rising expectations. Fueled by unprecedented activism in the civil sector and enabled by rapid developments in information technology, transparency has become the dynamic, immediate, and substantive force of modern corporate life. It enables any interested person to peer into product and service life cycles and find those impacts on society and nature that used to be hidden from public scrutiny. The third trend—rising expectations—invites companies to rethink the very essence of market demand. Investors, employees, and most importantly, consumers increasingly expect sound social and environmental performance. New parameters such as quiet, healthy, socially equitable, or environmentally friendly are becoming standard for every product and service in the economy. We don't want just any household-cleaning product; we want it nontoxic and biodegradable. We drink fair trade coffee and bring reusable shopping bags to the supermarket. And we no longer accept paying more for these attributes.

With these new pressures on our hands, what is business to do? How are companies to respond?

In response to these mounting pressures, the overwhelming majority of managers continue with the familiar approaches to sustainability in business, treating the new social and environmental demands as annoying obligations to be addressed by a random corporate social responsibility program. While there are some that now recognize social and environmental performance as business opportunity, most managers continue to bolt it on to existing strategy and operations like a poorly fitted Band-Aid. Remember all those solar panels and two-sided copying promoted at the office headquarters of a dirty manufacturing business? Way too often we just keep bolting it on!

Only a handful are choosing to embed sustainability into the very DNA of what they do, whereby social and environmental value is integrated into the products and processes across the entire value chain without compromises in price or quality—in other words, with no green or social premium. Take, for example, Nissan, a Global Compact member since 2004. It recently released Leaf, a 100% electric car named World Car of the Year 2011 (Blanco, 2011). Combined with the emerging infra-structure to recharge electric cars, Nissan's multibillion euro investment is driven by the quest for industry leadership, not selling eco-cars to environmentalists.

Unlike the omnipresent bolt-on approaches, embedded sustainability requires a fundamental shift across every dimension of the business system:

Bolt-On vs. Embedded Sustainability: Key Dimensions

	Bolt-On Sustainability	Embedded Sustainability
Goal	Pursue shareholder value	Pursue sustainable value
Scope	Add symbolic wins at the margins	Transform core business activities
Customer	Offer "green" and "socially responsible" products at premium prices or with diminished quality	Offer "smarter" solutions with no trade-off in quality and no social or green premium
Value chain	Manage company's own activities	Manage across the product or service life cycle value chain
Organization	Create a "scapegoat" department of sustainability	Make sustainability everyone's job

Source: Laszlo and Zhexembayeva (2011).

When embedded, sustainability becomes a source of a whole range of value creation opportunities, with radical innovation cutting across and enabling the other value-creating levels. Companies can use radical innovation to simultaneously lower costs, differentiate their products, and enter entirely new markets—all while creating a truly sustainable value for shareholders and stakeholders.

Managing risks and maximizing efficiencies are the lowest-hanging fruit for a company pursuing sustainable value. Alcoa, Global Compact newcomer of 2009, one of the leading integrated aluminum companies, has set up a number of energy efficiency projects, successfully identifying more than US$80 million in savings opportunities and reducing its operating costs by more than US$20 million (Berthon, 2008).

Product design and differentiation is another significant opportunity for companies pursuing sustainable value. At Timberland, Global Compact signatory of 2008, environmental metrics have been integrated into the key design platform, offering real-time information to designers as they select materials. In this way, Timberland has empowered its designers to consider the full-life impact of the materials they select. Fifty percent of consumers who read the environmental performance label carried by Timberland products indicated that it had "positively influenced their purchase" (Lacy et al., 2010).

As Natura Cosmeticos, which joined the Global Compact in 2000, shows us, brand and reputation offer another level of value creation. Natura, a US$2.3 billion São Paulo-based cosmetics and beauty products company, offers product lines designed around the sustainable use of natural resources, whereby 80% of the materials in all their products come from renewable plant sources. Placing sustainability at the core of its business strategy ensured Natura a significant advantage in promoting its brand and reputation, helping the firm to grow from a small local enterprise to Brazil's largest cosmetics firm. Revenues have grown by nearly 40% between 2007 and 2010—bottom-line growth by 44% over the same period (Lacy et al., 2010).

In addition to risk mitigation, efficiency, product differentiation, and brand and culture enhancement, other sources of value creation offer us a broad range of choices. Here is one way to visualize the entire seven levels of sustainable value creation available across products, services, processes, and strategies:

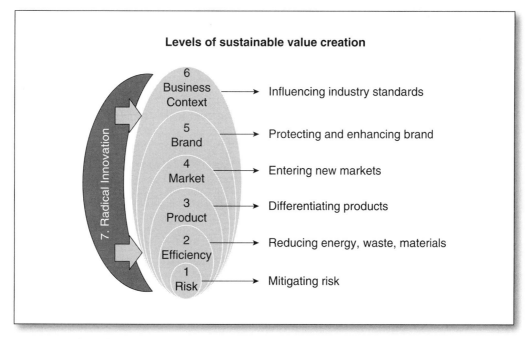

Source: Laszlo and Zhexembayeva (2011).

Sounds appealing, right? Indeed, the opportunities are plenty, but few manage to harvest the promising fruit. Embedding sustainability is a complex, multiactivity and multiactor challenge; no simple recipes are possible. Unlike the streamlined and often linear steps taken for bolt-on sustainability efforts, the task of embedding social and environmental value into the DNA of a business is iterative—repetitive and chaotic. It demands new thinking and unorthodox solutions that can spring from unlikely sources and in improbable ways. Having said this, the experience of market leaders suggests four interdependent and interconnected lines of action to help guide the journey from principles to high performance (Laszlo & Zhexembayeva, 2011):

1. *Getting the Right Start*: mobilizing, educating, and acting around specific low hanging fruits. Building momentum in the organization for sustainability projects that support existing business priorities and provide demonstrable payoff.

2. *Building the Buy-In*: aligning company, value chain, and all other stakeholders around the vision of embedded sustainability.

3. *Moving From Incremental to Breakthrough*: developing clear but unorthodox goals, designing the strategy and capturing value through cocreation and innovation.

4. *Staying With It*: managing learning and energy while making sustainability ubiquitous but largely invisible in the business practice.

With such a tall order on our hands, the good news is that new, radically holistic approaches to managing change toward sustainable value have already emerged, allowing us to engage the company and its entire value system across all required lines of action.

Large Group Methods as the Great Accelerator: The "AI Summit" and More

Too many organizational change efforts to embed a new strategic or operational way of life—whether it's a new IT system, a new culture or set of values, a new structure, a new platform of sustainability principles, or new big change of any kind—result in comments such as "why are we doing this?"; "what's this about?"; "here we go again!"; and " just flavor of the month" or "there are so many changes being announced—why don't they just let us do our jobs?" In many big organizations, cynicism is rampant—and understandably so—as many have seen new programs and initiatives launched to do what seems to have failed before.

What's becoming clear is that the vast majority of these efforts fall short of expectations for three very simple reasons:

1. The engagement challenge: key people—that is, all relevant and affected stakeholders—are not included in the designing and planning of the initiative;

2. The slow-to-the-point-of-ineffectiveness challenge: obviously timing matters, but too often the gap between strategy and implementation is so slow that inertia, politics, and timing in the marketplace become negatively comprised and often results in too little too late (this results in even greater cynicism about change); and

3. The fragmentation and turf challenge: this is where the system does things in such siloed and specialized ways—one small group handing it off to another group, or one level of the hierarchy not supporting the efforts at another level, or the inability to scale up what works in some smaller domain and spread it consistently and rapidly throughout the misaligned whole— that in each of these instances, the organization fails to optimize or leverage all the strengths, intelligence, cohesion, innovation, passion, engagement, and motivation that the whole could provide.

This is especially fatal in the embedded sustainability domain because, by definition, sustainable value is about higher levels of performance in the eyes and experience of an array of stakeholders. The formula *sustainability = innovation* is, therefore, almost synonymous with an equally important formula: new forms of stakeholder *engagement = innovation* (and the opposite is also true—separation, hierarchy, distance, or disengagement work against innovation). And it makes sense. Innovation happens when diverse assets or technologies or resources combine in unique constellations. That's why product designers spend time literally becoming their customers and vice versa, and that's why entrepreneurs spot breakthroughs in other industries and take them to create new combinations of their own. In each case, cross-fertilization is central: all innovation involves creative combinations.

So how do leading companies (see Waddock, Mirvis, & Ryu, 2008) embed the principles and turn environmental issues of energy, climate change, water, waste, depleted fisheries, and other natural resource depletions into bona fide business opportunities in ways that vitally and consistently benefit both business and the world? And how are leading Global Compact signatories embedding sustainability in ways that offset or overcome the engagement challenge, the slow-to-the-point-of-ineffectiveness challenge, and the fragmentation and silos challenge?

First, as we have shared, most leading companies are now using the language of sustainable value that includes the creation and measurement of stakeholder value and shareholder value. Many of the most successful approaches—for example at industry leading Green Mountain Coffee Roasters, award winning Fairmount Minerals, the city of Cleveland's "Green City on a Blue Lake" initiative, and the UN Global Compact itself—are discovering the power of the new large-group, whole-system-in-the room, planning and designing methods to set in motion the six levels of value creation (see, for example, Glavas, Senge, & Cooperrider, 2010). In the rest of this section, we will concentrate on one of those approaches that is particularly time tested and refined in terms of well-documented success factors. One CEO in a UN Global Compact Leaders Summit reports,

> I have been part of many global meetings of business and society leaders and I am convinced that the Appreciative Inquiry Summit approach, as we have seen it here, is the best large group planning method in the world today. (United Nations, 2004, p. 4)

It is called the "AI summit" method (where the term *appreciative inquiry* denotes the search for strengths and assets), and its power to scale up, its business-relevant speed, and its simplicity and reliability have made it the positive change method of choice for the domain of sustainable value (Laszlo & Zhexembayeva, 2011). Following the 2004 Leaders Summit with hundreds of CEOs from Tata Industries to Royal Dutch Shell and Hewlett-Packard, then secretary-general of the UN Kofi Annan wrote this to one of the authors (David Cooperrider):

> I would like to commend you more particularly for your methodology of Appreciative Inquiry and to thank you for introducing it to the United Nations. Without this, it would have been difficult, perhaps even impossible, to engage so many leaders of business, civil society, and government. (As quoted in Cooperrider & Whitney, 2005)

It's odd that after all these years we do not have a good term for the opposite of micromanagement. While we will leave it to historians to trace the shift from the micromanaging practice to macromanagement—what Peter Drucker described as "bringing in the meaningful outside"—it is clear that sustainability, with its search for new and unexpected sources of stakeholder value, is leading the way with its large group planning methodologies such as the AI summit.

To illustrate, let's start with a Global Compact company, Fairmount Minerals, at the launch of its commitment to embed sustainability principles into the core of its strategy, business operations, and innovation pipeline. The effort was led by its chief financial officer (CFO), Jenniffer Deckard, and CEO and president, Chuck Fowler. They selected the next generation AI summit method called "the sustainable design factory" that goes beyond grand visioning to the joint design of rapid prototypes of new products, operational improvements, and even the opening of new markets. And here, to make the descriptions of it even more concrete, we would like you to imagine that you are part of it. Imagine first of all that you are a concerned citizen and environmentalist. You are acquainted with Fairmount Minerals. And you have real questions about the next sand mine they might want to open. Then you receive an invitation letter from the CEO and CFO. You are invited not to be an observer, but to engage as a full collaborator in Fairmount's strategic planning and design summit. So imagine the start of the 3-day summit:

> You enter a grand ballroom. It is teeming with 350 people from the sand company. There is no central podium or microphone. As many as 50 round tables fill the room—each has a microphone, a flip-chart, and packets of materials including the summit's purpose, 3-day agenda, and a presummit strategy analysis and fact base. As an external stakeholder of the company, you've been invited to roll up your sleeves and participate in a real-time strategy and sustainable design session devoted to the future.
>
> You sit down at your assigned round table and you are struck by the complex configuration of individuals: the CFO of the company; a sand loader operator; a marketing specialist; a potential solar energy supplier (external); a product designer; a corporate lawyer; an IT professional; and a middle manager from operations. Soon the "whole-system-in-the-room" summit begins.
>
> The CEO of the company stands up from one of the 50 tables and speaks to the "state of the business" and the task of this strategic session. He speaks about the difference between being a sustainability leader versus a sustainability laggard and vows that this company will not be caught flat-footed by the future. He shares his support for and commitment to the UN Global Compact principles. An external moderator then calls attention to the key questions for the summit, each one designed to elicit discovery into strategic strengths, hidden opportunities, aspirations, and valued future scenarios—all with a focus on future results and game-changing industry possibilities. People are instructed to use the questions in the form of an interview with the person or key stakeholder sitting next to them. Within 30 minutes of the CEO's welcome, people are into deep exploration, sharing and listening. The Grand Ballroom is buzzing.
>
> The moderator, after almost an hour, calls people to reconvene and describes the 4-D cycle of Discovery, Dream, Design, and Deployment that will unfold over the 3 days. "The key point," states the moderator, "is that we are creating the innovation agenda together—this meeting is not about speeches or prenegotiated plans nor is it simply

about dialogue—this meeting is a codesign and collaborative creation of the future of the company . . . we need your best thinking."

An Appreciative Inquiry summit is a large group planning, designing, or implementation meeting that brings a whole system of internal and external stakeholders together in a concentrated way over 3 days to work on a task of strategic and, especially, creative value. Moreover, it is a meeting where everyone is engaged as designers, across all relevant and resource-rich boundaries, to share leadership and take ownership for making the future of some big league opportunity successful. The meeting appears bold at first, but it is based on a simple notion: that when it comes to embedding sustainability, there is nothing that brings out the best in human systems—faster, more consistently, and more effectively—than the power of "the whole." Flowing from a larger tradition called "strengths-based management" (Cooperrider & Godwin, 2011), the AI summit says that in a multistakeholder world it is not about (isolated) strengths per se, but about configurations, combinations, and interfaces. It's all about the chemistry of relationships—about the concentration effect of strengths—and it is surprisingly easy. As management thought leader Peter Drucker so insightfully remarked, the task of leadership is "ageless in its essence: the task of leadership is to create an alignment of strengths in ways that make a system's weaknesses irrelevant." And that's the focus of Appreciative Inquiry where the concept of appreciation means *to value* and to see what works, what's best and what's next; the word *appreciation* also means *to increase in value*. Start with your strengths; that's what the tools of Appreciative Inquiry enable stakeholders to do.

While at first it seems incomprehensible that large groups of hundreds of people in the room can be effective in unleashing systemwide strategies, making organizational decisions, and designing rapid prototypes, this is exactly what is happening in organizations around the world. Fairmount's experience was not an isolated or atypical triumph. And for you—an earlier critic of the company—the experience was eye-opening. First, you saw the integrity and sincerity of the company. Then you saw one new sustainable value business idea after another being discovered. One that amazed you most was the new multimillion dollar business that was designed to take old, spent sand—the material that is discarded after it is used in factories—and to turn that spent sand into clean biofuel for powering the company's heavy trucks. How could this be? Well, a chemist in your group shared how spent sand, when placed on farmland, has been shown to help grow higher yields of biomass. Another person observes that the company's sand mining facilities are located in rural locations near many farms. Between the two observations a light-bulb went off. The team asks, "How might we create a new business for spent sand? And why not create a new partnership with rural farmers—a partnership where sand-assisted biomass growth becomes the basis for lower cost, job creation, and green biofuels to power the heavy truck fleet?"

This single innovation, coupled with a dozen other win-win sustainability breakthroughs such as a low-cost sand water filter to clean putrid water in areas of the world where families have no access to clean healthy water, soon doubled Fairmount's already superior double-digit growth rates and set it on a pathway of differentiation unheard of in an industry that's just the opposite of Silicon Valley. Headlines in a Wisconsin business paper (Laszlo & Zhexembayeva, 2011) told the story in the article "The Tale of Two Sand Companies." It was about one sand company that failed. It had no commitment to advances in sustainable enterprise. The other company, part of the UN Global Compact, could communicate its progress with baseline measures, goals, achievements, stakeholder engagement methods, and several disruptive innovations. Today, Fairmount Minerals is speaking all over the world, sharing openly their discoveries. They convene whole systems in the room, codesigning processes in every new community they work with. They have learned how to bring in "the meaningful outside" not in adversarial terms, or even consultative terms, but as joint designers. They have shown how to turn sloganeering about participation into real engagement across the supply chain and across every level of the company. One sand loader operator on the company website film (http://www.fairmountminerals.com) showing the video of one of the large group design summits said, "It doesn't matter whether you're the CEO or Chairman or community member or a sand loader operator—everyone here just has a voice."

A leading companies report of the Global Compact (Waddock, Mirvis, & Ryu, 2008) documents the high engagement approach with many other companies, from Telephonica to Novartis and from Novo Nordisk to Royal Dutch Shell with their scenario planning. While each method might be slightly different, there is a formula emerging among leading companies that says *sustainability = innovation*. But the real question is how? Part of the shift involved is the important management innovation of whole system engagement. Embedding sustainability may be just this simple, fast, and far reaching. Do you want to embed? Then engage. This means to engage the universe of strengths. It also means to engage in profound and real ways. The lessons are becoming clear: sustainability and strategy together become a powerful tandem force for overcoming silos, making customers part of your team, speeding up the arithmetic of innovation, pushing the envelope on speed, and generating more leadership deep in the organization. For more on this issue, we recommend two books: *Appreciative Inquiry: A Positive Revolution in Change* (Cooperrider & Whitney, 2005) and *The Appreciative Inquiry Summit* (Ludema, Whitney, Mohr, & Griffin, 2005). Also, for more on the shift from micromanagement to macromanagement, see Tapscott and Williams (2010).

Scaling Up: How to Leverage UN Opportunities Through Issue-Specific Platforms

"A quantum leap in corporate sustainability action is needed. Yes, there are pockets of innovation and advanced performance. And it is promising to have mobilized thousands of companies around the world—large and small—towards sustainability. However, we are far from a critical mass, nor have we seen the depth of action needed to right the course and adequately address the world's most pressing challenges—poverty, climate, energy, water shortages and food security, as prime examples."

—Georg Kell, United Nations Global
Compact Annual Review 2010

"It's time to scale up. It's time to leverage our efforts through concerted, coordinated, cooperative global action. With the support and leadership of His Excellency Ban Ki-moon, the UN Global Compact gives us the structure and the focus to work together in ways that were difficult in the past . . . but demanded by the future."

—E. Neville Isdell, chairman and CEO,
The Coca-Cola Company, 2007

The final how to involves partnerships. In many ways there is not one single item on the global agenda for change that can be carried out by any single organization, sector, or even nation. In his keynote address at the UN in Switzerland at the 2007 Leaders Summit, the CEO and president of Coca-Cola, Neville Isdell, said, "It is time for all of us as CEOs to stand up, to step up, and to scale up." During this and other major speeches, Isdell (2007a) spoke about the power of partnerships and Coca-Cola's partnership with the World Wildlife Fund around several major environmental issues. Here is a rather extended passage from one of his speeches. It exemplifies the embedding of the UN Global Compact environmental principles while highlighting the how of partnership:

Because of the critical importance of water not just to our business, but to ecosystems, human health, progress and development, The Coca-Cola Company is focusing on conserving and protecting water for people, species and ecosystems throughout the world.

Much of the world is facing freshwater stress and scarcity. The loss of freshwater bio-diversity, with more than a 50% decline in species populations since 1970, makes this clear. Wetlands and rivers are the source of life and they are being destroyed at an alarming rate. More than half the world's wetlands, which cleanse water and help control flooding, have been lost in the last century alone. Many of the world's largest rivers often fail to reach the sea. And freshwater habitats and the species they support are among the most endangered in the world.

More than one billion people do not have access to safe water today; more than 2.5 billion lack adequate sanitation. And two-thirds of the global population will live in water-stressed areas by 2025. These are problems that need immediate solutions.

Climate change will only make the water challenges worse, with increased droughts, coastal flooding and more severe storms. Addressing water issues today is one of the most urgent climate adaptation priorities.

As I talk with people working on water issues I am inspired by their optimism and their unwavering commitment to finding solutions. Approaches grounded in a belief that conditions can and will improve helps people to see this problem not through a lens of near-term despair but rather through a lens focused on long-term progress.

As a company, we bring knowledge and expertise to water issues, operating nearly 900 plants throughout the world. . . .

Today, The Coca-Cola Company pledges to replace every drop of water we use in our beverages and their production; to achieve balance in communities and in nature with the water we use. . . .

This is a bold pledge—to return the water we use. We recognize that it can only be accomplished in partnership with others. Our ability to achieve this ambitious goal rests on the support of this expanding partnership with WWF along with our work with other conservation and development organizations. Our aim, ultimately, is to establish a truly water-sustainable business on a global scale. (Isdell, 2007a)

There is no question that embedded sustainability leads to bolder management innovation that is more macro, more outside-in, and more courageous than more traditional ways of managing. And this example of the wider horizons involved is not limited to Coca-Cola. This is hardly an isolated example. In 2010, three-quarters of companies reported in the Global Compact Implementation Survey that they too are taking actions to support UN objectives, both individually and in partnership with nongovernmental organizations such as the World Wildlife Fund. Drawing once again on the largest study on sustainability ever conducted with CEOs, the authors conclude,

Across the board, the CEOs we spoke to confirmed that partnerships and collaboration (e.g., with suppliers, nongovernmental organizations, government agencies, etc.) is now a critical element of their approach to sustainability issues. Businesses realize that today's global challenges are too broad and too complex to go it alone. Seventy-eight percent of CEOs believe that companies should engage in industry collaborations and multistakeholder partnerships to address development goals. (Lacy et al., 2010, p. 11)

Conclusion

In this chapter, we bring a special focus to the shifting question of "how?" and look to the state of the art of embedding the principles of environmental sustainability across the enterprise in a way where sustainability is not a bolted on program but becomes embedded into the heart of strategy, operations, and innovation. When embedded, sustainability becomes a source of a whole range of value creation opportunities, with radical innovation cutting across and enabling the other value-creating levels. Companies can use radical innovation to simultaneously lower costs, differentiate their products, and enter entirely new markets—all while creating a truly sustainable value for shareholders and stakeholders. To accelerate the movement from abstract principles to sustainable value creation, leading companies are turning to new management methods, including large group methods that bring whole systems into the room. The Appreciative Inquiry summit, for example, is a large group planning, designing, or implementation meeting that brings a whole system of internal and external stakeholders together in a concentrated way over 3 days to work on a task of strategic, and especially creative, value. Moreover, it is a meeting where everyone is engaged as designers, across all relevant and resource-rich boundaries, to share leadership and take ownership for making the future of some big-league opportunity successful. The meeting appears bold at first, but is based on a simple notion that when it comes to embedding sustainability, there is nothing that brings out the best in human systems—faster, more consistently, and more effectively—than the power of the whole.

Finally, companies are also reaping the benefits of partnership where they join together—often at the invitation of the United Nations as convener of major cross-cutting environmental issues such as water or climate change—across sectors, cultures, and nations "to unite the strengths of markets with the power of universal ideals." And while the sustainability agenda was barely to be found on the radar screen of most organizations a decade ago, today we are reaching a tipping point of historic significance.

Study/Discussion Questions

1. What leads Harmon to believe that business can be the new creative force?

2. What are three sustainability trends and how are they changing the way companies do business?

3. What are the key differences between *bolting on* sustainability versus *embedding* it? What are some of the complexities inherent in the latter?

4. What do you think it means when companies are accused of *greenwashing*? How does that differ from what the authors are proposing?

5. Waste, and in particular e-waste, is one the planet's biggest environmental issues. What might be a radical innovation by companies that could offer a sustainable solution?

6. What are the seven levels of sustainable value creation, and what might be examples of each?

7. Why do most efforts to change organizations fail?

8. What is the *Appreciative Inquiry methodology*? How can it be used to support the development of innovative, sustainable solutions?

9. How might companies align their environmental investment with the strategy of their company?

10. How can sustainability be a source of strategic advantage?

For Cases Relevant to Environmental Principles, See Pages 375 to 492

RBC—Financing Oil Sands (A)
Michael Sider, Jana Seijts, Ramasastry Chandrasekhar

Barrick Gold Corporation—Tanzania
Aloysius Newenham-Kahindi, Paul W. Beamish

Host Europe: Advancing CSR and Sustainability in a Medium-Sized IT Company
Rüdiger Hahn

Veja: Sneakers With a Conscience
Oana Branzei, Kim Poldner

Canadian Solar
Paul W. Beamish, Jordan Mitchell

Scandinavian Airlines: The Green Engine Decision
Jennifer Lynes

References

Berthon, B. (2008, October). *Embedded sustainability*. Paper presented at 2008 Futuropolis, Singapore. Retrieved from http://www.fulbrightacademy.org/file_depot/0-10000000/20000-30000/21647/folder/79004/Embedded+Sustainability-Bruno+Berthon.pdf

Blanco, O. (2011). *Nissan Leaf: 2011 world car of the year*. Retrieved from http://money.cnn.com/2011/04/21/autos/leaf_world_car_of_the_year/index.htm

Brundtland, G. H. (1987). *Our common future*. Oxford, UK: Oxford University Press.

Commodity Research Bureau. (2011). CRB BLS spot indices. Retrieved from http://www.crbtrader.com/crbindex/spot_background.asp

Cooperrider, D. L. (2007). New designs in transformative cooperation: The growing call and converging conversation. In S. Piderti, R. Fry, & D. Cooperrider (Eds.), *Handbook of transformative cooperation*. Stanford, CA: Stanford University Press.

Cooperrider, D. L., & Fry, R. (2010, April). Design-inspired corporate citizenship. *Journal of Corporate Citizenship*, 3–6.

Cooperrider, D. L., & Godwin, L. (2011). Positive organization development. *Oxford handbook of positive organizational scholarship*. Oxford, UK: Oxford University Press.

Cooperrider, D. L., & Laszlo, C. (2010). Creating sustainable value: A strengths-based whole system approach. In T. Thachenkery, D. Cooperrider, & M. Avital (Eds.), *Advances in appreciative inquiry* (Vol. 3). London, UK: Emerald Publishers.

Cooperrider, D. L., & Whitney, D. (2005). *Appreciative inquiry: A positive revolution in change*. San Francisco, CA: Berrett-Koehler.

Fish story: Big tuna sells for record $396,000. (2011, January 5). Retrieved from http://www.msnbc.msn.com/id/40921151/ns/world_news-asia_pacific/t/fish-story-big-tuna-sells-record/

Glavas, A., Senge, P., & Cooperrider, D. L. (2010, March 1). Building a green city on a blue lake: A model for building a local sustainable economy. *People & Strategy*.

Harman, W. (1991). *Creative work: The constructive role of business in transforming society*. San Francisco, CA: Knowledge Systems.

Isdell, E. N. (2007a). Remarks at the WWF Annual Conference. Bejing, China.

Isdell, E. N. (2007b). Speech at the Global Compact Leaders Summit, July 5, 2007. Retrieved from http://www.unglobalcompact.org/docs/summit2007/Opening_COCACOLA_Isdell.pdf

Lacy, P., Cooper, T., Hayward, R., & Nueberger, L. (2010). *A new era of sustainability: UN Global Compact-Accenture CEO study 2010.* Retrieved from http://www.unglobal compact.org/docs/news_events/8.1/UNGC_Accenture_CEO_Study_2010.pdf

Laszlo, C., & Zhexembayeva, N. (2011). *Embedded sustainability: The next big competitive advantage.* Stanford, CA: Stanford University Press.

Ludema, J., Whitney, D., Mohr, B. J., & Griffin, T. (2005). *The appreciative inquiry summit.* San Francisco, CA: Berrett-Kohler.

Schwab, K. (2003, May 5). Get back to business. *Newsweek.*

Sisodia, R., Sheth, J., & Wolfe, D. (2007). *Firms of endearment: How world-class companies profit from passion and purpose.* Upper Saddle River, NJ: Wharton School Publishing.

Tapscott, D., & Williams, A. (2010). *Macrowikinomics: Rebooting business and the world.* New York, NY: Penguin Press.

United Nations. (2004). *The UN Global Compact leaders summit: Final report.* New York, NY: Author.

United Nations Global Compact Office. (2010). *United Nations Global Compact annual review 2010.* New York, NY: Author.

Waddock, S., Mirvis, P., & Ryu, R. (2008). *United Nations Global Compact leading companies retreat summary report.* New York, NY: UN Global Compact.

World Wildlife Fund. (2008). *Living planet report.* Retrieved from http://assets.panda.org/downloads/living_planet_report_2008.pdf

Anti-corruption

Principle 10

The UN Global Compact principle relating to anti-corruption is

Principle 10: Businesses should work against all forms of corruption, including extortion and bribery.

8

The Challenges of Corruption in Business, Government, and Society

Peter Rodriguez

Darden School of Business, University of Virginia

W hen we cast our attention to a complex and important subject, what we seek more than anything else is the truth and an understanding of that truth. We seek to own, possess, and master the complexities of the truth in ways that offer us guidance toward bettering our lives and the lives of others. The enduring and, to some, irreducible presence of corruption in commercial and governmental transactions compels us to question whether and how corruption matters for development and for justice and also how we might effectively diminish or cope with its high social costs.

Unfortunately, the truth is often very hard to see or know or master. So it is with corruption. By nature, corrupt transactions are most often secreted or opaque. And yet, whether it takes the form of small, predictable grease payments or the abuse of power at the highest levels of government, corruption is a fundamental feature of living and doing business in virtually all economies. As a consequence, we are challenged by the question of whether such a pervasive and perhaps endemic socioeconomic institution exists because it fulfills some essential role in our lives and cultures and thus, cannot or should not be eliminated. The idea that corruption is better than the alternatives in many cases or that efforts to reduce it are poor investments is more common than one might imagine. And while heavy and thoughtful investments and efforts have been poured into anti-corruption laws and campaigns, the record for such works is mixed. The truth is that our knowledge about corruption and how to reduce it cannot yet deliver either a fully satisfying estimation of the costs of corruption or a compelling formula for combatting its ill effects, particularly in low-income economies. When it comes to corruption, we are not surrounded by the truth. At best, we are surrounded by facts. And facts or the sum or any particular combination of them are not the truth. A principal task of scholars and policymakers is to perpetually seek to establish and refine truth from facts, science, history, and wisdom about our world. So it is with the study of corruption and how we may address it so as to improve living standards through economic growth and the development of robust institutions.

The subject of corruption is critical to the maintenance and growth of living standards precisely because it threatens the legitimacy of private enterprise and governments in their beneficial roles as they promote economic development. Governments throughout the world seek to better living standards through changes in policies and laws and through the commercial, social, and political institutions that govern business. In turn, these institutions are central to firms' decisions regarding the attractiveness of business investment, domestic and foreign, and of portfolio holdings. Investments in developing economies in particular present firms with opportunities to realize substantial financial returns and contribute to economic growth but are fraught with unique challenges and risks. Moreover, these investments raise normative concerns regarding the role of business in society and the nature of globalization. Consequently, the careful examination of corruption, discussions of the measure of corruption and its effects, and the formulation of policies, laws, and institutions to combat corruption has never been more vital.

Definition and Measurement

The United Nations Global Programme Against Corruption defines corruption as the "abuse of power for private gain." That is the most commonly used definition perhaps because its breadth accommodates many corrupt acts and relationships. Despite this advantage, it is important to note that this definition neither specifies the source of the power that is being abused, nor does it describe what constitutes abuse of that power. Thus, the UN definition of corruption applies to the abuse of power by public officials such as elected representatives, by private parties such as CEOs, and by a combination of both in transactions that involve private parties and public officials. Under that general definition, any abuse of power is corruption.

For many purposes, the UN definition is ideal or at least highly serviceable. For others, such as forming the beginnings of comparative, cross-country analysis, the UN definition is too broad to permit a systematic, scientific search for the root causes and key effects of corruption. Many scholars, particularly those interested in economic development, focus their research on public corruption, which occurs at the interface of government(s) and private interests. Those scholars commonly define public corruption as the "misuse of publicly derived power for private gain" (Rodriguez, Uhlenbruck, & Eden, 2005). For those scholars, public corruption involves acts by politicians or bureaucrats that fall outside the definition or appropriate scope of their position and hence represents a misuse of the powers expressly or implicitly delegated to them by the public. For the most part, misuse of power is presumed to involve some form of private gain to the holder of publicly derived power. That definition of corruption does not deny that corruption between private parties matters, but it rather reflects a focus on the important role that governments play in enforcing laws and regulating competition in markets.

In addition to the UN definition and others that academics formulate to fit their own models of behavior, legal systems around the world promote slight variations on standard definitions of corruption. Among the most popular and versatile definitions used is this common legal definition: "an act done with the intent to give some advantage inconsistent with official duty and/or the rights of others" (Rodriguez, 2008). Most definitions of corruption are similar and differ only in their focus on particular types of corruption. What is common to all definitions is the qualification of some act as a misuse or abuse of power and some evidence of private gain by the corrupt actor.

All these definitions of corruption are flexible and satisfying, and yet, to some degree, they only push back the definition of corruption to other, equally challenging definitions. What exactly constitutes a misuse of power? What counts as a private gain? Those questions are difficult to answer with precision and confound efforts to measure corruption, to deter corruption through the law, and to implement managerial efforts to promote ethical behavior and limit a firm's engagement in corruption.

The ambiguity regarding what should count as corruption is a problem for many in society, including entrepreneurs, managers, and politicians. Moreover, ambiguity about the definition of corruption challenges everyday activities and transactions. For example, when should one consider a gift to be a bribe? Perhaps more relevant to managers in a corporate environment, when does lobbying cross the line into corruption? Is there a difference between a bribe that subverts the law and one that merely speeds along the bureaucratic process (e.g., speed money, a grease payment, or convenience fee)? Some argue that there is, and only such payments are hardly more costly to society than taxes. Everyone must pay, but no one is given undue access to government resources as a result of the payment. Indeed, while perhaps few corrupt transactions reflect this benign form of grease payment, contemplating what makes a corrupt transaction bad for society is essential for the design of anti-corruption policies and the proper prioritization of societal resources.

One common guidepost for measuring when a transaction or exchange is corrupt is the quid pro quo rule. *Quid pro quo* literally means "something for something" and is used to describe an arrangement or transaction in which something of value is given by one party with the understanding that something else of value will be given in return. Given this definition of quid pro quo, it is easy to differentiate the nature of a gift from that of a bribe. Gifts are differentiated from bribes or other political favors because gifts do not imply an obligation to offer a favor or something of value in return. Indeed, gift givers often make it clear that they expect nothing in return. Nevertheless, because determining whether an exchange is an act of corruption or a gift often depends upon the expectations of the parties involved, an identical object or act can be considered a gift in one circumstance and a bribe in another.

Some organizations resort to extensive lists of prohibited activities to deal with the ambiguity surrounding the definition of corruption, but such efforts are daunting and likely to be perpetually incomplete. Others ban gifts altogether but find that doing so is both difficult to enforce and sometimes awkward and bad for morale. Most firms and organizations have no official policy regarding corruption. They tacitly adopt an approach akin to U.S. Supreme Court Justice Potter Stewart's reasoning about obscenity: "I know it when I see it" (Rodriguez, 2008). An alternative is to take a middle path that seeks to identify corrupt transactions by their characteristics and implications. Asking questions like these can help determine whether a gift is just a gift or an act of corruption:

- Do I mind if others know or the press reports on what I do?
- Do I report my actions to others? Do they hold me to standards?
- Would I feel harmed if others did the same thing?
- Would it harm society if everyone engaged in acts such as these?

These are some of the acts commonly considered corruption:

- Bribery: A gift of money or favors given to influence the acts of a public official or one given power in a private organization
- Fraud: The use of deceit to avoid payments due to the government or a private organization

- Embezzlement: The theft of property from the government or the owners of a private organization
- Tunneling: The transfer of assets or property out of firms for the benefit of their controlling shareholders (a concept related to embezzlement)
- Nepotism: Notable favoritism that a public or private official gives to family or close friends in the awarding of jobs or contracts or the delivery of products or services

The Nature and Costs of Corruption

Corruption has rightly received notable attention from academics seeking to understand the forces of globalization and the interaction between firms, managers, and the environments in which they operate. Empirical work on the subject has received the most notice in journals despite significant handicaps of studying corruption: it's hard to define, hard to measure, and nearly impossible to observe. Empirical studies often proceed from general observations and presumed relationships without sound theoretical foundations. Thus, empirical studies of corruption may not seek to distinguish particulars of corrupt transactions or to carefully define the incentives that result from the nature of a corrupt environment.

Although some scholars have characterized corruption under entrenched regimes not so much as bribery but merely as a form of taxation or facilitating payment (Shleifer & Vishny, 1993; Wei, 1997), widespread press reports and broad reviews of corruption (Bardhan, 1997; Treisman, 2000) suggest that the full costs of corruption comprise far more than the monetary costs of bribery. Recent research shows that corruption results in a range of direct and indirect costs to firms and countries (Doh, Rodriguez, Collins, Uhlenbruck, & Eden, 2003) and thereby threatens the efficacy and legitimacy of private and public organizations.

The most prominent efforts to reduce corruption, which have been guided by international agreements that focus on high-level legal and bureaucratic interventions, have met with some modest success (Transparency International, 2001). Despite the numerous anti-corruption campaigns pursued by the United Nations, World Bank, Inter-American Development Bank, and other institutions (see Doh et al., 2003, for a review), corruption remains near or only slightly below historical levels in most developing countries. For example, after Argentina signed the Organization for Economic Cooperation and Development (OECD) Convention on Combating Bribery of Foreign Public Officials in International Business Transactions and adopted the Organization of American States Inter-American Convention Against Corruption, both in 1997, measured levels of corruption, already among the highest in the world, were higher seven years after these agreements were signed. Despite the potential criminal and civil consequences of violating the Foreign Corrupt Practices Act (FCPA), many U.S. companies appear to continue to engage in corrupt activities in many regions of the world.

Efforts to combat corruption work best when they begin with a robust understanding of how corruption is organized in a given context or region. Fundamentally, corruption is not simply about facilitating transactions but also about the maintenance and use of power. And the maintenance of power contributes to and persists when it is embedded within the mutually beneficial arrangements that arise in networks and other social organizations. The organizational structure of reciprocal corruption arrangements and regimes determines the nature of corruption and how public officials and private actors promulgate corrupt behavior. Efforts to adapt to and combat corruption can be successful only when guided by a deep understanding of how it manifests itself in a given environment.

Fifteen years ago, a burgeoning literature began to emerge regarding the causes and consequences of corruption, with virtually all empirical work based on cross-country data. These studies made important contributions to understanding causes and consequences of corruption. For instance, the studies showed that corruption slows economy-wide growth and total investment (Mauro, 1995), reduces foreign direct investment (Wei, 1997), drives firms out of the official economy (Kaufmann, 1998), and reduces both public sector budgets and the productivity of a country's infrastructure (Tanzi, 1998).

Country-level studies, however, since they only provide aggregate determinants, tell us very little about the relationships between corruption and economic agents. They especially cannot explain why individuals or firms facing identical institutional and policy environments can and do have very different experiences and behave differently in response to otherwise similar interactions with corruption. This issue raises an enduring challenge in all efforts to understand and reduce corruption, which is the issue of measurement. Just what counts as more or more severe corruption?

Groups like Transparency International typically measure the level of corruption within a given country through some combination of surveys of business leaders, politicians, and academicians. The cardinal rankings that result certainly capture a broad picture of the relative level of corruption across countries but may tell us very little about the likely implications of a particular level of corruption or even what it means for one country to be more corrupt than another. Moreover, there are good reasons to believe that the effects of corruption can be quite different among countries with the same broadly measured level of corruption. Bardhan (1997) notes that whereas country-level indices measure Indonesia and India as equally corrupt, most observers would agree that firms in the two countries have vastly different experiences with corruption. Understanding the particular nature of corruption and the consequent variegated effects is vital to the design of policies and other efforts aimed at reducing corruption, but it requires more detail than is available through one-dimensional measures.

A key challenge of using one-dimensional measures is reflecting the experience of corruption in regimes that operate very differently. Under some corruption regimes, the actions of those in the system are coordinated so as to preserve the status of corrupt officials and maximize aggregate bribe revenue. Through some combination of interpersonal and institutional controls, the organized system prevents opportunistic actions by individual actors and thereby curtails the cannibalization of downstream bribes by upstream agents. In such a system, the nature of the corrupt transaction is known: firms may pay bribes frequently, but the frequency itself is predictable. A greater degree of certainty surrounds the delivery of rights or state-provided services, and firms are rarely confronted with unexpected demands for bribes. As a result of predictable corrupt transactions, overall firm activity, demands for state-provided services, and total bribes are higher than under disorganized regimes.

In other environments, firms are confronted with substantial uncertainty regarding state-provided rights and services and may need to bribe multiple agents for the same service. Owing to this uncertainty, firms engage in fewer business activities and hence reduce their demands for the objects of bribery (e.g., contracts, business licenses, public services), thereby lowering the total amount of bribes paid and collected. The differences between the structured or loose arrangements that lie behind corruption suggest that the impact of corruption to firms derives as much from the uncertainty it creates as in the financial burden it imposes. Corrupt transactions within organized corruption regimes may be more akin to taxes—costly but predictable—whereas the same transactions in less predictable environments may be less expensive but perhaps even more debilitating because of the uncertainty that surrounds them.

For example, the experience of corruption in some environments hardly resembles that of others even when the corrupt transactions themselves are the same. The nature of corruption that existed under the rule of Indonesia's President Suharto typifies the behavior of a well-defined hierarchical structure of power throughout government. During Suharto's reign, Indonesia's highly centralized and stable political structure was complemented by an equally stable network of business groups and familial ties centering on the president's children. During this period, expatriate managers and local businesspeople described corrupt government officials who coordinated their actions in a predictable manner and who always consummated corrupt transactions as agreed. The business and political connections were based on long-standing family ties and were so well known that local consultancies sold "political roadmaps" and a "Suharto dependency index" to help foreign businesses (Fisman, 2001). Indonesian business groups, like those in many developing countries, controlled the lion's share of the economy and developed strong personal ties for carrying out legitimate and corrupt business dealings. Connections between the president, his children, and 23 allied business-group heads were entrenched and quite valuable; the social ties themselves, apart from any business group assets, were estimated to account for at least 20% of the value of the business groups (Fisman, 2001). Such was the corrupt environment in Indonesia: stable, predictable, and highly effective in ensuring compliance with spoken and unspoken norms of behavior.

Quite unlike the experience in Indonesia, a common experience with corruption in some states in India appears far less predictable. For example, the process of land consolidation in the Indian state of Uttar Pradesh reflects a much less stable distribution of the power to effect a corrupt transaction. Oldenburg (1987) describes the prominent role of brokers or *dalals* in the propagation of corruption during land consolidation. Dalals, who represent a large fraction of the corrupt actors in these networks, prey on the ignorance of important features of the corrupt environment and often act independently to obfuscate and complicate the process of bribery. They regularly fail to deliver on their promises—a failure that follows from the absence of a close connection to an authority with the power to grant the desired treatment to the briber. Moreover, the free entry of middlemen into the market for corruption clouds the workings of the system even to insiders, who cannibalize each other's efforts (Oldenburg, 1987).

These characterizations of corruption and its complexity speak to challenges of employing a uniform definition or simple technique for measurement. Whatever its nature where it occurs, the motivation behind the struggle to precisely define and accurately measure corruption is to come to a better understanding of corruption that will aid in the remediation of corruption's pernicious effects on economic development. In countries throughout the world, throughout history, and at all levels of economic development, corruption has been shown to slow economic growth, increase poverty, reduce material living standards, and undermine the establishment of sound social institutions.

Corruption's Costs

Corruption works through various channels to undermine the processes that lead to growth. Generally, corruption reduces the credibility of arm's-length transactions, particularly those between unfamiliar parties. Where corruption is prevalent, the institutions that govern or regulate transactions are seen as either unpredictable or easily manipulated by those willing to bribe officials. Consequently, corruption encourages individuals and firms to avoid transactions with unfamiliar parties, particularly those that utilize economic institutions and are managed by governments. By avoiding the market-based institutions that are designed to reduce some of the costs of transacting, individuals and firms are forced to internalize more of the costs of negotiating, regulating, and enforcing the terms of contracts costs that are at least partially borne by economic institutions where corruption is not prevalent.

By generally increasing transactions costs for all, corruption reduces the overall number and value of transactions that take place and thereby reduces the size of the economy. Moreover, fewer transactions translate into smaller customer bases, smaller, more localized markets, and less competition, which in turn deters the achievement of economies of scale, reduces the demand for new capital, and promotes less efficient production. Combined with a lack of trust in banks and the ill effects of slow growth and poverty, corruption does its part in deterring overall levels of investment both from within and in the form of foreign investment.

Among the most robust findings about corruption is that it reduces foreign direct investment (FDI), limits inward direct investment by firms, and even encourages citizens to invest their savings in less corrupt countries. By reducing investment and local savings, corruption slows capital accumulation, which is a vital component of any economy-wide growth strategy. Scholars have found support for many effects of corruption on firms and economies, most of which relate to the general effects described above. Some of the common effects of corruption are noted in Table 8.1.

For some firms, legal constraints discourage entry into environments where corruption is viewed as a serious threat. The FCPA enacted in 1977 imposes criminal penalties on any firm listed on a U.S. exchange whose employees bribe officials of foreign governments. In 1997, many of the nations of the OECD adopted the terms of a Bribery Convention patterned after the FCPA and also barring the bribing of foreign officials by firms based in OECD nations.

Even a cursory glance at indices such as the consumer price index hints that corruption and national income, more precisely gross domestic product per capita, go hand in hand. With few exceptions, corruption is perceived to be highest in low-income nations and lowest in high-income nations. What accounts for that apparent relationship between income levels and corruption? Is it merely correlation? Does corruption cause low income or the reverse? Are corruption and low income symbiotic?

Table 8.1   Social and Economic Costs Associated With Corruption

Cost	Explanation
Reduced and skewed public expenditures	Reduced taxes result from the general deterrence of business activity, the ability to avoid or reduce tax payments via bribes to tax officials, and the movement of firms to the unofficial economy. Officials seeking bribes or kickbacks may select privately beneficial and publicly costly expenditure projects where bribes are easily hidden. Construction projects are favored over service expenditures on wages, health care, and education where it is generally harder to hide bribes.
Weak physical infrastructure	Inadequate, expensive, and intermittently supplied infrastructure services such as telephony, electricity, and transportation. Weak infrastructure foments opportunities for small bribes to bureaucrats and technicians who control supply. Thus, there are incentives to maintain weak physical infrastructure. Inability to extract fair payment for services lowers resources available to maintain and expand services and lowers the return on investment in these sectors.
Squandered and/or misdirected entrepreneurial talent	Engagement of entrepreneurial and otherwise talented individuals into the socially unproductive avenues of advance afforded by corrupt environments. The challenges of business formation in corrupt environments deter would-be entrepreneurs from starting new firms. Investments in channels of influence to gain advantage in dividing up the benefits of economic activity; includes lobbying and more direct vote and influence peddling.
Macroeconomic weakness and instability	Reduced rates of macroeconomic growth, higher risks of instability in balance of payments, and greater susceptibility to financial crises.
Reduced investment	Reduced levels and growth rates in public and private investment flows; significantly lower rates of foreign direct investment and of business reinvestment by local firms.
Socioeconomic failure	Increased poverty, income inequality, and income growth for the poorest in society. It increases social demands on already weak central governments.
Red tape/ bureaucratic delay	Nonmonetary and opportunity costs of dealing with corrupt officials or of complying with the illegitimate bureaucratic requirements of corrupt regimes.
Corruption avoidance	Costs incurred in the process of avoiding and limiting the firm's exposure to extortionary behavior by corrupt officials, including hiding output and opting out of the official economy.
Forgoing market-supporting institutions	Costs imposed on the firm as a result of forgoing the use of courts for the enforcement of contracts, local financial operations, etc.
Engagement with organized crime or rackets	Monetary and nonmonetary costs imposed on firms as a result of willing or unwilling engagement with organized crime.

Perhaps the real issue is what counts as corruption. People commonly define corruption as bribe-seeking or -taking by bureaucrats and politicians. But what about subtler forms of influence that may be equally corrupt? For example, lobbying—the attempt to influence officials to take a certain action—is not considered to be corruption, though the line between rules-based influence and outright corruption is blurry at times. A review of top contributors to political parties in the United States reveals that firms spend hundreds of millions of dollars each year on lobbying. Moreover, it is plain that lobbying sometimes masks outright corruption.

Whether corruption is disease or symptom does matter for the design of laws, corporate strategies, corruption abatement efforts, and our understanding of the causes of sustained economic growth. Laws and international agreements like the FCPA and the OECD Bribery Convention are based on the idea that direct efforts to reduce corruption will promote equitable business environments and promote economic growth. Similarly, corporate codes of conduct and ethics guidelines intend to better society in part through reductions in corruption. Perhaps, corruption endures because the focus of laws and corporate codes has not treated its underlying causes. If institutional failures, such as a lack of democratic processes in government, cause corruption, efforts to reduce corruption directly will continue to fail. If corruption is a symptom of deeper problems that go unaddressed, what is the appropriate course of action for governments, nongovernmental organizations, and firms interested in corruption abatement? An enduring issue for academics and others interested in corruption abatement is the significance of the causality question and how it matters for efforts to cope with and reduce the ill effects of corruption.

Conclusion

Corruption is part of the landscape of human and organizational interaction all across the world. So far as anyone knows, it always has been. As a result, many question how corruption's many ill effects can be minimized and even whether it is possible to do so. It is clear that higher-income nations with long-tested and uniformly accessible institutions guaranteeing individual rights have notably less corruption than do low-income developing nations without such a history of individual rights. And yet, the pursuit of influence up to and perhaps crossing over into what may otherwise be considered corrupt never seems to fully fade. Though the right institutions limit or eliminate the most conspicuous and egregious forms of corruption, they also channel much of the motivation for undue influence into subtler interactions that blur the lines between what is appropriate and what is not.

Ultimately, the eradication of corruption is desirable, but what is far more important is steadily reducing the ability of some with power and influence to destroy the power of markets and of entrepreneurial energies to raise living standards. Doing so is the only way to promote the level of economic investment in infrastructure and education and to further the development of institutions that finally and fully secure those living standards.

Study/Discussion Questions

1. How does the United Nations define corruption? What is common to all definitions of corruption?

2. Why is understanding the origins of corruption so critical to eliminating it?

3. What is missing from the definition of corruption that challenges business managers?

4. How does the author distinguish between different types of bribery?

5. What does *quid pro quo* mean? Why does it matter?

6. How can one determine whether an exchange is a gift or a bribe? What are some questions to ask yourself when considering whether a gift is an act of corruption?

7. What are examples of acts that are commonly considered corruption?

8. What is the cost of corruption?

9. Why might corruption and low income be considered symbiotic?

10. What does the author identify as the enduring challenge of corruption? How does he suggest we combat it?

For Cases Relevant to the Anti-corruption Principle, See Pages 493 to 536

Phil Chan (A)
Paul W. Beamish, Jean-Louis Schaan

Medical Equipment Inc. in Saudi Arabia
Joerg Dietz, Ankur Grover, Laura Guerrero

Governance Failure at Satyam
Ajai Gaur, Nisha Kohli

References

Bardhan, P. (1997). Corruption and development: A review of issues. *Journal of Economic Literature, 35*, 1320–1346.

Doh, J., Rodriguez, P., Collins, J., Uhlenbruck, K., & Eden, L. (2003). Coping with corruption in emerging markets. *Academy of Management Executive, 17*(3), 114–127.

Fisman, R. (2001). Estimating the value of political connections. *American Economic Review, 91*(4), 1095–1102.

Kaufmann, D. (1998). Research on corruption: Critical empirical issues. In A. K. Jain (Ed.), *Economics of corruption* (pp. 129–176). Dordrecht, The Netherlands: Kluwer.

Mauro, P. (1995). Corruption and growth. *Quarterly Journal of Economics, 110*, 681–712.

Oldenburg, P. (1987). Middlemen in third-world corruption. *World Politics, 39*, 508–535.

Rodriguez, P. (2008). *A technical note on corruption* (Case No. UVA-BP-0502). Charlottesville, VA: Darden Business Publishing.

Rodriguez, P., Uhlenbruck, K., & Eden, L. (2005). Government corruption and the entry strategies of multinationals. *Academy of Management Review, 30*(2), 383–396.

Shleifer, A., & Vishny, R. (1993). Corruption. *Quarterly Journal of Economics, 108*, 599–617.

Tanzi, V. (1998). *Corruption around the world: Causes, consequences, scope, and cures* (Working paper No. 98/63). Washington, DC: International Monetary Fund.

Transparency International. (2001). *Corruption perceptions index 2001*. Berlin, Germany: Author.

Treisman, D. (2000). The causes of corruption: A cross-national study. *Journal of Public Economics, 67*, 399–457.

Wei, S.-J. (1997). *Why is corruption so much more taxing than tax? Arbitrariness kills* (Working paper No. 6255). Cambridge, MA: National Bureau of Economic Research.

Part III

Case Studies

The Ten Principles in Practice

In this section, we will use actual case studies to look at the *how* of corporate social responsibility: How do individual managers and corporations address issues involving human rights, labour, the environment, and corruption?

At an individual level, we'll consider how managers working globally address dilemmas where traditions, laws, and expectations are different and may be in direct conflict with how they do things at home. How can managers remain true to their own values, respect local traditions, and ethically create value for the business?

From a corporate perspective, we'll address how companies respond when asked to account for how they make things; who they engage with and how; what effect their production or investment has on the environment and the local community; how they sell and market their products; and in the end, how they dispose of the waste they have created.

We'll also examine how smart businesses see corporate responsibility as a way to set themselves apart from their competitors. From being green to instilling fair and equitable working conditions for workers, the more enlightened companies recognize both the moral and business imperative of responsible leadership, seeing it as a way to retain trust, enhance reputation, be a source of innovation, and in the end, build lasting value.

Human Rights

Killer Coke: The Campaign Against Coca-Cola[1]

Henry W. Lane

David T. A. Wesley

. . . the world of Coca-Cola, a world filled with lies, deception, immorality and widespread labor, human rights and environmental violations.

—Ray Rogers, Director, Campaign to Stop Killer Coke[2]

The people who are part of the [Killer Coke] campaign

are trying to use the [Coca-Cola] brand to advance a political agenda that has nothing to do with the company.

—Pablo Largacha, Communications Manager for Colombia, The Coca-Cola Company[3]

When Douglas Daft, CEO of Coca-Cola, arrived at the Hotel du Pont in

---

[1]This case has been written on the basis of published sources only. Consequently, the interpretation and perspectives presented in this case are not necessarily those of the Coca-Cola Company or any of its employees.

[2]"NYU students move to ban Coke products from college campuses,"" *Northeastern News*, December 7, 2005.

[3]"Diez universidades de Estados Unidos y Europa vetaron el consumo de Coca-Cola por presuntos nexos con 'paras'," *El Tiempo (Colombia)*, January 4, 2006.

Delaware to address the company's annual shareholders meeting, he was greeted by a crowd of protesters gathered near the hotel entrance. Most were there to denounce Coca-Cola's alleged complicity in the murders of union leaders in Colombia. The issue had garnered considerable media attention, and Daft knew that shareholders were wondering how the company planned to deal with the issue. He now hoped to put their concerns to rest. "Some in organized labor have been working overtime in college campuses to keep allegations about Colombia alive through misinformation and a twisting of the facts," he began.

> The charges linking our company to atrocities in Colombia are false and they are outrageous. Now what is happening in Colombia today is a tragedy. And during the past 40 years, 60,000 people have died as victims of terrorism and civil war there. We all know employees, colleagues, and friends, who have been victims of that violence, which we absolutely abhor. But the Coca-Cola Company has nothing to do with it.
>
> Our bottling partners have been good employers in Colombia for more than 70 years and have good relationships with a number of unions there. We contribute to an improved standard of living for Colombians, and that is why we continue to operate in that country.

Later, when Daft opened the floor to discussion, the first to the podium was Ray Rogers, a 60-year-old activist and director of the Campaign to Stop Killer Coke. "You lied about the situation in Colombia," he declared.

> You said that at no time was any union leader ever harmed by paramilitary security forces at any of your plants. Yet Isidro Gil was assassinated—murdered— in one of your bottling plants in Colombia. The next day, those same paramilitary security forces went into the plant and rounded up the workers. Coca-Cola managers in the plant had prepared resignation forms. Those workers were told that if they did not resign by 4 p.m. that day, they too would be murdered like their union officer, Isidro Gil. They all resigned en masse and the wages in that plant went from $380 a month down to $130 a month.

As Rogers continued to cite cases of alleged abuses, Daft interrupted. "Mr. Rogers, could you please finish?"

"I'm not done. I will finish very shortly," replied Rogers. When his microphone was cut off, Rogers raised his voice.

> Right now, there are five colleges and universities that have terminated Coca-Cola contracts over the Colombia issue. They have banned Coca-Cola products from all student-owned and operated facilities. Do stockholders know that? That was University College Dublin. Trinity College soon followed. In the United States, Carleton College, Lake Forest College and Bard College . . .

Suddenly Rogers was struck on the back by a security guard, followed by a number of others who forced him to the floor.

Appalled by what had happened, Daft pleaded with the security guards to "be gentle." He then turned to one of his executives and whispered, "We shouldn't have done that."

With Rogers ejected, the meeting was allowed to proceed. Civil rights activist Reverend Jesse Jackson rose to the podium and upbraided Daft for having Rogers silenced.

> Mr. Daft and members of the board let me say at the outset that while many disagreed with the first person making a comment, the violent removal was beneath the dignity of this company, it was by the security forces an overreaction and if he had been hurt and if he is hurt, that would be another lawsuit. It was an excessive use of power.

One by one, activist shareholders rose to rebuke Daft, many focusing on the human rights situation in Colombia. When one challenged Daft to "have an objective investigation," Daft rose to the company's defense.

> There have been objective evaluations and investigations. In every case, the company was cleared and any allegation was dismissed. The independent investigation has taken place.

The Republic of Colombia: A Brief History

Colombia was established as a colony of Spain in 1525. It remained under Spanish colonial rule until the early 19th century. The peace was broken in 1810 when several regions in the colony declared independence. The resulting civil war lasted 13 years and ended with independence for most of South America. It also firmly established a culture of internal conflict.

While Spain no longer governed Colombia, the Catholic church continued to exert great influence in political matters. A civil war between liberals, who opposed the influence of the church, and conservatives, who supported it, began in 1840 and lasted until 1903. When the liberal government confiscated all church-owned lands in 1861, a wide-spread guerrilla war erupted.

Between 1863 and 1885, Colombia saw more than 50 armed insurrections and 42 separate constitutions. "The army and the police force were kept small and weak to exclude them from politics, and as a consequence, law enforcement, especially in rural areas of the country, was left in private hands."[4] The war reached its climax between 1899 and 1903, following a collapse in the economy and increasing disparity of wealth under the liberal administration. By 1903, more than 100,000 lives had been lost and Colombia was in ruins.

Growing worldwide demand for coffee, oil and bananas helped Colombia to recover from the war and post strong growth during the next two and a half decades. In the early 1930s, a

---

[4]H. F. Kline, *Colombia: Democracy Under Assault,* Harper Collins, 1995.

liberal government confiscated dormant land from mainly conservative land owners. When the conservatives were returned to power in 1946, they quickly seized the opportunity to reclaim their land. Many desired to return to the "glories" of Spanish colonial rule and looked to Spanish president Francisco Franco "as the sole defender of Christian civilization."[5]

La Violencia

In rural areas of the country, liberal-backed guerrilla groups, which were the precursors for modern-day Marxist guerrillas, formed in order to violently defend land that conservative land owners were trying to reclaim. In 1948, they went on a rampage, burning churches in the colonial city of Santa Fe de Bogotá. This deeply offended the religious sentiments of many Colombians and created deep and long-lasting wounds. It also became the basis for the most violent period in Colombia's history, one that saw the loss of some 200,000 lives and became known as *La Violencia* (The Violence). "Toward the end of *La Violencia* a new generation of young Colombians who had been socialized to think that violence was a normal way of life . . . increasingly took to banditry."[6] In a successful effort to reestablish order, the military seized control of the country in 1953.

The military government offered amnesty to guerrillas who surrendered their weapons. And most did. However, liberal guerrilla groups included a large number of communists who refused to surrender their arms, but instead retreated to isolated areas of the country where they continued to operate with impunity.

The Revolutionary Armed Forces of Colombia

Civilian rule was restored in 1958 after moderate conservatives and liberals, with the support of the military, agreed to unite under a coalition known as the National Front. Meanwhile, communists successfully established their own government in a remote region of the country, known as the "republic" of *Marquetalia*. The government ignored the growing influence of communists until 1964 when, under pressure by conservatives, the Colombian army razed the communist controlled "republic."

Following the attack, the guerrillas reorganized under the banner *Fuerzas Armadas Revolucionarias de Colombia* (FARC). While the group officially came into existence in 1964, it continued to be led by former liberal guerrillas, and therefore "was the continuation

---

[5]Ibid.

[6]Ibid.

of the revolutionary movement that had begun in 1948."[7] As FARC continued to grow, it established itself throughout the country in semi-autonomous fronts.

FARC financed itself through kidnapping ransoms, extortion and protection of the drug trade. Fronts also overran small communities in order to distribute propaganda and, more importantly, to pillage local banks. Businesses operating in rural areas, including agricultural, oil and mining interests, were required to pay vaccines (monthly payments), which "protected" them from attacks and kidnappings. An additional, albeit less lucrative, source of revenue was highway blockades where guerrillas stopped motorists and buses in order to confiscate jewelry and money.

Over time, fewer recruits joined the organization for ideological reasons, but rather as a means to escape poverty. "FARC's narcotics-related income for 1995 reportedly totaled $647 million."[8] And per capita income for Colombian guerrilla fighters was at least 40 times the national average.[9]

By 1998, FARC's ranks had swelled to approximately 15,000 guerrilla fighters, up from 7,500 in 1992, and effectively controlled about half the country. They were also "better armed, equipped, and trained than the Colombian armed forces."[10] Over a period of 10 years, the war had cost the lives of an estimated 35,000 civilians and reduced the country's GDP by four per cent.[11]

United Self-Defense Forces of Colombia

The United Self-Defense Forces of Colombia (AUC)[12] was formed in April 1997 in an effort to consolidate local and regional paramilitary groups in Colombia. Its mission was to protect local economic, social and political interests from leftist rebels. While FARC and other guerrilla groups were obvious targets, the AUC also targeted trade unions, human rights workers and others suspected of having leftist sympathies. The AUC's paramilitary fighters were funded primarily through the production and sale of illegal narcotics and from businesses that paid the AUC for "protection."

---

[7]J. P. Osterling, *Democracy in Colombia: Clientelist Politics and Guerrilla Warfare*, Transaction Publishers, 1989.

[8]Drug Control: U.S. Counternarcotics Efforts in Colombia Face Continuing Challenges, United States General Accounting Office, February 1998.

[9]"Colombia: Guerrilla Economics," *The Economist*, January 13, 1996.

[10]"The Suicide of Colombia," Foreign Policy Research Institute, September 7, 1998.

[11]"Las FARC lamentan expectativas exageradas," *El Nuevo Herald*, April 22, 1999.

[12]Autodefensas Unidas de Colombia.

Trade unionists were frequently victims of paramilitary death squads. According to a U.S. State Department report on human rights in Colombia, 1,875 labor activists were killed between 1991 and 2002, and "labor leaders nationwide continued to be attacked by paramilitaries, guerrillas, and narcotics traffickers." Although the Colombian government "operated a protection program for threatened human rights workers, union leaders, journalists, mayors, and several other groups," AUC members acted with relative impunity. Accordingly, only five of the more than 300 labor-related murder cases investigated since 1986 resulted in a conviction.[13]

FARC was also implicated in the murder of unionists, albeit to a lesser extent. In 2002, leftist guerillas were linked to 19 murders of trade unionists, 17 attempted murders, 189 death threats, 26 kidnappings, and 8 disappearances.[14]

The human rights situation noticeably improved following the election of Álvaro Uribe Vélez in 2002. Under his administration, the government began to take a harder line against all armed groups in Colombia, including the AUC. With more than $3 billion in support from the United States under "Plan Colombia," Uribe significantly augmented military capacity. By 2004, homicides, kidnappings and terrorist attacks in Colombia decreased to their lowest levels in almost 20 years, resulting in unprecedented public support for the Colombian president.[15]

Coca-Cola Colombia

Coca-Cola Colombia was a wholly-owned subsidiary of the Coca-Cola Company (see Exhibits 1 to 3) with corporate offices in Bogotá. It was responsible for manufacturing and distributing Coke products to its Colombian bottlers. Major decisions concerning production, distribution and marketing came from the company's U.S. headquarters, while Coca-Cola Colombia was responsible for ensuring that these directives were carried out by the company's bottlers and other contractors.

Bebidas y Alimentos de Urabá (Bebidas) was a small corporation owned by two Florida residents, Richard Kirby and his son, Richard Kielland. Kirby was responsible for overall company strategy, while Kielland, as manager of plant operations, implemented company policy at the Colombian

---

[13]Colombia: Country Reports on Human Rights Practices, U.S. Department of State, Bureau of Democracy, Human Rights, and Labor, March 31, 2003.

[14]Ibid.

[15]Background Note: Colombia, U.S. Department of State, Bureau of Western Hemisphere Affairs, February 2005.

plants. The company operated one plant in Colombia, in Carepa, Urabá, a town of 42,075 inhabitants, located approximately 200 miles north of Medellín.

Coca-Cola beverages were also produced in 17 plants owned by Panamerican Beverages, a publicly traded corporation headquartered in Miami. In addition to its Colombian plants, Panamerican Beverages was the "anchor bottler" for Coca-Cola in Brazil, Costa Rica, Guatemala, Mexico, Nicaragua and Venezuela. In 2003, Panamerican Beverages was purchased by Coca-Cola FEMSA, a subsidiary of Coca-Cola U.S.A.[16]

The Case Against Coca-Cola and Its Colombian Bottlers

Background

Although union members at several Coca-Cola bottling plants were targeted by paramilitaries, Coca-Cola's troubles centered on the events at one particular plant, the Bebidas plant in Carepa, Urabá. According to an Amnesty International report, Urabá was one of the most violent regions in the country, a place where reprisal killings of civilians by communist guerillas and paramilitaries were commonplace.

In the mid-1990s, paramilitaries:

launched major offensives from the northern municipalities of the Urabá region of Antioquia and pushed southwards rooting out and killing those they considered guerrilla collaborators or sympathizers. FARC guerrilla forces, operating in alliance with dissident groups, responded by carrying out a number of massacres of [civilians] they considered to be supporting army or paramilitary forces.

Armed opposition groups have been responsible for forced displacement of communities who have fled their homes as a result of death threats or the deliberate and arbitrary killings of those accused of collaboration with the security or paramilitary forces. Many families have also fled their homes in order to escape forcible recruitment of their children by armed opposition groups.[17]

Torture Victims Protection Act Claim

In 2001, Sinaltrainal and representatives of several slain union leaders brought suit against Coca-Cola and Bebidas under the Alien Tort Claims Act (ATCA) and the Torture Victims

---

[16]Coca-Cola FEMSA was a joint venture between Mexican brewer Fomento Económico Mexicano, S.A. de C.V. (FEMSA) (46 per cent) and the Coca-Cola Company (40 per cent). The remaining shares were publicly held.

[17]Return to Hope, Forcibly displaced communities of Urabá and Medio Atrato region, Amnesty International Report 23/023/2000, June 1, 2000.

Protection Act (TVPA) (see Exhibit 4).[18] The petition, filed by lawyers from the International Labor Rights Fund and the United Steel Workers of America, argued that Coca-Cola and Bebidas "contracted with or otherwise directed paramilitary security forces that utilized extreme violence and murdered, tortured, unlawfully detained or otherwise silenced trade union leaders."[19] The suit also named Panamerican Beverages as a defendant for its alleged complicity in the kidnappings and murders of several union members and their relatives at three Panamerican plants in northern Colombia.

The use of ATCA in such cases was not without precedent. According to Michael Ratner, vice-president of the Center for Constitutional Rights, "courts in the United States pioneered the use of civil remedies to sue human rights violators."

> Litigation under the Alien Tort Claims Act and the Torture Victim Protection Act have resulted in billions of dollars in judgments, and have had an important impact on plaintiffs and human rights both in the United States and internationally. Such cases do not require official approval; they can be brought by individuals who have control over the lawsuits and thus are less subject to political vagaries.
>
> Civil remedies include damage awards for injuries and punitive damages meant to deter future abusive conduct as well as send a message to others that such conduct is unacceptable. In addition to any money that can be collected, these cases are important to the victims and their families. Plaintiffs are allowed to tell their stories to a court, can often confront their abusers, and create an official record of their persecutions. This in turn could lead to a criminal prosecution.[20]

The Murder of Isidro Segundo Gil

The plaintiffs sought compensation specifically for the murder of 27-year-old Isidro Segundo Gil, an employee of the Carepa plant, as well as other murdered union members at the Carepa plant and at three plants owned by Panamerican Beverages.[21]

In 1996, Bebidas hired Ariosto Milan Mosquera to manage the Carepa bottling plant. Mosquera allegedly began

---

[18]The Torture Victims Protection Act was enacted in 1992 and added as a provision under the Alien Tort Claims Act.

[19]"Coca-Cola Accused," *The New York Times,* July 29, 2001.

[20]Michael Ratner, "Civil Remedies for Gross Human Rights Violations," *PBS.org*, February 2, 1999 (www.pbs.org/wnet/justice/law_background_torture.html).

[21]Five of the eight murder cases cited by Coca-Cola opponents took place between 1994 and 1996 at the Carepa plant owned and operated by Bebidas & Alimentos de Urabá.

threatening to destroy the union. He allowed paramilitaries access to the plant and made a specific agreement with local paramilitary leaders to drive the union out of the Bebidas plant by using threats and violence, if necessary.

On September 27, 1996 Sinaltrainal submitted a letter to both Bebidas and Coca-Cola Colombia accusing Mosquera of working with the paramilitary to destroy the union and urging Bebidas to protect trade unionists from the paramilitaries who were threatening employees.

On the morning of December 5, 1996, two paramilitaries approached Gil as he arrived at work. They said they needed to enter the Bebidas plant. When Gil opened the door, the paramilitaries shot and killed him. Witnesses claimed the murderers were the same paramilitaries who had met with Mosquera at the plant. Two days later, paramilitaries arrived at the Bebidas plant, where they assembled the employees and told them that unless they resigned from the union, they would face the same fate as Gil. The employees then entered Mosquera's office and signed resignation forms that he had prepared. Many union members permanently fled Carepa after the forced resignations and continued to live in

hiding (for a more detailed summary of the Carepa events, see Exhibit 5).[22]

Coca-Cola's initial response was to deny any wrongdoing. "We adhere to the highest standards of ethical conduct and business practices and we require all of our companies, operating units and suppliers to abide by the laws and regulations in the countries that they do business," a company spokesperson explained.[23]

For nearly two years, both sides presented evidence to back up their cases. In 2003, the court agreed that Mosquera colluded with paramilitaries in an effort to break the union. It further argued,

Bebidas have not produced any evidence to refute the allegation that Bebidas had ties to Mosquera's decision to hire the paramilitary to impede Sinaltrainal's union activity at Bebidas.[24]

However, while the Bottler's Agreement between Coca-Cola and Bebidas granted Coca-Cola U.S.A. the right to supervise and control the quality, distribution and marketing of its products, including the right to terminate or suspend a bottler's operations for noncompliance with its terms and conditions, it did not give Coca-Cola direct

[22]The account of Gil's murder is summarized from: Sinaltrainal v. Coca-Cola Co., United States District Court for the Southern District of Florida, 256 F. Supp. 2d 1345; 2003 U.S. Dist. LEXIS 7145; 16 Fla. L. Weekly Fed. D 382, March 28, 2003, Decided, March 31, 2003.

[23]"Union Says Coca-Cola in Colombia Uses Thugs," *The New York Times,* July 26, 2001.

[24]Sinaltrainal v. Coca-Cola Co., United States District Court for the Southern District of Florida, 256 F. Supp. 2d 1345; 2003 U.S. Dist. LEXIS 7145; 16 Fla. L. Weekly Fed. D 382, March 28, 2003, Decided, March 31, 2003.

control over plant operations. As such, the court determined that Coca-Cola U.S.A. and Coca-Cola Colombia were not agents that conspired or acted jointly with the paramilitary through Bebidas. As such, the court dismissed Coca-Cola as a defendant because it lacked jurisdiction over Coca-Cola under ATCA.[25]

Bebidas and Panamerican Beverages, on the other hand, could be held liable as "an individual who, under color of law of any foreign nation, subjects another person to torture or extrajudicial killing," thereby overruling the company's defense that a private corporation is not an "individual" in the legal sense, and should not be held liable for acts of torture and killing in foreign countries.

The Anti-globalization Movement

The incidents at Coca-Cola's bottling plants in Colombia coincided with the rise of the anti-globalization movement, which targeted large multinational corporations as symbols of "the damaging effects of globalization." The movement's goals included labor rights, environmental protection, preservation of indigenous peoples and cultures, food safety and social welfare. It found wide support on

college campuses in North America and Europe, as well as from environmental organizations such as Greenpeace. Much of the criticism of globalization focused on alleged exploitation of workers in less-developed countries, such as the use of sweatshops by Nike, the Gap and others.

The Case of Nike: A Model for Change

Anti-globalization protesters viewed Nike, in particular, as a model for social change brought about through public pressure. In the 1990s, Nike came under scrutiny for alleged human rights violations by its outsourcing contractors in Asia. The company denied any wrongdoing and, to prove its case, hired Goodworks International, an Atlanta-based non-profit organization, to audit its Asian contractors. In early 1997, Goodworks director and former civil rights leader, Andrew Young, led the investigation. After a two-week tour of China, Vietnam and Indonesia, Young returned to the United States to report that Nike was "doing a good job."

> We found Nike to be in the forefront of a global economy. Factories we visited that produce Nike goods were clean, organized, adequately ventilated and well lit.[26]

---

[25]After Coca-Cola acquired a stake in Panamerican Beverages in 2003, the plaintiffs moved to have Coca-Cola reinstated as a defendant. The court agreed to consider the motion, but as of 2005 had not made a ruling.

[26]Andrew Young, and H. Jordan, *The Nike Code of Conduct Report*, Good Works International, June 27, 1997.

Young further cited Ernst & Young audits of particular plants.

> I did not find in the audit reports or in my own conversations with workers at these factories or in our other research a pattern of these factories violating national laws, local laws or the [Nike] Code of Conduct as relates to age or working conditions.[27]

Following Young's report, a widely criticized New York Times article reported "no evidence of widespread or systematic mistreatment of workers."[28] Medea Benjamin of San Francisco-based CorpWatch, who had expected Young to "maintain his credibility as a defender of the poor," was sorely disappointed.

A few months later, a disgruntled Nike employee handed CorpWatch a copy of one of the Ernst & Young audits. In contrast to Young's report, it cited gross human rights violations at company plants in Vietnam. Feeling that it had been misled, the New York Times lambasted Nike. A front page headline read, "Nike Shoe Plant in Vietnam Is Called Unsafe for Workers." It continued,

> In an inspection report that was prepared in January for the company's internal use only, Ernst & Young wrote that workers at the factory near Ho Chi Minh City were exposed to carcinogens that exceeded local legal standards by 177 times in parts of the plant and that 77 percent of the employees suffered from respiratory problems. The report also said that employees at the site, which is owned and operated by a Korean subcontractor, were forced to work 65 hours a week, far more than Vietnamese law allows, for $10 a week.[29]

Within months a proliferation of newspaper articles reported similar abuses at factories throughout Asia and Latin America. Almost overnight, anti-globalization organizers mobilized a worldwide movement against Nike that eventually forced the company to rethink its business practices.

Nike created a department to monitor suppliers in less-developed countries. Todd McKean, the company's new Director of Corporate Responsibility Compliance recognized that some Nike factories violated worker rights and that the company had to improve the way it monitored working conditions. "How much do we really know about issues in all of these factories?" he asked.

> Not enough. Every time we look closer, we find another thing wrong. Too much overtime. Wage errors. Too much heat. Involuntary pregnancy testing. An abusive supervisor. Every time we peel another layer off the onion we find another complex set of issues that our

---

[27]Ibid.

[28]"Nike's Asian Factories Pass Young's Muster," *The New York Times,* June 25, 1997.

[29]"Nike Shoe Plant in Vietnam Is Called Unsafe for Workers," *The New York Times,* November 8, 1997.

compliance and production people work with factory management to try to resolve.[30]

The company also hired independent agencies, such as the Fair Labor Association, to regularly monitor its 700 contract factories. When audits uncovered abusive practices, Nike required its contractors to implement changes or risk losing their contracts.

For CorpWatch, it was a major victory.

Student organizers demanding that universities doing business with Nike hold the company to higher standards kept Nike's labor practices in the spotlight. Meanwhile, faced with the increasing clout of activist groups, falling stock prices and weak sales, Nike announced major concessions to its critics in May, 1998.[31]

While some continued to criticize Nike's labor practices, most anti-globalization activists focused their efforts elsewhere.

Killer Coke Campaign

Shortly after the U.S. court dismissed Coca-Cola as a defendant in 2003, Ray Rogers mounted the Killer Coke campaign. The organization's website, killercoke.org (see Exhibit 6), dubbed Coca-Cola "the New Nike," and urged students to pressure colleges to cancel their Coca-Cola contracts. "Like Nike, Coke will only remedy its practices with significant pressure and the fear of a tarnished image," exclaimed a web article.[32]

Rogers, a long-time activist for labor rights, began his career as a labor organizer for the Amalgamated Clothing Workers of America. In 1978, the New York Times recognized Rogers as the moving force behind a successful campaign against J. P. Stevens, a large textile company, which forced the resignation the chairman of Stevens and the chairman of the New York Life Insurance Co. from each other's board of directors. "The important thing isn't just organizing people into unions," explained Rogers. "It's disorganizing the power structure."[33]

Rogers' early success allowed him to create Corporate Campaign, Inc., a public relations and labor strategy firm. In the 1980s, Corporate Campaign confronted Consolidated Edison Utilities, Hormel Foods, American

---

[30]Factory Monitoring Practices, Labor Practices, Nike, 2001.

[31]CorpWatch Takes on Nike, Sweatshops (www.corpwatch.org) February 17, 2006.

[32]Tremendous Victories on Campus, *Campaign to Stop Killer Coke Update*, May 20, 2005 (www .killercoke.org/nl0520.htm) February 17, 2006.

[33]"Rogers' Tough, Unorthodox Tactics Prevail in Stevens Organizing Fight," *The Wall Street Journal*, October 21, 2006.

Airlines, Bank of Boston, Campbell Soup, and International Paper, often winning important victories for labor unions. Tactics included walkouts, consumer boycotts, demonstrations and letter-writing campaigns. "I'd much rather see rich businessmen fight it out in the boardroom," Rogers asserted. "You can't embarrass them. You have to make them deal with real economic or political pressure."[34]

Rogers' strategy often pitted one company against another. For example, he encouraged trade unions to put pressure on financial institutions that managed union funds to withdraw support from companies opposed to union organizing activities. Other times he would target the largest company in an industry hoping that competitors would use it to their advantage.

> You have to create a situation where you're beating on one institution. They're taking heavy losses, and all the other institutions are standing behind them saying, "Whatever you do, don't set a precedent, don't give in." But finally the institution you're putting pressure on is going to say, "Hey, wait a minute. We're losing a lot of business. And where is that business going? It's going to you, our competitors, and to your banks. You're benefiting at our expense. So if you don't want to set a precedent, then don't you set it, but we're getting out of this thing."[35]

Killer Coke was a continuation of Rogers' tradition of activism, and it followed many of the same grass-roots tactics. Campaign flyers distributed to university students as part of the "Coke Organizing Manual" demanded that Coca-Cola,

- Denounce the violence that is occurring in the name of Coca-Cola in Colombia.
- Respect the fundamental rights to free association and to organize trade unions, as reflected in Colombian law, Article 22 of the International Covenant on Civil & Political Rights, as well as Conventions 87 & 88 of the International Labor Organization.
- Announce publicly in Colombia its intention to participate in an investigation of the violence at its bottling plants.
- Reinforce Coca-Cola's public stance against violence by directing all bottling plants in Colombia to stop dealing with any armed groups that are participating in violence against trade unionists.
- Establish a complaint and reporting process which will allow union members to report violations occurring in Coca-Cola bottling plants to an official of the company who will then investigate

---

[34]"Labor's Boardroom," *Time,* June 20, 1988.

[35]"An Interview with Ray Rogers," *Working Papers Magazine,* January/February 1982.

and take swift remedial action against these violations.

- Provide compensation to the known victims of violence at Coca-Cola bottling plants.[36]

Serving as a conduit of information, the website sought to foment support on college campuses. Pamphlets, banner templates, web icons, news links, and other resources were provided to help students put pressure on university administrators to suspend contracts with the Coca-Cola Company.

Coke Facts

When the Killer Coke campaign brought Coca-Cola increased notoriety among young consumers, some business analysts began to criticize the company's decision not to investigate the murders in Colombia.[37] Coca-Cola responded by sending high level executives to college campuses to explain its side of the story and by creating a company-owned website (cokefacts .org) to counter the Killer Coke website

(see Exhibit 7).[38] Finally, it hired Cal-Safety Compliance Corporation to audit its Colombian bottling plants.[39]

In an article on cokefacts.org, Ed Potter, director of Global Labor Relations for Coca-Cola, criticized the anti-Coke campaign. "I would stand our Company's labor relations practices alongside any other company on the planet," he wrote.

> These unjustified attacks do a disservice to the men and women of Coca-Cola; they mislead the public and impede progress for workers' rights worldwide. The Coca-Cola system is one of the most highly unionized multinational corporations in Colombia and throughout the world. Last year, the Company signed a joint statement with the IUF, the international organization for food and beverage unions, confirming that Coca-Cola workers are "allowed to exercise rights to union membership and collective bargaining without pressure or interference."

> Two different judicial inquiries in Colombia have found no evidence to support allegations that bottler management there conspired to intimidate or threaten trade unionists. An additional independent assessment conducted by

---

[36]Coke Organizing Manual, July 8, 2002.

[37]"The Real Story: How did Coca-Cola's management go from first-rate to farcical in six short years?" *Fortune*, May 31, 2004.

[38]Other company URLs, such as killercoke.com and stopkillercoke.org, redirected visitors to the cokefacts.org site.

[39]Cal Safety Compliance Corporation, a subsidiary of Specialized Technology Resources, Inc., was part of a worldwide organization "dedicated to ensuring the integrity of its clients' products and technologies." Services included compliance, inspection, and quality assurance testing. Specialized Technology Resources Inc. History & Highlights (www.struk.co.uk/comphistory.htm) February 23, 2006.

Cal-Safety Compliance Corporation [see Exhibit 8], an international social compliance auditor certified by the Fair Labor Association and Social Accountability 8000, confirmed that workers in Coca-Cola plants in Colombia enjoy freedom of association, collective bargaining rights and an atmosphere free of anti-union intimidation.[40]

According to Pablo Largacha, Communications Manager for Colombia, the problem was one of perception. Foreigners simply didn't understand the political reality that is Colombia. "In general," he explained, "Colombians have a better sense of what is happening."

We have a better understanding of the political situation and the history of armed conflict. The vast majority believe that these are unfounded accusations. Last year, in 2005, Coca-Cola was ranked in Portafolio magazine as the company with the third best reputation in Colombia, with the best marketing, and as one of the best places to work. Therefore, given the better understanding of the situation, that Coca-Cola is

an economic engine driving the advancement of this country, people here have a radically different opinion.[41]

An International Cause Célèbre

While the company attempted to defend its position, the Killer Coke campaign continued to gain momentum. On December 31, 2005, the University of Michigan joined Rutgers, NYU, and several other U.S. colleges in banning all Coke products from its campus.[42]

The university's board of directors had earlier rejected Coca-Cola's audit of its Colombian bottlers through Cal-Safety Compliance Corporation, calling it "problematic."[43] As a for-profit corporation hired by Coca-Cola to undertake the audit, Cal-Safety did not meet the university's definition of independent. The university essentially agreed with the United Students against Sweatshops, a U.S.-based network of college students working to

---

[40]The Coca-Cola Company Addresses "False and Inflammatory" Allegations Made by Teamsters, Cokefacts.org, February 7, 2006.

[41]Translated from an interview by El Tiempo. "Diez universidades de Estados Unidos y Europa vetaron el consumo de Coca-Cola por presuntos nexos con 'paras'," *El Tiempo (Colombia)*, January 4, 2006.

[42]"In the fiscal year 2005, the University of Michigan had 13 contracts for selling Coca-Cola products, totaling $1.4 million." Products sold by Coca-Cola included Sprite, Dasani water, Minute Maid juice and PowerAde. "U. of Michigan Becomes 10th College to Join Boycott of Coke," *The New York Times*, December 31, 2005.

[43]"University of Michigan seeks probe of Coke's Colombia operations," *Atlanta Journal-Constitution*, June 17, 2005.

end sweatshops. It noted Cal-Safety's documented history of giving favorable reports to factories that were later discovered to have been involved in gross human rights violations.[44] The fact that factory audits typically took three hours and involved interviewing employees in offices provided by plant managers was also deemed unacceptable.

Taking its cue from the United Students against Sweatshops, the University of Michigan demanded,

- Unannounced factory visits to deny management the opportunity to hide abuses.
- More extensive interviews of employees in off-site locations. "U.S. Department of Labor investigations take roughly 20 hours to complete," it noted. "Worker Rights Consortium investigations often take hundreds of person hours over a period of months."

- Audits conducted by non-profit organizations with "experience or expertise investigating violations of associational rights overseas."[45]

In its coverage of the Michigan decision, the Financial Times noted that "Coke's public relations offensive [had] so far failed to slow the [Killer Coke] campaign's momentum." Furthermore,

The value of the Coke brand has been edging down in recent years, following a series of blows to its reputation. Over recent years, the deaths [in Colombia] have become an international cause célèbre for labour rights groups and student activists, who accuse Coke of turning a blind eye to the murders. Anti-Coke campaigns have spread across more than 100 university campuses throughout the U.S., Canada and Europe, including the U.K., where activists are pushing for a nationwide student boycott.[46]

[44]United Students Against Sweatshops Statement, April 15, 2005 (www.killercoke.org/usascal.htm).
[45]Ibid.
[46]"Coke struggles to defend positive reputation," *The Financial Times*, January 6, 2006.

Exhibit 1   The Coca-Cola Company: Financial and Operational Performance
Highlights

The Coca-Cola Company and Subsidiaries					
Year Ended December 31 (In millions except per share data)	2006	2005	2004	2003	2002
SUMMARY OF OPERATIONS					
Net operating revenues	$24,088	$23,104	$21,742	$20,857	$19,394
Cost of goods sold	8,164	8,195	7,674	7,776	7,118
Gross profit	15,924	14,909	14,068	13,081	12,276
Selling, general and administrative expenses	9,431	8,739	7,890	7,287	6,818
Other operating charges	185	85	480	573	–
Operating income	6,308	6,085	5,698	5,221	5,458
Interest income	193	235	157	176	209
Interest expense	220	240	196	178	199
Equity income (loss) - net	102	680	621	406	384
Other income (loss) - net	195	(93)	(82)	(138)	(353)
Gain on issuances of stock by equity investees	–	23	24	8	–
Income before income taxes	6,578	6,690	6,222	5,495	5,499
Income taxes	1,498	1,818	1,375	1,148	1,523
Net income	$5,080	$4,872	$4,847	$4,347	$3,976
PER SHARE DATA					
Cash dividends	1.24	1.12	1.00	0.88	0.80
Market price on December 31	48.25	40.31	41.64	50.75	43.84
CASE VOLUME (millions)[1]					
Worldwide	21,400	20,600	19,800	19,400	18,700
North America	5,778	5,768	5,742	5,626	5,516
Africa	1,284	1,236	1,188	1,164	1,109
East, South Asia and Pacific Rim	1,722	1,854	N/A	N/A	N/A
European Union	3,424	3,296	N/A	N/A	N/A
Latin America	5,564	5,150	4,950	4,850	4,675
North Asia, Eurasia and Middle East	3,628	3,296	N/A	N/A	N/A

Source: www.thecoca-colacompany.com/investors/

[1]Coca-Cola redefined its European and Asian sales regions in 2005; therefore comparative data is unavailable for these regions prior to 2005.

Exhibit 2   Coca-Cola Timeline

Date	Event
1894	Coca-Cola is first produced in a candy store in Vicksburg, Mississippi.
1899	Exclusive bottling rights sold to three Chattanooga, Tennessee lawyers for one dollar.
1904	Coca-Cola becomes the most recognized brand in America.
1905	Cocaine is removed from the Coca-Cola formula.
1920–1939	First international plants were opened in France, Guatemala, Honduras, Mexico, Belgium, Italy and South Africa. By 1939, Coca-Cola had bottling operations in 44 countries.
1940	Coca-Cola Colombia is founded in Medellín. In its first year, Coca-Cola Colombia sells 67,761 cases of soda.
1945	"Coke" becomes a registered trademark of Coca-Cola.
June 1993	Coca-Cola acquires 30% of FEMSA Refrescos S.A. de C.V., a Mexican producer of carbonated beverages.
1994–1996	Paramilitary death squads murder five Sinaltrainal union leaders at a Coca-Cola bottling plant in Carepa, Colombia.
February 1996	Coca-Cola FEMSA acquires 100% of Coca-Cola's bottling operations in Argentina.
July 20, 2001	The United Steelworkers and the International Labor Rights Fund bring suit against Coca-Cola and its Colombian bottlers on behalf of Sinaltrainal, a Colombian union.
March 31, 2003	Coca-Cola is dismissed as a defendant in Sinaltrainal v. Coca-Cola Co., United States District Court for the Southern District of Florida
May 2003	Coca-Cola FEMSA acquires 100% of Panamerican Beverages, Inc. creating the second-largest Coca-Cola bottler in the world, accounting for almost 10% of Coca-Cola's global sales.
December 31, 2003	Coca-Cola ends the year with record net earnings of $4.3 billion on revenues of $21.0 billion.
April 13, 2003	Labor activist Ray Rogers begins "Killer Coke" campaign.
2004	Coca-Cola launches cokefacts.org to promote its side of the Colombia controversy. The site receives only 800 visitors a month compared with killercoke.org's 25,000 visitors a month.
July 21, 2005	Interbrand, the world's leading international brand consultancy, ranks Coca-Cola first among the world's leading brands for the fifth consecutive year. It estimates the company's brand value at $67.5 billion.
December 8, 2005	New York University bans Coca-Cola products from its campus.
December 29, 2005	University of Michigan bans Coca-Cola products from its campus.
December 31, 2005	Coca-Cola ends the year with record net earnings of $4.9 billion on revenues of $23.1 billion.

Exhibit 3   The Coca-Cola Company

Corporate Responsibility Policy

Strategic Vision

The health of our business depends on the health of our consumers, their communities and the environment. The people of The Coca-Cola Company work together with our bottling partners, our business partners and members of the communities where we operate—and even our critics—to identify and address existing and emerging social and environmental issues, as well as potential solutions.

With our technical and marketing expertise, our reputation and network of influence, and our global production and distribution system, we have a tremendous opportunity to make a meaningful difference in the more than 200 countries we call home. We believe that the greater our presence, the greater our responsibility.

Corporate Responsibility is an integral part of our mission, values, and actions.[1]

UN Global Compact

In March 2006, The Coca-Cola Company became a signatory to the United Nations (UN) Global Compact, affirming our commitment to the advancement of its 10 universal principles in the areas of human rights, labor, the environment and anti-corruption. Several of our bottling partners are also signatories.

Our 2006 Corporate Responsibility Review is our first communication on progress for the UN Global Compact and provides a cross-referenced index of the UN Global Compact principles.

Human Rights

Principle 1: Businesses should support and respect the protection of international human rights within their sphere of influence; and
Principle 2: make sure that they are not complicit in human rights abuses.

Labor

Principle 3: Businesses should uphold the freedom of association and the effective recognition of the right to collective bargaining;
Principle 4: the elimination of all forms of forced and compulsory labor;
Principle 5: the effective abolition of child labor; and
Principle 6: the elimination of discrimination in respect of employment and occupation.

Environment

Principle 7: Businesses should support a precautionary approach to environmental challenges;
Principle 8: undertake initiatives to promote greater environmental responsibility; and
Principle 9: encourage the development and diffusion of environmentally friendly technologies.

Anti-Corruption

Principle 10: Businesses should work against corruption in all its forms, including extortion and bribery.

---

[1]The company's full Corporate Responsibility guidelines are discussed in its *2006 Corporate Responsibility Review* (http://www.thecoca-colacompany.com/ourcompany/pdf/corporate_responsibility_review2006.pdf).

Exhibit 4   The Alien Tort Claims Act (28 USCA § 1350)

§ 1350.   Alien's action for tort

The district courts shall have original jurisdiction of any civil action by an alien for a tort only, committed in violation of the law of nations or a treaty of the United States.

HISTORY:
    (June 25, 1948, ch 646, § 1, 62 Stat. 934.)

HISTORY; ANCILLARY LAWS AND DIRECTIVES

Prior law and revision:
    Based on title 28, U.S.C., 1940 ed., § 41(17) (Mar. 3, 1911, ch. 231, § 24, P 17, 36 Stat. 1093).
    Words "civil action" were substituted for "suits," in view of Rule 2 of the Federal Rules of Civil Procedure.
    Changes in phraseology were made.

Other provisions:
    Torture Victim Protection Act of 1991. Act March 12, 1992, P.L. 102-256, 106 Stat. 73, provides:
    "Section 1. Short title
    "This Act may be cited as the 'Torture Victim Protection Act of 1991'.
    "Sec. 2. Establishment of civil action
    "(a) Liability. An individual who, under actual or apparent author-ity, or color of law, of any foreign nation:
        "(1) subjects an individual to torture shall, in a civil action, be liable for damages to that individual; or
        "(2) subjects an individual to extrajudicial killing shall, in a civil action, be liable for damages to the individual's legal rep-resentative, or to any person who may be a claimant in an action for wrongful death.
    "(b) Exhaustion of remedies. A court shall decline to hear a claim under this section if the claimant has not exhausted adequate and available remedies in the place in which the conduct giving rise to the claim occurred.
    "(c) Statute of limitations. No action shall be maintained under this section unless it is commenced within 10 years after the cause of action arose.
    "Sec. 3. Definitions
    "(a) Extrajudicial killing. For the purposes of this Act, the term 'extrajudicial killing' means a deliberated killing not authorized by a previous judgment pronounced by a regularly constituted court afford-ing all the judicial guarantees which are recognized as indispensable by civilized peoples. Such term, however, does not include any such

killing that, under international law, is lawfully carried out under the authority of a foreign nation.

"(b) Torture. For the purposes of this Act:

"(1) the term 'torture' means any act, directed against an individual in the offender's custody or physical control, by which severe pain or suffering (other than pain or suffering arising only from or inherent in, or incidental to, lawful sanctions), whether physical or mental, is intentionally inflicted on that individual for such purposes as obtaining from that individual or a third person information or a confession, punishing that individual for an act that individual or a third person has committed or is suspected of having committed, intimidating or coercing that individual or a third person, or for any reason based on discrimination of any kind; and

"(2) mental pain or suffering refers to prolonged mental harm caused by or resulting from:

"(A) the intentional infliction or threatened infliction of severe physical pain or suffering;

"(B) the administration or application, or threatened administration or application, of mind altering substances or other procedures calculated to disrupt profoundly the senses or the personality;

"(C) the threat of imminent death; or

"(D) the threat that another individual will imminently be subjected to death, severe physical pain or suffering, or the administration or application of mind altering substances or other procedures calculated to disrupt profoundly the senses or personality."

Exhibit 5   Court Filing (July 20, 2001)

The Events at Bebidas y Alimentos in Carepa (abridged)

In April of 1994, paramilitary forces murdered Jose Eleazar Manco David and Luis Enrique Gomez Granado, both of whom were workers at Bebidas y Alimentos and members of Sinaltrainal. The paramilitary forces in Carepa then began to intimidate other Sinaltrainal members as well as the local leadership of Sinaltrainal, telling them, upon threat of physical harm, to resign from the union or to flee Carepa altogether. The management of Bebidas y Alimentos permitted these paramilitary forces to appear within the plant to deliver this message to Union members and leaders. A number of Union members began leaving town as a result. And, in April of 1995, following more death threats, every member of the executive board of the Sinaltrainal local representing the Bebidas y Alimentos workers fled Carepa in fear for their lives.

In June of 1995, the Sinaltrainal local union elected a new executive board to replace the one that had fled. Isidro Gil was elected as a member of this new board as was an individual named Dorlahome Tuborquia. Shortly thereafter, in July of 1995, Bebidas y Alimentos began to hire members of the paramilitaries who had threatened the first Union executive board into fleeing. These members of the paramilitaries were hired both into the sales and production departments.

(Continued)

Exhibit 5 (Continued)

In September of 1995, Ariosto Milan Mosquera took over as the manager of the Bebidas y Alimentos plant in Carepa. Mosquera proceeded to discharge Dorlahome Tuborquia. Sinaltrainal challenged this discharge through the legal process, and a judge, finding the discharge to be unlawful, ordered Bebidas y Alimentos to rehire Tuborquia. He returned to work at Bebidas y Alimentos in December of 1995. Shortly after the return of Tuborquia, Mosquera announced that he had given an order to the paramilitaries to carry out the task of destroying the union. In keeping with these threats of Mosquera, the paramilitaries began to renew threats against Sinaltrainal members, including Dorlahome Tuborquia. Specifically, the paramilitaries threatened to kill Tuborquia. In response to these threats, Tuborquia fled Carepa and went into hiding. The paramilitaries then seized Tuborquia's home to use for their operations.

Throughout 1996, Sinaltrainal members witnessed Mosquera socializing with members of the paramilitary forces and providing the paramilitaries with Coke products for their parties. Meanwhile, Bebidas y Alimentos and Sinaltrainal began negotiating a new labor agreement. These negotiations included Sinaltrainal's proposals for increased security for threatened trade unionists and a cessation of Mosquera's threats against the union as well as his collusion with the paramilitaries. Defendant Richard Kirby Keilland personally participated in these negotiations on behalf of Bebidas y Alimentos and he flatly refused the union's requests.

In response, Sinaltrainal began a national campaign in August of 1996 to call upon Bebidas y Alimentos, as well as Panamco Colombia and Coca-Cola Colombia, to protect the Sinaltrainal leadership and members in Carepa from what it feared was the imminent threat of attack by the paramilitaries. By letter dated September 27, 1996, national leaders of Sinaltrainal accused Mosquera of working with the paramilitaries to destroy the union, and they urged that Bebidas y Alimentos ensure the security of the workers in the Carepa plant in the face of the paramilitary threats. Copies of this letter were contemporaneously sent to Coca-Cola Colombia as well as Panamco Colombia. In response to this letter, Mosquera told the union to retract its accusations.

On December 5, 1996, at 9:00 in the morning, two paramilitaries approached Isidro Gil, who was then involved in negotiations on behalf of the union with Bebidas y Alimentos, as he stood in the entrance of the Bebidas y Alimentos plant. The paramilitaries stated that they needed to go into the plant to talk to someone inside. Isidro Gil proceeded to open the door and the two paramilitaries then shot him to death inside the plant. That same night, these same paramilitaries went to the local union hall of Sinaltrainal and started a fire.

On December 6, 1996, paramilitaries approached several more members of the local Sinaltrainal executive board. These paramilitaries told the union board members that they killed Isidro Gil and burned the union office and that they would kill the remaining board members if they did not leave town. The paramilitaries also explained that they would have a meeting with the workers at the Bebidas y Alimentos plant the next day to tell them that they would have to resign from the union or face being killed.

On December 7, 1996 at 8:00 a.m., the paramilitaries appeared at the Bebidas y Alimentos plant as threatened. They assembled the workers and told them that Bebidas y Alimentos did not want the union at the plant. The paramilitaries explained that the workers had the option of either resigning from the union or leaving Carepa altogether lest they be killed. The paramilitaries then proceeded to direct the workers into the manager's office to sign resignation forms which were prepared by Defendant Bebidas y Alimentos itself. As a result of the threats of the paramilitaries, workers resigned en masse from Sinaltrainal.

In fear for their life, fourteen Sinaltrainal members, including the remainder of the local Sinaltrainal executive board, fled Carepa after this meeting on December 7, 1996. As a result of the flight of these individuals and the resignation of the other workers from the union, the local Sinaltrainal union in Carepa was destroyed. This union has never returned to Carepa. The Sinaltrainal members who fled Carepa on December 7, 1996 continue to fear for their lives and remain in hiding, moving frequently from house to house. Plaintiff Sinaltrainal, as it does for all such displaced members, helps provide support to these individuals.

After the murder of Isidro Gil, the paramilitaries presented themselves at the Bebidas y Alimentos plant with the medical cards of workers which they had taken from the local union office before they burned it. Bebidas y Alimentos paid the paramilitaries remuneration in the amount owed under these cards. The paramilitaries repaired the union office which they had burned and took it over for the purpose of storing their weapons. On December 26, 1996, the paramilitaries killed another Bebidas y Alimentos worker, José Herrerra. The same paramilitaries later killed the wife of Isidro Gil in 2000, leaving their two children without parents.

In 1997, Peggy Ann Keilland, a close relative of Defendants Richard I. Kirby and Richard Kirby Keilland, took over as the Manager of the Bebidas y Alimentos plant in Carepa. Very shortly after taking over, Ms. Keilland worked with the Chief of the Colombian military in the zone to ensure that the paramilitaries were kept out of the plant. Also in 1997, Defendants Richard I. Kirby and Richard Kirby Keilland asked Defendant Coke if they could sell the Bebidas y Alimentos business along with the Carepa plant. Defendant Coke denied them this request and these Defendants still maintain ownership of the Carepa operations, under the direction and control of Defendants Coke and Coke Colombia.

Exhibit 6   Killercoke.org Home Page

Exhibit 7   Cokefacts.org Home Page

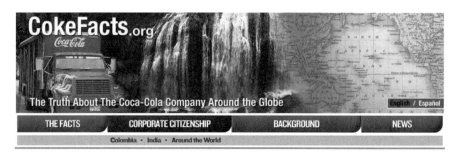

CokeFacts.org

The Truth About The Coca-Cola Company Around the Globe   English / Español

| THE FACTS | CORPORATE CITIZENSHIP | BACKGROUND | NEWS |

Colombia · India · Around the World

▸ **BREAKING NEWS :** ..SE AND INFLAMMATORY" ALLEGATIONS MADE BY TEAMSTERS. Click here to read more...

Colombia: Community Building

Working with Colombians to Create a Stronger Nation

The Coca-Cola Company has been operating in Colombia for more than 70 years. Our bottling partners distribute products to about a half million retailers, including everyone from supermarkets like the internationally owned Carrefour and the Colombian-owned Alkosto supermarkets, as well as the small, family-run bodegas that still control about 40 percent of the retail market in Colombia. As a community partner, our bottlers contribute significant resources – through donations and volunteer hours – to address such issues as hunger relief, education and the environment.

Over the past seven decades, Colombia has experienced internal conflict, which affects trade union activists and other civilians from all walks of life. Despite the volatile environment, The Coca-Cola Company and our bottling partners have maintained operations and worked to provide safe, stable economic opportunities for the people of Colombia.

Read More >>

Colombia: Rebuilding Shattered Lives – One Child at a Time

Reaching Across Continents to Help the Youngest Victims of War

No society can be made whole after decades of strife if the needs of its children are not addressed first. That's why The Coca-Cola Company is proud to be a founding sponsor of Colombianitos, the brainchild of a group of Colombian professionals living in Atlanta, Georgia, striving to rescue a generation of children whose lives have been shattered by Colombia's ongoing conflict. The plight of children in Colombia is acute. More than 6.5 million live in abject poverty, and children represent nearly a third of the victims of Colombia's countless land mines.

But Colombianitos is making a difference. Its land mine program provides prosthetic devices and the physical – and psychological – support required to master them. Additionally, scores of children are touched by other Colombianitos programs, which are helping turn back the tide on the drugs, violence and poverty that are robbing young Colombians of their childhoods. It is of course not possible to erase the past. But by matching resources with a passion for change, it is possible to rewrite the future – one child at a time.

FAST FACTS

Coca-Cola produces nearly 400 brands in more than 200 countries.

❖ LEARN MORE

GIVING BACK TO COMMUNITIES

Coca-Cola helped rebuild schools in Colombia that were destroyed after a devastating earthquake.

❖ READ MORE

SPREAD THE WORD

Enter friend's email address here.

❖ SEND

Exhibit 8   Cal-Safety Workplace Assessment Colombia (Overview)[1]

Perhaps most significant about the CSCC auditors' Colombia findings was what they did *not* find based on private interviews with employees.

Workers were not afraid to speak to outside auditors.

Employees did not ask to be excluded from interviews or for union representation during the interview process.

Auditors found no cases of improper disciplinary action against workers by plant supervisors and managers.

There were no threats by management discovered nor attempts to attack or intimidate a worker for being affiliated with a union, or for being a union organizer or for being a union official. Nonunion workers did not indicate that they were pressured to remain non-union and they were not pressured to join a union.

Security guards were not being used to harass, intimidate or threaten workers.

Auditors *did* find union officials of the plants able to operate in these facilities "free from obstruction and discrimination."

CSCC was told of demonstrations by some of our bottler's workers, all peaceful, all without reprisals.

Several of these demonstrations even involved employees showing their support for workers laid off at other plants within the Coca-Cola system. Both union and non-union workers felt free to exercise their rights of dissent and unionized workers referenced a number of examples

> It should be noted that in the assessment of our Colombian bottling partners' plants, not one worker was afraid to speak to the CSCC auditors; none asked for a union leader to be present during the interview; and no one showed any sign of concern about responding to very direct questions related to management labor relations during the interview process.

when they freely used the broad range of tools available to them under freedom of association and collective bargaining.

The auditors recorded several complaints about management not adhering to the terms of their collective bargaining agreements. The auditors examined each complaint, and in each instance they found documents indicating that plant managers followed proper procedures in dealing with disagreements with the union over contract terms, without intimidation or harassment on either side; thereby indicating compliance with the terms of collective bargaining agreements and adherence to proper procedures.

In addition, CSCC looked at the entirety of the workplace experience for workers at six facilities, five of which are owned by Panamco Colombia, S.A., a subsidiary of Coca-Cola FEMSA, S.A. de C.V., and the sixth by the family-owned company Bebidas & Alimentos de Uraba. Unfortunately, at a few of the plants, shortcomings were found that cannot be ignored. Areas that need attention and improvement have been highlighted in this report and a blueprint for improving plant conditions is provided. Our bottling partners have committed to addressing these findings immediately.

We will work diligently with our bottling partners as they take action to ensure compliance with all laws and regulations that apply to workplace practices and conditions.

[1] Workplace Assessments in Colombia, Conducted by Cal Safety Compliance Corporation for The Coca-Cola Company 2005.

Google in China[1]

Deborah Compeau
Prahar Shah

In less than 10 years of existence, Google had truly become a global success story. The internet giant had experienced unprecedented growth, wooed highly acclaimed talent from rival Microsoft and other competitors to join the company—including the "father of the internet," Vinton Cerf—and entered new markets across the world at a rapid pace. The company prided itself on its philosophy of "Do No Evil"—something that had served them well while operating in North America. However, in early 2006, they faced an ethical dilemma that put this philosophy to the test. According to some, Google's decision to censor search results in China left their motto "in smithereens."[2] The company faced intense international criticism and a backlash that made them question if their decision had been the right one.

The Birth of the Search Engine

Throughout the 1990s and into the new millennium, the world had seen the creation of a new "communications superhighway" which changed the way people accessed resources and shared knowledge. Perhaps the fastest-growing and farthest-reaching creation since the telephone, the Internet and the World Wide Web had forever changed the way people communicated and delivered information, products and services without any international boundaries. By 2005, almost 14.6 per cent of the world's population—close to one billion people—accessed it.[3]

During this time, as the web blossomed so did the need for a tool that enabled users to quickly and efficiently search the hundreds and thousands of isolated web-pages available online. Computer engineers and developers all over the world attempted to create a search engine that indexed these websites, and in 1990 the first tool to search the Internet, nicknamed "Archie," was introduced by McGill University student Alan Emtage. The program downloaded directory listings of all the files located on a File Transfer Protocol (FTP) site into a

---

[1]This case has been written on the basis of published sources only. Consequently, the interpretation and perspectives presented in this case are not necessarily those of Google Inc. or any of its employees.

[2]"Google move 'black day' for China," http://news.bbc.co.uk/2/hi/technology/4647398.stm, accessed August 2006.

[3]*Sergey Brin* and *Lawrence Page*, "*The Anatomy of a Large-Scale Hypertextual Web Search Engine*," *Stanford University*. 1998, accessed August 2006.

searchable database. Shortly thereafter, Mark McCahill and a team from the University of Minnesota launched "Gopher"—the first search engine that organized and enabled access to plain text files from across the web.[4]

As it became clear that this tool could quickly become a backbone of the Internet, investors and developers began simplifying, streamlining and marketing online search engines. Competition within the industry was intense, and with minimal barriers to entry and minimal capital required to launch a successful search engine, competitive advantage was not easily sustained. Between 1990 and 1997, dozens of Internet search engines were created, including Excite, Galaxy, Yahoo, WebCrawler, Lycos, Infoseek, AltaVista, Inktomi, Overture, AskJeeves and MSN Search. They each had their own algorithm of organizing, ranking and displaying search results and serviced a multitude of users. In 1998, two students at Stanford University—as part of a research project—launched Google, using a new and unique method of inbound links to rank sites.[5]

Google.Com

Co-founders Larry Page, president of products, and Sergey Brin, president of technology, brought Google to life in September 1998. By 2006, the company had grown to more than 5,000 employees worldwide, with a management team representing some of the most experienced technology professionals in the industry. Dr. Eric Schmidt joined Google as chairman and chief executive officer in 2001 while Vinton Cerf joined in 2005 as Google's vice-president and chief Internet evangelist.[6] While Page, Brin and Schmidt were largely responsible for the company's day-to-day operations and developing sustainable longer-term strategies, Cerf focused primarily on developing new ideas to launch products and find new sources of revenue apart from its search engine business. See Exhibits 1 and 2 for Google Inc.'s 2004 and 2005 financial statements.

Google's Business Model

Google's search engine used a pay-per-click (PPC) method to earn advertising revenue and provide companies with a vehicle to promote their products and services. According to wikipedia:

> Pay-per-click is often used to kick-start website visibility when a new website or page is promoted, and is basically a bidding system for advertisers who pay a fee to the promotion vehicle (search engine or directory) whenever a surfer clicks on their advertisement. The more the customer pays, the higher the bid, and the more highly placed—prominent—the advertisement appears.

[4]Ibid

[5]http://en.wikipedia.org/wiki/Search_engine, accessed August 2006.

[6]"Vint Cerf: Google's New Idea Man," http://www.wired.com/news/business/0,1367,68808,00.html, accessed August 2006.

Advertisers specify the words that should trigger their ads and the maximum amount they are willing to pay per click. When a user searches Google's search engine on www.google.com, ads for relevant words are shown as "sponsored link" on the right side of the screen, and sometimes above the main search results.[7]

The technology Google used to accomplish this was called AdWords. AdWords used a combination of pricing and relevance to place ads. If an ad was clicked through frequently, it would be displayed more prominently. An ad which fell below a threshold clickthrough rate would be deemed not relevant, and thus would be removed from that particular search. The key benefit of Google's approach was its targeting of ads. Ads were served in the places where they would be of most relevance to users, which had the dual effect of minimizing user frustration with advertising and optimizing clickthrough rates for advertisers.

Google's AdSense technology was created based on the success of AdWords. Google recognized a much more vast marketing opportunity and released a system for webmasters and site owners to publish Google advertisements on their websites. Essentially, a website owner could choose to have Google ads served up on its pages using the same process as Google used for its own sites. When users clicked through these ads, Google and the referring site shared the revenue.

Other Google Products

The AdWords promotional engine had catapulted the company's commercial worth into the multi-billion dollar league and funded development of spin-off search technology such as their desktop search. It had also led to further marketing opportunities for businesses as the search engine giant expanded into such areas as email and map marketing. In 2004, Google launched its first beta version of Google Desktop, a free downloadable application for locating one's personal computer files (including email, work files, web history and instant message chats) using Google-quality search. It also introduced Gmail in 2004, an email application service that received worldwide publicity during its launch. Gmail offered a powerful built-in search function, messages grouped by subject line into conversations and enough free storage to hold years' worth of messages.[8] Using AdSense technology, Gmail was designed to deliver relevant ads adjacent to mail messages, giving recipients a way to act on this information. By early 2006, Google offered a range of products (see Exhibit 3).

---

[7]Ad Words, http://en.wikipedia.org/wiki/AdWords, accessed August 2006.

[8]http://www.google.com/corporate/history.html, accessed August 2006.

Google in China

On July 19, 2005, Google announced the opening of a product research and development center in China, to be led by renowned computer scientist and industry pioneer Dr. Kai-Fu Lee. Dr. Lee served as the company's first president and hoped to exploit China's thriving economy, excellent universities and multitude of talent to help Google develop new products and expand its international business operations. "The opening of a research and development (R&D) center in China will strengthen Google's efforts in delivering the best search experience to our users and partners worldwide," said Alan Eustace, vice-president of engineering at Google. "Under the leadership of Dr. Lee, with his proven track record of innovation and his passion for technology and research, the Google China R&D center will enable us to develop more innovative products and technologies for millions of users in China and around the world."[9]

One of the company's goals was to revitalize the Google website and offer a search engine catered specifically to the Chinese population. As Andrew McLaughlin, senior policy counsel for Google, explained in January of 2006:

> Google users in China today struggle with a service that, to be blunt, isn't very good. Google.com appears to be down around 10 per cent of the time. Even when users can reach it, the website is slow, and sometimes produces results that when clicked on, stall out the user's browser. Our Google News service is never available; Google Images is accessible only half the time. At Google we work hard to create a great experience for our users, and the level of service we've been able to provide in China is not something we're proud of. This problem could only be resolved by creating a local presence, and this week we did so, by launching our website for the People's Republic of China.[10]

Google.cn

The launch of the new website and search engine, Google.cn, enabled the company to create a greater presence in the growing Chinese market and offered a customized region-specific tool with features (such as Chinese-language character inputs) that made the Chinese user experience much simpler. It also sparked the greatest controversy in the company's history. In order to gain the Chinese government's approval and acceptance, it agreed to self-censor and purge any search results of which the government disapproved. Otherwise, the new website risked being blocked in the same way the previous Google.com was blocked by the Chinese authorities. Google conceded. Type in "Falun Gong" or "Tiananmen Square" on Google.

---

[9]http://news.bbc.co.uk/2/hi/technology/4647398.stm, accessed August 2006.

[10]http://googleblog.blogspot.com/2006/01/google-in-china.html, accessed August 2006.

com and thousands of search results will appear; however, when typed into Google.cn all the links will have disappeared. Google will have censored them completely. Google's decision did not go over well in the United States. In February 2006, company executives were called into Congressional hearings and compared to Nazi collaborators. The company's stock fell, and protesters waved placards outside the company's headquarters in Mountain View, California.

Google's Defense

Google defended its position, insisting that while the decision was a difficult one, it served the greater advantage to the greatest number of people.

> We know that many people are upset about this decision, and frankly, we understand their point of view. This wasn't an easy choice, but in the end, we believe the course of action we've chosen will prove to be the right one.

> Launching a Google domain that restricts information in any way isn't a step we took lightly. For several years, we've debated whether entering the Chinese market at this point in history could be consistent with our mission and values. Our executives have spent a lot of time in recent months talking with many people, ranging from those who applaud the Chinese government for its embrace of a market economy and its lifting of 400 million people out of poverty to those who disagree with many of the Chinese government's policies, but who wish the best for China and its people. We ultimately reached our decision by asking ourselves which course would most

effectively further Google's mission to organize the world's information and make it universally useful and accessible. Or, put simply: how can we provide the greatest access to information to the greatest number of people?

> Filtering our search results clearly compromises our mission. Failing to offer Google search at all to a fifth of the world's population, however, does so far more severely. Whether our critics agree with our decision or not, due to the severe quality problems faced by users trying to access Google.com from within China, this is precisely the choice we believe we faced. By launching Google.cn and making a major ongoing investment in people and infrastructure within China, we intend to change that.

> No, we're not going to offer some Google products, such as Gmail or Blogger, on Google.cn until we're comfortable that we can do so in a manner that respects our users' interests in the privacy of their personal communications. And yes, Chinese regulations will require us to remove some sensitive information from our search results. When we do so, we'll disclose this to users, just as we already do in those rare instances where we alter results in order to comply with local laws in France, Germany and the U.S.

> Obviously, the situation in China is far different than it is in those other countries; while China has made great strides in the past decades, it remains in many ways closed. We aren't happy about what we had to do this week, and we hope that over time everyone in the world will come to enjoy full access to information. But how is that full access most likely to be achieved? We are convinced that the Internet, and its continued

development through the efforts of companies like Google, will effectively contribute to openness and prosperity in the world. Our continued engagement with China is the best (perhaps only) way for Google to help bring the tremendous benefits of universal information access to all our users there.

We're in this for the long haul. In the years to come, we'll be making significant and growing investments in China. Our launch of Google.cn, though filtered, is a necessary first step toward achieving a productive presence in a rapidly changing country that will be one of the world's most important and dynamic for decades to come. To some people, a hard compromise may not feel as satisfying as a withdrawal on principle, but we believe it's the best way to work toward the results we all desire.[11]

Dr. Lee, a Chinese citizen, also defended Google's decision to censor the search results for Google.cn, stating that the Chinese students he meets and employs "do not hunger for democracy." He claims that,

People are actually quite free to talk about the subject (of democracy and human rights in China). I don't think they care that much. I think people would say: "Hey, U.S. democracy, that's a good form of government. Chinese government, good and stable, that's a good form of government. Whatever,

as long as I get to go to my favorite web site, see my friends, live happily." Certainly, the idea of personal expression, of speaking out publicly, had become vastly more popular among young Chinese as the Internet had grown and as blogging and online chat had become widespread. But I don't think of this as a political statement at all. I think it's more people finding that they can express themselves and be heard, and they love to keep doing that.[12]

Google's management team, although publicly supporting their decision, were disturbed nonetheless by the growing anti-censorship campaign targeting Google. Led by groups such as the "Students for a Free Tibet" and Amnesty International, mass public rallies and demonstrations were staged outside Google offices, more than 50,000 letters were sent to Google CEO Eric Schmidt demanding the removal of search filters, and the company received intense negative publicity in the media.[13]

The web is a great tool for sharing ideas and freedom of expression. However, efforts to try and control the Internet are growing. People are persecuted and imprisoned simply for criticizing their government, calling for democracy and greater press freedom, or exposing human rights abuses, online.

---

[11]http://googleblog.blogspot.com/2006/01/google-in-china.html, accessed August 2006.

[12]Google – New York Times, http://www.nytimes.com/2006/04/23/magazine/23google.html?ei=5090&en=972002761056363f&ex=1303444800.&adxnnl=1&adxnnlx=1156925160-KvHRNCAA/InAFCXMUlz/+g, accessed August 2006.

[13]http://politics.slashdot.org/politics/06/02/20/0238233.shtml, accessed August 2006.

But Internet repression is not just about governments. IT companies have helped build the systems that enable surveillance and censorship to take place. Yahoo! has supplied email users' private data to the Chinese authorities, helping to facilitate cases of wrongful imprisonment. Microsoft and Google have both complied with government demands to actively censor Chinese users of their services.

Freedom of expression is a fundamental human right. It is one of the most precious of all rights. We should fight to protect it.[14]

As the debate continued, Google executives realized that statements such as "We actually did an evil scale and decided that not to serve at all was worse evil"[15] made by Schmidt were not resonating with the public. It wondered what the immediate and longer-term implications of their action would be, and whether they really were staying true to their motto "Don't Be Evil."

---

[14]http://irrepressible.info/about, accessed August 2006.

[15] http://www.rfa.org/english/news/technology/2006/02/01/china_google, accessed August 2006.

Exhibit 1 Consolidated Statements of Income (in thousands, except per share amounts)

	Year Ended December 31,		
	2003	2004	2005
Revenues	$1,465,934	$3,189,223	$6,138,560
Costs and expenses:			
Cost of revenues	625,854	1,457,653	2,571,509
Research and development.	91,228	225,632	483,978
Sales and marketing	120,328	246.300	439,741
General and administrative	56,699	139.700	335,345
Stock-based compensation[1]	229,361	278,746	200,709
Contribution to Google Foundation	–	–	90,000
Non-recurring portion of settlement of disputes with Yahoo	–	201,000	–
Total costs and expenses	1,123,470	2,549,031	4,121,282
Income from operations.	342,464	640,192	2,017,278
Interest income and other, net	4,190	10,042	124,399
Income before income taxes	346,654	650,234	2,141,677
Provision for income taxes	241,006	251,115	676,280
Net income	$105,648	$399,119	$1,465,397
Net income per share:			
Basic.	$ 0.77	$ 2.07	$ 5.31
Diluted	$ 0.41	$ 1.46	$ 5.02
Number of shares used in per share calculations:			
Basic	137,697	193,176	275,844
Diluted	256,638	272,781	291,874

	Year Ended December 31,		
	2003	2004	2005
Cost of revenues	$ 8,557	$ 11,314	$ 5,579
Research and development	138,377	169,532	115,532
Sales and marketing	44,607	49,449	28,411
General and administrative	37,820	48,451	51,187
	$ 229,361	$ 278,746	$ 200,709

Source: Google Inc. Annual Report 2005.

[1]Stock-based compensation is allocated as follows.

Exhibit 2   Consolidated Balance Sheets (in thousands, except par value)

	December 31,	
	2004	**2005**
Assets		
Current assets:		
Cash and cash equivalents	$ 426,873	$3,877,174
Marketable securities	1,705,424	4,157,073
Accounts receivable, net of allowances of $3,962 and $14,852	311,836	687,976
Income taxes receivable	70,509	–
Deferred income taxes, net	19,463	49,341
Prepaid revenue share, expenses and other assets	159,360	229,507
Total current assets	2,693,465	9,001,071
Property and equipment, net	378,916	961,749
Goodwill	122,818	194,900
Intangible assets, net	71,069	82,783
Deferred income taxes, net, non-current	11,590	–
Prepaid revenue share, expenses and other assets, non-current	35,493	31,310
Total assets	$ 3,313,351	$10,271,813
Liabilities and Stockholders' Equity		
Current liabilities:		
Accounts payable	$32,672	$115,575
Accrued compensation and benefits	82,631	198,788
Accrued expenses and other current liabilities	64,111	114,377
Accrued revenue share	122,544	215,771
Deferred revenue	36,508	73,099
Income taxes payable	–	27,774
Current portion of equipment leases	1,902	–
Total current liabilities	340,368	745,384
Deferred revenue, long-term	7,443	10,468
Liability for stock options exercised early long-term	5,982	2,083
Deferred income taxes, net	–	35,419
Other long-term liabilities	30,502	59,502

Exhibit 2   (Continued)

	December 31,	
	2004	2005
Commitments and contingencies		
Stockholders' equity:		
Class A and Class B common stock, $0.001 per value: 9,000,000 shares		
authorized at December 31, 2004 and December 31, 2005, 266,917, and		
293,027 shares issued and outstanding, excluding 7,605 and 3,303 shares		
subject to repurchase	267	293
Additional paid-in capital	2,582,352	7,477,792
Preferred stock-based compensation	(249,470)	(119,015)
Accumulated other comprehensive income	5,436	4,019
Retained earnings	590,471	2,055,868
Total stockholders' equity	2,929,056	9,418,957
Total liabilities and stockholders' equity	$ 3,313,351	$10,271,813

Source: Google Inc. Annual Report 2005.

Exhibit 3   Selected Google Products

Alerts

   – a service which provides emails of news and search results for a particular topic area

Answers

   – a service where users can post queries for which they are willing to pay others to do research; the user sets the price they are willing to pay

Blogs

   – Google's own blog site is "blogger"
   – They also provide a blog search utility

Book & catalog search

   – allows users to search the full text of books and to search and browse online catalogs for mail order businesses

Images and Video

   – Google's sites for searching pictures on the web and videos

Google Earth & Google Maps

   – global maps and driving directions
   – also includes the capability to search for various businesses etc. within a map and display the results graphically

Google Scholar

   – allows users to search academic papers

Google Groups

   – a site to allow users to create mailing lists and discussion groups

Google Desktop Search

   – uses Google's search technology to track information on the user's PC

GMail

   – Google's mail application

For a complete listing of Google products and services, see http://www.google.ca/intl/en/options/index.html

Ethics of Offshoring: Novo Nordisk and Clinical Trials in Emerging Economies

Klaus Meyer

On a warm day in early spring 2008, the telephone is ringing in the office of Anders Dejgaard, chief medical officer of Novo Nordisk, a leading developer and manufacturer of insulin and related products. A business journalist of the Danish national newspaper *Berlingske Tidende* is on the line and asking for an interview. Dejgaard knows her from several conversations relating to business practices in the pharmaceutical industry.

The journalist is investigating the off-shoring of clinical trials by Danish companies. A report recently published in the Netherlands alleges that multinational pharmaceutical companies routinely conduct trials in developing countries under allegedly unethical conditions. Also, the Danish National Committee on Biomedical Research Ethics has expressed concerns because Danish pharmaceutical companies are not obtaining ethical reviews in Denmark for such trials despite the offer from this committee. Thus, she wants to discuss Novo Nordisk's position on these issues.

Dejgaard reflects on how to react. Several articles on ethical aspects related to medical research in the Third World had appeared in the Danish press in recent months, creating an atmosphere of suspicion towards the industry.[1] Should he meet with the journalist and if so, what should he tell her? Or should he rather focus on his forthcoming business trip to new production facilities and send Novo Nordisk's press officer to meet the journalist? In his mind flashes the possibility of derogatory headlines in the tabloid press. As a company emphasizing corporate responsibility, the interaction with the media presents both opportunities and risks to Novo Nordisk.

Novo Nordisk[2]

Novo Nordisk A/S had been created in 1989 through a merger between two Danish companies, Novo Industri A/S and Nordisk Gentofte A/S. Both had been established in the 1920s as manufacturers of insulin, a crucial medication

---

[1]See in particular B. Alfter, "De fattige er verdens nye forsøgskaniner. Krav om kontrol med medicinalindustrien," *Information,* Feb. 26, 2008, pp. 4–5, and B. Lambeck and S.G. Jensen, "Halvdelen af al medicin afprøves i den tredje verden," *Politiken,* Oct. 6, 2007.

[2]This section draws on the company website, www.novonordisk.com, and an undated (circa 2002) document, "Novo Nordisk History," available via this website.

for diabetes. Over decades of fierce competition, they had become leading providers of insulin and related pharmaceutical products. Novo Industri had been pursuing an internationally oriented strategy from the outset, and by 1936 was supplying insulin to 40 countries. A significant step in the internationalization of the company was a major push into the U.S. market in 1979. At the time, Food and Drug Administration (FDA) regulations required Novo Industri to replicate its clinical studies in the United States to obtain the approval of the marketing of their new products. In 1989, the two companies merged and, in 2000, the merged company spun off the enzyme business "Novozymes."

In 2008, Novo Nordisk presents itself as a focused company within the healthcare industry and a world leader in diabetes care. It claims the broadest and most innovative diabetes product portfolio in the industry, including the most advanced insulin delivery systems. In addition, Novo Nordisk holds leading positions in areas such as haemostasis management, growth hormone therapy and hormone replacement therapy. Sales reached DKr41.8 billion (about US$8 billion) in 2007, of which DKr30.5 billion were in diabetes care and DKr11.4 billion were in biopharmaceuticals.

Innovation is considered pivotal to the success of Novo Nordisk, as it was to its predecessor companies. Continuous innovations allow the development of more refined, and thus more effective, insulin preparations, and new delivery systems, such as Novopen®, that facilitate the administration of the treatment, including self-administration by patients. In 2008, about 18 per cent of employees are working within research and development.

In 2008, Novo Nordisk holds market shares for insulin of about 56 per cent in Europe, 41 per cent in North America and 73 per cent in Japan and employs about 26,000 people, of whom 12,689 are located in Denmark, 3,411 in the rest of Europe, 3,940 in North America and the remainder in Asia Pacific and the rest of the world. Production facilities are located in six countries and products are marketed in 179 countries.

The shares of Novo Industri were first listed on the Copenhagen Stock Exchange in 1974 and on the London Stock Exchange in 1981 as the first Scandinavian company to be listed in London. In 2008, Novo Nordisk's B shares are listed on the stock exchanges in both Copenhagen and London, while its American depositary receipts (ADRs) are listed on the New York Stock Exchange.

Novo Nordisk emphasizes corporate social responsibility as part of its image, pursing a triple bottom line approach: environmental and social responsibility along with economic viability. This commitment is demonstrated through its values and its environmental and social responsibility policies that are reported on its website (see Appendix 1).

Critical milestones in Novo Nordisk's ambition to be recognized as a leader of corporate sustainability include the publication in 1994 of its Environmental Report. It was the first company in Denmark and one of the first in the world to do so. This was followed in 1999 by the first annual Social Report. In 2001, Novo Nordisk established the World Diabetes Foundation, a charity aiming to improve diabetes care in developing countries, where diabetes is becoming an epidemic as it had in Europe and North America a few decades earlier.

In recognition of its sustainability engagement, Novo Nordisk had been included in the Dow Jones Global Sustainability Indices, where it was ranked as "best in class" in the health-care category in 2007. At home, Novo Nordisk is frequently ranked as having the most highly regarded corporate image by Danish magazines *Berlingske Nyhedmagasin*, *Børsen* and *Ingeniøren*.

New Medications: Development and Approval

Novo Nordisk, like other pharmaceutical and medical companies, heavily invests in the development of new medications offering more effective, safe and user-friendly treatments. New product development involves the creation of new drugs or modifications in their use, for instance their dosage and the form of administration.

To bring new drugs or medical devices to market, they must be approved by the relevant authorities—the FDA in the United States and European Medicines Agency (EMEA) in the European Union. The approval of drugs and medical devices requires proof of their efficacy and their safety. Efficacy refers to scientific evidence that the drug improves patients' conditions as claimed by the manufacturer. Safety refers to the absence of substantive negative side-effects. Thus, to obtain approval, pharmaceutical companies have to provide scientific evidence that the drug improves the conditions of patients and is free of disproportional side-effects.

This evidence has to be based on, among other data, clinical trials in which the drug has been tested on actual patients. The clinical trials are normally conducted in four stages. Phase 1 involves a small number of healthy volunteers and serves to assess the kinetic properties and tolerability of the drug. Phase 2 is performed on larger groups of patients to assess how well the drug works and to establish the doses that give the desired effect and to continue its safety assessment. Phase 3 trials often involve thousands of patients and aim to provide a definitive assessment of how effective and safe the drug is. All data generated in the three phases form an essential part of submissions to the regulatory authorities (FDA, EMEA and their counterparts in other countries) for drug approval. With this approval, the drug can then be marketed for the approved indications. Further trials, in phase 4, may be required to obtain permission to extend the labelling of a drug to new indications (e.g., a different disease) or specific groups, such as children or pregnant women.

Phase 3 and 4 trials require a large number of patients with the specific disease that the drug is to improve. A typical approval process conducted by Novo Nordisk might require six to eight different phase 3 trials with different patient groups or combinations of the drug component, each involving about 400 to 800 patients. Such trials are often conducted as multinational studies involving up to 15 countries. With increasing requirements for patient exposure for approval and increasing numbers of drugs being tested, the recruitment of patients is often a major challenge. Typically, trials are conducted at multiple hospitals that all must follow the same trial protocol to ensure the consistency of data and compliance with existing "good clinical practice" (GCP) guidelines. Multi-site trials also facilitate the recruitment of patients with diverse backgrounds, for instance different ethnicities and diets, while helping to demonstrate their universal properties. Doctors and nurses but not patients are normally paid for this work and hospitals often find it attractive to participate in trials that allow access to new medications and front line research. Clinical trials, especially phase 3, are a major cost factor in the development of new medications and they often take many years to conduct (on average eight years).

In the early 2000s, major pharmaceutical industries increasingly moved parts of their trials, especially phases 3 and 4, to countries outside their traditional areas of operations, especially to Eastern Europe, South America, India and China. Hospitals in these areas provide access to qualified medical staff and larger numbers of patients with the specific conditions, while potentially being able to administer a trial at lower costs. Moreover, the efficacy of drugs may also vary across contexts, for instance due to genetic, dietary, climatic or other environmental conditions. In such cases, multi-site trials help to establish the efficacy of medications across contexts. Some countries, such as Japan, India and China, in fact require that trials are at least in part conducted locally to approve a new medication in the respective countries. However, the conduct of clinical trials in these areas also raises a range of ethical issues.

Ethical Issues in Medical Research[3]

Ethical issues in the pharmaceutical industry have received considerable

---

[3]This section draws in particular on E.J. Emanuel, D. Wendler and C. Grady, "What makes clinical research ethical?" *Journal of the American Medical Association,* 283:20, 2000, pp. 2701–2711, and Michael A. Santoro and Thomas M. Gorrie, *Ethics and the Pharmaceutical Industry,* Cambridge University Press, 2005.

media attention over several decades, as the industry has failed to live up to the expectations of some interest groups. In particular, clinical trials raise a number of widely recognized issues. Medical professionals, and with them many NGOs and media, focus on the medical ethics grounded in the Hippocratic oath that commits doctors to treat each patient to the best of their abilities, never to cause intentional harm and to maintain patient confidentiality. Scientists and approval authorities have been concerned about the scientific rigor of the tests to provide solid evidence of the effects of a new drug, and thus to protect potential future users of the drug. At the same time, pharmaceutical companies have to operate with limited financial resources and to satisfy shareholders and thus cannot spend more resources than expected future revenues would justify. Accordingly, the industry has been accused of performing trials in developing countries with lower attention to ethical principles—"ethical bribing," with patients acting as guinea pigs that do not understand and/or care about the risk involved but just want to get free medication and with investigators not meeting the competence requirements, etc. Allegedly, all this just serves to generate documentation for compounds that are to be sold only in developed countries.

Medical (Hippocratic) ethics concern primarily the individual patients that are participating in any experiment. The relationship between the doctor and the subject participating in a trial is thus governed by the doctor's responsibility to care for his or her patient. Past incidences where this principle had been violated continue to affect popular perceptions of medical research. Most infamously, the Tuskegee syphilis study left 400 impoverished and unwitting African-American men in Macon County, Alabama, untreated to study how they developed the disease—an experiment initiated in 1932 and terminated only in the 1970s.

To prevent such scandals, professional medical organizations have developed guidelines and principles of ethics to guide their research, notably the Helsinki Declaration of the World Medical Association (see Appendix 2). These widely accepted ethical principles aim to protect subjects, e.g., patients, participating in such research. These include:

- *Voluntary informed consent:* Each patient has to agree voluntarily to participate in the research based on being fully informed about the purposes of the study and potential risks for the individual. Sponsors and local site investigators thus normally write an "informed consent" document that informs potential subjects of the true risks and potential benefits, which is signed by each patient or their legal guardian before any trial procedure.

- *Respect of patients*: The privacy of the subject should be protected and they should be free to withdraw from the experiment at any time without reasoning. The doctor's professional responsibility to the patient should take precedence over any other considerations.
- *Independent review*: Any medical and pharmacological research has to be assessed on its scientific merits and ethicality by an independent review board (IRB) that is independent from those involved in or sponsoring the research.

Scientific ethics are concerned about the validity of the results of the scientific inquiry and thus the methodological rigour of the study. Thus, a study has to use valid measurements and statistical techniques and samples that are unbiased and sufficiently large that they can generate trustworthy and valid results.

Such scientific rigour is important to anyone who may in the future use an approved drug or medical device. Awareness of the need for rigorous tests prior to launching new medications had been triggered by various scandals of the 1960s, notably the Thalidomide scandal involving a pain killer used by women to ease sleep problems and pregnancy sickness. Due to side-effects of this medication, thousands of children worldwide were born with incomplete arms or legs, before the drug was withdrawn. In consequence to this and other scandals, the licensing and approval procedures for drugs have been tightened to ensure that only drugs with scientifically proven efficacy and safety are marketed.

Ethical businesses have to balance activities done in the interest of the wider society with their pursuit of profits. The late Nobel prize-winning economist Milton Friedman famously declared that the primary social responsibility of business is to make profits.[4] Under efficient markets, which he firmly believed in, this would generate the most mutually beneficial outcome. Thus, he argued, firms ought to give precedence to shareholders over any other interest groups.

Others argue that firms should engage in corporate social responsibility because it can be expected to benefit their bottom line in the long run, for instance through reputation effects. Yet others argue that firms have an intrinsic, normative responsibility to use their influence to do good for society and to aspire to the highest moral standards, independent of the profit motive. However, even so, their financial

---

[4]M. Friedman, "The social responsibility of business is to increase profits," *The New York Times Magazine,* September 13, 1970; reprinted in K.E. Meyer, *Multinational Enterprises and Host Economies,* Elgar, Cheltenham, 2009.

resources will be limited. Like organizations in the governmental or non-profit sector, businesses have to make critical decisions about how best to use their scarce resources.

Ethics of Placebo Experiments[5]

Particular concerns have arisen for placebo trials, that is, trials where a control group of patients receives a treatment without any active ingredient for the disease. The purpose of placebo trials is, normally, to provide evidence of product efficacy by showing statistically significant improvements of the conditions of patients receiving the active treatment, compared to those receiving a placebo treatment.

Placebo trials are especially important for diseases that are affected by the so-called placebo effect, that is, patients' conditions improving because of the positive effect of receiving a form of treatment rather than the specific medication. This has been shown to be quite substantive, for instance, for schizophrenia and other psychiatric conditions. Both American and European authorities thus often require placebo trials as prerequisite for the approval of new medications.

Alternatives to placebo trials include the use of active controls, in which the control groups receive a previously marketed medication with known properties. Yet these types of trials are often not sufficient to provide the required rigorous evidence regarding the efficacy of the medication.[6] Placebo trials may create risks for patients in the placebo group, in particular when patients are denied a treatment that is known to improve their condition. The Helsinki Declaration therefore requires avoiding placebo experiments unless very special reasons require them or no alternative treatment of the illness is available (see Appendix 2, item 29). Ethics review boards have become very restrictive in permitting placebo trials. There have been arguments from some

---

[5]This section draws on contemporary discussions in the medical literature, in particular E.J. Emanuel and F.G. Miller, "The ethics of placebo-controlled trials e—A middle ground," *New England Journal of Medicine,* 345:12, 2001, pp. 915–919, and R. Temple and S.S. Ellenberg, "Placebo-controlled trials and active-controlled trials in the evaluation of new treatments," *Annals of Internal Medicine,* 133:6, 2000, pp. 455–463.

[6]An active-control trial infers efficacy from non-significant differences of performance compared to the active-control drug. Such non-significance, however, can be caused by a number of other influences. Moreover, this test is problematic if the active-control drug is subject to large placebo effects varying with study designs. On the merits and concerns of active-control trials, see e.g., Temple and Ellenberg, "Placebo-controlled trials and active-controlled trials in the evaluation of new treatments," 2000, and B.T. Walsh, S.N. Seidman, R. Sysko and M. Gould, "Placebo response in studies of major depression: Variable, substantial and growing," *Journal of the American Medical Association,* 287:14, 2002, pp. 1840–1847.

groups that one reason for the pharmaceutical industry to place studies in developing countries is the possibility of performing placebo trials that otherwise can be difficult to get approval for in developed countries.

Novo Nordisk generally avoids placebo trials. Usually, they are used only in phase 1 trials in healthy volunteers when new drug candidates are being developed. These trials are normally located near its main research centres in Europe and rarely in non-Western countries.

Media Spotlights

In February 2008, a report from the Dutch NGO SOMO raised public awareness of placebo trials conducted by major pharmaceutical companies in developing countries.[7] The report was critical of trials that had been submitted to the FDA and the EMEA for drug approval. Its primary concern was that key information about ethical aspects of these clinical trials was not available to it as an external observer and it found incidences where patients suffered serious harm after receiving a placebo in a trial.

The report focused on three case studies of clinical trials for recently approved drugs conducted in Eastern Europe and Asia, based on publicly available information. It concluded that

> trial subjects in these countries are more vulnerable and their rights are less secured than in high income countries. Conditions such as poverty, illiteracy, poor health systems and inadequate research ethics committees result in international ethical standards not being met. Current EU legislation requires that results from unethical clinical trials . . . not be accepted for marketing authorization. With three case studies on recently approved drugs in the EU (Abilify, Olmetec, and Seroquel), SOMO demonstrates that this principle is being violated. European authorities devote little to no attention to the ethical aspects of the clinical trials submitted, and they accept unethical trials as well as trials of poor quality.[8]

In its conclusions, the report alleges that local regulation and the enforcement of ethical principles are less strict, partly because local independent review boards are less qualified and partly because they are less keen on restricting what is potentially a revenue earner. The authors thus advocate global harmonization of ethical criteria along the principles currently used by ethics committees in Europe: " . . . there must be no discrepancy between the ethical criteria used to approve research

---

[7]I. Schipper and F. Weyzing, "Ethics for Drug Testing in Low and Middle Income Countries: Considerations for European Market Authorisation," *Stichting Onderzoek Multinationale Ondernemingen* (SOMO), 2008, http://somo.nl/publications-en/Publication_2472, accessed October 2008.

[8]Ibid, abstract on the cover page.

protocols in Western Europe and in low and middle income economies to avoid the creation of 'easy countries.'"[9]

The media picked up, in particular, the case of a schizophrenic patient committing suicide while participating in a trial of the anti-schizophrenia medicine Seroquel by Astra-Zeneca. Moreover, media reported that 10 per cent of recipients in the placebo group had to be hospitalized because of worsening conditions. Careful reading of the original report suggests that 8.3 per cent (p. 64) of a group of 87 patients (p. 62) were affected, which adds to seven persons. No assessment of the likelihood of such incidents under alternative medication available at the time had been included in the report.

Concerns have also been raised by the Danish National Committee on Biomedical Research Ethics.[10] In particular, the committee criticizes the industry for not accepting the committee's offer to provide independent ethical reviews before submitting to local ethics committees as a service to the industry. The chairperson for the committee, Johannes Gaub, chief medical officer at Odense Hospital, told the media:

Like production companies locate their factories in low wage areas, the medical industry is outsourcing its scientific experiments in the same way. The costs of conducting medical trials in developing countries are only a fraction of what they are in the West because of the low wages . . . In the USA it costs about DKr 150,000 to move one patient through a trial. In Denmark, it costs DKr 80,000. I don't really know the price in developing countries, but it is a fraction of that.

Gaub also rejects the concern of the industry that hospitals in Denmark would not be able to conduct trials of the necessary scale, given the growing requirements worldwide to provide clinical trial data for approvals around the world:

We have considerable spare capacity in Denmark. Despite the high costs we have a well-functioning health system. We have data about patients because of our national identity number system, and there are many clinical researchers in the hospitals who would be happy to participate in the trials of new medications . . . It is actually worrying that we do not receive more applications in Denmark. We need clinical research to maintain the high level of health science that we so far have had in the country.[11]

---

[9]I. Schipper and F. Weyzing, "Ethics for Drug Testing in Low and Middle Income Countries: Considerations for European Market Authorisation," 2008, p. 68.

[10]For further information on the Danish National Committee on Biomedical Research Ethics, see www.cvk.im.dk/cvk/site.aspx?p=119.

[11]Both citations are from B. Erhardtsen, "Medicinalindustrien dropper frivillig etisk blåstempling," *Berlingske Tidende,* April 5, 2008, Inland section, pp. 6–7 (case author's translation).

Danish politicians also joined the debate. In a statement to the health committee of the national parliament, the minister for health emphasized that E.U. regulation for the approval of new medicines requires that trials conducted outside the European Union have been implemented in accordance with the European Union's own rules as well as with ethical principles such as the Helsinki Declaration. The minister thus concluded:

> I find no reason to take initiatives to constrain research projects by the Danish medical industry outside the EU. In this context, I consider it important to emphasize that all clinical trials that shall be used as a basis for applications for approval of marketing of a medication in the EU must comply with the EU's laws on good clinical practice and the ethical principles regarding medical research with human subjects.[12]

Also, other politicians joined the debate. For example, Member of Parliament Birgitte Josefsen (V)[13] urged Danish pharmaceutical companies to hold the ethical flag high: "The medical industry ought to be very careful about whom they use as test persons. That should be people who have resources to say 'no'. A poor Indian mother with three children is not the right one to become a test person." [14]

Novo Nordisk's Position on Clinical Trials

Anders Dejgaard is pondering the complexity of the ethical issues. As corporate sustainability features highly on Novo Nordisk's agenda, the ethically appropriate handling of clinical trials is important to the company. It conducts clinical trials globally to test the safety and efficacy of new drug candidates in order to obtain global marketing authorization. These trials always follow a common protocol and thus the same standards at all trials sites. Trials sites are selected based on a variety of criteria, including the quality of regulatory authorities, ethical review processes and medical practices. Moreover, drugs have to be tested on the types of patients who will later become users of the drug and trial subjects should have access to the drugs after the process has been completed. In addition, Novo Nordisk will only conduct trials in countries where it has affiliates with the necessary competence to arrange and monitor the trials.

---

[12]J.K. Nielsen, Besvarlse af spørgsmal nr. 20 (alm. del) som Folketingets Sundhedsudvalg har stillet til indenrigs - og sundhedsministeren (Written reply to a question in the health committee of the Danish parliament), January 9, 2008. (Archives of the Danish government: Indenrigs or Sundhedministeriet, Lægemiddelkontoret, J.nr. 2007-13009-599, Sagsbeh: nhj) (case author's translation).

[13](V) refers to Venstre, one of the parties of the minority government at the time.

[14]Berlingske Tidende website, www.berlingske.dk/article/20080403/danmark/704030057, April 3, 2008, accessed October 2008 (case author's translation).

In 2008, these criteria were met in about 65 countries worldwide.

Novo Nordisk has adapted the global guidelines and recommendations by all the professional bodies and publishes its policies on clinical trials on its website (see Appendix 3). This includes enhanced global exposure of investigated products through its own website as well as websites sponsored by the FDA (see Appendix 3). Novo Nordisk conducts research in therapies that require global trials and the inclusion of different ethnic populations. The company also anticipates a need to increase the number of clinical trials due to an expanding pipeline and more extensive global and local regulatory requirements. Its ethical principles and standard operating procedures, which apply globally, are designed to ensure due respect for the safety, rights, integrity, dignity, confidentiality and well-being of all human beings participating in Novo Nordisk-sponsored trials. Novo Nordisk is auditing 10 per cent of all trials, while at the same time the American and European authorities, FDA and EMEA, are making random checks of about one per cent of Novo Nordisk's clinical trials. These random checks have never identified ethical problems in clinical trials in developing countries. Since trials are normally conducted in multiple countries, the same standards are applied everywhere, for both ethical and scientific reasons (consistency of results).

At the same time, Dejgaard is irritated about the request for an additional ethics approval by the Danish National Committee on Biomedical Research Ethics. He estimates that it would add three months to the preparation of each new trial. In his own experience, the ethical reviews in those locations he worked in are as rigorous as in Western countries and he does not recognize an added benefit, as the Danish committee would be no better in assessing a trial than a local ethics committee. On the contrary, he finds the suggestion more appropriate for a colonial empire. Moreover, specific local issues, such as ethnic or religious minorities, would be better understood by local committees.

Yet various issues come to mind. Is Novo Nordisk doing its research and development in an appropriate manner or are there issues that could be done better in view of Novo Nordisk's triple bottom line commitments? Are Novo Nordisk's standard operating procedures being properly implemented in all developing countries that participate in the programs and how is such compliance to be monitored? How should Novo Nordisk manage its simultaneous relationships with various regulatory authorities, independent review boards at various sites and with the Danish National Committee on Biomedical Research Ethics?

Most pressing is the decision on how to handle the journalist. Should he meet her in person, send a public relations person or not meet at all and reply in writing, citing the corporate website? If he is to meet her, what should be the key messages that he should get across and how should he prepare himself for any questions she might raise during the meeting?

Klaus Meyer (www.ceibs.edu/faculty/cv/65579.shtml) is a professor of strategy and international business at the China Europe International Business School (CEIBS) in Shanghai.

Appendix 1   Corporate Sustainability at Novo Nordisk (Extracts)

At Novo Nordisk, we refer to corporate sustainability as companies' ability to sustain and develop their business in the long-term perspective, in harmony with society. This implies a more inclusive view of business and its role; one in which engagements with stakeholders are not just used to legitimise corporate decisions, but rather the foundation for how it conducts and grows its business. It is about innovation, opportunity and planning for the long term.

   The Triple Bottom is the principle behind our way of doing business. The company's Articles of Association state that it 'strives to conduct its activities in a financially, environmentally and socially responsible way.' This is a commitment to sustainable development and balanced growth, and it has been built into corporate governance structures, management tools and methods of assessing and rewarding individuals' performance . . .

The stakeholder dimension: Novo Nordisk needs to stay attuned to emerging trends and 'hot issues' on the global agenda in order to respond and to contribute to the debate. Stakeholder engagement is an integrated part of our business philosophy. We have long-standing engagements with stakeholders that are vital for building trust and understanding of a variety of issues. By involving stakeholders in the decision-making processes, decisions are better founded and solutions more likely to succeed. Stakeholders are defined as any individual or group that may affect or be affected by a company's activities.

Translating commitment to action: Corporate sustainability has made a meaningful difference to our business, and we believe it is a driver of our business success. This is best illustrated in three examples:

Business ethics: Surveys indicate that ethical behaviour in business is today the number one driver of reputation for pharmaceutical companies. Any company that is not perceived by the public as behaving in an ethical manner is likely to lose business, and it takes a long time to regain trust. While the Novo Nordisk Way of Management is a strong guide to our behaviour, we decided we needed more detailed guidance in the area of business ethics. In 2005 we therefore framed a new business ethics policy, in line with universally accepted high standards, backed by a set of procedures. Since then we have trained managers and employees, held workshops and offered e-learning on the new policy.

Climate change: We need to act to put a brake to human-induced climate change. While the implications of climate change pose major business risks, there are also opportunities. We have partnered with the WWF [World Wildlife Fund] in the Climate Savers programme and set an ambitious target to achieve a 10% reduction in our company's CO_2 emissions by 2014,

(Continued)

Appendix 1 (Continued)

compared with 2004 emission levels. This will occur through optimised production, energy savings, and greater use of renewable energy supplies.

The diabetes pandemic: Today, diabetes is recognised as a pandemic. Novo Nordisk responds to this major societal challenge by working in partnerships with many others to rally the attention of policy-makers and influencers to change diabetes. We have made a promise of **Changing Diabetes®** and have framed a **strategy for inclusive access to diabetes care**. We established the **World Diabetes Foundation**, and have made several initiatives to advocate for change and build evidence of diabetes developments. **The National Changing Diabetes® programme** and **DAWN** are examples of education and awareness programmes implemented by Novo Nordisk affiliates in their respective countries. Our **Changing Diabetes® Bus** that promotes Novo Nordisk's global Changing Diabetes® activities had reached 86,000 people by the end of 2007 during its world tour. Its primary goal is to support the **UN Resolution on diabetes**, which was passed in December 2006.

Source: www.novonordisk.com, accessed November 2008.

Appendix 2   Helsinki Declaration of the World Medical Association (Excerpts)

10. It is the duty of the physician in medical research to protect the life, health, privacy, and dignity of the human subject.

13. The design and performance of each experimental procedure involving human subjects should be clearly formulated in an experimental protocol. This protocol should be submitted for consideration, comment, guidance, and where appropriate, approval to a specially appointed ethical review committee, which must be independent of the investigator, the sponsor or any other kind of undue influence. This independent committee should be in conformity with the laws and regulations of the country in which the research experiment is performed. The committee has the right to monitor ongoing trials. The researcher has the obligation to provide monitoring information to the committee, especially any serious adverse events. The researcher should also submit to the committee, for review, information regarding funding, sponsors, institutional affiliations, other potential conflicts of interest and incentives for subjects.

14. The research protocol should always contain a statement of the ethical considerations involved and should indicate that there is compliance with the principles enunciated in this Declaration.

15. Medical research involving human subjects should be conducted only by scientifically qualified persons and under the supervision of a clinically competent medical person. The responsibility for the human subject must always rest with a medically qualified person and never rest on the subject of the research, even though the subject has given consent.

16. Every medical research project involving human subjects should be preceded by careful assessment of predictable risks and burdens in comparison with foreseeable benefits to the subject or to others. This does not preclude the participation of healthy volunteers in medical research. The design of all studies should be publicly available.

17. Physicians should abstain from engaging in research projects involving human subjects unless they are confident that the risks involved have been adequately assessed and can be satisfactorily managed. Physicians should cease any investigation if the risks are found to outweigh the potential benefits or if there is conclusive proof of positive and beneficial results.

18. Medical research involving human subjects should only be conducted if the importance of the objective outweighs the inherent risks and burdens to the subject. This is especially important when the human subjects are healthy volunteers.

19. Medical research is only justified if there is a reasonable likelihood that the populations in which the research is carried out stand to benefit from the results of the research.

20. The subjects must be volunteers and informed participants in the research project.

21. The right of research subjects to safeguard their integrity must always be respected. Every precaution should be taken to respect the privacy of the subject, the confidentiality of the patient's information and to minimize the impact of the study on the subject's physical and mental integrity and on the personality of the subject.

22. In any research on human beings, each potential subject must be adequately informed of the aims, methods, sources of funding, any possible conflicts of interest, institutional affiliations of the researcher, the anticipated benefits and potential risks of the study and the discomfort it may entail. The subject should be informed of the right to abstain from participation in the study or to withdraw consent to participate at any time without reprisal. After ensuring that the subject has understood the information, the physician should then obtain the subject's freely-given informed consent, preferably in writing. If the consent cannot be obtained in writing, the non-written consent must be formally documented and witnessed.

23. When obtaining informed consent for the research project the physician should be particularly cautious if the subject is in a dependent relationship with the physician or may consent under duress. In that case the informed consent should be obtained by a well-informed physician who is not engaged in the investigation and who is completely independent of this relationship.

29. The benefits, risks, burdens and effectiveness of a new method should be tested against those of the best current prophylactic, diagnostic, and therapeutic methods. This does not exclude the use of placebo, or no treatment, in studies where no proven prophylactic, diagnostic or therapeutic method exists.

Note of clarification on paragraph 29 of the WMA Declaration of Helsinki

The WMA hereby reaffirms its position that extreme care must be taken in making use of a placebo-controlled trial and that in general this methodology should only be used in the absence of existing proven therapy. However, a placebo-controlled trial may be ethically acceptable, even if proven therapy is available, under the following circumstances:

- Where for compelling and scientifically sound methodological reasons its use is necessary to determine the efficacy or safety of a prophylactic, diagnostic or therapeutic method; or

Appendix 2 (Continued)

- Where a prophylactic, diagnostic or therapeutic method is being investigated for a minor condition and the patients who receive placebo will not be subject to any additional risk of serious or irreversible harm.

All other provisions of the Declaration of Helsinki must be adhered to, especially the need for appropriate ethical and scientific review.

30. At the conclusion of the study, every patient entered into the study should be assured of access to the best proven prophylactic, diagnostic and therapeutic methods identified by the study.

Note of clarification on paragraph 30 of the WMA Declaration of Helsinki
The WMA hereby reaffirms its position that it is necessary during the study planning process to identify post-trial access by study participants to prophylactic, diagnostic and therapeutic procedures identified as beneficial in the study or access to other appropriate care. Post-trial access arrangements or other care must be described in the study protocol so the ethical review committee may consider such arrangements during its review.

Source: www.wma.net/e/policy/b3.htm, accessed October 2008.

Appendix 3 Clinical Trials: Novo Nordisk's Position

- Clinical trials sponsored by Novo Nordisk will always be conducted according to the Helsinki Declaration, which describes human rights for patients participating in clinical trials, and similar international ethical guidelines such as the Nuremberg code, the Belmont report and CIOMMS, and the International Conference of Harmonisation (ICH) guidelines for current good clinical practice (cGCP).
- The above guidelines and regulations are the foundation for our clinical Standard Operating Procedures (SOPs) including the SOP on the 'principles of clinical trials'. These standards are laid out to ensure the safety, rights, integrity, confidentiality and well-being of persons involved in Novo Nordisk trials globally.
- Novo Nordisk will apply the same procedures wherever we sponsor clinical trials. This means that all subjects enrolled in Novo Nordisk trials are protected by the same rights, high ethical standards and regulations irrespective of location of the study.
- The interest and well-being of the trial subject should always prevail over the interest of science, society and commerce.
- Novo Nordisk will not conduct clinical trials for drug development in countries where we do not intend to market the investigational drug. In any country where we do undertake clinical trials we will ensure that a proper internal organisation and a proper regulated external environment exist.
- Clinical trials should only be done if they can be scientifically and medically justified, and all Novo Nordisk-sponsored trials should be based on sound scientific methodology described

in a clear and detailed protocol. Placebo will only be used as comparator when scientifically and ethically justified.

- No trial activity in Novo Nordisk-sponsored trials will start before approval is obtained from external local ethics committees and health authorities.
- We will always ensure that investigators involved in Novo Nordisk clinical trials are skilled in the therapeutic area and are trained in GCP. No procedure involving a person undergoing clinical trial activities will take place before the appropriate freely given informed consent is obtained based on proper information on potential risk of participation in the trial. A patient can at any time withdraw from a clinical trial without giving any reason. In cases where trial subjects are incompetent, physically or mentally incapable of giving consent, or if the person is a minor, Novo Nordisk will follow local regulations for obtaining consent.
- Products used in Novo Nordisk-sponsored clinical trials will be manufactured and controlled according to international and local regulations and laws. Novo Nordisk will conduct frequent site monitoring to ensure that the study is executed according to the study protocol, and that data used in statistical analysis and reporting reflects the data obtained from the involved patients during the trial. Safety information from any Novo Nordisk trial will be monitored on a continuous basis and appropriate actions will be taken if risks of the investigational product outweigh the potential benefits.
- Patients participating in Novo Nordisk-sponsored clinical trials will always be offered best available and proven treatment after study termination. The treatment will be offered at the discretion of the responsible physician. If study medication is not marketed the responsible physician can apply for medication on a named patient basis. Post-study medication will be described in the protocol and informed consent.
- Novo Nordisk will ensure proper indemnification of trial subjects in case a trial product or procedures in a Novo Nordisk-sponsored trial cause bodily harm to a trial subject.
- Novo Nordisk strives to have all clinical trial results published according to accepted international guidelines, and we will always ensure transparency of our studies by publishing protocol synopses on the external website: **www.clinicaltrials.gov**. Study results from trials involving marketed drugs can be accessed via **www.clinicalstudyresults.org**. Furthermore, Novo Nordisk has its own online repository for clinical trials activities: novonordisk-trials.com. Novo Nordisk is collating all information about bioethics in the R&D area on **www.novonor disk.com/R&D/bioethics**.

Source: www.novonordisk.com, accessed November 2008.

Talisman Energy Inc.

Lawrence G. Tapp
Gail Robertson

At the August 2001 Talisman Energy Inc. (Talisman) meeting, the board of directors was updated on the company's activities in Sudan. Chief executive officer (CEO), Jim Buckee, and the board of directors (the board) participated in an ongoing review of the Sudan asset and its role in Talisman's portfolio. Throughout the three-year period during which Talisman had operated in Sudan, it had been criticized repeatedly by human rights, religious and social responsibility groups. On June 13, 2001, the United States House of Representatives had voted on a bill that would prevent Talisman and other foreign companies engaged in the development of oil and gas in Sudan from selling securities in the U.S. market. This action was the culmination of a broader-based effort resulting from pressure applied by various lobby groups in the United States.

The Sudan project continued to have good economic value and good production possibilities. As well, the contribution income from Talisman's interest in the Sudan project had been disproportionately high when compared to other Talisman properties; however, some downdrafts in the share price could be linked to events associated with Talisman's involvement in Sudan. A portion of the drop in the stock price in June and July of 2001 could be directly linked to the heating up of the Sudan issue and to the latest threat from the U.S. government directed at Talisman and other companies operating in Sudan. The question remained, however, whether the share price would continue to be adversely affected as issues pertaining to Talisman's Sudan interests unfolded. It was disturbing to Talisman's management that the entire company could be under attack due to decisions involving only 10 per cent of the business.

Talisman had gone to considerable lengths to develop and implement socially responsible policies regarding Sudan and believed the company had made a positive contribution toward improving the quality of life for the people of Sudan. In Sudan, the majority of the population was illiterate and access to the basics, such as clean water, was severely limited. Talisman executives believed that the economic development of Sudan was better left in the hands of ethical companies such as Talisman. It was the belief of Talisman executives that few companies would have contributed more to the economic development of Sudan than Talisman. While Talisman was not the sole operator of the Sudan operation, but rather a 25 per cent shareholder in the Greater Nile Petroleum Operating Company (GNPOC) operations, the influence of Talisman had prevailed with other shareholders in effecting socially responsible business practices in Sudan related to the GNPOC oil project.

Talisman's CEO was quoted in a Canadian national newspaper on June 19, 2001 as saying that Talisman was reconsidering its decision not to sell its interest in Sudan. This article was somewhat misleading as Talisman had always maintained that, in keeping with its role as a public company, at the right price, any asset, including its interest in the Sudan project, was for sale. The Sudan project had been highly successful to date, with substantial growth potential, and it had continually outperformed all plans. A key driver for the project was production growth, which was outstanding in this project. As a result, Talisman had continued to hold the asset to date.

The Sudan project had also outperformed expectations regarding political risk. The Talisman board of directors and management team had expected "typical" friction with local government in Sudan but had not anticipated the degree of domestic and North American political risk that had materialized since the acquisition. Nor had they anticipated the extent of public

outcry seen to date. The political system in the United States had provided Talisman with its greatest challenges to date. Some observers of the Talisman situation in Sudan were heard to speculate that Talisman, a Canadian company, was an easy target. It was suggested that by attacking Talisman, American politicians could take a stand on human rights issues in developing countries without hurting American corporations and important votes.

At the August 2001 board meeting, senior management and the board, in light of the external pressures brought to bear on the Sudan project, continued to be diligent as they sought to behave in a socially responsible manner. The board and management also continued to question whether the decision to operate holdings in Sudan was compatible with Talisman's mandate to operate in the best interests of the company and its shareholders.

The Energy Industry

Total energy costs in the world were approximately US$2 trillion annually in 2001, with the world consuming 28 billion barrels (bbls) of oil per year. Approximately two-thirds of the world's oil and gas reserves were located in the Middle East. Oil consumption accounted for 40 per cent of energy costs. New exploration discoveries replaced significantly less than half of this amount, though oil and gas were projected to provide two-thirds of the growth in energy demand over the next decade. Throughout the 1990s, oil prices averaged US$20 per barrel (/bbl), with global demand increasing by almost 10 million barrels per day. The majority of the increased supply came from the Organization of Petroleum Exporting Countries (OPEC). With world oil demand growing and production from major fields declining, it was felt that the long-term trend for oil prices was upward with dependence on the OPEC, especially in the Persian gulf, increasing.[1]

OPEC, a major force in the oil industry, was an international organization of 11 developing countries, all of which relied heavily on oil revenues as their main source of income. Membership was open to any country that was a substantial net exporter of oil and that held the ideals of the organization. In 2001, OPEC members included: Algeria, Indonesia, Iran, Iraq, Kuwait, Libya, Nigeria, Qatar, Saudi Arabia, the United Arab Emirates and Venezuela. Members met regularly to determine the organization's oil output level and to look at future considerations. OPEC collectively supplied about 40 per cent of the world's oil and was in possession of more than

three-quarters of the world's total proven crude oil reserves.[2]

Talisman's corporate strategy was based on the following beliefs about the oil and gas industry:

- The demand for oil and gas would continue to increase with population and economic growth.
- World-scale hydrocarbon discoveries were becoming increasingly rare; exploration risks could be mitigated by focusing on proved hydrocarbon basins.
- Corporate and asset acquisitions were viable ways to add value as long as they provided incremental exploration and development opportunities.
- Significant new oil developments would require a high level of technical, commercial and project management skills.[3]

Oil in Sudan was considered to be high quality oil. Canadian oil, in contrast, was heavier and had high sulfur content. Talisman's project in Sudan had been very successful by industry standards, as there had been less than two years' lead-time from the Arakis Energy acquisition in 1998 to production. The Sudan project had exceeded Talisman's

---

[1]Company sources.

[2]www.opec.org., November 2002.

[3]Company annual report.

expectations to date. Given that owner-ship of the pipeline would potentially gain incremental tariff revenues from third-party discoveries, the Sudan oper-ation was desirable for Talisman, with the huge oil exploration potential in Sudan. Thus, the Sudan project was considered to be a good fit with Talisman's corporate strategy.

History of Talisman Energy

Talisman, headquartered in Calgary, Alberta, was established in 1953 as BP Canada. The parent company, British Petroleum plc, sold off its Canadian interests in 1991. The new entity was renamed Talisman in 1992 and became an independent Canadian oil and gas producer, rather than a subsidiary of a major international corporation. Talisman continued, however, to have a major BP slant with its international management skills base. Talisman was listed as an independent on the Toronto Stock Exchange (TSE) in Canada, hav-ing previously been listed as BP, and was later listed on the New York Stock Exchange (NYSE) in the United States. Talisman was included in the Standard and Poor (S & P)/TSE 60.

Talisman had been successful and was now the largest Canadian oil and gas producer, with production growth averaging 17 per cent annually from 1995 to 2000 and cash flow per share growth averaging 27 per cent annually in the same period. Talisman's main

business activities included explora-tion, development, production and marketing of crude oil, natural gas and natural gas liquid. The company's main operating areas were Canada, the North Sea, Indonesia and Sudan. In 2001, Talisman directly employed more than 1,100 people and contracted ser-vices from approximately the same number of people.

Approximately half of Talisman's growth had been generic growth in production, with the other half based on acquisitions. Talisman's acquisition interests were

- Encor (1993)
- Bow Valley Energy (1994)
- Goal Petroleum plc (1996)
- Pembina Resources (1997)
- Arakis Energy (1998)
- Highridge Exploration Ltd. (1999)
- Rigel Energy Corporation (1999)
- Petromet Resources Limited (2001)
- Lundin Oil (2001)

The 1993 Encor purchase gave Talisman its first international interests, in Algeria and Indonesia. Talisman entered Sudan in 1998 through the acquisition of Arakis Energy Corporation, a move that resulted in Talisman obtaining a 25 per cent interest in the Greater Nile Petroleum Operating Company (GNPOC). In the summer of 2001, Talisman had its key international interests in Algeria, Colombia, Indonesia, Malaysia, Papua New Guinea, Trinidad, the United Kingdom, the United States and Vietnam.

Talisman had pursued international markets for growth as there was no significant growth potential in North America. The dilemma for smaller independents, such as Talisman, was that any new projects or acquisitions had to fit within the technical expertise of the organization as well as the financial capabilities. Such opportunities were limited.

Talisman Board of Directors and Management

The role of Talisman's board of directors in relation to the role of management was stated as follows:

> The principal role of the board of Directors is stewardship of the Company with the creation of shareholder value including the protection and enhancement of the value of its assets, as the fundamental objective. The stewardship responsibility means that the board oversees the conduct of the business and supervises management, which is responsible for the day-to-day conduct of the business. The board must assess and ensure systems are in place to manage the risks of the company's business with the objective of preserving the Company's assets. In its supervisory role, the board, through the Chief Executive Officer (CEO), sets the attitude and disposition of the Company towards compliance with applicable laws, environmental, safety

and health policies, financial practices and reporting. In addition to its primary accountability to shareholders, the board and the CEO are also accountable to government authorities, employees and the public.[4]

The board of directors of Talisman was elected annually by shareholders and consisted of a minimum of four directors and a maximum of 20 directors, as determined by the directors, the majority of whom were to be Canadian residents. At this time, the number of directors to be elected at shareholder meetings was fixed at nine, with four directors comprising quorum at any meeting.

At Talisman, the role of chairman of the board had been separated from the role of president and CEO. It was intended that the chairman should be independent from management and free from any interest and any business or other relationship that could interfere with the chairman's independent judgment other than interests resulting from company shareholdings and remuneration.

The CEO was responsible for leading Talisman. The CEO's primary function was the development of a long-term strategy for the Company. The CEO's leadership role also entailed ultimate responsibility for all day-to-day management decisions and for implementing the company's long- and short-term plans. The CEO, through the chairman,

---

[4]Internal company document.

acted as a direct link between the board and management of the company and acted as spokesman for management to the board. The CEO was also the ultimate spokesman on behalf of the company to government authorities, the public, shareholders, employees and other stakeholders and third parties.[5]

Chairman of the board in August 2001 was David Powell. Peter Widdrington had been chairman of the board during the time of the Arakis acquisition and for much of the Sudan controversy. Members of the board of directors are detailed in Exhibit 1. All but Larry Tapp and Douglas Baldwin had been directors under Peter Widdrington's leadership.

The senior executive management team at Talisman, under CEO James Buckee are also detailed in Exhibit 1. This senior management team was considered to be very strong. Many had significant tenure with the Talisman Corporation and its precursor and among them they had many years of experience in the oil and gas industry.

Talisman in Sudan

Talisman Energy (Talisman) owned a 25 per cent interest in the Greater Nile Petroleum Operating Company (GNPOC), covering four blocks in the Muglad Basin. The rest of the ownership in the GNPOC was distributed as follows: Chinese National Petroleum Company at 40 percent, Petronas (Malaysian corporation) at 30 per cent and Sudapet (Sudanese corporation) at 5 per cent.

Talisman also owned a 25 per cent interest in a 1,500 kilometre pipeline from the oil fields to Port Sudan on the Red Sea. Talisman's operations in Sudan accounted for approximately 10 per cent of Talisman's total business operations. Management and the board of directors of Talisman believed that the GNPOC was a good project for Talisman with excellent future exploration potential.

Operationally, the Sudan project continued to perform better than expected for Talisman. Total production reached a record 200,000 barrels/day (bbls/d) during 2000 against original design capacity (also known as nameplate capacity) of 150,000 bbls/day.

Highlights for the year 2000 in Sudan for the Talisman share of the project were

- Average production of 45,900 bbls/d in 2000 and 49,000 bbls/d in the fourth quarter;
- Spending of $70 million on exploration and development;
- Reserve additions of 26 million barrels, 152 per cent of production;
- Drilling 16 successful oil wells;
- Successful exploration well at Khairat, testing at 1,983 bbls/day;

---

[5]Internal company document.

- Drilling success at Munga and Bamboo, leading to development of these fields.

Talisman's objectives for 2001 in Sudan were

- Production of 50,000 to 55,000 bbls/day
- Startup of two new fields, Bamboo and Khairat
- Development of the Munga area for 2002 startup
- Capital spending of $120 million, including additional pumping capacity on the pipeline to increase nameplate capacity to 230,000 bbls/day and debottlenecking the central plant facilities at Heglig.
- Participation in 17 explorations and 25 development wells
- Drilling and testing a number of wells on Block 4 on the unexplored western side of the basin

Given that approximately five per cent of the GNPOC landholdings in Sudan were developed, Talisman believed there was great upside potential in the area. Talisman had operated in Sudan for three years and during that time had made a concerted effort to be a good corporate citizen and to enhance the quality of life of the Sudanese people.

Social Conditions in Sudan

The situation in Sudan was complex, and the people of Sudan faced many problems. There were approximately 500 tribes and 300 languages in Sudan and a history of internal conflict for generations. There had been almost continuous fighting between tribes as well as between the north and south since the British had left in the mid-1950s. The almost continuous fighting and famine in Sudan had created a human tragedy in this part of the world.

Despite the problems in Sudan, the United Nations recognized the government of Sudan as a legitimate government. Talisman was one of many companies from United Nations countries operating in Sudan.

The Canadian Department of Foreign Affairs and International Trade described Sudan as follows:

A civil war has raged in Sudan for most of the 43 years since independence in 1956. Although the origins of the conflict are found in the underdevelopment of the south during the colonial period, it is not longer simply north/south in scope. The Sudan Peoples' Liberation Movement (SPLM)—a southern-based movement—has been fighting consecutive, governing regimes. It has been joined by armed northern parties opposed to the current governing regime, led by the National Islamic Front (NIF), which seized power in a 1989 coup. Together they have formed a coalition called the National Democratic Alliance (NDA) that includes all the political parties that existed in the country prior to the 1989 coup, with the exception of the NIF, which retains power. Thus, the war has grown from a southern conflict to a complex crisis that is national in scale.

The principal factors now driving the conflict are disparities in the allocations of power, land and resources, the imposition of sectarian laws and the violation of the human rights of Sudan's marginalized people. Interstitial fighting was also widespread and a traditional activity. As is common in contemporary conflicts, civilians—particularly women and children—are the principal casualties. The human toll arising from war-related causes in Sudan, including famine is horrific. Nearly two million people, according to the United Nations, have died since 1983; in excess of four million people are internally displaced, dispossessed of their homes and separated from their families[6]

See Exhibit 2 for "Sudan Described by the World Bank" and "Sudan Described by the United States Energy Information Administration (EIA)."

The oil fields in Sudan were located on the 10th parallel; the dividing line between the north and south districts of the Anglo-Egyptian Condominium. Critics have stated that the oil revenue was fuelling the war there and that Talisman's presence lent legitimacy to the government. Rebels have stated that the oilfields were a legitimate target of war.

Public Pressure to Cease Operations in Sudan

Throughout the past three years in Sudan, Talisman had come under fire from many social, human rights, religious and government-based entities. North American and European human rights organizations had accused Talisman of supporting the Sudanese government by providing oil revenues that would then be used to support the government's civil war efforts. Following intense media scrutiny in the fall of 1999, the Canadian Department of Foreign Affairs and International Trade sent an envoy, John Harker, to Sudan on a fact-finding mission. According to Harker's final report on this mission, issued in February of 2000, the oil project was making the conflict worse.

In initial discussions with the Canadian government, Talisman had been told that its involvement in Sudan was acceptable, but the attitude of government appeared to have recently changed to one of uncertainty.

The United Nations Commission on Human Rights had also censured Sudan for its poor record in human rights protection, particularly with respect to the aerial bombing of civilian targets and the denial of food aid to needy populations. Further, it had been alleged that areas around the oilfields had become increasingly depopulated due to a "scorched earth" policy practiced by the Sudanese government. Several other organizations, including Africa Watch, Human Rights Watch, Doctors Without Borders, the Co-operative for American

---

[6]"Canada Announces Support to Sudan Peace Process," No. 232, October 26, 1999. www.dfait.maeci.gc.ca

Relief Everywhere Inc. (CARE) and the Inter-Church Coalition on Africa had repeated these assertions. Talisman executives had, in their possession, satellite photos taken at various times over decades that showed continuous development of communities surrounding the areas in which the GNPOC had its operations, not depopulation as was suggested by these organizations. Given the gravity of these issues, the past two Talisman annual general meetings and church-sponsored "town halls" (or town hall-styled meetings), had become focal points for individuals protesting Talisman's involvement in Sudan.

The Bush/Cheney administration in the United States appeared to be more supportive of oil holdings in the Middle East than the Clinton/Gore administration had been, but neither administration had approved of activities in Sudan. Bush had said he was opposed to capital market sanctions, as was Alan Greenspan, chairman of the U.S. Federal Reserve. Greenspan said that such measures could be "downright harmful" to the United States by pushing trade to other markets.[7]

Talisman and Corporate Responsibility

Talisman was committed to being a good corporate citizen worldwide and had participated in a number of initiatives to that end. Talisman had a history of being respectful of ethical issues in all of its operations. In light of the Sudan controversy, Talisman had added the International Code of Ethics for Canadian Business to its existing corporate Code of Ethics in December 1999, acting on a suggestion from Canadian Foreign Minister Lloyd Axworthy (see Exhibit 3).

Talisman believed that corporate responsibility should be a mainstream issue for the company and that corporate responsibility was intrinsic to all business. Talisman's CEO had repeatedly asserted that "ethically aware corporate engagement is the best way to improve the lives of people in the developing world, as opposed to isolation and sanctions." He based this assertion on the following:

- The generation of wealth in any country is a necessary precursor for progress and over time, has the potential to benefit the entire community.
- Corporations can do well in pursuit of their normal activities, such as: local job creation, expansion of infrastructure, building community capacity and creating opportunities for a better future for local people. In addition, it provides the opportunity to promote ethical

[7]Claudia Cattaneo, "Talisman Hopes to Dodge U.S. Sanctions," *Financial Post*, July 31, 2001.

business practices and advocates respect and tolerance.

- Corporate presence heightens international awareness and knowledge. Certainly, Talisman's presence in Sudan has greatly increased public awareness and debate about issues in Sudan.
- Public company presence leads to analyst coverage, quarterly reports, and press interest—all of which leads to international scrutiny. This produces the "external observer effect," which, like a police car on the highway, induces ethical behavior in the vicinity.
- Investment and trade lead to discussion and trust, exchange of ideas and resolution of differences.[8]

Dr. Buckee was fond of a quote by Kofi Annan, Secretary General of the United Nations and Nobel Peace Prize winner, that stated, "The only developing countries that really are developing are those that have succeeded in attracting significant amounts of direct foreign investment."

Talisman repeatedly made a strong business case for corporate social responsibility. In keeping with its commitment to corporate responsibility, in the year 2000, Talisman had set up a separate Corporate Social Responsibility Unit under the direction of Reg Manhas,

previously a member of Talisman's legal staff department.

Talisman's mandate in the area of corporate social responsibility included the following:

- Conducting activities in an economically, socially and environmentally responsible manner.
- Working together with stakeholder groups to identify constructive solutions to problems while bringing direct benefits to the communities in which they operated, including creation of jobs, expansion of infrastructure and support of community projects.
- Maintaining and promoting ethical business practices.
- Advocating respect and tolerance by and for all people.
- Advocating human rights to the Government of Sudan.[9]

Talisman held that the business case related to a number of factors:

- The corporation's ability to attract and retain top quality employees. In the case of Talisman, there was certainty that Canadian and British employees in the field in Sudan would not be party to unethical behavior on the part of Talisman or the GNPOC.

---

[8]Company files.

[9]Ibid.

- Most shareholders would also be attracted to corporations that acted in a socially responsible manner.
- Implementation of Corporate Social Responsibility (CSR) initiatives within an operating area would enable a corporation to manage risks to its assets and personnel in operating areas; an unpopular operation in the community could threaten security and financial performance.
- The benefit of a favorable reputation. Making the corporation an attractive business partner for other companies and host nations would increase business opportunities.

In Sudan, despite its commitment to corporate social responsibility, it was difficult for Talisman to operate in a corporately responsible manner to the extent it would want to, as it held only a 25 per cent share of the GNPOC project.

Talisman and Corporate Responsibility in Sudan

One reality of the oil business was the vast majority of known remaining conventional oil reserves were located in developing countries, more than three quarters of them in Muslim countries. As well, most oil investment was capital-intensive, had a 25-year life and couldn't be moved. Economic and operational realities dictated that oil production from a project could not simply be "stopped" as had been suggested of the Sudan project. In addition, oil business was often one of the largest foreign earners for host governments and thus had influence and importance. This influence and importance made the oil companies' relationships with communities and host governments extremely important, in that both must see the presence of the oil company as directly beneficial.

Difficulties, such as those experienced by Talisman with its Sudan operations, arose when projects become the focal point of unrelated social unrest. Despite this negative attention, and despite the fact that there was indeed a civil war ongoing and the oilfield revenues were disbursed to the Government of Sudan, Talisman held fast to the belief that walking away from Sudan was not the proper response to public outcry.

Instead, Talisman, with the support of its shareholders, developed a response in keeping with its business practices and beliefs. At Talisman's annual general meeting in May 2000, a number of shareholders presented a proposal to the shareholders of Talisman whereby they raised concerns about the Company's investment in Sudan. The proposal asked the board of directors to take a number of measures including the preparation of an independently verified report on the Company's compliance with the International Code of Ethics for Canadian Business within 180 days. In a second resolution, proposed by management, the board of directors was asked:

1. To cause the Company, in consultation with an independent third party, to develop and implement procedures for monitoring the Company's compliance with the International Code of Ethics for Canadian Business, including the human rights provisions thereof, with respect to the operations of the Company and its subsidiary in Sudan; and

2. To cause to be prepared annually an independently verified report on the Company's compliance with the International Code of Ethics for Canadian Business, with respect to such operations and to provide a summary of each such report to the shareholders, in conjunction with the Company's normal annual reporting to shareholders and to make a full report available to shareholders and the public on request.[10]

The shareholders accepted the resolution proposed by management and the Corporate Social Responsibility Report 2000: Sudan Operations was compiled (see Exhibit 4).

Peter Widdrington (chairman of the board of Talisman), in his introductory statement in the Corporate Social Responsibility Report 2000: Sudan Operations, reinforced the Talisman belief that corporate social responsibility must be a mainstream issue and intrinsic to all business. He indicated that Talisman, in response to public concern over the company's investment in Sudan, had enhanced its existing governance procedures to ensure accountability and control regarding corporate social responsibility issues. Talisman had endorsed and approved the Sudan Operating Principles, management structures and participation initiatives as outlined in the report and had endorsed the development of formal policies and procedures to implement codes of conduct and international standards that would define appropriate activities for business. Talisman was committed to providing to the board of directors comprehensive corporate social responsibility reviews and updates on Sudan twice a year, with other reports being made available throughout the year as deemed appropriate. A steering committee, consisting of the CEO, senior executives and senior people responsible for Corporate Responsibility, also met weekly to review issues related to Sudan and the implementation of the International Code of Ethics for Canadian Business.

In September 2000, Talisman had persuaded the GNPOC to adopt a code of ethics and proceeded to develop operating principles.

---

[10]Ibid.

As outlined in the Corporate Responsibility Report 2000, Talisman's commitment to corporate social responsibility in Sudan encompassed the areas of human rights, community participation, employee rights, business conduct and health, safety and environment.

Specific objectives in each of these areas were:

- HUMAN RIGHTS—a commitment to addressing human rights concerns arising from Talisman and GNPOC operations, supporting the Universal Declaration of Human Rights and advocating the beliefs with their joint venture partners and the Government of Sudan.
- COMMUNITY PARTICIPATION— ensuring that local communities received long-term sustainable benefits from Talisman operations; consulting with local communities, governments and non-governmental organizations and the joint venture business partners to identify suitable projects and initiatives.
- EMPLOYEE RIGHTS—Talisman endeavored to respect individual rights and to provide a safe and healthy working environment with meaningful employment opportunities for local people, competitive pay and a training/ development program for staff.
- BUSINESS CONDUCT—Talisman was committed to carrying out all business activities in accordance

with its Policy on Business Conduct, the Sudan Operating Principles and the International Code of Ethics for Canadian Business.
- HEALTH, SAFETY and ENVIRONMENT—Talisman was committed to maintaining high standards in occupational health, safety and environment, and saw these standards as being key to achieving efficiency and profitability in the oil and gas business.

Talisman, in keeping with its corporate social responsibility mandate had made significant contributions to the people of Sudan in each area, including:

- HUMAN RIGHTS
  - Extensive dialogue with the Government of Sudan expressing Talisman's support for the protection of human rights and supporting the peace process;
  - Development of a detailed human rights monitoring and investigation program manual to address concerns arising from GNPOC operations;
  - Introduction of a human rights awareness program for Talisman employees in Sudan;
  - Participation of the four most senior GNPOC security officials and Talisman's human rights Field Co-ordinator in human rights and modern peacekeeping training at the Lester B. Pearson

Canadian International Peacekeeping Centre.

- COMMUNITY PARTICIPATION
  - Completion of 15 independent community development projects for a total cost of Cdn$1 million;
  - Completion of 25 GNPOC community development projects for a total cost of close to Cdn$2 million;
  - Attainment of Sudanization targets: at December 31, 2000, Sudanese nationals held 72 per cent of all skilled and unskilled positions at GNPOC;
  - In the area of community development, Talisman's focus was on water, health, learning and capacity building. Talisman had constructed a 60-bed hospital in the concession area, had built four schools and provided or renewed 28 water wells in the concession area and along the pipeline. Talisman had also given mechanical and technical support for successful agricultural development in the concession area (see Exhibit 5).

- EMPLOYEE RIGHTS
  - Provided training to 1,159 participants in 67 different programs;
  - Formalized policies regarding: discrimination; screening of contractors; use of child and forced labor; respect for the cultural, spiritual and social needs of National employees; and a grievance and disclosure policy.

- ETHICAL BUSINESS CONDUCT
  - Implementation of an Ethical Business Conduct Management System;
  - Adoption by GNPOC of a Code of Ethics that deals with a wide range of issues including human rights and community participation.

- HEALTH, SAFETY AND ENVIRONMENT
  - Completion of an independent review of the GNPOC health, safety and environmental management system;
  - Provided over 600 person days of safety and loss control training to GNPOC employees.[11]

In addition to these achievements, Talisman had taken on an advocacy role at the highest levels of the Government of Sudan, discussing numerous issues including the protection of human rights, the peace process and the equitable distribution of oil revenues to all people and regions of Sudan. Talisman had also acted as a conduit for external opinion to the Government of Sudan. Talisman had seen positive results on all fronts, though many issues remained.[12]

[11]Corporate Social Responsibility Report 2000.

[12]Company files.

A major challenge facing Talisman in its efforts to bring CSR standards to the GNPOC project in Sudan was related to ownership. Despite the fact that each of the partners had its own CSR standards, Talisman had been very successful in implementing many of its CSR initiatives.

U.S. House of Representatives Sudan Resolution

On June 13, 2001, the United States House of Representatives voted to prevent Talisman and other foreign companies engaged in the development of oil and gas in Sudan from selling securities in the U.S. market. If approved, the new law would cost Talisman its stock market listing on the New York Stock Exchange.[13] The United States Senate passed the Sudan Peace Act (without the capital market provisions) on July 19, 2001, via a Unanimous Consent Agreement.

The next step in this process was the staging of a "conference," where representatives from the House and Senate would meet to reach a compromise between the conflicting versions of the Act that had been passed. Talisman had not yet been made aware of the timing of the conference or the names of the conferees (see Exhibit 6).

Financial Implications

Talisman was financially sound. In 2000, cash flow reached $2.4 billion ($17.51/share and a 97 per cent increase over 1999) and net income was $906 million ($6.41/share). Both cash flow and net income exceeded the company's previous record set in 1999. Talisman maintained targets for debt to cash flow of two times or less and 40 per cent or less for debt to debt-plus-equity. Talisman was well below these targets at year-end with a debt to cash flow ratio of 0.7 and debt to debt-plus-equity of 32 per cent (see Exhibits 7 and 8).

Talisman's share price had increased 51 per cent over the course of 2000. Talisman had consistently outperformed the oil and gas producers' index, the TSE 35 as well as the Dow Jones Industrial Average from its inception and continued to do so in 2000. Management was convinced that Talisman shares were still undervalued. The adverse publicity over Talisman's holdings in Sudan in 2001 had, however, an adverse effect on share price.

Lundin Oil—Acquisition Without Sudan Holdings

Talisman had announced on June 21, 2001, that a wholly owned Swedish subsidiary would make an offer to acquire all the outstanding shares and warrants of Lundin Oil AB (Lundin Oil). Talisman offered SEK36.5 (approximately US$3.43) for each Class A and Class B share of Lundin Oil. In addition, if the offer was successful, all of Lundin Oil's current

---

[13]Claudia Cattaneo, "Talisman Wavers on Sudan," *Financial Post*, June 19, 2001, p. C1.

interests in Sudan and Russia would be conveyed to a newly formed spinoff company (Newco) and the shares of Newco distributed to holders of Lundin Oil shares on a one-for-one basis. Newco would be managed by the current Lundin Oil management team.

Talisman, as a result of the deal, would retain Lundin's interests in the North Sea, Malaysia, Vietnam and Papua New Guinea at a cost of approximately US$344 million (Cdn$529 million) including debt and working capital. In a separate transaction, Lundin Oil's interests in Libya were to have been sold to a third party (Petro Canada) for US$75 million.

Subject to the satisfaction or waiver of all conditions to the offer, settlement was expected to begin on or about August 28, 2001.

The Decision

There had been ongoing frustration on the part of Talisman's management and board; 10 per cent of operations had been receiving a disproportionate amount of attention in the public eye, as well as a disproportionate amount of management time. In addition, the negative publicity surrounding Talisman's holdings in Sudan had been hard on staff morale.

Talisman CEO Jim Buckee had staunchly defended Talisman's position in Sudan and had taken steps to ensure the company continued to act responsibly in this area. In April 2001, Buckee said,

I think we are right...We are Canadians, we send Canadian values down into this area that needs it, and we are moving behavior, we are moving opinion by our presence, by our systems on health, safety, environment, human rights, corporate contributions.[14]

Despite its efforts, Talisman was in danger of losing U.S. capitalization if it did not sell off its interest in the GNPOC. One week after the U.S. House passed its version of the Sudan Peace Act, Buckee said, "We want to remain in compliance with laws, and we will. No asset is worth more than that." He indicated that Talisman was "taking prudent steps" that could result in Talisman selling its 25 per cent stake in the GNPOC. Buckee indicated that Talisman had been evaluating opportunities for new country entry in a new core area that was less politically controversial.

Steve Calderwood, an analyst from Salman Partners Inc., was reported to have said, after the U.S. government's decision was made, that Talisman had also considered dividending out to shareholders its Sudan interests as a separate company that would trade in Europe. Calderwood also indicated his belief that should Talisman get out of Sudan, because of pressure from peace advocates, claiming oil development was fueling the war and displacing people, these peace advocates would have a tougher time getting

---

[14]Claudia Cattaneo, "Talisman Wavers on Sudan," *Financial Post*, June 19, 2001, p. C10.

attention for their cause. He believed the oil operations would become less transparent and likely less relevant to the West. "If there isn't a North American or western company as a target from those interest groups, it's going to be tougher for them to make a case for oil development in Sudan to stop."[15]

A number of Middle East, Asian and Russian companies in need of oil holdings had expressed interest in Talisman's GNPOC interest. Talisman management and board were concerned, however, that selling their interest, while it may take the pressure off Talisman, could ultimately be harmful to the people of Sudan. The governments of the prospective buyers had not been strong advocates of human rights and corporate responsibility in the past, and Talisman had to question whether the sale of the GNPOC interest would be in keeping with its corporate social responsibility policies.

While Talisman had not named the potential buyers, members of the press and other industry followers speculated on which company or companies would be the most likely buyers:

- Talisman's partner in Sudan, China National Petroleum Co., which wanted to boost its production from Sudan;
- The French multinational, Total, which owned a vast concession south of Talisman's operations;

- Lundin Oil Corporation of Sweden's Newco, with current operations in Sudan;
- Petroliam Nasional Berhad of Malaysia, with operations in Sudan;
- ONGC Videsh Ltd. (OVL).

The Talisman board of directors and management team believed that the fundamental issue was that Talisman's investment strategy was driven by a business perspective. From both technical and strategic perspectives, Talisman had gained terrific stature from bringing about achievements in Sudan. It was clear that growth in the North American oil markets was not possible at this time. Only by expanding in international markets could Talisman continue to grow. The challenge of growth for a company the size of Talisman was to ensure that any projects undertaken fit both the technical expertise of Talisman and its financial capabilities.

Talisman's management and board had to make a decision: Should Talisman keep the property in Sudan and continue to try to make a difference through Talisman's corporate social responsibility initiatives? Would this action be sufficient to cause the share price to rebound? Or should Talisman sell its interest in the GNPOC property and maximize shareholder wealth in the short term?

---

[15]Financial Post, June 19, 2001.

Exhibit 1   Board of Directors

David Powell—Calgary, Alberta,
Chairman, Talisman Energy, Inc. since 1998

Chairman of the Board of the Company; Director of various corporations; Chairman of the Board of Petroleum Industry Training Service; from 1991 to 1995, President and Chief Executive Officer of Home Oil Company Ltd.

Douglas D. Baldwin—Calgary, Alberta,
Corporate Director since 2001

Director of various corporations; from 1999 to 2001, President and Chief Executive Officer of TransCanada PipeLines Ltd.; from 1992 to 1998, Senior Vice-President and Director of Imperial Oil Ltd.; from 1988 to 1992, President and Chief Executive Officer, Esso Resources Canada Ltd.

James W. Buckee—CEO, Talisman Energy Inc.

BSc Honors in physics from the University of Western Australia with first class honors; and a PhD in Astrophysics from Oxford University. Dr. Buckee held various petroleum engineering positions with Shell International and Burma Oil Company in the UK North Sea, Norway, Australia and New Zealand from 1971 to 1977. From 1977 to 1983, Dr. Buckee held various petroleum engineering posts with British Petroleum in Canada and the Middle East. In 1983, he became the Chief Reservoir Engineer with BP Exploration in London, England. In 1987, Dr. Buckee became Operations Manager for British Petroleum in Norway, and was subsequently appointed Vice President Development Programs for BP Alaska where he stayed until May 1989 when he moved back to London as Manager, Planning for BP Exploration. In September 1991, Dr. Buckee was appointed President and Chief Operating Officer for Talisman Energy Inc. and he was appointed President and Chief Executive Officer for Talisman Energy Inc. in May 1993.

Al Flood, C.M.—Thornhill, Ontario,
Corporate Director since 2000

Director of various corporations; from 1999 to 2000, Chairman of the Executive Committee of Canadian Imperial Bank of Commerce (CIBC); prior to June 1999, Chairman and Chief Executive Officer of CIBC and held various positions in the domestic and international operations of CIBC.

Paul Hoenmans—Director since 1998; Aspen, Colorado, Corporate

Director of various corporations; prior to September 1997, Executive Vice-President of Mobil Oil Corporation and Director and Member of the Executive Committee of Mobil Corporation and Mobil Oil Corporation; from 1986 to 1996, President, Exploration & Producing Division, Mobil Oil Corporation.

Dale Parker—Director since 1993; Vancouver, British Columbia

Public Administration and Financial Institution Advisor; Director of various corporations and public administration and financial institution advisor; prior to January 1998, President and Chief Executive Officer of Workers' Compensation Board of British Columbia; prior to November 1994, President of White Spot Ltd. and Executive Vice-President of Shato holdings Ltd.; prior to November 1993, Executive Vice-President and Chief Financial Officer of Shato Holdings Ltd.; prior to November 1992, Chairman and Chief Executive Officer of British Columbia Financial Institutions Commission.

Roland Priddle—Director since 2000. Saanich, British Columbia, Consultant

Consultant to public and private sector entities on policy and regulatory issues in oil and gas; advisor to the Energy Institute at the University of Houston; director of various corporations; prior to 1998, Chairman, National Energy Board of Canada.

Larry Tapp—Director since 2001; London, Ontario

Dean of The Richard Ivey School of Business, The University of Western Ontario since 1995; from 1992 to 1995, Executive in Residence of the Faculty of Management and Adjunct Professor, University of Toronto; from 1985 to 1992, Vice Chairman, President and Chief Executive Officer of Lawson Mardon Group Ltd.

Stella Thompson—Director since 1995, Calgary, Alberta

Principal, Governance West Inc.; President of Stellar Energy Ltd.; Director of various corporations; prior to June 1991,Vice-President, Planning, Business Information & Systems of Petro-Canada Products.

SENIOR MANAGEMENT

James W. Buckee

President and Chief Executive Officer; See Talisman Board of Directors.

Edward W. Bogle

Vice-President, Exploration. PhD in Geology from Queen's University in 1980. Dr. Bogle joined Talisman Energy Inc. (formerly BP Canada Inc.) in May, 1980. He has held positions of progressively increasing responsibility in the Company from 1980 to 1992. In June 1992, Dr. Bogle was appointed Vice President, Exploration for Talisman Energy Inc.

(Continued)

Exhibit 1 (Continued)

T.N. (Nigel) D. Hares

Vice-President, Frontier and International Operations. BSc Honors in Chemistry from the Polytechnic of North London. Mr. Hares worked for British Petroleum from 1972 to 1994. In August 1994, Mr. Hares became Vice President, International Operations with Talisman Energy Inc.

Joseph E. Horler

Vice-President, Marketing. Bachelor of Commerce from the University of Calgary; has completed a number of management and executive development programs. Prior to joining Talisman in 1987, Mr. Horler was Manager of Crude Oil Affairs with the Independent Petroleum Association of Canada, Manager of Crude and Product Supply with Husky Oil Operations, managed other assignments within the Supply and Transportation Department of Sun Oil. Mr. Horler represents Talisman Energy's shareholding as a member of the Board of Directors of Sultran, Ltd. and Pacific Coast Terminals Co. Ltd.

Michael D. McDonald

Vice-President, Finance and Chief Financial Officer; MA in Economics from the University of Calgary. Mr. McDonald worked on a broad spectrum of fossil fuel-based development projects for the Energy Resources Conservation Board beginning in 1979. He joined BP Canada in 1982 and has held positions of increasing responsibility in economics and corporate planning. In 1994, Mr. McDonald was seconded to Talisman Energy (UK) Ltd. in London, England and subsequently Aberdeen, Scotland. In 1995, he was appointed General Manager (UK) and was responsible for administration and management of Talisman's activities in the North Sea. In 1998, Mr. McDonald was promoted to Vice President, Business Development and in 2001 he was promoted to Vice President, Finance and Chief Financial Officer.

Robert W. Mitchell

Vice-President, Canadian Operations; BSc Honors in 1969 and PhD from University of Hull. Dr. Mitchell's early career was in teaching and research at Queen's University, Ontario. He entered the oil industry in 1971 and held a variety of petroleum engineering positions in Holland, Africa, the Middle East and the U.S. Dr. Mitchell joined BP International in Aberdeen in 1976 and held various engineering and management positions in the United Kingdom. In 1984, he transferred to BP Canada Inc. as Vice President Oil Sands and in 1990 became Vice President, Operations.

Robert M. Redgate

Vice-President, Human Resources and Corporate Services; Honors BSc from the University of Alberta; Masters in Environmental Design Planning and Management from University of Calgary. Mr. Redgate joined BP Canada Inc. in 1977 and held positions of increasing responsibility in Environmental Affairs, Health and Safety from 1977 to 1982. In 1982, he became the Manager, Personnel and Environmental Affairs and in 1985 he was appointed Manager,

Staff Planning and Development and in 1987, Manager, Personnel. In 1992, Mr. Redgate was appointed Vice President, Human Resources and Administration for Talisman Energy Inc. In 1996, he became Vice President Human Resources and Corporate Services.

M. Jacqueline Sheppard

Vice-President, Legal and Corporate Projects, and Corporate Secretary; Honors BA in Political Science from Memorial University, Newfoundland; Honors Jurisprudence BA and MA from Oxford University where she attended as a Rhodes Scholar; LLB (First Class Honors)from McGill University as a faculty scholar. Ms. Sheppard was partner at national law firm Blakes, Cassels & Graydon, based in Calgary, practicing in oil and gas, corporate/commercial and finance areas from 1981 through 1993, concentrating on corporate acquisitions, reorganizations, divestitures and public and private financings of energy companies. Ms. Sheppard joined Talisman in 1993 in her current role.

Exhibit 2   Two Descriptions of Sudan

Sudan as Described by the World Bank

Sudan gained its independence from Britain in 1956. The first episode in what has become an intractable civil war in southern Sudan occurred through a mutiny of southern forces in 1955. Civil strife escalated as southern demands for political expression and economic development were ignored by the ruling elite in the north. Sudan consequently endured a civil war that has spanned more than three decades. Since 1997, the Sudan People's Liberation Army (SPLA) has controlled much of the south. More recently, the southern-based rebels and the government have conducted direct negotiations under the auspices of the Inter-Governmental authority on Development (IGAD).

Economic progress has been constrained by the civil war, military expenditures, social dislocation, deterioration of basic infrastructure and lack of access to aid and foreign investments. Sudan is also vulnerable to external shocks, including floods and drought. As a result, poverty levels have risen despite growth.

Since 1996, GDP growth has averaged 5.5 per cent led mainly by agriculture which accounts for an estimated 45 per cent of GDP. Inflation has slowed from 133 per cent to 16 per cent. The general economic improvement has been helped by reforms supported by the IMF. These reforms emphasise containing fiscal deficits, and limiting monetary growth and inflation.

The key structural reforms aim at enhancing efficiency by liberalising the trade and exchange rate regime, phasing out price controls and privatising public enterprises.

More recently, Sudan has benefited from investment in oil production which is expected to reduce the country's import bill and improve the availability of foreign exchange for development financing.

COUNTRIES; SUDAN, SEPTEMBER 2000

Source: www.worldbank.org, September 2000.

(Continued)

Exhibit 2 (Continued)

Sudan as Described by the United States Energy Information Administration (EIA)

Sudan gained its independence from Egypt and the United Kingdom in 1956. The current government, led by General Omar Hassan Ahmad al-Bashir, came to power in 1989 after overthrowing a transitional coalition government. A new constitution was promulgated on January 1, 1999. Multi-party presidential and parliamentary elections are scheduled for December 2000.

Sudan is among the world's poorest countries. Its economy is primarily agricultural—a mix of subsistence farming and production of cash crops such as cotton and gum arabic. In the past four years, however, Sudan's economic performance has been strong; annual GDP growth has averaged 5.5 per cent, while inflation has slowed from 133 per cent to 16 per cent. Exports have grown by one-quarter to $780 million, while Sudan's current account deficit has dropped from nearly 8 per cent of GDP to 2.4 per cent. Sudan's real GDP growth rate is forecast at 6.5 per cent in 2000, while inflation is predicted to reach the 9 per cent year-end target set by the government. In May 2000, the International Monetary Fund (IMF) expressed its satisfaction with Sudan's implementation of a 1999–2001 structural adjustment program. However, representatives of the IMF advised the Sudanese government to move to full market liberalisation in the petroleum product sector as quickly as possible and to adopt full public disclosure of oil revenue data. In August 2000, the IMF lifted the suspension—in place since 1993—of Sudan's voting rights in the IMF.

Sudan recently has become more engaged in the global economy. In February 2000, Sudan opened its Red Sea Free Trade Zone, designed to encourage foreign direct investment, and in March 2000, Sudan publicly repeated its desire to join the World Trade Organisation. Since the end of 1999, Sudan has signed various trade and investment agreements with Saudi Arabia, Bahrain, Iraq, Kuwait, Ethiopia, and Syria, while simultaneously predicting that Malaysian investment in Sudan, particularly in the oil, gas and petrochemical industries, would exceed $1 billion by the end of 2000.

Despite its economic progress, Sudan still faces developmental obstacles, including a limited infrastructure and an external debt at the end of 1999 of nearly $24 billion, representing a debt-to-GDP ratio of 218.3 per cent. Furthermore, the government remains embroiled in the long-running conflict with rebel movements in the south of the country, inhabited primarily by non-Muslims. The conflict has maintained the scarcity of national development resources, despite the increase in government oil revenues. Over the past two decades, the civil war has claimed 1.5 million Sudanese lives.

SUDAN COUNTRY ANALYSIS BRIEF NOVEMBER 2000

Source: www.eia.doe.gov, November 2000.

Exhibit 3   Talisman Energy International Code of Ethics for Canadian Business

Vision

Canadian business has a global presence that is recognized by all stakeholders[1] as economically rewarding to all parties, acknowledged as being ethically, socially and environmentally responsible, welcomed by the communities in which we operate, and that facilitates economic, human resource and community development within a stable operating environment.

Beliefs

We believe that:

- we can make a difference within our sphere of influence (our stakeholders);
- business should take a leadership role through establishment of ethical business principles;
- national governments have the prerogative to conduct their own government and legal affairs in accordance with their sovereign rights;
- all governments should comply with international treaties and other agreements that they have committed to, including the areas of human rights and social justice;
- while reflecting cultural diversity and differences, we should do business throughout the world consistent with the way we do business in Canada;
- the business sector should show ethical leadership;
- we can facilitate the achievement of wealth generation and a fair sharing of economic benefits;
- our principles will assist in improving relations between the Canadian and host governments;
- open, honest and transparent relationships are critical to our success;
- local communities need to be involved in decision-making for issues that affect them;
- multistakeholder processes need to be initiated to seek effective solutions;
- confrontation should be tempered by diplomacy;
- wealth maximization for all stakeholders will be enhanced by resolution of outstanding human rights and social justice issues; and
- doing business with other countries is good for Canada and vice versa.

Values

We value:

- human rights and social justice;
- wealth maximization for all stakeholders;
- operation of a free market economy;
- a business environment which militates against bribery and corruption;
- public accountability by governments;
- equality of opportunity;

(Continued)

---

[1]Stakeholders include: local communities, Canadian and host governments, local governments, shareholders, the media, customers and suppliers, interest groups and international agencies.

Exhibit 3 (Continued)

- a defined code of ethics and business practice;
- protection of environmental quality and sound environmental stewardship;
- community benefits;
- good relationships with all stakeholders; and
- stability and continuous improvement within our operating environment.

Principles

Concerning Community Participation and Environmental Protection—We will:

- strive within our sphere of influence to ensure a fair share of benefits to stakeholders impacted by our activities;
- ensure meaningful and transparent consultation with all stakeholders and attempt to integrate our corporate activities with local communities as good corporate citizens;
- ensure our activities are consistent with sound environmental management and conservation practices; and
- provide meaningful opportunities for technology, training and capacity building with the host nation.

Concerning Human Rights—We will:

- support and promote the protection of international human rights within our sphere of influence; and
- not be complicit in human rights abuses.

Concerning Business Conduct—We will:

- not make illegal and improper payments and bribes and will refrain from participating in any corrupt business practices;
- comply with all applicable laws and conduct business activities in a transparent fashion; and
- ensure contractors', suppliers' and agents' activities are consistent with these principles.

Concerning Employee Rights and Health and Safety—We will:

- ensure health and safety of workers is protected;
- strive for social justice and promote freedom of association and expression in the workplace; and
- ensure consistency with universally accepted labor standards, including those related to exploitation of child labor, forced labor and non-discrimination in employment.

Source: Company files.

Note: The 'Code' is a statement of values and principles designed to facilitate and assist individual firms in the development of their policies and practices that are consistent with the vision, beliefs, values and principles contained herein.

Exhibit 4 Corporate Social Responsibility Report 2000: Sudan Operations: Timeline and Framework

| The International Code of Ethics for Canadian Business | Sudan Operating Principles | Key Stakeholder Concerns | Talisman Objectives | GNPOC Objectives | General Advocacy Objectives |

Talisman and GNPOC have developed policies and procedures under each of these headings which are capable of verification. As these policies and procedures are implemented Talisman's performance may be capable of verification.

December 1999
Adoption by Talisman of the International Code of Ethics for Canadian Business

March 2000
Establishment of Code of Social Responsibility

September 2000
Approval of the Sudan Operating Principles

January 2001
Gathering of formal Talisman stakeholder commentary

March 2001
Completion of external verification of this report

March 2001
Approval of the corporate social responsibility report by the Board of Directors

May 2001
Annual General Meeting

Exhibit 5   Major Talisman Community Projects in Sudan

- Construction of a 60-bed hospital in Heglig with a staff of four doctors, who see an average of 260 people per day in the 24-hour emergency department. Minor operations, dental care, x-rays, vaccinations and obstetric services are also provided free of charge to all patients.
- Construction, outfitting and staffing of five medical clinics and Abyei hospital. Environmental health classes are held for local community members from each clinic on a regular basis.
- Funding of medical treatments, including 15,000 vaccinations and an ongoing tuberculosis prevention program.
- Construction of four schools. Educational development and adult literacy programs in Paryang and Karkaria villages.
- Provision of new or restored water supplies in 28 communities. The program included well maintenance and repair training for local residents as well as an inventory of spare parts to keep the wells, usually hand pumps, in good working condition. Provision of six high-capacity water well systems (200-foot deep wells, storage containers and pumps/faucets) in Kummagon, Rubkona (2), Kailak Lake and Paryang (2).
- Provision of emergency relief for displaced people in Bentiu and Mayom including tents, mosquito netting, medication and an emergency medical clinic.
- Funding for an artificial limb camp in Khartoum, which has provided more than 2,000 lower limbs to amputees.
- Funding to support the development of entrepreneurial skills among 720 women in the internally displaced peoples (IDP) camps of Mayo and Shagara in Khartoum. Training in tailoring and pasta making provides opportunities to generate income. Flexible loans to fund business startup costs are also provided.
- Funding, mechanical and technical support for agricultural development in the concession including the tilling and seeding (dhura or sorghum) of 16,000 acres near Kailak Lake.
- A twice-weekly fruit program directed at the inmates of the Kober and Jaref Reformatories. This was the earliest of Project Health Opportunities for People Everywhere's (Project HOPE's) programs and ran for about 10 months.
- Provided beds and bedding to the Mother Theresa Orphanage as well as a cash donation towards food.
- The funding of capital costs for an orthopedic shoe fabrication facility at the Cheshire Home.
- The free distribution of 26 tricycles for disabled adults in Khartoum and 20 to a group of disabled people in Bentiu.
- The construction of two classrooms and the replacement of a roof covering two existing classrooms at the METADEC School.
- The purchase of tables and chairs for the children of the St. Joseph Kindergarten.
- Purchase of school text books for the Episcopal Church of Sudan (ECS) Basic and St. Phillips Basic schools.
- The provision of art supplies and musical instruments to a street boys' program.

Exhibit 6   Press Releases

Bush Admin, Greenspan Oppose Tighter Sudan Sanctions[1]

WASHINGTON—(Dow Jones)—President George W. Bush's administration and Federal Reserve Chairman Alan Greenspan have both voiced opposition to a proposed tightening of sanctions on Sudan that would restrict access to U.S. capital. Congress is considering preventing oil and gas companies operating in Sudan from listing equity shares or offering debt in U.S. markets. Last month, the House voted 422-to-2 in favor of a bill that would do just that.

Such capital markets sanctions "would significantly damage our relations with European and African countries that are essential to the peace process in Sudan," a Bush administration official familiar with U.S. sanctions policy told Dow Jones Newswires. The remark suggests Bush would veto any bill that restricts capital markets.

While the Bush administration official cited diplomatic concerns, Greenspan weighed in with concern about the economy. The Fed Chairman told the Senate Banking Committee Tuesday that the proposed capital market sanctions would "effectively move a considerable amount of financing out of the United States to London, Frankfurt, and Tokyo." The humanitarian goals of the Sudan bill are laudable but Greenspan said he is "most concerned that if we move in directions which undermine our financial capacity, we are undermining the potential long-term growth of the American economy."

The Senate and House have both passed versions of the Sudan Peace Act, legislation aimed at alleviating suffering in the war-torn African country. But the Senate's version has no capital markets sanctions. The two versions must be reconciled in conference between House and Senate negotiators.

Bush Admin Differs With Religious Freedom Commission[2]

U.S. companies are barred from operating in Sudan. But affiliates of companies listed on U.S. exchanges—including Canada's Talisman Energy Inc. (TLM) and China's Petrochina Co. (PTR)—have major stakes in Sudan's burgeoning oil industry.

Talisman and Petrochina, an affiliate of state-owned China National Petroleum Company, have been targets of human rights activists and religious groups that say their investments support the Sudanese government's military campaign against religious and ethnic minorities.

In March the Congressionally established U.S. Commission on International Religious Freedom recommended tighter sanctions on companies like Talisman and CNPC for their roles in Sudan, as well as a complete prohibition on U.S. import of Sudanese gum Arabic, a food additive in soft drinks and candy. The Bush administration has demurred. The administration official

(Continued)

---

[1]Campion Walsh, "Bush Admin, Greenspan Oppose Tighter Sudan Sanctions," *Dow Jones International News*, July 25, 2001.

[2]Campion Walsh, "Bush Admin Differs With Religious Freedom Commission," *Dow Jones International News*, July 25, 2001.

Exhibit 6 (Continued)

said the House bill's proposal of more stringent disclosure requirements for companies seeking financing in the U.S. "has a lot of potential to damage U.S. capital markets and undermine the authority of the Securities and Exchange Commission."

In May the SEC said it was requiring more-detailed reporting by non-U.S. companies offering securities on U.S. financial markets, a move that largely preempts the disclosure provision in the House's bill.

As for restricting access to U.S. capital markets, the Bush administration official said, "it wouldn't reduce oil revenues to the Sudanese Government and therefore wouldn't affect the ability of that country to fund the war against its own people."

Sanctions Would Affect Subsidiaries, Parents[3]

As proposed in the House bill, companies operating in Sudan would have a hard time avoiding sanctions through "firewalling" techniques such as using affiliates for investments.

A spokesman for Rep. Spencer Bachus, R-Ala., who sponsored the capital markets amendment, said sanctions would apply to parent companies, subsidiaries and affiliates of companies operating in Sudan. "This is similar to how it's worded in the Iran-Libya Sanctions Act: it applies to both subsidiaries and their parent companies," the spokesman said.

Sudan is the scene of one of the world's bloodiest and longest civil wars. The Khartoum-based government has fought non-Muslim separatist groups in the country's southern regions where its major oil fields are. The war has claimed an estimated 2 million lives over two decades.

Since an export pipeline was finished in 1999, Sudan has become a significant oil producer. Output rose to more than 200,000 barrels a day last year, while exports reached 180,000b/d.

The oil exports have raised hopes in some quarters that one of the world's poorest countries will make rapid economic progress. But human rights advocates say oil sales have also funded bombing campaigns by the Khartoum government against southern rebels and civilians.

In February 2000, the U.S. imposed financial sanctions on Greater Nile Petroleum Operating Co., the joint venture producing most of Sudan's oil. But those sanctions don't apply to the individual members of the venture, including Talisman, CNPC and state-owned Malaysian company Petronas (P.PDG).

---

[3]Campion Walsh, "Sanctions Would Affect Subsidiaries, Parents," *Dow Jones International News*, July 25, 2001.

Exhibit 7   Financial Statements 2000 for Years Ending December 31

(millions of Canadian dollars except per share amount)	2000	1999	1998
Revenue			
Gross sales	**4,835.9**	2,317.6	1,533.6
Less royalties	**945.8**	389.0	213.5
Net sales	**3,890.1**	1,928.6	1,320.1
Other (note 11)	**98.8**	46.2	50.6
Total revenue	**3,988.9**	1,974.8	1,370.7
Expenses			
Operating	**826.9**	603.5	581.0
General and administrative	**94.9**	70.1	58.9
Depreciation, depletion and amortization	**1,152.6**	746.6	614.8
Dry hole	**77.3**	50.6	91.2
Exploration	**99.6**	79.5	102.4
Interest on long-term debt (note 5)	**135.9**	119.6	91.0
Other (note 5 and 12)	**15.8**	(60.6)	143.7
Total expenses	**2,403.0**	1,609.3	1,683.0
Income (loss) before taxes	**1,585.9**	365.5	(312.3)
Taxes (note 13)			
Current income tax	**333.5**	48.8	14.6
Future income tax (recovery)	**196.5**	109.2	(87.9)
Petroleum Revenue Tax	**149.6**	30.7	19.8
	679.6	188.7	(53.5)
Net income (loss)	**906.3**	176.8	(258.8)
Preferred security charges, net of tax	**22.5**	13.3	–
Net income (loss) available to common shareholders	**883.8**	163.5	(258.8)
Per common share (Canadian dollars) (note 8)			
Net income (loss) available to common shareholders	**6.41**	1.31	(2.31)
Diluted net income (loss) available to common shareholders	**6.32**	1.30	(2.31)
Average number of common shares outstanding (millions)	**137.8**	124.6	111.9

Source: Company files.   *(Continued)*

Exhibit 7 (Continued)

Consolidated statements of cash flows for years ending December 31 (millions of Cdn$)			
	2000	**1999**	**1998**
Operating			
Net income (loss)	**906.3**	176.8	(258.8)
Items not involving current cash flow (note 14)	**1,406.9**	854.5	787.5
Exploration	**99.6**	79.5	102.4
Cash flow	**2,412.8**	1,110.8	631.1
Changes in non-cash working capital (note 14)	**321.5**	(179.4)	(64.1)
Cash provided by operating activities	**2,734.3**	931.4	567.0
Investing			
Corporate acquisitions (note 2)	–	(79.2)	(28.4)
Capital expenditures			
Exploration, development and corporate	**(1,194.4)**	(1,013.0)	(1,158.7)
Acquisitions	**(430.8)**	(481.7)	(65.4)
Proceeds of dispositions			
Resource properties	**81.0**	132.5	157.2
Investments	**0.2**	3.2	–
Investments	–	–	0.1
Changes in non-cash working capital	**(406.9)**	379.9	76.4
Cash used in investing activities	**(1,950.9)**	(1,058.3)	(1,018.8)
Financing			
Long-term debt repaid	**(2,880.3)**	(1,422.7)	(740.8)
Long-term debt issued	**2,367.2**	1,249.5	1,029.0
Common shares (purchased) issued	**(172.8)**	19.1	8.7
Preferred securities issued	–	428.0	–
Preferred security charges	**(40.1)**	(23.7)	–
Deferred credits and other	**(35.7)**	83.9	(5.0)
Changes in non-cash working capital	**0.3**	(150.7)	150.3
Cash (used in) provided by financing activities	**(761.4)**	183.4	442.2
Net increase (decrease) in cash	**22.0**	56.5	(9.6)
Cash (bank indebtedness), beginning of year	**54.0**	(2.5)	7.1
Cash (bank indebtedness), end of year	**76.0**	54.0	(2.5)

Exhibit 7 (Continued)

SEGMENTED INFORMATION

	Canada			North Sea			Indonesia			Sudan			Other			Total		
	2000	1999	1998	2000	1999	1998	2000	1999	1998	2000	1999	1998	2000	1999	1998	2000	1999	1998
Revenue																		
Gross sales																		
Oil and liquids	**798.9**	450.7	307.2	**1,513.0**	583.0	380.6	**288.9**	261.3	203.7	**588.9**	133.7	–	–	–	–	**3,189.7**	1,428.7	891.5
Natural gas	**1,215.6**	609.0	466.4	**159.4**	128.4	148.6	**227.1**	121.8	8.1	–	–	–	–	–	–	**1,602.1**	859.2	623.1
Synthetic oil	**41.3**	28.3	20.0	–	–	–	–	–	–	–	–	–	–	–	–	**41.3**	28.3	20.0
Sulphur	**2.8**	1.4	(1.0)	–	–	–	–	–	–	–	–	–	–	–	–	**2.8**	1.4	(1.0)
Total gross sales	**2,058.6**	1,089.4	792.6	**1,672.4**	711.4	529.2	**516.0**	383.1	211.8	**588.9**	133.7	–	–	–	–	**4,835.9**	2,317.6	1,533.6
Royalties	**510.8**	223.5	131.0	**70.4**	16.7	6.7	**112.7**	118.6	75.8	**251.9**	30.2	–	–	–	–	**945.8**	389.0	213.5
Net sales	**1,547.8**	865.9	661.6	**1,602.0**	694.7	522.5	**403.3**	264.5	136.0	**337.0**	103.5	–		–	–	**3,890.1**	1,928.6	1,320.1
Other	**18.9**	18.0	19.5	**78.1**	26.8	28.6	**2.7**	–	0.3	**0.7**	0.9	0.4	**(1.6)**	0.5	1.8	**98.8**	46.2	50.6
Total revenue	**1,566.7**	883.9	681.1	**1,680.1**	721.5	551.1	**406.0**	264.5	136.3	**337.7**	104.4	0.4	**(1.6)**	0.5	1.8	**3,988.9**	1,974.8	1,370.7
Segmented expenses																		
Operating																		
Oil and liquids	**97.5**	73.4	70.2	**374.1**	250.4	266.4	**39.9**	52.5	54.9	**63.8**	22.4	–	–	–	–	**575.3**	398.7	391.5
Natural gas	**155.4**	127.7	115.9	**25.3**	31.9	39.5	**15.7**	15.8	3.7	–	–	–	–	–	–	**196.4**	175.4	159.1
Synthetic oil	**16.5**	12.5	13.0	–	–	–	–	–	–	–	–	–	–	–	–	**16.5**	12.5	13.0
Pipeline	**3.5**	3.1	3.0	**35.2**	13.8	14.4	–	–	–	–	–	–	–	–	–	**38.7**	16.9	17.4
Total operating expenses	**272.9**	216.7	202.1	**434.6**	296.1	320.3	**55.6**	68.3	58.6	**63.8**	22.4	–	–	–	–	**826.9**	603.5	581.0
DD&A	**477.9**	368.7	306.7	**512.3**	282.7	253.0	**83.0**	71.8	54.9	**79.3**	23.2	–	**0.1**	0.2	0.2	**1,152.6**	746.6	614.8
Dry hole	**29.1**	12.7	22.5	**14.9**	26.4	48.2	**17.2**	1.3	3.9	**3.3**	2.0		**12.8**	8.2	16.6	**77.3**	50.6	91.2
Exploration	**53.9**	39.8	39.9	**13.1**	8.5	37.5	**6.4**	8.1	10.0	**8.2**	11.6		**18.0**	11.5	12.5	**99.6**	79.5	102.4
Other	**9.9**	(61.0)	(57.8)	**(4.1)**	(2.4)	190.3	**5.6**	(0.4)	7.7	**(0.5)**	2.8		**4.9**	0.4	4.1	**15.8**	(60.6)	143.7
Total segmented expenses	**843.7**	576.9	513.4	**970.8**	611.3	849.3	**167.8**	149.1	135.1	**154.1**	62.0	1.9	**35.8**	20.3	33.4	**2,172.2**	1,419.6	1,533.1

(Continued)

231

Exhibit 7 (Continued)

SEGMENTED INFORMATION

	Canada			North Sea			Indonesia			Sudan			Other			Total		
	2000	1999	1998	2000	1999	1998	2000	1999	1998	2000	1999	1998	2000	1999	1998	2000	1999	1998
Segmented income (loss) before taxes	**723.0**	307.0	167.7	**709.3**	110.2	(298.2)	**238.2**	115.4	1.2	**183.6**	42.4	(1.5)	**(37.4)**	(19.8)	(31.6)	**1,816.7**	555.2	(162.4)
Corporate expenses																		
General and administrative																94.9	70.1	58.9
Interest on long-term debt																135.9	119.6	91.0
Total corporate expenses																230.8	189.7	149.9
Income (loss) before taxes																**1,585.9**	365.5	(312.3)
Property, plant and equipment	**3,658.0**	3,369.8	2,304.7	**2,483.9**	2,217.6	1,537.1	**516.3**	553.4	579.6	**748.3**	768.4	523.9	**94.1**	73.8	51.5	**7,500.6**	6,983.0	4,996.8
Segmented assets	**4,057.1**	3,497.6	2,393.3	**2,873.1**	2,475.6	1,654.9	**714.4**	808.8	701.6	**824.6**	853.2	553.5	**101.4**	78.8	55.9	**8,570.6**	7,714.0	5,359.2
Add corporate																105.1	94.1	88.5
Total assets																**8,675.7**	7,808.1	5,447.7
Capital expenditures																		
Exploration	**252.4**	106.2	126.9	**45.6**	39.2	101.9	**30.1**	18.1	32.9	**33.1**	35.8	4.3	**45.6**	38.4	47.4	**406.8**	237.7	313.4
Development	**434.0**	217.0	276.8	**257.2**	256.3	263.9	**3S.7**	36.1	146.7	**36.8**	245.1	144.4	**5.5**	3.8	–	**772.2**	758.3	831.8
Exploration and development	**686.4**	323.2	403.7	**302.8**	295.5	365.8	**68.8**	54.2	179.6	**69.9**	280.9	148.7	**51.1**	42.2	47.4	**1,179.0**	996.0	1,145.2
Acquisitions																430.8	481.7	65.4
Proceeds on dispositions																(81.0)	(132.5)	(157.2)
Corporate																15.4	17.0	13.5
Net capital expenditures																**1,544.2**	1,362.2	1,066.9

232

Exhibit 8 Financial Results Q.2, 2001

| | Three months ended March 31 | | Six months ended June 30 | | |
	2001	2000	2001	2000	
Financial (millions of Canadian dollars unless otherwise stated)					
Cash Flow[1]	**640.9**	572.7	**1,404.6**	1,144.1	
Net income[1]	**237.2**	213.9	**582.7**	420.1	
Exploration and development	**474.4**	278.5	**848.3**	517.2	
Per common share (dollars)					
Cash flow[1] - Basic	**4.73**	4.14	**10.37**	8.27	
- Diluted	**4.64**	4.07	**10.18**	8.17	
Net income[2] - Basic	**1.71**	1.51	**4.22**	2.96	
- Diluted	**1.68**	1.48	**4.14**		2.92
Production (daily average production)					
Oil and liquids (bbls/d)	**224,085**	252,372	**232,271**	245,452	
Natural gas (mmcf/d)	**980**	978	**987**		1,000
Total mboe/d (6mcf = lboe)	**387**	415	**397**		412

1) Amounts are reported prior to preferred security charges of $10.5 million ($5.9 million, net of tax) for the three months ended June 30, 2001

   (2000 - $10.0 million; $5.6 million, net of tax).

2) Per common share amounts for net income and diluted net income are reported after preferred security charges.

   Cash flow for the quarter ended June 30, 2001 increased 12% to $640.9 million ($4.73/share), compared to 2000. Cash flow for the first six months was $1.4 billion ($10.37/share). Significantly higher North American natural gas prices and higher Canadian gas production were offset by reduced North Sea oil and natural gas production. Net income per share increased to $1.71, an increase of 13% over 2000. Revenues for the quarter were $1.3 billion, with crude oil and natural gas accounting for 60% and 40% of the total, respectively.

(Continued)

Exhibit 8 (Continued)

	Three months ended March 31		Six months ended June 30	
	2001	2000	2001	2000
Production (daily average production)				
Oil and liquids (bbls/d)				
Canada	**66,624**	66,177	**66,456**	65,775
North Sea	**85,751**	119,376	**95,533**	114,816
Indonesia	**18,502**	20,874	**18,628**	20,850
Sudan	**53,208**	45,945	**51,654**	44,011
	224,085	252,372	**232,271**	245,452
Natural Gas (mmcf/d)				
Canada	**792**	735	**791**	751
North Sea	**99**	135	**103**	138
Indonesia	**89**	108	**93**	111
	980	978	**987**	1,000
Total mboe/d (6mcf = lboe)	**387**	415	**397**	412

Labour

Netcare's International Expansion

Saul Klein
Albert Wöcke

As he reviewed the National Health Amendment Bill that had just been introduced in Parliament in June 2008, Dr. Richard Friedland, who had led Netcare Limited ("Netcare" or "Group") since 2005, wondered how pressures at home would affect the company as it strived to become a global player in the health-care industry. The proposed legislation would pave the way for regulated prices and collective bargaining between medical schemes and health service providers such as hospitals and doctors, and it could change the entire industry structure in South Africa going forward.

For a company with a market share in South Africa in excess of 28 per cent, growth at home by acquisition was always going to be limited and subject to stringent scrutiny from competition regulators. Potentially strong organic growth options at home, however, were on the horizon. At the same time, Netcare was itching to demonstrate its skills and abilities on a wider international platform.

One of Netcare's key long-term goals was to deliver innovative, quality health-care solutions to patients in every continent of the world. The recent acquisition of the General Healthcare Group (GHG) in the United Kingdom had propelled Netcare from a predominately South African operation into one of the largest private hospital groups in the world. Political pressures in South Africa, however, could only further complicate the difficult decisions to come in defining how to execute the group's strategy. What lessons, Friedland pondered, could be learned from the GHG acquisition, how could he leverage the group for further growth internationally, and which continent was best suited for expansion?

Netcare Overview

Netcare, founded in 1994, was listed on the Johannesburg Stock Exchange in December 1996 with six hospitals. Several small and independent hospital groups in South Africa were acquired soon thereafter, including Clinic Holdings Limited and Excel Medical Holdings Limited. In 2001, Netcare acquired Medicross, a managed health-care provider network of 75 medical and dental centers across South Africa. In 2006, Medicross then acquired Prime Cure Holdings, a provider of primary care services for the emerging market with a further 25 centers and 130,000 managed care customers.

By 2007, with 18,877 employees, Netcare was demonstrating strong growth (see Exhibit 1 for Netcare's financial statements). Netcare was providing the following key services in South Africa (see Exhibit 2 for a map of locations):

- Private hospital and trauma services through equity interests in 56 hospitals with more than 9,546 beds, 358 operating theatres and 86 retail and hospital pharmacies;
- Netcare 911, the largest private emergency service with more than 7.5 million members and a fleet of 246 response vehicles and ambulances, three helicopters and two fixed-wing air ambulances; and

- Ancillary health-care services including primary care services through Medicross and Prime Cure, and diagnostic services through an interest in a nation-wide administration and logistical services infrastructure servicing 290 high-tech pathology laboratories and depots.

The South African Health Care Industry

South Africa is often characterized as two countries living side by side, with a largely black, poor population with limited access to health care and a low standard of living, on the one hand, and a wealthy, predominantly white population utilizing a world-class private health care system, on the other. The poor rely on a public health-care system that is focused on primary health care and the management of HIV/AIDS, tuberculosis, malaria and other diseases afflicting the poor such as malnourishment. In contrast, the private health-care sector resembles that of a developed country and patients are typically older and require tertiary-level care.

Health-care spending in South Africa in 2004 was 8.6 per cent of GDP, which equated to a *per capita* spend of roughly US$390 per annum[1] of which about 60 per cent went towards private health

---

[1]World Health Organization, 2006.

care. Approximately 14 per cent of the population had private medical insurance, while 40 per cent used private sector health services, as outpatients or otherwise.[2] Compared to other countries, the private health care system in South Africa ranked near the top in terms of access and quality, while the public sector ranked near the bottom (see Exhibit 3).

In South Africa, the hospital groups generally did not employ physicians or medical specialists but rather competed on the basis of attracting doctors to practice in one of their hospitals. Private patients saw their local doctor or specialist, who then referred them to the hospital of their choice to perform operations and the like. The private hospital then billed a medical insurance scheme directly. In a sense, the traditional business model was doctor-driven, with the hospital "renting" facilities and nursing hours to doctors. To attract the busiest doctors to practice in their hospitals, the organizations competed to have the latest and best medical technology, the best nursing staff and world-class facilities.

The overwhelming majority of private patients in South Africa were covered by medical insurance schemes, which had tended to increase tariffs above inflation rates. This was leading to increased spending on private health, but at the same time, encountering resistance from consumers. Meanwhile, the growth of traditional private sector medical schemes had been slow. In response to these circumstances, the South African government had explored options for broadening social health insurance to the general population. Its first two initiatives were the introduction of a broad-based medical scheme for the 1.1 million public servants in the country and making health insurance compulsory for all formally employed South Africans. These initiatives would increase the pool of insured people by between seven and 10 million and free up public resources to concentrate more on expanding primary health care and on HIV/AIDS management and prevention. For service providers, such as Netcare, the major implication was a shift from traditional low-volume, high-margin operations to high-volume, low-cost, low-margin ones. The structure of the health-care market in South Africa is depicted in Exhibit 4.

During the Apartheid era, the private hospital sector served the minority white population almost exclusively, while the majority black population had to use public hospitals. To address social and economic inequities, the South African government developed a regulatory environment to drive national and sectoral transformation. The Broad-Based Black Economic Empowerment Act,

---

[2]Statistics South Africa, General Household Survey, 2005.

promulgated in 2004, allowed the government to issue Codes of Good Practice for private sector firms.

The Codes provided a core set of indicators and criteria to define and measure Black Economic Empowerment (BEE) and guidelines on how to establish sector transformation charters and targets to achieve meaningful, effective and broad-based BEE. Central to the Codes was a balanced scorecard approach, which measured an enterprise's BEE contribution across a range of indicators, as follows:

	Weighting
Equity ownership (by historically disadvantaged individuals)	20%
Management control (by historically disadvantaged individuals)	10%
Employment equity (achievement of affirmative action targets)	15%
Skills development (of historically disadvantaged individuals)	15%
Preferential procurement (from firms owned by historically disadvantaged individuals)	20%
Enterprise development (of firms owned by historically disadvantaged individuals)	15%
Socio-economic development	5%

[3]US$1 = R7.80.

The BEE Charter for the Healthcare Sector (the Health Charter) sought to manage a myriad of health-care challenges effectively and ensure a healthy workforce that could participate productively in the economy. While the Health Charter had not yet been finalized, the development process had entailed information sharing and open discussion between the public and private sectors and had fostered partnerships in a previously fragmented industry.

What differentiated the draft Health Charter from other sectoral charters was that improved access was considered equally as important as broad-based black economic empowerment.

Proposed Legislation

In her 2008 budget speech in the National Assembly, the Minister of Health, Dr. Manto Tshabalala-Msimang, noted that:

Of the R118 billion[3] that was spent in the health sector in 2007/08, R66.4 billion (or 56.3%) was private sector expenditure, which serves about 7 million people, while R51.6 billion (43.7%) was utilised in the public health sector, which provides services to about 40 million people. Over the past years, the private health sector has been unable to increase access and also appears to be unable to contain cost escalations. . . . The National Health Amendment Bill has been submitted to this House for consideration. The Bill provides for the appointment of a facilitator to work with funders and providers to seek agreement on tariffs for healthcare services provided by the private health sector. This process should bring some transparency into the process of tariff setting in the private healthcare sector and assist us to contain costs (June 5, 2008).[4]

Industry representatives regarded the Bill as a price-setting mechanism, while the Department viewed the Bill as creating a regulatory framework through which prices were negotiated, as happened in many developed countries. The country's third-largest private hospital group said the minister should rather work with the industry to find alternative mechanisms to price controls to make health-care services available to more people: "Medi-Clinic maintains the opinion that the draft bill objectives are already covered by extensive legislation. It is undesirable that the Health Act be amended to introduce additional regulatory controls."[5]

South Africa's private health-care industry warned that the proposed changes could hasten the emigration of doctors and nurses and undermine investment in the country. Private hospitals were highly capital-intensive and if returns were not sufficiently appealing,

the capital would be routed elsewhere.[6] Indeed, Medi-Clinic noted that it and Netcare had already made significant investments offshore. Medi-Clinic had recently completed the acquisition of a Swiss hospital group (Hirslanden Finanz) at a price of $2.36 billion. Concern from investors was also cited as causing downward pressures on company share prices, and Netcare shares were trading at around R8.00, down from a peak of more than R13.00 some six months earlier.

Netcare's Strategy

Netcare's philosophy and approach to its health-care business was characterized by a strong performance-driven culture with a fanatical attention to detail. With a reputation in the South African health-care industry for innovation and an obsession with measurement, Netcare maintained world-class standards in patient care, staff competence and relationships with medical practitioners.

Netcare's strategy was based on six major themes:

Organizational Growth

Netcare saw its presence in South Africa and the United Kingdom as an

[4]Minister of health budget speech 2008 at www.info.gov.za/speeches/2008/0806051 5451001.htm.

[5]Medi-Clinic CEO Koert Pretorius, *Business Day*, June 4, 2008.

[6]*Sunday Times*, May 25, 2008.

opportunity to combine the expertise and experience of senior teams from both countries to drive sustainable growth across two major private and public health-care markets. In South Africa, organizational growth had come from expansion of existing hospitals and the building of new hospitals, with four being completed in 2006. Additionally, it had secured large contracts for its Netcare 911 emergency and ambulance service. Netcare was expanding into new emerging markets by providing a low cost, high volume service to private patients who previously could not afford the traditional private hospital offering. In the United Kingdom, Netcare's operations were reorganized into regional structures, and three new National Health Service (NHS) contracts were awarded in 2007.

Operational Excellence

An ongoing focus on building and sustaining a culture of excellence at every level of operations characterized the Group. It was committed to driving efficiencies and containing costs in ways that did not compromise quality. In South Africa this had led, for example, to the implementation of a Systems, Applications and Products (SAP) system, the accreditation of all hospitals and a drive to implement shared-services centers. In the United Kingdom, 28 hospitals were IT-enabled for the NHS Extended Choice Network, and back-office functions were integrated.

Physician Partnerships

General practice physicians and specialists were the most critical part of the private hospital business model, and Netcare focused on providing them with state-of-the-art facilities, skilled nurses and the latest technology. Netcare had invested heavily in facilities and technology and nursing and doctor training. These initiatives led to Netcare attracting an additional 162 medical specialists to its facilities in 2007. In the United Kingdom, Netcare had launched partnership schemes with doctors and expanded to more than 60 Practice Development Groups across their hospitals.

Best and Safest Patient Care

Netcare introduced a clinical governance program to define clinical pathways, which in turn led to reduced variability in service and thereby safer patient care. Netcare also formed a Medical Advisory Ethics Committee and had its own clinical governance guidelines for trauma, ICU and infection control. The Group boasted of having the lowest hospital infection rate in South African recorded history. Netcare experienced a 5.9 per cent increase in admissions in 2007 over 2006 (to one million), and a 9.4 per cent increase in primary care visits (to 3.6 million in 2007). Netcare also enjoyed a 1.7 per cent increase in total cases handled in the United Kingdom to 1.1 million.

Passionate People

Netcare's HR strategy was a critical component of its overall business. South Africa was suffering a critical shortage of skills, including nurses. Aggravating the skills shortage was a brain-drain of nursing skills from South Africa to countries such as Saudi Arabia, the United Kingdom, Canada and Australia. Netcare believed that it needed to be an employer of choice to attract and retain nurses and related skilled workers, as well as to increase the training of nursing students to overcome these problems. Netcare participated in initiatives by South African companies to recruit expatriates back to South Africa. Netcare also trained 3,700 nurses and paramedics in 2007, at a cost of R100 million.

Transformation

Under the leadership of founder Dr. Jack Shevel, Netcare had adopted a largely confrontational approach to the government and regulators in the industry.[7] Netcare left the Hospital Association of South Africa (HASA) when HASA wanted to follow a consultative lobbying approach with the health minister over new pricing regulations. Netcare broke ranks and launched a controversial court challenge. Ultimately, the court challenge was successful but relations with the government were considerably soured.[8]

When Richard Friedland took over as CEO in 2005, he immediately ordered a strategic review and Netcare's approach to government changed significantly. Friedland recognized that government was an important stakeholder in the health industry and that regulations had a strong impact on a health operator's ability to make a profit. Netcare's current approach was to engage early and regularly with the government so that it was seen as a partner in health care.

Friedland embraced the Health Charter and Netcare currently had 17.3 per cent black equity ownership and seven per cent women ownership. The majority (61.4 per cent) of the company's workforce was from previously disadvantaged groups, and Netcare had spent R37 million on corporate social investment, including R18 million covering indigent patients. On a well-respected scale of BEE commitment, Netcare was rated at the highest level.

Friedland's vision for Netcare's vision in South Africa was to be able to provide a tiered system that could provide access to all South Africans:

> The top tier is already well-serviced and there is a high degree of competitive rivalry between the private hospital groups to service this market. Netcare is the leading hospital group in this highly

---

[7]"Cool operator Shevel looks back on R10bn adventure," *Business Day*, May 13, 2005.

[8]"Rivals speak on Netcare's move," *Business Day*, August 11, 2004.

competitive sector of the market and intends for this to remain so. For future growth, however, Netcare has to take risks and develop new models to service the rest of South African society. This is not only the only alternative for organic growth in South Africa, but is also a social imperative. Netcare is well-placed to offer a holistic solution to the formally and informally employed who can not currently afford private healthcare. The future lies in a new funding model and efficiencies in service provision. Netcare is well-positioned to serve this market with its primary healthcare offerings of Medicross and Primecure—51% of patients using Primecure in 2007 paid for services out of their own pockets. The reason for this was primarily a lack of trust in the public service healthcare, or the desire for a more efficient experience. This will also remove a substantial burden from the South African public healthcare.

International Expansion

Netcare began to expand outside South Africa in 1997. The United Kingdom was chosen as one destination, based on its low penetration of private sector operators and its attractive demographics in terms of an aging population. (See Exhibit 5 for an overview of the relationship between demographics and health-care spending.)

The U.K. Health System

In 1997, when the Labour Party came to power, the National Health Service (NHS) was in disarray as a result of severe under-funding and lack of modernization. There were waiting lists of more than one million patients, with five per cent waiting for more than 12 months to see a doctor. Increases in health expenditure fluctuated between zero per cent in some years to six per cent in others and, since the 1960s, real spending per annum averaged 3.6 per cent of GDP, while the average for OECD countries was 5.5 per cent.[9] Compared to other developed countries, the United Kingdom had fewer doctors and health-care professionals per capita, and investment in health care technologies and facilities was low. Many buildings predated the formation of the NHS in 1948. The problems were exacerbated by poor morale amongst staff and severe staff shortages.

In response to these challenges, the U.K. government set a series of ambitious targets for the NHS in 2000,[10] including:

- Maximum wait for inpatient treatment of six months by 2005;
- three-month maximum wait for outpatient treatment;

---

[9]NHS Plan 2000, Department of Health, United Kingdom.

[10]www.dh.gov.uk.

- Primary care access to a general practitioner within 48 hours by 2004;
- A wait of no more than 18 weeks from general practitioner consultation to hospital treatment; and
- Patients to have a choice of four to five practitioners by 2006 and open choice of health care providers by the end of 2008.

The Labour government hoped that the initiatives would result in more choice to patients, more value for money by the introduction of market forces, the creation of a sustainable independent health sector market, increased capacity in difficult areas and innovation in the NHS. In doing so, it also intended to change the balance between public and private funding (see Exhibit 6) and thereby open the way for public/private partnerships.

Netcare's Entry Into the United Kingdom

Netcare entered the U.K. market in 2002 to provide specialized health-care services on contract to the NHS. Netcare had seen an opportunity to use the skills that it had developed in South Africa to win tenders with the NHS in the United Kingdom. According to Friedland:

Initially Netcare's hope was to take advantage of the NHS waiting lists and

fly UK patients into South Africa for treatment, but this was not feasible due to the nature of the UK market. In rural England many people had not even traveled to London and it was unlikely that they would want to travel to South Africa. Instead Netcare decided to send South African medical professionals to the UK to test whether they could operate efficiently within these boundaries. Netcare introduced systems that were regarded as novel and groundbreaking by patients such as the patient making one visit and having a complete diagnosis with all services such as x-rays and other assessments available on the spot.

Netcare's first tender was a five-year contract with the NHS (worth GBP 42 million[11]) to perform 44,737 cataract procedures. Netcare enjoyed almost immediate success, as it was able to adapt its home-grown efficient methods to the U.K. environment. Realizing that it could not perform all of the procedures from a single location, Netcare developed mobile ophthalmic units that rotated between different locations, offering pre-operative assessments, surgery and post-operative care. Each unit had a staff complement of 30.

Netcare innovated in the development of "factory services," where economies of scale were achieved by scheduling a large number of similar operations together. The resulting efficiencies allowed Netcare to perform 22 cataract surgeries per day per surgeon,

[11]GBP1 = US$2.

while the best practice in the United Kingdom was 12 per day.

A South African entrant into the U.K. health-care market did not go unnoticed and elicited some concern from the general public, but this quickly dissipated with direct experience. The 10,000th patient had the following to say about the service:

> I was a bit apprehensive before the cataract procedure with Netcare, but I was delighted with how it went. The staff were fantastic. I liked the cleanliness of the unit. There was no pain. I hope the NHS continues using partnerships like this.

Success with the cataract contract led to other opportunities, such as running a surgical centre in the Greater Manchester area. This facility had 48 beds, three laminar flow theatres, a rehab department, clinical support services and 120 staff. The period of the contract for the surgical centre was for five years, from 2005 to 2010, and would lead to 44,863 procedures for which the NHS paid Netcare GBP 85 million. The quality of the service provided is reflected in the comment by a patient of the centre:

> Everyone was so lovely and understanding at the centre, I know that they have operated on hundreds of knees but I felt very special and certainly not just an operation number. Since I have returned home I have been able to take up bowling again and although I still feel the odd ache and pain I can just ring up my surgeon and have a consultation.

Netcare subsequently won a tender to run primary health care facilities in Leeds. All services were provided through Netcare UK, an established independent service provider to the NHS.

In focusing on publicly funded health-care services, Netcare realized that it could apply its knowledge and modern processes in additional areas such as renal, dental, diagnostics and others. Netcare UK's stated strategy was to become the provider of choice amongst patients, general practitioners and commissioners for an increasing range of health-care services. In charge of U.K. operations at the time, Friedland felt that by working together with Primary Care Trusts, Acute Trusts and Strategic Health Authorities, Netcare could provide additional capacity and capability, and contribute to a quality public health service, delivered at or below NHS tariffs.

Growth Through Acquisition

In May 2006, Netcare acquired a controlling interest (52.6 per cent) in GHG. GHG's business unit, BMI Healthcare, was the largest private acute care hospital provider in the United Kingdom, operating 48 acute care private patient hospitals with more than 2,606 beds, 152 operating theatres and 37 pharmacies, and was supported by 4,200 medical specialists.[12] These various facilities functioned autonomously, and Netcare saw an opportunity to enhance their efficiency through implementation of the Group's standardized systems. In the financial year ending September 2007, Netcare UK/GHG admitted 230,000 patients and served 892,500 outpatients. (See Exhibit 7 for a map of BMI's geographical coverage.)

In explaining the reasons for the GHG acquisition, Friedland commented:

> We're confident of achieving strong organic growth in South Africa, but given our size it had become difficult to make significant acquisitions. We've built a good base in the UK, learnt about that market and have also been involved in several unsuccessful acquisition attempts there before.[13]

> Having served the needs of the UK healthcare market, we have gained invaluable insight into the challenges and opportunities that exist in this market. We have targeted the UK healthcare market for expansion, as the long-term demographic trends and prospects for development of the private acute care market as well as partnership with the NHS, offer significant future growth potential.[14]

The GHG acquisition provided Netcare with infrastructure, property and facilities, a strong group management team, local connections, purchasing power and an opportunity to build the Netcare brand outside South Africa on a quality platform. Additional benefits included:

- Leveraging the combination of best practices from both organizations;
- Providing opportunities to grow the U.K. private market and take advantage of further NHS partnerships;
- Providing a natural hedge within a changing market;
- Providing Netcare with the capability of transforming health-care delivery in the United Kingdom and South Africa through combining skills; and
- Positioning Netcare as a leading international health-care solutions company.

The acquisition was a creatively structured transaction where Netcare, in consortium with three partners, successfully bid GBP 2.2 billion for GHG. This price was equivalent to 13.4 times

---

[12]"General Health Care," BC Partners, 2007, www.bcpartners.com/bcp/cases/generalhealthcare.

[13]"Netcare Bids 2.2 Bln Pounds for General Healthcare (Update 6)," Bloomberg, 2006, www.bloomberg.com/apps/news?pid=10000087&sid=aIeXsX_VriY4&refer=top_world_news.

[14]"Network Healthcare Holdings Limited acquires leading private hospital group in UK," Apax, April 25, 2006, www.apax.com/en/news/story_general-healthcare-group-limited.html.

GHG's EBITDA (earnings before inter-est, tax, depreciation and amortization) of GBP 164 million in fiscal 2005. The consortium included Apax Partners Worldwide (one the world's largest pri-vate equity partners, with a particular interest in health care), London & Regional Properties (one of the largest private property companies in Europe, with investments in the United Kingdom, Sweden, Finland, Germany, Denmark and Lithuania) and Brockton Capital LLP (a U.K.-only opportunity fund, with significant experience in real estate and private equity).[15]

Netcare received 52.6 per cent of GHG in return for a payment of GBP 219 million and the injection of its U.K. operation into the transaction. The con-sortium partners received 47.4 per cent in exchange for their contribution of GBP 303 million. The balance of the purchase price was debt-financed, and secured by the property that was acquired. GHG management received a performance-based equity interest which may equate to approximately seven per cent of the equity over a period, but Netcare's share may not dilute to less than 50.1 per cent as a result of the participation.[16]

In explaining the transaction to South African investors, Netcare addressed concerns about exposure of the South African operation to foreign debt. Netcare noted that its share of the pur-chase price was funded using new debt facilities provided by Dresdner Bank, which were raised for the purposes of the acquisition. GHG was restructured to form an operating company and property company, OPCO and PROPCO, respectively. OPCO had a ring-fenced debt of GBP 265 million of secured and unsecured mezzanine debt with no recourse to Netcare South Africa. (This was a condition for the deal from the South African Reserve Bank due to exchange controls.) PROPCO had GBP 1.650 million debt secured over land and buildings.[17]

Questions Raised

The GHG acquisition raised ques-tions at home about Netcare's commit-ment to its South African base. Friedland, however, argued that the deal in no way detracted from Netcare's operations in South Africa, which con-tributed 47.7 per cent and 46.1 per cent to revenue and operating profit, respec-tively, and employed approximately 18,900 employees:

> Netcare remains fully committed to providing affordable, quality healthcare

---

[15]Ibid.

[16]Friedland presentation to MBA students, GIBS, June 7, 2007.

[17]Ibid.

to more South Africans. We fully embrace the Department of Health's drive to achieve equity and access in healthcare. As one of the largest hospital and managed healthcare operators in South Africa, there are [simply] limited acquisition-based expansion opportunities on offer to Netcare domestically.

Further, Friedland noted that GHG had a strong management team to partner with Netcare to drive the development of the U.K. business forward. As a result, the acquisition of GHG would not denude Netcare South Africa of resources or management capability.[18] It was not at all clear, however, that the South African government saw things the same way.

Other International Expansion

The United Kingdom was not Netcare's only foray into international markets, and other initiatives had less favorable results. For example, Netcare began its international expansion with an entry into Rwanda in 1997, following that country's genocidal civil war. When the Rwandan government privatized a polyclinic, Netcare invested R60 million into converting it into a hospital that was able to provide world-class specialized services. The King Faizel Hospital had previously been used as a refugee camp.

The venture enjoyed a high profile at the time, being officially opened by the president of Rwanda, and the hospital was world class. The project, however, was a disaster for three main reasons. First, the project was dependent on doctors who had fled Rwanda and the African lake region, returning once stability had returned. These doctors, however, were seen as highly skilled and experienced and consequently were in great demand almost everywhere. To fill the gap, Netcare had to employ and fly in South African doctors.

The second problem was a lack of understanding and appreciation for the enormity of the social and cultural trauma that Rwanda had recently gone through. Netcare came from a South African experience that was fundamentally different to the Rwandan one. Rwanda at the time was a country recovering, as opposed to a recovered country. The differences and animosity between Hutus and Tutsis were still very much in evidence. For example, when Netcare put a Hutu in charge of eight Tutsi receptionists, the hatred and distrust was so evident that it was almost impossible to run the operation. Netcare failed to appreciate the diversity in the situation. According to Friedland, "We came out of South Africa in 1994 (the first democratic elections in South Africa) and had forgotten about

---

[18]"Network Healthcare Holdings Limited acquires leading private hospital group in UK," *Apax*, April 25, 2006, www.apax.com/en/news/story_general-healthcare-group-limited.html.

Apartheid. Black South Africans had been extremely gracious and forgiving. Rwanda wasn't like that at all."

The third reason the King Faizel Hospital project failed was because the $85 million in aid provided by the United Nations and other agencies for the provision of health and infrastructure was never spent on these services.

Netcare also looked at opportunities in Tanzania and Kenya and at building hospitals elsewhere in Africa, but these efforts did not come to fruition. Its investigations revealed that the South African model had little opportunity of success in these countries, as there was no social funding and limited private medical insurance in Africa.

Through an international division, Netcare was expanding marketing activities beyond South Africa's borders. The primary focus of Netcare International was patient referrals, offering patients who resided outside of South Africa the opportunity to benefit from Netcare's excellent network of hospitals and health-care services. The division was currently involved in a number of health-care projects in sub-Saharan Africa and the Middle East and negotiations were in progress in several other countries. A referral network of more than 200 agents throughout Africa worked closely with Netcare International's Central Referral Office to offer a comprehensive referral service. This included hospital bookings, full travel and accommodation requirements and recuperative care.

The African initiatives had focused on securing patient referrals and the marketing of insurance and health-care packages. Netcare International contributed approximately R80 million to hospital revenues in 1999, mainly through patient referrals from countries in Africa.

Netcare was also looking for public-private partnerships, such as in an 18-year contract Netcare acquired in 2008 to rebuild a large hospital in Lesotho and run most of the Lesotho health-care system, including its primary clinics. This project was funded by the Lesotho government and the World Bank. Netcare had also built and commissioned hospitals in Saudi Arabia and Bahrain.

Following its initial experience in the United Kingdom (prior to acquiring GHG), Netcare was on the lookout for other markets that were unconsolidated, and it bid for a group of hospitals run by the Red Cross. These hospitals were later withdrawn from sale at the last stage of the bidding. In Portugal, Netcare tried to buy into a network of hospitals but was similarly unsuccessful.

New Opportunities

Netcare was also considering expansion into other countries, either by making acquisitions or partnering with other health-care providers. Globally, health-care expenses varied considerably, even between OECD countries (see Exhibit 8), and many countries faced pressures from aging populations.

One of the countries under active consideration was Brazil, where Friedland saw large demand as well as an opportunity to consolidate the industry through the offering of an integrated health-care model.

Brazil, the largest country in South America, had a population of 184.2 million, with GDP in 2006 of US$1.1 trillion and a total labor force of 75 million. The private health-care system had 36.6 million members (approximately 20 per cent of the population), geographically concentrated in major cities. Total premiums paid in 2005 amounted to US$18.7 billion. Private hospitals were not required to serve the general public.[19]

The public health-care system provided universal coverage through a large delivery network of hospitals and clinics. There were no charges for usage, as the system was entirely funded by taxation. The public system faced substantial capacity and quality challenges. (Additional information on the Brazilian market is shown in Exhibit 9.)

Challenges and Future Expansion

As he contemplated an upcoming retreat with his executive team, Friedland wondered how to proceed. He noted that his team had previously developed what he termed the Big Hairy Audacious Goal (BHAG) of having a presence on all continents. Netcare saw its core competence in consolidating fragmented markets and introducing efficiencies to them. It had not, however, established any timeline for further expansion, or any priorities for further market entry.

As of September 30, 2007, the Group managed 107 private hospitals and clinics, equipped with more than 12,240 beds. It had consolidated revenues of R19billion, operating profits of R3billion, and total assets of R50billion, with a market capitalization of R22billion. Netcare had clearly made much progress, but could it continue to grow as before? In doing so, would the South African market represent an opportunity or a hindrance, and where should the Group focus its efforts?

---

[19]Merrill Lynch, Brazilian Healthcare Market.

Exhibit 1   Netcare Financial Performance

Five year review, years ending September 30 in millions of South African Rands (Rm):

Balance sheet	2007	2006	2005	2004	2003
ASSETS					
Non-current assets					
Property, plant and equipment	**26,683**	27,246	3,109	2,880	2,704
Goodwill and intangible assets	**16,380**	17,016	350	227	170
Associated companies, investments and loans	**298**	255	791	597	491
Financial assets—Derivative financial instruments	**1,453**	834			427
Deferred taxation	**514**	396	19	43	41
Total non-current assets	**45,328**	45,747	4,269	3,747	3,833
Total current assets	**5,211**	4,791	2,013	1,759	1,949
Total assets	**50,539**	50,538	6,282	5,506	5,782
EQUITY AND LIABILITIES					
Ordinary shareholders' equity	**4,132**	2,237	3,342	2,722	2,867
Preference share capital and premium	**644**	644			
Minority interest	**3,806**	3,355	76	74	72
Total shareholders' equity	**8,582**	6,236	3,418	2,796	2,939
Non-current liabilities					
Long-term debt	**28,944**	29,224	493	793	922
Financial liability—Derivative financial instruments	**1,156**	2,152			
Post-retirement benefit obligations	**115**	294	65	55	44
Deferred lease liability	**63**	64	159	153	141
Deferred taxation	**6,073**	6,399	62	203	227

Balance sheet	2007	2006	2005	2004	2003
Total non-current liabilities	36,351	38,133	779	1,204	1,334
Total current liabilities	5,606	6,169	2,085	1,506	1,509
Total equity and liabilities	50,539	50,538	6,282	5,506	5,782

Note: The financial results of the Group have been prepared in accordance with International Financial Reporting Standards (IFRS) from the beginning of the 2005 financial year.

(Rm = Millions of South African Rands)						
Income statement	Compound growth %	2007	2006	2005	2004	2003
CONTINUING OPERATIONS						
Revenue	32.6	18,607	11,152	7,534	6,853	6,013
Cost of sales		(10,856)	(6,376)	(3,651)	(3,490)	(2,753)
Gross profit		7,751	4,776	3,883	3,363	3,260
Other income, administrative and other expenses		(4,761)	(3,198)	(2,693)	(2,416)	(2,337)
Operating profit	34.2	2,990	1,578	1,190	947	923
Financial income and expenses	87.4	(2,135)	−927	−138	−102	−173
Attributable earnings of associates		32	28	63	25	
Profit before taxation	4.3	887	679	1,115	870	750
Taxation		99	−229	−300	−216	−169
Profit for the year from continuing operations	14.1	986	450	815	654	581

(Continued)

Exhibit 1 (Continued)

		2007	2006	2005	2004	2003
DISCONTINUED OPERATION						
Profit for the year from discontinued operation		**109**	87			
Profit for the year		**1,095**	537	815	654	581
Attributable to:						
Ordinary shareholders		**927**	729	813	652	580
Preference shareholders		**30**	12			
Minority interest		**138**	−204	2	2	1
		1,095	537	815	654	581
Stock exchange performance						
Market prices per share						
– at September 30	cents	**1,193**	1,240	655	495	410
– highest	cents	**1,677**	1,318	670	535	440
– lowest	cents	**1,150**	611	470	400	265
– weighted average	cents	**1,368**	950	560	463	337

Exhibit 2   Netcare Locations in South Africa

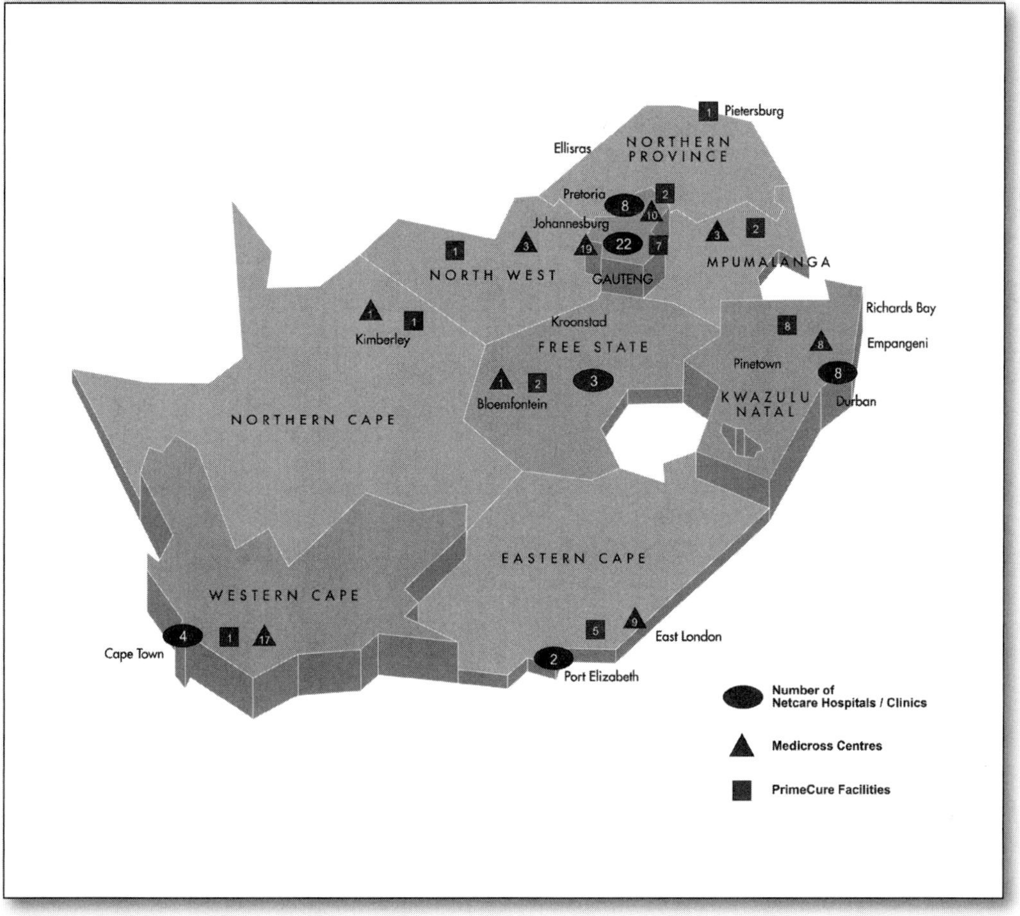

Source: Netcare.

Exhibit 3   Health-Care System Performance on Access and Quality

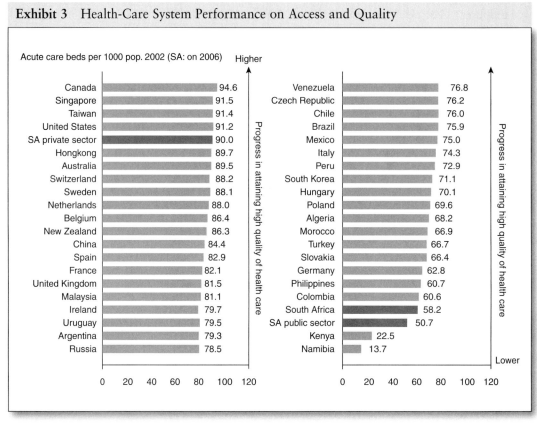

Source: Monitor Group, January 2004.

Exhibit 4   Health Care in South Africa

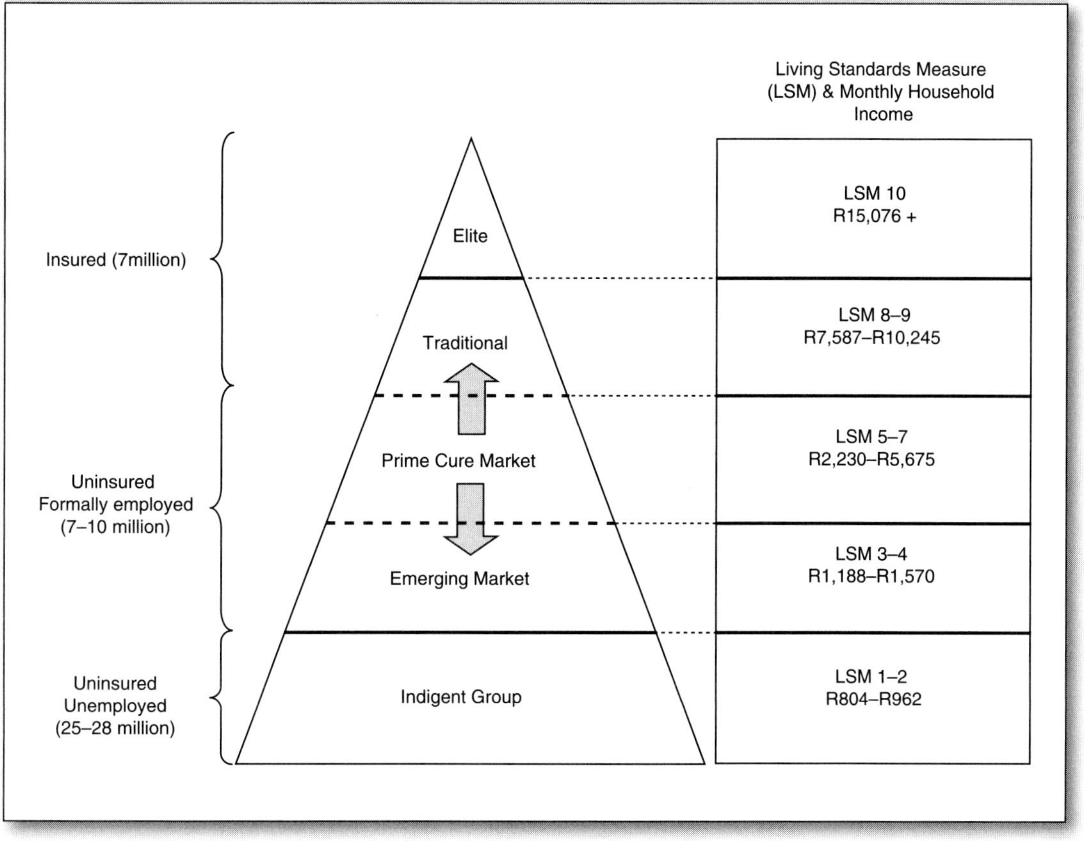

Living Standards Measure
(LSM) & Monthly Household
Income

Insured (7million)

Uninsured
Formally employed
(7–10 million)

Uninsured
Unemployed
(25–28 million)

Elite

Traditional

Prime Cure Market

Emerging Market

Indigent Group

LSM 10
R15,076 +

LSM 8–9
R7,587–R10,245

LSM 5–7
R2,230–R5,675

LSM 3–4
R1,188–R1,570

LSM 1–2
R804–R962

Source: SAARF Trends, 2002–2006.

Exhibit 5   Effects of Aging Populations

Average revenue per age band (indexed) for South Africa's Major Private Hospital Groups (similar to developed country profiles)

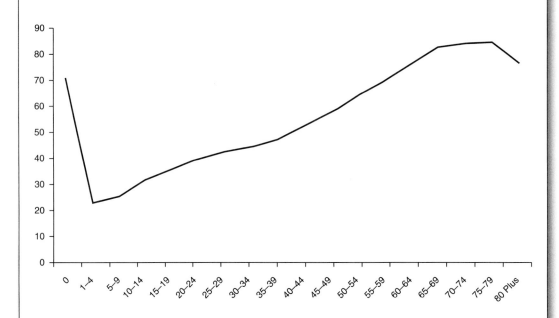

- The average age of a patient in a private sector hospital was 42.5 years old in 2006, compared to 36.9 years in 2002. This trend translates to an approximate "age creep" of 1.4 years per annum.

- There is a strong linear relationship between age and hospital billings.

- The average "cost creep" due to "age creep" cost medical schemes in South Africa was R936 million from 2002 to 2006.

Source: Hospital Association of South Africa (HASA), 2007.

Exhibit 6   The Changing Balance of Public/Private Funding and Provision in the United Kingdom

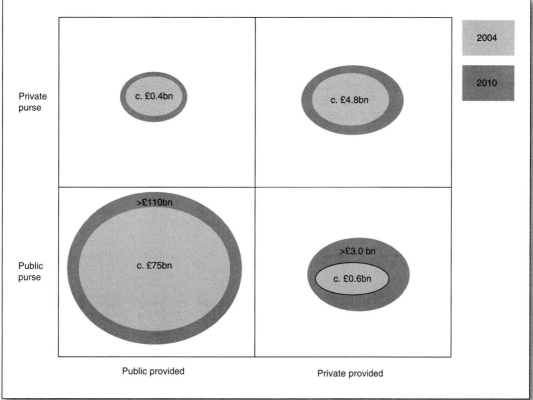

Source: NHS, 2000, & Netcare UK.

Exhibit 7   BMI Locations in the United Kingdom

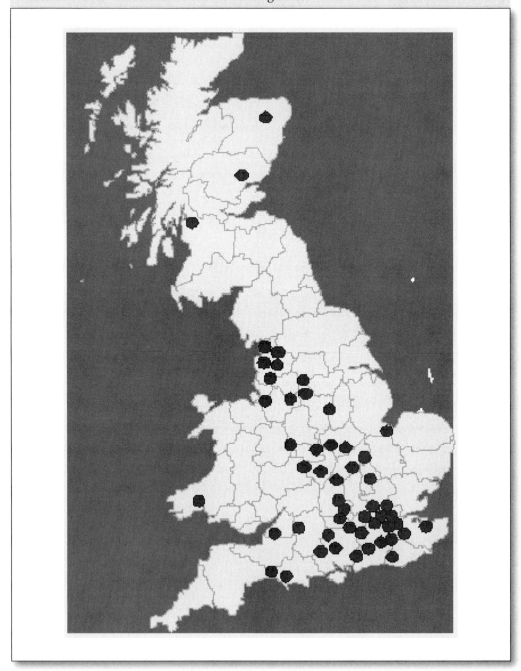

Source: Netcare.

Exhibit 8   Health Care Expenditures (Selected Countries) (USD = US Dollars)

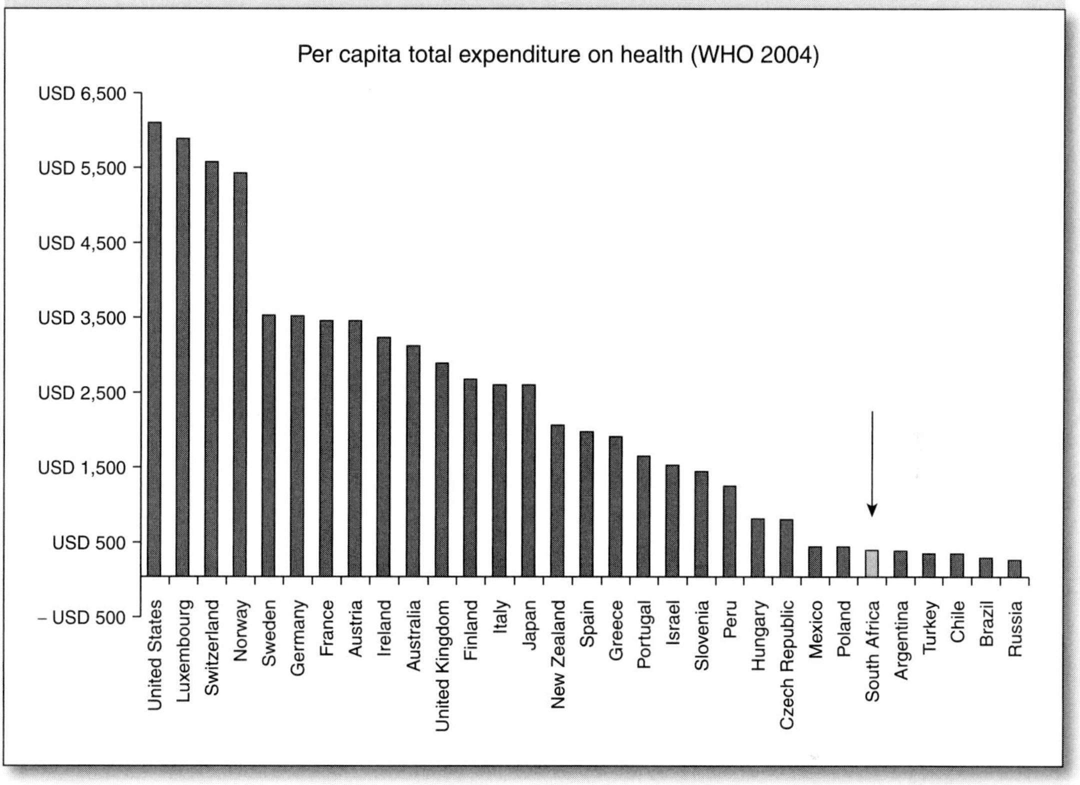

Per capita total expenditure on health (WHO 2004)

Exhibit 9   Fact Sheet: Opportunities in Brazil

- Brazil has several private hospitals that can compete with top American and European hospitals
- Lower levels of consumer spending power have forced private hospital managers to seek new ways to deliver high-quality care from fewer resources. Notable examples are:

  - The creation of purchasing groups to manage relationships with suppliers
  - A variety of services have been outsourced
  - Partnerships have been formed with real estate developers and investment funds to make hospital expansions viable
  - There has been an increased focus on illness prevention, the use of day-hospitals and homecare nursing programs to reduce costs
  - Safety and quality of care have received attention, with 34 hospitals in Brazil receiving accreditation by 2004
  - Health-care insurance plans are responsible for between 80 and 90 per cent of hospital revenue

HOSPITAL STATISTICS (Public and Private)

Hospitals	7,687
Hospital Beds	483,495
Average Number of Beds per Hospital	63
ICU Beds	20,462
MRIs	341
CT Scanners	1,497

Source: Research commissioned by Netcare.

Nestle's Nescafe Partners' Blend: The Fairtrade Decision (A)

Niraj Dawar
Jordan Mitchell

Introduction

In early February 2005, Hilary Parsons, head of corporate affairs, Nestlé UK was on a train heading from Geneva, Switzerland, to Nestlé SA's head office in Vevey. As the train chugged along Lac Léman with a dramatic view of the mountain scenery, Parsons thought about the current decisions relating to Nestlé UK's Nescafé Partners' Blend initiative. With roots tracing back to the late 1990s, the Partners' Blend project involved developing a soluble instant coffee for the expanding "ethical" coffee segment in the U.K. market. Over the past two years, Parsons, along with several other managers at Nestlé UK and at Nestlé's head office in Switzerland, had been working on developing the product, brand positioning, consumer messaging and, importantly, a traceable and transparent supply chain linking back to individual smallholder farmers in Ethiopia and El Salvador.

Throughout the process, Parsons had been in touch with members of the Fairtrade Foundation, an independent body that awarded its Fairtrade mark to products (not companies) that abided by its set of standards aimed at guaranteeing a better deal for third-world growers. Fairtrade had expressed interest in certifying the yet-to-be launched Nescafé Partners' Blend. The two parties had agreed to convene in Switzerland, in February 2005, to discuss the possibilities of releasing Nescafé Partners' Blend with the Fairtrade mark.

As Parsons approached the familiar mountain range at Vevey, she pondered the issues for the meeting between Nestlé's managers and Fairtrade Foundation's representatives. As the largest buyer of coffee beans in the world, would Nestlé SA change its historical position on not accepting Fairtrade certification of its coffee products?

The Global Coffee Market

Coffee was widely consumed throughout the world in forms ranging from canned coffee drinks common in Japan to elaborate half-caf, low-fat, iced-mocha frappés in North America. Worldwide coffee consumption represented an approximate retail value of

US$33 billion, accounting for 57 per cent of all hot drinks consumed, and beating out tea as the number one hot beverage of choice.

Arabica and Robusta were the two basic types of coffee. Arabica had a caffeine content between 0.6 and 1.5 per cent, while Robusta's was 1.5 to three per cent. Arabica, typically grown at 800 to 2,400 meters above sea level, at temperatures ranging from 17 to 23 degrees Celsius, had a strong aroma, tasty acidity and less body. Robusta, grown between zero and 800 meters above sea level, at average temperatures between 18 to 27 degrees Celsius, was known for its low-acid content and strong body. Arabica accounted for 64 per cent, while Robusta made up the remaining 36 per cent of all coffee produced.

Coffee trees took between three and four years to reach a state where their red berries could be harvested.[1] Mature coffee trees yielded coffee during two to three months each year, save unforeseen periods of frost or drought. Each cherry contained two coffee beans. Green beans were packaged and traded in industry-standard 60-kilogram bags. Approximately 120 million bags (7.2 million tonnes) of coffee were produced annually across 50 countries. Approximately 63 per cent of coffee was produced in the Americas, 24 per cent in Asia and 13 per cent in Africa.

The top five coffee-producing countries were Brazil (34.9 per cent of worldwide production), Vietnam (11.8 per cent), Colombia (10.1 per cent), Indonesia (6.6 per cent) and Ethiopia (3.8 per cent). See Exhibit 1 for production by country.

More than 80 per cent of all coffee was produced by approximately 25 million smallholder farmers worldwide, each tilling two hectares or less of coffee fields. As a rule of thumb, one hectare yielded 10 bags (600 kilograms). Farmers' decision to grow coffee rather than bananas or corn, for example, was based on a combination of factors, including climate, market opportunity, trading prices, yield and family tradition. A study by TechnoServe and McKinsey estimated the production cost of a pound of coffee ranged between 17 and 30 cents for non-washed Robusta green beans (between 37 and 66 cents per kilogram). Washed Arabica beans in Colombia, on the other hand, could cost between 70 and 90 cents per pound (between $1.54 and $1.98 per kilogram). See Exhibit 2 for details.

Farmers sold the green bean to middlemen or wholesalers. The opportunity to sell green beans varied greatly by country and even by specific location. But most coffee-producing countries had hundreds of independent middlemen, some were farmers themselves. In some locations, farmers organized

---

[1] "The Nestlé Coffee Report: Faces of Coffee," *Nestlé Report,* March 2004, p. 12.

themselves into cooperatives, which frequently dealt directly with wholesalers or exporters. Middlemen frequently bought directly from farmers. The beans were then taken to wholesale-buying stations and sold for an on-the-spot price based on the quality of the bean and market factors. In Ethiopia, for example, approximately 15 family-run wholesale companies gathered and re-sold between 200 and 800 bags each. Wholesalers dealt with large coffee export companies. Three major companies—British ED&F Man/Volcafé, German Neumann Kaffee Gruppe and Spanish Ecom—controlled more than 30 per cent of the worldwide coffee export market. In some instances wholesalers were also exporters.

Exporters brought green bean coffee to foreign markets. Green bean coffee was a traded commodity on the London International Financial Futures Exchange (LIFFE) and the New York Board of Trade. See Exhibit 3 for a chart of coffee trading prices. Prior to 1989, coffee prices had been protected from price fluctuations through the International Coffee Agreement (ICA), which documented specific export quotas and helped smallholders by set price bands.[2] In 1989, the United States withdrew from the agreement, and

eventually the ICA collapsed.[3] Throughout the mid-1990s, coffee prices fluctuated substantially moving from US$0.50 per pound in 1990 to more than US$0.75 per pound in 1994, due to frost and drought in Brazil. In 1997, a dip in the supply of Arabica caused the price to race from less than $1.25 per pound to nearly $3.00 per pound.[4] The trend reversed again, when from 1998 to 2002, the supply was greater than demand, pushing coffee prices down to record lows. In 2001, Robusta hit an all-time low of 25 cents per pound. Record low coffee prices sparked a number of actions. First, many coffee farmers stopped producing coffee and switched to other crops. Many of those who could not switch were left with earnings below sustenance levels. Second, nongovernmental organizations (NGOs), such as Oxfam, Fairtrade and a number of other groups, published reports and launched high-profile media campaigns highlighting the plight of small growers. Major consumer-brand coffee producers, too, looked for ways to build sustainable projects in coffee producing communities.

Four multinationals—Nestlé, Kraft, Sara Lee and Procter & Gamble—represented approximately half of the

---

[2] "The Nestlé Coffee Report: Faces of Coffee," *Nestlé Report*, March 2004, p. 4.

[3] Ibid.

[4] Ibid.

worldwide value of retail coffee. Other significant players were Tchibo from Germany, Starbucks from the United States and Italian-based brands, such as Lavazza, Segafredo and Illy. Roast and ground coffee (also referred to as fresh coffee) made up 84 per cent of worldwide volume and 61 per cent of value sales in 2003. The remaining percentage represented instant coffee. Volume consumption of coffee worldwide had grown by more than 10 per cent between 1998 and 2003. Growth was underpinned by developing nations' migration from tea to coffee, while consumption in mature markets had plateaued. From 1998 to 2003, the retail value of coffee had decreased at a 0.5 per cent compound annual rate.[5] Retail value had rebounded slightly from 2002 to 2003, but only as a result of more premium products in both the fresh and instant coffee markets.

Approximately 76 per cent of worldwide sales of coffee were through retail outlets, such as supermarkets and other shops. The remainder was sold through food service spots, such as cafes and restaurants. Foodservice sales growth had outpaced retail sales in many mature markets, due to the growing prevalence of premium coffee bars, such as Starbucks. To transfer the experience of an authentic café to the home, all four major coffee producers had teamed up with appliance makers to launch branded coffee machines to produce high-quality brewed coffee from pod-like contraptions in less than a minute.

Another major trend in mature coffee markets was the adoption by several retailers and brands of certifications from Fairtrade, the Rainforest Alliance and Utz Kapeh. Throughout 2003, for example, more than 100 companies in the United States were certified by these organizations. It was estimated that certified coffee had grown at 75 per cent compound annual growth rate (CAGR) from 1998 to 2003. Mainstream multinationals, such as Dunkin' Donuts, had introduced a Fairtrade espresso beverage; Procter & Gamble had launched a Mountain Moonlight Fairtrade coffee and Kraft had released a Rainforest Alliance beverage during 2004. Some activists had criticized Kraft for its launch of a Kenco "Sustainable Development" brand with the Rainforest Alliance certification in 2004. Criticisms mounted because under the Rainforest Alliance certification, Kraft did not pay fixed prices, but rather a 10 to 12 cent premium above the traded coffee price, leaving farmers vulnerable to market volatility.[6] Also, Fairtrade representatives stated that the Rainforest

---

[5] "The World Market for Hot Drinks," *Euromonitor Report,* October 2004, Table 49, p. 17.

[6] Jim Winslet, "Coffees with a Conscience," *The Financial Times,* October 18, 2005, p. 13.

Alliance label generated confusion in the marketplace.

The U.K. Coffee Market

The U.K. coffee market was worth approximately £1 billion[7] as of early 2005, split into 84 per cent instant (soluble) coffee, and 16 per cent fresh (roast and ground) in terms of value. Approximately 85 per cent of all coffee was purchased at retail locations, and 15 per cent was purchased through foodservice outlets, such as coffee chains, measured by value. Over the last 10 years, cafés such as Starbucks, Costa Coffee and Caffe Nero had grown rapidly throughout the country. Consumption at most out-of-home locations however was still largely (65 per cent) instant coffee. At retail locations, for example, supermarkets and shops, instant coffee made up 90 per cent of all coffee purchased. Fiona Kendrick, managing director, Beverage Division of Nestlé UK explained the split between instant and fresh coffee: "This is an instant market for the simple fact that we are a tea drinking nation." Exhibit 4 shows market data on coffee consumption in the United Kingdom, and Exhibit 5 shows the average cost breakdown of 100 grams of instant coffee.

The Fairtrade Movement in the UK

A growing trend in the grocery business in the United Kingdom was the certification of products by NGOs, such as the Fairtrade Labelling Organization. The Fairtrade Labelling Organization determined the standards required for classification as a Fairtrade product and worked with nation-specific groups, such as the United Kingdom's Fairtrade Foundation, to grant the Fairtrade mark. Many products were often referred to as "fair trade," although that description did not necessarily mean that they had been approved by the Fairtrade Labelling Organization. Other descriptions, such as "ethical" and "sustainable" were also used to denote products that could be linked to a supply chain in which farmers were either given fixed prices or where certain ethical conditions were met. Words such as "organic" and "free-range" (for livestock and poultry products) referred to how the product was grown or raised. Some of the most popular Fairtrade certified products in the United Kingdom were Green & Black Fairtrade chocolates and Café Direct Fairtrade coffee. Other "certified" products included tea, fruits, vegetables and even footballs.[8]

---

[7]In this case, billion refers to the North American definition, which is 1,000 millions. The average exchange rate for the first month of 2005 was GBP1.00 = US$1.88.

[8]In the United Kingdom, footballs refer to what North Americans call soccer balls.

In addition, there were a number of organizations, including the NGO Oxfam, which aimed to support growers in third-world countries. Oxfam was very active in the coffee sphere, organizing profile-raising events. The NGO had published the high-circulation MUGGED report in September 2002, which called for a Coffee Rescue Plan (see Exhibit 6) to aid smallholder coffee producers after the price freefall from 1997 to 2002. Oxfam had even helped set up coffee shops in the United Kingdom, which were partly owned by growers' cooperatives in Honduras, Ethiopia and Indonesia.[9]

Other efforts ranged from small-scale university student union donation programs to the 500-organization strong Make Poverty History campaign (of which Fairtrade was a member). Make Poverty History aimed to apply pressure to governments to reassess trade, aid and debt with developing countries. World-famous musicians, such as Bono, Stevie Wonder, Sir Paul McCartney and notable others, would be brought together by Sir Bob Geldolf to play at Live 8 during the summer of 2005—a mega-concert that would take place simultaneously in eight countries around the world to raise money for poverty-stricken African nations.

The Fairtrade Foundation and the Fairtrade Labelling Organization (FLO)

The concept of Fairtrade Labelling began in Holland in the late 1980s. In 1988, the Max Havelaar Foundation was the first entity to launch a Fairtrade-approved coffee originating from Mexico. The Fairtrade Foundation was set up in 1992, in the United Kingdom, by the Catholic Agency for Overseas Development (CAFOD), Christian Aid, New Consumer, Oxfam, Traidcraft and the World Development Movement. Later, the Women's Institute joined the organization. Fairtrade Foundation was registered as both a charity and company. As of early 2005, the Fairtrade Foundation had 13 charity shareholder organizations, 32 permanent staff and 15 volunteers. The Fairtrade Foundation was the U.K. representative of Fairtrade Labelling Organizations International (FLO)—a nongovernmental organization based in Bonn, Germany—which united 20 national Fairtrade initiatives in Europe, Japan, the United States, Canada, Mexico, Australia and New Zealand.

The Fairtrade Foundation granted the Fairtrade mark to products in the United Kingdom, which abided by standards laid out by the FLO in Germany. The brand-owner was required to sign

---

[9]"The World Market for Hot Drinks," *Euromonitor Report*, October 2004, p. 16.

the Fairtrade Foundation's Licence Agreement and paid a licensing fee of two per cent of revenues. The Fairtrade Foundation did not certify individual farmers, but rather farmers' cooperatives or a democratically organized group of workers. To grant the license, the Fairtrade Foundation needed to certify the actual raw material sources. Fairtrade required that a stable price be paid to the growers. The Fairtrade Foundation explained on its website:

> The problems experienced by poor producers and workers in developing countries differ greatly from product to product. The majority of coffee and cocoa, for example, is grown by independent small farmers, working their own land and marketing their produce through a local co-operative. For these producers, receiving a fair price for their beans is more important than any other aspect of fair trade. Most tea, however, is grown on estates. The concern for workers employed on tea plantations is fair wages and decent working conditions. To address this there are two sets of generic producer standards. The first set applies to smallholders organised in co-operatives or other organisations with a democratic, participative structure. The second set applies to organised workers, whose employers pay decent wages, guarantee the right to join trade unions and provide good housing when relevant. On plantations and in factories, minimum health and safety as well as environmental standards must be complied with, and no child or forced labour can occur.[10]

To certify producers, Fairtrade charged cooperative coffee sellers between US$3,000 and US$5,000 for the initial certification plus a renewal fee of $500 per year and a 0.45 per cent volume fee, based on the export price of the volume sold under Fairtrade terms.[11] Fairtrade Labelling Organization provided financial assistance to producer groups who wished to become certified. In other situations, producers received financial support from the trading partner, a national Fairtrade Labelling Organization member or another source. See Exhibit 7 for financial information on the Fairtrade Foundation.

Fairtrade Products and Fairtrade Coffee in the United Kingdom

In the United Kingdom, the first three Fairtrade certified products were launched in 1994. By the end of 2004, there were 1,000 Fairtrade products from 150 companies on supermarket shelves in a number of product categories. The retail value of Fairtrade products was estimated at £145 million annually, having grown 40 per cent year-on-year since 1999. Unaided consumer awareness of Fairtrade was

[10]Fairtrade Foundation website, About Us, www.fairtrade.org.uk, accessed April 14, 2006.

[11]Ibid.

estimated at 50 per cent of the population, with the highest recognition in the 25- to 34-year-old age group. Awareness was aided by high-profile sippers, including British Prime Minister Tony Blair who had made it public that they consumed only Fairtrade-certified coffee while in parliament.

Within the United Kingdom, approximately 18 per cent of all fresh coffee sold was already Fairtrade. In the instant coffee segment, 1.9 per cent was Fairtrade-certified. The total volume of Fairtrade instant coffee had grown from 327,000 kilograms in 2003 to 458,000 kilograms in 2004. The value of Fairtrade instant coffee in the country grew from £8.1 million to £10.6 million. The branded player Café Direct held 91.6 per cent share in volume and 94.8 per cent share in value in early 2004. Café Direct had been established in 1991, by Oxfam, Traidcraft, Equal Exchange and Twin Trading to combat unstable coffee prices.[12] However, as other competitors entered, Café Direct's share fell to 69.4 per cent in volume and 77 per cent in value by 2005. Café Direct was priced at £2.69 per 100 grams at retail. The second group of competitors were private labels from major supermarkets, such as Tesco and Co-op. Other supermarkets, such as Sainsbury's and Morrison's, were formidable competitors in the Fairtrade fresh coffee segment, but as of early 2005, did not offer Fairtrade instant coffee products. Collectively, private labels controlled 28.1 per cent of the volume and 20.5 per cent of the value as of early 2005. The remaining share of 2.6 per cent in volume and 2.5 per cent in value was attributed to the small brand Percol. Private labels and Percol were priced similarly to the market leader, Café Direct. As of early 2005, none of the major instant coffee brands had a Fairtrade product.

Brief Corporate History of Nestlé

Nestlé's roots stretched back to 1843, when Henri Nestlé purchased a food and beverage factory in Vevey, Switzerland. In 1867, he developed a substitute for mother's breast milk by combining cow's milk and wheat flour in the form of powder. In 1905, the company merged with Anglo-Swiss, another prominent food company in Switzerland, and the merged entity continued overseas expansion. In the 1920s, the company acquired a number of companies, one of which was a condensed milk factory in Brazil. Brazilian coffee growers suggested the company develop a water-soluble "coffee cube." By 1938, Nestlé released its first instant coffee product, and it was an immediate success with households around the

---

[12]Café Direct website, http://www.cafedirect.co.uk/about/company.php, accessed April 16, 2006.

world. The company expanded through new product launches, including the Crunch candy bar in 1938 and Quick chocolate drink mix in 1948; and through acquisitions, notably prepared meal producer Stouffer's, condensed milk producer Carnation, Rowntree Chocolates (creators of Kit Kat), Buitoni pastas, Butterfinger and Baby Ruth chocolates, Perrier water, energy snack company PowerBar, pet-food producer Ralston Purina and ice-cream maker Mövenpick.

Nestlé in 2005

By 2005, Nestlé was the largest food company and the largest coffee producer in the world, in terms of annual revenue. Nestlé SA's worldwide sales amounted to US$69.9 billion in 2004, representing an increase of 6.8 per cent over the prior year.[13] The company posted an earnings before interest, taxes, depreciation and amortization (EBITDA) of US$8.8 billion and a net profit of US$5.4 billion in the same year. Nestlé was organized by the following product groups: beverages (25.1 per cent of total sales in 2004); milk products, nutrition and ice cream (27.2 per cent); prepared dishes and cooking aids (18.3 per cent); chocolate, confectionery and biscuits (11.8 per cent); pet

care (11.4 per cent); and pharmaceutical products (6.1 per cent). Beverages, which included Nescafé, Nestlé Waters and a whole host of other drinks, was the leading earnings contributor making up 35.3 per cent of the overall company's EBITDA. The company had 500 factories and 247,000 employees across 83 countries. Exhibit 8 shows the company's financial highlights.

"Good food, good life" guided Nestlé's strategy, which was founded on four pillars: operational efficiency, innovation and renovation, consumer communication, and product availability. Operational efficiency meant that Nestlé focused local resources on consumers and centralized back office functions at a regional level. Innovation and renovation called for Nestlé employees to keep all products relevant to consumers through new product introductions, packaging, channel sales, distribution and logistics. Consumer communication supported a move towards greater interactive marketing. To make the transition, the company had consolidated its media buying with two agencies aiming to improve the payback and efficiency from all media spending. Product availability promoted the concept of Nestlé products "whenever, wherever, however." This concept meant that Nestlé would continue building its relationships

---

[13]Nestlé SA's sales in Swiss francs (its home currency) declined by 1.4 per cent, partly due to negative currency swings of 3.5 per cent.

with small retailers and kiosks in developing nations and would increase its presence in the European "hard-discounter" channel.[14]

Social Responsibility at Nestlé

Nestlé's chief executive officer (CEO) and chairman, Peter Brabeck-Letmathe articulated how Nestlé viewed corporate social responsibility:

> To us, corporate social responsibility is not something that is imposed from the outside, but is an inherent part of the Nestlé business strategy and *Nestlé Business Principles,* which guide the way we operate. As stewards of large amounts of shareholders' capital, it is my firm belief that, in order for a business to create value of its shareholders over the long term, it must also bring value to society . . . we believe that the true test of a business is whether it creates value for society over the long term. This is particularly true in developing countries, where we often need to improve business conditions, improve the capabilities of farmers, create a skilled workforce and develop improved standards in order to operate successfully. Nearly half our factories are in the developing world; they must meet the same standards for food quality, safety and business practices that we have in the developed world. [15]

One of the most challenging moments in Nestlé's history was dealing with boycotters and government officials in Europe and North America in the late 1970s who claimed that Nestlé was harming children in developing nations by unethically marketing its infant baby formula to low-income mothers. Campaigners argued that low-income consumers did not have access to safe drinking water causing infants to become ill when consuming powdered milk. In 1981, Nestlé's management met with critics and the World Health Organization to form guidelines governing the marketing of breast milk substitutes under the *International Code of Marketing of Breast-milk Substitutes.* As of 2005, Nestlé continued to face criticisms from groups such as Baby Action Milk, which actively promoted boycotts of Nestlé products through public demonstrations and its website.

Since the early 1980s, the company had developed a number of country-specific programs aimed at improving nutrition, environmental standards and the agricultural supply chain. One example of a nutrition program was in Nigeria, where the company sponsored the Duchess Club, which held nutrition classes for 4,000 women who sold food in open-air markets. Environmentally, one of the company's central areas of

---

[14]Nestlé Management Report 2004, December 31, 2004, p. 11.

[15]"The Nestlé concept of corporate social responsibility as implemented in Latin America," *Nestlé Report,* March 2006, p. 2.

concern was water management. The company had reduced water usage throughout its factory network by 8.9 per cent CAGR since 2000. Efforts to improve agricultural conditions throughout its supply chain involved Nestlé's co-founding of the Sustainable Agriculture Initiative (SAI) with two other giant food multinationals, Danone and Unilever. SAI had since grown to include more than 20 other major multinationals. The company was also active in more than 50 projects under the United Nations Millennium Development Goals for poverty reduction.[16]

Nestlé created a framework for Creating Shared Value, which involved three major parts of its value chain: agriculture and sourcing, manufacturing and distribution, and products and consumers. See Exhibit 9 for the framework.

Nestlé's Global Procurement and Production of Coffee

Nestlé was the largest buyer and seller of coffee in the world with about a 20 per cent worldwide market share by retail value.[17] The company purchased approximately 12.5 million bags (750,000 tonnes) of green coffee per year, or about 12 per cent of the world's annual production through two channels: 84 per cent through the open market and 16 per cent through direct procurement. Nestlé had direct procurement operations in seven countries: Mexico, Côte d'Ivoire, Thailand, Indonesia, Vietnam, Philippines and China. Direct purchases were not shipped to other countries, but rather were used in that country's coffee roasting operations.

In addition to direct buying, Nestlé employed coffee agronomists, who worked with growers and their cooperatives to improve the quality of the green bean. The company's agronomists channeled support such as technical assistance and the early growth of coffee plantlets from Nestlé's large-scale research facility in Tours, France, to farmers. Nestlé also encouraged growers to diversify their crops to shield them from fluctuations in coffee prices.

The company had 27 instant coffee factories, of which 11 were in coffee-producing nations. Nestlé produced 55 per cent of all of its coffee in 15 developing nations. Exhibit 10 shows a world map indicating Nestlé's coffee direct procurement and production facilities.

Nescafé in the United Kingdom

The United Kingdom was one of the largest markets for Nescafé products

---

[16]Nestlé Management Report, December 31, 2004, pp. 20–23.

[17]"The World Market for Hot Drinks," *Euromonitor Report*, October 2004, Table 57, p. 20.

within Nestlé's global footprint. In the United Kingdom, Nescafé played only in the instant coffee segment with sales of £400 million[18] per year in the United Kingdom, which represented approximately 20 per cent of Nestlé's overall U.K. sales of £2 billion.

In the soluble (instant) market, the company had about 60 per cent of the U.K. market. Nestlé looked at the U.K. soluble market as made up of five primary consumer segments: economy, regular, premium, connoisseur and specialty. Nescafé did not play in the economy segment, which was dominated by private labels at prices between £1 and £1.50 per 100 grams. Nescafé Original in the regular segment retailed at £1.78 per 100 grams, and held about 70 per cent market share. Nescafé Original accounted for 30 per cent market of the overall soluble market. It competed against Kraft's Kenco Rappor brand, Maxwell House and private labels.

The premium segment consisted of coffee with a higher Arabica content and crystals that were freeze-dried rather than the lower cost powder used in the economy and regular segments. Nestlé's main offering in the premium category was Nescafé Gold, which dominated the segment and enjoyed a market share of 13 per cent of the overall soluble coffee market in the country. Nescafé Gold was priced at approximately £2.50 per 100 grams and positioned against Kraft's Kenco and Douwe Egberts. In the connoisseur segment, Nestlé sold Nescafé Ultra Premium with several brand extensions, including Cap Colombie and Kenjara. All coffee in this segment was 100 per cent Arabica. Connoisseur offerings ranged between £2 and £4 per 100 grams depending on the blend and were targeted at top-end coffee drinkers who sought out quality and exciting new tastes. Finally, the specialty segment comprised a mix of soluble products, such as cappuccinos, frappés, lattés and café-mochas. Nescafé had products in each sub-category of the specialty segment and held 68 per cent of the segment. The specialty market represented only three per cent of the volume of the overall soluble market, but 10 per cent of the value. Prices in this segment ranged from £2 to £3 per box of 10 sachets.

The Development of the Partners' Blend Label

The idea to develop a consumer coffee product for the U.K. ethical coffee segment arose for a number of reasons. First, Nestlé executives saw that the ethical coffee segment was attractive as it had grown at a CAGR of 75 per cent

---

[18]This is not an official Nestlé UK sales figure. This figure is the case writer's estimate, based on a market share of 40 per cent × £1 billion market size = £400 million.

since 2001. Second, Nestlé UK saw that nearly all of the growth had occurred in the roast and ground market, leaving the door open for a major player to enter with an ethical soluble product. The ethical category in the instant market had only grown by 25 per cent CAGR in the same period. Third, Nestlé UK and Nestlé SA had received feedback both in formal consumer panel testing and through letters to the company requesting a product in the ethical category. In response, Nestlé UK executives believed that the company could integrate its multiple sustainability initiatives into a consumer product. As one Nestlé SA executive stated: "we were hearing from honest consumers who said, 'we like your brand, we like your product, but we can't understand why you don't have a "fairtrade" option.'"

Nestlé S.A. gave approval to Nestlé UK to begin developing a Nescafé product aimed at the ethical segment. Parsons explained the first step:

We knew if we wanted to launch the product we would have to develop a traceable and transparent chain back to the individual farmer. We were looking to find farmers who were heavily affected by the falling price of coffee. After considering a number of factors, we decided to focus our initial efforts on Ethiopia and El Salvador.

While several observers believed fixed price guarantees to farmers were the most beneficial, Nestlé SA's corporate position was to offer assistance through other means, such as its direct procurement program, providing technical assistance to farmers, building schools in coffee-producing communities and helping farmers diversify their crops. Niels Christiansen, vice-president of corporate affairs at Nestlé SA explained:

Our focus is to give the farmers more value, but it does not work on the same principles as offering a fixed price. By buying a portion of green beans directly from the farmer, our value proposition is that it offers additional help to the farmers. However, by offering just a fixed price we could run the risk of over-stimulating farmers to grow more coffee. In turn, that could lead to an over-supply, which would be counter-productive to helping the farmers secure a reasonable price for their coffee.

Sourcing

Parsons sought out the assistance of Patrick Leheup, commodity sourcing manager, Coffee and Beverages SBU from Nestlé SA, who joined the Partners' Blend development team with the central task of sourcing green beans directly from farmers in Ethiopia and El Salvador. Leheup requested proposals from major exporters and negotiated agreements with Ecom in El Salvador and VolCafe in Ethiopia. Leheup and Parsons visited both countries where they met with individual farmers, wholesalers, cooperatives and representatives from VolCafe and Ecom. In Ethiopia, the Partners' Blend project started with 3,100 farmers at the country's main cooperative, Oromia Coffee Farmers Co-operative Union. In El Salvador, there were 157 farmers at four worker cooperatives under the larger cooperative union Proexcafe. For the first year, Nestlé estimated that they would purchase 5,000 bags (300 tonnes) from each country.

In coordination with purchasing, Nestlé planned on offering assistance through several other initiatives. In Ethiopia, Nestlé planned to build facilities for water distribution, install new environmentally friendly pulping and washing equipment, provide payments to farmers during off-season and assign full-time agronomists to work with the farmers to improve quality. In El Salvador, Nestlé's plans involved assigning agronomists from an NGO called Semi Empresariales de Meso America (SEM) to work with farmers to improve coffee quality while helping farmers diversify their sources of income. In both communities, Nestlé was contributing funds to social improvements, such as a potable water supply in Ethiopia and co-op workers' housing and a training/medical center in El Salvador. The initiatives were estimated to cost £500,000 over three years.[19]

Product and Price

Labeled Nescafé Partners' Blend, the product would be available in 100-gram containers to start. Originally, the product was to be placed in Nescafé's signature ergonomically shaped glass jar. But feedback from top Nestlé executives suggested that the product take on a more rustic and distinctive look. The Partners' Blend team shifted to a recyclable can wrapped in brown paper with black and white pictures of El Salvadorian and Ethiopian farmers. Exhibit 11 shows the label design. The coffee was 100 per cent Arabica content and was freeze-dried. The intent was to provide a high-quality coffee comparable in taste to the Nescafé Gold product line. All coffee would be roasted at the freeze-dried production line at Nestlé's factory in Girona, Spain. Packaging would be done by an external co-packing plant.

The product would be priced at £2.69 per 100 grams at retail. Retailers' and Nestlé's margins were estimated to be between 15 and 25 per cent each.[20] Kendrick talked about the decision to price Partners' Blend at £2.69:

> We were very careful that we didn't want to price the product up. It was very important that we weren't perceived to be taking a higher margin

---

[19]All financial details of the project have been disguised to protect confidentiality.

[20]Ibid.

on the product. The Fairtrade labels are between £2.59 and £2.79, so we went right down the middle. This product is quite reasonably priced considering that it is 100 per cent Arabica coffee.

Channels of Distribution

The team forecast that Partners' Blend would be distributed 80 per cent through supermarkets and convenience stores and 20 per cent through out-of-home channels, such as the educational, governmental and leisure sectors. Nestlé would make the product available at all supermarkets where it sold other Nescafé lines, such as Tesco, Asda, Sainsbury's and Co-op.

Promotion

Nestlé planned on promoting the product through four strategies: press advertorials, public relations coverage, wet sampling and a website named Grow More than Coffee. The company did not foresee promoting through trade discounts. Nestlé planned to spend £500,000 at the launch date and an additional £500,000 five to six months after the launch to reinforce the message. The team estimated 45 per cent coverage of the target audience with a 1.5 opportunity to see. For wet sampling, the company estimated 25 sampling days and the distribution of 37,500 one-serving sachets. Kendrick talked about the strategy:

The ad plan is very specific and it attempts to tell a clear story. The spend will be directed to editorial, sampling and the website to give more information. This allows consumers to learn and to contact us with any questions. We always use the press where we can and in the Ultra Premium segment, we often appeal to the Connoisseur market that way. Editorials work where you have more information to communicate and explain. As a brand, we have only 50 per cent on TV. We typically use billboards, both 48 sheet and 6 sheets, and they are used in integrated campaigns to reinforce the message. We've put about £250,000 towards sampling. It's very costly to set up a big booth and get the samples out there, but it's very important. We also have an up-to-date database of one million Nescafé consumers through our loyalty scheme. We provide these consumers samples and communicate through quarterly magazines.

Consumer Segments

With research dating back to 1999, Nestlé's marketing department had identified three consumer stances with respect to the ethical product category: the Global Watchdog, the Conscientious Consumer and Do What I Cans. The Global Watchdog was estimated to represent less than five per cent of the U.K. population and was a group actively campaigning and scrutinizing details of products. The Global Watchdog was likely to have boycotted the use of certain company products and tended to skew towards leftist politics. The

Global Watchdog was likely to drink only an independent brand of certified coffee. The Conscientious Consumer was a considerably larger group, representing approximately 20 per cent of the population and included individuals who were informed and engaged in human rights issues, but involved to a lesser extent in active campaigning than the Global Watchdog. The Conscientious Consumer was likely to be a *Guardian*[21] reader and purchased a mixture of Fairtrade, Oxfam, free-range, organic and mainstream products. The Do What I Cans were the bulk of consumers (the remaining 75 per cent) who took actions to be responsible whenever they could. These individuals were not active campaigners, but they were predisposed to Fairtrade, Oxfam, free range and other ethical products.

The Partners' Blend team felt that they would target the Do What I Cans, who were the largest group of consumers in terms of size. While the Do What I Cans spanned a number of age categories, two primary age groups had been identified: a group in their mid- to late 40s who had reached a life-stage where they wanted to give something back; and, a group in their 30s with young families who wanted to make a real effort to act responsibly and would purchase Fairtrade products to demonstrate responsible actions.

The team predicted that approximately 57 per cent of Partners' Blend consumers would be women.

The Fairtrade Consideration

During the development of the Partners' Blend product, Parsons, Kendrick and several others at Nestlé UK and Nestlé SA had talked about the possibility of certifying the product with the Fairtrade Foundation. By certifying Partners' Blend with Fairtrade, Nestlé would agree to pay a minimum fixed price of US$1.26 per pound of coffee to the farmer cooperatives. If the traded price of coffee rose above $1.26 per pound, then Nestlé would pay a $0.05 premium over the market rate. Under FLO guidelines, US$0.05 of the US$1.26 would be re-invested back into the farmers' communities for infrastructure, education, improvement of growing techniques or diversifying into other crops. Nestlé would also pay two per cent of revenue to Fairtrade for the licensing of the Fairtrade mark.

The alternative was to release the Partners' Blend without an external certification. Under this alternative, Nestlé would continue with its existing program, under which the assistance would not be in the form of a fixed coffee price but rather through providing

---

[21]The Guardian is a popular U.K.-based newspaper that is renowned for its thought-provoking articles and left-leaning political view.

financial aid to improve coffee quality; diversify into other crops; enhance water management; build schools, homes and roads; and offer payments to farmers during the off-season.

There were a number of consider-ations for Nestlé. Executives wanted to ensure that the Fairtrade program was in line with Nestlé's philosophy about offering assistance to coffee farmers. One executive at Nestlé SA commented:

The main friction [has been] how to provide better income for the farmers and our position [has been] that fixed price programs stimulated demand for farmers to grow more coffee, and yes that benefited some—but only two per cent of the entire group.

Many people are not aware of what Nestlé does in coffee—for example, the fact that we purchase 15 per cent directly, the help we offer with agronomists throughout the world, the sustainability initiatives that we're involved in or the fact that 55 per cent of the production is done in developing nations.

Parsons reflected on the Nescafé Partners' Blend initiative:

I think one of the interesting things about this project is it has brought together marketing, corporate affairs and production on issues that had pre-viously not been discussed together. And, the marketing and brand manager needed to deal with several issues that had previously been dealt with by cor-porate affairs.

One of the realities that we face is that there's a great deal of cynicism in the U.K. We don't want to have consumers perceiving us as not being serious about helping out the farmers. We are serious about it and we need to engender that understanding.

Exhibit 1   Key Coffee-Producing Countries

Country	2003–04	2004–05 Est	%
Arabica/Robusta - in 000s 60-kg bags			
Brazil	38,238	39,883	34.9%
Vietnam	15,520	13,450	11.8%
Colombia	11,300	11,500	10.1%
Indonesia	6,500	7,500	6.6%
Ethiopia	4,200	4,400	3.8%
India	4,900	4,200	3.7%
Guatemala	3,700	3,800	3.3%
Honduras	3,100	3,600	3.1%
Mexico	3,900	3,400	3.0%
Uganda	2,600	2,400	2.1%
Costa Rica	2,100	2,000	1.7%
Ivory Coast	2,300	2,200	1.9%
El Salvador	1,500	1,400	1.2%
Smaller	15,150	14,575	12.8%
Total	115,008	114,308	100.0%

Source: Company files.

Exhibit 2   Production Costs

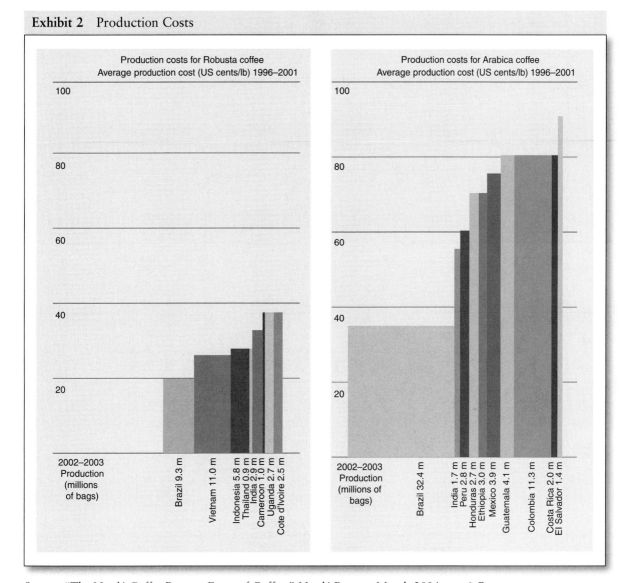

Source: "The Nestlé Coffee Report: Faces of Coffee," Nestlé Report, March 2004, pp. 6–7.

Exhibit 3   Coffee Prices

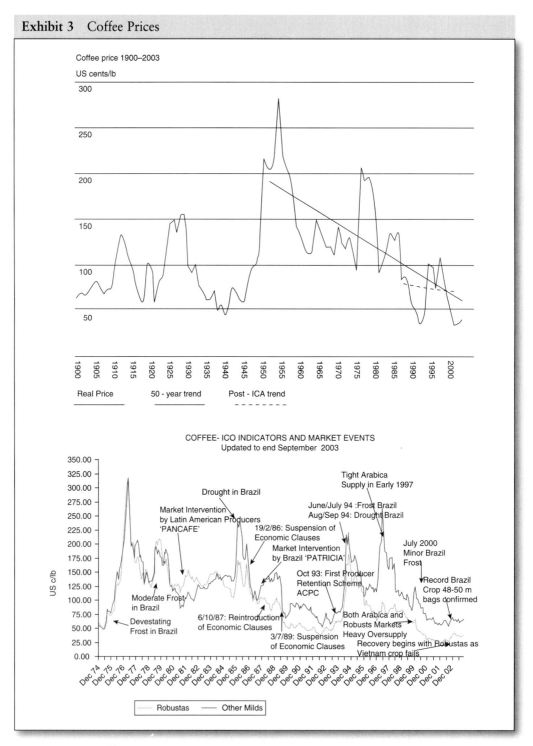

Source: Company files.

Exhibit 4   Coffee Consumption in the United Kingdom

Sales of Hot Drinks by Sector: Volume 1999–2004

Tonnes	1999	2000	2001	2002	2003	2004
Coffee	48,330.0	48,235.0	48,355.0	48,475.0	48,378.2	48,545.2
Tea	129,885.0	127,528.2	125,920.0	126,113.0	121,712.9	119,053.2
Other hot drinks	21,755.7	22,093.7	21,184.7	20,857.4	20,995.5	21,355.2
Hot drinks	199,970.7	197,856.9	195,459.7	195,445.4	191,086.6	188,953.5

Sales of Hot Drinks by Sector: Value 1999–2004

£ million	1999	2000	2001	2002	2003	2004
Coffee	775.7	770.7	746.6	725.2	734.6	733.6
Tea	789.6	800.3	809.8	828.9	810.5	799.1
Other hot drinks	155.3	161.5	156.3	155.2	152.1	153.9
Hot drinks	1,720.6	1,732.5	1,712.7	1,709.3	1,697.2	1,686.6

Source: "Hot Drinks in the UK," *Euromonitor,* November 2005, Section 2.1, Tables 1–2, pp. 2–3.

Retail Sales of Coffee by Type: Volume 1999–2004

Tonnes	1999	2000	2001	2002	2003	2004
Fresh coffee	11,430.0	11,505.0	11,975.0	12,445.0	12,888.0	13,352.2
Fresh ground coffee	11,000.0	11,070.0	11,510.0	11,950.0	12,362.7	12,796.4
Fresh coffee beans	430	435	465	495	525.3	555.8
Instant coffee	36,900.0	36,730.0	36,380.0	36,030.0	35,490.2	35,193.0
Instant standard coffee	33,400.0	33,250.0	32,930.0	32,605.0	32,013.6	31,629.4
Instant decaffeinated coffee	3,500.0	3,480.0	3,450.0	3,425.0	3,476.6	3,563.5
Coffee total	48,330.0	48,235.0	48,355.0	48,475.0	48,378.2	48,545.2

(Continued)

Exhibit 4 (Continued)

Retail Sales of Coffee by Type: Value 1999–2004						
£ million	1999	2000	2001	2002	2003	2004
Fresh coffee	99.8	100.9	105.3	112.1	115.7	120
Fresh ground coffee	94.2	95.3	99.6	106	109.2	113.2
Fresh coffee beans	5.6	5.6	5.7	6.1	6.5	6.9
Instant coffee	675.9	669.8	641.3	613.1	618.9	613.6
Instant standard coffee	595.5	590.5	565	540	544.6	537.4
Instant decaffeinated coffee	80.4	79.3	76.3	73.1	74.3	76.2
Coffee total	775.7	770.7	746.6	725.2	734.6	733.6

Source: "Hot Drinks in the UK," *Euromonitor,* November 2005, Section 3.2, Tables 21–22, p. 23.

Coffee Company Shares 2000–2004					
% retail value rsp					
Company	2000	2001	2002	2003	2004
Nestlé UK Ltd	42.8	41.4	39.4	39.4	39.7
Kraft Foods UK Ltd	22.9	22.1	22.1	22	21.5
Douwe Egberts UK Ltd	4.9	5.7	6.1	6.3	6.4
Cafédirect Ltd	2.5	2.3	2.4	2.7	2.9
Betty & Taylors of Harrogate Ltd	1.3	1.4	1.6	1.6	1.6
Lavazza Coffee Ltd	0.9	1.1	1.2	1.3	1.3
Gala Coffee & Tea Ltd	1	1	1.1	1.1	1.1
RGB Coffee Ltd	0.5	0.6	0.6	0.6	0.6
Private label	17.5	16.8	16.6	16.5	16.7
Others	5.6	7.5	8.9	8.7	8.2
Total	100	100	100	100	100

Source: "Hot Drinks in the UK," *Euromonitor,* November 2005, Section 3.2, Table 23, pp. 23–24.

Exhibit 5   Average Cost Breakdown of 100 Grams of Instant Coffee in the United Kingdom

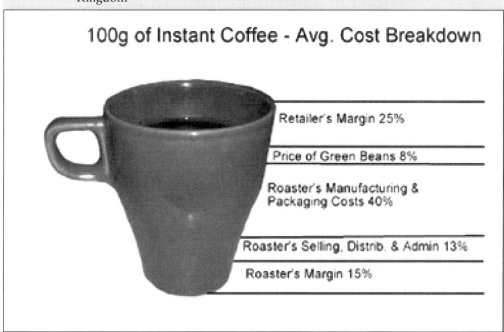

Source: Photo and graphic by case writer.

100g Instant Coffee Cost Breakdown	In £	
Retailer Price	2.00	
Roaster Price to Retailer	1.50	
Retailer Margin	0.50	25.0%
Roaster Price	1.50	
Roaster Costs		
Green Beans*	0.15	
Manufacturing & Packaging Costs	0.80	
Selling, Distr. & Admin - Direct	0.25	
Total Roaster Costs	1.20	
Roaster's Margin	0.30	20.0%

Source: Estimated by case writer based on general industry data. This does not refer to any particular retailer or roaster.

Note: The cost of Green Beans fluctuates based on the prices of world markets.

Exhibit 6   Excerpt From Oxfam's Mugged Report—Coffee Rescue Plan: 2002

Until now, rich consumer countries and the huge companies based in them have responded to the crisis with inexcusable complacency. In the face of human misery, there have been many words yet little action. Existing market-based solutions—Fair Trade and the development of specialty coffees—are important, but only for some farmers. They can help poverty reduction and the environment. However, a systemic, not a niche solution, is needed.

The challenge is to make the coffee market work for all. The failures of previous efforts at intervention in the market must be understood and lessons learned. But so too must the lessons of the moment. The low coffee price creates a buyers' market, leaving some of the poorest and most powerless people in the world to negotiate in an open market with some of the richest and most powerful. The result, unsurprisingly, is that the rich get richer and the poor get poorer. Active participation by all players in the coffee trade is needed to reverse this situation.

The next year is critical. Coffee-producing governments have agreed to a plan that aims to reduce supply by improving the quality of coffee traded. This will only work if it is backed by the companies and by rich countries and is complemented by measures to address long-term rural underdevelopment. Within one year the Rescue Plan, under the auspices of the International Coffee Organization, should result in:

1. Roaster companies paying farmers a decent price (above their costs of production) so that they can send their children to school, afford medicines, and have enough food.

2. Increasing the price to farmers by reducing supply and stocks of coffee on the market through:
   - Roaster companies trading only in coffee that meets basic quality standards as proposed by the International Coffee Organization (ICO).
   - The destruction of at least five million bags of coffee stocks, funded by rich-country governments and roaster companies.

3. The creation of a fund to help poor farmers shift to alternative livelihoods, making them less reliant on coffee.

4. Roaster coffee companies committing to increase the amount of coffee they buy under Fair Trade conditions to two percent of their volumes.

The Rescue Plan should be a pilot for a longer-term Commodity Management Initiative to improve prices and provide alternative livelihoods for farmers. The outcomes should include:

1. Producer and consumer country governments establishing mechanisms to correct the imbalance in supply and demand to ensure reasonable prices to producers. Farmers should be adequately represented in such schemes.

2. Cooperation between producer governments to stop more commodities entering the market than can be sold.

3. Support for producer countries to capture more of the value in these commodities.

4. Financed incentives to reduce small farmers' overwhelming dependence on agricultural commodities.

5. Companies paying a decent price for all commodities, including coffee.

Source: "Mugged: Poverty in Your Coffee Cup," *Oxfam Report Summary*, September 2002, p. 3.

Exhibit 7   Fairtrade Foundation Financial Statements

Fair Trade Foundation		
Full Amounts in Pounds Sterling	**2003**	**2004**
Incoming Resources		
Donations and similar incoming resources		
Donations and miscellaneous income	81,606	134,159
Grants for general charitable purposes	99,600	103,355
Actitivites to further the charity's objects		
Grants receivable	415,212	309,892
License and distributor fees	766,119	1,396,858
Sale of promotional items	48,327	54,884
Interest received	6,936	11,449
Total incoming resources	1,417,800	2,010,598
Cost of Generating Funds		
Fundraising	29,758	41,665
Total cost of generating funds		
Net incoming resources available for charitable application	1,388,042	1,968,933
Charitable Expenditure		
Costs of activities in pursuit of charitable objects		
Certification, licensing and product development	617,227	816,869
Public education and awareness	565,418	638,648
Management and administration	51,262	86,926
Total charitable expenditure	1,233,907	1,542,443
Total resources expended	1,263,665	1,584,108
Net income / (expenditure)	**154,135**	**426,490**
Transfers between funds		
Fund balances brought forward	151,250	305,385
Fund balances carried forward	305,385	731,875

Source: Fairtrade Foundation Annual Report and Financial Statements, December 31, 2004, p. 11.

Exhibit 8   Nestlé SA Financial Highlights

In Millions USD	2003	2004	Change %
Sales	65,460	69,918	6.8%
EBITDA	10,171	11,083	9.0%
EBIT	8,189	8,840	7.9%
Net profit	4,623	5,413	17.1%
Equity	29,742	34,707	16.7%
Market capitalization, end Dec	96,674	101,980	5.5%
Per share			
Net profit	11.95	13.93	16.6%
Equity	76.85	89.35	16.3%

Source: Nestlé Management Report, December 31, 2004, p. 14.

By Product Group				
In Millions USD				
Sales	**2003**	**2004**	**% of Total**	**Change %**
Beverages	23,520	21,793	25.1%	−7.3%
Milk products, nutrition and ice cream	23,283	23,582	27.2%	1.3%
Prepared dishes and cooking aids	16,068	15,878	18.3%	−1.2%
Chocolate, confectionary and biscuits	10,240	10,258	11.8%	0.2%
Pet care	9,816	9,934	11.4%	1.2%
Pharmaceutical products	5,052	5,324	6.1%	5.4%
Total	87,979	86,769	100.0%	−1.4%
EBITDA				
Beverages	4,038	3,867	35.3%	−4.2%
Milk products, nutrition and ice cream	2,796	2,682	24.4%	−4.1%
Prepared dishes and cooking aids	1,884	1,924	17.5%	2.1%
Chocolate, confectionary and biscuits	1,047	1,153	10.5%	10.1%

Pet care	1,444	1,446	13.2%	0.1%
Pharmaceutical products	1,329	1,532	14.0%	15.3%
Sub-total	12,538	12,604	114.9%	0.5%
Unallocated items	−1,532	−1,634	−14.9%	6.7%
Total	11,006	10,970	100.0%	−0.3%

Source: Nestlé Financial Statements, December 31, 2004, p. 22.

Exhibit 9   Framework for Creating Shared Value

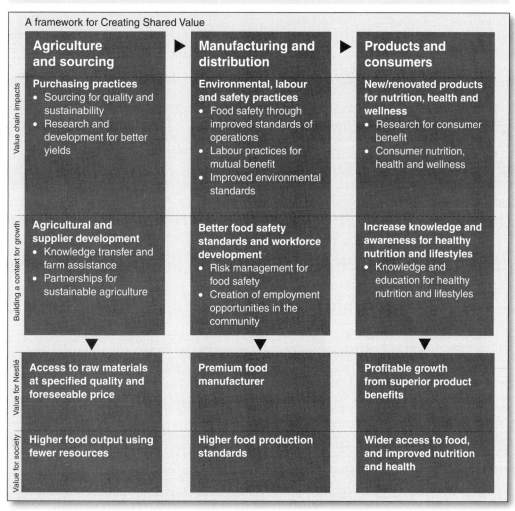

Source: "The Nestlé Concept of Corporate Social Responsibility as Implemented in Latin America," *Nestlé Report*, March 2006, p. 6.

Exhibit 10   Nestlé's Worldwide Coffee Procurement and Production

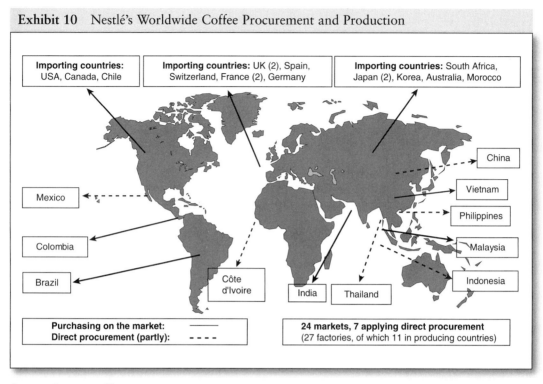

Source: Company files.

Exhibit 11   Partners' Blend Images

Source: Company files.

Jinjian Garment Factory:
Motivating Go-Slow Workers

Tieying Huang

Junping Liang

Paul W. Beamish

On December 15, 1999, at 11 p.m., Mr. Lou Baijin, the owner and managing director of Jinjian Garment Factory, was still in his Shenzhen office in deep thought and red-eyed from lack of sleep. In the adjacent workshop were more than 200 of his factory workers. Like Mr. Lou, they had been working 12 hours a day for seven days, non-stop, in order to finish in time a large Christmas order for an important European customer. From his experience, Mr. Lou could tell from the speed and sound of the sewing machines in the workshop that the workers had slowed their pace. Although they might be tired because of the long hours of overtime they had worked the last week, it was more likely that their slowness was deliberate. As a general practice in this industry, the workers had a tendency to slow their working pace in order to force management to increase the price of their piecework. If the orders were not delivered on time, Mr. Lou would have to ship the order by air freight at extra expense or risk losing valuable customers. The question of how to motivate workers, which

had haunted Mr. Lou for a long time, became more urgent now. When he glanced at the entrepreneurship book, which had been on his desk for more than a month and which he had read several times, Mr. Lou forced a smile and painfully realized that the book had not provided a solution.

Lou Baijin and His Garment Factory

Mr. Lou was born in the town of Louta in Zhejiang province in 1956. He graduated from junior high school in 1973 and was expected to make his living as a farmer. In 1976, he became a mineworker in a neighboring province. Then, in the early 1980s, Mr. Lou returned to his home town and became a salesman. He travelled extensively in China to promote the use of raw chemical materials for the enterprise sponsored by his village.

In 1991, Mr. Lou came to Shenzhen (the most prominent special economic zone of China) and searched for jobs there. He wasn't very lucky at first. In order to save on living expenses, he lived on two boxes of fast food each day for half a year. Mr. Lou finally became a commission-based salesman for an electronic factory.

By 1996, manufacturing costs in Shenzhen for garments were very high; consequently, many factories migrated to the hinterland of Mainland China. Unlike those factories' owners, Mr. Lou saw an opportunity. He took his life savings and bought 30 secondhand sewing machines at a very low price and established his first factory in Shenzhen.

In the beginning, the factory employed about 50 workers. The main business came from taking small orders, as a subcontractor, from larger factories that had direct access to Hong Kong and overseas garment buyers. Mr. Lou's business grew very fast from that point forward. By 1999, Mr. Lou's factory had 150 sewing machines and more than 250 workers and had begun to compete directly with surrounding factories for the orders of Hong Kong and overseas customers.

The Garment Manufacturing Industry in Shenzhen

Shenzhen was one of the most advanced garment manufacturing centres in the world. Garments produced there were sold at department stores in many upscale locales, including Bloomingdale's and Nordstrom in the United States. The garment manufacturing industry had prospered along with the development of the Shenzhen special economic zone during China's broad economic reforms that began in 1980. Hong Kong was the centre of the world garment-manufacturing industry during the 1980s and 1990s. When China opened its economic door to foreign investment, Shenzhen was the first place in China for Hong Kong garment manufacturers to transfer this labor-intensive industry. Hong Kong had been gradually losing its competitive advantages to other Southeast Asian countries because of the increased production costs there.

Shenzhen was inexpensive in terms of land and labor but also manageable since it was a neighbor of Hong Kong, and people spoke the same language. Hong Kong business people could go to work in Shenzhen as commuters because of the location and convenient transportation.

In less then a decade, more than a thousand garment factories were established in Shenzhen. The majority of the garment factories were either owned or managed by Hong Kong residents. The Shenzhen garment industry was literally a direct extension of the Hong Kong garment industry.

Working Environment

Hong Kong was a capitalist society known in Mainland China for its minimal social welfare and labor protection laws. Because Hong Kong was the model of the Shenzhen garment industry, the management system of the garment industry in Shenzhen copied the factory environment found in Hong Kong in the 1970s. These were known as "sweatshops" by economists and sociologists.

Workers in the Shenzhen garment industry were willing to work overtime during the peak season, and the average workday was more than 12 hours. The workers rested for only one or two days each month during the six-month peak season because they were able to work only four to five hours per day, if at all, during the slow season. Over 90 per cent of the wages were based on piecework performance, which closely linked individual effort and reward. Because the other 10 per cent of wages given by the employers (such as food subsidy, holiday allowance and special bonus for overtime) barely covered the living expenses for workers themselves, the piecework wage fostered strong motivation for workers to work long and fast. The laws for minimum wage and labor protection in China had been established for less than a decade and had not been strictly adhered to because of the difficulty of enforcement, especially in private sectors such as the garment industry. In particular, 95 per cent of the garment workers in Shenzhen were peasants who did not have permanent residency status in the city. (China was one of the few countries in the world with a resident permit system among its citizens.) If a person was not a permanent resident, it was virtually impossible to get social welfare or labor protection from the local government.

The average monthly income for a skilled garment worker in Shenzhen was US$150 during the peak season. The average living accommodation for each person was three to four square metres, with usually eight or more people sharing one room. In spite of such conditions, the promise of a job in the industry still attracted many peasants to Shenzhen. In fact, some workers even gave monetary deposits to their factory just to retain the opportunity to work. Once they found a job in Shenzhen, most did not choose to raise a family there since they could not afford the high living cost. Instead, they went back to their home province after eight to 10 years of hard work in Shenzhen, and their savings enabled them to build a new house and live a relatively easy life.

Garment Manufacturing

Shenzhen garment manufacturing was a labor-intensive industry with a relatively low capital investment required for entry. About 90 per cent of the garment-making equipment in Shenzhen was imported from Japan, but even with the most advanced garment manufacturing equipment, the work still involved a lot of manual labor (sewing, ironing and button tacking, etc.) that could not be automated, especially with ladies' clothing, which required more dedication than men's clothing. In most garment-making procedures, workers had to operate the machine by hand. Usually the work was divided into more than 10 procedures to efficiently produce even a simple shirt. Hence, a garment factory needed many workers.

The capital requirement of garment manufacturing was very low compared to the labor requirement. "You can be a boss for only US$5,000," said Mr. Lou. Setting up required a small amount of capital to buy several sewing machines, rent a house (even an apartment) and hire several workers. The industry continued to attract numerous new entrepreneurs.

Seasonality and High Workforce Turnover

Although the supply of garment workers was unlimited, some of the workers were unskilled as they were peasants coming straight from the farm. Skilled workers were a valuable and scarce resource during peak time, September to February.

The need for work in the factories was seasonal. During peak time, garment factories in Shenzhen usually work 12 hours a day, 28 days per month to produce clothing for Christmas and spring seasons when consumers purchased most of their wardrobes. During other times of a year, even skilled workers did not have sufficient work.

During the peak season, proficient workers were so scarce that factories would do almost anything to keep them. The factories knew that having more skilled workers would make them more competitive. Therefore, retaining skilled workers was one of the most pressing problems the factories faced. Because of insufficient orders and furious competition in the slow season, factories were usually unprofitable, even when paying minimum wage to workers and this usually meant a bottom-line loss for the company. Large factories with long-term views usually could keep a minimum stable work force during the slow season, while small factories usually closed in order to save costs. The tricky part was that no one could tell for sure whether the losses in the slow season would be recovered during the coming peak season since 90 per cent of the garments produced in Shenzhen were exported to foreign markets, and garment factories in Shenzhen had little knowledge or control over demand.

Many workers had a long holiday during the slow season when they usually went back to their home town. When they came back at the beginning of the peak season, some might find a new job in a different factory if they were not satisfied with the existing one. The turnover rate of the workers was very high because of the unstable nature of the garment industry.

Effective Management of Workers

Production costs, which were derived from cutting, manufacturing and trimming a garment, were known in the trade as CMT. Because of competition within the industry in Shenzhen, the CMT of Shenzhen had decreased almost by half in the past 10 years. Foreign garment buyers usually imported the fabric and provided design patterns for the factories to produce apparel for a particular foreign market. The cost of the fabric was usually higher than the CMT. This put the garment manufacturers in Shenzhen at risk because the expensive fabric could sometimes be destroyed in the process of making a garment, and CMT received from the order was usually not enough to recoup such losses.

Because of the labor-intensive nature of the industry, normally the wage of the workers was about 60 per cent of CMT of a garment, which meant that 60 per cent of the revenue of a garment factory went to workers as wages. Mistakes such as destroying fabric in the garment making process or late shipments meant the owners did not make a profit, since they had to bear the cost of the fabric and high air transportation costs when a job was not completed on time for sea shipment. Therefore, effective management of workers, who not only accounted for 60 per cent of the revenue but who also decided the fate of an order, had become central to survival in the garment-making business.

Because of the nature of the export-oriented garment business in Shenzhen, the normal order size was relatively small, while the number of orders was large. The typical size of a Shenzhen garment factory ranged from 100 to 200 employees, and a typical factory could produce about 200 orders per year. In order to satisfy the most current fashion, most designers liked to alter their patterns at the last minute, which gave the manufacturers very short production lead-times. This meant that the garment factories in Shenzhen had to be able to produce a new style of clothing on an average of every three to four days.

In spite of such a short production time, the factory had to achieve two aims: (1) produce the garment according to a quality standard acceptable to customers, and (2) ship the product on time. (Late fashion is no fashion!) These two factors were also essential for a garment factory to survive.

The Piecework System

The piecework system employed by the factories in Shenzhen was well suited to the nature of the work. For example, the retail price of a lady's dress might be US$30, and the cost of CMT (cutting, making and trimming) for it in Shenzhen might be US$3 (the fabric, accessories and patterns were supplied by the customer). The manufacturing process of this dress had more than 15 procedures, and the three dollars was distributed to the workers first. The price of sewing the collar might be five cents, the price of fitting on a sleeve might be three cents, the ironing of the dress might cost four cents, etc. Each worker was assigned to a specific job and earned an exact amount derived from the number of finished pieces times the price of that particular job to finish the procedure (piecework). One's pay was strictly linked with one's performance. Normally, more skilled and more industrious workers earned more than average workers did.

Due to the nature of division of garment-making processes, a garment factory was made up of several self-contained work units, called production teams, which usually contained 10 to 15 sewing workers and were able to produce a garment independently. A team leader, appointed by management, had absolute authority to assign the different working procedures of making a garment among the team members. Besides the unit price of piecework and the efficiency of a worker, production team leaders might also have some influence on the income of workers, as they could assign good jobs, more often, to their favored team members at the cost of jeopardizing the morale of the teams. This situation was more severe in Shenzhen's garment factories than in other cities because Shenzhen was a migrant city and many factory workers might come from the same village town or may even be related to each other.

After the deductions of the workers' cost, the balance of the US$3 CMT

was distributed to the overhead of the factory. What was left was the profit for the factory owner.

Determining the Price of Piecework

Because each procedure for making a particular style was unique, the price of the same procedure when making a garment could vary. For example, the work required to make a round-shaped collar was different from that of a square-shaped collar so the prices for these two jobs were different. The same worker might earn $0.03 for making one round collar and $0.02 for a square one, although the two jobs belonged to the same production procedure.

Even for the same style of garment, if the order size was different, the price of making the garment might also vary. Generally speaking, productivity was increased when workers became more familiar with a particular garment. Larger orders were easier to produce than smaller ones owing to the learning curve associated with each order. Thus, owners and management (customers also required lower CMT price for larger orders) would lower the piecework price for each production procedure of a larger order and increase the prices when the order was small. The prices might also be different based on different fabrics for the same orders. For example, silk garments were normally more difficult to make than polyester ones.

In theory, if garment factories had enough time and resources, it was possible to accurately predetermine the piecework price of every procedure for every style based on the complexity, average daily salary of workers and the manufacturing efficiency of average workers. This was similar to what Frederick Taylor did in the early 1900s in the United States when he objectively measured the actions necessary for each work task. In reality, until the production of a garment order was finished, it was impossible for a garment factory to make an accurate and fair determination on the piecework price for a procedure due to the nature of the fashion business. This was because the quantity of most of the garment orders was relatively small (which was uneconomical to measure accurately), the short production lead-time of garment manufacturers offered no time for accurate measurement, and non-standard products for each fashion season had too many different styles, which were too difficult to measure reliably.

Therefore, it was a general practice for garment factories in Hong Kong and Shenzhen to decide the piecework price after the completion of an order. Usually at the end of the month, when workers received their salary, they knew the exact price of the piecework for a particular order they had finished.

Though it was difficult to know the exact price of piecework for an order before production, both management and workers, owing to past experience, would have a rough idea of the range for the prices before they began. Thus, how to divide the slim CMT fee of a garment among them was a prime focus of workers and owners, and each side tried to get a larger share because a few cents difference on a piecework price would make a big difference, both to owners and workers.

Because of the norm of "work first; pay later" in this trade, disputes over piecework prices between workers and factory owners happened quite often. Workers always believed management would take advantage of them by lowering the price of their piecework if they worked too fast since no owner was willing to pay more to workers than their market salary.

Yet, the piecework system still did not necessarily favor the factory owners. Workers knew they might offer more work for less pay if they worked too fast. They were too smart to be cheated. Sometimes the workers deliberately and collectively slowed their working pace in order to get management to increase the piecework price because of their low productivity. Therefore, factory owners often found themselves in the dilemma of either being late for sea shipment, which led to an expensive airfreight fee, or paying more to workers by increasing the price of piecework.

Severe Punishment Policy of Quality Assurance System

Stern punishment policies prevailed in Shenzhen to control for quality problems arising from the process of garment manufacture. Because the income of the workers mainly came from piecework, to increase their income, they had to work longer hours at a faster pace. But increases in production efficiency could, to some extent, decrease quality because it tended to increase the occurrence of errors. So, to assure the quality of the garments, factories in Shenzhen adopted severe punishment systems (such as deduction of a worker's own salary) to compensate for the damage induced by the worker. This policy played a crucial role in assuring quality, on-time delivery and low waste rates.

To avoid punishment for errors, workers usually tried to cover their mistakes and avoid responsibility. Whenever a mistake was discovered, the parties involved blamed each other. When the workers were caught, the factory could then deduct the wages to compensate the loss to the company.

Quality problems could not always be easily traced to the responsible parties. In fact, the management of a factory usually caused more mistakes due to mismanagement. Workers, owing to the piecework salary system, had no way of receiving compensation for the loss of their working time due to management mistakes. That was one of the major reasons the job satisfaction among garment workers was among the lowest and turnover rate the highest of all industries in Shenzhen.

What Can Mr. Lou Do to Motivate His Workers to Work Faster?

Mr. Lou's factory was a typical Shenzhen garment factory. He had the same agonizing experiences in managing workers as others in the industry. As he listened painfully to the slow pace of the sewing machines, Mr. Lou knew that he would be responsible for a US$15,000 air freight cost to this customer because there was no way for his factory to catch up to meet tomorrow's deadline for this order. What a waste! US$15,000 was one-fifth of his total profit last year. Mr. Lou had to do something to change the deliberate slowing down of his workers. Otherwise he would have to consider selling the factory and changing to another profession. What could he do about this?

Textron Ltd.

Lawrence A. Beer

Introduction

Gary Case, executive vice-president of Textron Ltd., sat at his desk and slowly drew a circle around the words *ethics* and *social responsibility*. Above the circle he wrote in bold letters the phrase "public opinion," and sat back to ponder his symbolic illustration of a potential problem that only he seemed to envision.

Case was thinking ahead and letting his mind focus on an issue that seemed out of the realm of the tenets of basic managerial principles that his undergraduate and MBA studies had prepared him for during his scholastic years. While he well appreciated the strategic decision-making concepts of running a transnational business, he felt himself personally wondering how to approach the complex subject of applying global ethics and social responsibility to an international venture that was being pushed on his company.

Background

Textron Ltd. was a 65-year-old, family-held business based in Youngstown, Ohio. As a producer of cotton and sponge fabricated items for the beauty trade, selling to intermediate users as components in their make-up compact cases as well as direct to the retail trade for onward sale to consumers, the company was under constant attack from Far Eastern manufacturers. The need to enter into some type of offshore manufacturing enterprise was now evident in order to maintain a cost competitive position for the firm to continue to prosper and grow.

As a maker of cotton puffs for the application of make-up cosmetics, the company had grown from a loft in Brooklyn, New York, back in the mid-1930s to a medium-sized enterprise with sales of $25 million and pre-tax earnings of $1 million plus. In the category of cosmetic applicators, Textron's fine reputation had been built on years of excellent service to the trade with attention to detail. Using at first the hand sewing abilities of seamstresses from the garment centres of lower Manhattan, the company had been a pioneer in developing customized machinery to produce quality cotton puffs to the precise custom requirements of modern cosmetic manufacturers. Today, 100 per cent virgin cotton rolls would enter Textron's factory at one end and exit as soft velour pads in numerous shapes, contoured sizes and colors at the other end of the process.

These puffs would be either sewn or glued with ribbon bands and satin coverings bearing the well-known brand names of the major franchised cosmetics companies of the world from Revlon, Estee Lauder, Maybelline and Max Factor as well as numerous others. They might also contain the names of retail store house brands or the internationally recognized trademarks of their own company. Currently, a new collection had been created through a licensing arrangement bearing the name of a highly respected fashion beauty magazine, whose instant recognition with the teenage trade was propelling the company to new sales levels. While historically Textron Ltd. primarily had produced components, supplying cosmetic companies with custom applicators tailored to their cosmetic ingredient requirements, the growth of its retail business in this sub-category was developing at a rapid pace. Major drug store chains, supermarkets and specialty shops featured Textron brands and their lines were becoming synonymous with the best in cosmetic applicators and assorted beauty accessories. With the launch of an additional range under the guise of a high fashion authority, featuring highly stylized "cool shapes" and "hot colors" designed to entice younger adolescent buyers, their reputation was achieving enhanced public notice. Such products using uniquely descriptive trendy phrases evoked an image of "hip to use applicators" and a whole new generation of teenage users was being developed.

The firm also was a key purveyor to the entertainment industry directly servicing the Hollywood movie and TV production companies, Broadway and the theatrical community, along with indirect sales to professional make-up artists and modeling studios thanks to the quickly developing beauty store trade. All in all, the future for Textron Ltd. was most promising.

Gary Case, a college friend of the company's president and principal owner, was brought into the business because of his experience at the retail sales and marketing level. The chief executive officer, who possessed an engineering background was more than capable of overseeing the manufacturing side of the business; however, the strong movement of the organization into direct consumer goods, coupled with the overall expansion of the company, necessitated Case's hiring.

As the company began to prosper in the early 1970s, other stateside competitors emerged, but none could match the quality and inherent reputation of Textron Ltd. Their attention to detail and expertise of their original equipment manufacturer (OEM) sales staff servicing the franchise cosmetic companies gave Textron a competitive edge. They were called upon to work closely with their industrial customers to develop cotton puffs that matched the trends in new cosmetic ingredients and application methods at the research and development (R&D) stage of such developments. Such progressive fashion-oriented but facially skin-sensitive cosmetic formulas required applicators that matched the demanding specifications of these new advances in the cosmetic field. Cotton materials were needed to sustain the look on the skin and provide the user with the same result that the cosmetic cream, lotion or powder promised. While women, the prime purchasers of such products, wanted to obtain the dramatic results the franchise cosmetic companies advertised, professional make-up artists had long known that the choice of applicators to transfer the pressed powder in the compact, the lotion in the bottle or the cream in the jar, was the key to the process. The right puff was therefore needed to complement the make-up process.

In the late 1980s, Far Eastern manufactures of cosmetic applicators began to emerge, offering cheaper versions of such items. While the detailed processing of the raw cotton material used in such production was inferior to the quality and exacting details of those manufactured by Textron Ltd., the cost considerations necessitated a strong consideration of their offerings by the company's clients. As textile manufacturing began to develop in the Indochina region and more and more American firms brought their expertise to the area, the overall quality of goods as well as the base materials used began to improve. As an outgrowth of improvements in the generic textile business

emerged, better methods of production, selection of raw materials and attention to quality filtered down into the cosmetic cotton applicator category.

Case, along with the president of the company, David Grange, and the head of product development group, Nancy Adams, had made periodic trips to the Hong Kong Beauty Exhibition to constantly gauge Far Eastern competitors. For many years, they observed a display of poor offerings and found themselves returning from such trips confident that the threat of offshore competition was not yet emerging as a viable alternative for their clients. Their regular customers, both beauty companies and retailing organizations, were rarely evident at such conventions and hence their positive feelings were continuously strengthened.

Current Issues

Over the last few years, however, it became evident that startup companies, beginning as derivative plants of the large textile manufacturers throughout China, Taiwan, Korea and Thailand, could become a real danger to their ever-growing global business. While many of these enterprises still produced inferior merchandise, Textron noticed that a number of their American competitors were now forming alliances with such organizations. These associations brought with them the knowledge of how to deal with the beauty industry both in America and Europe, instilling in them a deep appreciation for quality and endurance of raw materials to work with the new cosmetic preparations. Once such considerations took a foot-hold and a reputation for delivering such competitively detailed quality merchandise with vastly lower costs was discovered by Textron's clients, the company could be in for some rough times ahead. During the last visit to the Hong Kong show, Grange had bumped into a number of his key franchise cosmetic component buyers as well as a few of his retail chain merchandise managers. They had all acknowledged the quality advances made by these emerging new players. It was felt however that the distance of such suppliers from their own factories and key decision-making staffs and the fact that the shapes and designs were still not up to the innovative expertise of the Textron company created a hesitation among clients wanting to deal with them. Grange knew full well however that with advanced global communication technology and the alliances with American-based representative organizations, the gap would be closed shortly. If such alterations were made and a fully competitive quality product could be offered with the inherent deep labor and overhead cost advantages that Far Eastern firms possessed, Textron was due for some major sales competition in the future.

After their last trip to the Asian convention in September of 1999, Grange and Case spent the hours on the return trip discussing strategic alternatives for the company in the years ahead. This wasn't the first time such matters were approached and, in fact, two years earlier, the company entered into an alliance with a United Kingdom manufacturer for the production on a joint basis of cosmetic sponges. Grange had always been reluctant to place his production facilities out of his geographical everyday domain. He was a "hands on" entrepreneur who felt strongly that all facets of one's business should be at arm's reach. Grange was deeply committed to his people and his door was always open to everyone in his organization. He was involved in every area of the business and it was not until Case joined Textron that Grange began to relinquish control over selective daily operations. This desire to closely preside over and monitor his people was born out of a heritage of family involvement as exemplified by his father. His dad had instilled in Grange a great empathy for workers and staff, and even today the company's culture still carried such roots of benevolent carrying.

When the firm had moved from the greater New York area to Youngstown, key personnel were given liberal incentives to move to the new location, and great care was given to those who could not make the journey. Still today, the company showed great pride in its relationship with employees. Textron's human resources department was not merely a conduit for processing applications for employment and overseeing payroll but a large fully functional multitalented group that ran off-site improvement seminars and cross training exercises. Besides offering a full array of benefit packages, the company had a well-supervised child-care facility on the premises at no charge to employees. The human resources director attended all managerial meetings, thereby maintaining a strong presence in all company decision-making and the position was considered on par with senior management executives. The commitment to maintaining hands-on control of his organization and the strong, caring relationship with his people made for a close-knit family and a kind of patriarchal role for Grange. He prided himself on the fact that union attempts to organize his factory labor force never got off the ground, as his employees felt that they were best represented by Grange himself.

Years ago, a satellite retail packaging assembly plant and distribution facility in San Antonio, Texas, which had been part of the purchase of a small professional beauty applicator business, was dissolved in favor of consolidating all operations in Youngstown. All personnel at this redundant factory were given an opportunity to relocate in Youngstown or they received good termination benefits.

The United Kingdom alliance was finalized due to Grange's long and valued friendship with the principal of that company. The two also shared similar feelings about managing people and a common cultural background. Both parties had spent many years working together and enjoyed a special relationship, which had been fostered by the fact that the U.K. managing director's family resided in Ohio, thereby bringing the two executives together on a monthly basis as the Englishman came home often. Grange also visited the British facility every two months and the two executives spoke weekly on the phone. Both men viewed the alliance as more of a partnership than an arm's length sourcing arrangement.

Grange always felt that one of his prime differentiated product marketing characteristics was that up until the U.K. association for sponge material applicators, all his products were made in the United States. He believed that such designation symbolized quality of material and manufacturing excellence as well as innovative styling and technologically advanced, state-of-the-art compliance. Even with the English sponge production unit, all the cotton puff applicators were still made in the States. To drive home this important selling issue, all packages of retail cotton finished goods bore the American flag proudly stamped on them next to the words "Made in the U.S.A." Grange had recently seen consumer products bearing the slogan "Designed in America" as well as "Product Imported From China and Packaged in the U.S.A." but felt that the global customer still valued the U.S.A. slogan indicating the country of origin on his retail line. But in Grange's recent discussions with component buyers in the cosmetic and fragrance industry, such designation did not seem so important, given the fact that both the sponges and cotton puffs were slightly undistinguishable or hidden parts in the total presentation of the makeup compact, the accent being on the brand name, ingredients and plastic case; imported items could be utilized if quality was maintained. The recent acceptance of the sponges made in England by Textron's clients gave credence to the fact that quality, price and service were the prime criteria for the industry, rather than the country of origin.

Decision-Making Time

Following the conference on the plane ride home from the Orient, Grange and Case had assembled their managerial staff and charged them with putting together a preliminary plan to form an association with a Far Eastern manufacturer of cotton puffs. At the initial briefing meeting, samples of cotton puff merchandise collected from a variety of Far Eastern producers were evaluated by the manufacturing quality control people as well as by representatives of the marketing and sales groups from the retail and OEM divisions. The immediate consensus was that with a little direction in fashion styling composition and adjustment in

fixative dyes to sustain color in the cotton velour, a quality comparative range to supplement their domestic manufacturing output could be produced abroad. When Case presented the factory cost quotations for the samples being reviewed, the vice-president of finance exclaimed, "Such values were way below our own manufacturing standard costs before administrative overhead." He further added that "even with anticipated duty and freight via containerized shipments, the projected landed price at our door would eclipse our costs by a good 20 per cent or more reduction." When Case noted that "These foreign price quotations were based on minimum quantities and could be subject to economies of scale discounting," all participants quickly realized that their projected stock keeping unit (SKU) sales for 2000 would easily allow for even greater margins.

When the meeting broke up, Chris Jenkins, the vice-president of finance, cornered Grange and Case in the hallway.

> Guys, if these numbers can be confirmed, and if future production of these Chinese puffs can be modified to accommodate our quality stability color standards and slightly altered for design modification, we need to jump on this as soon as possible. Better still, if we can manufacture over there ourselves via our own factory or through a joint venture, our profit potential would be magnified at least three times.

Alternative Proposals

It was now six months since that initial meeting. In the interim, Case had been back and forth a number of times, holding substantial discussions with what was now a short list of two potential alliance candidates, both of which were co-operative ventures, with local Chinese governmental bodies holding a share in them. While these companies' abilities to alter their production to accommodate changes in the color additive process and make design modifications were verified, and the exchange of cost quotations was proceeding well, Case had not yet proposed the final type of alliance he wanted.

In the back of his mind, Case wanted to form his own subsidiary but felt that such initial market entry strategy was both costly and risky, given the large investment required. Besides Case and Grange, the company did not have any other executives familiar with managing abroad. Given such considerations, Case's discussions to date with his Chinese associates had produced only two feasible alternatives to begin the relationship:

(1) An initial three-year guaranteed outsourcing purchase agreement wherein, following the detailed specifications of Textron Ltd., supplies of cotton powder puffs would be produced at base prices. Such quotations would be subject to preset quantity discounting

but offset slightly by an inflationary yearly adjustment. The right to pre-approve the samples of each and every shipment before departure would also be included in the arrangement. In essence a simplistic arm's-length purchasing association was contemplated.

(2) The creation of a joint venture wherein Textron Ltd. would own 48 per cent of the company and the alliance partner would own the rest. Textron would be primarily responsible for sales and marketing worldwide along with periodic on-site technical assistance as to product design, quality assurances and engineering considerations by their technical staff. The plant facility, the manufacturing process itself and everyday operations would be under the direct control of the Chinese partner. Textron Ltd. would contribute a yet-to-be-finalized small dollar investment to help upgrade machinery and in general modernize the physical facilities. The partners would share the revenue generated by the sales efforts of Textron for the items produced in the plant.

Although exacting details of either proposed strategy needed to be worked out, with the former option requiring more legal and regulatory considerations, Case was confident that both situations could be accomplished. With the additional help of some local Chinese alliance specialists whom Case had utilized during the days when he had actually lived and worked in Hong Kong for a former employer, all seemed to be progressing nicely. Case knew he had to give additional thought to many other operational and administrative issues, and he wanted to obtain some sound advice from his internal teams before deciding which alternative to pursue. Questions as to the capital investment and how such funds would be utilized would require more discussions with the potential partners if the joint-venture route was chosen, but such issues would be addressed during Case's next trip to the Far East.

China as the Prime Choice of Supply

The focus on China was due mainly to Case's familiarity with the people and business environment. He felt very comfortable, given his prior experiences in the region and his knowledgeable appreciation of the culture and the way relationships were constructed. Beyond Case's personal considerations, the Chinese manufacturers he had encountered already had the necessary machinery and were well versed in the production of cotton puffs. Many already supplied the worldwide beauty trade, but did not possess the sophisticated marketing and sales competencies practised by Textron, nor had they

gained the reputation Textron historically enjoyed with the franchise cosmetic industry. An alliance with Textron would enhance the Chinese manufacturers' technical abilities and provide them with a wider entrée to the trade. The annual beauty show in Hong Kong attracted a global following, which would allow Textron to even create an offshore sales office and showroom close to the prime production facility to entertain prospective clients. Besides the Chinese connection, Case had opened initial discussion with makers of sponge applicators and other beauty accessories in Japan and Korea so that his trips to China could be combined with other business opportunities he wanted to pursue in the Far East.

Case had entertained pursuing a Mexican manufacturer, as he had had prior dealings with companies producing a variety of cotton products in Mexico. Given the background of many of them in the cotton and aligned textile trade, this seemed a natural consideration, especially given the NAFTA accords and geographical proximity to Textron's major market, the United States. All potential companies Case visited, however, were located in the central part of the country, none near the border where the *Maquiladoras* were available. Case's Mexican contacts were not familiar with the specific production of cotton puff applicators as their cotton experience was in the manufacturing of surgical dressings, bandages, feminine hygiene pads and simple cotton balls. They would need to buy machinery and train a staff in such manufacturing operations. If Textron would fund such investment and provide technical assistance, a number of them agreed to manage such a facility on the U.S.-Mexican border through a joint venture. Case was hesitant to provide the funding, and he was worried that starting up a new plant would not let Textron achieve the inherent historical benefits that the more mature existing production in China would instantly allow.

Besides the economic considerations, Case found the Mexican manager's attitude a bit troublesome. Textron had once used a Mexican plant to supply, in final packaged form, cotton pads for the removal of facial cosmetic make-up. While his dealings with the principals of this family owned and operated business were most cordial and personally gratifying, Case had found that their attention to manufacturing details left much to be desired. The quality inspection of the raw cotton coming into their plants had given Case cause for concern. Many openly told him they mixed first quality fibres with "seconds" and remnants from the textile manufacturers in their local areas to achieve cost efficient production. As Textron always claimed its materials for cotton puff applicators were of "100 per cent virgin cotton," such an assertion might be difficult to enforce and supervise, given the pronouncements by his prior supplier. When

discussions as to the importance of schedules to insure timely supply arose, the Mexican sources seemed to give the impression that they would do their best to comply. This slight hesitation bothered Case, as his component buyers demanded on-time delivery and were always changing specifications at the last minute.

Case had deep reservations on the business competencies exhibited by such Mexican firms, as his communications with them in the past, wherein days would go by before he heard from them, had left a poor impression on him. Many times, when he had repetitively inquired by e-mail, fax and telephone as to shipping dates for packaged finished products, he was eventually told that third-party suppliers of the packaging materials for the cotton pads caused the assembly delay. Inquiring further, during a visit with his Mexican supplier, Case learned that when local Mexican firms contract with each other, time promises are flexible and it seemed that an attitude of "when they are available, we get them" took precedence over definite schedules. During the year the company utilized the Mexican supplier, not one shipment was dispatched within the required period, and Case had given up contacting them, even paraphrasing the Mexican explanation when queried by his own inventory/warehouse manager.

The decision to go with a Chinese partner in some format seemed to be the best solution.

Case's Personal Reflections

As Case pondered what other matters needed to be resolved, his mind began to focus on his three-year posting, back in the early 1990s in Hong Kong, with an electronics manufacturer to oversee their Chinese network of suppliers. When Case and his family had first arrived in the then-British colony, the excitement of this new foreign land and its unique culture had made a lasting impression on him. He had marveled at the sights, sounds, smells and overall ambience of the city state that mixed East and West. Coming from a middle class American lifestyle, the treatment the family received was like being transformed into a rich conclave of the elite. His children went to a specialized English-type boarding school and rarely mixed with local natives of their own age. In fact, such young Chinese children were lucky to get a basic elementary school education before being forced out into the real world and into the working community. The outskirts of the city, and even sections within, contained deep pockets that were below some extreme poverty levels Case had seen in other depressed regions of the world. Within a severely overpopulated area that was strained every day with new immigrants from the mainland, the concept of work, any job, took on a new meaning. People would work for what seemed like slave wages to Case, and he wondered how they survived, just attaining a mere sustenance level.

His wife could afford household maids and cooks that were more like indentured servants than domestic employees. They worked long hours at meagre wages and never complained.

During Case's visits to plants in mainland China, both during his expatriate posting years and subsequent trips back in the mid-1990s, the conditions at such facilities had initially deeply disturbed him. The environments he witnessed were nothing like he had ever seen in the United States. Factories were like prison compounds. The laborers seemed to toil at their job stations never looking up, never smiling and always looked like they were staring out with blank facial expressions. Rarely had Case seen them take a break, with many workers eating lunch at their desks and at their worktables or machinery. He seldom witnessed the laborers even taking bathroom breaks. The air in the facilities was always stale with no ventilation except for a few fans, and it was always very hot or very cold, depending on the outside temperature. He witnessed children, younger it seemed that his two adolescent kids, toiling in the plants alongside the elderly. He watched infants placed alongside their mothers on the floor of the factories being rocked by feet as the mothers' hands moved on the table above them. As these visits become more frequent, Case's disdain for such initially horrific working conditions began to lessen and he began to accept what he saw.

Many times, in social conversations with other executives and managers, Case had voiced his concerns about the treatment of the workers. He listened as they tried to get him to understand and appreciate that while the conditions were terrible, the alternative might be even worse. With the expanded population, growing at a massive rate, the supply of people outstripped employment opportunities. In order to survive, people would take any job and children as well as the elderly all had to work. Public governmental assistance was not only inadequate but almost impossible to administer, even if the resources could be found. The old communist philosophy of all society working for the good of the common proletariat, and hence the state, had been indoctrinated with the birth of the Mao regime; people saw it as their duty and obligation to endure hard times.

Case's Chinese friends had often remarked that if China were to catch up to the Western capitalistic nations and be a participant in the world's expanded trading economies, its people were its greatest competitive asset. In order to be a member in the world community and to provide enrichment for future generations, sacrifices had to be made. Capital for the improvement of factory environmental conditions was secondary to the need to update basic machinery and gain technology. The government had to build a sound internal infrastructure of roadways, rail and port facilities to ship its goods before the physical welfare of its people could be considered. With power still a scarce commodity, any electricity flowing into a factory needed to be first used to run the machinery and not for hot or cool air to be produced. The only way to achieve the goal of making mainland China competitive with the rest of the world was through the exportation route which was founded in the country's ability to produce cheaper goods than the rest of the globe. This simple fact necessitated low labor and overhead operating costs that contributed to poor working conditions in the factories.

Obviously, Case understood this economic argument was the main reason his company—and therefore he himself—had come to the region. In order for his own organization to remain competitive in the cotton puff business both at home and abroad, it would have no choice but to locate a portion of its operations in China or some other emerging nation.

Case had seen the TV footage of the protesters at the 2000 WTO conference in Seattle who had destroyed that meeting and in later months had done the same in Washington, D.C., and Ottawa, Canada. He heard them voicing and physically demonstrating their deep concerns against governments and transnational companies as to worker rights and environmental conditions in emerging and developing nations. Case was well aware of the attention the press gave to large multinational companies like Levi Strauss, Reebok and others over their treatment of employees accusing them of almost slavelike practices in their foreign factories. Even personalities that lent their names to the labels of garments, like Kathy Lee Gifford, had come under strong pressure for allowing their third party licensees in the United States to operate sweat shops and mistreat workers. Companies that did not even have a direct relationship wherein they exercised straight control over employee conditions were still questioned about the suppliers they used abroad as the social conscience of the world seemed to be focused on these issues.

Although Case himself deplored the hiring of adolescent children, he understood the economic and social context that existed in China for their use. China wasn't America. Young kids grew up much faster and much more was expected of them as contributors to the family unit. Even with the government mandate, made within the framework of the message of a collective good of the nation for families to have only one child, did not alleviate the problem. In fact, in many families it just made the burden deeper. Most Chinese families were made up of extended relatives who grouped together to pool their resources for their common survival. In these family units, all members had to work. The simple luxury of going to a public school, playing games and watching TV, as American children enjoyed, was not part of their world. In numerous families, children, mostly young girls, were sent away from their rural villages to emerging urban industrial centres to look for work. After paying large portions of their meagre weekly salaries back to their employers for dormitory housing and food within the confines of the factory compound, any amount left over was sent to the family.

Even the elderly felt such pressure to work, as retirement after years of service and a reasonable pension was almost a non-existent consideration. No true governmental program like social security existed, and the family had to care for the elderly in their homes, putting a great burden on the whole extended unit. Political dissidents and even criminals were conscripted into the labor force to help offset the cost of the State having to provide for them. Plant conditions, treatment of workers and even caring about the environment were not primary issues for an emerging country trying to first find work for its population during the transformation process into a competitive world economic nation.

Case pondered if it was time for the company to prepare a written corporate moral compass. Should it publish a code of ethics, as many transnational firms had been doing? What should it consist of, what specific criteria defining norms of behavior should be stated? and should it be incorporated as an obligation in the arm's length purchasing agreement being considered with the Chinese supplier? If the announced provisions were violated, should this be viewed as an automatic right for Textron to terminate the agreement, or should there be a time frame in which to cure such conditions? Case also wondered how his firm could monitor such matters to ensure compliance. If the alternative joint venture were chosen, how should such values be incorporated into the partnership agreement and how should Case process such matters during the negotiation?

Case was comfortable with discussions on costs, quality and delivery specifications as they had a finite measurable logic to them. Social responsibility and ethics touched upon many emotional areas that were harder to define. He had seen firsthand how different cultures approached them from divergent viewpoints, and he had gained a respect for the saying "when in Rome do as the Romans do." He also, however, maintained the feeling that there were core human values that at times transcended such local traditions and social context.

Moral Dilemmas—
Unanswered Questions

What worried Case was even if the business decision were the right one, could the company be entering a relationship that might some day backfire? If a factory that Textron bought merchandise from or, because of the joint venture, was more deeply involved in was alleged to be mistreating employees, would public opinion injure the company's reputation? Was the focus of the world now on China and its historic practices of human rights abuse? Would someone be watching companies more closely that associated themselves with Chinese partners in any form?

What if Textron's buyers of components, the franchised cosmetic houses, were themselves chastised for using slave-type labor in the supplies used in their own manufacturing of their brand named products? Would they in turn cease to buy from Textron Ltd.? What if consumers of the retail packaged lines decided to boycott the products for similar reasons? What if the licensor of the new collection felt that such foreign sourcing of items bearing their trademark was injurious to their image and reputation, and they objected?

Given his company's strong traditional organizational culture of placing employees first, Case also wondered what effect any such ethical and social responsibility issues stemming from a Chinese association could have on his own domestic operational employees.

He wondered about such matters again as he thought to himself that going global was more than just an exercise in financial, legal and operational logistical decision making; it involved taking a moral position in Textron's commercial relationships with overseas entities.

Bayer CropScience in India (A): Against Child Labour

Charles Dhanaraj

Oana Branzei

Satyajeet Subramanian

January 27, 2007 was not business as usual for many Bayer executives converging in Hyderabad, India. Michael Schneider, manager Corporate Social Responsibility at Bayer CropScience, located in Germany, along with Suhas R. Joshi, head of Strategy at Bayer BioScience Pvt. Ltd., India, had to recommend an approach on how best to tackle the issue of child labor in the company's contracted cotton seed production in India. Several non-governmental organizations (NGOs) had lodged complaints against Bayer at various public forums in India and Europe, citing the company for sanctioning the use of child labor. Though the company took immediate action after becoming aware of the situation in early 2003, from 2003 to 2006 the issue had escalated, including complaints to Organization for Economic Co-operation and Development (OECD) and media campaigns. Bayer had co-founded an industry-level group, but collective action had not been effective. Bayer had also taken independent action, and several strategies were

showing promise. In this dilemma, Bayer had to decide whether to stick with other multinationals sharing the blame or to move ahead on its own. The Hyderabad meeting brought together senior executives from the Germany-based corporate headquarters of Bayer CropScience, executives in charge of the seed business from its France-based BioScience group, and representatives from its Mumbai-based India headquarters to weigh in on this decision (see Exhibit 1).

Bayer had been operating in India for more than a century[1] and worked on crop protection since 1958, when it established Bayer Agrochem Pvt. Ltd. In 1963, the company was renamed to Bayer India Ltd. However, it has only been involved in the fast-growing agriculture seed industry for about four years. In December 2002, the Bayer Group completed the acquisition of Aventis CropScience SA. This acquisition brought onboard a well-known Indian company, Proagro Seed Pvt. Ltd., which had operations in amongst others

---

[1]Bayer in India, http://www.bayergroupindia.com/bayerin_india.html, accessed April 1, 2010.

the cotton seed industry. Child labor was widespread in the cotton seed industry and taken for granted by Indian farmers. However, it caught Bayer CropScience unaware. They learned about the incidence and prevalence of child labor in its newly acquired India-based cotton seed operations during the few months post acquisition. They took immediate steps to raise awareness that Bayer does not tolerate child labor with the farmers starting in April 2003. In the following years, Bayer worked collaboratively with a few other multinational companies, the seed industry association and a group of activist NGOs to eliminate child labor within its sphere of influence.

Bayer's stance against child labor had been, and remained, unequivocal. The company had a long tradition of corporate social responsibility. Bayer had been actively involved in and triggered several societal and environmental programs since its inception. One of its decisive strategic steps toward sustainability took place in 1988[2] when the group adopted the "Ecological Evaluation of New Investments," a procedure that promoted responsible investments. By July 1999, the company had introduced several guidelines concerning legal compliance and corporate responsibility. Among these, a supplier code of conduct required all its suppliers to adhere to ethical principles.[3] In 2000, Bayer became one of the founding members of the United Nations Global Compact, one of the world's largest corporate citizenship and sustainability initiatives.[4] In 2005, the company published a Sustainable Development Policy[5] and was reporting annually on its sustainability initiatives.[6] A year later, the company released a Human Rights Position.[7]

Many in India still considered child labor as a necessary evil that enabled survival in poor and rural communities, rather than a business issue. The

[2]*Bayer, Sustainable Development Report 2001—Production, Development pointing the way forward,* http://www.sd2001.bayer.com/produktion/umweltministerium_en.html, accessed April 1, 2010.

[3]*Procurement-Supplier Code of Conduct,* http://www.beschaffung.bayer.com/procmt/byc_cpstd_en.nsf/LPSNavigationLUByContentID/HWER-7B5BZZ?OpenDocument&nav=nav65225316, accessed April 1, 2010.

[4]United Nations Global Compact, "Participants & Stakeholders: Participant Information," www.unglobalcompact.org/participant/1212-Bayer-AG, accessed April 1, 2010.

[5]*Bayer, Bayer Sustainable Development Report 2005, Sustainable Development Policy,* http://www.sd2005.bayer.com/en/Sustainable_Developement_Policy.aspx, accessed April 1, 2010.

[6]http://www.sustainability2007.bayer.com/en/homepage.aspx, accessed June 17, 2010.

[7]*Bayer, Bayer Sustainable Development Report 2006—Bayer Human Rights Position,* http://www.sustainability2006.bayer.com/en/human-rights.aspx, accessed April 1, 2010.

vast majority of Bayer's local competitors in cotton seed production (roughly 90 per cent of the market) considered child labor business as usual. However, Bayer had a zero-tolerance policy for child labor. Consequently for the company having identified the issue in its supply chain, two options are arising: Start actions to minimize child labor or consider to exit the business. Concerning the cotton seed production, the situation was as such that Bayer had been working with the farmers for several years to implement a full scale comprehensive system of penalties and incentives as part of a collaborative industry approach. In January 2007, Schneider and Joshi had to recommend for decision making whether to opt out or continue with this collaborative industry association initiative as before. On the one hand, the project had shown some encouraging results where many other options had failed. On the other hand, child labor was a pervasive and deep-rooted problem within rural communities in India. Even if something could be done, many of those from the company involved in the collaborative industry approach questioned whether Bayer should be the one taking action. The Indian government or non-governmental organizations seemed much better suited for the task. Some executives questioned

why Bayer would go to such an extent to support a business that, from the perspective of its shareholders, was not of any significant volume, market share or profit—yet posed significant reputation risks. For these critics, a more financially sensible approach could be to simply exit the cotton seed business altogether and put the whole issue behind Bayer.

Bayer: Science for a Better Life

Friedrich Bayer and Johann Friedrich Weskott founded Bayer in 1863 in Barmen, Germany. The company initially manufactured and sold synthetic dyes for the textile industry and later diversified into pharmaceuticals. From its inception, Bayer had emphasized scientific research, a commitment that had led to the development of several leading products, including Aspirin, launched in 1899, now considered the "drug of the century." By the early 1900s, Bayer had developed into a multinational company with operations in the United Kingdom, the United States, Russia, France and Belgium. More than 80 per cent of its revenues came from exports.[8]

After the Second World War, the company established its business activities globally. Over the years, the company expanded around the world through a

---

[8]History: *Becoming an international company (1881–1914)* http://www.bayer.com/en/1881-1914 .asp, accessed April 1, 2010.

combination of acquisitions and organic growth. On December 6, 2001, the company's management announced plans to establish independent operating subsidiaries under the umbrella of a management holding company. Along with the holding company, three subgroups were created: Bayer HealthCare AG, Bayer CropScience AG and Bayer MaterialScience AG. To support business activities, three service companies were also launched: Bayer Business Services, Bayer Technology Services and Currenta, a joint venture of Bayer and its spun-off chemical business, LANXESS. The reorganization into a holding company was finalized in 2003[9] (see Exhibit 2).

In 2001, Bayer acquired Aventis CropScience SA, for €7.25 billion, making it a world leader in crop protection. By 2006, the Bayer group operated in 120 countries, had a global workforce of 106,000 employees and net sales of €28,956 million.[10,11] Globally, Bayer ranked 10th[12] in the chemical industry. The year 2006 also marked the acquisition of Schering AG for approximately €17 billion, which made the new Bayer Schering Pharma AG one of the world's leading suppliers of specialty pharmaceuticals.[13]

Bayer's corporate mission statement[14] underscored its commitment to shape the future by generating innovations that benefit humankind and emphasized new products emerging from the company's active substance research (e.g., in the health care business, the growth markets of Asia and new areas such as biotechnology and nanotechnology). The corporate mission statement also contained an ethical code of conduct, which was binding for all its employees. The company professed five core values, all five emphasizing strong personal commitment:

1. **A will to succeed** by a personal commitment to goals; to win by adhering to a standard of excellence; to pursue goal achievement with energy, drive, and

[9]*Bayer-1996-2009, Highlights in the recent history of the Bayer Group,* http://www.bayer.com/en/1996-2009.aspx, accessed August 25, 2010.

[10]*Bayer, Science for a Better Life: Bayer Annual Report 2006,* www.bayer.com/en/GB-2006-en.pdfx, Bayer Group Key Data, p. 53, accessed April 1, 2010.

[11]In 2006, 1€ equivalent to $1.26 approximately, http://www.x-rates.com/d/USD/EUR/hist2006 .html, accessed June 14, 2010.

[12]Patricia L. Short, "Global Top 50," Chemical & Engineering News, July 23, 2007, pp. 13–16, http://pubs.acs.org/cen/coverstory/85/8530cover.html, last accessed on May 25, 2010.

[13]*Bayer, Science for a Better Life: Bayer Annual Report 2006,* www.bayer.com/en/GB-2006-en.pdfx, Chairman's Letter, p. 4, accessed April 10, 2010.

[14]*Bayer-Mission Statement* (published in July 2004), accessed April 10, 2010.

determination; to not give up, especially in the face of resistance or setbacks.

2. **A passion for stakeholders** (customers, employees, shareholders, suppliers and communities), promoting a personal commitment to deliver value for all the stakeholders; striving for mutual understanding; and balancing the interests of the stakeholders.

3. **Integrity, openness and honesty** encouraged employees to become role models for all the company values by accepting accountability for actions and results; being open to ideas of others; and complying with laws, regulations and good business practices.

4. **Respect for people and nature** spoke to valuing people and their different perspectives and cultures; ensuring a high level of health, safety and environmental protection; utilizing natural resources in a responsible way.

5. **Sustainability of actions** referred to acting in a way that balanced the economic, ecological, and social needs of current and future generations by reconciling short-term results with long-term requirements as well as contributing to the continued evolution of Bayer's unique identity.

Bayer CropScience

Headquartered in Monheim, Germany, Bayer CropScience was formed in October 2002,[15] driven by a belief that innovation in agriculture could help to overcome the growing pressure on food resources, exacerbated by the increase in global population, the shortage of arable land, and the growing affluence of consumers in emerging countries, which was boosting the demand for high-quality foods and animal protein. Bayer CropScience invested and does so today significantly in research and development to find solutions for agricultural challenges providing innovative products for crop protection as well as seeds and traits.

Bayer CropScience included three distinct business groups. Bayer Crop Protection, which marketed insecticides, herbicides and fungicides, was the company's largest revenue earner in 2006. Bayer BioScience marketed high-quality seeds, for both agricultural crops (e.g., rice, cotton and canola) and fruit and vegetable crops (e.g., watermelons, hot peppers and tomatoes). Bayer Environmental Science specialized in pest control products for a wide range of applications, including public health. Both Bayer Crop Protection and BioScience focused on the farming sector; Environmental Science did not (see Exhibit 3 for Bayer CropScience financial statements).

---

[15]http://www.bayercropscience.com/bcsweb/cropprotection.nsf/id/History, accessed April 10, 2010.

Bayer India

Bayer had a history of more than 100 years in the country, dating back to its first wholly owned subsidiary that had been set up in Mumbai in 1896. In 2006, the Bayer group in India had total sales of €149 million and a total workforce of 1,020 employees.[16]

Mirroring its three-pronged global structure, Bayer CropScience in India operated three business segments— Crop Protection, BioScience and Environmental Science—that offered a wide range of products and extensive service backup both for modern, sustainable agriculture and for non-agricultural applications. Its operations in India were focused on crop protection, seeds biotechnology and non-agricultural pest control; Bayer India also had seven production centers including facilities located in Thane, Himatnagar and Ankleshwar. The Mumbia-based headquarters also oversaw Bayer's activities in India's neighboring countries of Sri Lanka, Pakistan and Bangladesh.

Bayer India's Crop Protection business was the biggest revenue earner, with activities focused on five areas: herbicides, insecticides, fungicides, seed treatment and plant growth regulators. Its extensive, well-balanced portfolio of more than 50 high-performance products and an exciting pipeline,[17] continued to respond effectively to a wide range of market needs. By 2006, it had captured a good market position in India by offering holistic crop protection solutions for key crops (cotton, rice, pulses, oilseeds, chilies, tea, fruits and vegetables).

Bayer India's BioScience business division, headquartered in Hyderabad, focused on agricultural seeds and vegetable seeds. To cater to the specific needs of the Indian farmers, BioScience hybrid seeds offered a wide product range, including hybrid rice, cotton, pearl millet, corn and grain sorghum in addition to open pollinated (OP) research varieties of mustard. The BioScience division also specialized in vegetable seeds through its group company, Nunhems India Pvt. Ltd. Committed to delivering value for its customers, this company also followed Bayer CropScience's "seed to harvest" concept, which offered farmers a wide range of agricultural products. The "seed to harvest" concept combined

[16]*Bayer CropScience Limited, India, Annual Report 2006*, http://www.bayergroupindia.com/pdf/ Bayer%20Annual%20Report%202006.pdf, accessed April 10, 2010.

[17]According to Thomson Reuters, Bayer India's crop protection products brands include Confidor/ Admire, Calypso, Decis, Temik, Oberon, Antracol, Baycor, Folicur, Monceren, Atlantis, Basta, Topstar, Whip Super, Gaucho, Raxil, Bayfolan zinc, Ethrel and Planofix, http://www.alacrastore .com/company-snapshot/Bayer_CropScience_Limited-1063444, accessed June 17, 2010.

high quality seeds with crop protection products to deliver customized and comprehensive crop management for farmers.

Bayer India's Environmental Science (BES) was a leader in non-crop pest management and weed control. It was involved in diverse activities such as controlling rodents and roaches, combating the vectors of the deadly Malaria parasite, preventing termites from damaging homes, and protecting stored grains against pest attack.

Bayer India and the Cotton Seed Business

Bayer India entered the cotton seed business by acquisition factually in December 2002, when along with other Aventis-owned Indian companies, the Hyderabad-based company Proagro Seed Pvt. Ltd. was actually integrated in Bayer India's CropScience portfolio.

At first sight, hybrid seed production and marketing complemented well Bayer India's "seed to harvest" approach. But the activities involved in hybrid seed production stood in stark contrast to the centralized production of crop protection products—chemicals manufactured in large quantities in closely controlled conditions in only a handful of factories. Hybrid seed production was dispersed among thousands of small farms who had different needs across seeds and seasons. By 2006, Bayer India's CropScience had contracted nearly 30,000 farmers in the states of Andhra Pradesh, Karnataka and Tamil Nadu to supply rice, cotton, mustard, sunflower, vegetable and corn seeds. As many other companies working in seed production—Bayer India relied on "seed organizers," who selected the farmers, contracted with the farmers on behalf of the company and inspected the contracted farms to ensure that farmers followed the industry-prescribed agricultural practices (see Exhibit 4).

In India, cotton accounted for almost 50 per cent of the sales of the total seed industry for agricultural crops. With the introduction of Bt[18] cotton hybrid seed in 2002, the Indian government approved the commercial planting of its first genetically modified (GM) crop-insect-protected Bt Cotton hybrids developed by the U.S. company Monsanto and its Indian partner, Maharashtra Hybrid Company (Mahyco).[19]

---

[18]Bacillus thuringiensisor Bt was a naturally occurring soil bacterium that produced a toxin that farmers used to control Lepidopteran insects. Through genetic engineering, scientists had isolated the gene responsible for making the toxin and introduced it into a range of crops, including cotton.

[19]K.S. Jayaraman, "India Approves GM Cotton," Nature Biotechnology, May 2002, p. 415, www .nature.com/nbt/journal/v20/n5/full/nbt0502-415.html, accessed April 15, 2010.

By 2006, the Indian cotton seed market had grown to an estimated €140 million[20] and about 200 companies. Local companies such as Nuziveedu and Rasi each had approximately 25 per cent of the market share; many others had much smaller shares and were competing fiercely. Monsanto and Bayer accounted for barely 6 per cent of the production area for cotton seed. Several other multinational corporations such as Pioneer Hi-Bred (a Du Pont company) decided against entering the cotton seed market. Others were divesting. By mid-2006, Syngenta had divested all its cotton seed business globally:[21] Syngenta sold its global cotton seed business to the U.S. cotton seed company Delta and Pine Land. Monsanto acquired Delta and Pineland in 2007.[22]

Cotton seed production was a profitable venture for farmers. Each season, the average Bt cotton seed farmer would invest nearly Rs 56,000 (approximately $1,206) per acre[23] and achieved a 60 to 65 per cent profit margin.[24]

Production of hybrid cotton seed was labor-intensive, complex and time-consuming. Cotton seed farming required approximately 10 times more labor days than ordinary commercial cotton production. Hybrid cotton seed production required approximately 1,000 labor days per acre. Cross-pollination, a crucial stage in the farming process was done manually and continued for six months, constituting approximately 90 per cent of the total labor cost and 45 per cent of the total capital investment.[25] To help with the cross-pollination stage, farmers frequently contracted extra labor. Children were often preferred because their nimble fingers were useful in carrying out the emasculation and cross-pollination and their height matched the height of the cotton plant. Children were also more agile than adults and made fewer demands than adults.

Child Labor in India

According to various sources, the magnitude of child labor in India undoubtedly is vast:

- The 2001 Government of India national census report estimated

---

[20]Interview at BCS Headquarters, Monheim, Germany, April 8, 2010.

[21]"Director's Report: Syngenta India Ltd.," The Economic Times, http://economictimes.indiatimes.com/dirreport.cms?year=2006&companyID=3323, accessed April 15, 2010.

[22]http://www.agrow.com/multimedia/archive/00083/Agrow_583_83042a.pdf, accessed December 17, 2010.

[23]One acre is equal to approximately 4,050 square meters or 0.4 hectares.

[24]Interviews with company-contracted cotton seed farmers, used with permission.

[25]Ibid.

12.6 million[26] working children, out of the total 210 million children aged 5 to 14 years.

- Prof. Shanta Shina, as a chairperson of the Indian National Commission for Protection of Child Rights stated in 2007:

> According to the National Sample Survey estimates of 2004–05, there are around 5.6 million children working in agriculture. . . . Children working in agriculture sector constitute two third of all child labor force in India and their percentage in rural child labor force is more than 75 per cent.[27]

The state of Andhra Pradesh had one of the highest incidences of child labor, with 1.36 million children working in 2001.[28] The majority of child laborers were working on farms and plantations, often from sunup to sundown, planting and harvesting crops, spraying plant protection products and tending livestock on rural farms.[29]

In 2006, the International Labour Organization (ILO) reported that India had the largest number of working children in the world.[30] Child rights activists estimated that 20 per cent of India's economy was dependent on children under the age of 14.[31] Child labor in India was the result of a complex set of supply and demand factors, including parental poverty, illiteracy, unemployment, social and economic circumstances, lack of access to basic education and skills, and deeply ingrained cultural values.[32]

Growing pressure from national and international civil society and development agencies that decried the employment of children in apparel sweatshops had triggered regulatory responses. In October 2006, the Indian government introduced a new amendment to its

---

[26]ILO: *Child Labor Facts and Figures—An analysis of the Government of India National Census*, 2001, http://www.ilo.org/public/english/region/asro/newdelhi/ipec/responses/india/index.htm, accessed June 17, 2010.

[27]*Child Labor in Agriculture*, http://ncpcr.gov.in/Reports/Chairperson_Address_on_Child_Labour_in_Agriculture_at_ILO _Conference_on_12_June_2007_Delhi.pdf, accessed April 15, 2010.

[28]http://www.ncpcr.gov.in/Reports/Magnitude_of_Child_Labour_in_India_An_Analysis_of_Official_Sources_of_Data_Draft.pdf, accessed August 25, 2010.

[29]International Labour Organization, "International Programme on the Elimination of Child Labour: Agriculture," www.ilo.org/ipec/areas/Agriculture/lang--en/index.htm, accessed April 1, 2010.

[30]International Labour Organization, ILO Report: *The End of Child Labor: Within Reach*, International Labour Organization, Geneva, 2006.

[31]"Taking Action Against Child Labor," VOA News, May 15, 2010, www1.voanews.com/learning english/home/world/Taking-Action-Against-Child-Labor-93892309.html, accessed June 1, 2010.

[32]International Labour Organization, *A Decade of ILO-India Partnerships: Towards a Future without Child Labor 1992–2002*, International Labour Organization, New Delhi, 2004.

1986 Child Labor (Prohibition and Regulation) Act.[33] This amendment banned the employment of any children younger than 14 years of age in Domestic work or work as servants and work in so called "Dhabas" (roadside eateries), restaurants, hotels, motels, tea shops, resorts, spas or other recreational centers. However, exempted in the legal provision are family-owned enterprises. Many factories circumvented the law by claiming that the child was a distant family member. This regulation did not even address child labor in agriculture (except: Processes in agriculture where tractors, threshing and harvesting machines are used and chaff cutting).

Local Tradition

Child labor has long been an industry-wide practice. Ananda UVL, Bayer India's manager of Public Affairs and Communications recalled that "child labor in India was never seen as a problem issue. It was a culturally accepted thing to do."

She adds: "We had to address the issue in several layers. [...] Our challenge was to devise an external communication strategy that would highlight the ills of child labor and at the same time encourage farmers to refrain from using children on their farms. Internally, we had to deal with company staff in India that felt that child labor was an unsolvable issue as they had grown up with this tradition. Many still believed that dealing with the issue was the primary responsibility of the Indian government."[34]

Global Expectations

Shanta Sinha, a renowned anti-child labor activist and recipient of the internationally renowned 2003 Ramon Magsaysay Award for community leadership, did take issue with child labor:

> It has been proven time and again, beyond doubt, that the powerful global players who claim to uphold themselves to their codes of conduct and corporate social responsibility have flouted all norms of human rights and values.[35]

In 2002, Sinha along with representatives of India Committee of the Netherlands (ICN) and other international NGOs—including the Netherlands Confederation of Trade Unions (Federatie Nederlandse Vakbeweging, or FNV), Novib and Amnesty International, Netherlands—began investigating two Dutch corporations: Unilever and Advanta. Their report focused squarely on the cotton seed industry in Andhra Pradesh and

---

[33]http://labour.nic.in/cwl/ChildLabourAct.doc, last accessed August 25, 2010.

[34]Interview with company executives at BCS Headquarters, Monheim, Germany, April 8, 2010.

[35]"Suhasini," One World, October 6, 2004. Available at www.globalpolicy.org/component/content/article/221/46956.html, accessed April 10, 2010.

lamented that "social, economic and political developments in the West influence the daily lives of millions of Indians."[36] A second report by Dr. Davuluri Venkateswarlu, director of Glocal Research and Consultancy Services (GRCS), a social research organization in Hyderabad, also released in 2002, linked the broader issue of child labor with the production of hybrid cotton seeds.[37] This report estimated that 247,800 children worked for farmers supplying seeds to multinationals. Disturbed by the findings, Amnesty International pleaded that companies "recognize their full responsibility for the human rights of all involved in their supply chains."[38] A third report was released in April 2003, evocatively titled Child Labor and Transnational Seed Companies in Hybrid Cottonseed Production.[39] This report mentioned child labor on Bayer-contracted (formerly Proagro-contracted) farms.

Rude Awakening

Bayer was quickly challenged on the child labor issue on its home turf. The Coalition against Bayer Dangers, GermanWatch and the Global March against Child Labor gave the public in Germany an ear-full. In the United Kingdom, the Anti-Slavery Society took similar issue with Unilever. In the United States, the International Labor Rights Forum (ILRF) and the International Center on Child Labor and Education (ICCLE) focused on Monsanto.[40]

Bayer executives were the first to counter these reports:

We follow a clear "zero tolerance to child labor" policy in our business operations worldwide. We do not tolerate child labor in our supply chain either, where we take action against known cases of violations. Our efforts to fight against child labor are consistent with the ILO's[41] [International Labour

---

[36]Julia Brümmer, Think Locally, Act Globally? An Actor-Oriented Case Study on the Transitional Cooperation of NGOs on Bayer and Child Labour in Andhra Pradesh, India, master's thesis, University of Maastricht, Maastrickt, Netherlands, March 2007, www.indianet.nl/pdf/thinklocally .pdf, accessed March 20, 2010.

[37]Davuluri Venkateswarlu, Seeds of Bondage: Female Child Bonded Labour in Hybrid Cottonseed Production in Andhra Pradesh, www.indianet.nl/sob.html, last accessed March 20, 2010.

[38]Simon Fraser, "Unilever Denies Child Labour Link," BBC News Online, May 6, 2003, http://news .bbc.co.uk/2/hi/south_asia/3005059.stm, accessed March 14, 2010.

[39]DavuluriVenkateswarlu, Child Labour and Trans-national Seed Companies in Hybrid Cottonseed Production in Andhra Pradesh, www.indianet.nl/Cotton_seeds.doc, accessed March 10, 2010.

[40]Julia Brümmer, Think Locally, Act Globally? An Actor-Oriented Case Study on the Transitional Cooperation of NGOs on Bayer and Child Labour in Andhra Pradesh, India, master's thesis, University of Maastricht, Maastrickt, Netherlands, March 2007, www.indianet.nl/pdf/thinklocally .pdf, accessed March 1, 2010.

Organization] core labor standards and the United Nations Global Compact principles.[42]

Dr. Uwe Brekau, then Manager, International Chemicals Policy, Corporate Center, Bayer AG, Germany,[43] explained that under no circumstances should children be allowed to work for Bayer.

> Farmers are like any of our other business suppliers and the same conditions of no child labor applies to them as well. We simply cannot allow children to work just because they have no other options. As a responsible company, we need to help create new and better options and ensure that children have a better future.[44]

However, as the international campaign of the non-governmental organizations gained momentum, mainly through publicity in national and international written media, correspondence and dialogues with companies and pressure by social investors and public opinion, Bayer was additionally pressured to speed up its response to the "inherited" child labor issue in its newly acquired business and to address the problem head-on.

Growing Challenge

Clive Pegg, managing director of Proagro, was tasked to act. Pegg, who had worked across continents before being sent by Aventis CropScience to head Proagro, was familiar with the reputational damage that Marks and Spencer, IKEA and Nike had undergone after reports of child labor in their global supplier factories.

> The issue of child labor in the supply chain of Proagro, our Indian Seed Company acquired in 2002, was the most challenging task that I personally had to face in over 30 years of working in the agricultural supply industry. With our relatively few contract farms for cotton seed production in India, compared to the enormous number of Indian cotton seed farms, we had to create islands free of child labor in a sea of widespread child labor practice. We were challenged to change attitudes and behavior in a country with a completely different social structure and culture to that of Bayer with its headquarters in the heart of Europe. This required new thinking in developing our strategies along with determination and significant resources in implementation. In addition, we needed to develop

---

[41]Minimum Age Convention 1973; (No. 138); Worst Forms of Child Labor Convention, 1999, (No. 182), International Labor standards, http://www.ilo.org/ilolex/english/convdisp1.htm, accessed March 10, 2010.

[42]*Bayer Sustainable Development Report 2006—Bayer Human Rights Position* http://www .sustainability2006.bayer.com/en/human-rights.aspx, accessed March 10, 2010.

[43]Dr. Uwe Brekau later joined Bayer CropScience, Germany in July 2008 as Head, Corporate Social Responsibility.

[44]Interview with company executives at BCS Headquarters, Monheim, Germany, April 8, 2010.

partnerships with various organizations which could actively support us, with a long-term commitment, to enable us to meet our responsibilities in this area.

Pegg brought in Suhas R. Joshi, an MBA, then head of Strategy, Bayer BioScience India, to outline an action plan. Joshi started with a first-hand understanding of the problem.

> We started to spend more time finding children and ensuring that they stayed out of the farms. We had to be careful not to pressurize farmers beyond a limit; farmers had the option of working with other companies, which did not expect them to follow any social standards whatsoever. Farmers and company field staff did not understand at that time that Proagro was now Bayer and accordingly there was a need to change the way business was done.

Bayer CropScience at that time felt that collective action along with other seed companies would be an ideal approach as the issue was very complex and Bayer had a very small market share in the cotton seed business.

The Child Labor Elimination Group (CLEG)

In 2003, Bayer CropScience and the Indian Association of Seed Industry

(ASI) co-founded a coalition called the Child Labor Elimination Group (CLEG). Two other multinationals, Syngenta (Switzerland) and Monsanto (United States), which were facing similar pressure from activist groups, also joined CLEG. Although these three multinationals combined had only 10 per cent share of total cotton seed production acreage in India, they had been at the centre of the controversy. Several prominent activist organizations were co-opted. Both the MV Foundation and Venkateswarlu, vocally against multinationals were part of the initial multi-stakeholder approach.

This industry-wide coalition stirred further controversy. Rather than seeing such collective action as a step towards addressing the problem, media reports criticized Bayer, Monsanto and Syngenta for, allegedly, conspiring to skirt the issue. An open letter dated December 2003, co-signed by a group of European NGOs, threatened the Bayer Group chief executive officer (CEO) with a complaint to the Organization for Economic Co-operation and Development (OECD)[45]—unless Bayer acted swiftly (see Exhibit 5).

In the meantime the program had been further developed: Bayer had scaled up its awareness activities to communicate the message that Bayer does not tolerate child labor to reach

---

[45]An intergovernmental organization that helped governments tackle economic, social and governance challenges, stating a non-compliance with the guidelines for multinational enterprises.

nearly 10,000 farmers. For weeks in a row, educational rallies and road shows were organized across several villages in Andhra Pradesh.

This positive development however did not stop fellow CLEG member, Venkateswarlu, who in October 2004 published a new report—Child Labor in Hybrid Cottonseed Production in Andhra Pradesh: Recent Developments.[46] His report vividly described how children were forced to work with no food for long hours in the heat.

The NGOs which had co-signed the open letter made good on their earlier threat. GermanWatch, Coalition against Bayer Dangers and Global March against Child Labor prepared a joint complaint against Bayer for violating the OECD Guidelines for Multinational Enterprises.[47] They approached the national contact point for these guidelines in the German Federal Ministry of Economics and Technology, because according to Cornelia Heydenreich, then senior advisor for corporate accountability of GermanWatch:[48]

> We have been trying for over a year to talk to Bayer's Indian subsidiary Proagro in order to solve the problem of child labor, so far without any success. This is why we are now submitting a complaint to the Federal Ministry: we have to increase pressure on the company by involving the official German authorities.

The successful solution of a complex challenge, which, among other aspects, requires a complex change in mindset, does not come with the turn of a switch. Bayer was well on track on its learning curve and as a consequence from the lessons learned in the fields, the collaborative program called CLEG was continuously further developed: Its structure was revamped to increase effectiveness. Three committees were established at the state, district and field levels. The district and field committees visited the farms and monitored the labor composition. They were also made responsible for planning and implementing field activities. These monitoring reports were sent back to the State committee for further analysis and decision making. Further, an auditing firm was commissioned by Bayer to independently conduct unannounced visits to randomly selected farms over the crop season to verify the monitoring efforts. The main objective

---

[46]Davuluri Venkateswarlu, *Child Labour in Hybrid Cottonseed Production in Andhra Pradesh: Recent Developments*, www.germanwatch.org/tw/bay-stua.pdf, accessed April 20, 2010.

[47]GermanWatch, Coalition against Bayer Dangers and Global March against Child Labor, "OECD Complaint against Bayer Because of Child Labor in India," joint press release, Berlin/Cologne, October 11, 2004, www.germanwatch.org/presse/2004-10-11e.htm, accessed March 1, 2010.

[48]Ibid.

of the state committee was to involve the government agencies, strengthening the multi-stakeholder approach.

To further promote dialogue and learning, Bayer CropScience shared information related to its production plans (e.g., the names of farmers, farm sizes, locations, etc.) with CLEG-member NGOs. These NGOs were welcome to organize unannounced visits and as long as representatives of Bayer India could also participate in these visits to gain first-hand information. Results of the visits were shared in monthly group meetings. However, CLEG-member NGOs complained that they were not being given full freedom to operate. On the flip side, Bayer CropScience—as well as Monsanto—resented the policing attitude of CLEG-member NGOs.

CLEG continued to monitor child labor, but trust among partners continued to erode, as did their commitment to find a common solution. MVF left the coalition disenchanted a few months after. Joshi explained:

> Results under the CLEG cooperation were slow due to complex agreement process and the many parties involved. We had the will and the vision but unfortunately the program was not giving us the desired results. Coordinating with all stakeholders was taking away our major attention.

Incentives and Sanctions

Still under the CLEG cooperation, Bayer announced a 5 per cent bonus on the procurement price paid to farmers who complied with the new contractual provision and did not engage child labor.[49] As an additional component for its farmers, Bayer CropScience introduced an industry-first productivity improvement training program, called "Target 400," which helped increase crop productivity from the average 260 packets of cotton seed per acre towards the ambitious goal of 400 packets per acre.[50]

But the additional income did not motivate all farmers. For some, hiring child labor meant a low cost of production and better labor management. Such farmers faced sanctions. A first-time violation of the new contractual provision resulted in a warning. If the farmer was found employing child labor a second time, the company cut 10 per cent of the procurement price. A third violation terminated the contract.

Bayer also decided to launch a set of innovative educational projects to tackle poor access to education—one of the undisputed factors that perpetuated child labor in rural India.

Most children found working on cotton seed farms had either dropped out of school or had never attended

---

[49]All Bayer CropScience contracts included an additional clause for cotton seed farmers in India explicitly prohibiting any use of children younger than 15 years of age in any production activity.

[50]Each packet contains 750 grams of seed.

formal school. In some communities, there were no alternatives to farm work. Bayer launched programs for the construction of schools and funded educational materials. One such program was started in March 2005. Bayer contracted the Naandi Foundation, a children's educational organization, to take the children who were found working on the farms and enroll them into regular schools. The project established 23 Creative Learning Centers (CLCs) for such children in 19 villages in Andhra Pradesh. CLCs operated for two to three hours every day and provided children with academic support prior to joining regular schools. The project also placed considerable emphasis on motivating parents and mobilizing the community at large to support education for all children.

Escalation

In April 2006, NGOs staged a protest at Bayer's annual shareholder meeting in Germany. The Norwegian pension fund, one of Bayer's larger investors, started an inquiry process in spring 2006 (see Exhibit 6):

The negative media caught the attention of The Norwegian Bank Investment Management (NBIM) within the Norwegian State Bank. NBIM ran the investments for the state pension fund, which was one of Bayer's larger institutional investors. The pension fund had its own Council on Ethics, with the authority to recommend divestment for any acts or omissions that constituted an unacceptable risk that the fund contributed to one or more social ills, including child labor. In 2005 and 2006, the fund had divested its investment from several well-known companies, such as Walmart, Raytheon, Freeport and Honeywell. Its Council on Ethics now scrutinized Bayer's actions to address the child labor issue.[51]

Working Together

News of child labor in the Indian operations of Bayer CropScience spread like wildfire in political and media circles. Steffen Kurzawa, Head of Corporate Communications at Bayer CropScience who had been driving the international Corporate Social Responsibility Strategy in his previous function at Bayer AG, was not satisfied with the speed at which the Child Care Program was progressing. He thus assigned Dr. Michael Schneider, then manager Corporate Social Responsibility at Bayer CropScience fully to the project. Schneider, who had an international professional background and previously worked at ICI and CIBA/Novartis, was

---

[51]"The Good Capitalist," Nordic World, www.nordicworld.tv/news/22/news/item/null, accessed May 18, 2010.

well trained to handle demanding matters including complex certification procedures. Schneider explained how he made the decision to work full time on the child labor issue:

> I had dealt with complex issues before and understood that a huge challenge like child labor needed dedication and focused attention. In a country like India western company ethics could not simply be put to work without major efforts. Though our company including our India unit were trying its best to respond to the situation, there was a good chance to fail with all negative consequences to our reputation and brand. I took the next flight to India to understand the situation myself. I spent the whole day but managed to only cover four small farms in three villages. The area was vast and the challenge was how to effectively monitor thousands of such farms on a regular basis. Even more important [was how it would] be possible to win the hearts and minds of farmers who saw no wrong in using children for labor.

Schneider visited India for the first time in October 2006. His four-day visit to India marked a new beginning. He recalled that, when he first attended a CLEG meeting, he "could see [the] suspicion in the room between all the partners":

> The whole process lacked trust and the will to address the problem like a team. Arguments were driven by emotions and not based on facts. If we had to succeed, we had to improve internal

functioning and each member had to realize that the success of CLEG had global implications.

Schneider understood the dimension of the child labor issue and the implication for the reputation of Bayer. Global management had to get involved along with the Indian organization. On his return, he started to explain the situation on the ground and the NGO campaign to his colleagues at Bayer's headquarters. He brought the relevant managers from various departments of the cotton seed business together with legal teams in Lyon, France; the colleagues from the investor relations department in Leverkusen, Germany, and the management team in Mumbai. At a telephone conference with international executives on December 7, 2006, Schneider advocated for a new approach and organizational set-up, a well managed process and for a separate budget so the project could be professionally run and hire a dedicated field team to manage various elements of the project in the field.

Schneider started to talk to NGOs to understand the civil society's position on child labor and, in particular, their expectations of Bayer. He traveled extensively across Indian farms, which enhanced his understanding of the cultural norms and then social conditions in India. He established two-way communications to facilitate a better understanding of the prevailing Indian conditions by his colleagues in the

European head office, while helping Bayer India staff understand the expectations of their Europe-based colleagues.

The Decision

With full support of the Bayer Group's top management, Schneider had facilitated formation of a steering committee, which met for the first time in January 2007 in Hyderabad, to take stock of the progress and chart the future path to addressing the child labor issue in its India-based cotton seed farms. Schneider along with Joshi advocated against a collective initiative, which had been slow and only partially effective. Instead, they proposed a standalone, systematic program—Bayer CropScience Child Care Program (BCS-CCP).

Bayer CropScience Child Care Program (BCS-CCP)

Schneider and Joshi recommended a standalone program which would "strengthen our educational projects and monitoring and improve our farmer incentive packages." The program strategy was restructured in three pillars of communication, implementation and education. Each pillar had a well defined action plan. This proposal would give them direct control and follow a more systematic approach.[52] CCP would also provide the company with accurate and precise data and information on child labor cases by directly identifying and monitoring the use of child labor. Ernst & Young Private Limited would independently conduct unannounced field visits to randomly selected farms over the crop season to verify Bayer's efforts. The incentive and sanction plan would be revised. A set of innovative educational projects would also be developed to tackle poor access to education—one of the undisputed factors that perpetuated child labor in rural India.

The Richard Ivey School of Business gratefully acknowledges the generous support of Bayer CropScience AG in the development of these learning materials.

---

[52]Bayer India management instructed their field monitoring teams to verify the ages of the child laborers through collection of some documentary evidence (e.g., a school certificate)—not to rely on the physical appearance of the child laborer or verbal statements from the farmer. Farmers could obtain age certificates from the school, but these were not issued unless the farmer was present. To get an age certificate issued, the farmer would have to forego a day of work on the farm. The interruption was unproductive but acted as a deterrent to employing children.

Exhibit 1   Bayer CropScience's Child Care Program (CCP) Steering Committee

1. Aloke Pradhan, *head, Corporate Communication, Bayer Group, India*, managed all internal and external branding and corporate communications. He was a commerce graduate and held an MBA in Advertising.

2. Ananda UVL, *manager, Public Affairs and Communication, India,* had begun her career as a journalist in 1994, working with leading publications in India. She held a master's degree in Mass Communications & Journalism and a Certificate in Business English.

3. Charles Grange, *Global Cotton business manager, Bayer BioScience, Lyon*, had worked with leading agribusiness companies across Europe. He was a trained agronomy engineer with degrees in Plant Biology and Physiology.

4. Frederic Arboucalot, *head, BioScience, Agricultural Crops Asia / Pacific*, had extensive experience in strategy formulation and implementation and operational marketing. He held a master's degree in Agronomy.

5. Jens Hartman, *head, Bayer CropScience, South Asia*, has been with Bayer for two decades and has held key positions globally. He held an MBA with a specialization in Economics.

6. Kai-Uwe Brueggen (Dr.), *head, Project Management & Technical Development, Bayer CropScience, India*, joined Bayer AG in 1990. Since then, he had key positions in the crop protection business across continents. He held a PhD in Entomology & Plant Protection.

7. Mahesh Girdhar, *head, Bayer BioScience, India*, had diverse experiences in the Indian crop protection and seed industry spanning more than a decade. He held a master's degree in Agricultural Science.

8. Michael Schneider (Dr.), *manager, Corporate Social Responsibility, Bayer CropScience, Germany*, had been trained as a banker and an agricultural scientist. He had worked with leading companies in the United States and Europe and in agriculture in the Near East and Cyprus.

9. Steffen Kurzawa, *global head, Corporate Communication, Bayer CropScience, Germany*, had been with Bayer for more than 15 years. He had led key communications and media relations assignments around the world and incepted the global Corporate Social Responsibility Program at Bayer in 2003/2004. He held a degree in Economics.

10. Suhas R Joshi, *head, Child Care Program, India*, managed commercial functions with India's leading agribusiness companies. He held a graduate degree in Agricultural Sciences and an MBA.

Source: Company documents, used with permission.

Exhibit 2   Organizational Structure of the Bayer Group

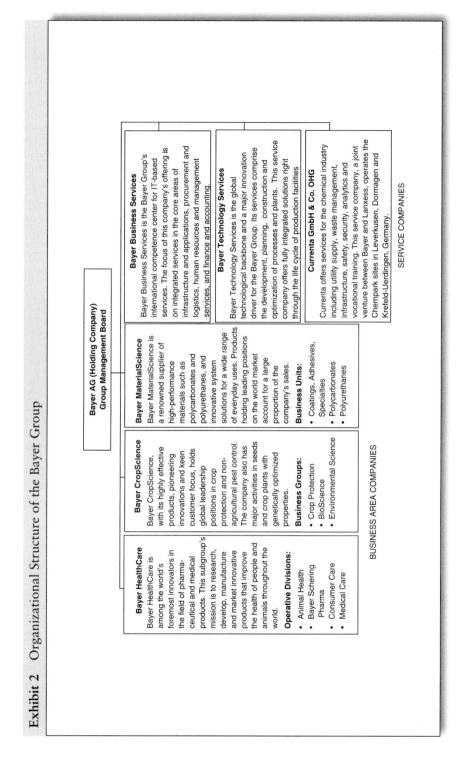

Bayer AG (Holding Company)
Group Management Board

BUSINESS AREA COMPANIES

Bayer HealthCare

Bayer HealthCare is among the world's foremost innovators in the field of pharmaceutical and medical products. This subgroup's mission is to research, develop, manufacture and market innovative products that improve the health of people and animals throughout the world.

Operative Divisions:

• Animal Health
• Bayer Schering Pharma
• Consumer Care
• Medical Care

Bayer CropScience

Bayer CropScience, with its highly effective products, pioneering innovations and keen customer focus, holds global leadership positions in crop protection and non-agricultural pest control. The company also has major activities in seeds and crop plants with genetically optimized properties.

Business Groups:

• Crop Protection
• BioScience
• Environmental Science

Bayer MaterialScience

Bayer MaterialScience is a renowned supplier of high-performance materials such as polycarbonates and polyurethanes, and innovative system solutions for a wide range of everyday uses. Products holding leading positions on the world market account for a large proportion of the company's sales.

Business Units:

• Coatings, Adhesives, Specialties
• Polycarbonates
• Polyurethanes

SERVICE COMPANIES

Bayer Business Services

Bayer Business Services is the Bayer Group's international competence center for IT-based services. The focus of this company's offering is on integrated services in the core areas of infrastructure and applications, procurement and logistics, human resources and management services, and finance and accounting.

Bayer Technology Services

Bayer Technology Services is the global technological backbone and a major innovation driver for the Bayer Group. Its services comprise the development, planning, construction and optimization of processes and plants. This service company offers fully integrated solutions right through the life cycle of production facilities

Currenta GmbH & Co. OHG

Currenta offers services for the chemical industry including utility supply, waste management, infrastructure, safety, security, analytics and vocational training. This service company, a joint venture between Bayer and Lanxess, operates the Chempark sites in Leverkusen, Dormagen and Krefeld-Uerdingen, Germany.

Source: Bayer—Profile and Organization, company documents, used with permission.

329

Exhibit 3   Bayer CropScience AG: Financial Statement (in millions of euros)

	FY 2004[1]	FY 2005[2]	FY 2006[3]
Sales	5,946	5,896	5,700
EBITDA[4]	1,219	1,284	1,166
EBITDA (before special items)	–	1,273	1,204
EBIT[5]	492	690	584
R & D	–	664	614
Gross cash flow	893	964	900
Net cash flow	778	904	898
Employees at year end[6]	19,400	18,800	17,900

Source: Bayer CropScience, Corporate Brochure 2007/2008: Strengthening Crops—Securing Yields, p. 29, www.bayercropscience.com/bcsweb/cropprotection.nsf/id/EN_Corporate_Brochure/$file/Image_ englisch_neu.pdf, accessed May 1, 2010.

Notes: December 31, 2004: 1 euro = 58.8 INR.

[1]Bayer, Science for a Better Life: Annual Report 2004, www.bayer.com/en/en_ar_complete_2004 .pdfx, accessed May 1, 2010.

[2]Bayer, Science for a Better Life: Annual Report 2005, www.investor.bayer.com/user_upload/485, accessed May 1, 2010.

[3]Bayer AG, Annual Report 2007, http://www.annualreport2007.bayer.com/en/homepage.aspx, accessed May 1, 2010.

[4]EBITDA = EBIT (earnings before interest and taxes) plus amortization of intangible assets and depreciation of property, plant and equipment. EBITDA, EBITDA before special items and EBITDA margins are not defined in the International Financial Reporting Standards and should therefore be regarded only as supplementary information. The company considers underlying EBITDA to be a more suitable indicator of operating performance since it is not affected by depreciation, amortization, write-downs/write-backs or special items. The company also believes that this indicator gives readers a clearer picture of the results of operations and ensures greater comparability of data over time. The underlying EBITDA margin is calculated by dividing underlying EBITDA by sales.

[5]EBIT as shown in the income statement.

[6]Bayer, "Subgroups and Service Companies," Science for a Better Life: Sustainable Development Report 2005, pp. 54–65, www.investor.bayer.com/user_upload/626, accessed May 1, 2010.

Exhibit 4 Hybrid Cotton Seed Farming Process

SELECTION

Independent agents known as "seed organizers," acting on behalf of the company selected farmers on the basis of their capability (both financial and technical) and the size of the farmer's landholding. "Seed organizers" also employed their own staff to conduct field visits to ensure quality standards.

CONTRACTS

The formal contract with the farmer included two agreements: one between the farmer and the company and a second one between the "seed organizer" and the company. These contracts were written in the local language and included detailed terms and conditions, such as the payment terms, the quality of seed specifications and the procurement rate.

SOWING

The process began with the growing of female and male parent plants separately in the ratio of 5:1. Sowing the seeds took place on small plots spread over hundreds of villages. Hybrid cotton seed production was labor-intensive and required, on average, 1,000 workdays for a one-acre plot. Farmers were responsible for hiring labor and purchasing crop protection products. Where required, financing was provided by the "seed organizer" or through nationalized agri banks.

EMASCULATION AND CROSS-POLLINATION

As the season advanced, the production process required two important operations: emasculation and cross-pollination. These stages were *the most labor-intensive, and child labor was often hired during this stage.* The process of emasculation involved removing the petals of the female parent's flower first by hand, along with anthers and filaments, without damaging the stigma, style or ovary. Each individual flower bud then needed to be emasculated and pollinated by hand.

PICKING

The crop was picked over a period of two months as the bolls ripened. The picking stage also had high labor requirements. The unwanted materials (i.e. leaves and the remains of the cotton boll), called "trash" were left behind. The cotton bolls that were too young to harvest were left for a second and third picking.

QUALITY TESTING

The final seed lots were collected and sent to the company for quality testing. A series of quality tests were conducted, including moisture and germination tests. Seeds that did not meet the quality requirements were rejected.

PAYMENT

The farmer was paid for the seeds after passing all quality tests.

Exhibit 5   Open Letter to Bayer

December 18, 2003

To: Werner Wenning, CEO of Bayer AG and Dr. Jochen Wulff, CEO of Bayer CropScience AG

Dear Mr Werner Wenning, Dear Dr. Wulff,

We, the Coalition against BAYER-dangers, Germanwatch and the Global March against Child Labor, are writing to express our deepest concern at the intense employment of children in the planting of cotton seeds in India. Your Bayer affiliate, ProAgro, is one of the beneficiaries of this process. To prevent ongoing harm to children we urge you to take immediate steps against this practise. The research of the "Glocal Research and Consultancy Services" (GRCS) institute in Hyderabad/India, published under the title "Child Labor and Transnational Seed Companies in Hybrid Cottonseed Production" (translated into German in July 2003), proves the employment of the children at the suppliers of ProAgro, Monsanto, Unilever and other companies. This is a violation of the ILO-basic working conditions conduct, as well as of other international standards such as the OECD-Guidelines on Multinationals. One of the companies benefiting is ProAgro, which has been a Bayer affiliate since 1999.

Bayer has committed itself to the abolition of child labor, for example by joining the UN Global Compact. Your company has meanwhile admitted the problems with the Indian seed suppliers. But only in September 2003 a meeting took place between the seed suppliers involved and the Indian initiative on children['s] rights, the Mamidipudi Venkatarangaiya Foundation (MV Foundation) in Hyderabad/India. At this meeting companies, including ProAgro, took over responsibility on children's working conditions at their suppliers. Since then there has been much delay without putting the commitments into place. On December 13th 2003 another meeting of the MV Foundation and the companies involved took place where a specific plan of action with detailed activities has been created and agreed upon.

We expect from BAYER and its affiliate ProAgro to take up all required actions to end the employment of children and to immediately implement the plan of action. In addition we urge you to finance an education programme for the children who have suffered from child labor at your suppliers. This education programme should be developed together with the local authorities. Your commitment to the abolition of child labor at BAYER companies, as well as your contract clauses on preventing your suppliers [from] using child labor, are not enough in order to fulfil the target. Agreements made with local contractors need to be monitored. In order to

Exhibit 5 (Continued)

prevent your suppliers from using child labor, the prices paid for their products need to be high enough so that employment of adults is profitable to the suppliers.

Educational re-integration for children who have been forced to drop school in order to work is seldom successful. After each employment period with an average duration of seven months the children concerned—basically girls—do not get any further formal education. These children are at the age of six to fourteen. Through the work for the suppliers of Bayer/ProAgro, who depend on the contracts, the children have lost their options for the future. Their health is also endangered as the labor protection laws, such as when using herbicides, are not applied. We are in close co-operation with our partners in India, the MV Foundation. From Germany we will observe carefully the steps taken [by] Bayer/ProAgro and the implementation of the plan of action. As Bayer/ProAgro working methods violate the OECD Guidelines for Multinationals, we are presently evaluating the possibility of a complaint to the relevant authorities.

What are the steps that you, as well as those responsible at ProAgro, will take in order to immediately stop all use of child labor at your suppliers?
We look forward to your answer.

Yours sincerely,

Sd.-   Sd.-   Sd. -

         Philipp Mimkes   Cornelia Heydenreich   Rainer Kruse

Coalition against BAYER-dangers   Germanwatch e.V.   Global March against Child Labor/Germany

Source: http://www.cbgnetwork.org/345.html, accessed April 15, 2010.

Exhibit 6   Timeline of Events

PHASE I: 2002–2003	PHASE II: 2004–2005	PHASE III: 2006–2007
December 2002: Bayer completed the acquisition of Aventis CropScience business in India. Alongside this acquisition, Proagro Seeds, a leading seed company in India, joined Bayer CropScience.	April 2004: GermanWatch protests carried out at Bayer's annual stockholders' meeting.	January 2006: In Germany, ARD-Monitor (German TV) broadcasted a story about child labor at Bayer. The European Commission, European Parliament and investor groups took note and began to enquire about the situation.
January 2003: Within weeks of the takeover, Bayer informally found out about child labor in its contracted cotton seed farms in the state of Andhra Pradesh. An awareness drive on Bayer's no child labor policy was launched for all contract farmers to stop the employment of children younger than 15 years of age.	October 2004: Dr. Venkateswarlu released a report titled *Child Labor in Hybrid Cottonseed Production in Andhra Pradesh: Recent Developments*. The study was commissioned by The India Committee of the Netherlands, Coordination against Bayer Dangers, GermanWatch and EINE WELT NETZ NRW (EWN NRW).	April 2006: The Eine Welt Netz NRW (EWN NRW) protested at Bayer's annual stockholders' meeting. Stockholders started frequent enquiries about the issue with company managers.
April 2003: NGOs released the report *Child Labor and Trans-National Seed Companies in Hybrid Cottonseed Production in Andhra Pradesh*. The study was commissioned by The India Committee of the Netherlands (ICN). The report mentioned child labor in Bayer-contracted farms, which created a major stir in the press.	October 2004: CBG, GermanWatch and Global March Against Child Labor submitted a complaint against Bayer to the National OECD (Organisation for Economic Co-operation and Development) Contact Point at the German Federal Ministry of Economics and Technology.	June 2006: The Norwegian Investment Pension Fund, one of Bayer's larger institutional investors, started an enquiry process. The fund's ethical unit, the Council on Ethics, began a systematic investigation.

Exhibit 6 (Continued)

PHASE I: 2002–2003	PHASE II: 2004–2005	PHASE III: 2006–2007
May 2003: Deutsche Welthungerhilfe (DWHH) together with several other NGOs started the international campaign "Stop child labor! School is the best place to work." This organization partnered with the MV Foundation, ICN and Global March against Child Labor.	October 2004: Südwind organized a conference on ethical investment in Bonn. Dr. Venkateswarlu was among the participants.	September 2006: Activists wrote an open letter to the Prime Minister of Finland (then Acting President of European Union) urging him to discuss with India the child labor in cotton seed supply chain, among other issues, during the European Union-India Summit.
September 2003: Association of Seed Industry in India passed a resolution to proactively discourage child labor in hybrid cotton seed production.	February 2005: Eine Welt Netz NRW (EWN NRW) started a campaign under the slogan "Wer hat mit Kinderarbeit und Kopfschmerzen zu tun . . . und reimt sich auf MAYER?" ("Who has to do with child labor and headaches and rhymes with MAYER?")	January 2007: Child Care Program (CCP) Steering Committee meeting held in Hyderabad, India.
December 2003: Coordination against Bayer Dangers (CBG), GermanWatch and Global March against Child Labor wrote an open letter to the Bayer Group CEO. Bayer replied on February 4, 2004.	April 2005: The EINE WELT NETZ NRW (EWN NRW) protested at Bayer's annual stockholders' meeting. Stockholders started frequent enquires about the issue with company managers.	Should Bayer go it alone and scale up the CCP, continue with CLEG, or should it exit the hybrid cotton seed business altogether?
Bayer became a founding member of Child Labor Elimination Group (CLEG), a coalition formed within the Association of Seed Industry which also included Monsanto India, Syngenta India and local NGOs.	Bayer launched a system of farmer incentives and sanctions. It started a multi-level field program which placed greater emphasis on field monitoring and awareness programs.	Proposed an independent, in-house program called Bayer CropScience Child Care Program.

L'Oréal S.A.: Rolling Out the Global Diversity Strategy

Cara C. Maurer
Ken Mark

Introduction

It was the morning of January 15, 2007, as Sylviane Balustre-D'Erneville, Europe diversity director for L'Oréal S.A. (L'Oréal), the largest cosmetics and beauty company in the world, looked out over rue Martre from her Paris office. As she contemplated the next 12 months, Balustre-D'Erneville wondered how to focus her communication effort and her actions to build support and momentum for the global rollout of L'Oréal's diversity strategy, which encompassed dimensions such as nationality, ethnic origin, socio-economic background, gender, disability and age (see Exhibit 1).

Diversity had taken on strategic importance for L'Oréal, whose corporate goals were to eliminate all forms of discrimination anywhere in its operations around the globe and to increase the overall diversity of the entire multinational corporation. In 2004, L'Oréal France had signed a Charter of Diversity, committing to a series of principles related to improving diversity in the workplace (see Exhibit 2). To implement its diversity strategy globally, L'Oréal had put in place a diversity team headed by Jean-Claude Le Grand, L'Oréal's global diversity director.

George-Axelle Broussillon, L'Oréal's corporate diversity manager, worked with Balustre-D'Erneville to implement the firm's diversity strategy. Broussillon discussed the importance of diversity to the corporation:

> Diversity for L'Oréal is a requirement that goes way beyond being "politically correct." . . . Diversity is a richness that has to be reflected in all that we do. Why? Because the diversity of talents is the driving force behind creativity and innovation. And then, it should also be remembered that product diversity ensures that there is something in it for every single one of us. . . . Having said that, globalization teaches us every day that common aspirations and values do indeed exist over and above the differences. They have to be accessible to all at L'Oréal, respecting them and sharing them day-in, day-out.

Balustre-D'Erneville's work with the various country units (see Exhibit 3) informed her that some regions were more advanced than others in their embrace of the need for a global diversity strategy that is adopted locally. From her analysis thus far, the biggest issues facing L'Oréal seemed to be neither legal nor regulatory in nature. Instead, Balustre-D'Erneville believed the main obstacles to be cultural differences between countries and a low-level awareness of the benefits that a diversity strategy could bring.

L'Oréal S.A.

L'Oréal, headquartered in Clichy, France, sold a range of makeup, perfume, and hair and skin care products in 130 countries and employed a workforce of 52,000 in 2006. L'Oréal's family of brands included such well-known names as L'Oréal Paris, Biotherm, Cacharel, Garnier, Giorgio Armani, Diesel, Innéov, Lancôme, SoftSheen Carson, Shu Uemura, Maybelline New York and La Roche-Posay.

In 2006, L'Oréal earned €1.8 billion on revenues of €15.8 billion.[1] The foundation of the company had been its strong sales in Europe and North America, growing 12 per cent per year for the past five years. However, L'Oréal's sales growth in emerging markets was much higher, at 37 per cent per year for the same period. By 2006, emerging markets contributed 22 per cent of L'Oréal's overall sales. Each of L'Oréal's country units operated independently, with full profit and loss responsibility at the country level. Country results were then consolidated at the group level. Although each country manager was responsible for running his or her country unit as if it were a stand-alone corporation (though with the ability to seek best practices and procure product lines from other L'Oréal country units), frequent meetings took place between each country manager and L'Oréal's senior management team, which was based in Paris.

L'Oréal's products were targeted at the general market and, increasingly, at multicultural consumers. The company's first foray into the multicultural product space was the acquisition of SoftSheen-Carson, a manufacturer of products for people of African origin. Lindsay Owen-Jones, L'Oréal's chairman, stated:

> In our business, it is absolutely vital to be in tune with your consumers. And it's by listening very carefully to our consumers all around the world that we've come to understand the extreme diversity of their needs. You have to understand that we at L'Oréal, we do not try to export or impose a single view of beauty on the world. On the contrary, all our brands must reach out to people—very different types—all around the world. But additionally— and this is quite original for a company like ours—we have developed a unique portfolio of brands, each one with a different cultural origin to better satisfy the differences in sensitivities of people around the world.

---

[1]At the end of 2006, the Euro to U.S. dollar exchange rate was €1 = US$1.32, http://www.x-rates .com/cgi-bin/hlookup.cgi.

To promote products to its multicultural consumers, L'Oréal used a variety of approaches: employing ethnically diverse spokespeople, advertising in ethnic magazines and partnering with agencies focused on marketing to specific ethnic groups. As the company made inroads into non-European markets, L'Oréal saw diversity in its markets and its employees as a competitive advantage it could cultivate. Jean-Paul Agon, L'Oréal's chief executive officer (CEO), explained the firm's approach to implementing its diversity strategy:

> Firstly the very nature of our business makes diversity absolutely vital for us. Being a global company that serves customers with different sensitivities all over the world, our desire to innovate is based on understanding and respecting difference. As you all know, a major part of our success is due to the diversity of the brands in our portfolio. Building further on this, we now have research centres not only in Europe, but also in North America, in Asia and soon in Latin America to better understand the diversity of hair and skin types across five continents. It is our belief that beauty has many faces.

> Secondly, diversity is key to L'Oréal being a "Great Place to Work in." As Sir Lindsay Owen-Jones said, "In order to be global, we must be global from within." Being truly global from within,

however, has more to it than simply attracting diverse profiles. We must go beyond representation and strive for equitable management in order to ensure that everyone has an equal opportunity of realizing their potential. It is my conviction that happy and fulfilled employees are more productive and creative. This is why it's so important for managers to lead with human sensitivity.

> Thirdly, our experience shows that variety breeds more creativity and innovation, both of which are paramount to our success. Teams made up of diverse profiles cover any issue from multiple angles and thus come up with more holistic approaches.

> Lastly, diversity is a mirror of the ever changing world in which we live and, as such, prepares us to meet the challenges of the 21st century. A diverse workforce is better equipped to deal with change. It's all about being in tune with the environment.

L'Oréal's Diversity Strategy

Diversity at L'Oréal was not narrowly focused on ethnic origins or gender differences and was not merely about compliance with legal standards. L'Oréal defined diversity as follows:

> Diversity is a mosaic of visible[2] and invisible[3] differences . . . of similarities

---

[2]According to L'Oreal, visible differences included ethnic origin, gender, disabilities, physical appearance and age.

[3]According to L'Oreal, invisible differences included cultural origin, socio-economic status, education, experience, religious beliefs, political or philosophical convictions, sexual orientation and values.

and interactions which influence attitudes, behavior, values and ways of working of both men and women within their professional environment.

The concept of diversity was not entirely new to the company; back in 2000, it had put in place an Ethics Charter (see Exhibit 4), which touched on issues of diversity. In addition, L'Oréal had already made significant progress since its adoption of the Ethics Charter (see Exhibit 5). Le Grand stated:

> There had been several important milestones for L'Oréal's diversity program in the six years since it adopted its Ethics Charter in 2000. There had been policies put into place, executives appointed to posts specifically overseeing diversity initiatives, employees had received diversity training, and the company had participated in career fairs promoting diversity.

L'Oréal took an active approach to diversity, seeing it as an investment in its future success. L'Oréal aimed to be a responsible "corporate citizen of the world," to attract and retain top talent and to position itself as a "brand of choice" for consumers. The diversity strategy was part of L'Oréal's ongoing efforts to deliver on its commitment to diversity. Broussillon commented:

> As you can see, our diversity initiatives have come in waves. First, there was a movement to implement the Ethics Charter in 2000. Then in 2002, we created the first position for diversity in the U.S.—a vice-president was assigned to the task. Owen-Jones, who was our

CEO at the time, started to diversify the portfolio of brands we owned, purchasing brands with different cultural origins. Then the challenge was to recruit people to manage these brands with different cultural origins—that's why intercultural management became so important for us.

In 2004, L'Oréal France signed the Diversity Charter with 35 large French corporations. As a further signal of the importance of diversity to the firm, L'Oréal promoted its head of recruitment, Jean-Claude Le Grand, to global diversity director. Le Grand was committed to diversity at L'Oréal. He explained the rationale behind L'Oréal's people policy:

> Since its inception, L'Oréal has made diversity one of its guiding principles. Whether in terms of the people it employs or the products it develops, L'Oréal has always viewed diversity as a key concern. The diversity of our human resources, our balance of male and female employees and our mix of talents, is one of the keys to L'Oréal's success. At all levels and in all arenas, teams made up of a wide variety of people lead to greater creativity and a better understanding of every type of consumer. The Group therefore intends to continue hiring a diverse range of people and completely rejects any form of discrimination, be it on the grounds of sex, age, disability, ethnic or social origin, religious, national or cultural beliefs, etc.

A team was assembled at L'Oréal to continue the rollout of the firm's diversity strategy. The company was also careful to note that the strategy was not about lowering standards for its workforce. Diversity was about "recognizing, accepting and valuing differences and capitalizing on differences to increase performance." Ultimately, diversity at L'Oréal was at the core of the organization with strong support from top leadership.

Putting L'Oréal's Diversity Strategy Into Action

Agon described how the firm communicated the need for diversity to its thousands of managers across the world:

> In order for diversity to work, and thus to enable us to meet current and future challenges, it is necessary to go beyond words. At L'Oréal, we've initiated several actions over the years to promote diversity. Today, we have a 5-line diversity strategy that takes into consideration: Recruitment & Integration; Management; Career Management; Communication; and, last but not least, Training.

> Accordingly, we have set up a 2-day training program for over 8,000 managers in 32 countries across Europe. This program is a cornerstone of our overall diversity policy. As our collective commitment must be reflected in each and everyone's day-to-day actions, your personal action plan at the end of the training program is indispensable: "What will you do to promote and manage diversity within L'Oréal?"

Balustre-D'Erneville's team aimed to deliver diversity training to 8,000 managers in 32 countries before the end of

2010. The intent of the training was to "prepare managers to approach their role and responsibility as a team leader in a new way, based on who they are and want to be as a manager."

These managers would participate in a one-and-a-half day diversity seminar that would clarify the meaning and importance of diversity for L'Oréal; help them to understand the concept of diversity; help them to identify personal, team and organizational barriers to diversity; and enable them to establish an individual action plan. An overview of the seminar can be found in Exhibit 6. Once the training was completed, managers were expected to return to their day-to-day operations with a better understanding of diversity.

After the seminar, managers were appointed to lead diversity initiatives in their offices. These appointees were expected to assess the state of diversity in their workplace and to develop a diversity strategy tailored to their particular situation. This diversity strategy would then be approved by the local director prior to implementation. By the end of 2006, approximately 4,000 managers had attended this training seminar.

While the number of attendees met Balustre-D'Erneville's expectation, she learned that the content of the training seminar and the new expectations afterward had generated both positive reactions and significant pushback from managers. The following are a selection of the comments Balustre-D'Erneville's team received:

"I think that the seminar was useful and we will make an effort to be more understanding in our workplace."

"The objective is to be tolerant of different ideas and I learned that this might require a change in the way I perceive others."

"I don't understand why we need to attend these sessions because we're not discriminating against any employees to begin with."

"Diversity is ingrained in our beliefs as it is. A diversity seminar would be great for senior managers but may be of less value to younger employees."

"We have too many things to do in a day as it is and there is no time for yet another 'flavour of the month' program. Is this really necessary?"

"We understand the need for diversity and there is little value to be gained in spending two days on the topic."

"I understand and support the need for diversity as a strategy. But implementing it when there are day-to-day pressures is going to be tough even if I support it wholeheartedly."

"Is this another way of saying we now have an 'Affirmative Action' program?"

"This is more of a French concept and some of the directives may not be relevant in some regions."

"I don't understand why the definition of diversity is so broad—it practically encompasses everything."

"I did not know before the seminar that I was discriminating but it seems that I was. I will change the way I manage my people."

Balustre-D'Erneville wondered how to react to the feedback her team had received from managers about the relevance of a diversity strategy and the diversity training program.

Clear geographical differences affected how L'Oréal's global units viewed the idea of implementing a diversity strategy. In comparison with other country units, the United States was the farthest along in its acceptance of the need for diversity. The U.S. management team was diverse—the percentage of ethnic minorities in L'Oréal's U.S. workforce was 32 per cent of the total—and included a vice-president in charge of diversity.

On the other end of the scale, some Asian country units, characterized by very homogenous workforces from an ethnic and cultural perspective, had not given high priority to the diversity of their workforce. In some cases, local management had given very little attention the matter even after having attended the diversity seminars.

The Diversity Team Takes Action to Motivate the Attendees

Balustre-D'Erneville looked at the range of issues facing her team. She was committed to implementing L'Oréal's diversity strategy as efficiently and effectively as possible. But local management in each of these country units had to understand and buy into L'Oréal's overall diversity strategy before they would even think of developing and implementing a diversity strategy of their own. Broussillon, who was present for the seminars, described how her team was facing as they worked to encourage managers to change their behaviors:

> Our task is to explain to employees that diversity is not only an external subject, that it's not just "affirmative action." What we are saying at the moment is that diversity is key to our success and we can show the link that exists between diversity and performance. Our communication is backed up by commitments from our CEO and Chairman.

Balustre-D'Erneville knew that the stakes of this issue were high and that she had to take action to prevent the rollout of L'Oréal's diversity strategy from getting stuck in its tracks. She wondered what her diversity team's strategy should look like in the next year and beyond.

Exhibit 1   L'Oréal Diversity Strategy

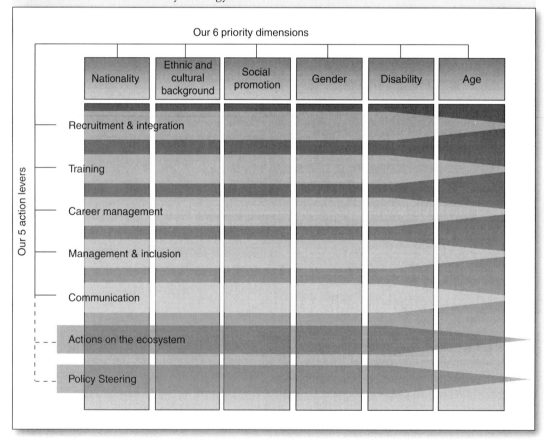

Source: Company files.

Exhibit 2   The French Diversity Charter

Promoting pluralism and seeking diversity through recruitment and career development is an opportunity for companies to progress. Such strategies improve efficiency and contribute to a better social climate. They can also have a positive impact on the way a company is viewed by customers, suppliers and consumers, in France and overseas.

The Charter of diversity, adopted by our company, is intended to demonstrate our commitment, in France, to cultural, ethnic and social diversity within our organisation.

In accordance to this Charter, we undertake to:

1. Raise awareness of non-discrimination and diversity issues among top management and staff involved in recruitment, training and career development and to educate them in these matters.

2. Respect and promote the application of all aspects of the principle of non-discrimination at every stage of the human resources management, in particular in the recruitment, training, promotion and career development of employees.

3. Endeavour to reflect, the diversity of the French society particularly in its cultural and ethnic dimension at every level of our workforce.

4. Make all our employees aware of our commitment to non-discrimination and diversity, and keep them informed of the practical results of this commitment.

5. Make the development and implementation of the diversity policy a subject of a dialogue with the employees' representatives.

6. Insert a chapter in the annual report describing our commitment to non-discrimination and diversity including details of the measures implemented, our internal procedures and the results achieved.

Source: Company files.

Exhibit 3   L'Oréal Country Units

Europe	North America	Africa, Orient, Pacific
Belgium	Canada	Australia
Bosnia	USA	Bahrain
Bulgaria		Egypt
Croatia	**Latin America**	India
Czech Republic	Argentina	Israel
Denmark	Brazil	Jordan
Finland	Chile	Kazakhstan
France	Colombia	Kuwait
Germany	Guatemala	Lebanon
Greece	Mexico	Morocco
Hungary	Panama	New Zealand
Iceland	Peru	Oman
Ireland	Puerto Rico	Pakistan
Italy	Uruguay	Qatar
Latvia	Venezuela	Saudi Arabia
Netherlands		South Africa
Norway	**Asia**	United Arab Emirates
Poland	China	Yemen
Portugal	Cambodia	
Romania	Hong Kong	
Serbia-Montenegro	Indonesia	
Slovakia	Japan	
Slovenia	Malaysia	
Spain	Philippines	
Sweden	Singapore	
Switzerland	South Korea	
Turkey	Taiwan	
Ukraine	Thailand	
United Kingdom	Vietnam	

Source: Company files.

Exhibit 4   L'Oréal Code of Business Ethics, Values and Guiding Principles

L'Oréal enjoys a world-wide reputation for the performance and safety of its products, as well as for the frequency and originality of its innovations and for the quality of its staff.

L'Oréal stands out through continual progress in its economic performance, its international expansion and the ever-increasing reputation of its brands.

L'Oréal is highly regarded for its business ethics: respect for the consumer, partnership with suppliers, clients and distributors, sincerity and openness in the information provided on its business operations and for its range of environmentally friendly products.

L'Oréal is appreciated for the quality of its human and social policy which is built upon mutual trust, high standards of performance and respect for the individual.

The men and women who have built L'Oréal's success and reputation have applied themselves to the Company's development with rigour, commitment, the will to succeed and the firm conviction that the aspiration to beauty and well-being is universal.

It is the professionalism and loyalty of these men and women that ensure the continued prosperity of the Group.

The lasting nature of the trust between L'Oréal and its partners stems from its respect for simple rules of conduct based on shared principles.

The aim of this document is to draw to the attention of each and every one of us the importance of these rules and principles; it is a guide to every individual within the Group in determining appropriate behaviour when confronted with situations that are sometimes complex.

[Only the selected sections "Respect for the law," "Respect for the individual," and "Principles of loyalty and integrity" are shown here.]

Respect for the Law

It is incumbent upon all the Group's subsidiaries and individual employees, in the performance of their duties, to respect the laws of the countries in which L'Oréal operates.

L'Oréal attaches particular importance to respect for the spirit and the letter of the laws governing:

- Social legislation: prohibition of child labour and forced labour; observance of hygiene and safety standards, and of anti-discrimination laws; provisions governing working time and remuneration; employees' collective representation;
- Taxation, notably concerning accurate communication of financial information;
- Competition, in line with international legislation and the World Trade Organisation's recommendations;
- The environment.

Each individual, at whatever level of responsibility, should ensure that these principles are respected by all persons and should, in this matter, monitor the respect for these principles in all legally established bodies with which L'Oréal has dealings.

Respect for the Individual

Respect for the individual is a fundamental principle. It is applied daily at L'Oréal and is the focus of human relations within the company.

(Continued)

Exhibit 4 (Continued)

L'Oréal believes in the value of difference and diversity for the development of its human assets. L'Oréal categorically rejects all forms of discrimination, both in thought and deed, notably concerning sex, age, physical disability, political and philosophical opinion, union activity, religious conviction, as well as race and social, cultural and national origins.

Each individual has the right to respect and human dignity; all behaviour or acts likely to create a hostile working environment and, in particular, any form of sexual harassment, will not be tolerated.

Respect for the individual is also demonstrated by L'Oréal's commitment to its employees and to those management values upon which the Company sets great store. Respect for the individual is maintained through an ongoing dialogue between individuals and management. Thus, recruitment and career development are based on competence and quality, appraised objectively in relation to the Company's needs.

The Group's Training and Development programmes play a vital part in the development of each employee's skills and potential.

L'Oréal is committed to facilitating the professional integration of those who require special attention: young adults, persons from disadvantaged backgrounds and those with special physical needs.

Principles of Loyalty and Integrity

"Two-way loyalty" is an expression of fundamental importance to L'Oréal.

It articulates a deeply-held set of values that includes, for example, support for employees who might find themselves in difficulty.

L'Oréal's practical commitment to "two-way loyalty" is a policy of long-term personal development for each employee, based on the Company's growth and economic performance.

L'Oréal respects each employee's right to privacy. Each individual has a duty to ensure that he or she speaks in his or her own name in private life, refraining from making any remarks that might be interpreted as reflecting L'Oréal's official position.

Similarly, no employee must use L'Oréal's name for personal reasons or to obtain any personal gain whatsoever through his or her position in the Company or through information acquired, by whatever means.

It is forbidden to accept or to offer invitations or gifts for which the value exceeds those customary in the particular country.

Everyone is under an obligation to act in the best interests of the Group, with the constant aim of protecting its assets, maintaining its image and good name and keeping all information or know-how confidential, whatever its nature.

As a general rule, employees must avoid situations where personal interests might come into conflict with the interests of L'Oréal or which might be prejudicial to the Company.

L'Oréal encourages the exchange of ideas and respects freedom of speech. It is naturally incumbent, however, upon each employee to refrain from any form of denigration of his or her colleagues, of the Group, its customers, its suppliers or its competitors.

Integrity both in day-to-day business activities and in overall behaviour is a requirement that is enshrined in the values of L'Oréal.

Source: Company files.

Note: The full document shows several sections, but only three sections (i.e., "Respect for the Law," "Respect for the Individual" and "Principles of Loyalty and Integrity") are included here.

Exhibit 5   L'Oréal Diversity Milestones

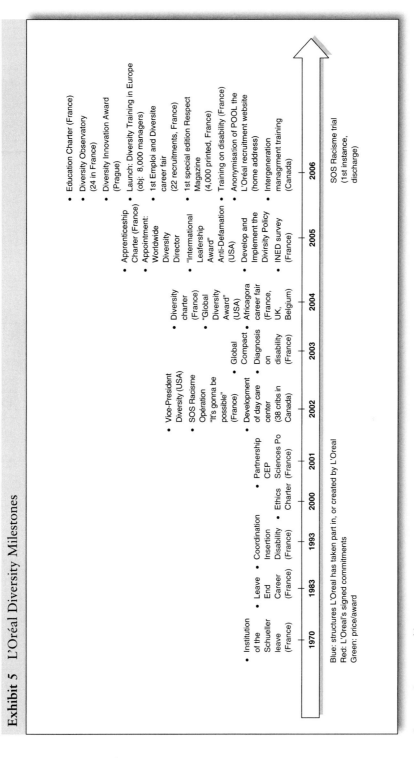

Source: Company files.

347

Exhibit 6 L'Oréal Diversity Seminar

The Seminar

Day 1

Sequence A
The World Around Us
- Understand diversity in society at large and at work
- Diversity filters

Sequence B
The Employee
- My awareness
- Communication and inclusive management

Day 2

Sequence C
The Team
- L'Oréal: Our Diversity Policy, Our Expectations and Aspirations Presentation by L'Oréal Senior Manager
- Diversity and team dynamics
- Individual Action Plan

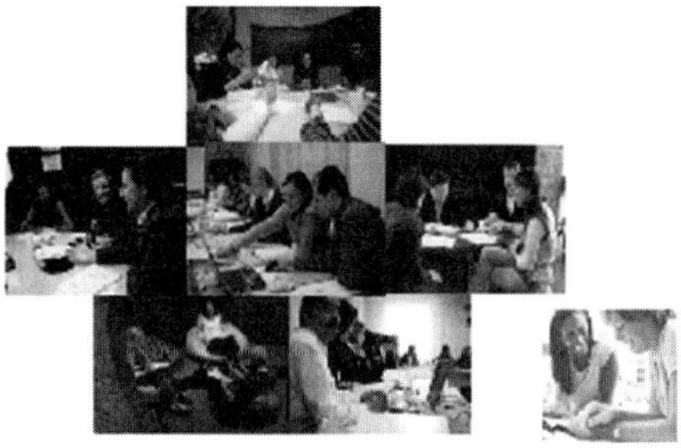

Source: L'Oréal—Celica Thellier document, accessed from ec.europa.eu/social/BlobServlet?docId-1825&langID=en.

Huxley Maquiladora

Paul W. Beamish

Jaechul Jung

Joyce Miller

On Monday, June 24, 2002, Steve Phillips, head of the Huxley Maquila project team, had to make a recommendation about moving production to Mexico. The final report of the team, outlining the results of six months of investigation, was on his desk. The task now was to recommend at Thursday's board of directors meeting whether to establish a manufacturing plant, and if so, where and how.

Company Background

Huxley Manufacturing Co. was part of the materials technology division of a holding company based in the eastern United States, which had interests in chemicals, aluminum, packaging and aerospace. Huxley employed 1,800 people in three defence-related businesses and recorded $472 million in annual sales in 2001. Huxley headquarters were located in San Antonio, Texas, a city that had a strong Mexican influence; over 50 per cent of its population was Hispanic. A U.S. military base and hospital were also located in the area.

Huxley took pride in its cutting-edge engineering technologies in raw material processing and part assembling. It had demonstrated superiority in the use of aluminum hybrids, ceramics and composite metals to increase the survivability of military equipment. These materials met tough performance standards for weight, size and durability, all of which were critical characteristics for military applications. Only two or three of Huxley's competitors whose manufacturing facilities were confined to the U.S. were capable of designing, processing and assembling to the same standards.

Huxley's three businesses had historically been managed separately, with little information sharing and communication among the units. This corporate need for separation had resulted from the secrecy that had been required in Huxley's work for the defence industry.

During the 1990s, Huxley faced several factors that converged to profoundly reshape the U.S. defence industry. The first factor was the increasing "knowledge intensity" of defence products, resulting in higher development costs. These rising costs could be attributed primarily to the increasing technological complexity of almost all types of military systems, and to the rapid pace of technological innovation. Higher costs of research and development (R&D) for each generation of weapons caused absolute costs to rise, and the increasingly knowledge-intensive nature of weapon production had the effect of rendering even the largest multi-divisional firms incapable of funding R&D independently.

Furthermore, the forecast was uncertain for the political environment in which defence firms in the United States were operating. With the end of the Cold War, high funding levels for equipment in the American defence budget fell. There were declining numbers of military personnel and a debate on the most appropriate force structure and roles for the American armed forces in the new era. In such a political environment, the U.S. economic decline of recent years only exacerbated the situation facing U.S. firms in the defence industry. As well, the September 11, 2001 attacks had highlighted the need for greater intelligence gathering, not necessarily more hardware. These factors combined to reduce U.S. government spending on defence to 2.4 per cent of the gross domestic product (GDP) in 2000, compared with the 6.4 per cent under the Reagan administration.

In order to deal with this adverse environment, the U.S. government had moved away from the use of sole vendors to more competitive bidding for contracts to supply military equipment. As a result, price had become a more important selection criterion. U.S.-based firms were still the major suppliers, but some foreign-produced goods were also purchased by the U.S. armed forces.

The Ground Transportation Business

Under such transforming environment pressure, Huxley began searching for feasible solutions to reduce its production costs in its ground transportation unit (GTU). Technological developments in composite materials, hybrid electric power systems, integrated vehicle survivability and other features positioned Huxley's GTU at the forefront among competitors.

The GTU had operations near San Diego, California and Dallas, Texas, and was negotiating to acquire a $30 million sales company in Denver, Colorado, which would function similarly to the plant in San Diego. The GTU manufactured steering column components (SCCs) at its California site. The production of SCCs for combat vehicles generated annual revenues of about $130 million. There had been continual demands for replacement SCCs, in addition to new purchases during the annual procurement wave.

Although the production of SCCs required heavy capital investment, labor-intensive processes made up the major portion of production costs. Examples included the processes of lamination and filing: by adhesively bonding thin, composite metal layers and filing them to fit specifications, the finished assembly combined strength and lightness, which were critical characteristics for successful maneuvering. Machines were currently available to complete these vital processes, but manual processing still turned out a superior product.

Filing by hand required enormous patience and precision and had been done by females who worked 42 hours a week and received an average wage of $12.30 per hour. The GTU provided a 30-hour job training program before a newcomer began in SCC production. Even after training, some of the new workers found they could not master the required job skills and quit during the three-month probationary period. The rejection rate had been around 10 per cent monthly. Aside from being required to meet specified performance standards in precision, working with metals, requiring physical strength and patience, made this job unattractive. As a result, in spite of the comparatively high wages for women, the turnover rate in this position had always been relatively high—up to 11 per cent monthly. Robert Chan, the chief executive officer (CEO) of Huxley, once stated, "Such labor-intensive tasks are excellent candidates for us to attempt offshore production." Many U.S. companies had gained their competitive advantages by running their labor-intensive operations in developing countries, which provided well-educated labor forces at low wage costs.

Along with the worsening external environment, Chan's participation in a business conference in Mexico in 2001 triggered him to seriously consider Mexico as a strong candidate to transplant Huxley's SCC manufacturing plants. After evaluating the manufacturing processes in the GTU, Huxley's management then identified several labor-intensive activities in the large San Diego plant related to SCC manufacturing and agreed provisionally to move the plant. As a subsequent step, Chan launched the Huxley Maquila project team, composed of five members chosen from various backgrounds and led by Phillips. During the six months prior to the June 2002 report, Phillips sent three team members to Mexico to gather local information.

The Maquiladora Program

The term *maquiladora* came from the Spanish term *maquila* (to perform a task for another; to assemble). During the Mexican colonial period, the miller kept a certain amount of a farmer's corn after he ground it for him. The payment was known as the *maquila*. The current use of the term *maquiladora* referred to any Mexican company that assembled imported, duty-free components and then re-exported them as finished products.

In May 1965, the *maquiladora* industry began, with a border industrialization program. The new policy allowed machinery, equipment, material and component parts to be imported duty free on an "in-bond" basis. The posting of a bond with the Mexican Customs Bureau guaranteed that assembled or manufactured products were exported to the country from which they had first been exported or to a third country. *Maquiladoras* had grown during the years to become the industrial backbone of the country's northern border, with more than 3,500 plants now employing 1.2 million people. Most of the plants were concentrated in Ciudad Juarez, Chihuahua, across from El Paso, Texas, and Tijuana, Baja California, across from San Diego, California (see Exhibit 1).

Maquiladora handled a variety of tasks from textile, automobile, and electronics production to the assembly of toys and sporting goods. In the 1960s and '70s, many U.S. firms transferred the labor-intensive and assembly portions of their manufacturing activity to these companies. The most prominent advantage to setting up a *maquiladora* was access to cheap Mexican labor. From the 1960s to the '70s, Mexican manufacturing wages were about 15 per cent to 25 per cent of those in the United States. Yet Mexican wages were higher than those in many Asian countries like Singapore and South Korea. However, in the 1980s, subsequent currency devaluations decreased Mexican hourly wages to well below those of Hong Kong, South Korea, Singapore and other low-wage competitor countries. Mexican wages dropped to about 10 per cent of U.S. wages at that time.

Currently, there were still countries like China providing lower wage labor forces than Mexico. Wages for Mexican garment workers were approximately double those in China, but the benefits of faster delivery and lower shipping costs often outweighed this difference. Mexican products could reach the U.S. market within two or three days, compared with the three to four weeks required for shipment from China. Combined with access to the U.S. market, the wage levels of the 1980s established *maquiladora* manufacturing as one of the most competitive manufacturing platforms in the world. Finally, the regions became a portal for Asian and European firms to enter the North American market (see Exhibit 2).

NAFTA (The North America Free Trade Agreement)

The North America Free Trade Agreement (NAFTA) was launched in 1994 by Mexico, Canada and the United States. NAFTA participants planned to phase out all tariffs among the three countries over a 15-year period. Since its implementation, tariffs had been eliminated on 84.5 per cent of all non-oil and non-agricultural Mexican exports to the United States and on 79 per cent of exports to Canada. In order to receive preferential NAFTA tariffs, a minimum of 50 per cent of product content had to come from one of the three countries for most products. For autos and light trucks, the requirement level was stricter, at 62 per cent.

The content requirements and tariff reductions, coupled with the already existing *maquiladora* laws in Mexico, made *maquiladora* manufacturing much more competitive under NAFTA. By 2001, Mexico had received $108.7 billion in foreign direct investment (FDI). Among the FDI, U.S. and Canadian firms made up 71 per cent, with most from the United States (see Exhibit 2). NAFTA, as well, had nurtured a rapid increase in Mexican exports. The export total of $60 billion in 1993 had soared to $182 billion by 2000 (see Exhibit 3). Between 1993 and 2000, Mexico's annual average exports to the United States increased 19 per cent, while those of the rest of the world grew only eight per cent. In 2000, trade between Mexico and the United States totalled $263 billion, three times that of 1993.

Currently, Mexico had free trade agreements (FTAs) with 32 countries. In particular, trade with Latin American partners was rapidly growing. In fact, Mexican exports to Costa Rica and Venezuela in 2000 had grown by 259 per cent and 303 per cent, respectively, since 1994.

Mexico

Mexico was a country of approximately 100 million people and 1,958,000 square kilometres, sharing a 3,200-km border with the United States. Prior to the Mexican-American War in the mid-19th century, Mexico governed what was now the southwestern United States. Even after annexation of half Mexico's territory by the United States, Mexicans continued to live in the area and their number had substantially increased through emigration. Mexico's current relationship with the United States was largely economic, stimulated by NAFTA. Although the Mexican economy was currently experiencing recession triggered by U.S. economic decline, it had grown steadily since its economic crisis in 1994.

On the political side, the Mexican Revolution in the early 20th century had shaped Mexico's economic, political and social life since that time. The Institutional Revolutionary Party (PRI) continued its dominance as a governing party up to recent years, providing political stability. Based on its stable political leadership, Mexico showed rapid economic growth and became one of the most industrialized countries in Latin America. However, as in other Latin American countries, Mexico was now undergoing rapid transformations in economic and political spheres. The changes in the economic environment and the economic crisis of the 1980s resulted in a rejection of old economic models and an acceptance of new economic policies. The new model was based on opening Mexico's economy to foreign trade and investment reducing government intervention in the economy. Participation in NAFTA was one manifestation of this change. Economic changes had, in turn, brought about a process of democratization that finally reached a major milestone in July 2000 as Vicente Fox of the National Action Party (PAN) was elected the country's president, ending the 71-year hegemony of the PRI.

On the other hand, the temporarily duty-free import programs of NAFTA were eliminated as of January 1, 2001, on trade between Mexico, the United States and Canada (Article 303 of the NAFTA). Hence, *maquiladoras* could not continue to benefit from access to duty-free import materials and they had to change their sourcing strategies. Responding to this change, the Mexican government introduced the Sectorial Promotion Program (PROSEC), which allowed low import taxes (zero per cent to five per cent) on parts or materials intended for assembly and export to the United States or Canada.

The Huxley Maquila Project Report

The Huxley Maquila project team focused on the tasks of creating feasibility studies for operating in Mexico, location and site selection, and appraisal of various entry modes. The three team members stationed in Mexico played major roles in sourcing necessary data. The project report was submitted to Phillips, director of the project team, on June 19, 2002. Regarding transferring the SCC manufacturing process of the GTU, the report predicted that the 57 workers directly affected would be absorbed in other Huxley operations or terminated with a severance package. The report suggested that a 25,000-square-foot plant would be adequate and could still accommodate a possible worker increase of at least 50 per cent in the future. Much equipment would be required, including benches, steel tables, holding fixtures and so on. The report noted:

The SCCs assembly processes are labor intensive and had documented description of the method, sequence and dimensions for initial training, and would qualify for favorable PROSEC treatment. The San Diego plant had a significant problem with high turnover rate because working with metals was a dirty job. With appropriate training, young Mexican women would probably perform these tasks better than their counterparts in the U.S. since they are more patient. Even by taking a conservative figure like $2.10 as the fully fringed hourly pay, the direct labor savings would be considerable.

After investigating numerous sites, the Huxley Maquila project team gave its attention to Coahuila, Mexico's third largest state, lying to the south of Texas. Coahuila shared 512 kilometres of border with the state of Texas. Its geographical proximity made Coahuila the crossing point between the United States and the central and southern regions of Mexico. Prior to NAFTA's implementation, 156 *maquiladoras* were operating in the Coahuila state. As of November 2001, 267 *maquiladoras* were up and running (see Exhibit 1). The project report noted that Coahuila's geographical closeness to Huxley's headquarters in San Antonio, Texas, and the SCC plant in Dallas, Texas, was one of the merits of the location.

Among several attractive spots for a new plant, the project team members considered Ciudad Acuna, the best border site and Saltillo, the capital of Coahuila, as the best site in the interior. A border location minimized transportation costs, facilitated trouble-shooting by managers and engineers based in U.S. headquarters, and permitted factory managers to live in the United States and commute across the border. However, the influx of *maquiladora* operations had strained the infrastructure of many border cities. Public services could not cope with the population growth in Ciudad Acuna. The city's annual budget was insufficient to keep up the pace, resulting in a city with quite a large portion of its streets unpaved

and water and sewage systems lacking in many of its makeshift neighborhoods. The most significant problem was the housing shortage, which stemmed from the flood of migrants from the interior of Mexico seeking *maquiladora* jobs. A team member of the project commented:

> People are lured from the interior by the promise of a job. They move in with relatives or friends, then quit when they can't find permanent accommodation. The Mexico government doesn't have enough resources to fund construction of sufficient low-cost housing. The current housing situation will not be improved soon.

The shortage of housing created a significant labor problem for *maquiladora* operators. Turnover rates ranged from seven to 13.5 per cent per month along the border. While interior regions offered a more stable labor force and cheaper Mexican material, these advantages came with higher transportation costs and a lower quality of life for foreign managers. Infrastructure, including roads, housing, utilities and especially communications in the interior, would have to be carefully evaluated. Exhibit 4 details various factors that needed to be considered for location selection of the SCC plant.

The project report included three options for operating in Mexico as a *maquiladora*. These were subcontracting, shelter operation and wholly owned subsidiary.

Subcontracting

The easiest way to operate as a *maquiladora* was to subcontract the manufacturing services of a Mexican company. Under this arrangement, a Mexican service firm manufactured items according to the specifications of the foreign-based client. The client provided the raw materials, components and specialized equipment, and the subcontractor was responsible for all the manufacturing and assembly work as well as the import-export process. The foreign client rarely supplied a plant manager.

The Mexican subcontractor was generally paid for each product based upon a per-piece price agreement. This subcontracting arrangement made sense for well-documented operations requiring a small number of employees. The client could enjoy a reduction or elimination of capital expenditures for facilities, equipment and management. The Huxley Maquila project team report estimated that a Mexican firm could be subcontracted at a rate of about $5 per direct labor hour. To start contracting product assembly in Mexico took 30 to 45 days.

Shelter Operation

A "shelter" was an intermediary option. Under such a program, the non-Mexican manufacturer was "sheltered" from most of the legal and financial exposure of operating in Mexico.

Among the non-Mexican manufacturers operating in the *maquiladora* industry, about 10 per cent were shelter operations. Under this arrangement, the Mexican service firm provided foreign manufacturers with customized administration. This allowed the client to maintain complete control over the Mexico production management while ensuring that all administrative requirements were being met by the offshore operation. The shelter service provider supported 1) administration: accounting and tax service, licences and permits, and performance monitoring; 2) human resource management: Mexican personnel administration and payroll services; and 3) import and export service: customs services related to Mexican and U.S. government requirements. The foreign company controlled the production process and provided equipment, raw materials, components and plant managers.

Billing of operation was directly related to the number of hours provided by the service firm. The fully burdened hourly rate for a shelter operation was around $3.50. Depending upon the complexity of the setup, it generally took 45 to 120 days from receipt of authorization to production startup. The shelter operation was attractive for several reasons. First, it allowed fast, easy startup with little capital investment. At the same time, it provided complete control over the quality of the work. In addition, if the client wished, the shelter operation could be converted to a "full-blown presence" in Mexico as the company grew, or control could be turned over to the shelter partner to form a contract operation.

Wholly Owned Subsidiary

Known as a "stand-alone," a wholly owned subsidiary offered potentially the lowest operating costs, as long as overheads were strictly controlled. Such an operation was often the best alternative when significant engineering and/or product development support was required. This approach was the most complex of the three options. To set up a wholly owned *maquiladora*, foreign firms had to 1) search, select and negotiate to get a plant site; 2) staff and recruit employees; 3) implement

systems, controls and procedures; and 4) get government permits and licences. The foreign firm needed to establish relationships at local, state and federal government levels and had to understand and manage the details of doing business in Mexico, which could be particularly burdensome in the areas of hiring, compensating and terminating labor. Before starting operations as a *maquiladora*, the company had to ensure that it had in place all the required licences and permits. The Secretary of Commerce agency in Mexico (SECO) permitted firms to operate under the *maquiladora* program. It generally took anywhere from six months to one year to set up a wholly owned *maquiladora*. Some typical costs for operating a wholly owned subsidiary in Mexico were:

Feasibility consulting fee	$18,000
Mexican legal fee	$7,000 to $10,000
Construction for shell building including land with improvement	$14 to $25 per square foot
Annual leasing of factory space	$3.68 to $5.47 per square foot
Developed land price, in case of purchasing land	$1.05 to $2.30 per square foot
Average hourly wage for unskilled labor (including fringes)	$1.80 to $2.20 per hour
Average plant manager wage (including fringes)	$84,000 per year

In addition to these costs, the report included transportation and a few more cost factors, which were applied commonly to the three operation options. Most maquiladora machinery,

raw materials and semi-finished products entered and left Mexico by truck. The average round trip rate from Ciudad Acuna to the U.S. border was around $150. In the case of Saltillo, the cost rose to $1,000. American and Mexico broker fees accounted for an additional $625 per round trip shipment. Each day a round-trip truckload shipment was expected from Monday to Friday, except on the eight national holidays throughout the year. The report estimated that miscellaneous costs and Mexican corporate tax would be annually $43,050 and $12,500 in the case of shelter operation and wholly owned subsidiary. The one-time operation startup in Mexico would cost approximately $97,000, which contained training a manager, visits from California staff and a facility upgrade.

Remaining Issues

In its final section, the project report added several concerns regarding operating in Mexico as a *maquiladora*. The report pointed out that fulfilling the financial, legal and logistic requirements would merely enable a *maquiladora* to operate. Managing the human relations aspects would determine its success or failure. The report stated:

> Managing a maquiladora is not at all the same as managing a plant in the United States. The maquiladora management has to become acquainted with the cultural values and customs of its workers, and this understanding has to be carried over to home office.

Despite benefits enjoyed by government and industry, the situation for the low-wage *maquiladora* workers themselves was not bright. Since the late 1990s, labor groups had protested the low wages, unsafe working conditions, and sexual and other forms of harassment that took place. For instance, in 1997 the Han Young de Mexico plant in Tijuana was enveloped in a strike that attracted international attention. Protesters claimed that there were many companies along the borders that treat their employees "like trash." These conflicts appeared to originate from an excessive exploitation of Mexican employees and a misunderstanding of Mexican cultural values.

> The U.S. Department of Labor's National Administrative Office in January 1998 concluded, after investigating a complaint filed by Human Rights Watch, that maquiladoras administer medical tests to weed out pregnant applicants and harass pregnant workers to coerce their resignation. This practice violates Mexican labor law and the US asked Mexico to investigate. Mexico responded that administering pregnancy tests to job applicants was not illegal because Mexico's labor laws protect workers only after they have been hired. Refusing to hire women because they are pregnant violates Mexican law.

> Labor militancy is spreading to Central American maquiladoras. Some 2,800 workers employed at the Chentex Garment factory in the Las Mercedes Free Trade Zone in Managua, Nicaragua

went on strike January 26, 1998 to protest the firing of 21 of the 90 workers who had signed papers in support of a union in the factory.[1]

These mistreatments by foreign-owned *maquiladoras* put those firms at risk and added to the housing shortage, employee recruitment and training problems. To attract new employees and lessen the expressed anger of existing workers, some of the *maquiladoras* had come up with their own solutions, like supporting the local government in housing initiatives, running commuter buses and introducing high-cost training programs.

Phillips' Recommendation

Based on the report's comments, Phillips concluded that entry-into-Mexico decision should be implemented carefully if Huxley wanted to take full advantage of low-cost production. A successful launch and management of the plant would require special attention. The plant would need to be run not only to the standards of its own headquarters, but also considering Mexican cultural values and practices. Launching and managing a plant in a foreign country would be a different experience for Huxley's managers, who were accustomed to U.S. management practices.

On Thursday, June 27, a board of directors meeting would be held regarding the transfer of the San Diego plant. Phillips was scheduled to present a briefing on the *maquiladora* project report and to provide his recommendations on this plant transfer decision. He fully understood Chan's eagerness for "testing offshore waters" and, at the same time, the complexity of launching and managing a plant in a neighboring foreign country. He had only three more days to reach his final conclusion and prepare for the coming briefing.

[1]*Source*: "Mexico: Wages, Maquiladoras, NAFTA," Migration News, February 1998, Volume 5, Number 2.

Exhibit 1   Mexico's Network of Maquiladoras in November 2001

State	Number of Maquiladoras
1. Baja California	1,226
2. Baja California Sur	7
3. Sonora	246
4. Chihuahua	432
5. Sinaloa	10
6. Durango	73
7. Coahuila	267
8. Nuevo Leon	169
9. Tamaulipas	401
10. Zacatecas	20
11. San Luis Potosi	15
12. Aguascalientes	72
13. Jalisco	131
14. Puebla	116
15. Distrito Federal	29
16. Edo. Mexico	47
17. Yucatan	121
18. Guanajuato	68
19. The rest of the country	77
Total	3,527

Source: INEGI.

Exhibit 2   Foreign Direct Investment in Mexico by Country and Sector Between 1994 and September 2001 (%)

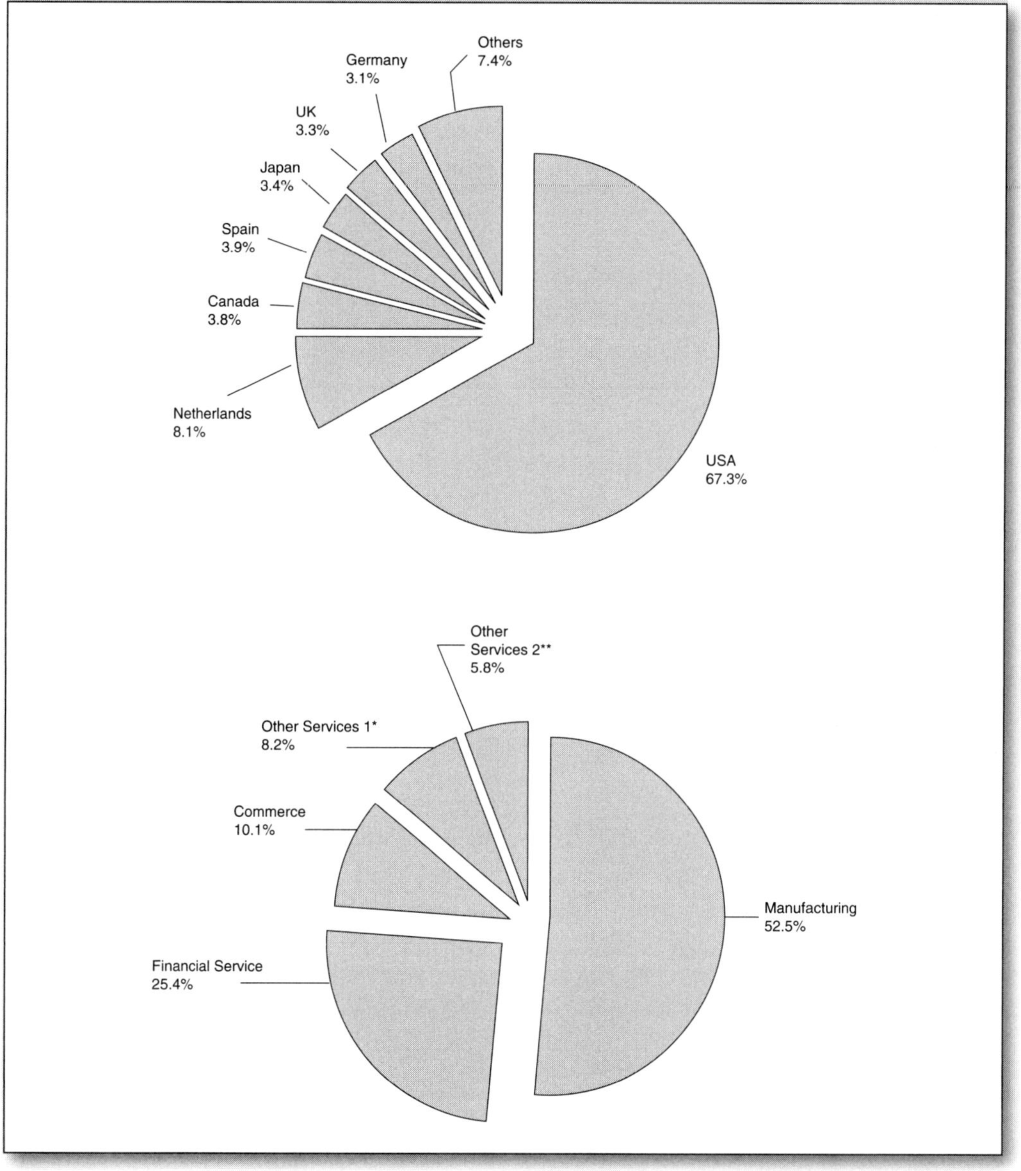

Source: Ministry of Economy, Mexico.

*Other Service 1 Agricultural, mining, constructing, electricity, transportation and communication, and water.

**Other Service 2 Social and communal service: hotels and restaurants, professional, technical and personal.

Exhibit 3　Mexico's Export Increase

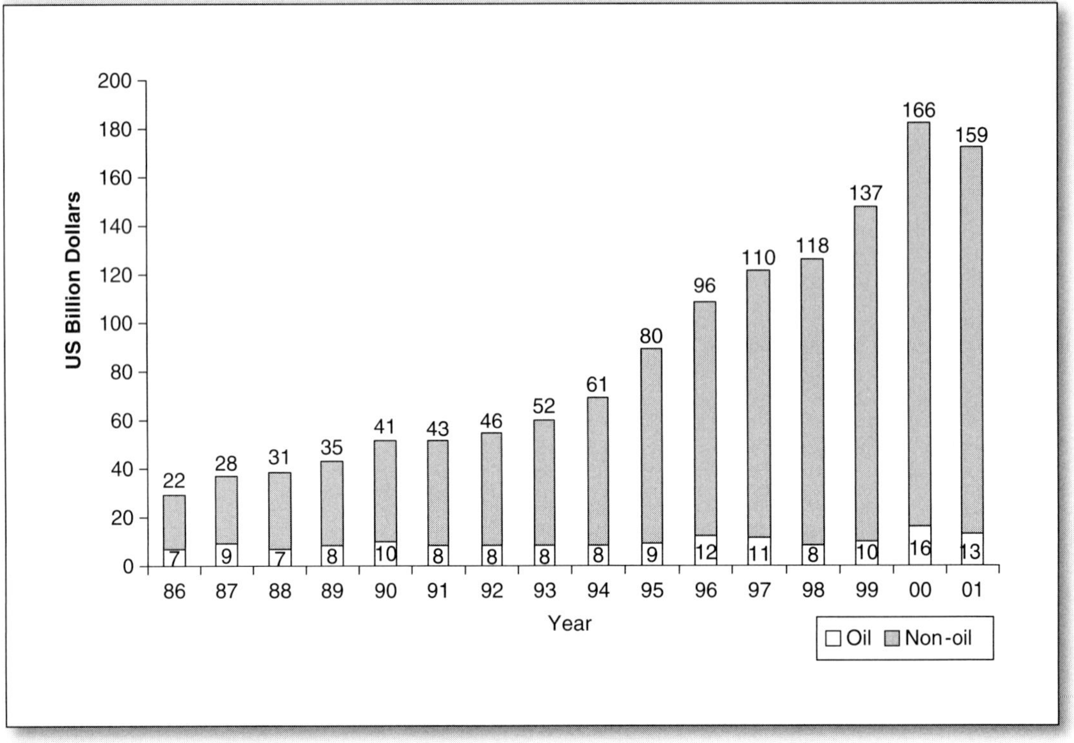

Source: Ministry of Economy, Mexico; BANXICO.

Exhibit 4　Location Profiles: Border Site (Ciudad Acuna) Versus Interior Site (Saltillo)

		Border Site: Ciudad Acuna	Interior Site: Saltillo
Demographic Aspects	Total Population	78,232	577,352
	Males	39,564	285,507
	Females	39,668	291,845
Aviation Service	Nearest Airport	Piedras Negras International Airport - 83 km away	Plan de Guadalupe International Airport - 13.5 km away
	Flights	• Monterrey	• Mexico, D.F. • Houston, TX. • Dallas, TX.
	Frequency	Monday–Sunday	Monday–Sunday
	Capacity	19 to 33 passengers	51 to 101 passengers
	Cargo Service	None	Daily, 100 tons and up

		Border Site: Ciudad Acuna	Interior Site: Saltillo
Highways	Federal Highway	• Hw. 2 reaches Nuevo Laredo, Tamps through Piedras Negras	• Hw. 57 connects with Piedras Negras, Queretaro, Qro. and Mexico City. • Hw. 40 connects Torreon, Coah. with Reynosa, Tamps. and Mazatlan, Sin. through Saltillo
Railroads		The Northern railroad connects Ciudad Acuna and Zaragoza.	The railroad connects Parras, General Cepeda, Saltillo and Ramos Arizpe.
Industrial Park		Three industrial parks	Five industrial parks
Primary Industry		Automobile, aluminum blinds, material lamination and electrical harnesses	Automobile harnesses, plastic lids, aircraft harnesses, electronic cards, agro-chemical and appliances
Labor cost (Hourly wage for general laborer)	Manufacturing	$0.94	$1.38
	Assembly	$0.65	$1.06
Water	Water ($/m^3)	$0.97	$1.30
	Drainage	$0.24	$0.32
Electricity	Less than 25KW	$2.54	Same
	More than 25KW	$11.52	Same
Telephone	Local	Base rate: $0.16 Day rate: $0.16 Evening rate: $0.16	Same
	National Long Distance	Base rate: $0.27 Day rate: $0.24 Evening rate: $0.12	Same
	Long Distance to U.S.A.	Base rate: $1.00 Day rate: $0.88 Evening rate: $0.59	Same
Education	Professional Technical School in the near region	13	36
	Universities in the near region	10	19

(Continued)

Exhibit 4 (Continued)

		Border Site: Ciudad Acuna	Interior Site: Saltillo
Commerce and Services	Hotels	10	20
	Shopping Centres	3	10
	Banks	8	63
	Hospitals	11	12

Source: Secretariat of Planning and Development Government of the State of Coahuila.

Exhibit 5   Mexican Minimum Wage for Unskilled Workers in 2000 (in U.S. dollars)

	Minimum Wage
1. Regional minimum hourly wage[1]	$0.51
2. Annual salary (365 days)[2]	$1,117.92
3. Christmas bonus (Aguinaldo-15 days) and vacations (5 days)	$64.21
4. Employer's payroll taxes and state taxes	$44.71
5. Average fringe benefits	$254.69
6. Total Annual Cost (= 2 + 3 + 4 + 5)	$1,481.53
7. Fully Fringed Hourly Cost[3]	$0.68

Source: International Labor Organization; BANCOMEXT.

Note: The minimum wage (salario minimo) is the income level determined by the federal government to be adequate to meet the basic needs of a typical family.

---

[1]Including social security contributions, the INFONAVIT worker's housing fund and the retirement savings plan.

[2]Considering weekly working hours (44) and annual working days.
        (300 = 365 – Sundays (52) – legal holidays (8) – vacations (5)).

[3]Fully Fringed Hourly Cost = Total Annual Cost/Annual Working Hours (2,192).

Staffing Wal-Mart Stores, Inc. (A)[1]

Alison Konrad
Ken Mark

Introduction

In 2003, an executive vice-president (EVP) at Wal-Mart Stores, Inc. (Wal-Mart) wondered about Wal-Mart's employment equity record. For the past few years, Wal-Mart consistently appeared on Fortune's list of the 100 best companies to work for in the United States, most recently ranking 94 in 2002. Although the EVP was aware of several lawsuits against the company alleging gender discrimination, Wal-Mart's published practices indicated that the organization was committed to fair practices. The EVP wondered what employment-related information should be requested from the People Division.

Wal-Mart Stores, Inc.

In 2002, Wal-Mart was the world's largest employer and the world's largest company. With net income of US$8 billion on sales of US$247 billion, Wal-Mart was the subject of countless newspaper features and journal articles praising its dominance and success. For a look at Wal-Mart's selected financial information, see Exhibit 1. One of the many reasons for this success was that, unlike its retail counterparts in the grocery industry, Wal-Mart remained a non-unionized company, working incessantly to fend off organizing attempts in the United States and around the world.

Wal-Mart's Workforce

Available data showed that by 2001, Wal-Mart employed 930,000 people in its domestic U.S. stores, and this employment figure was up 50 per cent since 1996. But during the same period, the percentage of women employed decreased from 67 per cent to 64 per cent. The number and composition of people at Wal-Mart was of keen interest to company officials because of the sheer size of their workforce and how employment costs affected the company's financials. Analysts who examined the company's stores and financial performance estimated that payroll expenses accounted for 50 per cent of Wal-Mart's total operating, selling, general and administrative expenses.

---

[1]This case has been written on the basis of published sources only. Consequently, the interpretation and perspectives presented in this case are not necessarily those of Wal-Mart Stores, Inc. or any of its employees.

At Wal-Mart, there were retail store employees (including hourly and salaried workforce), the store management, and high-level managers such as district managers and regional vice-presidents (see Exhibit 2). In 2001, management employees earned about $50,000 on average while hourly employees earned $18,000.

Operations

There were four types of domestic retail stores at Wal-Mart in 2002: discount stores, supercentres, SAM's Club, and Neighborhood Markets. A quick overview of key 2001 store statistics is provided in Exhibit 3.

There were five levels of operations at Wal-Mart:

Level	Description
Corporate	Total Wal-Mart including domestic and international
Division	Division One stores (discount stores, supercentres, Neighborhood Markets) and SAM's Club make up Wal-Mart's two key domestic divisions
Region	There were 41 regions in the United States
District	Each region contained five to six Districts on average
Store	Each District contained 10 to 15 stores

Corporate-wide human resource policy was the responsibility of Wal-Mart's People Division. Primary and secondary people policy committees met with representatives from each of the company's operating divisions and representatives from home office in Bentonville, Arkansas, to formulate policies. This process was overseen by the EVP of the people division. The EVP described his duties as "overall responsibility for getting, keeping and developing Wal-Mart talent worldwide." He reported to Wal-Mart's president and chief executive officer (CEO) and sat on the corporate executive committee. The company's senior human resource executives all had "dotted-line" reporting relationships to the EVP of the People Division. For example, the senior vice-president of People for the SAM's Club division would report both to the president of that division and to the EVP of the People Division.

Human Resources Reporting Relationships for Domestic Divisions

Wal-Mart had similar human resources (HR) policies across its domestic divisions, i.e., Division One and SAM's Club. The HR function was organized hierarchically: in Division One, the over 2,600 stores were organized into five or six divisional areas, with five or six regions within each area and 80 to 85 stores within each region. Each store had an hourly employee, the personnel manager, who co-ordinated hourly recruiting and performed payroll functions. Thirty-five regional personnel managers (RPM) based in Bentonville oversaw these personnel managers. These RPMs reported to one of three People Directors in the home office; in turn, these People Directors reported to the vice-president of People at Division One.

The company had a computerized information system that made personnel policies and guidelines available to its staff. In addition to relying on information generated by reports at store, district, regional and divisional levels, store visits by district managers and RMP were frequent; district managers visited stores once every two weeks and RPMs visited stores weekly. Reports from each visit were immediately submitted to the regional vice-president.

Organizational Culture

Wal-Mart prided itself on its strong culture, with numerous references to Sam Walton's personal biography, the history of the company and how Walton's personal values became core beliefs for the company. Wal-Mart public information indicated that its customer-focused culture stemmed from the company's pursuit of everyday low prices (EDLP) and "genuine customer service." Founder Sam Walton had three basic beliefs on which the company was built: Respect for the Individual; Service to Our Customers; and Strive for Excellence. In addition, there were two key "rules" at Wal-Mart that supported the three basic beliefs: the sundown rule (attending to requests the same day they were received); and the Ten-foot Rule (offering greetings whenever one was within 10 feet of a customer). In his autobiography, Walton outlined his Rules for Building a Business (see Exhibit 4).

New employees learned the "Wal-Mart Way" by viewing videos about the company's history, completing computer-based learning modules about elements of the culture and reading the associate handbook. At each store, a daily meeting, held at shift changes, allowed managers to discuss company culture and encourage employees to perform the Wal-Mart cheer.

The company indicated in its promotional literature that it received letters from customers praising individual associates for exceptional service, citing examples of employees who had gone above and beyond the call of duty. Walton had once asked associates to practice what he called "aggressive hospitality"—striving to be the most friendly, giving better service over what customers expected, and generally exceeding customers' expectations. This hospitality also extended to the community in which Wal-Mart operated.

The company frequently provided charitable assistance, raised funds for organizations and provided scholarships to students.

Ongoing training for store managers and home office employees consisted of weekly Saturday morning meetings (the first meeting of the month was devoted to a culture topic). In addition, instruction and orientation on the Wal-Mart culture was given to managers at all levels of the company.

Rewards and Promotions

Annual pay increases were tied to performance evaluation ratings, with a percentage increase guideline specified by the home office. Typically, an annual merit increase of four per cent or five per cent was the maximum given, although this amount could not be granted within 90 days of an annual performance increase or raise due to promotion.

Before 1998, higher-level jobs were not posted. In 2002, these and any other openings were typically posted at stores and were usually available online, but there were exceptions. Store managers could circumvent this process and rely on filling positions with lateral moves. In addition, store managers had the authority to waive minimum requirements regarding time in current position in order to promote employees.

When employees were promoted to higher-level jobs, there was an implicit expectation that they would be moved to other stores, districts or regions, as much as business need required. For example, a district manager in Northern California asked employees applying for the management training program to certify in writing that they were willing to transfer "to any location within the Wal-Mart trading area" to receive training and were willing to relocate post-training. A former regional vice-president required co-managers to be open to relocate "whenever and wherever we need them." See Exhibit 5 for relocation statistics by job type.

In the late 1980s, Wal-Mart implemented and formalized a policy of creating resident assistant manager positions for individuals who were eligible to be assistant managers but were not able to relocate. These resident assistant managers could move into co-manager positions without relocating. One company official stated that the program had been phased out by 2002. Another official stated that the program still existed but only on an "as requested" basis.

In his 1992 autobiography, Sam Walton discussed the changes he had made to his original management philosophy of requiring managers to be extremely flexible:

> Maybe that was necessary back in the old days (that one had to be ready to relocate on a moment's notice to move into management), and maybe it was more rigid than it needed to be. Now, though, it's not really appropriate anymore for several reasons. First, as the

company grows bigger, we need to find more ways to stay in touch with the communities where we operate, and one of the best ways to do that is by hiring locally, developing managers locally, and letting them have a career in their home community—if they perform. Second, the old way really put good, smart women at a disadvantage in our company because, at the time, they weren't as free to pick up and move as many men were. Now I've seen the light on the opportunities we missed out on with women.[2]

Addressing Disparities

Wal-Mart established the goal that the percentage of women employed should reflect the community—50 per cent of the workforce. This was a well-known target throughout the organization, and all managers insisted they were aware of it and were striving to meet it. In fact, numerous company memos since 1999 had raised the issue of employment equity and urged managers to address inequalities if they existed.

The executive vice-president wanted to know what types of information should be requested to evaluate the state of Wal-Mart's employment practices. Simply asking for "everything" would be illogical as there were literally thousands of documents that could be retrieved, requiring months, if not years, to sift through.

---

[2]Sam Walton, "Sam Walton with John Huey" Made in America, Bantam Books, New York, 1992.

Exhibit 1   Wal-Mart Historical Financials (years ending January 31) (US$ millions, except per share data)

	1994	1995	1996	1997	1998	1999	2000	2001	2002	2003
Selected Financial Information										
Net revenues	67,977	83,398	94,765	106,152	119,248	139,025	166,628	193,116	219,671	246,525
Cost of sales	53,444	65,586	74,505	83,510	93,438	108,725	129,664	150,255	171,562	191,838
Operating, selling and general and administrative expenses	10,333	12,858	15,021	16,946	19,358	22,363	27,040	31,550	36,173	41,043
Net income	2,333	2,681	2,740	3,056	3,526	4,430	5,377	6,295	6,671	8,039
Shareholders' equity	10,753	12,726	14,756	17,143	18,503	21,112	25,834	31,343	35,102	39,337
Return on shareholders' equity	21.7%	21.1%	18.6%	17.8%	19.1%	21.0%	20.8%	20.1%	19.0%	20.4%
Total number of associates (000)	528	622	675	728	825	910	1,140	1,244	1,383	1,400
Shares outstanding (millions)	2,299	2,298	2,294	2,266	2,240	4,450	4,454	4,470	4,451	4,386
Book value per share	4.68	5.54	6.43	7.57	8.26	4.74	5.80	7.01	7.89	8.97

Source: Company files.

Exhibit 2 Job Hierarchy at Wal-Mart

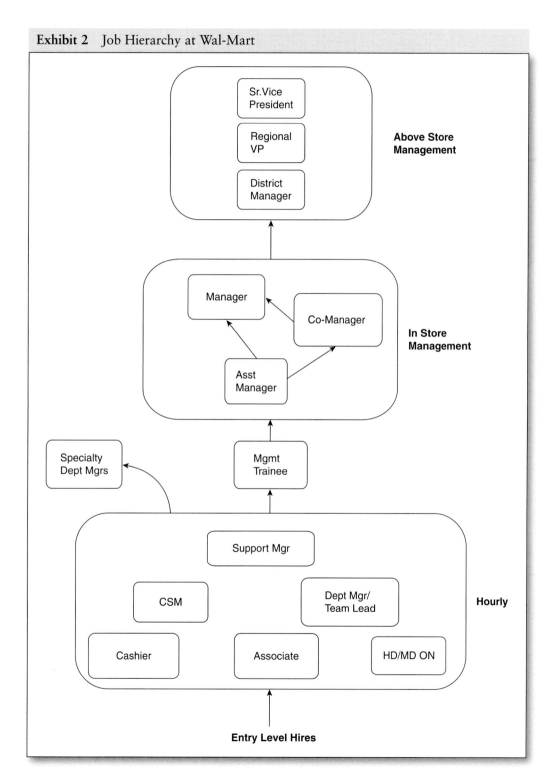

Exhibit 3   2001 Store Statistics

Store Type	Division	Number of Domestic Stores	Average Size (in Square Feet)	Annual Sales per Store (US$ Millions)	Operations Expense (% of Store Sales)	Average Number of Employees per Store (Estimate)	% of Workforce Full-time
Discount Stores	Division One	1,736	125,000	39	15.0	207	85
Supercenters	Division One	888	200,000	75	15.7	540	85
SAM's Club	SAM's Club	475	135,000	60	14.5	172	85
Neighborhood Markets	Division One	19	30,000	14	16.0	81	85

Source: Company files.

Exhibit 4   Sam's Rules for Building a Business

Rule 1

Commit to your business. Believe in it more than anybody else. I think I overcame every single one of my personal shortcomings by the sheer passion I brought to my work. I don't know if you're born with this kind of passion or if you can learn it. But I do know you need it. If you love your work, you'll be out there every day trying to do it the best you possibly can, and pretty soon everybody around will catch the passion from you—like a fever.

Rule 2

Share your profits with all your Associates, and treat them as partners. In turn, they will treat you as a partner, and together you will all perform beyond your wildest expectations. Remain a corporation and retain control if you like, but behave as a servant leader in a partnership. Encourage your Associates to hold a stake in the company. Offer discounted stock, and grant them stock for their retirement. It's the single best thing we ever did.

Rule 3

Motivate your partners. Money and ownership alone aren't enough. Constantly, day-by-day, think of new and more interesting ways to motivate and challenge your partners. Set high goals, encourage competition, and then keep score. Make bets with outrageous payoffs. If things get stale, cross-pollinate; have managers switch jobs with one another to stay challenged. Keep everybody guessing as to what your next trick is going to be. Don't become too predictable.

Rule 4

Communicate everything you possibly can to your partners. The more they know, the more they'll understand. The more they understand, the more they'll care. Once they care, there's no stopping them. If you don't trust your Associates to know what's going on, they'll know you don't really consider them partners. Information is power, and the gain you get from empowering your Associates more than offsets the risk of informing your competitors.

Rule 5

Appreciate everything your Associates do for the business. A paycheck and a stock option will buy one kind of loyalty. But all of us like to be told how much somebody appreciates what we do for them. We like to hear it often, and especially when we have done something we're really proud of. Nothing else can quite substitute for a few well-chosen, well-timed, sincere words of praise. They're absolutely free—and worth a fortune.

Rule 6

Celebrate your successes. Find some humor in your failures. Don't take yourself so seriously. Loosen up, and everybody around you will loosen up. Have fun. Show enthusiasm—always. When all else fails, put on a costume and sing a silly song. Then make everybody else sing with you. Don't do a hula on Wall Street. It's been done. Think up your own stunt. All of this is more important, and more fun, than you think, and it really fools the competition. "Why should we take those cornballs at Wal-Mart seriously?"

Rule 7

Listen to everyone in your company. And figure out ways to get them talking. The folks on the front lines—the ones who actually talk to the customer—are the only ones who really know what's going on out there. You'd better find out what they know. This really is what total quality is all about. To push responsibility down in your organization, and to force good ideas to bubble up within it, you must listen to what your Associates are trying to tell you.

Rule 8

Exceed your customers' expectations. If you do, they'll come back over and over. Give them what they want—and a little more. Let them know you appreciate them. Make good on all your mistakes, and don't make excuses—apologize. Stand behind everything you do. The two most important words I ever wrote were on that first Wal-Mart sign, "Satisfaction Guaranteed." They're still up there, and they have made all the difference.

Rule 9

Control your expenses better than your competition. This is where you can always find the competitive advantage. For 25 years running—long before Wal-Mart was known as the nation's largest retailer—we ranked No. 1 in our industry for the lowest ratio of expenses to sales. You can make a lot of different mistakes and still recover if you run an efficient operation. Or you can be brilliant and still go out of business if you're too inefficient.

Rule 10

Swim upstream. Go the other way. Ignore the conventional wisdom. If everybody else is doing it one way, there's a good chance you can find your niche by going in exactly the opposite direction. But be prepared for a lot of folks to wave you down and tell you you're headed the wrong way. I guess in all my years, what I heard more often than anything was: a town of less than 50,000 population cannot support a discount store for very long.

Source: www.walmart.com, accessed June 5, 2003.

Exhibit 5   Relocation Statistics by Job Type

Percent of Promotions Where Employee Changes Store, District, or Region 1996 and Later

Target Job	Changed Store	Changed District	Changed Region
Store Manager	91.2	69.4	35.6
Co-Manager	81.3	57.0	32.6
Assistant Manager	63.3	40.2	22.0
Management Trainee	62.2	32.5	17.0
Area Manager, SAM's	17.4	5.4	2.8
Support Manager	4.8	7.6	6.0

Average Number of Changes in Store, District, and Region After Entering Store Management Jobs

Target Job	Changed Store	Changed District	Changed Region
Store Manager	3.6	2.8	1.7
Co-Manager	3.0	2.2	1.3
Assistant Manager	2.8	2.0	1.2
Management Trainee	3.0	2.0	1.2
Area Manager, SAM's	1.2	0.6	0.5
Support Manager	0.8	0.6	0.4

Source: Richard Drogin, "Statistical Analysis of Gender Patterns in Wal-Mart Workforce," Drogi, Kakigi & Associates, February 2003.

Environment

RBC—Financing Oil Sands (A)

Michael Sider

Jana Seijts

Ramasastry Chandrasekhar

In early August 2009, Sandra Odendahl, director of Corporate Environmental Affairs, Royal Bank of Canada (RBC), Canada's largest commercial bank (see Exhibit 1: Top Ten Banks in Canada by Assets), was asked to prepare a briefing paper and strategy proposal for the head of Corporate Citizenship, a department that oversaw RBC's strategy and programs on environment and corporate responsibility. The head of Corporate Citizenship wanted a briefing on the growing backlash over the bank's financing of companies involved in the extraction of crude oil from oil sands located in the province of Alberta in Canada. Some environmental activists wanted the bank to stop financing these companies because the extraction process consumed freshwater, generated waste and emitted carbon dioxide (CO_2). The activists also believed strongly that oil sands extraction had a negative impact on the ecosystem of First Nations communities living near, and downstream from, the extraction sites.

As Odendahl compiled alternatives for review, she knew that the decision of the Corporate Citizenship Department would not be an easy one. The choices would involve dilemmas in which the core issues were ambivalent.

One week earlier, the Rainforest Action Network (RAN), an environmental activist group headquartered in San Francisco, California, had draped a 15-foot banner on RBC's headquarters building in downtown Toronto, appealing to Janet Nixon, wife of the bank's chief executive officer (CEO), Gordon Nixon, to "pressure" her husband to "pull RBC out of funding oil sands." The appeal was followed by RAN's bombardment of the e-mail accounts of executives in RBC's Corporate Citizenship Department. It was against this volatile backdrop that Odendahl had to brief the head of Corporate Citizenship on the various implications of financing businesses operating in Alberta's oil sands.

Said Odendahl:

> There are several components here. There is the strategic component. Is our lending to the oil sands sector, per se, flawed? Do we need to change the basics of our lending strategy? There is the communications component. Have we adequately portrayed our track record, of over a decade now, as an environment-friendly bank? Have we let the agenda slip out of our hands? There is the customer component. Do our customers, internal and external, concur with our lending to oil sands? If so, shouldn't we stand by them? There is the component of globalization. Can we be an island unto ourselves in an interconnected and interdependent world? Can we take a call, in a social vacuum, on cutting out the flow of credit to a customer segment? There is also the element of our identity and our raison d'être. Who are we as a bank? Are we in the business of lending or in the business of allocating sectoral credit?

Oil Sands Sector

Alberta had oil reserves trapped in intricate amalgamations of sand, water and clay, called oil sands. Also known as tar sands, they had been formed by the same forces of nature that had shaped the province's other landmark, the Rocky Mountains.[1] Light crude had been buried in the depths of southern Alberta for millennia, and geological pressures had been driving it toward the northern regions of the province. During the course of migration, bacterial intervention had converted the crude into bitumen, a viscous oil rich in carbon and in a solid state. Over time, bitumen had saturated the sand deposits left over from the rivers in the region and now lay buried under 140,000 square kilometers of pristine boreal forest in northern Alberta and Saskatchewan, an area larger than the provinces of New Brunswick, Nova Scotia and Prince Edward Island combined. The oil sands had proven reserves of 179 billion barrels of oil, second only to Saudi Arabia. The total "estimated" reserves were, however, of the order of 1.7 trillion to 2.5 trillion barrels.

Although deposits of natural bitumen were found in many other countries, they did not lend themselves to the scale essential for commercial

---

[1]Oil Sands Discovery Centre, "The Oil Sands Story," www.oilsandsdiscovery.com/oil_sands_story/story.html, accessed November 3, 2009.

production. The only exception was Venezuela's Orinoco Belt, which had not only reserves of oil sands but also production facilities.

Alberta had three designated oil sand areas (OSAs): Athabasca Wabiskaw-McMurray, Cold Lake Clearwater and Peace River Bluesky-Gething. Contained within these areas was a total of 15 oil sands deposits (OSDs) in specific geological zones, together covering 140,000 square kilometers (see Exhibit 2: Map of Main Oil Sands Region in Alberta).

In the early 1920s, the first efforts were made to extract oil from oil sands in the Alberta region. But it was not until the late 1960s that large-scale commercial operations made extraction economically viable. Suncor Energy was the first company to enter the oil sands business in Alberta in 1967, followed by Syncrude Canada in 1978.

The process used was known as open-pit mining, prevalent even today and contributing to 82 per cent of production from oil sands in 2008. In this process, trees were cleared, and the top layer of the earth was removed to expose the slurry that would be moved by trucks to a separation facility. The slurry was mixed with water to be segregated into three layers: sand, water and bitumen. The bitumen was then skimmed off for further processing. The trucks used for transporting the slurry each had a 400-ton capacity, as large as a house. The process was continuous, 24/7 and 365 days a year.

Open-pit mining dislocated vast tracts of flora and fauna and generated waste—both liquid and solid—which was difficult to treat. Two tonnes of material needed to be mined to produce one barrel of oil. Open-pit mining was not viable as a long-term alternative because more than 80 per cent of the oil sands in Alberta were buried deep. Open-pit mining skimmed only the surface, tapping deposits buried to 75 meters.

The process of open-pit mining had led to so-called in situ mining, which was gaining ground, and could be used to recover the deeper reserves of bitumen. The technology used was known as Steam-Assisted Gravity Drainage (SAGD). Steam was injected to heat the oil sand directly without mining it. The heat lowered the viscosity of bitumen, and the hot bitumen migrated to the surface, leaving the sand "in place" (*in situ*, in Latin). SAGD was expensive and required minimum conditions, such as a nearby water source. Low-cost methods of in situ recovery were in different stages of development.

The processing of bitumen involved four stages to remove the carbon and add hydrogen: coking (for removing the carbon), distillation (sorting hydrocarbon molecules into various components), catalytic conversion (transforming hydrocarbons into high-value forms) and hydro-treating (adding hydrogen). The end product was synthetic crude oil (also known as syncrude) that was refined further into jet fuels, gasoline and other petroleum-based products such as plastics.

Inputs

Extraction of oil from oil sands required two major inputs: water and natural gas. Water was required to steam up the oil sands and reduce the viscosity of bitumen so that it could be segregated. Three barrels of freshwater were needed to produce one barrel of oil. In Alberta, the Athabasca River was the primary source of water for production facilities; however, climate change and a variety of industrial and agricultural demands for water from the Athabasca River had lowered its flows to critical levels during certain times of the year. The average summer flow of the river had declined by 29 per cent between 1970 and 2005. Although more than 90 per cent of the water extracted could be reused, ultimately only five to ten per cent of the extracted water was returned to the river. The rest was too toxic.

On a broader plane, Canada had a relative abundance of water, possessing nine per cent of the world's renewable freshwater to meet the needs of only 0.5 per cent of the world's population. Canada also had more lake area than any other country in the world, with approximately eight per cent of its territory covered by lakes. One-third of Canadians depended on groundwater as their freshwater source. But increased evaporation of surface water under warmer climates and altered precipitation patterns were causing summer droughts in the interior of southern Canada. In the past several years, 25 per cent of Canadian municipalities had experienced water shortages. With each passing year, the shortages had become more frequent and of longer duration. In Western Canada, the shortages were likely to worsen. The alpine glaciers, which were providing much of the freshwater input in regional streams and rivers in summer, were gradually disappearing due to global warming.

Extraction of oil from oil sands was an energy-intensive activity. Energy, in the form of natural gas, was needed to make energy. In 2007, 412 billion cubic feet of natural gas was consumed by oil sands producers, representing 13 per cent of total Canadian demand for natural gas.[2]

A related issue was the need to establish pipelines, consistent with the expansion plans of mining and oil companies, to supply natural gas to the oil sands and transport crude to nearby ports for the onward journey to various

---

[2]Natural Resources Canada, "Executive Summary," *Canadian Natural Gas: Review of 2007/08 and Outlook to 2010,* http://www.nrcan-rncan.gc.ca/eneene/sources/natnat/revrev-sumsom-eng.php, accessed January 8, 2010.

processing facilities. Two projects were under review by a joint territorial and federal review board. The first was a $42-billion Alaska natural gas pipeline to transport the gas from Alaska's Arctic Slope region, across the Yukon to Alberta and eventually to Chicago, a total distance of 5,600 kilometers. The second was a $16.2-billion proposal—by a consortium including Imperial Oil, Royal Dutch Shell and ConocoPhillips—to lay a 1,200-kilometer gas pipeline through the Mackenzie Valley. The World Wildlife Fund (WWF), a leading conservation organization based in the United States, was of the view that the pipelines would cut through wetland eco-regions and affect the lives of native communities irreversibly. WWF had proposed what it called a "Conservation First" approach, which would establish a network of protected areas functioning at an ecosystem level prior to any exploitation of mineral resources.

Output

In addition to oil, oil sands also generated several other end products. The waste water, amounting to 95 per cent of the input, was diverted to tailings ponds, which each covered approximately 50 square kilometers. Dam structures, among the largest in the world, were constructed over the tailing ponds. Even after decades of oil sands operations, no evidence had shown that reclamation of tailing ponds was possible. The tailing pond water contained high levels of residual naphthenic acids, making it toxic to aquatic life. Toxins connected to oil sands production were found as far downstream as the Athabasca Delta, one of the largest freshwater deltas in the world. Oil sands extraction also emitted up to three times more greenhouse gases (GHGs) than conventional oil extraction.

The end product left a large environmental footprint: open-pit mine holes, disrupted supplies of freshwater, tailing ponds filled with toxic waste water and CO_2 emissions.

Expansion Plans

Canadian oil sands production was pegged at 1.7 million barrels per day (bpd) in late 2008 (see Exhibit 3: Bitumen Production at Alberta Oil Sands). Strategy West, a Calgary-based consultancy firm, had forecast that oil sands production would increase to up to seven million bpd by 2030 (see Exhibit 4: Existing and Proposed Commercial Projects at Alberta Oil Sands). The expansion plans of all the 23 operators in the oil sands—including the transcontinental pipelines—had been valued at more than US$125 billion. Nineteen of the operators had firmed up plans to produce 5.45 million bpd by 2020 (see Exhibit 5: Current and Planned Output at Alberta Oil Sands by Company).

The expansion plans were a lightning rod for environmentalists.

Said Brant Olson, oil campaign director, RAN:

> Business success is no longer about profits alone. There is an ethical dimension to conducting business. The concept of Corporate Social Responsibility is catching up. Triple Bottom Line reporting is becoming a way for businesses to demonstrate they have strategies in place for Sustainable Development. People, planet and profits are widely accepted as the three integrated metrics for measuring corporate performance. Banks can not take decisions in an ethical vacuum. They have to take a stand. The current developments in sustainability are a great opportunity for them to lock in their reputation and their brand value on a differentiating platform of sustainability. Making a conscious choice about not lending to oil sands is a great way for a bank to build its brand equity. A bank like RBC should be leading by example.

Context

For environmentalists, their concern over the funding of oil sands by banks was escalating in an atmosphere in which business models were changing worldwide, both in the services and manufacturing sectors. The triggers for the change were twofold—the subprime mortgage crisis of September 2007 and the October 2007 awarding of the Nobel Peace Prize jointly to the Intergovernmental Panel on Climate Change (IPCC), a body established by the United Nations, and to Al Gore, a former U.S. vice president.

The subprime mortgage crisis had been precipitated by the launch of innovative products aimed at niche markets, which had failed the litmus test of risk tolerance. Sensing a demand for loans to borrowers with fractured credit, banks had developed customized products, generating a perception among borrowers that the more they borrowed, the more they earned. The superstructure of credit started collapsing when a few minor defaults in payments snowballed into larger defaults, and the loans were recalled. The collapse of the credit structure had quickly led, in many parts of the world, to a decline in customer confidence, the pillar of the banking system. Banks were shrinking in size or disappearing altogether in the United States, the United Kingdom and Asia.

Canadian banks were much less affected by the global trend because their lending practices were more conservative and they had managed risk well. Their asset leverage was low and their capital stock was of high quality. Canada's banks were also regulated effectively under the Bank Act, with oversight by the Office of the Superintendent of Financial Institutions (OSFI) and the Financial Consumer Agency of Canada. Unlike their counterparts in G8 countries,[3] Canadian banks did not

---

[3]G8 comprised USA, UK, West Germany, Japan, Italy, France, Canada and Russia.

seek capital infusion from the government. They had not only endured the crisis but had grown and maintained their dividends. Even in the worst year for global banking in decades, RBC had posted record profits.

Despite the resilience of the Canadian banking system, the financial crisis had a spinoff in the form of a recession, which had affected the Canadian economy. Although Canadian banks were insulated from the global financial crisis, they were being pulled in opposite directions by the recession. They were under a general mandate—by the federal government and the Bank of Canada—to loosen up on lending to facilitate the flow of credit and stimulate spending. They were also under pressure—from regulators, analysts, shareholders and rating agencies—to exercise prudence to preempt a crisis.

The awarding of the Nobel Peace Prize to the IPCC and Al Gore had galvanized, into a worldwide movement, the concept of sustainable development, defined as "development that meets the needs of the present without compromising the ability of future generations to meet their own needs."[4] At the same time, banks and financial institutions were being increasingly recognized as lenders to the energy industry, which positioned them to lead the movement. As the 2008 Report by the Carbon Disclosure Project, an independent not-for-profit organization holding the largest database of primary corporate climate change information in the world, noted: "[The financial services sector's] greatest risk from climate change and its greatest opportunity to reduce the advance of global warming is through its investment and lending portfolios."[5]

Said Brant Olson, RAN's oil campaign director:

The recent banking crisis has shown how the financial markets can totally misjudge both the risks and values inherent in company balance sheets. Major banks are financing a growth in GHG emissions that could lead to a catastrophic climate crisis that will negatively impact us all. When banks chase short term profits, they risk overreaching the long range carrying capacity of the planet. Financing oil sands at Alberta will prove to be the sub-prime lending of the oil industry. It will be a financial and environmental disaster rolled into one.

Banks were now under pressure from new quarters to revisit financing that

---

[4]United Nations General Assembly, "Report of the World Commission on Environment and Development," December 11, 1987, http://www.un.org/documents/ga/res/42/ares42-187.htm, accessed December 15, 2009.

[5]PricewaterhouseCoopers, *Carbon Disclosure Project Report 2008: Global 500*, https://www.cdproject.net/CDPResults/67_329_143_CDP%20Global%20500%20Report%202008.pdf, p. 85, accessed January 8, 2010.

had already been committed. Activist groups were asking banks to redirect their resources to building a low-carbon and climate-friendly business environment. According to these groups, the top-five Canadian banks were adopting, with regard to oil sands, the same "short-sighted and myopic"[6] lending strategies of American banks that had caused the meltdown in global financial markets in 2007 (see Exhibit 6: Canadian Banks' Loan Portfolios, 2008).

Some, like Rajendra Pachauri, chairperson of the IPCC, had called for an extreme position: "Canada should consider closing down the controversial oil sands projects in northern Alberta."[7]

In 2008 and 2009, a wide range of opinion and disagreement emerged among the scientific, academic, nongovernmental organization (NGO), government and industry communities regarding the actual environmental implications of oil sands development, with each group citing sources that would bolster its own viewpoint.

As a result, the Academies of Arts, Humanities and Sciences of Canada (also known as the Royal Society of Canada), a think tank, was planning to commence a study entitled "Environmental and Health Impacts of Canada's Oil Sands Industry."[8] Scheduled to be released in the spring of 2011, the study was expected to provide definitive answers to the dilemmas in oil sands development faced by policy makers, businesses, bankers, consumers of energy and the general public.

RBC's stance in this regard was explained by Gordon Nixon, CEO:[9]

> We do everything we can, as a corporation, to do things the right way such as containing our environmental footprint, when it comes to our own buildings, or ensuring our lending practices are responsible. It's easier to do this if you are a financial institution than if you are a mining company or an oil company.
>
> Looking at sustainable value, we take a view that you can't over-emphasize the environment at huge cost to the economy and, at the same time, you cannot do things economically that are a huge cost to the environment. The middle ground is the answer. Take the development of Northern Alberta. It's important economically and in

---

[6] http://understory.ran.org/2009/02/26/rbc-get-out-of-the-tar-sands/statement_of_brant_olson, referenced December 15, 2009.

[7] "Canada Failing in Fight against Climate Change, UN Panel Says," *Montreal Gazette*, September 21, 2009, http://www.montrealgazette.com/business/Canada+failing+fight+against+climate+change+panel+says/2016158/story.html, accessed January 8, 2010.

[8] http://www.rsc.ca/updates/5October2009/, accessed December 15, 2009.

[9] Gordon Nixon, in an interview with Diane Francis, "Building Sustainable Value at RBC," *Financial Post*, September 9, 2009, p. FP3.

terms of energy security, but it has to be done responsibly from an environmental viewpoint.

Energy Security

Since 2002, Alberta had been experiencing the strongest period of economic growth ever recorded by any province in Canadian history.[10] The average growth in Alberta's gross domestic product (GDP) of 12.7 per cent per annum was the fastest among the provinces of the developed world and compared favorably with China's GDP growth of 14.8 per cent. The growth was being driven by Alberta's unique competitive advantage as an exporter of natural resources. Crude oil and natural gas accounted for 65 per cent of Alberta's exports, and coal and petrochemicals accounted for ten per cent. The provincial government, based in Edmonton, had been collecting approximately one-third of its fiscal revenues from lease sales and royalties on fossil fuel extraction, including from the oil sands. Because Alberta was running a surplus budget, it had become the center of jobs creation in Canada. Calgary, the province's commercial capital, had become the energy hub of North America.

Energy security was a crucial component of a country's geo-political leverage and power play, worldwide. Canada was already the largest supplier of crude oil to the United States. Exports to the United States from oil sands in Alberta comprised more than a million barrels per day and were expected to increase progressively to five million barrels per day by 2020, coinciding with the ongoing expansion plans in Alberta. The oil sands projects in Alberta were forecast to generate $500 billion for the North American economy and 5.4 million person years of work between 2009 and 2020.[11] The energy security and economic benefits offered by the oil sands businesses were too promising for either the federal government of Canada or the provincial government of Alberta to even consider cutbacks in oil extraction. The stakes were running high.

Environmentalists, however, had a different view of the issue. Said Olson:

> The extraction of oil from oil sands is not a sustainable model of economic development. It is tactical and shortsighted. The benefits will not last beyond a generation or two. But the damage will harm many generations to come. Once the assets are depleted, mining and oil companies will not be able to bring profitable products to the

[10]Philip Cross and Geoff Bowlby, "The Alberta Economic Juggernaut," *Canadian Economic Observer*, September 2006, Section 3.1 Statistics Canada catalogue no 11-010.

[11]Jon Entine, "Sifting Oil Sands for Grains of Truth," *Ethical Corporation*, November 2009, http://www.jonentine.com/ethical_corporation/2009_11_Oil%20_Sands.pdf, accessed January 8, 2010.

market. The investments will be stranded. Alberta is a region of compelling environmental concern in the world today because of both the size of investment being committed by banks in oil sands projects and the scale of its impact on the ecosystem.

RBC had been providing credit and financing services to the energy industry for more than 50 years. Its clients were in both the decades-old petroleum-based sectors (such as oil extraction and processing) and the emerging renewable energy sectors (such as wind farms). Several of RBC's clients had been involved in oil sands projects (the first category of investment) since the late 1960s.

Social Costs

CO_2, methane, nitrous oxide and fluorinated gases were collectively known as greenhouse gases (GHGs). Emitted largely as the result of industrial processes, GHGs trapped the heat in the atmosphere, leading, over time, to a phenomenon called global warming.[12] Governments all over the world were trying to reduce the GHG emissions from their respective geographies, as part of an attempt to reduce global warming. The emissions of CO_2, in particular, were being monitored through a metric called "a carbon footprint." Narrowed down to individual business enterprises, the carbon footprint was the sum total of CO_2 emissions as a result of an organization's various business activities.

A study released by Statistics Canada in June 2009 had shown that Canada's GHG emissions had risen from 592 million tons in 1990 to 721 million tons in 2006. The increase, of 21.7 per cent, was the biggest percentage increase among G8 countries over the same time period.[13] The trend was contrary to the commitment made by Canada, as a signatory to the Kyoto Protocol, to reduce its GHG emissions by six per cent by 2012 over 1990 levels[14] (see Exhibit 7: Canada's GHG Emissions 1990–2006).

The Alberta Department of Environment had estimated that the oil sands contributed four per cent of Canada's overall GHG emissions[15] amounting to approximately 30 million tonnes in 2006.

---

[12]U.S. Environmental Protection Agency, "Greenhouse Gas Emissions," http://www.epa.gov/climate change/emissions/index.html www.epa.gov, accessed December 15, 2009.

[13]Statistics Canada, "Human Activity and the Environment: Annual Statistics," Catalogue no. 16-201-X, June 2009.

[14]David Suzuki Foundation, "Kyoto Protocol," http://www.davidsuzuki.org/climate_Change/Kyoto/, accessed November 9, 2009.

[15]Government of Alberta, "FAQ—Oil Sands," http://environment.gov.ab.ca/info/faqs/faq5-oil_sands.asp, accessed December 15, 2009.

In calculating their own carbon footprints, banks traditionally considered emissions from activities such as business travel, energy consumption and employee commutes, which were quantifiable and measurable.

However, RAN had a different perspective on the carbon footprint of banks. It not only considered emissions associated with running the bank offices (known as "operational emissions") but also those resulting from the megaprojects the banks were financing (which it called "financed emissions"). RAN had thus calculated that Canada's five largest banks were financing carbon emissions totaling 625 million tonnes of CO_2.[16]

The oil sands projects in Alberta were being funded by not only the five leading Canadian banks but also other banks, including three British commercial banks: Barclay's, HSBC and the Royal Bank of Scotland. However, RBC had come under particular spotlight on the part of RAN, which felt that, as the largest among Canadian banks, RBC was in a position to influence the pace of lending to the oil sands projects by its Canadian peers. RBC could also, as the 13th largest bank in the world (see Exhibit 8: Top Global Banks Ranked by Market Capitalization), shape the thinking of global peers towards ecological and social accountability.

Said Odendahl:

There is no question that we are responsible for our own carbon footprint just as our customers are responsible for theirs. It is not fair, though, to combine the bank's footprint with our customers' footprints and hold the bank accountable for both. Where would we draw the line? We have 18 million clients, and every individual and company that we lend to emits CO_2. It is illogical to expect banks to track, report on, and be accountable for their customers' CO_2 emissions. Furthermore, there are many environmentally significant emissions other than CO_2. Would banks eventually be expected to track, report on and be accountable for client emissions of all pollutants? Clearly, this is ridiculous.

Royal Bank of Canada

Established by a group of private traders in 1864 at Halifax, Nova Scotia, The Merchants Bank, as it was then called, financed fishing, timber and retail businesses. The bank obtained a royal charter in 1869. After opening a branch in 1887 in Montreal, the hub of Canadian finance at the time, the bank expanded into Western Canada and changed its name to The Royal Bank of Canada in 1901. By 1925, it had grown, mainly through acquisitions, to

---

[16]Rainforest Action Network, *Financing Global Warming: Canadian Banks and Fossil Fuels*, November 2008, p. 5, http://climatefriendlybanking.com/fileadmin/materials/comms/mediacontent/reports/executive_summary.pdf, accessed January 8, 2010.

become Canada's largest bank with 668 branches and a staff of 8,500.

In 2008, RBC was still Canada's largest bank as measured by assets. It was also the 13th largest in the world as measured by market capitalization. RBC provided personal and commercial banking, wealth management services, insurance, corporate and investment banking and transaction processing services on a global basis. RBC had offices in Canada, the United States and 48 other countries, employing more than 80,000 full- and part-time staff who served more than 17 million personal, business, public sector and institutional clients.

RBC's commitment to sustainable development could be traced to at least 1991, when it released its first corporate policy on environment. The bank had received annual recognition for its approach to sustainability. RBC had been included in the Dow Jones Sustainability World Index (a listing of the top 10 per cent of the largest stocks in the Dow Jones Global Index in terms of their sustainability and environmental practices) since the Index's inception in 1999; The Dow Jones North American Sustainability 40 Index (which tracked the performance of the largest sustainability leaders in North America); the Jantzi Social Index (comprising Canadian companies meeting environmental, social and governance rating criteria) and the FTSE4Good Index (which measured the performance of

companies meeting globally recognized corporate sustainability standards).

In 2007, RBC published an "Environmental Blueprint" outlining its priorities pertaining to operations, business activities, products and services, employees, compliance, reporting transparency and partnerships. The Environmental Blueprint articulated three clear goals: to reduce the bank's own environmental footprint (by focusing on energy use, paper consumption, employee travel, water use and procurement); to promote environmentally responsible business activities (by reorienting its lending and investment policies) and to offer environmental products and services (such as e-statements and energy saver mortgages). In all, the Economic Blueprint presented 44 medium- and long-term environmental commitments and pledged to report on their progress annually.

Issues in 2009

RBC risked that any of its responses might seem to provide a spin to its own products and policies to create an illusion of sustainability. The perception of "greenwash," as it was commonly referred to, would undo the recognition RBC had gained as an organization focused on sustainable development.

The other risk to consider was the vacuum that would be created if RBC, or other Canadian banks, stopped financing the non-renewable energy sector. It might only be a matter of time before overseas banks with less robust environmental risk management practices would attempt to take business away from Canadian banks on Canadian soil. For example, Chinese banks were eager to bankroll investments in Alberta oil sands by Chinese oil companies. PetroChina, the investment wing of China National Petroleum Corp, an oil company owned by the Chinese government, was planning to bid for a 60 per cent stake in two key bitumen operations in Alberta (the MacKay River and the Dover projects) for $1.7 billion. Its application would need to receive mandatory approval by the federal government. Under the provisions of the Investment Canada Act, any non-Canadian firm acquiring controlling interest of a Canadian company with assets more than $312 million required clearance from the federal government.[17] The federal government of the day, however, was

known to favor international investment in general; and thus, was unlikely to discourage overseas bankers from playing a role in Alberta oil sands.

Said Odendahl:

RBC is only one of the many constituents with a stake in oil sands projects. They include the federal government, provincial government, oil companies, mining companies, local businesses, indigenous communities, consumers of energy and the public at large. But, let us say, for the sake of argument, that RBC stops financing energy companies which are active in the oil sands on the ground that environmentalists consider oil sands hazardous. What happens when an interest group decides that the use of pesticides on farms is wrong or that genetically modified foods are unethical? Should banks stop lending to the agriculture sector? Should banks stop providing car loans to customers who buy large cars which are gas guzzlers? Should banks disallow mortgages to smokers? Where does one draw the line? There are no clear cut answers.

The Richard Ivey School of Business gratefully acknowledges the generous support of the Royal Bank of Canada in the development of these learning materials.

[17]Jason Fekete, "China's $1.98 Bid in Oilsands Sparks Energy Security Debate," *Calgary Herald*, http://www.calgaryherald.com/business/China+oilsands+sparks+energy+security+debate/1949947/story.html, accessed November 30, 2009.

Exhibit 1   Top Ten Banks in Canada by Assets

Ranking			Total Assets (in US$ million)	
2008	2007	**Bank**	2008	2007
1	1	Royal Bank of Canada	723,859	600,346
2	2	TD-Canada Trust	563,214	422,124
3	3	Bank of Nova Scotia	507,625	411,510
4	4	Bank of Montreal	416,050	366,524
5	5	Canadian Imperial Bank of Commerce	353,930	342,178
6	6	National Bank of Canada	129,332	113,085
7	7	HSBC Bank of Canada	69,687	65,153
8	8	ING Bank of Canada	25,921	24,264
9	9	Laurentian Bank of Canada	19,559	17,787
10	10	Citibank Canada	18,070	19,028

Source: "Canadian Banks 2008—Perspectives on the Canadian Banking Industry," PricewaterhouseCoopers, March 2009, page 68.

Exhibit 2   Map of Main Oil Sands Region in Alberta

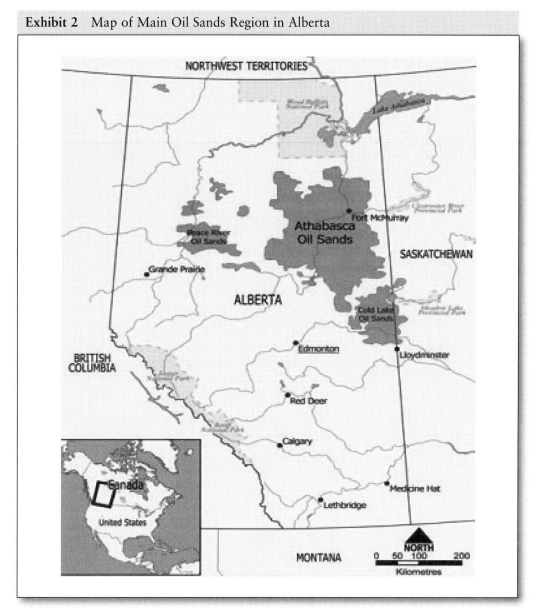

Source: "Unconventional Oil: Scraping the Bottom of the Barrel?" The Cooperative Group of UK in association with World Wildlife Fund, 2008, page 9.

Exhibit 3   Bitumen Production at Alberta Oil Sands

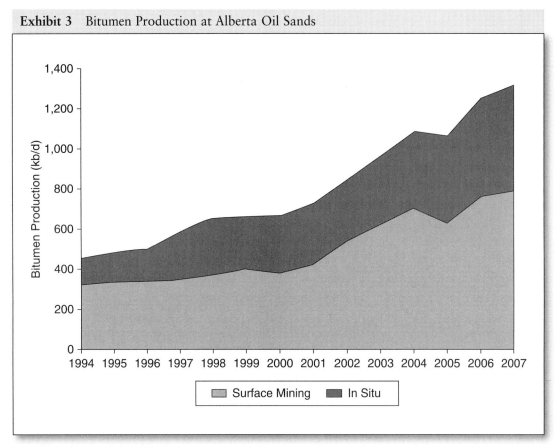

Source: R. B. Dunbar, www.strategywest.com/Canada's_oil_sands/oil_sands_industry_outlook/pdf, "Canada's Oil Sands Industry: Production and Outlook," December 2008, page 6.

Exhibit 4   Existing and Proposed Commercial Projects at Alberta Oil Sands

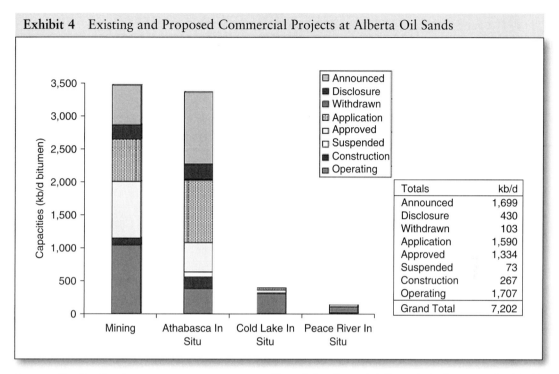

Source: R. B. Dunbar, www.strategywest.com/Canada's_oil_sands/oil_sands_industry_outlook/pdf, "Canada's Oil Sands Industry: Production and Outlook," December 2008, page 10.

Exhibit 5   Current and Planned Output at Alberta Oil Sands by Company

Company	Mining ('000s of barrels per day)		In Situ ('000s bpd)		Total ('000s bpd) (2020)
	2006	Planned (2020)	2006	Planned (2020)	
CNRL	0	577	50	240	817
Suncor	276	324	66	376	700
Shell	155	570	12	100	670
Syncrude	291	593	–	–	593
Encana		–	50	500	500
Exxon/Mobil/Imperial		300	140	170	470
PetroCanada		190	34.5	274.5	464.5
Total/Deer Creek		200	2	42	242
BP/Husky		–	–	230	230
OPTI/Nexen		–	2.5	218.5	218.5
Statoil/North American		–	–	160	160
Synenco		100	–	–	100
ConocoPhilips		–	–	100	100
Devon		–	–	70	70
JECOS		–	10	60	60
MEG		–	–	25	25
Black Rock		–	0.5	20.5	20.5
Connacher		–	–	10	10
Orion		–	2	–	–
Total	722	2,854	371.5	2,596.5	5,450.5

Source: "Unconventional oil: Scraping the bottom of the barrel?" Report published by The Cooperative Group of UK in association with World Wildlife Fund, page 33 of 52.

Exhibit 6   Canadian Banks' Loans Portfolios, 2008

#		Royal Bank of Canada		Bank of Montreal		Bank of Nova Scotia		Canadian Imperial Bank of Commerce		Toronto-Dominion Bank	
		2008	%	2008	%	2008	%	2008	%	2008	%
A	**Segment-wise loans**										
1	Residential mortgages	122,991		49,343		115,084		90,695		63,003	
2	Personal and credit card loans	69,660		45,857		50,719		42,953		86,997	
3	Business and government loans	99,104		84,151		125,503		39,273		71,160	
4	Allowances for credit losses	(2,215)		(1,747)		(2,626)		(1,446)		(1,536)	
	Total loans	289,540		177,604		288,680		171,475		219,624	
B	**Business loans by industry category**										
1	Agriculture		4.9		3.9		3.8		6.7		3.3
2	Commercial mortgages & real estate		21.4		21.2		10.6		25.3		34.1
3	Communications		–		1.5		3.4		1.8		2.3
4	Financial institutions		13.1		24.7		22.4		13.3		10.4
5	Government (including social services)		2.3		0.9		5.4		6.5		7.2
6	Manufacturing		8.4		9.7		7.1		5.5		7.4
7	Media and entertainment		3.0		–		2.2		1.4		2.9
8	Natural resources		12.3		10.8		12.5		14.8		11.1
9	Service industries, retail & wholesale		6.9		19.5		17.3		17.8		8.0
10	Transportation		3.9		3.5		9.4		5.7		4.6
11	Others		23.8		4.3		5.9		1.2		8.5
	Total		100.0		100.0		100.0		100.0		100.0

Source: Canadian Banks 2009: Perspectives on the Canadian Banking Industry published by PricewaterhouseCoopers March 2009 pages 58 and 59 (for segment-wise loans in dollar amounts) and pages 66 and 67 (for percentages of industry-wise business loans).

Exhibit 7   Canada's GHG Emissions, 1990–2006

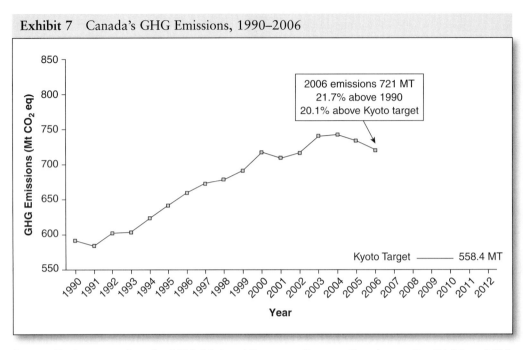

Source: Environment Canada, 2008. National Inventory Report, Greenhouse Gas Division, 2008. http://www.ec.gc.ca/pdb/ghg/inventory_report/2006/tab_eng.cfm Referenced November 24, 2009.

Exhibit 8   Top Global Banks Ranked by Market Capitalization

| Ranking | | | | Market Value as of Dec 31, 2008 |
2008	2007	Name of the Bank	Country	(in US$ millions)
1	1	Industrial and Commercial Bank of China	China	130,207
2	6	JP Morgan Chase and Co	USA	117,681
3	2	HSBC Holdings	UK	115,217
4	–	Wells Fargo & Co	USA	98,028
5	4	Bank of China Ltd	China	77,403
6	7	Banco Santander SA	Spain	75,009
7	3	Bank of America Corp	USA	70,647
8	–	Tatra Banka AS	Slovakia	46,769
9	–	Bayerische Hypo-Und-Vereinsbanken AG	Germany	45,832
10	–	Banco Bilbao Vizcaya Argentaria SA	Spain	45,119
13	24	The Royal Bank of Canada	Canada	40,881
22	37	The Toronto Dominion Bank	Canada	29,782
28	38	The Bank of Nova Scotia	Canada	27,155
44	63	Canadian Imperial Bank of Commerce	Canada	15,759

Source: "Canadian Banks 2008—Perspectives on the Canadian Banking Industry," PricewaterhouseCoopers March 2009.

Barrick Gold Corporation—Tanzania[1]

Aloysius Newenham-Kahindi
Paul W. Beamish

By March 2009, Canadian mining company Barrick Gold Corporation (Barrick) had only been operating in the Lake Victoria Zone in Tanzania for a decade. In the same year, Barrick had adopted a new name for its business in Tanzania, African Barrick Gold plc (ABG), which was also listed on the London Stock Exchange. The company was widely considered to be one of the more "responsive" global corporations in the mining industry.[2] Its extensive mining activities in the region employed thousands of local people, and Barrick was engaged in social development projects in various Tanzanian communities.[3] By October 2010, the company operated four main gold mining sites in the country.[4]

Despite Barrick's efforts to support social development initiatives in the Lake Victoria Zone over the past decade, discontent and resistance at one of its mining sites in North Mara still

remained. This area posed challenges. A key question was why the tension and violence had not stopped in certain mining sites in the North Mara mining area, and whether there was much more Barrick could reasonably be expected to do to resolve the problem.

Background on Tanzania

Tanzania was a developing country located in East Africa, with a total land size of 945,087 square kilometres. It had one of the highest levels of unemployment and poverty in Sub-Saharan Africa. Its economy was heavily dependent on agriculture, which accounted for half of the gross domestic product (GDP), provided 85 per cent of the country's exports and employed 90 per cent of the work force. Topography and climatic conditions, however, limited cultivated crops to only four per cent of

---

[1]This case has been written on the basis of published sources only. Consequently, the interpretation and perspectives presented in this case are not necessarily those of Barrick Gold Corporation or any of its employees.

[2]www.barrick.com/CorporateResponsibility/BeyondBorders/default.aspx, accessed March 24, 2009.

[3]www.barrick.com/News/PressReleases/PressReleaseDetails/2010/Barrick-Named-to-Dow-Jones-Sustainability-World-Index-for-Third-Consecutive-Year/default.aspx, accessed September 27, 2010.

[4]www.tanzaniagold.com/barrick.html, accessed October 1, 2010.

the land area. Industry was mainly limited to processing agricultural products and light consumer goods.

Like most developing nations, Tanzania had a very weak national institutional and legal system. It also had a very high rate of corruption.[5] The country needed support from foreign direct investment (FDI) and transnational corporations (TNCs) in order to promote businesses, employment, and other opportunities for its citizens. Tanzania wanted its institutions to be more transparent and accountable and to regulate the activities of FDI and TNCs in addressing the country's social and ecological issues. Both local and international not-for-profit organizations (NFOs), however, had continued to create a significant impact with respect to promoting responsive behaviour in corporate governance practices, positively influencing all involved stakeholders and other social actors to address social issues.

Following independence in 1961, Tanzania opted for a socialist command economic and institutional system, with socialist policies (*"Ujamaa"* in Swahili) being implemented in 1967. The emphasis of these policies was to promote co-operative institutions and collective villages with the aim of building an egalitarian society, eliminating ethnic and gender barriers, and creating a common language of Swahili for all.

Within the practice of Ujamaa, the country had managed to unite its ethnic groups under a common language, with the result that the central government had created strong post-colonial nationalistic ideologies, unity, ethnic harmony and peace among its people. Compared to many post-colonial Sub-Saharan African countries that went through civil and ethnic strife and conflicts after independence in the 1960s and 1970s, Tanzania under Ujamaa appeared to be a successful model.

Towards the end of the 1980s, however, Tanzania began to experience significant economic stagnation and social problems. To combat these issues, in the early 1990s the government sought to privatize its economy and reform its institutions in order to attract foreign investment. The introduction of the famous post-Ujamaa Investment Act of 1997 was intended to encourage free market and trade liberalization in the country. Investment in various private sectors such as mining, tourism, fishing, banking and agriculture under foreign-owned TNCs served to bolster the country's reforms by creating employment opportunities for the local economy.

As the country continued to privatize and reform its national institutional and legal systems, many foreign companies sought to invest in its economy. The Tanzania Investment Centre (TIC)

---

[5]See data on Tanzania at www.transparency.org.

was created in the early 2000s as a tool for identifying possible investment opportunities and aiding potential investors in navigating any procedural barriers that might exist during the process of investment in the country.[6] The liberalization of the banking industry in 2002, for example, saw the former Ujamaa Cooperative and Rural Development Bank replaced by the Commercial Rural Development Bank (CRDB) and the National Microfinance Bank (NMB), which promoted community investments across the country. In February 2009, the Tanzania Private Sector Foundation (TPSF) was created with the aim of strengthening the entrepreneurial culture among its citizens by providing communities and individuals across the country with entrepreneurial business ideas and grants. In June 2009, the government started an ambitious national resolution under the so-called "Kilimo Kwanza" policies (meaning "Agriculture First" in Swahili) to boost the standard of living among the *eighty per cent* of citizens who relied on agriculture for their livelihood.[7] It was based on Green Revolution principles aimed at boosting Tanzania's agriculture into the modern and commercial sector, and mobilizing for-profit organizations (FPOs) such as local private businesses and foreign-owned TNCs in

the country to increase their investment engagement with the agriculture sector, both at the macro and micro levels (i.e. along with local communities).

In order to ensure that there was sufficient security and peace for private and foreign-owned investors (i.e. TNCs), in 2005 the government introduced a new entity called "Tanzania Security Industry Association." The association was based on local, professional private security firms and groups whose main tasks were to safeguard business firms' activities rather than letting the firms rely on local police forces. The largest and best-known local security firm was "Moku Security Services Limited," based in Dar Es Salaam, which had over 13,000 employees across the country. Other security groups with over 400 employees were "Ultimate Security Company," "Dragon Security," "Tele-security Company Limited," and "Group Four Security Company." Private security employees were mainly retired army and police officers; young people who had lost their previous jobs following the collapse of the Ujamaa policies that provided "jobs for everyone and for life"; and individuals who sought better remuneration in the security sector than in the government public sector. However, due to increased demand for

---

[6]www.tic.co.tz, accessed April 1, 2009.

[7]www.actanzania.org/index.php?option=com_content&task=view&id=121&Itemid=39, accessed February 12, 2010.

better security across businesses, many foreign-owned TNCs sought the services of security firms from abroad, mainly from South Africa's professional security firms such as the South African Intruder Detection Service Association (SAIDS). Some security personnel had combat experience, which helped them handle sophisticated forms of crime and intrusion.

The Tanzanian economy continued to grow and create job opportunities, training and innovative development prospects for its people. Earlier, the country had introduced new mining legislation such as the Mining Act of 1998 and the Mining Regulation Act of 1999 in order to harmonize investment relations between FDI and local interests. However, in April 2010 the government passed another new mining Act, following consultations with civil society groups such as the Foundation for Civil Society Tanzania (FCST), companies and other stakeholders. The legislation of a new mining Act imposed a new form of royalties that required all TNCs and local companies to be listed in the country and gave the state a stake in future projects.[8]

The country possessed vast amounts of natural resources like gold, diamond, copper, platinum, natural gas, and zinc deposits that remained underdeveloped. It was one of the more peaceful countries in Sub-Saharan Africa. In order to attract and protect the interests of FDI and TNCs and, of course, its own people, Tanzania had attempted to harmonize its investment practices and labour legislation. In order to create responsible institutional policies, in February 2010 the National Assembly of Tanzania enlisted a group of local environmental and toxicity experts to investigate environmental and toxic effects on the people and livestock in the North Mara gold mine in Tarime District, Mara Region, by the Tigithe River.[9]

For a number of reasons, Tanzania was a willing host nation for FDI. The country needed the input of TNCs in order to create employment and prosperity. In return, Tanzania could provide TNCs with low-cost labour and a readily available labour force. Low labour costs were an opportunity to support a host nation's development policy in attracting FDI and ultimately in creating a knowledge-based society in the midst of the globalization challenges that were faced by so many developing countries. Furthermore, Tanzania continued to create a local business environment in conjunction with various TNCs' global business interests in order to generate sustainable development policies and practices. It also engaged in market development

---

[8]www.mining-journal.com/finance/new-tanzanian-mining-act, accessed September 27, 2010.

[9]www.dailynews.co.tz, accessed February 10, 2010.

initiatives that represented innovative learning opportunities and entrepreneurship ventures for its citizens.

Lake Victoria Background Tanzania's Lake Victoria was surrounded by the three East African countries of Kenya, Tanzania and Uganda. The lake itself was named after the former Queen of England, Queen Victoria, and stood as the world's largest tropical lake and the second-largest freshwater lake after Lake Superior in North America. Covering a total of 69,000 square kilometres, the lake was as large as the Republic of Ireland and lay in the Rift Valley of East Africa, a 3,500-mile system of deep cracks in the earth's crust, running from the Red Sea south to Mozambique. Lake Victoria was the source of the Nile River, which passed through the Sudan and Egypt and finally reached the Mediterranean Sea.

Lake Victoria Zone in Tanzania

The Lake Victoria Zone consisted of the three regions of Mwanza, Mara (formerly called Musoma) and Kagera (formerly called Bukoba), and was one of the most densely populated regions in Africa. Population growth around Lake Victoria was significantly higher than in the rest of Sub-Saharan Africa. During the last five decades, population growth within a 100-kilometre buffer zone around the lake had outpaced the continental average, which had led to growing dependency and pressure on the lake's resources.

Prior to the mining extraction boom in the early 1990s and following the collapse of Ujamaa, most people living in this region were mainly engaged in rudimentary forms of fishing, agricultural farming and keeping cattle, as well as other forms of co-operative activities that had been engineered by the country's former Ujamaa policies. Irrigation was limited to a small scale and often used rudimentary technologies to support both individual and co-operative farming activities. Noted for its temperate climate, the area had a mean temperature of between 26 and 30 degrees Celsius in the hot season and 15 and 18 degrees Celsius in the cooler months. The area was rich with tropical vegetation and fruits such as bananas, mangoes, corn, pineapple and many others. The lake was essential to more than 15 million people, providing potable water, hydroelectric power, and inland water transport, as well as support for tourism and wildlife.

The area remained one of the most fertile for farming activities and continued to attract immigrants from other regions of the country, as well as from Tanzania's neighbors in the war-torn populations of Burundi, Rwanda and the Democratic Republic of Congo. The presence of hundreds of TNCs engaged in various activities in the area was the main "draw" for these immigrants, who came seeking employment and new sources of livelihood.

The resulting population increase in the Lake Victoria Zone created several problems with respect to the lake and the environment. According to a report by World Watch Institute in Washington, D.C., the once clear, life-abounding lake had become murky, smelly and choked with algae. It had been reported that:

> The ecological health of Lake Victoria has been affected profoundly as a result of a rapidly growing population, clearance of natural vegetation along the shores, a booming fish-export industry, the disappearance of several fish species native to the lake, prolific growth of algae, and dumping of untreated effluent by several industries. Much of the damage is vast and irreversible. Traditional lifestyles of lakeshore communities have been disrupted and are crumbling.[10]

As a result of the overuse of natural resources in the area, the traditional lifestyles of the lakeshore communities were significantly disrupted, a situation that prompted both social and ecological concerns for the area and its residents.

The fishing industry was badly affected in the region following the introduction of Nile perch (Lates Niloticus) and Nile tilapia (Oreochromis Niloticus) into the lake. For example, in the 1980s a survey of the lake revealed an abrupt and unexpected increase in numbers among the Nile perch, constituting 80 per cent of all fish in the lake. In spite of working harder, local fishermen caught fewer fish since the populations of smaller fish, which traditionally had been the fishermen's primary source of livelihood, became decimated. In addition, the big oily Nile perch, generally referred to as "Mbuta," swam too far out in the open waters for the little local fishing boats and was too big to be caught in the locals' unsophisticated nets.

In response to an increased international demand for the Nile perch, commercial fishing fleets owned by foreign firms displaced local fishermen and many women in lakeside communities who worked as fish processors. The processing of fish, traditionally performed by women, was gradually taken over by large filleting plants. The women resorted to processing fish waste, commonly referred to as *mgongowazi*, or "bare-back" in Swahili. The waste, comprised of fish heads, backbones and tails, was sun-dried and then deep-fried and sold to local people who were drawn to its low price and nutritional value. Many fishermen were forced to look for alternative sources of livelihood, mainly seeking employment in extractive mining corporations and other industries as manual labourers.

---

[10]www.cichlid-forum.com/articles/lake_victoria_sick.php, accessed April 1, 2009.

The water hyacinth posed another threat to the health of Lake Victoria. With the deceptive appearance of a lush, green carpet, the hyacinth was in fact a merciless, free-floating weed, reproducing rapidly and covering any uncovered territory. First noticed in 1989, the weed spread rapidly and covered areas in all three surrounding countries. It formed a dense mat, blocking the sunlight from reaching the organisms below, depleting the already-low concentrations of oxygen and trapping fishing boats and nets of all sizes. The hyacinth was also an ideal habitat for poisonous snakes and disease-carrying snails that caused bilharzias. The government, in partnership with other international agencies, had tried desperately to control the weed. Its most promising approach involved harvesting the hyacinth and using it either for compost or for biogas production.

The health implications associated with the declining state of the lake were extensive. Dumping untreated sewage in the lake and nearby rivers exposed people to waterborne diseases, such as typhoid, cholera and diarrhea, and chronic forms of malaria. The Lake Victoria Zone was known to have the most dangerous types of malaria in the world. As fish prices soared, protein malnutrition became a significant threat for communities living in the zone. Lack of regular income also meant that many people in the area could not afford to be treated for waterborne typhoid, yellow fever, and various forms of tropical worms such as tapeworms and hookworms.

Mining in Tanzania

Gold mining activities around the Lake Victoria Zone in Tanzania started during the German colonial period in 1894, when Tanzania was called Tanganyika. The First and Second World Wars accelerated the demand for gold production in the region and, following the introduction of Ujamaa in 1967, mining became a state-directed activity. By nationalizing the industry, the government hoped to capture more benefits from mining through the creation of local employment, direct spending on social services for mining communities, and higher budget revenues from having a direct stake in the business. However, despite these high hopes, the mining sector failed to stimulate the industrialization of the country's economy. During Ujamaa, the production of gold declined significantly due to limited government funding and limited technological know-how within the industry. Mining activities that were performed illegally by small-scale operators contributed to several environmental and social problems.[11]

---

[11]www.douglaslakeminerals.com/mining.html, accessed February 26, 2009.

The collapse of Ujamaa in the 1990s, however, resulted in new opportunities for the country to attract mining companies from Canada, the United Kingdom, Australia and South Africa, all of whom were interested in gold exploration and development activities. Following successful exploration mining activities that began in 1995, Barrick invested in Tanzania in 1999 at the Lake Victoria Zone. It acquired gold reserves in the Bulyanhulu mine, located in northwest Tanzania, East Africa, approximately 55 kilometres south of Lake Victoria and approximately 150 kilometres from the city of Mwanza; Buzwagi near Kahama District; Tulawaka in Biharamulo, Kagera Region; and later at the North Mara gold mine in the northwestern part of Tanzania in Tarime District of Mara Region, approximately 100 kilometres east of Lake Victoria and 20 kilometres south of the Kenyan border.

According to the Tanzanian Mineral Authority and Tanzania Chamber of Minerals and Energy (TCME), since 2000 production of gold had been growing, making the Lake Victoria Zone one of the most attractive areas for employment opportunities as well as for business opportunities in other industries. Tanzania was Africa's third-largest producer of gold, after Ghana and South Africa.[12] Tanzania was also richly endowed with other minerals, including cobalt, copper, nickel, platinum group metals, and silver, as well as diamonds and a variety of gemstones. The energy sector was dominated by natural gas. Commercial quantities of oil had yet to be discovered. In 2008, TCME reported that a total of US$2 billion in the past decade had been injected into the Tanzanian economy by mining TNCs, and in total mining TNCs had paid the government over US$255 million in taxes within the same period.[13]

In 2002, Tanzania joined the African Union's development blueprint, an endeavour that was governed by the New Economic Partnership for African Development (NEPAD), to oversee an African Mining Partnership (AMP) with global mining corporations. The goal of this partnership was to promote sustainable development and best-practice guidelines for African governments as a way to ensure that their mining laws protected ecological and community welfare while maximizing remittances from the mining TNCs to the government budgets in a transparent and accountable way.

The country did, however, develop competitive tax packages and incentives to attract TNCs to invest in high-risk and complex exploration areas

---

[12]www.mineweb.co.za/mineweb/view/mineweb/en/page67?oid=39782&sn=Detail, accessed May 1, 2009.

[13]Ibid.

such as the Lake Victoria Zone. The government did not devise a practical and engaging strategy to utilize mining resources and revenues paid by TNCs to support the local communities that were situated around mining sites and who had lost their livelihood, homes, health, natural resources and recreation with little or no compensation.[14] Also, the government did not come up with a concrete strategy to deal with the chronic sewage and environmental issues in the area.

Like any TNC engaged in extractive mining activities in a developing country such as Tanzania with so many social problems and legal and institutional weaknesses, Barrick had faced conflicting pressures with regard to the way it engaged in locally based community social partnership (see Exhibit 1). Such partnerships were meant to address the social problems of unemployment, poverty, diseases and environmental concerns in a sustainable way. Barrick strictly followed Western legal and property approvals to legitimize its mining activities in the country. It also continued to face challenges with respect to its efforts to strike a balance between its global strategies and those of the local subsidiary operations in Tanzania. Mineral wealth continued

to fuel and prolong violent behaviour by local communities mainly in North Mara, thus failing to diversify economic growth and contribute to the development of communities in the Lake Victoria Zone. Corruption and weak institutional capabilities to enact or enforce the democratic, transparent and agreed-upon rules and laws that governed the operation and taxation of mining activities were a source of ongoing problems.[15] Also, some local communities did not see the potential benefits of large corporations in their communities.

Barrick Gold Corp in Tanzania

As a gold producer on the world stage, Barrick used advanced exploration technological systems for its mining development projects.[16] The company owned one of the world's largest gold mineral reserves and a large land position across its subsidiary mining extraction activities. These were located across the five continents of North America, South America, Afric, Australia and Asia. As one of the largest Canadian mining companies, Barrick shares were traded on the Toronto and New York

[14]"The Challenge of Mineral Wealth in Tanzania: Using Resource Endowments to Foster Sustainable Development," International Council on Mining & Metals, 2006.

[15]www.revenuewatch.org/our-work/countries/tanzania.php, accessed May 1, 2009.

[16]www.tanzaniagold.com/barrick.html, accessed May 1, 2009.

stock exchanges and on other major global stock index centres in London, as well as on the Swiss Stock Exchanges and the Euronext-Paris. It was a shareholder-driven firm. Barrick invested in Tanzania in 1999, following the completion of exploration activities that had started in 1995. The company's initial mining activities were limited to Bulyanhulu in Kahama District until 2004, when it expanded to other areas surrounding the Lake Victoria Zone.

Socialization was part of the corporate culture used to manage human resources (HRM)[17] in Tanzania. Each mining site had a training department. Barrick recruited university graduates who worked on administrative activities in corporate offices, and assigned manual labourers to mining sites to work along with expatriates and locals who had experience in mining activities. Also, the company was involved in developing the so-called Integrated Mining Technical Training (IMTT) program, a joint project with the Tanzania Chamber of Minerals and Energy and the Tanzanian government. The goal was to offer locals the skills they needed to participate in the country's burgeoning mining sector and to reduce the industry's reliance on foreign-trained expatriates.[18] Barrick used its Global Succession Planning Program (GSPP) that provided expatriates with a chance to increase their knowledge and expertise by transferring them into assignments at other Barrick sites in Tanzania, and sites in other countries where the company operated.[19] The major role of GSPP was to instill the corporate culture through the training of employees regarding various mining technology skills and to run the company's daily practices in accordance with the corporate business interests of the company.

Mission, Vision and Values

Given the questionable reputation of some global mining corporations with respect to sustainable development projects in developing societies, Barrick's core vision and values were to continue finding, acquiring, developing and producing quality reserves in a safe, profitable and socially responsible manner. Barrick claimed to promote long-term benefits to the communities in which it operated and to foster a culture of excellence and

[17]www.barrick.com/CorporateResponsibility/Employees/AttractingRetaining/default.aspx, accessed April 24, 2009.

[18]www.barrick.com/Theme/Barrick/files/docs_csr/BeyondBorder2008July.pdf#page=4, accessed September 27, 2010.

[19]www.barrick.com/CorporateResponsibility/Employees/AttractingRetaining/default.aspx, accessed September 27, 2010.

collaboration with its employees, governments and local stakeholders.

The company followed global corporate social responsibility standards as part of its larger global business strategies, using the vocabularies of business ethics, human rights and development. Among these strategies, the company placed significant emphasis on its social relationships with local communities and the right to operate in their land.[20]

Building Social Development Initiatives

Barrick was committed to making a positive difference in the communities where it operated. The company focused on responsible behaviour as its duty, as well as creating opportunities to generate greater value for its shareholders, while at the same time fostering sustainable development in the communities and countries where it operated. As a global TNC, Barrick strove to earn the trust of its employees, of the communities where its subsidiary operations were based, of the host nations' governments, and of any other persons or parties with whom the company was engaged in the sustainable development of mineral resources.[21]

In 2008, the corporation established a locally based mining institution in Moshi, Kilimanjaro Region. The aim of the institute was to provide training skills and opportunities for Barrick's mining sites and other mining TNCs in the country.[22] Local individuals involved in the training program included fresh university graduates in engineering and geology, and dedicated individuals from local communities where Barrick operated. Such an initiative supported Barrick's sense of corporate responsibility towards these two groups of people by providing tangible benefits to their communities in the form of employment opportunities and co-operative relationships.

Yet among community leaders and NFOs, there was clear discontent regarding the various foreign companies:

"The government has not addressed the role of foreign companies in our communities. Some communities have been compensated by the government to clear land for the mining company, but some did not receive any money. Most communities would tell you what was given to them by the government, which is very little. They cannot build a house and send children to school and so on. They feel their livelihood is gone forever."

"The mining corporation does not compensate people nor does it explain

[20]www.barrick.com/CorporateResponsibility/OurCommitment/default.aspx, accessed September 27, 2010.

[21]www.barrick.com/CorporateResponsibility/default.aspx, accessed March 25, 2009.

[22]www.ippmedia.com/ipp/guardian/2008/04/11/112164.html, accessed February 13, 2009.

why it is operating in our communities. Of course, these companies have official binding contracts and the right to operate in our communities from the government. Local communities are in despair . . . the government is nowhere to be seen! The people are angry with the government and the mining company."

"People are not happy with the government. They are aware of the extent of corruption among the government officials in the region and districts, but they cannot confront the government the way they are now confronting the mining company. They think that the company might be more sympathetic to them than the government would be with respect to offering them jobs and other opportunities."

"The company has initiated several development projects in our communities [North Mara] in education, health and infrastructure. But we do not have jobs to access these better equipped services (education and health) nor essential means to support us to build community enterprises where we could apply our local skills in many activities. Though the company is doing very good projects here, we are still unhappy with the company. Our problems are long-term; they need serious engagement with us."

"The company discharges water to the land, which is causing lots of environmental problems on our farms such as land erosion and polluting of the rivers. We have more mosquitoes, snakes and snails at the moment than any time in our lives because of stagnant water caused by the company's water discharge. The exploration and explosive activities conducted at night on mining sites have caused shockwaves, panic and sleepless nights among neighborhood villages, making big cracks on community farms and land."

Two community leaders (representing local stakeholders' interests) commented:

"The other night we were all suddenly shaken by the mining blast tremor. Initially, we thought it was the so-called earthquake ('Tetemeko la Ardhi' in Swahili). What is on all the people's minds here in Bulyanhulu is 'When will all this end?'"

"We need a mutual partnership with foreign companies investing in our communities. There are so many potential benefits we can get from the company with respect to jobs and skill development; also, the company can learn a lot from us when it comes to negotiation strategies with our communities. If the company responds positively to our concerns, we will strive to protect its business interests here and it will operate in harmony in our communities. But the government needs to sit with local communities and tell them why the government has allowed the company to come to practice mining in their land and tell us what potential benefit it will bring in our communities. For the time being, the company is left to itself to address these issues with the local communities."

Amid this climate of discontent among the native Tanzanians, Barrick's mining operations were subject to some hostilities from local stakeholders. In response, the company put into place several CSR initiatives that were aimed at developing sustainable benefits within the communities and around its business operations in the core mining sites of Tulawaka, Bulyanhulu and Buzigwa. Two NFO officials in Mwanza cut to the nature of the problem:

"The company initially attempted to collaborate with local communities and the local government to address the social and ecological issues during its initial stage of entry into the country. But it was not easy to find serious stakeholders right away. Because of the nature of the local institutions, it was also not easy to have things done quickly due to the degree of bureaucracy and the culture of corruption."

"The recent protests in North Mara from local communities can be resolved only if the government, company and other social awareness groups sit together to address this situation. Shooting protestors, closing the mining site and sending employees home without pay won't solve the problem in the long run. And the company's legal insistence of its right to operate in the communities isn't enough to convince these angry communities."

"The company is not wrong at all . . . it has followed all legal procedures and has the right to be here [in the Lake Victoria Zone], but for local communities, legal papers are NOTHING. The company finds people very unpredictable. The answer is so simple: it is all about deep understanding, integration, and building a trusting relationship."

"Mining companies are granted too many tax contracts and subsidies in order to create jobs. During this process, it is very possible for companies to avoid paying taxes that would actually benefit poor countries. There are often 'secret contracts' with corrupt government officials. The lack of institutional capacity is also a major problem; the people have not been made to see how these companies can benefit our poor societies. That's why there is still so much poverty, and that's why communities around the mining sites are angry and desperate."

Several local communities felt they were isolated when it came to the social issues that concerned them, e.g., land issues, compensation, employment, and how the presence of the company in their communities would benefit them generally. According to community leaders, few projects were initiated by the company within the various neighbourhood communities, and the ones that were enacted showed a lack of any significant sense of local ownership and influence; they did not possess the diverse forms of institutional infrastructure that fostered accountability values in communities and in the management of the company itself. As a consequence, local communities lost interest in pursuing most of the developmental projects that Barrick had initiated.

Following community tensions with Barrick between 2007 and 2009, a different strategy was developed. Implementing a locally based interaction model that promoted mutual partnership with communities seemed like the best strategic legitimacy approach. In early 2009, Barrick encountered discontent from the local communities, as well as from the local media, activists groups and lobby groups, who felt that the company had not done enough to promote sustainable and inclusive development in the communities where it operated. Barrick's new mining site at North Mara was featured several times in the media.[23] Two local NFOs commented on the dispute:

> "The government needs to educate its people as to what benefits TNCs would bring to its citizens; the mining company is extracting our natural resources, causing environmental degradation and pollution, and displacing people, all with a lack of accountability, and is not doing enough for the host communities to create prosperity, jobs, local innovation and entrepreneurship initiatives."

> "The source of discontent is from local communities and small-scale miners who feel neglected by the government. We strongly feel that their livelihoods have been destroyed with little or no compensation. They also feel that the government and local authorities have been giving foreign investors much attention at the expense of local people. Corruption and lack of accountability on the government side is the source of all these problems. The company is caught in the middle!"

Creating a Corporate Responsive Agenda

Barrick developed a responsive initiative to deal with the company's challenges in its international business activities abroad, including Tanzania. It established a community department in all four mining areas to oversee development initiatives. It also adopted standardized global CSR strategies as part of its larger international and localization business strategies, stating that "as a global corporation, we endorse the definition of Corporate Social Responsibility as proposed by the World Bank—Corporate Social Responsibility is the commitment of business to contribute to sustainable economic development—working with employees, their families, the local community and society at large to improve the quality of life, in ways that are both good for business and good for development."[24]

1. Education in partnership with local communities

Through its newly established community department, Barrick had made a concerted attempt to identify self-employment opportunities to the communities around the Bulyanhulu gold

---

[23]Several protests by local communities against Barrick's mining activities in Tanzania had been reported. See www.protestbarrick.net/article.php?list=type&type=12, accessed February 17, 2009.

[24]www.barrick.com/CorporateResponsibility/Ethics/PoliciesStandards/default.aspx, accessed February 17, 2009.

mine. In partnership with local governments, NFOs and communities, the company had used educated locals to promote a broad array of social entrepreneurship skills in a variety of areas such as finance, accounting and marketing (see Exhibit 2).

The communities surrounding the mine needed a great deal of support in terms of education in order to be able to exploit the area's potential. By 2008, Barrick had committed to working closely with eight villages before expanding to another eight villages along the Bulyanhulu-Kahama road in Bulyanhulu. Seven of the eight villages were in the Bugarama ward and one was in the Mwingilo ward, but all were located in the Bulyanhulu mining area.

2.   Community-based entrepreneurship

In collaboration with local community authorities, Barrick went on to assist several community groups that already possessed local skills and entrepreneurship initiatives and which had local resources to generate business activities. Other community development projects had also been started and were engineered under the same procedure of governance.

3.   Health

Barrick committed itself to upgrading the Sungusungu Health Centre into what became called the Nyamongo Hospital in the Bulyanhulu area under the so-called phase I. Organized by the Evangelical Lutheran Church in the area, several NFOs had entered into an agreement with the local District Office and the Village Councils to provide health care that was affordable to the many local residents to treat diseases such as malaria, waterborne diseases, typhoid, yellow fever and other epidemiology problems. The community trust committed $30,000 towards beds and fittings and for a general upgrade to the hospital. Barrick's overall objective was to make health services available to many disadvantaged communities, and to attempt to curb the number of deaths that occurred among pregnant women when they travelled from the poor communities to the district hospital.

4.   Environment

The Lake Victoria Zone was one of the most densely populated areas in Sub-Saharan Africa, but it was also one of the most polluted and environmentally affected places in the world. Barrick, in cooperation with local government authorities, had been working to provide opportunities to the residents of the mining areas to orient themselves with mining operations. The company was creating environmental awareness in order to create local "ambassadors" who could then go out and speak positively about the mining sites to other communities. Adequately addressing the issues of water toxins on rivers and the lake and land degradation had been the major challenge for Barrick.

Protests from so-called "secondary" stakeholders that included local communities, artisanal miners, peasant farmers and their families, and local not-for-profit organizations (NFOs) had occurred to address specific social, environmental, and land heritage and resettlement issues. All these stakeholders had widely varying claims, interests and rights. In addition, subgroups and individuals with multiple and changing roles and interests existed. They included manual mining workers who had felt unfairly dismissed from their jobs with little or no compensation and felt unjustly treated by either Barrick or the Tanzanian labour court system. Local communities also had expressed anger at the level of noise caused by heavy machines during mining explorations at night and the extent of the company's impact on land in their neighborhoods. There were also individuals, mainly unemployed youths, who were engaged in intrusion, vandalism and theft at the mining sites.

Barrick had relied on the Tanzanian anti-riot police force, known as "Field Force Unit" (FFU), to quell large-scale mob criminal behaviour and demonstrations at the mining sites. Also,

Barrick had relied on the Tanzanian legal system and government to protect its business activities in the region. However, the behaviour of the FFU, the weak government institutional system, and the loyalty of administrative workers to Barrick had increased anger, frustration, and resentment among communities, small-scale artisan miners and NFOs. The FFU had been regarded by local communities as brutal and uncompromising during confrontations. Responses by the FFU had even led to death,[25] long-term imprisonment of community campaigners' leaders, intimidation and harassment.[26] The government had been viewed as lacking vision and leadership to reap the benefits of the mining activities in the region and had been criticized for failing to protect the interests of its citizens.

Conclusion

By 2010, a variety of corporate social responsibility (CSR) initiatives were established based on ABG's commitment to building a sustainable relationship with local communities. The overall aim was to ensure that the company would build mutual respect, active partnerships, and a long-term commitment

---

[25]A recent incident at a Barrick mining site in the Mara region had led the Tanzanian FFU to kill an intruder (see www.protestbarrick.net/article.php?list=type&type=12, accessed April 17, 2009).

[26]For the behaviour of Tanzania's FFU in quelling demonstrations, see www.protestbarrick.net/article.php?id=369, accessed April 17, 2009.

with its secondary stakeholders who tended to have disparate goals, demands and opinions. Mutual respect, it was argued, was important if such relationships were to be lasting, beneficial and dynamic. In addition, the company had used its social development department in each of the mining sites to develop practical guidelines in order to facilitate the implementation of its organizational values and mission, including building long-term relationships of

mutual benefit between the operations and their host communities, and to avoid costly disputes and hostilities with local stakeholders.[27] Although significant progress and successful collaborations had evolved across local communities at its mining sites, African Barrick Gold still faced serious, unique problems and increased pressure to manage conflicts and reconcile stakeholders' demands in places such as North Mara.

Exhibit 1 Three Types of Engagement Behaviors

Dimension	Transactional	Transitional	Transformational
Corporate Stance	"Giving Back" Community Investment	"Building Bridges" Community Involvement	"Changing Society" Community Integration
Communication	One-Way	Two-Way	Two-Way
# of Community Partners	Many	Many	Few
Nature of Trust	Limited	Evolutionary	Relational
Frequency of Interaction	Occasional	Repeated	Frequent
Learning	Transferred from Firm	Transferred to Firm	Jointly Generated
Control over Process	Firm	Firm	Shared
Benefit & Outcomes	Distinct	Distinct	Joint

Source: F. Bowen, A. Newenham-Kahindi and H. Irene, "Engaging the Community: A Synthesis of Academic and Practitioner Knowledge on Best Practices in Community Engagement," Canadian Research Network for Business Sustainability, Knowledge Project Series, Ivey School of Business, 1:1, 2008, pp. 1–34.

[27]Further CSR programs are available at www.barrick.com/CorporateResponsibility/default.aspx, accessed February 24, 2009.

Exhibit 2   Barrick Spending on Corporate Social Responsibility in Tanzania

Bulyanhulu
US $1.2 Million

North Mara
US $0.8 Million

Tulawaka
US $0.1 Million

☐ Donations in US$

■ Infrastructure Development in US$

▨ Community Intitatives in US$

Value Added in 2006 (USD)

Donations	$321,000
Infrastructure Development	$1,110,000
Community Initiatives	$655,000
Local/Regional Procurement	$104,900,000

2006 Environmental, Health and Safety Performance

Source: www.barrick.com/Theme/Barrick/files/docs_ehss/2007%20Africa%20Regional%20Rpt .pdf, accessed April 30, 2009.

Note: Total amount of money in U.S. dollars spent on health & safety training and emergency response training in 2006.

Exhibit 3 Total Amount of Money Spent on Community Development Projects, 2006

Community	2006	2005	2004	2003
Donations in US$				
Bulyanhulu	20,193	14,000	410,000	485,000
North Mara	294,220	50,000	0	0
Tulawaka	6,778	7,662	5,894	n/a
Infrastructure Development in US$				
Bulyanhulu	631,222	3,570,000	4,374,000	572,000
North Mara	389,384	360,000	350,000	100,000
Tulawaka	89,020	43,697	6,250	n/a
Community Initiatives in US$				
Bulyanhulu	519,793	609,000	0	0
North Mara	135,015	0	not measured	
Tulawaka	304	0	0	n/a
Regional Purchases of Goods & Services in US$				
Bulyanhulu	65,600,000		not measured	
North Mara	37,700,000		not measured	
Tulawaka	1,600,000		not measured	

Source: www.barrick.com/Theme/Barrick/files/docs_ehss/2007%20Africa%20Regional%20Rpt .pdf, accessed April 30, 2009.

Host Europe: Advancing CSR and Sustainability in a Medium-Sized IT Company

Rüdiger Hahn

In 2009, Host Europe, the third largest webhosting company in the German-speaking markets, set the course for the further development of its sustainability and corporate social responsibility (CSR) strategy. The company was founded in 1997 and since then had grown steadily to more than 160 employees catering to more than 175,000 private and business customers in Germany, Austria and Switzerland.[1] It operated three data centres in the German city of Cologne to provide its customers with Internet hosting services.[2] Apart from an impressive increase in customers and revenues, the company had also matured as a good corporate citizen in the last few years. It had not only actively improved its energy efficiency and environmental performance but had also invested substantial efforts to live up to its CSR. Recently, the first sustainability report had been launched, covering projects such as the building of a new eco-efficient data centre in 2007, the switch to renewable energy supplies, the introduction of various employee-related measures (e.g. the building of a company nursery school) and certain philanthropic activities.

A lot had been done to integrate CSR into the day-to-day business in the last few years but there was still room for improvement. Some sustainability-related issues, such as certain aspects of "green IT," environmental standards and certification, the gender ratio in the IT sector, awareness raising for sustainability issues among employees and recruiting of skilled professionals, remained on the agenda, and so the management had to decide how to further proceed on Host Europe's course to becoming a sustainable and responsible IT-service provider.

The ICT Sector in Europe and Germany

The worldwide economic crisis of 2008/2009 seemed to hit the information and communication technology

---

[1] www.hosteurope.de/content/Unternehmen/Die-Host-Europe-GmbH, accessed December 3, 2009.

[2] That means that the company ran Internet servers and provided organizations and individuals with the opportunity to serve content to the Internet. The various levels and kinds of service are explained below.

(ICT) industry less hard than other areas of the economy. According to industry experts, the European markets for ICT would again stabilize in the next few years. In 2010, the overall market for information, telecommunication and consumer electronics was expected to slightly decrease by 0.5 per cent following a decline of 2.2 per cent in 2009.[3] Specifically, the IT sector (which included hardware, software and services) was even expected to grow by 0.6 per cent in 2010 to more than €300 billion following a growth of three per cent in 2008 and a decline of 2.6 per cent in 2009.

In Germany, the ICT sector was one of the leading industries, with 800,000 people directly employed in the industry itself and a further 650,000 working with non-ICT companies (e.g. in companies' ICT service departments).[4] Two-thirds of all Germans used the Internet and around 80 per cent of households owned at least one PC. In terms of general ICT usage in Europe, Germany directly followed Great Britain as the country with the widest dissemination of ICT. The total revenues of the industry accounted for roughly €150 billion. This represented approximately six per cent of the world market, making it the third largest ICT market worldwide (following the United States and Japan) and the most significant market in Europe.

The IT service industry, to which Host Europe belonged and which traditionally was the fastest-growing segment in the German ICT sector, was expected to grow by 3.3 per cent in 2009 to roughly €28 billion.[5] In the mid-term perspective, market researchers expected an annual growth rate of 4.7 per cent for the next three years. However, some areas were expected to outperform others. While project-oriented services, such as consulting or custom application management, could stagnate, other areas, such as outsourcing or cloud computing,[6] could even benefit from the difficult overall economic situation since they might open

---

[3]*BITKOM* (Federal Association for Information Technology, Telecommunications and New Media in Germany), "Europäischer ITK-Markt stabilisiert sich im Jahr 2010," Press Release, Berlin, Germany, November 8, 2009.

[4]www.bmwi.de/BMWi/Navigation/Wirtschaft/branchenfokus,did=197728.html, accessed December 3, 2009.

[5]www.heise.de/newsticker/meldung/Ausblick-IT-Service-Markt-waechst-2009-nur-gut-3-Prozent-196832.html, accessed December 3, 2009.

[6]"Cloud computing is a model for enabling convenient, on-demand network access to a shared pool of configurable computing resources (e.g. networks, servers, storage, applications and services) that can be rapidly provisioned and released with minimal management effort or service provider interaction." P. Mell and T. Grance, "The NIST Definition of Cloud Computing," Version 15, October 10, 2009.

up opportunities for a cheaper and more flexible usage of IT services. The marketing of training and maintenance services, on the other hand, could become even more difficult since these activities were regularly bound to sales of hardware and software, which often decline in economic hard times.

CSR and Sustainability in the IT Sector

In recent years, CSR, and especially sustainability issues, increasingly came to the agenda within the whole IT sector. Following the public discussions and concerns about climate change, companies from all parts of the economy thought more and more about how to measure (and eventually reduce) their carbon footprints to prevent or reduce public pressure or to proactively anticipate possible national regulations. Against this background, the IT sector was in a unique position. On the one hand, it might help to contribute to such a reduction of the greenhouse gas emissions of its clients by offering chances to substitute transports and commuting with teleworking and virtual conferences. On the other hand, however, the ICT industry itself was a major source of CO_2 and other greenhouse gases.

Energy Issues[7]

Computer, printer and communication devices, including basic technology grids, supposedly accounted for roughly two per cent of worldwide carbon dioxide emissions.[8] The German Öko Institut calculated that it took 20 large-scale power plants just to run the worldwide Internet.[9] The global energy usage for IT had doubled between 2000 and 2005 and was still growing with increasing speed. In 2050, the total use of energy in ICT could even quintuple compared to 2005. In Germany, data centres alone were estimated to use around 1.6 per cent of electricity and by 2020, 45 per cent of domestic energy usage was predicted to be consumed by ICT. Consequently, CO_2 emissions often stood in the middle of discussions about "green IT."

A large share of energy usage in IT was not productive. In most data centres, merely a quarter of power was used for core functions. Nearly 50 per cent of the energy did not even reach the servers since it was used for cooling purposes and other peripheral functions. Therefore, data centres had a high fixed

---

[7]*BITKOM*, "High Tech—Low Carbon," Berlin, Germany, March 2008.

[8]*Gartner Inc.*, "Gartner Estimates ICT Industry Accounts for 2 Per cent of Global CO2 Emissions," Press Release, Stamford, United States, April 26, 2007.

[9]D. Quack, "Green IT," Öko-Institut, Freiburg i. Br., Germany, March 3, 2008.

power demand regardless of their capacity utilization. In addition, businesses tended to heavily oversupply hardware to cope with potential spikes in demand. Furthermore, infrastructure management often seemed to be poorly conducted since sometimes servers were not actively monitored and managed. Moreover, cooling mechanisms or insulations were often sub-optimal, and poor asset management could even lead to situations in which servers were running despite not functioning at all. All in all, the number of data centres was growing fast, with data capacity doubling approximately every 18 months. To reduce the high energy burden, new "green" data centres introduced energy-efficient measures in the construction phase. New and efficient insulation and cooling systems, green architecture and power-saving hardware could all contribute to better energy efficiency. Virtualization was another option to increase performance, especially for Internet hosting services. A virtual server provided hosting services similar to a physical server and ran an operating system and applications like a real computer. The main difference, however, was that several virtual servers shared mutual hardware resources. That meant several virtual servers could be consolidated onto one physical computer without interfering with each other.

In fact, they behaved as if they were individual machines, which enabled a more efficient use of each single computer. This strategy could result in power savings well in excess of 50 per cent.

E-waste Issues

A relative decoupling, however, might not be enough to absolutely reduce the environmental burden in the IT sector. According to the widely cited coherence of Moore's law, the capacity and capability of various IT systems have doubled approximately every two years.[10] This has led to the constant renewal of hardware, a trend that was predicted to continue in the future. Such short investment cycles not only introduced more powerful hardware but also produced piles of unused (and usually still functional) computers, servers, consumer electronics and the like. Such "rebound effects" could negate improvements in energy efficiency by proliferation and a tendency to introduce ever bigger and better systems. Redundant computer systems turned into so-called e-waste. In e-waste, bulk materials such as aluminium, plastics and glass usually accounted for more than 80 per cent of weight that could potentially be recycled.[11] However, other materials of significant value and hazardous materials

---

[10]D.C. Brock, "Reflections on Moore"s Law," *Understanding Moore's Law*, Chemical Heritage Foundation, Philadelphia, United States, 2006, pp. 87–108.

[11]http://ewasteguide.info/facts_figures, accessed December 3, 2009.

were part of discarded hardware, too. While the recycling of gold, silver, copper, platinum, etc. could be a lucrative business opportunity, the recycling (or dumping) of toxic substances such as lead, cadmium or arsenic posed serious health and environmental risks. In the European Union (EU), each citizen generated around 18 kilograms of waste electrical and electronic equipment (WEEE) per year. In the EU, legislation restricting the use of hazardous substances and promoting the recycling of WEEE had been in force since February 2003.[12] However, two-thirds of e-waste still went to landfills or to sub-standard treatment sites outside the EU with potentially major environmental and health risks, and illegal trade continued to be widespread. Consequently, e-waste was also a frequently discussed issue in the IT sector, especially since a legal framework, collection systems, logistics and other services were often still lacking in large parts of the world.

The Digital Divide

Apart from these largely ecological and health-related aspects, the "digital divide" refers to a specific social issue within ICT. It illustrates unequal access to computers and the Internet by different groups of people that can be classified based on gender, income, age or location. The digital divide encompasses imbalances in physical access to ICT infrastructure as well as in capabilities and resources or necessary skills to use these technologies.[13] The digital divide is mostly cited when talking about deficits, especially for the poorest of the poor in developing countries. However, it may also be relevant in developed countries since differences in education or lack of (financial) resources can substantially hamper access to ICT for certain groups within these societies, too.

Host Europe

Company History

Host Europe was founded as "ONE-2-ONE GmbH"[14] in 1997.[15] In February 2001, the company changed its name to "Host Europe GmbH" (Host Europe) and became part of the London-based Internet-hosting company Host Europe

---

[12]http://ec.europa.eu/environment/waste/weee/index_en.htm, accessed December 3, 2009.

[13]J. James, *Bridging the Global Digital Divide*, Edward Elgar, Cheltenham/Northampton, England, 2003.

[14]A "GmbH" is a type of enterprise that is very common in German-speaking countries. One of the main characteristics is that the owners are not personally liable for the company's debts.

[15]Host Europe, "Die Host Europe PLC ist neuer Mehrheitsgesellschafter der ONE-2-ONE GmbH," Press Release, Cologne, Germany, March 14, 2001.

PLC, which acquired a stake of 51 per cent. With this move, a time of accelerated growth began. Already in 2002, Host Europe moved its German head office to a different location within the city of Cologne due to capacity reasons.[16] The new site was rented by a third party, and not only provided office space but also a 400-square-metre (sqm) data centre. In April 2004, PIPEX PLC, one of Great Britain's leading Internet service and broadband providers, took over Host Europe PLC for £31 million.[17] In the following three years, growth continued and Host Europe opened a second data centre in Cologne, thus bringing the company's total server capacity to 10,000 servers in July 2005.[18] On April 2, 2008, the ownership changed again when PIPEX sold its entire hosting business (consisting of Host Europe GmbH in Germany as well as 123.Reg and Webfusion in Great Britain) together with the network specialist Vialtus Solutions to the private equity fund Oakley Capital for a total of £120 million.[19] All four companies operated under the roof of Host Europe

WVS Limited. Within this structure, Host Europe GmbH was still independently run by its management and so managing director Uwe Braun stated: "The new independent holding enables Host Europe to pointedly develop its position as a high-quality provider for Internet solutions."

Products

Host Europe provided server space to its customers. The product lines could be divided into five main segments:[20]

1. Webhosting, domains and e-shops: Host Europe offered easy-to-handle hosting products and online shops (e-shops) for private and commercial websites. Web hosting products differed mainly according to storage capacity and traffic and were offered from €0.99 to €14.99 per month. E-shops ranged from €9.99 to €29.99 per month and differed by the number of allowed product categories and overall product items offered.

---

[16]Host Europe, "Partnerschaft zwischen Host Europe und KPNQwest," Press Release, Cologne, Germany, March 14, 2002.

[17]www.theregister.co.uk/2004/07/20/host_europe_pipex, accessed December 3, 2009.

[18]Host Europe, "Host Europe mit zweitem Datacenter und erweitertem Backbone," Press Release, Cologne, Germany, July 4, 2005.

[19]*Oakley Capital*, Annual Report and Accounts 2007, June 2008, www.oakleycapitalinvestments .com/pdf/OCIL_2007_Annual_Report.pdf, accessed December 3, 2009.

[20]www.hosteurope.de, accessed December 3, 2009.

2. Virtual server or virtual private server (VPS): These were offered in Windows, Linux and managed server[21] versions. VPSs act as individual servers although several of them share the hardware of a particularly powerful real server. Prices ranged from €12.99 to €44.99 per month. For Host Europe, VPS was a fast-growing business field. In the first half of 2009, the company gained 75 per cent more customers compared to the same period in 2008. It provided more than 25,000 virtualized servers in mid-2009.[22]

3. Dedicated server: These servers could be leased by clients without sharing the hardware with anyone. Host Europe offered Dell servers running in Linux, Windows and managed server versions. Prices ranged from €79 to €300 or more per month.

4. Cloud hosting: Cloud hosting or cloud computing refers to a set of pooled IT resources delivered over the Internet. By handling security, load balance and hardware resources virtually, the hosted service has access to the processing power of several computers, which increases flexibility and reliability. Host Europe offered individual cloud computing solutions for its clients.

5. Managed hosting: Since especially high-performing websites or critical applications often reach a high complexity, they not only require powerful hardware but also professional personal resources. Host Europe catered to these needs by offering customized hosting services and solutions that included all necessary hardware and software as well as technical support.

For a while, Host Europe also offered broadband Internet access to end consumers, but this product segment proved to be unsuccessful. All services came with a guaranteed availability of 99.9 per cent and even the smaller products for private customers included 24/7 support via email as well as a toll-free phone service.

There is a growing demand for secure, scalable and cost-effective hosting solutions that do not require large capital and personnel expenditures from the customers, even more so in times like

---

[21]Managed servers were fully maintained by Host Europe. The customer had easy access via a graphic interface while the system including all security measurements was managed by Host Europe.

[22]Host Europe, "Host Europe bleibt weiter auf Erfolgskurs," Press Release, Cologne, Germany, July 14, 2009.

these. Moreover, customers benefit in particular from the many years of experience the specialized experts from Host Europe have in their field of business. Optimization of existing hosting solutions often results in astonishing cost savings when migrating to Host Europe.

Uwe Braun, Managing Director

Customers

Since the foundation of Host Europe, its customer base had grown steadily. In January 2007, the company could not only celebrate its 10th anniversary but also its 100,000th customer.[23] One and a half years later, already 150,000 customers were registered. In the first half of 2009, the company signed more than 10,000 new customers, and customer number 175,000 was welcomed after just another 10 months in June 2009.[24] Apart from serving private clients and countless small- and medium-sized businesses, Host Europe also provided numerous DAX-listed[25] corporations with products and services and hosted several high-capacity websites. The company's hosting products, as of 2009, served nearly 500 major customers.

Examples included the entire customer relationship management system for 450 German Renault car dealers and the German kids TV channel Super RTL's website, www.toggo.de, which generated more than 100 million clicks per month. Also, Europe's largest amateur photo community, www.foto community.de, and Europe's largest tire database, www.tyre24.de, were hosted by Host Europe servers.[26] According to regular surveys, customer satisfaction continuously reached the highest levels.

Six of ten new customers come to us based on the recommendation of one of our existing customers. We are a number one choice thanks to this high satisfaction when our corporate customers need complex and service-intensive hosting solutions. We continuously develop our products and services and set high standards concerning quality, reliability, and service in the highly price sensitive hosting market.

Uwe Braun, Managing Director

Employees

Along with the customer base, the number of employees also grew steadily:

---

[23]Host Europe, "Host Europe feiert 10-jähriges Jubiläum und 100.000 gewonnene Kunden," Press Release, Cologne, Germany, January 17, 2007.

[24]Host Europe, "Host Europe startet Cloud Hosting," Press Release, Cologne, Germany, September 25, 2008; Host Europe, "Host Europe bleibt weiter auf Erfolgskurs," Press Release, Cologne, Germany, July 14, 2009.

[25]The DAX (Deutscher Aktienindex) is the most important German stock index and comprises the 30 largest German companies.

[26]www.hosteurope.de/content/Unternehmen/Referenzen, accessed December 3, 2009.

From 2005 to 2009, the workforce doubled (from 89 in 2005 to almost 180 at the end of 2009). As in most high-tech companies, the age average was comparably low, with the average age of Host Europe's employees being just 29 years.[27] Less than 20 per cent of all employees were women (while more than half of all inhabitants in Cologne, where Host Europe was based, were female) and most of them worked in administrative roles rather than pursuing a technical career. These figures corresponded to the overall picture in Germany, where 86 per cent of all IT jobs were held by men. Of the 33 executive positions, six were held by women. Although this was just 18 per cent of management positions, it roughly corresponded to the overall ratio of women in the company.

Flat hierarchies and an open-door policy enabled a constant exchange between employees and management. Regular employee surveys showed a high level of job satisfaction. In 2008, 75 per cent of the respondents were proud to work for Host Europe.

Financial Situation

Host Europe had seen remarkable growth since its foundation in 1997. In the last three years, revenues had grown continuously (see Exhibit 1). In 2005, revenues passed the €10 million mark for the first time. In 2006, the company recorded a growth in sales of 31 per cent, leading to a total of almost €14 million in 2006.[28] This was mainly achieved due to the high growth rates in the core hosting business. The managed hosting segment was especially successful, with growth of more than 50 per cent. By the end of 2006, these services already accounted for 25 per cent of total sales (from zero per cent two years before). In 2006, the company achieved an increased EBITDA of €2.91 million (up from €2.07 million in 2005). The EBITDA margin grew from 19 to 20 per cent. The 2006 EBIT, however, fell by 16 per cent to €0.2 million (from €0.23 million in 2005) due to increased investments.

In 2007, revenues again increased significantly by 31 per cent to €18.18 million and therefore substantially exceeded the projected growth of 20 per cent.[29] The EBITDA grew by 70 per cent to €4.96 million (EBITDA margin 26 per cent) while the EBIT increased to €0.77 million (EBIT margin four per cent). Significantly, total assets went from €15.66 million on December 31,

[27]Host Europe, "Nachhaltigkeitsbericht 2009," Cologne, Germany, July 2009.

[28]Host Europe, "Jahresabschluss zum 31. Dezember 2006," *Elektronischer Bundesanzeiger*, November 27, 2007.

[29]Host Europe, "Jahresabschluss zum 31. Dezember 2007," *Elektronischer Bundesanzeiger*, July 25, 2008.

2006 to €21.97 million on December 31, 2007 (see Exhibit 2). The substantial growth in tangible assets from €12.56 million to €18.55 million mainly resulted from increased investments in the area of managed hosting and dedicated servers as well as from the construction of a new data centre.

In 2008, revenues again grew by 30 per cent to €23.68 million with an increased EBITDA of €7.23 (plus 46 per cent), which represented a margin of 31 per cent.[30] EBIT skyrocketed to €2.31 million, achieving a margin of 10 per cent. In 2009, tangible assets were reduced substantially to €12.24 million. This reduction resulted from the sale of a data centre to the Cologne Data Center GmbH, which was, like Host Europe, a subsidiary of Oakley Capital Investment Limited. These assets had a book value of €7.84 million.[31] With the transfer of Host Europe from PIPEX Ltd. to Oakley, the accompanying liabilities also passed over to the Cologne Data Center GmbH in April 2008.

In the first half of 2009, revenues again rose by 19 per cent compared to the same period in 2008.[32] Due to this positive development even in a difficult market, Host Europe anticipated yearly revenues of almost €30 million for 2009.

CSR and Sustainability at Host Europe

In 2009, sustainability was officially introduced as part of the corporate mission statement.[33] In the same year, CSR was developed as an organizational unit run by one fulltime employee. In the past, one major effort in the area of environmental sustainability was the construction of a new energy-efficient data centre.

Energy and the New Green Data Centre

The new energy-efficient building was opened in May 2007 after less than a year of construction time. It housed a 2,500-sqm data centre on the ground level and 2,500 sqm of office space on the first floor.[34] After the second

---

[30]Host Europe, "Jahresabschluss zum Geschäftsjahr vom 01.10.2008 bis zum 31.12.2008," *Elektronischer Bundesanzeiger*, June 30, 2009.

[31]Host Europe, "Jahresabschluss zum 31. Dezember 2007," *Elektronischer Bundesanzeiger*, July 25, 2008.

[32]Host Europe, "Host Europe bleibt weiter auf Erfolgskurs," Press Release, Cologne, Germany, July 14, 2009.

[33]Host Europe, "Nachhaltigkeitsbericht 2009," Cologne, Germany, July 2009.

[34]Host Europe, "Host Europe erweitert 'grünes' Rechenzentrum in Köln," Press Release, Cologne, Germany, July 7, 2009.

expansion stage in 2009, the "green data centre" had a power usage effectiveness value (PUE) of just 1.35, which means that for one kilowatt hour (kWh) of effective computing power, 1.35 kWh energy was needed. Traditional data centres usually consumed up to two kWh energy for computing and cooling purposes. The plans to build a new data centre were first discussed in November 2005, when it was obvious that the two other data centres were soon reaching full capacity.[35] The final decision to build a green data centre was made in May 2006. A ground-breaking ceremony took place at the new site at Welserstraße near Cologne-Bonn airport in August 2006.

The construction phase was divided into several sections. At first, a 650-sqm data centre area and the full 2,500-sqm office space were developed. The investment volume for this phase was €7.28 million. In a second phase, the remaining data centre space was completed according to requirements, leading to a total investment for the whole data centre of about €11 million.[36] Since Host Europe could not find a construction company that offered a satisfying overall solution for an energy-efficient building, it cut its

own path and did the whole project management on its own initiative. Together with a Dresden-based engineering consultancy, specialists from various areas, such as structural engineering, power supply, air-conditioning technology, fire extinguishing technology and building security, were contracted. To ensure the highest-quality standards, the sub-contractors were committed to undertake maintenance for the first five years after completion.

> Generally, suppliers offer ready-made solutions which reflect the status quo of a usual data centre. Everything that goes beyond that standard has to be insistently requested. At the beginning, we approached things a little naive and only after a while we learned what was ecologically feasible.
>
> Patrick Pulvermüller,
> Managing Director

The results had been impressive. A whole plethora of measures had led to a server energy-efficiency ratio of 75 per cent, which was unheard of before. Large savings had been accomplished by using the latest cooling technologies, for example infinitely variable ventilators or up-to-date compression technologies.[37] Inside the highly insulated

---

[35]C. Egle, "Ein grünes Rechenzentrum," *PC Welt Linux Pro*, No. 3, 2008.

[36]Host Europe, "Jahresabschluss zum 31. Dezember 2006," *Elektronischer Bundesanzeiger*, November 27, 2007.

[37]Host Europe, "Grünes" Rechenzentrum von Host Europe geht ans Netz," Press Release, Cologne, Germany, May 23, 2007.

building, exhaust heat was used to heat the offices, thus reducing the need to revert to community heating. In the data centre, a new concept of separating cold corridors from warm corridors saved additional energy. All servers were installed back-to-back, leading to cold corridors that were used to absorb cold air and warm corridors that were used to emit exhaust air. This separation effectively avoided the mixing of cold and warm air, thus improving cooling efficiency.[38] Up to an outdoor temperature of 17° Celsius (~62.6° Fahrenheit), no artificial cooling was needed. This added up to a total of 60,000 hours or 250 days per year without additional cooling. In sum, all these and many more measures had led to additional construction costs of 15 to 20 per cent. However, they also pushed energy usage down by 30 per cent. When running at full capacity, these costs would amortize in about 2.5 years due to reduced electricity bills.[39]

> There were many things [about which] we thought, "There must be a better way to do that." Efficiency should really be higher, because we did feel the pain of the electricity bill every month.
>
> Patrick Pulvermüller,
> Managing Director

In terms of energy usage, the new data centre saved 3.2 million kWh compared to a conventional data centre, while the use of exhaust heat saved an additional 0.28 million kWh in heating energy, leading to total CO_2 savings of roughly 1,300 tons per year.[40]

> Our green data centre provides a blueprint for sustainable and customer-oriented management in the hosting industry. Since energy adds up to 15 per cent of hosting costs, we are able to offer attractive conditions for our hosting solutions even with rising energy prices in the long run.
>
> Patrick Pulvermüller,
> Managing Director

To express its ongoing commitment, Host Europe also joined "The Green Grid," a global industry syndicate that promoted energy-efficiency in the IT sector by establishing energy saving standards and best practice examples in power management.[41] Moreover, the company also supported a research project conducted at the well-known RWTH Aachen University, Germany's largest university of technology, to explore new scenarios to reduce energy usage for servers.

However, even with the new data centre, overall power consumption was

---

[38]Host Europe, "Nachhaltigkeitsbericht 2009," Cologne, Germany, July 2009.

[39]Host Europe, "Host Europe schaltet um auf grünen Strom," Press Release, Cologne, Germany, May 28, 2008.

[40]www.energieeffizienz-online.info/index.php?id=11964, accessed December 15, 2009.

[41]www.thegreengrid.org/en/about-the-green-grid/member-list.aspx, accessed December 3, 2009.

still significant at Host Europe (see Exhibit 3). The company was Cologne's second largest consumer of electricity just after car manufacturer Ford, whose main German plant was located in the Cologne suburb of Niehl.[42] The estimated 2009 power usage of 14.5 million kWh was equivalent to the consumption of more than 3,200 four-person households in Germany.[43] Therefore, it was only an expected step for the management to completely transfer Host Europe to renewable energy with regard to its sustainability efforts. Since May 2008, all electricity used was certified according to the international Renewable Energy Certificate System (RECS) and came from hydroelectric power generated in Norway, thus potentially saving more than 9,000 tons of CO_2 annually.[44] However, the company also looked for other options to actively contribute to an overall CO_2 reduction.

> We saved a total of four million kWh of energy last year. If you don't control your energy usage, you do not even recognize how much energy you could save. I'm investing 20 per cent of my working hours in this topic. One employee was hired to work solely on this issue. We calculated that it would be financially feasible to exchange each computer every two years because of energy savings. Due to the generated e-waste, however, we are doing it only every four or five years.
>
> Patrick Pulvermüller, Managing Director

Virtualization

Another strategy to increase energy efficiency was virtualization. Virtualization enabled providers to combine several virtual servers on one physical server, therefore allowing a better utilization of the existing hardware with distinct advantages for customers:

> The processor usage of a non-virtualized server seldom exceeds 15 per cent. By using virtualization technology, the utilization can be raised to 60 to 80 per cent while still using the same amount of energy. These gains in efficiency not only reduce energy costs per customer, the intensified hardware usage is also the basis for cheaper hosting solutions.
>
> Uwe Braun, Managing Director

At the same time, VPS offered high flexibility, scalability and possibly even increased stability and reliability compared to dedicated servers. In 2009, Host Europe was one of the largest providers of virtual servers worldwide. At

---

[42]H. Hamm, "Grüner Surfen," *natur+kosmos*, August 2009.

[43]The average four-person household consumed roughly 4,500 kWh per year. www.ea-nrw.de/_info-pool/page.asp?InfoID=4106, accessed December 3, 2009.

[44]Host Europe, "Host Europe schaltet um auf grünen Strom," Press Release, Cologne, Germany, May 28, 2008.

the end of 2008, the company promoted the virtualization technology to its customers by offering new customers the first three months of hosting free of charge. Despite the mentioned advantages and substantially lower prices, many customers were still reluctant to change to virtual servers.

> There are still customers who say, "Virtualisation, I don't like it." But their numbers are getting smaller all the time. Our server utilisation was still 15 per cent at the beginning of 2007; it rose to about 40 per cent by mid-2008.
>
> Patrick Pulvermüller, Managing Director

Apart from energy usage, further ecological issues were also on the agenda. Since 2007, for example, waste paper was separated from other waste in a company-wide initiative. However, social issues also stood in the middle of Host Europe's sustainability thinking.

Employees and Workplace Measures

> Host Europe is a high tech company but despite all technological aspects we are highly dependent on the quality and commitment of our employees.
>
> Uwe Braun, Managing Director

This statement reflects the importance of workplace measures for the overall CSR of Host Europe. The multitude of related measures included ergonomic workplaces with adjustable desks, ergonomic office chairs and flicker-free flat screens.[45] Free courses on preventive back pain training helped employees to learn about optimal seating positions and individual adjustments of their workplaces. Smokers found support for quitting and enduring withdrawal. In addition, Host Europe offered subsidized memberships for a local gym but this measure was suspended due to low demand. A healthy food supply also catered to the needs of the young workforce and included a subsidized soup and salad buffet, free organic fruit, weekly assortments of pastries and sandwiches and free drinks such as coffee, tea, cocoa and water.

Other voluntary non-financial measures included special leaves of absence (e.g. for weddings, childbirth or moving), full compensation of overtime, the possibility to pursue secondary employment where possible and usually flexible working times. Host Europe also actively conducted staff development. In 2009, an average of €750 per employee was spent on professional training. The number of apprentices grew steadily to a total of nine in the same year. However, only four of the planned eight to ten new apprentice positions could be filled since some

---

[45]Host Europe, "Nachhaltigkeitsbericht 2009," Cologne, Germany, July 2009.

candidates did not show up to work or cancelled on short notice.

Host Europe was proud of its trusting work atmosphere and the open contact between employees and management, which was backed by an open-door policy. Through an idea database, every employee was able to contribute to the overall development of Host Europe. They could voice opinions and ideas on new products, procedures, social initiatives or otherwise, and all ideas were directly passed to the top management.

Family Friendliness at Host Europe

> Open communication, idea management, professional development and work life balance go without saying. This of course includes support in childcare.
>
> Uwe Braun, Managing Director

Apart from flexible working patterns, the company also tried to enhance family friendliness by introducing alternative working schemes where possible, such as telework. Since the average age of 29 years was comparably low, many employees were actively engaged in family planning. In 2008, six children were born, a number that was expected to increase in 2009.

> The idea to introduce some kind of company childcare was initiated by the company management. An employee survey affirmed the emerging demand and thus we got active.
>
> Janine Poullie, CSR Manager

In February 2009, the company's own daycare centre, "Die Krabbelkäfer,"[46] opened its doors.[47] It provided 10 places for children up to three years of age directly in the Cologne headquarters and included 100 sqm of indoor space as well as an outdoor terrace including a sandbox and playground equipment. With three full-time nursery teachers, it was open Monday to Friday from 8 a.m. to 5:30 p.m. In the first two years, 50 per cent of operating expenses (with a maximum of €6,000 per year and child) would be covered by a program from the European Social Funds. An employee summarized the benefits of this new institution:

> The biggest plus of the "Die Krabbelkäfer" is that my kids are nearby and I can see them during the day. I use short breaks to go to see how my son and my daughter are doing. Before the day-care centre was installed, I was working part time. Seeing how smoothly this worked probably has eased the decision of some of my colleagues to have children.

---

[46]This roughly translates as "the crawling beetles."

[47]Host Europe, "Host Europe eröffnet Betriebskindergarten "Krabbelkäfer" in Köln," Press Release, Cologne, Germany, May 29, 2009.

Social and Community Engagement

Host Europe also engaged in the wider community. Since 2005, regular donations constantly increased. In 2007, Host Europe donated roughly €5,000 to non-profit organizations.[48] In addition, a Christmas fund-raising campaign was conducted annually. During Christmastime 2009, for example, a donation box was placed prominently inside the office building. The company added double the amount that was donated by the employees, and the donation was handed to the "Kölner Tafel," a local charity organization that used City Harvest in the United States as its role model. Moreover, instead of handing out gifts to large customers or suppliers, Host Europe donated money or goods for social purposes. In January 2009, 10 projectors (with an original price of €500 each) and a used server rack (with a book value of €470) were donated to the Erich-Gutenberg-Berufskolleg (a local vocational school).[49] Apart from these direct donations, indirect donations were also made to charity projects by supplying hosting products free of charge. The number of beneficiaries of those products also rose

constantly to 33 in 2009.[50] In October 2009, a company-wide initiative to donate blood was conducted.

In 2009, Host Europe also participated in "Girl's Day" for the first time. Girl's Day was an annual nationwide initiative to introduce young women to jobs in engineering, IT and natural sciences, which traditionally had been dominated by male employees. On April 23, 2009, 20 girls aged between 12 and 15 years visited Host Europe to observe the working routines in an IT company and to learn about job prospects.[51] One of the girls even applied for an internship later on. Although this could have been a good opportunity to take a closer look at Host Europe's work, the girl was rejected since technicians sometimes encountered the X-rated content of clients' web pages and, therefore, minors were not allowed to work in some departments.

The Challenges Ahead

Despite these many efforts, there were still some challenges but also opportunities for an improved CSR of Host Europe. An issue constantly discussed was the low proportion of women

[48]Host Europe, "Jahresabschluss zum 31. Dezember 2007," *Elektronischer Bundesanzeiger*, July 25, 2008.

[49]Host Europe, "Jahresabschluss zum Geschäftsjahr vom 01.10.2008 bis zum 31.12.2008," *Elektronischer Bundesanzeiger*, June 30, 2009.

[50]Host Europe, "Nachhaltigkeitsbericht 2009," Cologne, Germany, July 2009.

[51]Host Europe, "Girls' Day bei Host Europe," Press Release, Cologne, Germany, April 27, 2009.

currently working for the company, although this was in line with the overall ratio in the IT industry. Applications from women were especially welcome, although the company announced that gender would not be a decisive criterion in hiring new staff. Moreover, highly specialized employees were constantly needed in the fast-growing ICT sector. Another topic connected with the employees was raising awareness of ecological issues. For example, further waste separation in potential recyclables, glass, etc. was not regarded as feasible at the time due to logistical reasons but also because an extended understanding among personnel still needed to be built. The same applied to other areas such as a sensible use of printer and copying machines, for example by avoiding stand-by time with technical equipment. Raising awareness could also be an issue when pushing virtualization. Despite being a cost-efficient alternative, many customers still preferred their own dedicated servers.

Since energy usage was one of the major areas of commitment at Host Europe, obtaining an energy-efficiency certification could also be an option, but so far no widely accepted standard was available. Moreover, a general certification of the company's environmental management system could be considered. Up until 2009, Host Europe regularly participated in competitions and award programs that focused on ecology, quality, social health and/or

sustainability in order to receive feedback on its efforts (see Exhibit 4).

To achieve a broader sense of sustainability, supply chain responsibility was also in question. However, a complete control of the whole supply chain of purchased products regarding sustainable production, humane working conditions or a ban on child labour seemed to be difficult at best. Measures to improve transparency and accountability in the supply chain would be needed but usually extended far beyond the reach of single corporations. At the end of product life cycles, aspects of disposal (and possible recycling) of used IT equipment might be considered. Furthermore, Host Europe negotiated with Deutsche Post on its "Go Green" program for a CO_2-neutral shipping of all mailings and shipments.

Options for an increased social commitment were also being discussed, for example voluntary work of the employees and participation in different awareness-raising days and events. Consequently, the team was constantly searching for feasible opportunities to embrace its corporate social responsibility.

The main questions for Uwe Braun, Patrick Pulvermüller and their team were: What would an even more complete CSR engagement look like? Which kind of measures could be introduced to further improve the ecological and social aspects of sustainability without jeopardizing economic success at Host Europe but maybe even enhancing it?

Exhibit 1   Income Statements, 2006–2008 (in 000 €, Years' End)

	2008	2007	2006	2005
1. Revenues	23,683	18,178	13,876	10,599
2. Production for own fixed assets capitalized	259	275	159	148
3. Other operating income	544	307	202	154
4. Cost of purchased materials and services	−3,329	−3,357	−2,989	−2,338
5. Personnel expenses				
a) Salaries and wages	−5,695	−4,415	−3,541	−2,596
b) Social security and other pension costs	−1,028	−820	−653	−479
6. Depreciation and amortization	−4,920	−4,181	−2,713	−1,833
7. Other operating expenses	−7,204	−5,212	−4,143	−3,419
8. Interest and other income	38	21	22	16
9. Interest and other expenses	−446	−524	−220	−49
Profit/loss from ordinary activities	**1,902**	**272**	**−1**	**201**
11. Taxes on income	−386	−161	−16	−69
12. Other taxes	−1	−1	−1	−1
13. Profits passed over due to profit-pooling agreements	−734	0	0	0
Net income/loss	**781**	**110**	**−18**	**131**

Source: Host Europe, "Jahresabschluss zum 31. December 2006," *Elektronischer Bundesanzeiger*, November 27, 2007; Host Europe, "Jahresabschluss zum 31. Dezember 2007," *Elektronischer Bundesanzeiger*, July 25, 2008; Host Europe, "Jahresabschluss zum Geschäftsjahr vom 01.10.2008 bis zum 31.12.2008," *Elektronischer Bundesanzeiger*, June 30, 2009 (translations by the author). Data for 2005 and 2006 rounded off.

Exhibit 2   Comparative Balance Sheets, 2005–2008 (in 000 €, Years' End)

	2008	2007	2006	2005
Assets				
A. Fixed assets				
I. Intangible assets	477	607	634	221
II. Tangible assets	12,239	18,552	12,557	5,345
III. Financial assets	502	390	302	2

(Continued)

Exhibit 2 (Continued)

	2008	2007	2006	2005
B. Current assets				
I. Receivables and other assets				
1. Trade receivables	769	738	508	361
2. Amounts due from related companies	449	213	243	–
3. Other assets	241	213	540	247
II. Cheques, cash in hand, bank balances	1,825	373	235	1,511
C. Prepayments and deferred charges	2,026	880	637	412
	18,528	**21,966**	**15,656**	**8,099**
Liabilities				
A. Equity				
I. Subscribed capital	35	35	35	35
II. Capital reserves	3,789	3,789	2,539	2,039
III. Retained earnings	1,003	222	112	130
B. Accrued liabilities				
1. Tax accruals	387	125	55	103
2. Other accruals	1,106	836	592	275
C. Liabilities				
1. Amounts due to banks	–	6,930	4,721	26
2. Trade accounts payable	7,394	5,465	4,142	2,666
3. Amounts due to related companies	512	1,347	867	504
4. Amounts due to shareholders	190	–	–	–
5. Other liabilities	459	219	152	409
D. Prepayments and deferred charges	3,653	2,998	2,441	1,912
	18,528	**21,966**	**15,656**	**8,099**

Source: Host Europe, "Jahresabschluss zum 31. Dezember 2006," *Elektronischer Bundesanzeiger*, November 27, 2007; Host Europe, "Jahresabschluss zum 31. Dezember 2007," *Elektronischer Bundesanzeiger*, July 25, 2008; Host Europe, "Jahresabschluss zum Geschäftsjahr vom 01.10.2008 bis zum 31.12.2008," *Elektronischer Bundesanzeiger*, June 30, 2009 (translations by the author).

Exhibit 3   Total Electric Power Consumption of Data Centres Exclusively Used by Host Europe Including Office Space (in kWh)

Source: Host Europe, "Nachhaltigkeitsbericht 2009," Cologne, Germany, July 2009.

Exhibit 4   Host Europe GmbH, Awards and Achievements

2005	Named "Best Hosting Provider" by the Association of the German Internet Industry
2006	Named best webhosting company in the categories "Technology/Performance" and "Usability" by the readers of PC Professional
2007	Eco Award 2007 in the category "Hosting Provider for Business Clients" by the Association of the German Internet Industry
2008	Named best practice example for energy-efficient data centres by the German Federal Ministry for the Environment, Nature Conservation and Nuclear Safety
2008	Award for sustainable medium-sized businesses ("Förderpreis Nachhaltiger Mittelstand") from the Ethikbank
2009	Third place at the Cologne Entrepreneurship Award ("Kölner Unternehmerpreis") of the Cologne Business Club (Wirtschaftsclub Köln)
2009	Eco Award 2009 in the category "Datacenter" by the Association of the German Internet Industry
2009	Green data centre labelled as "Good Practice Energy Efficiency" by the dena (German Energy Agency)

Source: www.hosteurope.de/content/Unternehmen/Auszeichnungen-und-Zertifizierungen, accessed December 3, 2009.

Veja: Sneakers With a Conscience

Oana Branzei

Kim Poldner

The First Five Years

Sébastien Kopp and François-Ghislain Morillion (see Exhibit 1), recent business graduates in their twenties, had traveled the planet looking for a cool way to do business.[1] In 2005, they settled in Brazil, where they founded Veja,[2] the first ethical sneaker company in the world. The Veja sneakers were made from wild latex sourced from the Amazon River area (Amazonia) to mitigate rubber tree deforestation, from Brazilian organic cotton to enhance biodiversity and from vegetable-tanned leather to prevent water pollution. These sneakers not only made consumers look good but also prompted them to take a closer look at bigger issues, such as the use of pesticides, genetically modified crops and fair-trade labor practices.

Kopp and Morillion had designed and produced several sneaker collections, had launched brand extensions (e.g. Veja Baby and Veja Kids), had opened offices in London and had established a distinctive presence online (see Exhibit 2). In 2005, the company started off aiming to sell its sneakers—with a conscience—in conventional stores, right next to iconic brands such as Nike. By 2010, Veja was selling more than 100,000 pairs annually, in 200 stores worldwide, including 80 in France. Customers included singer Lilly Allen and actress Angelina Jolie, whose baby had been recently photographed wearing Veja running shoes.[3] Veja sneakers had been on display at the Ethical Fashion Show (EFS) in Paris, the biggest eco fashion event that brought together 100 brands from around the world. Perhaps even more impressive, Veja had created, from scratch, a global chain that emphasized solidarity and the environment and linked small producers in Brazil to the European catwalks.

---

[1]Their world journey is featured at the Juste Planet website; available at http://www.justeplanete.org/index.php, accessed on September 26, 2010.

[2]In Brazil, Veja means "look." For the company, "veja" symbolized looking around to develop a conscience about what is going on in the world.

[3]Ana Santi, "From Fashion to Rubber," Born in Brazil: Bringing Brazil to the UK, blog entry, posted August 22, 2010; available at http://www.borninbrazil.co.uk/2010/08/from-fashion-to-rubber.html, accessed on September 26, 2010.

Hold or Fold?

Kopp and Morillion had been at the forefront of a rapidly changing industry. Large companies wanted a share of the rapidly increasing market that valued ecologically and socially responsible fashion. Small ethical fashion brands such as Veja were hot buys. Since 2007, several small eco-fashion pioneers had been taken over by bigger brands. These deals enjoyed great media coverage and stirred vivid debates on the future of fashion.

New ethical fashion brands were popping up in attempts to copy Veja's successful business model.[4] For example, France-based Loic Pollet, the founder of Sébola,[5] who had launched his first collection in the fall of 2008, commented: "Looking at success stories like Veja, we felt inspired to start our own brand." Since 2009, Canada-based Tal Dehtiar, founder of Oliberté, had begun working with producers in Ethiopia to launch a competing eco-sneaker.[6] In March 2010, the sneaker brand Sawa shoes launched its first collection, made in Cameroon.[7] Ethical fashion companies such as Simple Shoes[8] and Patagonia[9] had also added eco-sneakers to their offerings. Multinationals such as Nike and Adidas[10] had also recently launched their own limited editions. For example, Nike's Trash Talk sneaker, co-developed with Phoenix Suns basketball star Steve Nash, was made from factories' leftover materials.[11] Veja faced even greater competition for its accessories, such as Veja's newly launched bags (see Exhibit 2). The competitors were keenly watching Veja's next move.

---

[4]Eco Fashion World, "Guide"; available at http://www.ecofashionworld.com/Brands-/listA.html, accessed on September 26, 2010.

[5]Interview with Loic Pollet, October 1, 2009, used with permission; further information at http://www.sebola.fr, accessed on September 26, 2010.

[6]Oliberté Limited, "This Is Africa"; available at http://www.oliberte.com/, accessed on September 26, 2010.

[7]Sawa, available at http://www.sawashoes.com/eng/, accessed on September 26, 2010.

[8]Simple Shoes, available at http://www.simpleshoes.com/, accessed on September 26, 2010.

[9]Patagonia, Inc., available at http://www.patagonia.com/web/us/search/sneakers, accessed on September 26, 2010.

[10]Kim Poldner, "Adidas Green," *Eco Fashion World*; available at http://www.ecofashionworld.com/Trends/ADIDAS-GREEN.html, accessed on September 26, 2010.

[11]Nike, "Steve Nash and Nike Turn Garbage into Trash Talk," media release, February 13, 2008; available at http://www.nikebiz.com/media/pr/2008/02/13_Nash.html, accessed on September 26, 2010.

Ethical Fashion Deals

On December 4, 2006, Timberland acquired Howies Limited (Howies), an active sports brand created less than a decade ago to serve as "a voice and mechanism for communicating a core environmental and social conscience, to ask a different question and show the world that there is another way to do business."[12] Jeffrey Swartz, Timberland's president and chief executive officer (CEO) welcomed Howies to the family: "I want people to believe in the power of the marketplace to make things better."[13] Swartz also pledged that "Together we will leverage our complementary strengths to bring our brands to new consumers and new markets."[14] Timberland's media release commended the ethical fashion brand for innovation, authenticity and integrity. The co-founders of Howies, David and Claire Hieatt, had built a company they

were proud of. They would stay onboard to help the Howies brand grow within Timberland, citing their commitment to "make better and lower impact products, to give a better service and to do more good as we go about our business. Those are our rainbows to chase. They always will be."[15]

On May 18, 2009, "the world's largest luxury conglomerate [the Louis Vuitton Group], paid an undisclosed amount to secure a minority stake in Edun, a prominent ethical fashion line"[16] founded just four years earlier by Ali Hewson and her husband, Bono, U2's lead singer and a political activist, with designer Rogan Gregory. Edun had used "star power and edgy designs to bring worldwide attention to important ethical fashion principles."[17] Although critics wondered whether the acquisition could "green" the conglomerate, Louis Vuitton soon created a special bag for Edun (which sold for

---

[12]David Hieatt, "Exciting News," December 4, 2006; available at http://www.howies.co.uk/content .php?xSecId=56&viewblog=557, accessed on September 26, 2010.

[13]PSFK, available at http://www.psfk.com/2006/12/ethical_entrpre.html, accessed on September 26, 2010.

[14]Fibre2fashion, "USA: Timberland Acquires Howies, UK-based Active Sports Wear Brand," December 4, 2006; available at http://www.fibre2fashion.com/news/company-news/timberland-company/newsdetails.aspx?news_id=27033, accessed on September 26, 2010.

[15]David Hieatt, "Exciting News," December 4, 2006; available at http://www.howies.co.uk/content .php?xSecId=56&viewblog=557, accessed on September 26, 2010.

[16]Ethical Style, "Louis Vuitton Buys Minority Stake in Edun," Ethical Style blog entry, May 18, 2009; available at http://ethicalstyle.com/2009/05/louis-vuitton-buys-minority-stake-in-edun/, accessed on September 26, 2010.

[17]Ibid.

US$4,900) and agreed to donate all proceeds from the bag sales to the Conservation Cotton Initiative—an organization advocating for the development of eco-friendly, organic cotton farming to improve incomes and increase economic growth.[18] The bag was adorned with charms—distinctive bunches of ebony and bone spikes—that were produced in co-operation with Made,[19] a fair-trade brand of jewelry and accessories expertly finished by craftspeople in Kenya; these bag charms were Louis Vuitton's very first "made in Africa" product.[20] In exchange, Bono and his wife appeared in the latest Louis Vuitton campaign.[21]

On September 10, 2009, the Vivarte Group (known for such brands as Naf Naf and Kookaï) partnered with Les Fées des Bengales; Vivarte's share remained undisclosed. The ethical fashion brand Les Fées des Bengales had been founded in 2006 by two sisters, Sophie and Camille Dupuy, and their friend Elodie le Derf, after a voyage in poverty-stricken yet beautiful rural India. Sophie Dupuy recalled the trip as having been a revelation. She was captivated by the brightly colored saris and equally struck by the trying work conditions and the know-how she observed in the traditional workshops. Les Fées de Bengales was mainly set up to work with women in India.[22] Seventy per cent of its output was produced in India but the company had recently acquired new partners in Portugal, Tunisia and France to grow its output. Post-partnership, both design and production remained in the hands of the founders: "We are continuing with our strategy and now we even guarantee the eco-friendly production line."[23]

---

[18]EDUN, "EDUN Launches the Conservation Cotton Initiative—Joining Forces with the Wildlife Conservation Society," news release, July 31, 2007, PR Newswire; available at http://www.prnews-wire.com/news-releases/edun-launches-the-conservation-cotton-initiative—joining-forces-with-the-wildlife-conservation-society-52788817.html, accessed on September 26, 2010.

[19]Made, available at http://made.uk.com/, accessed on September 26, 2010.

[20]Trend Hunter Fashion, "Tribal Designer Bags: The Louis Vuitton for Edun Keepall 45 Duffel Is Stunning"; available at http://www.trendhunter.com/trends/louis-vuitton-for-edun, accessed on September 26, 2010.

[21]High Snobiety, "Louis Vuitton x Edun Keepall 45 Tavel Duffel Bag," September 20, 2010; available at http://www.highsnobiety.com/news/2010/09/20/louis-vuitton-x-edun-keepall-45-travel-duffle-bag/, accessed on September 26, 2010.

[22]Les Fées de Bengale, available at http://www.lesfeesdebengale.fr/v3/fr/la-marque/lhistoire, accessed on September 26, 2010.

[23]Barbara Markert, "Vivarte Partners with Les Fées de Bengale," *Sportswear International Magazine*, September 10, 2009; available at http://www.sportswearnet.com/fashionnews/pages/protected/VIVARTE-PARTNERS-WITH-LES-FES-DE-BENGALES_1877.html, accessed on September 26, 2010.

The Ethical Fashion Industry

The global apparel, accessories and luxury goods market generated total revenues of $1,334.1 billion in 2008.[24] In 2005, the industry employed approximately 26 million people and contributed to 7 per cent of world exports.[25] Fierce competition and lack of supply chain transparency kept driving costs down—at a high social and environmental burden that included the use of child labor, unfair practices and disruption of natural ecosystems.

Ethical fashion was booming. Some predicted that, by 2015, certain practices, such as the use of organic cotton, would become mainstream.[26] Nearly every big label, including H&M, Guess and Banana Republic, had developed a "green" line. Nike and Adidas had integrated ethical principles into their core business, and leading retailers, such as Wal-Mart and Marks & Spencer, had made ethical sourcing a centerpiece of their new strategy.[27] For example, Wal-Mart had become the biggest buyer of organic cotton in the world. Although the quantity of organic cotton produced was still minuscule—in 2009, 175,113 metric tonnes of organic cotton were grown, representing 0.76 per cent of the cotton production[28]—the organic cotton segment was growing at an impressive 20 per cent per year.

Several established fashion brands were working together with non-governmental organizations (NGOs) to add organic fibers to their collections. For example, Vivienne Westwood[29] used her catwalk shows as platforms to campaign for less consumption and a more sustainable lifestyle. Since 2005, eco fashion designs had been shown during New York Fashion Week by such fashion brands as Versace, Martin Margiela and Donna Karan. Instead of using traditional fabrics, such as silk and cashmere, many fashion designers now preferred to use fabrics such as sasawashi (a Japanese fabric made from

---

[24]*Consumer Goods: Global Industry Guide*, Datamonitor, March 2009, accessed on September 26, 2010.

[25]HM Customs & Excise, Provided by the British Apparel & Textile Confederation (2005) provided to Defra: www.defra.gov.uk, accessed on September 26, 2010.

[26]cKinetics, *Exporting Textiles: March to Sustainability*, April 2010; available at http://www.ckinetics .com/MarchToSustainability2010/, accessed on September 26, 2010.

[27]Organic Exchange, *Organic Cotton Market Report 2007–2008*; available at www.organicex change.org, ccessed on September 26, 2010.

[28]Organic Exchange, *Organic Cotton Farm and Fiber Report 2009*; available at www.organicex change.org, accessed on September 26, 2010.

[29]Vivienne Westwood is a well-known fashion designer, whose four decade career remains highly influential, http://www.viviennewestwood.com/flash.php, accessed on September 29, 2010.

paper and herbs), hemp and peace silk (a silk produced in such a way that silk worms lived out their full life cycle).

In 2003, the Ethical Fashion Show (EFS) was launched in Paris. It was the first and biggest event to focus exclusively on ecological, socially responsible and environmentally friendly garment production. In 2008, EFS began expanding to other cities, from Milan to Rio de Janeiro. In April 2010, the Messe Frankfurt (also known as the Frankfurt Trade Fair)—the world's market leader in trade shows, which hosted 31 textile fairs around the world—took over the EFS. The acquisition meant that Messe Frankfurt, the combined fair and exhibition company, now covered the world's entire supply chain in the sector of textile fairs.

As the ethical fashion movement picked up,[30] it brought together like-minded stylists, activists, models, journalists, stores, celebrities and events. Eco boutiques on the web encouraged online shopping and drove change in the retail industry. Fashion schools stimulated their students to consider this issue through the introduction of special topics within the curriculum. Governments played their part by regulating destructive practices and transforming the mindset of consumers. NGOs developed systems to trace each item back to its origins. Others campaigned and lobbied to create more general awareness on ethical fashion and to help create eco fashion brands that could become successful examples of public-private partnerships.

The main actors in the ethical fashion movement, however, were the small eco-fashion brands, many of which had been born less than four years earlier. By 2010, more than 500 ethical fashion brands were in business around the globe. In the majority of the brands, the founder (and the founder's small team) worked directly with people in developing countries to source and produce socially and environmentally responsible fashion items. These ventures were no longer just designing an item to wear; they were crafting stories that signaled how individuals felt about big issues, such as poverty and deforestation. Wearing eco-fashions made a statement all right, but it was no longer just about the clothes—or shoes.

Eco-fashion was still in its infancy. Despite the financial crisis, sales of organic and ethical fashion were

---

[30]Entrepreneurs in ethical fashion were from a variety of backgrounds. They ranged from NGO workers to business people, and only a small percentage had been trained as fashion designers. Many of them had altruistic reasons for starting their brand, such as to help a specific community in a developing country. In the beginning, the focus of these brands was often not on design, but more on survival and philanthropic goals. This focus changed as an increasing number of entrepreneurs hired professional stylists who created ever more beautiful collections.

shooting up, growing by 50 per cent each year.[31] Although the industry was small—eco-fashion represented just 1 per cent of the sales in the broader fashion industry—it was growing momentum. Eco-fashion was particularly popular among a segment known as "cultural creatives,"[32] who were highly educated consumers who had an interest in spirituality, actively participated in society through voluntary work, advocated a conscious lifestyle and were motivated by a high need to strive for a better world. More than 50 million cultural creatives spent $230 billion on everything from yoga gear to organic apples to hybrid cars. This trend was evident not only in fashion-forward countries, such as France, the United Kingdom, Germany and the United States, but also in BRIC countries, such as Brazil, which were characterized by increasing numbers of customers seeking a green lifestyle.[33] Awareness for eco-fashion brands was growing rapidly: 18 per cent of consumers had heard of eco fashion brands, three times the number four years earlier.[34]

Business Model

Kopp and Morillion started their company without a clue about the fashion industry. After graduating from Paris business schools, Kopp and Morillion took off for a one-year journey around the world. They visited and studied sustainable development projects in different industries, from Chinese factories to South African mines to the Amazon rainforest, witnessing firsthand problems such as deforestation, exhaustion of natural resources and labor exploitation. When they returned to France, they knew they needed to act and to act now. They first tried consulting and recommended to companies such as supermarket Carrefour: "Stop charity, but instead have a close look within your company at what is wrong

---

[31]Organic Trade Association, "Industry Statistics and Projected Growth," June 2010; available at http://www.ota.com/organic/mt/business.html, accessed on September 26, 2010.

[32]Cultural Creatives, available at http://www.culturalcreatives.org, accessed on September 26, 2010.

[33]Hartman Group, *The Hartman Report on Sustainability: Understanding the Consumer Perspective, 2007*; available at www.hartman-group.com, accessed on September 26, 2010. Consumers in many major markets want more green product choices. Studies show that 50 per cent of women want mass retailers to carry more green goods, and 11 per cent of these consumers see themselves as "extremely green" today, and 43 per cent say that they will be "extremely green" in five years.

[34]Forum for the Future, "Fashion Futures 2025: Global Scenarios for a Sustainable Fashion Industry," February 24, 2010; available at http://www.forumforthefuture.org.uk/projects/fashion-futures, accessed on September 26, 2010.

in the countries where you work and try to do something positive about it."[35] Then they realized they had to do something themselves: "Let's pick a product and try to put as much sustainable development in it as we can."[36]

Both Kopp and Morillion were sneaker addicts. They knew from the start what they wanted to create: good-looking shoes that had a positive impact on both the planet and society, as opposed to the negative impacts that characterized the big sneaker manufacturers. The two friends took the path of fair trade because they felt it would be the most effective way to integrate environment and dignity into everyday products. They set out to "invent new methods of work."[37] Veja was built on three main values: using ecological inputs, using fair trade cotton and latex and respecting workers' dignity.

Getting Started

Kopp and Morillion's journey around the world had opened their eyes to the rich variety of countries and cultures. They chose to operate in Brazil. Kopp and Morillion loved Brazil, its climate, its language and culture, and they imagined themselves living in Brazil. Here, they had met many people from NGOs and social movements working collaboratively to protect the sensitive Amazonian eco-system; connecting with these players, they felt, would help them scaffold the entire value chain.

After calculating the budget needed to produce their first sneaker collection, Kopp and Morillion were able to negotiate a bank loan. They then moved to Brazil, set up their company and began producing the collection. They presented their first sneaker collection at a conventional trade fair in Paris. "Who's next?"[38] always had extra space available to feature new designers, and Kopp and Morillion managed to secure a spot to showcase their new sneakers. They learned on the go:

I remember running out the tradeshow to buy some paper on which we could write down the orders people placed. But then you talk to your neighbours and you pick up quickly how it works.[39]

It was a Cinderella story. Kopp and Morillion identified the stores where they wanted to place their sneakers and

---

[35]Interview with François Morillion, October 2, 2009, used with permission.

[36]Ibid.

[37]Veja, "Is Another World Possible?," available at http://www.veja.fr/#/projets/VISION-26, accessed on September 26, 2010.

[38]http://www.whosnext.com/, accessed on September 29, 2010.

[39]Interview with François Morillion, October 2, 2009, used with permission.

then invited those buyers to see their collection. People came, loved the product and started buying. Their product was so successful that the first collection sold out, and Veja was able to pay back its bank loan within a year. Veja had enough money to produce a second collection. Since then, the company grew ten-fold by following the same approach: they took little risk, produced small quantities and focused on the product. Morillion commented:

> We had a plan for the first year, then we had a plan until we presented the shoe and after that we discovered a whole world we didn't know about. We basically went learning by doing, making many mistakes.[40]

Morillion was in charge of production and finances, and Kopp ran the commercial side of the company, but they did most of the work together. "We fight every day," [Morillion] confessed. In the first few years

> . . . every day there was a new problem because we really had no clue about the shoe business. It was definitely the biggest challenge in building Veja, to learn how to make proper shoes.[41]

Kopp and Morillion initially spent half of the year in Brazil. Then they hired a shoemaker who had all the expertise they needed and who later

became the manager of the Veja team co-located in Porto Alegre, the eleventh most populous municipality in Brazil, the centre of Brazil's fourth largest metropolitan area and the capital city of the southernmost Brazilian state of Rio Grande do Sul. The Brazil-based team took care of quality, administration, logistics (e.g. shipping) and the entire raw material process of buying and paying for the cotton, rubber and leather. The founders were in touch with the Brazilian team daily, via Skype, and traveled to Brazil four or five times a year to meet with their Brazilian co-workers. In addition, the team manager traveled to Paris twice a year to see the new stores where the sneakers were sold and to meet customers and colleagues in the headquarters in Paris.

Distribution Chain

Since the beginning, Veja had aimed to place its product in trendy sneaker boutiques next to other (non-ethical) brands. Veja did not see the need to promote its ethical approach to customers who were already convinced about the importance of purchasing ethical products. Instead, the company wanted to inspire customers who were accustomed to buying trendy sneakers. Veja sneakers sold in premium venues, such as the Galeries Lafayette in Paris

---

[40]Ibid.

[41]Ibid.

and Rien à Cacher in Montreal. Veja sneakers were available in selected shops across Europe and Canada, but most sneakers were sold in France, Spain and the United Kingdom.

In France, Veja collaborated with the Atelier Sans Frontières association (ASF), which facilitated work for socially marginalized people,[42] by helping them to build a new life and by promoting their social, professional and personal development. Since the founding of Veja, ASF had received all the finished sneakers from Brazil, stored them and prepared all the orders, which were dispatched to the retail stores where Veja sneakers were sold. ASF logisticians had recently started managing the functional portion of Veja's online store, the Veja Store.[43] ASF was in charge of printing, preparing, packing and sending all online orders.

Production

Veja sneakers were manufactured in a factory close to Porto Alegre. Most of the employees traced their roots to a community of German descendants who had arrived in Brazil at the end of the 19th century. All employees owned houses with running water and electricity, and 80 per cent were union members. Sixty per cent of the workers lived in the towns and villages surrounding the factory (the farthest being located 47 km away), while the remaining 40 per cent live near the factory. The factory pre-arranged coach services ensure all employees could travel safely and comfortably to work.

Veja complied with the core International Labour Organization (ILO) labor standards but felt more was needed to guarantee dignity at work. For example, Veja cared about workers' freedom to gather and uphold their rights, their standard of living and purchasing power, their social benefits and their rights of free speech. The average wage of the factory workers was approximately €238 each month, 16 per cent higher than Brazil's legal minimum wage for the shoe industry of €205 each month. In addition, Veja paid overtime and an annual bonus. The factory employees were entitled to four weeks of paid holiday, and they did not work on bank holidays. During the peak season, each employee worked a maximum of two hours extra per day, on average. Each employee contributed seven to 11 per cent of their salary to INSS (Instituto Nacional do Seguro

---

[42]Beyond this partnership with Veja, ASF tried to involve its employees in other tasks, such as collecting old sports material and computers and repairing them. All the work is adapted to the people depending on their skills and experience. The aim is to aid the employees in (re)building their lives and careers.

[43]Veja, http://www.veja-store.com/, accessed on September 26, 2010.

Social, Brazil's governmental pension scheme), which provided an additional safety net for the employees.

When Kopp and Morillion were in business school, they had taken internships in investment banking and consultancy companies, where they learned about hard work and earning a lot of money. Morillion commented: "In these places, we saw how people were stressed and didn't like their jobs, but just came home happy because of the money. This is definitely not our culture."[44] At Veja, employees started their work at 9:30 in the morning and left the office before 7 p.m. On Friday afternoons, everyone went home at 4:30 p.m., and the founders themselves often went out of town for the weekend. Keeping the balance between work and private life was at the core of Veja's approach of creating a company that cared about the employees.

Each year, each new member of the Veja team was given the opportunity to travel to Brazil to meet the producers. For the founders, involving their employees in the entire Veja story was essential, instead of simply letting them work in an office in the center of Paris. Morillion explained:

> We travel a lot and meet many different people, but our employees don't get that chance. If we don't involve them in the whole process, they will get bored

and might want to leave the company. [We created] different experiences for our employees and they loved it.[45]

Certification

As part of the fair trade certification process, the main shoe factory in Porto Alegre underwent two social audits. The different departments of the factory and the fabrication workshops (which housed the cutting, sewing, soles, assembling processes) were audited in 2008 and 2009, in accordance with the Fairtrade Labelling Organization-Certification (FLO-Cert) standard requirements. The auditor raised 52 non-compliances in May 2008 and 16 non-compliances in February 2009; in April 2009, the certification of the factory was officially confirmed.

While the fair trade certification was increasingly important to consumers, for it was a means to a greater end, it was a starting point in Kopp and Morillion's path to improve the bigger picture. Veja sought to establish higher standards and strive toward loftier social and environmental objectives. To help the farmers gain additional credibility, Kopp and Morillion supported the cooperatives in the process of obtaining certification, but their personal relationships with the farmers extended beyond certification. The founders cared about social equity, and saw their venture as

[44]Interview with François Morillion, October 2, 2009, used with permission.

[45]Ibid.

one means to improve farmers' lives by supporting traditional livelihoods.

Supply Chain

Kopp and Morillion created a supply chain that was based on sustainable relationships (see Exhibit 3). They viewed the company's connection to its producers as one not just of trade but of cultural exchange. Whereas the fashion industry was accustomed to contracting new parties as soon as a factory could deliver on time or cut costs, Veja tried to improve living conditions and to work cooperatively with supply chain to jointly develop the best product they could imagine. Veja bought raw materials directly from producers. The company paid a fixed price, which, though higher than the market price, was calculated by the farmers and allowed them to live in dignity. Veja was happy to pay extra. Kopp and Morillion viewed fair wages as a means of re-establishing social justice.

Cotton

The canvas for the Veja sneakers was organic cotton. With help from Esplar,[46] an NGO that had been collaborating with Brazilian farmers for 30 years, Veja started working with 150 families to grow cotton under agro-ecological principles (i.e. without the use of agro-chemicals or pesticides); Veja now sourced cotton from 400 families in the state of Ceará in north-eastern Brazil.

Veja purchased 90 per cent of the organic cotton it used from ADEC, a new association of rural farmers who followed agro-ecological principles. The strong interdependence made Veja vulnerable. Changes in weather and natural disasters, such as insect plagues and violent rains, could deplete the supply of organic cotton. Production needed to adapt to the availability of organic cotton, which still varied considerably. Depending on the extent of the harvest, Veja sometimes needed to reduce the quantities of sneakers ordered by retailers.

Rubber

The Amazon was the only place on earth where rubber trees still grew in the wild. The survival of the Amazonian rainforest depended on sustainable management of its resources, including the latex extracted from rubber trees. Since the 1960s, the increasing use of synthetic rubber derived from petroleum had lowered both the demand and price for natural rubber. Thus, the inhabitants of the Amazon forest had moved from rubber tapping to more profitable activities, such as cattle-raising and wood extraction, which

---

[46]Esplar, available at http://www.esplar.org.br/, accessed on September 26, 2010.

both required the clearing of land. As a consequence of deforestation, the soils were no longer protected by the cover of vegetation, leaving them vulnerable to accelerated erosion and desertification.

Inside the Chico Mendès Extractive Reserve, located in the Brazilian state of Acre, Veja worked with Amopreab[47] (Associação de Moradores e Produtores da Reserva Extrativista Chico Mendes de Assis Brasil), an association of seringueiros, or rubber tappers (see Exhibit 3). Beatriz Saldanha, who had lived and worked with the seringueiros for 10 years, helped Veja to make the connection. By 2010, Veja was working with 35 rubber tapper families. Paying a fairer price for latex not only guaranteed a better income for the rubber tappers but also provided an incentive for conserving the rubber trees.

Leather

After two seasons of relying on organic cotton and rubber, Veja started researching the qualities of leather and its impact on the environment. The typical tanning process used heavy metals, such as chrome, making leather one of the least sustainable raw materials. Chrome allowed for quick tanning, but was a dangerous product and accounted for three problems: 1) it affected the people who tanned the leather, 2) it polluted the water and 3) it was not biodegradable. Sustainable processes, however, were available. In Italy, for example, factories often used vegetal tanning techniques and worked with companies such as Gucci and Chanel. Veja searched for companies that worked with alternative tanning processes, eventually locating a factory that tanned leather the way it was done 100 years ago. At that time, tanners did not work with chrome, so going back to basics helped to overcome the problem. Veja collaborated with this traditional factory to produce only eco-tanned leather created from a vegetable extract such as acacia. To obtain a consistent color without staining, Veja used conventional dying approved by Eco-Label.[48] To continuously improve the quality of the natural dyes, Veja undertook a collaboration with a Brazilian specialist in the field of vegetable and non-polluting color pigments.

Cost Structure

Veja's fabrication costs were seven to eight times higher than other footwear brands because its shoes and bags were produced in a principled way. Veja's price for organic cotton was twice the world market price. In 2009, Veja

---

[47]"Portal do Meio Ambiente"; available at http://www.portaldomeioambiente.org.br/index .php?option=com_content&view=article&id=2560:vencedores-do-chico-mendes-recebem-premiacao-em-dezembro&catid=40:comunicacao-ambiental-&Itemid=733, accessed on September 26, 2010.

[48]http://www.eco-label.com/default.htm, accessed on September 29, 2010.

bought Brazilian wild rubber (produced according to FDL—folha desfumada liquida, or liquid smoked sheet) at €2.33 per kg. The price of planted natural rubber from São Paulo varied between €1.60 per kg to €1.90 per kg. The price of synthetic rubber, determined by the oil price, ranged between €1 per kg and €1.2 per kg.

A large part of Veja's current profits funded research and development (R&D), such as developing new applications to work with organic cotton, rubber and leather. Veja also invested in collaborations with a Brazilian dyeing specialist to help improve the vegetal tanning techniques. Veja had just started collaborating with other French-Brazilian brands, such as Envão and Tudo Bom, to work together on improving the supply chain and jointly sourcing raw material to be able to meet the quantity criteria. The Veja founders welcomed other small brands interested in sourcing from Brazil because Kopp and Morillion felt "it makes them stronger and reduces the risk for both them and their producers."[49]

Zero Ads

Generally, 70 per cent of the cost of sneakers was dedicated to marketing. Veja, however, had a "no advertising" policy. Regardless, the company's products had been endorsed by the media and appreciated by the public since the company's creation. Veja benefitted widely from media coverage, blogs, forums and word of mouth. Morillion commented:

> That is really the most rewarding thing in running this company, to see people walking down the streets on our sneakers. Last week I saw someone with a Veja bag, which is a very new product just in stores. He was not even a friend of us, but a complete stranger who had already picked up this product![50]

Zero Stock

The popularity of Veja's products paid off: most outlets had fewer Veja sneakers than they could sell. Veja did not produce extra; it produced only according to orders placed six months in advance. Veja was not about large volumes but about profitability—with a conscience.

Environmental Footprint

CO_2 Emissions

Veja looked at every aspect of its supply chain and adjusted the company's methods of transportation, organization, production and distribution. All

---

[49]Interview with François Morillion, October 2, 2009, used with permission.

[50]Ibid.

Veja shoes were transported by boat from Porto Alegre, Brazil, to Le Havre in France. Upon arrival in Le Havre, the shoes traveled in barges along the canals to the Parisian suburbs. Veja's packaging was made from recycled and recyclable cardboard, and it used shoe boxes that were sized down to optimize efficiency. Finally, Veja's headquarters used Enercoop (a green electricity cooperative) instead sourcing electricity from Électricité de France (EDF, the French national nuclear energy supplier).

Limitations

Veja was open, both about its limitations and its work to overcome them. Kopp and Morillion were open about the remaining shortcomings of Veja's production processes and explained how they kept working to become more sustainable. For example, because production was still low, Veja did not need many pairs of shoelaces and could thus not afford to create the laces from organic cotton. The moss used to maintain the ankle was a synthetic, oil-based product. The shoes' sole contains between 30 per cent and 40 per cent of rubber, whereas the insole contained only 5 per cent of rubber. The insole also had technical properties (i.e. comfort and resistance), which required additional components, such as synthetic rubber. The eyelets in the shoes did not contain nickel but were composed of metal whose origin was not controlled. The sneakers were shipped by boat from Brazil to France, but American and Asian stores and clients continued to be serviced by plane. Veja also aimed to recycle the sneakers, thereby further increasing their lifespan.

Message

Since day one, Veja had produced more than sneakers. It also crafted art events as a way of connecting to customers and inspiring its own employees. The company's communication team reached out, and Veja sponsored art installations made by local artists they befriended in the French and Brazilian urban art scenes.[51] For example, for the 2006 Fashion Fair "Who's next?" Veja invited the art collective Favela Chic to perform. In an example of Veja's own creativity, São Paulo's 2006 ban on advertising inspired Veja to create an installation in the window display of the Parisian store French Trotters.[52]

The most recent exhibition (in October 2009), suggestively titled "São Paulo, Mon Amour," showcased the

---

[51]Although the event was a co-production between Veja and several other parties, the company deliberately chose to not be visible in the event's promotion and publicity.

[52]Veja, "Urban Archeology," March 25, 2009; available at http://blog.veja.fr/en/site/comments/urban_archeology/, accessed on September 26, 2010.

vision of São Paulo artists on their city.[53] The pieces conveyed messages about social inequality and pollution in Brazil's capital (Brasilia) and raised awareness about these issues. The exhibition, which was held in a public space in Paris, attracted 3,000 people in two weeks' time and was jointly sponsored by the Brazilian Ministry of Culture and the Municipality of Paris. Veja chose a discreet approach to promote the event by inviting the company's contacts, who would thus associate the brand with an interesting and beautiful exhibition.

Art was also a driver in the various special collections Veja developed in collaboration with other companies and organizations. For example, in 2007, the company launched a collection designed by the young French fashion designer Christine Phung.[54] In July 2009, the Veja Kids, a line of sneakers for children, landed exclusively in Bonpoint stores around the world.[55] Using the motto "Sell your car, get a bike," the company launched the Cyclope collection in the Cyclope shop in Paris in November 2009.[56] In January 2010, the Veja + Merci became exclusively available in the Merci store, a lifestyle and fashion emporium in Paris. All proceeds from the Cyclope collection were donated to charity.[57]

The Decision

When Veja had started, Kopp and Morillion were in their mid-twenties. They had never worked for anyone else, commented Morillion:

> By now I don't think we can ever work for another company, since Veja allows us so much freedom to do what we want and to strive for our dreams. [58]

They had many ideas, but took things step by step and tried to take as little risk as possible. At the moment they were focusing on their first range of accessories, like bags, wallets and computer cases. In another five to 10 years, they could save enough to open their own flagship store.

---

[53]Veja, "São Paulo, Mon Amour," blog entry, posted September 9, 2009; available at http://blog .veja.fr/en/site/comments/megapole_insensee_mon_amour/, accessed on September 26, 2010.

[54]Curitiba 75, "Veja," video clip; available at http://www.youtube.com/watch?v=h__qANp3g8U& feature=player_embedded, accessed on September 26, 2010.

[55]Veja, "Veja and Bonpoint, One to Watch this Winter," blog entry, posted July 17, 2009; available at http://blog.veja.fr/en/site/comments/veja_and_bonpoint/, accessed on September 26, 2010.

[56]http://blog.veja.fr/fr/archive/200912, accessed on September 26, 2010.

[57]Veja, "Vega + Merci," blog entry, posted January 12, 2010; available at http://blog.veja.fr/en/site/ comments/veja_merci/, accessed on September 26, 2010.

[58]Interview with François Morillion, October 2, 2009, used with permission.

We're always thinking about the next project, but not really about the one after. It comes as it goes.[59]

Kopp and Morillion's social change ambitions held strong. Veja's website portrayed the company as one drop in the ocean, offering the following call to action:

> Day after day, prophets of all kind are pulling the emergency cord, the entire economy is turning green and sustainable-developementising speeches are spreading around.
>
> Actions remain scarce but words abound.
>
> Beyond movies about the environment, beyond multinational companies building green windows to hide disasters, beyond the Copenhagen speeches filled with words and political promise.
>
> And despite this green-fronted economy, let's try to offer a different vision which combines fair trade and ecology and links together economy, social initiatives and the environment.
>
> A vision that proposes cultural change.[60]

Kopp and Morillion's vision for social change had already extended beyond their company. Kopp and Morillion coached new eco-fashion brands, which then started men's collections; they tried to give them direction:

> Many people call us and we meet them and give them advice. What is lacking in the ethical fashion field, is strong men's brands and this is where Veja tries to make a difference.[61]

Kopp and Morillion also aimed to influence existing brands to convert to organic and fair-trade practices. Sometimes they felt it might be easier to change existing brands because they had already created the style that people wanted to wear, whereas ethical fashion brands often lacked the right aesthetics.

> I think the ethical fashion world is still missing a bit of fashion and that's why it doesn't grow as fast as we all hope. Our product came at the right time at the right place. If we would have done the same product without the fair-trade and organic [angle], it might have brought us the same success. It's sad, but I think it is true.

They had a lot of work ahead: "Right now I still haven't found cool ethical T-shirts and jeans and I just hope that I can wear only ethical one day."[62]

---

[59]Ibid.

[60]Veja, "Veja Is Just a Drop in the Ocean," http://www.veja.fr/#/projets, accessed on September 26, 2010.

[61]Interview with François Morillion, October 2, 2009, used with permission.

[62]Ibid.

Exhibit 1   Veja Founders

François-Ghislain Morillion	Sébastien Kopp
Production & Finances Born July 25, 1978 MSc HEC Paris, 2002 Passion: electronic music	Sales & Marketing Born July 16, 1978 MSc DESS, 2002 Passion: writing

Source: Prepared by the case writer on the basis of company documents and interviews. Photo credits: Veja, used with permission.

Exhibit 2 Veja Collections

2005: Volley	2006: Tauá	2007: Grama	2008: The Grid	2009: SP, MA	2010: Bags, Veja+Merci

VEJA MILESTONES

2005	2006	2007	2008	2009	2010
Feb: Launch Veja	Feb: Collaboration Agnes b.	June: launch Veja + Christine Phung	March: Launch Veja Kids	March: Launch bags+wallets	Jan: Launch Veja+Merci
Sept: Launch Veja website	July: Launch Veja blog	Sept: Veja @ Ethical Fashion Show (EFS)	Aug: London office open	Sept: Expo SP, Mon Amour	Feb: Veja+Bonpoint Merci
Nov: Launch Veja Baby	Nov: 1st rubber collection	Dec: Veja lands in Madrid	Oct: Launch online store	Nov: Launch Veja+ Cyclope	May: Snippet expo London

ETHICAL FASHION MILESTONES

2005	2006	2007	2008	2009	2010
Ethical Fashion Forum is founded in the UK	1st Esthetica in London	Organic Exchange turns 5 years old[1]	5th EFS in Paris	EFS launches in other cities like Milan	Messe Frankfurt acquires EFS
Launch of Made-By				Launch NY Greenshows and TheKey.to Berlin	

Source: Prepared by the case writer on the basis of company documents and interviews.

[1]http://cogent.controlunion.com/cusi_production_files/SISI_files/FL_011210114219_Market_Report_08-_Executive_Summary.pdf, accessed September 28, 2010.

Exhibit 3   Veja's Sourcing of Cotton, Rubber and Leather

The state of Ceará in northeast Brazil has vast wealth inequalities, fragile soils and a tendency toward drought. It also works with a producers' cooperative in Paraná, a relatively more productive area located in the center of Brazil. In contrast to the predominant monoculture farming system, a group of small producers grow cotton and food plants as rotational crops. For these small-scale farmers (one hectare of land on average), farming development goes hand-in-hand with environmental protection. But there were setbacks. After a caterpillar attack, producers panicked and decided to spray pesticide to protect their harvest. Veja had committed itself to purchase the harvest and could not ask the producers to lose their entire harvest. Therefore, these 12 tons of "infected" organic and ethical cotton were used to make the shoes' lining and as a double layer for the Projet Numero Deux accessories (see http://www.veja.fr/#/projets/Coton-15 for the process). The photo at left shows the Porto Alegre team manager checking the cotton.

Seringueiros (derived from the word *seringueira*, or the rubber plant) extract natural latex directly from the trunk of the rubber tree (Hevea brasiliensis), by making small cuts in the bark. At least five hours are needed to fill a tiny container with latex, and two years must pass before new cuts can be made on the same tree. To process the liquid rubber into sheets that can be used to make rubber soles, the seringueiros use a new technology developed by Professor Floriano Pastore of the University of Brasilia, called FDL (folha desfumada liquida, or liquid smoked sheet). FDL allows the rubber tappers to transform latex into rubber sheets without any industrial intermediary processes. Once extracted, filtered and purified, the latex is stretched and "spread" in six layers onto canvas of organic cotton, and then subjected to a curing process in the open air, which allows it to dry and results in a high-quality product. To produce a pair of slabs, the seringueiros must first tap into material extracted from at least 10 rubber plants. The FDL technology permits the seringueiros to sell semi-finished products and receive a higher income. The sheets of rubber are directly sent to the factory and shaped into soles for the Veja shoes. Not only does the production of vegetable rubber represent an instrument for environmental protection, but it also provides an economic alternative for seringueiros, who wander the heart of the Amazon forest during six months a year engaged in the extraction and processing of this material. This practice safeguards the culture and traditions of autochthonous populations, who are the true guardians of the forest (see http://www.tyresonfire.com/amazonlife.com/index.php?id=60 for a clip of seringueiros at work). The photos at left show a seringueiro and Beatriz Saldanha, the woman who connected Veja with the seringueiros.

Leather is typically not made under fair trade principles because it is difficult to work directly with leather producers, and it is often difficult to confirm the leather's origin and the cattle's treatment. The breeding of cattle also requires vast fields and the relevant financial inputs. Veja chose not to marginalize leather producers but instead sought to make a positive change within this specific industry. Veja ensured that the leather it sourced did originate from the cattle from the Amazon, where cattle breeding remains a main contributor to deforestation. The company's main objective was to be knowledgeable and in control of the entire leather supply chain, from the cows' nurturing and living conditions to the tanning and dyeing process of the leather. Veja used only eco-tanned leather created with vegetable extracts such as acacia. Unlike modern tanning procedures (which use chromium and other heavy metals), ecological tanning decreases pollution in the water surrounding the tannery plant.

(See http://www.veja.fr/#/projets/Cuir-14 for a video clip of the process). The photo at left shows one step in the leather veggie-tanning process.

Source: Prepared by the case writer on the basis of company documents and interviews; photos used with permission.

Canadian Solar

Paul W. Beamish

Jordan Mitchell

In late September 2009, Dr. Shawn Qu, CEO, president, chairman and founder of Canadian Solar, was constantly on the move. His company, a NASDAQ-traded solar cell and module manufacturer, had grown at a compound annual growth rate (CAGR) of 135.7 per cent over the last five years from $9.7 million in revenues in 2004 to $705 million in 2008 (see Exhibit 1 for key financials). The strong growth had been spurred by an increasing number of government incentive programs to encourage the adoption of solar photovoltaic (PV)[1] technology. For the past couple of years, solar energy was seen to be the world's fastest-growing industry. However, the credit crunch and global economic downturn combined with changes to Spain's incentive program had put the worldwide PV industry into oversupply for the first half of 2009. During the summer, demand changed again. Forecasts were exceeded, causing a temporary undersupply of ready-to-install solar modules. The fluctuating solar demand had caused analysts to change their financial outlook for Canadian Solar several times

throughout 2009. In mid-2009, a Deutsche Bank analyst had predicted full-year sales to come in at $395 million with net losses at –$18 million, only to revise the outlook two months later to sales of $574 million and net income of $49 million.

Part of the increasing positive outlook was attributed to government incentive programs. Of particular interest to many players, including Canadian Solar, were proposed incentive programs in China and Canada. In Ontario, for example, the details of the provincial government's incentive program for green energy—the Feed-in Tariff (FIT) program—had just been released with specific requirements for domestic content. Although registered as a Canadian company, Canadian Solar had the bulk of its production operations in China; namely, seven facilities dedicated to the manufacture of different solar PV components. And, even though the company's "bases" were in China and Canada, 89.5 per cent of 2008 revenues came from Europe. Company management expected that to change rapidly as they were planning

---

[1]Solar photovoltaic (PV) technology is one of the main types of solar electric power. It is the main focus of this case.

or had already established new sales offices in South Korea, Japan, China, Italy, Spain, Germany, the United States and Canada.

When looking at the relatively nascent and rapidly growing solar PV industry replete with a mix of diverse competitors, Qu and other Canadian Solar senior managers wondered how best to compete in the increasingly "global" PV industry.

Solar Energy

Solar energy was divided into three main categories: solar electric, solar thermal and concentrating solar. Solar electric converted the sun's energy into electricity and solar thermal used the sun for heating or cooling. Concentrating solar power mixed solar electric and solar thermal as it used small optical mirrors to collect solar energy and convert the sunlight to heat. The heat was then applied to a liquid or gas to turn a turbine, thereby creating electricity.

The other important distinction in solar energy was between "grid-tied" and "off-grid" applications. Grid-tied applications were solar-electric systems that were connected to an electricity utility grid (in nearly all jurisdictions, electricity utility grids were heavily regulated by government bodies and were often separate from electricity providers). Grid-tied applications were either "ground mount" or "rooftop"—ground mount applications were typically in a field or desert area and were either solar PV or concentrating solar power. Grid-tied rooftop projects ranged from one kilowatt to 10 kilowatts (kW) on residential homes to larger projects of 10 kilowatts to five megawatts (MW) on commercial buildings.

Off-grid applications were defined as a system completely independent of the main electricity grid. Off-grid applications ranged from tiny solar cells in pocket calculators to solar-thermal systems for hot water tanks in residential homes. In the last few years, off-grid applications had become popular for road lights, signs and parking meters whereby a solar module was placed on top of the apparatus to provide power at night through a battery. Off-grid applications were also seen as one solution to providing power in isolated rural areas.

Photovoltaic Cells[2]

The main tenet of solar-electric power was the photovoltaic (PV) cell, which used the "photovoltaic effect" to generate electricity. When sunlight hit a PV cell, electrons bounced from negative to positive, thus producing electricity. In

---

[2]This section draws upon SBI, "The U.S. Solar Energy Market in a World Perspective," March 2008, pp. 2–30.

order to generate electricity, a PV cell required a semiconductor material and positive and negative poles.[3]

The most common semiconductor material for PV cells was silicon.[4] For most solar applications, the silicon was refined to 99.9999 per cent purity, which was known as 6N silicon (the number "6" referred to the number of "9s"). Companies such as Canadian Solar had commercialized products with lower grades of silicon for solar applications. For example, upgraded metallurgical-grade silicon (UMG-Si) was one such type of lower grade silicon. It was 99.999 per cent pure (or 5N for five "9s"). UMG-Si was a bi-product of the aluminum smelting business and historically had been less expensive than 6N silicon.

The three types of PV cells were polycrystalline ("poly"), monocrystalline ("mono") and amorphous ("thin-film"). Poly PV cells used silicon in its refined state whereas mono took the refinement a step further, thus creating higher efficiency (the drawback with mono PV was the higher cost of production vs. poly). The third type, thin-film, was substantially different in that it did not have crystalline silicon, but rather a painted or printed semi-conductor. There were six main types of materials used in thin-film, although three had not yet been proven to be commercially viable.[5]

The basic process of constructing a crystalline PV cell began by forming cylindrical ingots from the semi-conductor material. The ingots were then cut into very thin disc-shaped wafers. The wafer was etched with hydrofluoric acid and washed with water, creating a PV cell. To create a usable "solar module" (also called a "solar panel"), a series of PV cells were placed in between a sheet of glass held in by an aluminum frame and plastic backing connected to a cable plug. In most installations, a number of modules were used to make up an array. The array was then connected to an inverter (to convert the electricity from direct current (DC) to alternating current (AC)).

Solar modules were rated by their capacity in watts (W). Most solar PV modules were rated between 80W and 250W. Larger solar modules (200W+) weighed approximately 20 kilograms and were sized 1.6 meters long, one

---

[3]Phosphorous was often used as the negative pole and boron was often used as the positive pole.

[4]Silicon was found in sand, rocks or soil as silicon oxide (SiO_2); the process for manufacturing silicon involved heating silicon oxide with a carbon material like coke or coal at high temperatures to remove the oxygen.

[5]The six types of materials used in thin-film technology were: amorphous silicon (a-Si); copper indium diselenide (CIS); copper indium gallium diselenide (CIGS); cadmium telluride (CdTe); gallium arsenide (GaAs); and thin-film silicon.

meter wide and four to five centimeters thick. Solar efficiency—the amount of sunlight energy converted to electricity—ranged between 12 and 18 per cent for most PV modules. However, breakthroughs were constantly being achieved—as of mid-2009, the highest PV cells had efficiency ratings slightly above 23 per cent. As a general rule of thumb, one to two per cent efficiency was deducted from the rating of the cell to determine the rating of the module (i.e. an 18 per cent efficient cell would have a 16–17 per cent efficient module).

The cost of PV cells was a constantly moving target. In securing contracts with large volumes, it was common for PV manufacturers to offer discounts of 10–30 per cent on the price of a module. In large-scale projects, many buyers saw PV modules more as a commodity product and were largely concerned with the price per watt. From 2007 to 2009, the selling price of a solar PV (from a PV module manufacturer to a customer) had increased slightly from $3.50 per watt to around $4 before dropping to approximately $2.50 per watt (put another way, the price for one 200W solar PV crystalline module was about $500 as of mid-2009).

A major driver behind the price of solar PV was the price of silicon. A temporary silicon shortage around mid-2008 pushed the spot price of silicon to over $500 per kilogram (up from around $25 per kilogram in 2004). However, by mid-2009, that price had fallen to around $60 per kilogram.[6] As the supply for silicon increased along with greater manufacturing efficiencies, the cost for crystalline PV modules was expected to fall below $1 per watt in two to three years.

Many industry insiders debated whether thin-film modules held more promise given their lower cost versus poly and mono modules. As of August 2009, the price of thin-film was reported at $1.76 per watt versus $2.50 per watt for silicon modules.[7] Despite silicon's current higher price, crystalline silicon supporters often pointed to the fact that thin-film would have trouble competing as the price of crystalline modules dropped. Additionally, poly and mono crystalline silicon modules typically enjoyed higher efficiencies than thin-film and required less space, fewer mounting systems and less cabling for the same power output.

In addition to the cost of the module itself, the cost of installation ranged from $4 to $8 per watt. Developers of utility-scale PV projects also had to be mindful of the real estate cost and electricity transmission costs. All tallied,

---

[6]Edgar Gunther, "Solar Polysilicon Oversupply until 2013?" August 3, 2009, http://guntherportfolio .com/2009/08/solar-polysilicon-oversupply-until-2013, accessed August 18, 2009.

[7]Quote from www.solarbuzz.com, accessed August 11, 2009.

the cost of solar PV was between 0.15 and 0.35 per kilowatt-hour (kWh) versus non-renewable sources of energy between 0.03 and 0.15 per kWh. As scale efficiencies grew along with technological breakthroughs, many insiders felt that the cost of solar would be competitive with non-renewable sources in a three to five year time horizon (this was referred to in the industry as reaching "grid parity").

The Global Solar Industry

In 2008, solar PV experienced its largest increase to date by growing 5.6 gigawatts (60.8 per cent) to 14.73 gigawatts (GW) in 2008.[8] (On a global level, solar power accounted for under one per cent of all electricity generation.) Geographically, total installed capacity was split: 65 per cent in Europe, 15 per cent in Japan and eight per cent in the United States. In 2008, the strongest market was Spain, which represented nearly half of the installations due to its aggressive Renewable Energy Feed-in Tariff (referred to as REFIT or FIT) program, which guaranteed electricity rates for certain renewable projects. Even though Spain dominated the PV market in 2008, the Spanish government had placed a 500MW cap on annual installations for

the next two years, given uncontrollable growth. Thus, Spanish PV installations were expected to drop substantially in 2009. Germany was the second largest market, capturing 26.7 per cent of worldwide installations during the year (Germany was one of the first countries in the world to introduce a FIT program). Other leading solar countries were the United States (six per cent of worldwide installations), South Korea (five per cent), Italy (4.9 per cent) and Japan (four per cent).

The future of the global PV market largely hinged on government initiatives and renewable support schemes. The European Photovoltaic Industry Association (EPIA) predicted two scenarios: a moderate scenario without heavy government incentives and a policy-driven scenario with some support initiatives present. Under the first scenario, EPIA projected that cumulative solar PV power would equate to 54.8GW in 2013 (representing a CAGR of 30 per cent). The second scenario resulted in global installed PV power being 85.8GW by 2013 (CAGR of 42.3 per cent). Exhibit 2 shows some highlights from different world markets and Exhibit 3 gives EPIA's moderate and policy-driven scenarios for the top 13 markets.

Germany was expected to be the top market for the next few years, given

---

[8]By comparison, the global installed capacity of wind power grew by 29 per cent from 93.9GW in 2007 to 121.2GW in 2008.

the government's continuing Renewable Energy Law (*Erneuerbare-Energien-Gesetz* or EEG). As a successor to an earlier law passed in 1991, the EEG came into effect in 2000 as part of Germany's aim to derive 12.5 per cent of the country's energy from renewable sources by 2010 (the goal was surpassed in 2007 when Germany reached 14 per cent and was modified to reach a new goal of 27 per cent renewable by 2020). In 2009, the EEG was updated—for PV solar, the feed-in rates were between €0.33 and €0.43 per kWh ($0.46 to $0.60 per kWh) depending on the size of the project. The EEG called for those rates to decrease by eight to 10 per cent in 2010 and nine per cent after 2011 but guaranteed the rates for a period of 20 years.[9] Despite the decreasing feed-in rates over the next few years, the EPIA believed that the rates were sufficient to encourage installations. Furthermore, PV solar was expected to remain strong as a result of high public awareness and support of renewables, the skilled PV industry and accessible financing

opportunities through Kreditanstalt für Wiederaufbau (KfW).[10]

The story of Spain's boom and subsequent bust had become a hot topic in the solar industry. Through laws in 2004 and 2007, the Spanish government created an attractive Feed-in Tariff (FIT) giving up to €0.44 per kWh ($0.62 per kWh) for solar projects installed before September 2008. In spite of the original cap of 400MW, the country was flooded with demand for projects and in an 18-month period (from the passing of the 2007 law to September 2008), about 3GW of PV solar energy were installed. The heavily unanticipated installations were estimated to cost taxpayers about $26.4 billion, causing a public backlash against the government.[11] In 2008, the Spanish government placed a new cap of 500MW on installations and backed off the Feed-in Tariffs to €0.32 to €0.34 per kWh ($0.45 to $0.48 per kWh).[12] Despite the new cap, Spain was seen as a key market in the long term due to its government's high renewable target (the government

---

[9]"Act Revising the Legislation on Renewable Energy Sources in the Electricity Sector and Amending Related Provisions—Renewable Energy Sources Act—EEG 2009," www.erneuerbare-energien.de/inhalt/42934/3860, accessed August 18, 2009.

[10]European Photovoltaic Industry Association (EPIA), "Global Market Outlook for Photovoltaics until 2013," March 2009, p. 7.

[11]Paul Voosen, "Spain's Solar Market Crash Offers a Cautionary Tale About Feed-In Tariffs," August 18, 2009, www.nytimes.com/gwire/2009/08/18/18greenwire-spains-solar-market-crash-offers-a-cautionary-88308.html?pagewanted=2, accessed August 18, 2009.

[12]"Spain Makes Changes to Solar Tariff," September 29, 2008, www.renewableenergyworld.com/rea/news/article/2008/09/spain-makes-changes-to-solar-tariff-53698, accessed August 18, 2009.

wanted 20 per cent of consumed energy to come from renewables by 2020).[13]

Prior to the boom in Germany and Spain, Japan had had one of the strongest solar PV markets in the world up until 2006, when the government stopped supplying subsidies. The majority of its PV installations were in residential applications (different from other markets where commercial applications were the norm). Recently, the government had set new targets of reaching over 50GW of installed PV power by 2030 and had implemented national and regional support mechanisms. The country's Feed-in Tariff schemes promised an initial rate of 50 yen per kWh ($0.50 per kWh) for solar installations.[14]

The U.S. market also held great promise given President Obama's support of renewable energy and several state programs targeted at rolling out renewables. California, Arizona, New Mexico, Texas, Vermont and several other states had or were in the process of enacting incentives and stimulus programs. In 2010 many expected that the United States would enact a federal incentive program—one source suggested that the bill would guarantee a 10 per cent return over 20 years for renewable projects under 20MW.[15] Nearly all of the PV manufacturers had set up offices in the United States given the future potential in what many believed would become the world's largest market by the middle of the next decade.

A number of other policies and support mechanisms had also been implemented or were in the design phase in countries as far-reaching as Italy, Greece, France, Israel, South Korea, China and Canada.

In Canada, the main program was Ontario's FIT, announced in early 2009 with a start date of October 1, 2009. Ontario's FIT would replace the 2006 Standard Offer Program, which gave PV solar rates of Cdn$0.42 per kWh and other renewable sources rates of Cdn$0.11 per kWh.[16] As North America's first FIT program, renewables could garner between Cdn$0.08 and Cdn$0.802 per kWh depending on

[13]"Plan de Energías Renovables 2011–2020," http://www.plane.gob.es/plan-de-energías-renovables-2011-2020, accessed August 17, 2009.

[14]*Energy Matters*, "Japan Announces Solar Feed In Tariffs," February 25, 2009, www.energymatters.com.au/index.php?main_page=news_article&article_id=335, accessed August 17, 2009.

[15]James Murray, "US lawmakers outline plan for feed-in tariff bill," *Business Green*, August 5, 2009, http://www.businessgreen.com/business-green/news/2247352/lawmakers-outline-plan-feed, accessed August 19, 2009.

[16]"Ontario's Standard Offer Contracts," March 22, 2006, www.energyalternatives.ca/content/SOC.htm, accessed August 18, 2009.

the scale of the project. Smaller-scale solar rooftop systems for residential homes would receive the highest rates, between Cdn$0.539 and Cdn$0.802 per kWh. Larger-scale solar (less than 10MW) would receive Cdn$0.443 per kWh. The program called for domestic content to make up 40 per cent on projects less than 10kW and 50 per cent of the project cost on projects over 10kW (after January 1, 2011, domestic requirements would rise to 60 per cent). See Exhibit 4 for more details on Ontario's FIT program.

In July 2009, the Chinese government announced major subsidies for utility-scale solar projects. The conditions of receiving the subsidies required that the project have a minimum of 300kW peak, and be built in one year with longevity of 20 years. The subsidy would be 20 yuan ($4) per watt with the overall goal of reaching 10GW of installed power by 2020.[17]

Players in the Global PV Market

Globally, there were hundreds of PV cell and module manufacturers. On the supply side of PV manufacturers, there were raw material suppliers for goods such as silicon, glass, substrates, metal and cables as well as specialized equipment manufacturers to make solar components such as furnaces, sawing machines, printing machines and laminators. On the buyer side of PV manufacturers, there were several potential customers. Consumer electronics, automotive and industrial product companies integrated solar cells into their products for resale (examples ranged from solar cells in garden lamps through to cells used on marine buoys). For grid-tied applications, the typical customers were project developers, utility companies, solar installation companies, distributors, wholesalers, governments, construction companies and building owners.

Barriers to entry were considered fairly low due to the low capital requirements and medium-low technological know-how to make a PV module. However, product warranties were one barrier that was becoming more important. For example, smaller manufacturers struggled to sell modules for use in bank-financed large-scale projects because of requirements from the banks for greater assurances that 25-year product performance warranties would be upheld. Some analysts also predicted more vertical integration both from silicon producers, specialized suppliers of PV cells and customers (such as project developers). Complementary players such as inverter manufacturers or rack suppliers were not considered to pose an immediate vertical integration threat.

---

[17]Jim Bai and Leonora Walet, "China offers big solar subsidy, shares up," *Reuters*, July 21, 2009.

The top 10 producers accounted for 55.3 per cent of PV module sales in 2008. Exhibit 5 shows the market shares of both PV module and PV cell producers. Some observers divided the market into three groups based on geography, market strength, size and quality perception. The first group competed on the basis of price and used China as a manufacturing base, the second was made up of up-start companies with a point of technological differentiation, and the third consisted of Japanese electronic firms with established brand names. The market could also be divided simply into more recent start-ups and established incumbents.

A powerful contingent of emerging PV module companies were the four companies which used China as their primary manufacturing base: Suntech, Yingli Green, Trina Solar and Canadian Solar. All were vertically integrated in that they produced ingots, wafers, cells and modules and used their access to low-cost labor for a cost advantage. Canadian Solar's management believed its company to be unique in that it combined elements of Western management and engineering with a low-cost Chinese production base.

Of the specialized start-ups, two main groups of companies existed: those producing complete PV modules and those focusing on the production of PV cells only. PV module start-ups competed more on tailored propositions, customer relationships and service,

technological differences and price. For example, First Solar used Cadmium Telluride as a semi-conductor, which allowed it to deliver a lower price per watt. SunPower competed by offering solar systems complete with inverters for easy residential and commercial installation. Both U.S. companies had the majority of their production in low-cost Asian countries, namely Malaysia and the Philippines.

Up-starts such as Germany's Q-Cells and Solar World, Taiwan's Motech and Gintech and China's JA Solar produced PV cells only and sold the cells to module producers. Q-Cells had surpassed Sharp in terms of total PV cell production in the last couple of years. The five PV cell companies competed on technology, relationships with module producers and price.

Of the incumbents, Japanese electronics multinationals such as Sharp, Kyocera and Sanyo all had long histories developing PV solar. They typically competed on the strength of their brand recognition, research and development, strong distribution and in some cases, exclusive rights with large-scale customers. Sharp had begun developing PV solar in 1959 and had dominated the world market for much of the last 50 years. While Sharp had historically sold mono and poly crystalline PV, they had begun investing in thin-film technology in 2005. In addition to its four plants in Japan, the company produced PV solar products in the United States, the United Kingdom and Thailand. To expand production even further, Sharp was seeking joint venture partners to build solar module factories in other countries (in late 2008, the company inked a deal with Italy's Enel for a joint venture plant in Italy).

Japan's second largest PV solar producer, Kyocera, produced a range of PV products in a network of factories split between Japan, China, the Czech Republic and Mexico. Japan's third major player, Sanyo, produced nearly all of its PV offerings in its home country. It had invested heavily in developing its own thin-film technology (called HIT for Heterojunction with Intrinsic Thin-layer), which it claimed had the highest efficiency of any solar PV cell in the world (its efficiency was 23 per cent).[18] Sanyo sold its complementary batteries with its PV solar products and had reorganized its business to satisfy its master plan of becoming a "leading provider of environment and energy-related products."[19] Sanyo's strong position in PV solar and related

products was one of the key reasons for Panasonic taking a key ownership stake in Sanyo in late 2008.[20]

Other multinationals also participated in PV solar, namely, Japan's Mitsubishi, Britain's BP and U.S. companies General Electric and Chevron. Mitsubishi began developing PV solar technology in the 1970s and offered complete packages including the PV module and inverter. As of 2009, Mitsubishi claimed to have one of the highest efficiencies of any poly PV cell (18.9 per cent).[21] Its production capacity was about 200MW. BP Solar also had about 30 years of history in the solar industry. With a capacity of 200MW, it produced poly and mono PV cells and modules in five plants located in Australia, Spain, the United States, India, and China. However, in a recent move to focus on its core business of petroleum, its parent company, BP, had announced that it would be closing factories in Australia, Spain and the United States and shifting to a mix of its lower cost plants

---

[18]"Sanyo Develops HIT Solar Cells with World's Highest Energy Conversion Efficiency of 23.0%," May 21, 2009, http://us.sanyo.com/News/SANYO-Develops-HIT-Solar-Cells-with-World-s-Highest-Energy-Conversion-Efficiency-of-23-0-, accessed August 16, 2009.

[19]Sanyo Annual Report 2008, December 31, 2008, p. 9.

[20]"Panasonic and SANYO Agree to Capital and Business Alliance," http://sanyo.com/news/2008/12/19-1.html, accessed August 17, 2009.

[21]"Mitsubishi Electric Breaks Own Record With World's Highest Conversion Efficiency Rate Of 18.9% For Multi-Crystalline Silicon Photovoltaic Cells," February 18, 2009, www.mitsubishi electricsolar.com/news, accessed August 19, 2009.

and sub-contractors in China.[22] (Shell divested its solar operations in 2006 and 2007—the majority of the assets were purchased by Germany's SolarWorld.[23])

Background on Canadian Solar

Canadian Solar was established by Qu in October 2001 in Markham, Ontario. In tandem, a production facility in Changshu, China, registered as CSI Solartronics was set up as a wholly owned subsidiary. Qu, a graduate of applied physics at Tsinghua University (B.Sc.) and the University of Manitoba (M.Sc.), had completed a doctoral degree in material science from the University of Toronto (Ph.D.) and extensive post-doctorate work on semiconductor optical devices and solar cells. In 1996, he joined Ontario Hydro (now Ontario Power Generation) as a research scientist, where he worked on the development of a next-generation solar technology called Spheral Solar™. In 1998, he joined ATS (Automation Tooling Systems), working in several capacities such as product engineer, director for silicon procurement, solar product strategic planning as well as technical vice president for one of ATS's subsidiaries.

Qu left ATS to establish Canadian Solar; he commented on the opportunity he saw at the time:

> In 2001, solar was still a very small industry. A lot of my colleagues from the PhD program in applied physics were involved in fibre optics for the telecommunications industry. I believed that solar had great prospects and thought I could easily spend my career in the solar industry. Because solar was such a small part of ATS, it did not get a lot of management attention. Around 2000, I started thinking of starting my own company and worked on the business plan. At that time, the major players were small solar divisions in multinationals. My idea largely focused on areas that I felt they were not addressing: rural electrification with solar, the low-cost production of solar cells and solar modules, building integrated solar products and consumer solar products. It just so happened the first product was a consumer solar product for the automotive industry.

Canadian Solar's first contract was to manufacture and sell a solar charger to Audi-Volkswagen for use in its automobiles being manufactured in Mexico. Audi-Volkswagen required that Canadian Solar became ISO9001 and ISO16949 certified. Management saw the certification as an essential part of raising Canadian Solar's quality

---

[22]Ed Crooks, "Back to petroleum," *Financial Times*, July 7, 2009.

[23]Terry Macalister, "Big Oil lets sun set on renewables," *The Guardian*, December 11, 2007, www.guardian.co.uk/business/2007/dec/11/oil.bp, accessed August 19, 2009.

credibility in the early stages of the company. Canadian Solar established two additional solar module manufacturing plants in Suzhou, China, incorporated as separate companies: CSI Solar Technologies in August 2003 and CSI Solar Manufacturing in January 2005. The company purchased solar cells and silicon raw materials from a small group of companies such as Swiss Wafers (Switzerland), Kunical (United States), Luoyang Zhong Gui (China) and LDK (China).

While continuing to supply Audi-Volkswagen (eventually receiving the accolade of class A supplier), Canadian Solar's management saw a great opportunity to develop solar modules for electricity generation for residential and commercial applications in 2004. Qu commented:

> In early 2004 with the change of Germany's FIT program, I identified a major increase in demand for solar PV modules for buildings. Within three to four months, we were able to switch gears to large solar modules. The decision to spin-off the company from ATS in 2001 when we did was vital—had I waited until 2004, I would not have had the time to build the team and capabilities to make this switch into larger solar modules.

By the end of 2004, nearly three-quarters of Canadian Solar's sales were derived from selling standard solar modules to distributors and system integrators based in Germany, Spain and China. The company made initial contact with its customers through international trade shows. By the end of 2005, the top five customers accounted for 68.2 per cent of total sales. Most sales were made with non-exclusive, three-month sales contracts. It was normal that the customer paid 20 to 30 per cent of the purchase as prepayment and the remainder in advance of the shipment from China. In China, sales of solar modules were associated with development projects in conjunction with Chinese governmental organizations and the Canadian International Development Agency (CIDA)—for example, in the spring of 2005, the company installed a demonstration power plant in a rural area of the province of Jiangsu.

With sales of standard solar modules accelerating, Canadian Solar turned to venture capital (VC) funding. Qu stated: "Up until 2005, we had grown without any VC involvement. We received an investment from HSBC and Jafco Ventures [a VC from Japan with $350 million under management] and then started preparing for an IPO." In November 2006, the company listed on the Nasdaq, raising $115.5 million. The proceeds were to be used to purchase and prepay for solar cells and silicon (35 per cent); expansion into solar cell manufacturing (45 per cent); and general funding purposes (20 per cent). The initial public offering (IPO) enabled it to expand into solar cell manufacturing, resulting in the following facilities:

CSI Solarchip for solar cells and modules; and CSI Advanced and CSI Luoyang for solar modules. By the end of 2007, the company had established four solar cell production lines, taking total cell capacity to 120MW.

Canadian Solar's management established a sales office of two people in Phoenix, Arizona, and a European office of three people near Frankfurt, Germany in December 2007. All sales in Spain were done through an independent distributor. As Qu said: "We serviced these growing markets from China and Canada. The decision to open up the offices in 2007 was a logical move given that the majority of sales were coming from those markets." On the production side, the company expanded to seven factories including a solar module manufacturing site in Changshu and an ingot and wafer manufacturing site in Luoyang. The continued expansion in China was complemented by a high-profile BIPV (Building Integrated Photovoltaic) module roof project as part of the Beijing 2008 Olympic Games. At the close of 2008, the company was recognized as one of the top 10 fastest-growing companies in China by Deloitte Asia, given its sales had more than doubled from $302.8 million in 2007 to $705 million in·2008.

In 2009, the company underwent a number of changes in its international configuration. To respond to market opportunity in South Korea, it established a two-person sales office. In Canada, it established an international development office of three people in Ottawa to focus specifically on projects in Latin America and the Middle East, given its working history with CIDA. In the United States, the company moved the Phoenix office to San Ramon, California, to be located closer to the heart of the U.S. solar movement and to take advantage of the favorable Californian incentives. It opened a warehouse at the office site to store finished solar modules. In China, it opened a PV research and development facility at its head office in Suzhou. As of the end of 2008, the company had 3,058 employees: 2,742 in manufacturing, 251 in general and administrative, 36 in research and development and 29 in sales and marketing.[24]

Canadian Solar's Model

The company described itself as an "inverted flexible vertical integration business model." This meant that the company had higher capacity as it went further downstream in the manufacturing process of each component of a solar module. Graphically, this could be illustrated as:

---

[24]Canadian Solar Annual Report 2008, 20-F, www.sec.gov, December 31, 2008, p. 74.

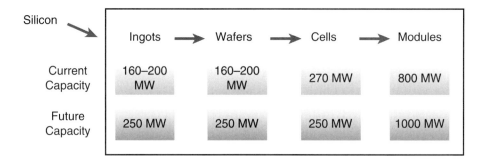

The rationale behind the "inverted vertical integration" model was to allow for flexibility in short-term demand shifts by purchasing ingots, wafers and cells from other manufacturers and to free the company from the capital investment required to have equal capacity of each component. The company believed that it would lead to a lower manufacturing cost base in the long term as well as superior production yields, better inventory control and efficient cash management.

Canadian Solar also had been one of the first solar companies to initiate a recycling process for reclaimable silicon from discarded, broken or unused silicon wafers and ingots at two of its plants in Suzhou and Changshu. The process involved a substantial amount of labour and analysts believed that Canadian Solar had a competitive advantage in recycling silicon. However, in the 2008 Annual Report, the company stated: "As a result of the oversupply of silicon materials that developed in the fourth quarter of 2008, we expect this aspect of our operation to be less significant in the foreseeable future."[25] The company also became a member of the Belgian organization PV CYCLE in mid-2009. PV CYCLE promoted a take-back and recycling of PV modules that had reached the end of their useful life.[26]

Products

Canadian Solar offered a portfolio of products ranging from 0.3W to 300W. It split its offerings into two main divisions: standard and specialty. The company used both its own branding and manufactured white label products for other OEMs. With a few exceptions, all products were standardized for the global market.

[25]Canadian Solar Annual Report 2008, 20-F, www.sec.gov, December 31, 2008, p. 30.

[26]"Canadian Solar Becomes Member of PV Cycle," July 21, 2009, http://phx.corporate-ir.net/phoenix .zhtml?c=196781&p=irol-news, accessed November 20, 2009.

The company offered three types of products:

1. Standard: Standard modules were used for both ground mount and rooftop systems and were available in both mono and poly.

2. e-Modules: e-Modules were a recent product introduction which were aimed at providing a lower-cost product for smaller rooftop systems. e-Modules were lower cost because they used upgraded metallurgical-grade silicon (Umg Si) instead of pure silicon.

3. BIPV (Building Integrated Photovoltaic). Finally, BIPV were intended to be used as a building material in a roof, skylight or façade.

Standard modules were all tested and certified by various international standards. Product performance warranties were normally 25 years depending on the product. Prices were negotiated on the quantity ordered but were between $2 and $3 per watt. Margins ranged from 13 to 18 per cent for standard and e-Modules and were 15 to 20 per cent on BIPV products. Canadian Solar's strategy was to maintain comparable prices to its primary Chinese competitors.

Specialty products included items to be used in battery chargers, GPS tracking systems, street and traffic lights, garden lights, marine lights and other home systems. Prices varied greatly depending on the level of customization—margins were usually around 15 to 20 per cent for specialty items.

Production Facilities

The company produced all of its products in its seven plants in China. The seven factories had been set up because of Chinese government incentives to establish operations in specific jurisdictions. For example, the Luoyang factory, located approximately eight hours by road from the central offices of Suzhou, was set up at the request of the government-owned silicon supplier in Luoyang.

In late 2008, Canadian Solar's then vice president of corporate and production development, Robert Patterson, was asked if production facilities would be opened closer to areas of demand:

> Not yet. We got our hands full in terms of how fast we're growing and also our capital requirements going into our current plants. We'd probably have to stabilize our current supply stream and then we would address whether we'd want to do assembly plants in various locations. If you're based in China, you have an advantage on an assembly basis, mainly because of the labour content of a solar cell or solar module. So, it would be a future thing, not ruled out.[27]

[27]Interview with Robert Patterson, VP corporate & production development, by Mark Osborne, Photovoltaics International, December 3, 2008, www.pv-tech.org/solar_leaders_video_clips/_a/canadian_solar_vp_robert_patterson_talks_umg_si_product_lines_150mw_plus.

Sales Offices

Canadian Solar had seven sales offices outside of China (domestic Chinese sales were done primarily from Suzhou and Shanghai). In mid-2009, the company opened an office in Kitchener, Ontario, and shifted its official headquarters there from Markham. The Kitchener office (eight people) was responsible for the development of Canadian sales with a focus on the Ontario market, given the recently introduced FIT program. The Ottawa office (four people) was the international sales office for projects in the Middle East and Latin America and initially also housed the company's investor relations manager. Opportunities in the Middle East and Latin America were developed through a combination of trade shows, bids on public tenders and CIDA-sponsored development projects.

The United States was primarily covered through the 10-person facility in San Ramon, California, which included business development managers and a warehouse. Additionally, there was a sales representative located in a satellite office in New York State.

The company's office in Munich, Germany, was responsible for the coordination of all sales efforts in Europe. The top five German customers accounted for just over half of the company's corporate sales. The customers were utility-scale developers and distributors of rooftop solar projects. With a total of 15 people, the office was responsible for managing the independent sales agent in Spain as well as establishing new offices.

Canadian Solar served the Asian market through its sales forces at the principal Chinese office in Suzhou and offices in Seoul, South Korea (two people), and Tokyo, Japan (eight people). In Japan, due to the popularity of solar PV in residential applications, Canadian Solar was developing a complete systems package, which included the solar PV modules, racking systems, inverter and monitoring devices.

Marketing

Due to the small size of the PV industry, the company focused on building its brand through industry tradeshows and publications such as *Photon International* and *PV Technology*. In early 2009, the company had recently rebranded itself to emphasize its "Canadian" roots by changing its logo to read "Canadian Solar" instead of the previous "CSI" (standing for "Canadian Solar International"). Hanbing Zhang, the company's director of global marketing, explained:

> No one really understood what CSI meant—with Canadian Solar, we don't need to explain. As a country, Canada is well received around the world. People from all over have a connection to Canada; for example, Koreans send their kids to learn English in Canada and many Europeans have relatives in Canada. It is seen as a peaceful and environmentally aware country. By

emphasizing the Canadian image, we can further differentiate from the other Chinese manufacturers.

Development Projects

In addition to its role as a producer, Canadian Solar was becoming more active in the development of both ground-mount and rooftop commercial projects. Typically, Canadian Solar partnered with a solar developer, system integrator or utility to carry out the tasks involved in commercial solar development such as engineering, construction, financing, negotiation of the power purchase agreements (PPAs) and the operation of the solar project.

In its largest project to date, in 2009 Canadian Solar formed a strategic alliance with China-based Guodian Power Development to build and operate two 50MW PV power plants in China. Historically, most of Canadian Solar's development projects had been focused on providing power to rural areas in China.[28]

Financials

For the past three years, Canadian Solar posted losses. In 2008, the net loss was $9.4 million. The global economic crisis caused the company to have higher than normal interest expenses on short-term loan facilities, increases in the allowance for doubtful accounts and a major inventory write-down (caused by both a weakening in demand and the rapidly declining price of silicon).

In June 2009, Deutsche Bank analysts projected Canadian Solar's revenues to be $395 million with a loss of $18 million and wrote:

> [Canadian Solar] is a smaller, upstream solar PV company, struggling with weak fundamentals in a highly competitive industry where capital is still a constraint for its solar PV customers amidst a credit contraction environment. Upside risks include: a rapid demand rebound, minimal average sales price declines, a weakening U.S. dollar and more favorable policy and incentive programs. Downside risks include: gauging end demand for company products amidst industry demand destruction, rapid average sales price declines/ high input costs dislocating business model assumptions, capital constraints hindering operational flexibility and managing currency dislocations.[29]

However, by August 2009, Deutsche Bank had raised its estimates to revenues of $574 million and net income of $49 million for 2009, stating:

> Canadian Solar posted 2Q09 results well ahead of expectations on strong shipments growth [in markets like the Czech Republic, Korea and Italy], further aided by favorable FX trends (i.e., $0.14 contribution to EPS) and prior inventory

---

[28]Canadian Solar Prospectus, October 12, 2009, www.sec.gov, p. 5.

[29]"Canadian Solar: Notes from the Deutsche Bank alternative energy conference," *Deutsche Bank*, June 10, 2009, p. 3.

write-downs . . . we believe the company is gaining share in new markets.[30]

Deutsche Bank rated the stock a "hold" and Oppenheimer rated it an "outperform." As of September 25, 2009, Canadian Solar's stock price closed at $16.74 (the 52-week range was from $3.00 to $19.91).

Considerations Going Forward

Some industry observers believed that the solar PV industry needed to regroup and get back to basics. Consultants from BCG wrote:

> In order to thrive in and not merely survive the harsh reality of today's market, PV suppliers need to take a critical look at their business model and operations. . . . To negotiate this far more challenging environment, PV suppliers will need to refocus their attention on the basics: relative cost position, go-to-market effectiveness, and an understanding of key market segments and channels.[31]

Having been on a track of dynamic growth since inception, it was now Canadian Solar's opportunity to strategically think about any changes to its international strategy. Qu stated:

> In terms of the solar industry, the first step is to determine the market and follow the renewable policies closely.

For the next two to three years, we've determined that we will be focusing on 10 countries: Canada, China, Germany, Spain, Italy, France, Czech Republic, South Korea, Japan and the United States.

There is plenty of competition. First, the established players such as Sharp and Sanyo have powerful brands. From a technology standpoint, a company like FirstSolar clearly has a different product with their thin-film technology and the question is, "Which technology wins?" The other U.S. competitor is SunPower, which has high efficiency and a high price premium. Out of the Chinese producers, Suntech is slightly different than others since they combine Australian engineering with Chinese production much like we combine Canadian engineering with Chinese production. The other potential threat is the possibility that some upstream silicon makers will adapt their business models to start producing modules downstream. After the financial crisis, I think the industry realizes that silicon is not precious and there could be an increasing trend for silicon producers to move downstream to capture more value.

When I look back at my original business plan, we've greatly exceeded our initial revenue projections. The business has changed substantially from its initial focus—this illustrates that one of the key skills in this industry, and any start-up for that matter, is the ability to see changes in the marketplace and adapt the business accordingly.

---

[30] "Canadian Solar: New market penetration drives solid shipments," *Deutsche Bank*, August 6, 2009, p. 1.

[31] "Back to the Basics: How Photovoltaic Suppliers Can Win in Today's Solar Market," *The Boston Consulting Group*, p. 1.

Exhibit 1   Canadian Solar Financials

USD million, Years ended Dec. 31	2006	2007	2008
Net Revenues	**68.2**	**302.8**	**705.0**
Cost of revenues	55.9	279.0	634.0
Gross Profit	**12.3**	**23.8**	**71.0**
Operating expenses:	0.0	0.0	0.0
Selling expenses	2.9	7.5	10.6
General and administrative expenses	7.9	17.2	34.5
Research and development expenses	0.4	1.0	1.8
Total operating expenses	11.2	25.7	46.9
Income (loss) from operations	**1.1**	**−2.0**	**24.1**
Other income (expenses):			
Interest expense	−2.2	−2.4	−11.3
Interest income	0.4	0.6	3.5
Loss on change in fair value of derivatives	0.0	0.0	0.0
related to convertible notes	−8.2	0.0	0.0
Gain on foreign currency derivative assets	0.0	0.0	14.5
Debt conversion inducement expense	0.0	0.0	−10.2
Foreign exchange gain (loss)	−0.5	2.7	−20.1
Other—net	0.4	0.7	0.0
Income (loss) before income taxes	−9.0	−0.4	0.5
Income tax benefit (expense)	−0.4	0.2	−9.9
Net loss	−9.4	-0.2	−9.4
Loss per share—basic and diluted	−0.5	0.0	−0.3
Shares used in computation—basic and diluted	19.0	27.3	31.6
Total current assets		219.9	339.0
TOTAL ASSETS		**284.5**	**570.7**
Total current liabilities		59.2	172.7
TOTAL LIABILITIES		**158.2**	**238.6**
Total stockholders' equity		126.3	332.2
TOTAL LIABILITIES AND STOCKHOLDERS' EQUITY		**284.5**	**570.7**

Source: Canadian Solar Annual Report, 20-F, www.sec.gov, December 31, 2008, p. 54.

Exhibit 2   Highlights From World Markets

Country	Comments
Germany	Leading market for solar PV with strong financing available
	Over 40,000 people were employed in the PV sector
	The Renewable Energy Law (Erneuerbare-Energien-Gesetz or EEG) promised rates of $0.46 to $0.60 per kWh for solar PV with digression in 2010 and 2011
	The country had some of the world's largest solar parks (e.g. the 40MW Waldpolenz Solar Park)
	Over 100,000 rooftop solar PV applications had been installed
Spain	Historical strength had been on utility-scale solar parks
	The Spanish market would undergo a major decrease in 2009 and 2010 due to the government's cap of 500MW
	Potential growth beyond 2013 was still seen to be strong due to experience with renewables and long-term targets
Japan	Historical strength had been with solar PV on residential homes due to the "Residential PV System Program," which ended supplying subsidies in 2006
	In December 2008, the government was renewing its focus on solar with the aim to have solar power installed on 70 per cent of new homes. Furthermore, it wanted 14GW of installed PV power by 2020
United States	The Investment Tax Credit (ITC), state programs and the potential of a federal-level FIT were expected to boost solar PV in 2010 and beyond
	The challenge was seen to be a lack of financing
	The United States had some of the world's largest solar PV parks (e.g. Nellis Solar Power Plant, NV 15MW)
	California was the leading state for solar roof installations due to programs such as the "Million Solar Roofs" vision and the "California Solar Initiative"
Italy	The country had a competitive FIT program and a net-metering scheme (allowing PV system owners to get credits for their produced electricity)
	Italy had no cap for PV installations
South Korea	The country's FIT program was seen as promising; however, the devaluation of the Korean currency and the placement of a cap of 500MW on the FIT in October 2008 were expected to dampen the number of installations
	Observers believed that strong political support for solar PV still existed and expected the market to grow in 2010
France	The government had a favorable FIT program for BIPV; however, the growth had been stalled by long administrative procedures to connect the systems to the grid
	France was expected to adopt a FIT program for non-BIPV applications for commercial roofs, which would be the source of its growth over the next few years

(Continued)

Exhibit 2 (Continued)

Country	Comments
Czech Republic	The Czech government introduced a FIT program in 2008 and was one of the premiere Eastern European growth countries for solar PV
Portugal	Portugal had several large-scale PV and concentrating solar power plants but had not yet introduced a FIT program or similar incentive scheme
Greece	Greece was seen to have one of the most favorable FIT programs in Europe The country had a pipeline of 3.5GW of PV projects Bureaucracy and lengthy administrative procedures were seen to be barriers for installations in 2008
Israel	Solar-thermal (solar water heaters) were very popular, being present in 90 per cent of Israeli homes Israel was extensively used for research and development due to the country's high level of solar irradiance A FIT scheme was passed in 2008 and the market was expected to grow
India	India was expected to develop slowly but held great potential due to efforts for both on and off-grid projects (off-grid projects were a specialty area for project developers—e.g. Shell Solar had had a division dedicated to off-grid solar PV development in India)
China	The new incentive program was expected to boost solar PV applications both for residential, commercial and utility-scale applications
Canada	Ontario's solar PV applications were expected to grow under the proposed FIT program The FIT program required that for projects up to 10kW, the minimum domestic content was 40 per cent and for projects greater than 10kW, the domestic content was 50 per cent for projects with a commercial operation date prior to January 1, 2011. For projects thereafter, domestic content needed to be 60 per cent

Source: Compiled by case writer.

Exhibit 3   EPIA Predictions by Market

Country	Type	2006	2007	2008	2009E	2010E	2011E	2012E	2013E
Belgium	EPIA Moderate	2	18	48	100	70	80	90	100
	EPIA Policy-Driven				175	125	130	140	160
Czech Republic	EPIA Moderate	0	3	51	80	90	110	140	170
	EPIA Policy-Driven				100	160	200	220	240
France	EPIA Moderate	8	11	46	250	340	600	900	1,000
	EPIA Policy-Driven				300	500	850	1,200	1,400
Germany	EPIA Moderate	850	1,100	1,500	2,000	2,000	2,300	2,600	3,000
	EPIA Policy-Driven				2,500	2,800	3,200	3,600	4,000
Greece	EPIA Moderate	1	2	11	35	100	100	100	100
	EPIA Policy-Driven				52	200	450	700	900
Italy	EPIA Moderate	13	42	258	400	600	750	950	1,250
	EPIA Policy-Driven				500	800	1,100	1,400	1,600
Portugal	EPIA Moderate	0	14	50	40	50	100	160	230
	EPIA Policy-Driven				50	80	800	350	1,500
Spain	EPIA Moderate	88	560	2,511	375	500	500	550	800
	EPIA Policy-Driven				375	500	600	650	500
Rest of Europe	EPIA Moderate	12	17	28	120	140	200	300	450
	EPIA Policy-Driven				250	325	400	525	625
Japan	EPIA Moderate	287	210	230	400	500	700	1,000	1,100
	EPIA Policy-Driven				500	1,000	1,200	1,500	1,700
USA	EPIA Moderate	145	207	342	340	1,000	1,200	1,500	2,000
	EPIA Policy-Driven				1,200	3,000	3,400	3,900	4,500
China	EPIA Moderate	12	20	45	80	100	300	600	1,000
	EPIA Policy-Driven				100	150	600	1,200	2,000
India	EPIA Moderate	12	20	40	50	60	80	120	300
	EPIA Policy-Driven				100	200	250	300	600
South Korea	EPIA Moderate	20	43	274	100	150	220	300	400
	EPIA Policy-Driven				200	350	450	700	1,000
Rest of the world	EPIA Moderate	153	125	126	250	300	300	300	350
	EPIA Policy-Driven				400	600	800	1,000	1,600
TOTAL	**EPIA Moderate**	1,603	2,392	5,559	4,620	6,000	7,540	9,610	12,250
	EPIA Policy-Driven				6,802	10,790	13,810	17,385	22,325
CUMULATIVE	**EPIA Moderate**	6,770	9,162	14,730	19,350	25,350	32,890	42,500	54,750
	EPIA Policy-Driven				21,532	32,322	46,132	63,517	85,842

Source: European Photovoltaic Industry Association (EPIA), "Global Market Outlook for Photovoltaics until 2013," March 2009, p. 6.

Exhibit 4 Ontario's Feed-in Tariff (FIT) Program

Renewable Fuel	Size tranches	Contract Price Cent/kWh
Biomass	≤ 10MW	13.8
	> 10MW	13.0
Biogas		
On-farm	≤ 100kW	19.5
On-farm	> 100kW ≤ 250kW	18.5
Biogas	≤ 500kW	16.0
Biogas	> 500kW ≤ 10MW	14.7
Biogas	> 10MW	10.4
Waterpower	≤ 10MW	13.1
	> 10MW ≤ 50MW	12.2
Landfill gas	≤ 10MW	11.1
	> 10MW	10.3
Solar PV		
Any type	≤ 10kW	80.2
Rooftop	> 10kW ≤ 250kW	71.3
Rooftop	> 250kW ≤ 500kW	63.5
Rooftop	> 500kW	53.9
Ground mounted	≤ 10MW	44.3
Wind		
Onshore	Any size	13.5
Offshore	Any size	19.0

Domestic Content Requirements: The minimum requirements of Ontario-based content: 40% for MicroFIT (projects less than 10kW) and 50% for FIT (projects over 10kW) for projects reaching commercial operation by the end of 2010. For projects with commercial operation after January 1, 2011, domestic content increases to 60%.

	Designated Activity	Qualifying Percentage
1.	Silicon that has been used as input to solar photovoltaic cells manufactured in an Ontario refinery.	10%
2.	Silicon ingots and wafers, where silicon ingots have been cast in Ontario and wafers have been cut from the casting by a saw in Ontario.	12%
3.	The crystalline silicon solar photovoltaic cells, where their active photovoltaic layer(s) have been formed in Ontario.	10%
4.	Solar photovoltaic modules (i.e. panels), where the electrical connections between the solar cells have been made in Ontario, and the solar photovoltaic module materials have been encapsulated in Ontario.	13%

(Continued)

Exhibit 4 (Continued)

	Designated Activity	Qualifying Percentage
5.	Inverter (to convert the electricity from direct current (DC) to alternating current (AC)), where the assembly, final wiring and testing have been done in Ontario.	9%
6.	Mounting systems, where the structural components of the fixed or moving mounting systems have been entirely machined or formed or cast in Ontario. The metal for the structural components may not have been pre-machined outside Ontario other than peeling/roughing of the part for quality control purposes when it left the smelter or forge. The machining and assembly of the mounting system must entirely take place in Ontario (i.e. bending, welding, piercing, and bolting).	9%
7.	Wiring and electrical hardware that is not part of other designated activities (i.e. items 1, 2, 3, and 5 of this table), sourced from an Ontario supplier.	10%
8.	All on- and off-site labour and services. For greater certainty, this designated activity shall apply in respect of all contract facilities.	27%
	Total	**100%**

Source: Ontario Power Authority, http://fit.powerauthority.on.ca, accessed October 30, 2009.

Exhibit 5   Market Shares and Gross Profits by PV Module Producers

2008 Rank	PV Supplier	HQ	2008 % of Total MV Shipments	2008 Gross Profit (%)
1	Suntech	China	7.2	23.7
2	Sharp	Japan	7.2	16.0
3	First Solar	U.S.	6.9	54.4
4	Yingli Green Energy	China	4.4	21.9
5	Kyocera	Japan	4.2	25.9
6	Sunpower	U.S.	3.4	25.3
7	Trina Solar	China	3.3	19.7
8	Sanyo	Japan	2.8	15.8
9	Canadian Solar	Canada/China	2.6	10.7
10	Solar World	Germany	2.6	N/A
	Top 10 Total		**44.7**	
	Others		**55.3**	
	Total Module Shipments in GWs		**6.3**	

Source: IMS Research and company files.

N/A = not available   *(Continued)*

Exhibit 5 (Continued)

Market Shares PV Cell Producers

2008 Rank	2007 Rank	PV Supplier	HQ	2007 % of Total MW	2008 % of Total MW	08/07 % Change	2007 % of Total $	2008 % of Total $	08/07 % Change
1	1	Q-Cells	Germany	10.9	9.4	48	14.5	12.2	43
2	4	First Solar	U.S.	5.8	8.3	144	6.2	9.0	147
3	2	Suntech	China	10.2	8.2	37	9.0	7.2	36
4	3	Sharp	Japan	9.0	8.0	51	8.0	7.3	56
5	6	Motech	Taiwan	4.9	4.8	67	4.1	4.0	70
6	5	Kyocera	Japan	5.7	4.6	37	5.0	4.0	38
7	10	JA Solar	China	3.7	4.6	108	4.6	5.8	117
8	9	Yingli Green Energy	China	4.0	4.5	93	3.3	3.8	95
9	12	Gintech Energy	Taiwan	3.1	4.4	144	2.6	3.6	141
10	8	Solar World	Germany	4.7	4.0	44	4.9	3.8	32
		Top 10 Total		62.0	60.8	67.0	62.0	60.6	67.0
		Others		38.0	39.2	75	38.0	39.4	77
		Cell & Panel PV Total		3.57GW	6.0GW	70	$8.1b	$13.85b	71

Source: "Japanese solar cell manufacturers losing market share, says IC Insights," July 22, 2009, www.pv-tech.org/news/_a/japanese_solar_cell_manufacturers_losing_market_share_says_ic_insights.

Scandinavian Airlines: The Green Engine Decision

Jennifer Lynes

Introduction

In the spring of 1995, the five members of the senior management team of Scandinavian Airlines (SAS) were sitting around the boardroom table listening to Bengt-Olov Nas, SAS's director of aircraft and engine analysis. Senior management were discussing the decision to update the airline's fleet, and Nas had just finished introducing his specification wish-list for the new fleet of 55 Boeing-737s that SAS was about to purchase.

The decision to add or remove aircraft from a fleet is one of the most important to be made within an airline because of both the significant cost of replacement and the long-term consequences that result from the choice of aircraft. An average fleet would last an airline between 25 and 35 years. The environmental performance of an airline is also strongly related to the age and makeup of its fleet. The type of aircraft an airline chooses to purchase has to serve the airline in the regulatory, market and technological environments predicted to exist within the life of the fleet. As one can imagine, the decision for SAS was complex and

involved analysis, prediction and perhaps even a gamble to come up with an aircraft fleet most suited to the coming needs of the airline. Nas and his team of aircraft analysts had spent several years researching the type of aircraft SAS needed for its new fleet.

Unlike cars, the body and engine of large commercial aircraft does not come as one unit. Generally, an airline chooses the aircraft body from one manufacturer and the engine from another. For SAS, while the decision to buy the Boeing 737 model had already been made, the airline had yet to decide on an engine. After much discussion with aircraft and engine manufacturers, Nas had come up with an option for SAS to purchase a "green" engine for its new fleet of Boeing-737s. This two-stage dual annular combustor (DAC) engine produced significantly lower NO_x emissions and would represent a strong commitment to the future environmental improvement of the airline. However, the DAC engines added kr3.5 million[1] per aircraft onto the total cost of the new aircraft fleet (which was estimated to be kr12 billion). At the time of the meeting, Nas could not provide specific figures on the economic

---

[1] kr = Swedish Kronor. At time of print, approximately kr7 = CDN$1; kr9 = US$1; kr11.5 = €1.

payback of these engines. Forecasters anticipated increased emissions charges and taxes for the European airline industry, however, the future regulatory structure of the industry was too uncertain to make any clear predictions. Nas was presenting this idea largely on intuition that purchasing these engines would have positive financial payback for SAS, as it minimized the risk of future operational limitations.

Nas had only one meeting to convince the management team to approve the procurement of the proposed DAC engines for the new Boeing-737s.

The Airline Industry

The airline industry has played a key role in shaping modern society. With 1.6 billion passengers using air transport each year worldwide, the airline industry has facilitated globalization, both in economic and social terms. Passengers are traveling more frequently and for longer distances than ever before. Low-cost airlines have also increased the proportion of people that could afford to fly.

On a global scale, the airline industry has experienced almost continual growth in passenger numbers. Over the past 50 years the commercial airline industry has almost consistently sustained positive rates of growth.

The industry had gone through significant changes in recent times, including deregulation and increased security concerns.

Airline Industry Trends

The 1980s were a period of prosperity for the airline industry, however, in the 1990s things started to change when the industry began to deregulate. In mid-2001, the industry began experiencing an economic downturn that was further fuelled by the terrorist attacks of September 11, the SARS[2] outbreak in Asia in 2003 and political unrest in the Middle East. The companies that had kept or increased market share during these turbulent times have been those that have best been able to adapt to these challenges.

Liberalization of the skies has allowed more airlines to fly to airports that were previously restricted to a nation's flag carrier. These changes have contributed to the growth of airline travel (by making it less expensive for the passenger) but have also increased competition between carriers. Moreover, particularly in Europe, airlines do not only compete with other airlines but also with other forms of transportation—especially the high-speed railway networks. The past decade has seen a large increase in the number of low-cost air carriers. These

---

[2]SARS: severe acute respiratory syndrome.

low-cost airlines have forced major national and international carriers to change the way they operated.

To remain in business, many airlines have tried to improve competitiveness through increased efficiency.[3] The resultant strategic realignment and search for resource efficiency has resulted in a consolidation of domestic carriers, as well as a movement towards the development of international alliances. These alliances allow airlines to share flights and also to optimize connections between international flights.

The Major Environmental Concerns in the Airline Industry

It is estimated that 90 per cent of an airline's environmental impact comes from its flight operations (e.g. fuel consumption, air and noise emissions), five per cent from cabin operations (e.g. meal service and cleaning the aircraft cabin) and five per cent from ground operations (e.g. aircraft maintenance and operation of vehicles on the ground).[4] Although the rate of CO_2 and NO_x emissions from aircraft are comparable to other forms of transport such as road and rail, studies have shown that the impact of the emissions from aircraft at high altitudes are thought to have a global warming effect three times greater than on the ground.[5] While there have been significant improvements in aircraft technology over the past few decades, the sheer growth in airline travel makes it difficult for the industry to reduce overall aircraft emission levels.

Increasingly, pressure has been mounting from governing structures, such as the European Union, for the airline industry to respond to environmental challenges—particularly in the areas of noise and emissions. Growing public awareness of the environment has further encouraged airlines and airports to address these issues.

Greenhouse gases are an unavoidable part of airline operations. It is a major challenge to seek solutions to minimize aviation's climate impact. Although aviation contributes approximately three per cent to global emissions of carbon dioxide, international flights are currently exempt from the Kyoto Protocol.

[3]IATA (International Air Transport Association), "Urgent to get out of financial abyss," April 8 press release detailing the opening address by IATA director general and CEO Pierre J. Jeanniot to the Airline Financial Summit, New York, April 8, 2002.

[4]SAS Environment Report, 2000.

[5]J. Penner, D. Lister, D. Griggs, D. Dokken and M. McFarland (eds), "Summary for Policy-Makers: Aviation and the Global Atmosphere. A Special Report of IPCC Working Groups I and III in Collaboration with the Scientific Assessment Panel to the Montreal Protocol on Substances that Deplete the Ozone Layer," Intergovernmental Panel on Climate Change (IPCC), Cambridge University Press, Cambridge, 1999.

The altitude and distance aircraft travel make it difficult for emissions from international flights to be attributed to a specific geo-political boundary. Airlines are also unique from other sectors in that they are usually based out of one country but operate "cross-nationally" in the sense that they might fly to many countries. Airlines are therefore subject to the regulatory structure of their home base as well as that of each country to which they fly.

Environmental Policy and Regulation for Airlines in Sweden

The regulatory milieu of commercial aviation is complex. In general, the airline industry is governed by a combination of international, federal, regional and local legislation. Although the majority of control has traditionally been at the federal and international level, local governments have been granted increased power in recent years, and many airports have now been privatized. Commercial air transport remains highly regulated with respect to air traffic control, airspace, safety and security. International environmental standards regarding air and noise emissions have been developed by the United Nations' International Civil Aviation Organization. Exhibit 1 outlines the major environmental impacts of commercial air travel.

The International Air Transportation Association (IATA), the industry body

of the international commercial aviation industry, has recognized the environment as a key consideration for the industry by publishing a report for the airline industry that discusses the impacts, the tools being used to improve environmental performance and the challenges facing the industry (IATA, 2000). More recently, it has created five management positions that focus on the environmental management and performance of the industry.

The government body that deals with aviation in Sweden is "Luftfartsverket," which translates in English to the "Swedish Civil Aviation Administration" (Swedish CAA). The Swedish CAA is the government's "expert" in aviation and has the responsibility of ensuring that Sweden's interests in aviation are fulfilled on a national and international level. Sweden is a leader in management of environmental impacts related to air travel and is one of only two countries (Switzerland being the other) to favour charges in aviation as a tool for encouraging airlines to improve their environmental performance. The Swedish CAA argues that charges and taxes are an effective way to get airlines to use the best available technology.

The largest airport in Sweden, Stockholm-Arlanda, uses charges and taxes as a mechanism to reduce noise and fuel emissions. It has even implemented a cap on NO_x and CO_2 emissions— meaning that once NO_x or CO_2 emissions reach a certain level, the airport will not allow an increase in traffic flow. This was one of the conditions that formed part of an agreement to allow the airport to build a new runway in the 1990s. As SAS's main hub is Stockholm's Arlanda airport, this is a significant factor affecting SAS's day-to-day operations.

Background of SAS— The Company

Walking into the headquarters of SAS in Frösundavik, a suburb of Stockholm, there was a feeling of both serenity and efficiency. Passive solar light and ergonomic furniture were key ingredients to each office. Equality of employees, a fundamental component of Swedish culture, was visibly present; for instance, the office of the deputy CEO did not look much different than that of a middle manager.

Scandinavian Airlines (SAS) was the largest airline in Scandinavia and had bases in Stockholm, Denmark and Oslo, serving 32 million passengers per year on domestic, inter-Scandinavian, European and Intercontinental routes. The airline was part of the larger SAS Group, which included hotels, other airlines as well as airline support services. The holding company, SAS Group, was 50 per cent state-owned (Sweden 21.4 per cent, Norway 14.3 per cent, Denmark 14.3 per cent), with the remaining 50 per cent being publicly

traded. SAS Group was Europe's fourth largest airline group, demonstrating that it was an important player in the global airline market.

The airline had a reputation in the commercial aviation industry for being forward-thinking and had pioneered such steps as being the first major Western airline to have a female pilot (1969), to offer business class on board its flights (1981) and to have its environmental report audited and verified by a third party (1996). The company's management realized that key issues involved in developing polices, strategies and decision-making were cost reduction, the company's image as well as the ability to anticipate market and regulatory changes and be able to plan ahead of time.

The Evolution of Corporate Greening at SAS

In 1995, environmental management was elevated to a strategic level at SAS. The environment had become part of the overall policy-making structure for SAS, evident through the establishment of environmental visions and goals and a commitment to publish environmental reports on an annual basis (SAS, 1996). At the forefront of this strategic change was the then-president and CEO, Jan Stenberg.

In 1995, Stenberg appointed SAS's first environmental director, Niels Eirik Nertun, who, since then, had been an influential player in the role that environmental management had taken in decision-making within SAS. Once in the position as environmental director, Nertun was able to justify the expense of developing environmental initiatives such as reporting mechanisms by arguing to upper management that competitors such as British Airways were reacting to environmental pressures and big (corporate) customers were demanding it. A look through SAS's Environmental Reports from 1995 onwards showed the rapid evolution of SAS's environmental programs.

Despite the economic downturn of the industry in 2001, the CEO announced in the 2001 Environmental Report that SAS's commitment to the environment would remain firm. Since then, however, the environmental department of SAS had faced cutbacks in economy and staff—albeit no more than other departments within the airline. This had resulted in a reduction of staff from four to two people working directly on environmental issues and an environmental report that, instead of being a separate report (as it was for seven years), was now integrated into the overall annual report for SAS.

Exhibit 2 shows a timeline of significant events in relation to corporate greening at SAS, including awards it had received for its environmental reports, changes in the company's leadership and the evolution of its corporate environmental policies.

Environmental Management at SAS

SAS had been identified as a leader in environmental commitment by its suppliers and other airlines as well as by representatives of international organizations such as the Air Transport Action Group and IATA.[6] SAS was committed to implementing sound environmental management practices that ensured minimal environmental impacts, adopting best available technologies as well as commitment to continual improvement and promoting awareness of environment-related aspects of the industry to external parties. The former CEO of SAS, Jan Stenberg, expressed that the reasons behind this commitment were not solely idealistic reasons:

> We believe that companies which have an impact on the environment and ignore their responsibility will disappear from the market within a decade . . . A sound environmental profile is profitable. But it is more that that. It is our contribution to a sustainable society and to future generations.

---

[6]Based on communications with well (former) head of sustainable business unit, British Airways, November 4, 2002; environmental manager, Qantas, October 17, 2002; executive director, Air Transport Action Group, June 28, 2002; IATA representative, June 6, 2001.

SAS stated in its environmental reports that what was driving it to strive for enhanced environmental performance was a combination of ethical principles, economic efficiencies, passenger interest, better company image, and liability concerns of banks and insurance companies, as well as the potential of gaining a competitive edge. The airline had implemented a comprehensive environmental management system and had introduced a number of tools and mechanisms to report environmental performance. These included:

- Annual public and audited environmental reporting since 1995.
- An environmental index that measured economic efficiencies derived from implementing environmental measures, e.g., eco-efficiencies.
- Corporate environment policy obligating all managers to conduct an environmental assessment as part of their decision-making documentation. SAS also supported product stewardship programs and would only deal with suppliers who had environmental policies and management systems.
- An online emissions calculator for passengers that provided a destination specific calculation of CO_2 generated.

A series of environmental goals, also established in 1995, had been revised over the years and expanded to include an "eco-political vision" (SAS's message to environmental policymakers), policy, overall and communication goals and strategy. Largely these environmental goals and policies involved:

- Achieving profitability while minimizing environmental impact;
- Being a forerunner in the development of internal environmental standards;
- Desiring various forms of transport to be equally governed by the "polluter pays principle";
- Harmonizing production, financial and "qualitative" goals;
- Communicating SAS's environmental performance and promoting stakeholder discussion;
- Increasing environmental awareness throughout the organization by conducting environmental activities at all levels and in all decisions; and
- Utilizing the methods that resulted in the lowest possible impact.

The leadership role that the CEO, Jan Stenberg, took in making the environment a strategic priority had had strong impacts on how SAS managed environmental issues, described the vice-president of procurement at SAS:

I believe SAS's environmental agenda was driven, or at least heavily supported by our previous CEO Mr. Stenberg . . . because he was *aware* of the importance of this. He did very much and he implemented quality measures and criteria for that. I would say he was the driving force behind that.

Every manager with decision-making authority and budget responsibility was required to include an environmental impact assessment in the decision-making data, as stated in SAS's environmental strategy. The airline had an integrated environmental management system in the total operations and management of the airline (TQM—Total Quality Management). See Exhibit 3 for an overview of SAS's environmental policy.

Each year SAS measured both the overall and environmental image of the airline (see Exhibit 4). This measurement was based on a Customer Satisfaction Index. When the environment moved up to a strategic level in 1995, the environmental image was not as strong as the overall image. But gradually over the years, SAS's environmental image had helped boost the overall image of the airline. There were several motivations embedded in this quest for a positive environmental image such as boosting the overall image of the company, improving the "brand" of SAS and living up to the spirit of the Scandinavian people. "What is the value of a brand?" asked Niels Eirik Nertun, environmental director for SAS. "How do you quantify the increase in business because of a positive environmental image? If the overall image of SAS is improved because of our environmental image, then the cost of having an environmental department is justified."

SAS management cited other reasons that it was important to maintain a positive image with respect to environmental commitment and performance such as:

- Negative publicity as a result of a poor environmental report from human rights/environmental organizations could have dramatic and immediate effects on the company's bottom line—even if it was a result of a supplier and not the company itself;
- A growing need for environment, ethical and social accountability through transparency and reporting;
- As a tool for negotiation with government and NGOs;
- Establishing a leadership role in dialogues about the regulatory environment; and
- Reacting to increasing pressure from corporate clients who were seeking ISO 14000 certification and who, as a result, were demanding environmentally responsible suppliers.

The reasons why image and being a good corporate citizen were important to SAS may be associated with a deeper set of values and beliefs embedded in Scandinavian culture about the importance of caring for the environment. This was an important, yet indirect, influence on SAS's pursuit of environmental commitment. "As a Scandinavian company," described a former chief operating officer for SAS, "we reflect the Scandinavian outlook on life. An outlook that's always been strongly connected with the environment. That's why it's rather natural for SAS to focus on the environment." Another senior manager strongly expressed the importance of culture as a driver of environmental stewardship:

> I think that the society of the Scandinavians are simple, honest people. And from time to time we could be perceived as being a little bit naïve in the international interaction. But the upside of it is that we do things like that because we like to be that way, and I think that's a driving force that's definitely being stimulated by corporate policies. The Scandinavian culture, the spirit if you like, appreciate having a company doing that. I think we would be hated by Scandinavian people, they wouldn't fancy having a company like SAS behaving badly, not in the environmental sector, not in other sectors. And the airline is always a very public type of business, everybody has a view on it and everybody has tried it and everybody is a customer as well. So it is probably from that perspective, even more important compared to other types of business. But that is on the rational side of it. Regardless of that, it is a matter of doing what you believe is good for society.

The environmental director of the Swedish CAA remarked that a few years ago Boeing said that, on a scale of one to ten, Scandinavian countries were a "twelve" with respect to environmental commitment. The executive director of the Air Transport Action Group believed that it was not just about realities, it was about *perception*. SAS

would be a big promoter of the environment because of Scandinavian culture. Culture played a strong role in shaping SAS's reaction to the environmental challenges that it faced within the airline industry.

The DAC Engine Decision

The decision to purchase the 55 new aircraft was a long time in the making. Negotiations with various aircraft and engine manufacturers spanned over almost five years.

Sweden was considering tightening charges on airport emissions. The choice of aircraft was therefore critical to meet anticipated future regulatory requirements. The decision to fit these aircraft with "green engines," however, was not an easy one.

Background of the Decision

In the early 1990s, as SAS was establishing itself as a leader in the airline industry in terms of environmental commitment, the airline developed an environmental policy stating that the company was committed to using the best available environmental technology. With regards to aircrafts, best available technology referred mainly to selecting the best combined noise and emissions reduction technology. Updating the fleet provided the first major test of this commitment. While honoring the commitment would cause increased expenditure, not complying with this policy could cost the airline its reputation as an industry leader in environmental management. SAS had worked hard to build its green reputation—an image that was also important to the Scandinavian people.

Furthermore, the government-imposed emissions cap at the Stockholm airport had to be considered. Up to that point, SAS had paid the tax related to CO_2 emissions but the director of aircraft and engine analysis at SAS felt that the emissions cap could become a potential problem. If SAS, for example, had a fleet of planes that it could not fly into the airline's main hub because of poor aircraft environmental performance, then the financial implications of that decision could quickly become very serious.

The next step was to evaluate potential aircraft with respect to noise and emissions and communicate SAS's requirements for environmental performance to the manufacturing industry. The challenge was to create an optimal balance between the levels of noise, NO_x and CO_2. Nas encouraged the manufacturers to offer an engine with superior environmental performance. Nas described how the process went:

> So we challenged the airline manufacturer—actually we strongly encouraged two manufacturers—to offer the two-stage combustors [as one option]. The combustors had been developed as a

research effort back in the 1970s, so the manufacturers understood the technologies and techniques to reduce NO_x even though it had not been commercialized.

Since the B-737 had never been produced or sold with the dual combustor engine, technical hurdles had to be overcome before the manufacturer could finally offer the product to SAS. Two manufacturers could offer the DAC technology for the engines to fit the B-737, but at significant additional cost for the engine.[7] Nas also had to convince management to adopt a technology that had never been used with the B-737 aircraft, knowing that using new technology could have unanticipated complications and added costs.

The DAC engines represented just one of the many options the company had for outfitting the new fleet of aircraft. There were many other decisions that also needed to be made regarding the B-737s. "So you have to decide," Bengt-Olov Nas explained, "do I want the forward air stairs so passengers can walk onto the plane from the ground? That's an option, but it has a price and it also adds weight to that plane. So you have to evaluate that. The list goes on and on." The opportunity cost of other options SAS would not be able to have on the new aircraft fleet because of the substantial extra cost of the engines also had to be considered. To push the DAC engines to the top of the

---

[7]The other engine powered another aircraft that competed with the B-737.

"must have" list required additional drivers.

Nas knew that a strong case had to be made for the engines. Talking to the management team was going to be tough—while the chief executive officer thought that the environment had moved up to a strategic level for the airline, some of his colleagues were not convinced, particularly the chief financial officer and deputy CEO. Nas knew he only had one chance to convince the management team to purchase the green DAC engines for the new fleet.

Exhibit 1   Summary of Environmental Impacts Generated by Airlines

Environmental Issue	Summary of Impact	Factors Affecting Management
Air Emissions Air transport accounts for 3% of global CO_2 emissions and 12% of transportation CO_2 emissions	• Carbon dioxide (CO_2) • Carbon monoxide • Hydrocarbons (HC) • Oxides of nitrogen (NO_x) • Oxides of sulphur (SO_x) • Condensation trails (contrails)	• Airline's choice of aircraft • International standards developed by the International Civil Aviation Organization (ICAO) • Individual countries can impose emissions-related charges and taxes • Emissions of international flights do not fall under the present Kyoto Protocol
Noise Emissions Exacerbated by increasing residential development near airports and under flight paths	• Most prominent during landing/take off cycle (LTO) • Affects local residents and wildlife	• Airline's choice of aircraft • Standards developed by ICAO (starting in the 1960s) • Landing charges for noise emissions at some airports
Congestion Up to 10% of aircraft fuel use could be reduced through more efficient air traffic management	• Increased fuel use (and thus emissions) caused by circling busy airports and longer taxiing on the ground	• Regional/national governments and their NGOs develop more effective air traffic management systems • Partly caused by national air space rules that sometimes prevent aircraft from flying the most direct route
Waste Solid and hazardous wastes	• Solid waste from inflight service and aircraft grooming • Waste generated from airline administration offices • Hazardous waste from aircraft maintenance (e.g. petroleum products) and de-icing of aircraft (glycol)	• Local rules developed by each municipality or airport authority for waste disposal/treatment of tarmac run-off

Exhibit 2 Timeline of Important Events, Achievements and Leadership in Relation to Corporate Greening at SAS, 1994–2004

	1994	1995	1996	1997	1998	1999	2000	2001	2002
Environmental Reporting and Achievements		SAS's first environmental report (1995)	Awarded best environmental report in Norway and Sweden (1996)	First year environmental report externally audited (1997)		Mercury Award for best overall service—cabin operations (1999)	Awarded best environmental report in Europe (2000)		Best performance thus far in SAS's environmental index (2002)
Environmental Leadership		Appointment of environmental director (1995)	Creation of joint Star Alliance environmental forum (1996)			Signing of Star Alliance joint environmental forum (1999)		Expansion of environmental department to 4 personnel (2001)	Creation of passenger emissions calculator (2002)
Management Decisions	First discussion of developing an environmental policy (1994)	Environment moves up to a strategic level (1995)	Unanimous support from board to adopt environmental strategy at SAS (1996)				Forced reduction of environmental department due to cutbacks (2000)		

Exhibit 3   SAS's Environmental Policy as of 1995

- Within the framework of SAS's financial and qualitative goals, all operations shall be conducted so as to have the least possible environmental impact.
- Through a long-term program, SAS shall become one of the airline industry's leading companies in the environmental sector.
- Environmental work shall be conducted at all levels and within all units of SAS, thus creating increased environmental awareness throughout the organisation.
- Environmental aspects shall be included in all material on which decisions are based.
- SAS shall utilize or introduce methods which enable production with minimum environmental impact, characterised by low energy consumption, recycling potential, and minimal emissions.
- SAS shall account for its environmental work in a separate annual report.
- SAS shall encourage external parties to understand the role and environmental impact of air.

Exhibit 4   SAS's Environmental and Image Index 1996–2006

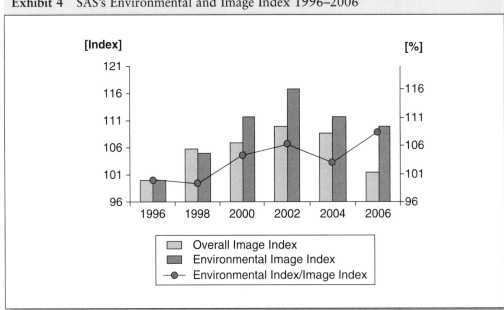

Anti-corruption

Phil Chan (A)

Jean-Louis Schaan

Paul W. Beamish

Saturday, February 16, 2008. "We're getting there!" thought Phil Chan as the Air France flight took off from Paris on its way to Lagos, Nigeria. Phil Chan was the Vice-President Marketing of Basic Software, a middle-sized software producer. He was going to Lagos to close a business deal that Allen Lee, the owner of Basic Software, had been negotiating in the preceding weeks. Phil had left his home sixteen hours earlier and he looked forward to reaching his final destination.

Phil decided to review one more time the specifics of the deal and the strategy that he would follow in the next day's meeting with his Nigerian partners. This was his first trip to Africa, and he was somewhat uncertain about local business practices. Since he would be in Lagos for a short stay, he wanted everything to go smoothly.

The Deal

The deal required Basic Software to facilitate a financial transaction involving an international transfer of funds and would earn the company over $5 million, their 35 per cent share of the US$14.3 million deal. Allen Lee had been approached a month earlier by Tokunbo Jacobs with the business proposal (see Exhibit 1 for a copy of Mr. Jacobs' initial letter to Mr. Lee). Intrigued by the prospect, he entered into discussions with Mr. Jacobs. Mr. Lee was in the process of negotiating a sale in Bahrain on the Persian Gulf and thought that Africa could offer additional prospects for his company:

"Business is all over the world for us. You have to adapt yourself to the fact that conditions are different in other countries from how they are here. This is just part of living in today's world."

In response to his inquiries, he received further details on the deal (see the two faxes in Exhibit 2 and Exhibit 3) and decided to send Phil Chan to Nigeria to complete the negotiations with the Nigerians.

The Nigerian Context

Nigeria offered significant business opportunities (for a profile on Nigeria, see Exhibit 4). With 144 million people, Nigeria was the giant among Africa's 55 countries. Home to both Christians and Muslims, it possessed great assets. Nigeria's Gross Natural Product was the fifth largest on the African continent (in 2005 it amounted to US$73 billion). However, on a per capita basis it was only about $650. The country was endowed with significant resources. For example, Nigeria was among the world's largest producers of peanuts and rubber. It also produced important quantities of cotton, cocoa, yams, cassava, sorghum, corn and rice.

Nigeria was a major producer and exporter of petroleum. Oil revenues were channeled towards the creation of an industrial base and the strengthening of the agricultural sector. Other important industries included mining (natural gas, coal) and processing (oil, palm, peanuts, cotton, petroleum).

Phil's Position

Phil Chan wondered how to approach the negotiations with the Nigerians and resolve a few issues which had not been addressed. He wanted the deal to go through without upsetting his partner. Phil had recently read a business publication which emphasized the need to be "skillful in the art of bargaining" when dealing with Nigerians (see Exhibit 5).

Phil and Allen had agreed on what should be obtained from the Nigerians. They believed that five per cent (i.e., US$715,000) was more than sufficient to cover the contingencies associated with the completion of this deal. They wanted the contingency fund reduced from 10 per cent to five per cent and their share raised from 35 per cent to 40 per cent.

Phil's plan was to negotiate the financial commitments to be made by both sides prior to the release of funds in order to minimize Basic Software's exposure. To have a clear picture of the expenses to be incurred in the implementation of the deal and of the respective contributions expected from each side, he wanted to examine the pro-forma financial statements prepared by Mr. Tokunbo. His objective was to modify them to Basic Software's advantage.

In a phone conversation with Mr. Tokunbo, Phil had found that in order to do business with the Nigerian government and its agencies, it was necessary to be registered in the official list of pre-qualified suppliers. Various approvals and stamps were required in the registration process. The US$48,000 requested in the September 21st fax was for that purpose.

Phil also wanted to obtain a written commitment that all expenses and advances incurred by Basic Software would be reimbursed from the contingency fund including his travel and accommodation expenses that amounted to just over $6,000.

Phil brought with him all the documents requested by the Nigerian partners, including a power of attorney signed by Allen Lee, which authorized him to conclude the deal on behalf of Basic Software.

As he closed the Nigerian file and put it back in his briefcase, Phil wondered how he should conduct the negotiations in order to achieve his objectives without jeopardizing the relationship.

Exhibit 1   Initial Letter Sent by Tokunbo Jacobs to Allen Lee

22 January 2008

Tokunbo Jacobs
32 Falkar Street, Lagos, Nigeria
Tel. 234-1-874235, FAX 234-1-442157
TELEX *37854* RT NG

Dear Mr. President,

I am Mr. Tokunbo Jacobs, a staff of Nigerian National Petroleum Corporation (NNPC) and a member of the "Tenders Committee" of same corporation. I got your contact address through a close relation who is the corporate affairs manager of Nigerian Export Promotions Council. The transaction which is detailed below is being presented to you based on mutual trust and confidentiality.

After due consultation with other members of the Tender Committee, I have been specifi- cally mandated to arrange with you the remittance of US$14.3M. being an over estimated sum resulting from contract executed by an expatriate contractor. The original value of this contract was purposely over inflated by us (Tender Committee) with the sum of $14.3M. Now that the firm have received their supposed payments accordingly and the projects commissioned, I want you to nominate an account into which this money will be paid for division between us and you.

Sharing terms are: 35% to you as the owner of the account into which the money will be paid, 55% to the officials of the three parastatals. 10% is set aside for contingencies. The big bosses of the three parastatals involved in this transaction namely: Nigerian National Petroleum Corporation (NNPC) Federal Ministry of Finance (FMF) and Central Bank of Nigeria (CBN) are aware and behind the deal.

Meanwhile, you are required to indicate your interest through my <u>FAX LINE</u> or <u>TELEX</u> or by <u>personal call</u>. Please in your reply include your personal telephone, fax and telex numbers for easy communications.

You can be rest assured that within few weeks of my receipt of your positive reply this amount will be remitted into your nominated account.

May I demand with the highest respect for the code of business morality and secrecy that under no circumstance should you circumvent or share with any uninvolved person the contents of this letter and other vital documents that may arise in the course of this noble transaction until it is accomplished.

I look forward to your pragmatic conformity to this mutual proposition.

Yours faithfully,

TOKUNBO JACOBS

The text of the letter is original. The address, phone, FAX and TELEX numbers have been disguised.

Exhibit 2   February 2 Fax From Jacobs to Lee—2 February 2008

FROM: TOKUNBO JACOBS

ATTENTION: ALLEN LEE

Thanks for your fax of 22 January 2008 accepting to do this business with us. As you rightly mentioned there must be some responsibilities from your company to see this deal through. As a matter of fact you will be required to send to us some basic documents regarding your company to enable us process payment to your account.

These requirements are:

Two of your company's letter headed papers
Two of your company's proforma invoices
Bank particulars in which the said money will be transferred to:
the name of the bank, the account number, the telex number of the bank

On receipt of these above requirements the money will be remitted within twenty one working days.
   Allen, I will suggest you visit us with the requirements to expedite this deal and to enable the officials involve in this transaction meet with you person to person for more confidence and to enable to meet who we are entrusting our money. Furthermore I want your personal home phone number for easy communications. Remember we will not hesitate to ask for your assistance financially if the need arises which will be duely deducted from the 10% set aside as contingencies during the process of this transaction. All request needed by you will be given proper attention.

Note: There is no risk whatsoever in this transaction putting into consideration our good home work and calibre of people involve in this deal.
   Acknowledge receipt of this message through my fax number 442157.

Thanks and God bless.

TOKUNBO JACOBS

Exhibit 3   February 11 Fax From Jacobs to Lee

FAX: 11TH FEBRUARY 2008

FROM: TOKUNBO JACOBS
ATTENTION: ALLEN LEE

Consequent to our telephone discussions, these are the required information. When you despatch those documents via DHL courier service, including your company's catalogues fax the air way bill number to me to enable me pick them up in earnest.

I want you to realize that there are some expenses which we cannot afford to ignore if this transaction must succeed highfreely. We will need US$48,000.00 in order to off-set these expenses. We therefore solicit you to assist us with the already set aside amount. As regards the account:

Beneficiary:	Larry Olunitgo
Bank Name:	National First Bank of Nigeria PLC
	Broad Street, Branch Lagos
	Nigeria
Account Number:	1554

Below is the format for the attorney:

The Governor of Central Bank of Nigeria
Tinubu Square Lagos

Dear Sir,
Letter of Authority

I wish to inform you that I Mr. Allen Lee, the president of Basic Software Company hereby authorize barrister Eze Bakoto to sign on my behalf for the release of the sum of US$14.3 million U.S. dollars being payment for contract completed in 2004 for N.N.P.C. This is due to my present indisposed condition.

I look forward to your anticipated co-operation.

Yours faithfully,

Allen Lee (President).

N.B.:   The about format should be typed on your company's letter-headed paper and should be included with the courier documents.

Exhibit 4   Nigerian File

1963	The establishment of the Republic of Nigeria.
1966	Military coup. The Biafran war begins, lasting two years and causing several million deaths of which approximately two million were Biafran.
1983	Military coup. Benral Buhari overturns President Shagari.
1984	Demonetization operations; bank notes are no longer in circulation and are replaced by a new currency.
1985	State coup. General Ibrahim Babangida replaces General Buhari.
1986	End of the flat exchange rate. Seventy per cent devaluation of the Naira and currency fluctuations.
1990	Unsuccessful state coup against President Babangida. 42 military shot after aborted state coup of April 22nd, 1990.
1991	Riots provoked by Shiite fundamentalists cause two hundred deaths.
1993	Civilian elections held. Results annulled by Babangida, who then steps down and gives power to an interim government.
1994	General Abacha overthrows government. Widespread strikes against regime of Abacha, who arrests union leaders.
1995	Dissident writer Sara-Wiwa hanged. International pressure on Abacha builds.
1996	National Election Commision of Nigeria names five political parties allowed to participate in future elections.
1997	Commonwealth fails to make good on promise to expel Nigeria for human rights violations and not restoring democratic processes.
1998	Following the death of Abacha, successor General Absulsalam Abubakar promises to end military rule and restore democratic processes within one year.
1999	Former President Obsanjo re-elected in Nigeria's first democratic election since the end of military rule.
2000	Several northern states adopt Islamic, or Sharia law. Clashes between Muslims and Christians break out.
2002	Nigerian government attempts to suppress EU report implicating it in fuelling violent clashes between ethnic and religious groups in the area that have killed thousands.
2003	Obsanjo re-elected in first legislative elections since 1999. Election marked by delays and accusations of ballot rigging.
2004	State of emergency declared after religious clashes result in the death of 200 Muslims.
2005	Lenders agree to write off $20 billion of Nigeria's $30 billion debt.
2006	Obsanjo denied the ability to stand for a third term as senate refuses to alter constitution.

Exhibit 5   Doing Business in Nigeria

Greetings: In Nigeria, greetings are highly valued among the different ethnic groups. Refusing to greet another is a sign of disrespect. Due to the diversity of customs, cultures, and dialects that exist among the different ethnic groups in Nigeria, English is widely used in exchanging greetings throughout the country. Visitors are advised and encouraged to greet while in Nigeria. "Hello" is the most popular greeting. More formal greetings, such as "Good Morning," "Good Afternoon," and "Good Evening" are also appropriate. Avoid the use of casual or colloquial greetings and phrases such as "Hi" or "What's happening?" In addition, visitors are also encouraged to be courteous and cheerful when exchanging greetings. Do not be arrogant. Nigerians treat visitors with respect and, in return, expect to be treated with respect. Personal space between members of the same sex is much closer than in North America. This may cause discomfort to those not accustomed to conversing at close quarters.

Visiting: Nigerians try very hard to please their guests. Although Nigerians are generally not too concerned with time, they know about the western habit of punctuality and expect their western friends to arrive at the appointed time. Most Nigerians prefer "African time" to western punctuality. Nigerians treat their guests with congenial respect and expect their guests to respond in the same manner. Nigerians possess a rich heritage and hope for a bright future as a modern African nation, and thus can be offended by the "superior" attitude of some visitors.

Tipping: A dash (from the Portuguese word das, meaning "give") is a common Nigerian form of compensation in money, goods, or favours for services rendered. With the exception of services performed by waiters or bellhops, a "dash" is normally paid before the service is given. If the service offered is not desired, a firm refusal is usually necessary. The government is officially committed to discouraging certain kinds of "dash" that resemble bribery, such as payments for help in clearing customs, getting visas, or obtaining preferential treatment from government officials. But the custom is widespread and one has to be skillful in the art of "bargaining."

Personal Appearance: Dress varies according to the area and the culture. In the Muslim north, dress is very conservative for both men and women. Dress is more casual in the non-Muslim east and west. Shorts are not considered appropriate attire for Nigerian adults. For men, a shirt and tie are appropriate for formal and most other semi-formal occasions. Visitors will be most comfortable in cotton clothing—polyester is too warm. Traditional Nigerian men's dress is loose and comfortable. Although women in the cities and young girls often wear western dress, most women wear traditional long wraparound skirts, short-sleeved tops and head scarves. The fabric is renowned for its color and patterns.

Gestures: Nigeria is a multicultural nation and gestures differ from one ethnic group to another. Generally, pushing the palm of the hand forward with the fingers spread is a vulgar gesture and should be avoided. One should not point the sole of the foot at a person. Using the left hand in eating (unless left-handed) or in receiving something from someone has a bad connotation. The Yorubas (a large major ethnic group), in addition to the Ibibios and Igbos (two smaller, although major ethnic groups) will wink if they want their children to leave the room.

General Attitudes: Individual Nigerians are proud of the unique cultural heritage of their particular ethnic group. There is some ethnic tension, but continuing efforts are gradually unifying the nation. The Nigerians are striving to create a modern industrial society that is uniquely "African," and not "western." Because of negative connotations attached to the word "tribe," Nigerians avoid its use and "ethnic group" is often used in its place. Life in Nigeria moves at a relaxed pace with the exception of Lagos which can be very frenzied. People are generally not as time-conscious as in the west.

Language: English is the official language in Nigeria. However, because of the Nigerian mother tongue influence, spoken English may be difficult to understand. Pidgin English (broken English) is widely spoken by uneducated Nigerians, although even educated people widely use Pidgin English as a medium of informal conversation among themselves. Each of the over *250* ethnic groups also has its own distinct language. Hausa, Yoruba, and Ibo are widely spoken. Educated Nigerians usually are fluent in several languages.

Religion: In very general terms, Nigeria can be said to be divided between the Muslim North (47%) and the Christian South (34%), with a strong minority of traditional religions throughout the country (18%). However, it is important to note that both the Christians and the Muslims have strong missionary movements all over the whole country making the division of faiths into particular regions not exactly accurate. In addition, Nigerians may claim membership in a particular religion but may also incorporate traditional worship practices and beliefs into their daily life.

Family: Although the technical details of family structure vary from culture to culture, Nigerian families are generally male-dominated. The practice of polygamy is common throughout the country. The protected status of Muslim women in Nigeria is similar to other Muslim countries; however, most other Nigerian women enjoy a great degree of freedom by influencing family decisions and engaging in open trade at the market place, where the money they make is their own. Large families traditionally help share the workload at home. Nigerians pay deep respect to their elders. Children are trained to be quiet, respectful, and unassertive in their relations with adults. Marriage customs vary, but the payment of bridal wealth (money, property, or service traditionally given to the family of the bride by the husband) is common throughout the country.

Social and Economic Levels: Nigerians have the third highest average income in sub-Sahara Africa, but are still very poor by western standards. The average home consists of 1.4 rooms and more than three people per room. About 30% of the people live in absolute poverty. Nigeria once had the ninth lowest crime rate in the world, but without current statistics, it is difficult to determine the country's rank today.

Business Schedules: Most businesses are open from 8:00 AM to 12:30 PM, and then reopen from 2:00 to 4:30 PM. Government offices are open from 7:30 AM to 3:30 PM Monday through Friday. Many establishments and shops are also open on Saturdays with shorter hours. Every fourth Saturday is "Sanitation Day" (where no one is allowed on the street before 10:00 AM) and shops normally are not ready to receive business before noon. Sunday is the normal day of rest. Business appointments must be made in advance. Due to the poor telephone communication, business is often discussed on a person-to-person basis rather than via the telephone. Westerners are expected to be prompt, even though they may have to wait for some time after arriving.

Source: Canadian High Commission, Lagos

Medical Equipment Inc. in Saudi Arabia

Joerg Dietz

Ankur Grover

Laura Guerrero

On Wednesday, October 25, 2006, Ankur Grover, a recently hired U.S.-trained sales account manager at Medical Equipment Inc. (Medical Equipment), returned to his office after a meeting with Dr. Matthew Saxman, head of the Cardiology Department at the Prince Khalid Specialist Hospital and Research Centre in Jeddah, Saudi Arabia. Although Grover had worked very hard to secure his first sale (US$725,000 for healthcare equipment), he felt disheartened. Saxman had told Grover that the hospital's purchasing director, Sulaiman Al Humaidi, apparently intended to give the order to Hamad Najjar from Wilson's Surgical Supply Company (Wilson's), Medical Equipment's main competitor in the deal. Najjar and Al Humaidi had known each other for 10 years, and Saxman implied that Al Humaidi might accept side payments from Najjar. Grover knew that Medical Equipment's product was technically superior and wondered how he could secure the order without having a history with Al Humaidi and without engaging in practices he found ethically questionable.

Saudi Arabia

In 2006, the population of Saudi Arabia was estimated at between 23 million and 26 million, with an approximate annual growth rate of 2.7 per cent.[1] Approximately two-thirds of the population consisted of Saudi nationals, and the remaining one-third were foreign workers and their dependents. Among Saudi nationals, approximately 90 per cent were Sunni Muslims, and the remainder were Shi'a Muslims (legally, only Muslims could hold Saudi citizenship). Saudi Arabia occupied most of the Arabian Peninsula. As the world's largest oil exporter, possessing 25 per cent of the world's proven petroleum reserves, Saudi Arabia played a leading role in the Organization of the Petroleum Exporting Countries (OPEC). In 2004, the petroleum sector accounted for

---

[1]Economist Intelligence Unit, "Factsheet" (Saudi Arabia), available at http://www.economist.com/countries/SaudiArabia/profile.cfm?folder=Profile-FactSheet, accessed July 24, 2007.

roughly 75 per cent of state budget revenues, 45 per cent of gross domestic product (GDP) and 90 per cent of export earnings. The GDP per capita was US$12,650.

The Kingdom of Saudi Arabia also housed two of the holiest cities of Islam: Mecca and Medina. Annually, Mecca welcomed approximately two million pilgrims who traveled there for the Hajj (the pilgrimage). Saudi Arabia was divided into 13 provinces and had 45 major cities. The largest city was Riyadh (population 3.6 million), followed by Jeddah (population 2.7 million) and Mecca (population 1.5 million) (see Exhibit 1). Approximately 83 per cent of the population lived in urban areas, and 17 per cent lived in rural areas.

Saudi Arabia was founded in 1932 by King Abdul Aziz Al Saud. Since then, the Al Saud Royal Family had remained in power. King Abdullah bin Abdul Aziz Al Saud had been Saudi Arabia's King and Prime Minister since 2005.[2] The family's legitimacy and power were supported by the clerics and their Wahhabi-based interpretation of Sunni Islam. Wahhabism was an Islamic movement named after Muhammad bin Abd al Wahhab (1703–1792). Since the

discovery of large oil reserves in the Kingdom, the distribution of oil revenue had become another source of influence for the Royal Family.[3]

Many foreign businesses operated in Saudi Arabia. Furthermore, approximately 5.5 million foreign workers worked in Saudi Arabia. Foreign employees made up about 67 per cent of Saudi Arabia's workforce and occupied about 90 per cent to 95 per cent of private sector jobs. In contrast, the unemployment rate for Saudi nationals was between 25 per cent and 30 per cent. Eighty-five per cent of foreign workers had low-skill jobs. Most of the low-skilled foreign workers came from South Asia and Southeast Asia (i.e. Bangladesh, Pakistan, India and the Philippines). In the high-skilled foreign workforce, Westerners from the United States and England dominated.[4]

For highly qualified expatriates, job opportunities generally offered high salaries and excellent benefits, including free housing, extended vacation time, airline tickets to return home several times per year, relocation allowances and—unless it was restricted by the expatriate's own country—tax-free income. Most of the North American

[2]Central Intelligence Agency, "Saudi Arabia," *The World Factbook*, available at https://www.cia.gov/library/publications/the-world-factbook/geos/sa.html, accessed July 24, 2007.

[3]Economist Intelligence Unit, "Factsheet" (Saudi Arabia), available at http://www.economist.com/countries/SaudiArabia/profile.cfm?folder=Profile-FactSheet, accessed July 24, 2007.

[4]Divya Pakkiasamy, "Saudi Arabia's Plan for Changing Its Workforce," available at http://www.migrationinformation.org/Feature/display.cfm?id=264, accessed July 24, 2007.

multinationals in Saudi Arabia pre-ferred to fill their senior-level positions with North American graduates who had relevant work experience. However, the number of North American expatriates had been shrinking. One reason was that living in an Islamic monarchy required significant lifestyle adjustments for Westerners. The King governed by Islamic law (Shari'ah), with the Quran (holy book of the Muslims) and the Sunna, which contained the sayings or Hadith of the Prophet Mohammad, as the country's constitution. Therefore, the possession of items such as pork products, alcohol, drugs and pornography were considered crimes in Saudi Arabia. Other crimes included criticizing Islam or the Royal Family and socializing with a member of the opposite sex to whom one was not closely related.[5] Punishment for certain crimes could be very severe, including detention, floggings, amputations or death, whereby the Shari'ah judges had significant latitude in their decisions.[6] Furthermore, the U.S. Department of State website extensively warned of the possibility of anti-Western attacks in Saudi Arabia.[7] Since the 1990s, the Saudi government had started the process of "Saudiization," the practice of forcing businesses to hire more Saudi nationals to reduce unemployment among Saudi nationals.[8]

The Saudi Arabian Healthcare Sector

Saudi Arabia was the largest market for medical equipment and healthcare products in the Persian Gulf. The healthcare sector in Saudi Arabia was expected to grow for several reasons. First, due to record-high oil prices, the government had been able to make large investments in health care. Second, the government was working toward the goal of providing free access to health care to everyone living in Saudi Arabia. Third, the population was growing.

In 2001, the healthcare sector of Saudi Arabia comprised 314 hospitals with 45,730 beds and 1,756 specialist centers and clinics that spread across the

---

[5]U.S. Department of State, "Consular Information Sheet, Saudi Arabia," available at http://travel.state.gov/travel/cis_pa_tw/cis/cis_1012.html, accessed August 14, 2007.

[6]Expat Focus, "Saudi Arabia—Overview," available at http://www.expatfocus.com/expatriate-saudi-arabia-overview, accessed July 24, 2007.

[7]U.S. Department of State, "Consular Information Sheet, Saudi Arabia," available at http://travel.state.gov/travel/cis_pa_tw/cis/cis_1012.html, accessed August 14, 2007.

[8]Divya Pakkiasamy, "Saudi Arabia's Plan for Changing Its Workforce," available at http://www.migrationinformation.org/Feature/display.cfm?id=264, accessed July 24, 2007.

country, including in rural areas.[9] The healthcare sector was divided into three sub-sectors: Defense/National Guard, Ministry of Health (MOH) and Private.

The defense hospitals, which accounted for only 10 per cent of the hospitals, were designated for the use of military staff and their families. These hospitals were known to have some of the most modern equipment and facilities worldwide. King Fahd Specialist Hospital, for example, was built in Dammam in April 2005. This hospital not only featured the latest medical technology and equipment, but also had a nuclear protection dome for protecting staff and patients in the event of a nuclear attack. The estimated amount spent in constructing and equipping this hospital was SAR1.092 billion (about US$291.2 million). These defense hospitals directed most of their purchases through their purchasing departments and the rest through formal tenders.

The MOH hospitals accounted for approximately 65 per cent of the hospitals and clinics. All major purchases in these hospitals were controlled by the MOH through tenders or individual equipment purchases. The goal was to centralize the purchasing function for all these hospitals to achieve economies of scale.

The remaining 25 per cent of the hospitals and medical facilities were owned and operated privately by Saudi businesspeople or doctors. Private hospitals were less likely to invest in expensive new equipment because of budgeting constraints.

Medical Equipment

Headquartered in the United Kingdom, Medical Equipment employed more than 20,000 people worldwide. Medical Equipment's mission was to serve healthcare professionals and their patients in more than 80 countries by providing innovative medical technology products. Medical Equipment's expenditures on research and development were close to US$750 million annually. Revenue had grown at an average rate of 140 per cent from 2000 to 2006, when it reached US$13.5 billion.

Medical Equipment was a recognized industry leader in the healthcare sector, in terms of both innovation that led to improvements in existing equipment and in the provision of innovative medical technologies and services. Medical Equipment's expertise included medical imaging and information technologies, medical diagnostics, patient-monitoring systems, drug discovery and biopharmaceutical manufacturing technologies. Medical Equipment's broad range of products and services were utilized, among other things, in

[9] "About Saudi Arabia," SaudiaOnline, available at http://www.saudia-online.com/saudi_arabia .htm, accessed April 11, 2007.

the diagnosis and treatment of cancer, heart disease, neurological diseases and other conditions in their early stages.

Medical Equipment Clinical Systems

Medical Equipment Clinical Systems was a primary business unit of Medical Equipment. This business unit provided a wide range of technologies and services for clinicians and healthcare administrators. These technologies and services helped improve the consistency, quality and efficiency of patient care with product innovations in areas such as ultrasound, electrocardiogram (ECG), bone densitometry, patient monitoring, incubators and infant warmers, respiratory care and anesthesia management. Some cardiology equipment developed by Medical Equipment Clinical Systems is shown in Exhibit 2.

Medical Equipment— Saudi Arabian Operations

The sales and service division of Medical Equipment Clinical Systems in Saudi Arabia employed approximately 25 staff (see Exhibit 3 for an organizational chart). Medical Equipment Clinical Systems Saudi Arabia was divided on a regional basis into three main areas: the Northern-Central region (with Riyadh as the center), the

Eastern region (with Dammam at the center) and the Western-Southern region (with Jeddah as the center). The combined operations of all regions of Saudi Arabia were very important for the company: the revenue generated from the Saudi market almost equaled the revenue generated by the whole European region. The company was able to reach this level of revenue in Saudi Arabia because of the booming healthcare industry. This boom had resulted in the construction of numerous new hospitals and clinics, and others were in the development phase. The European market, on the other hand, was almost saturated and had low potential for growth.

Ankur Grover

Ankur Grover, who was 25 years old, was born in India and came from a Hindu background. When he was 10, his family moved to Saudi Arabia where he lived in an expatriate compound until he completed his high-school education at an Indian school.

In 2000, he moved to the United States to obtain his bachelor's degree of science in computer engineering at the Georgia Institute of Technology in Atlanta. While pursuing his engineering degree, Grover worked on three internships. His first internship with Medical Equipment Clinical Systems in Paris, France, took place in the summer semester of 2001. It gave him an initial exposure to Medical Equipment. Grover's second internship was with Synchrologic, Inc. in Atlanta during the spring semester of 2002. Grover interned as a quality assurance engineer for software applications. The third internship was again with Medical Equipment in its Atlanta branch during the summer semester of 2002. This time, Grover worked as a field service engineer on multi-vendor medical equipment.

When he graduated in 2006, Grover decided to accept a position in the Cardiology Sales department of Medical Equipment Clinical Systems in Saudi Arabia. As a sales account manager, he would be responsible for the Western-Southern region of the country. He was the third employee for this region; the other two employees had responsibilities for other products. Grover had a basic knowledge of sales and cardiology, and he received one week of product training. He had previously lived in Saudi Arabia and wondered whether his former experiences would translate to the work environment of Saudi Arabia. Grover was enthusiastic about having the opportunity to work toward a successful career in Medical Equipment.

Grover's starting base salary was US$50,000 with a target of US$1,200,000 in 2006 sales. If Grover exceeded this target, commissions would be paid as a percentage of the base salary, depending on the percentage of the target achieved. For example,

meeting 100 per cent of his target resulted in commission payments equal to 50 per cent of his base salary.

The Current Situation

Grover's Arrival in Saudi Arabia

Grover arrived in Saudi Arabia in early July 2006. At this time of the year, it was very hot in Jeddah, with temperatures often reaching 40°C (equivalent to 104° Fahrenheit) or hotter by noon. His employer paid for the move and for an initial four-day stay at a hotel. Grover had arranged the move himself and found an apartment in Jeddah within a week.

At work, Grover was expected initially to compose a database of potential customers. After one week, Grover was sent into the field to work on sales. Grover enjoyed the work environment. He felt that he had a very good mentor in the Riyadh general manager with whom he frequently communicated. Grover also often spoke with his colleagues. He quickly developed relationships with them although he was the only employee who was non-Arab and non-Muslim. As Grover noted, "I was the odd one out, but I was able to mingle well with them."

Grover's First Sales Opportunity

Being assigned as the only cardiology sales account manager for the

Western-Southern region, his first opportunity to work on a sale came from the Jeddah branch of the Prince Khalid Specialist Hospital, a Defense/National Guard hospital. This hospital had almost exclusively purchased its cardiovascular equipment from Medical Equipment's main competitor Wilson's. It was a "Wilson's account" as Grover said. The hospital came to Medical Equipment only for small parts that Wilson's did not have.

The total potential sale was US$725,000, a significantly sized order for Grover and Medical Equipment. Grover knew that the lead time on this sale might be several months and that it would take numerous visits to the hospital to secure the order. The order included the following (refer to Exhibit 2 for illustrations of the equipment):

Equipment	Quantity
1. Stress Test	3
2. Holter Monitoring	1
3. Holter Recorder	6
4. High-end ECG	1
5. ECG	5
6. Defibrillator	3

Grover's Sales Approach

The approach when making sales of this type was to make frequent visits to the Cardiology, Biomedical Engineering and Purchasing Departments. Grover had to carefully study the needs of the hospital and then analyze those needs against the vast range of software options and equipment offered by Medical Equipment to determine which options needed to be included in the quote. Inadequate analysis at this step could result in the loss of the order. If he offered a quote with more options than those that were necessary, the price of the equipment would be high. If he offered a quote with fewer products and software than those required, the bid might be rejected because it would not meet the hospital's criteria. Thus, the sales position required Grover to have a clear understanding of the needs of the client. He perceived his role to be that of a consultant with the ability to evaluate the customer's needs against the solutions that could be offered.

The sales process would require Grover to obtain initial approval from several hospital departments. First, the Cardiology Department had to approve the quote. Grover would then need additional approval from the Biomedical Engineering Department. To complete the sale, he had to obtain approval from the purchasing director, who had the final authority on all major purchasing decisions of medical equipment.

The Competition

The competitor for Medical Equipment in this deal was Wilson's. Wilson's was not usually far behind Medical Equipment in terms of technology, but for this particular order, Medical Equipment had a much better solution because of recent advances in its software. The new software offered better features including automatically generated ECG diagnoses. However, the price offered by Wilson's included substantial discounts and was very competitive. Grover also felt he had to compete with the sales account manager at Wilson's, Hamad Najjar. Najjar had worked in the region for more than 10 years and had developed strong relationships with the local customers. Najjar was of Syrian background and appeared to understand the Saudi culture well (both the Syrian and Saudi cultures were Arab cultures). During their sales activities, Grover and Najjar at times bumped into each other by accident. They had a "hi-hello" relationship.

Meetings With the Cardiology Department

August 3, 2006

Grover began by meeting with the cardiologists. Most of the cardiologists were Western expatriates. As the primary users of the equipment, they wanted to know the clinical details of the equipment and the software the hospital was going to purchase. When Grover met with Dr. Saxman, a U.S. national, and the other cardiologists, he explained the benefits of the equipment and the software. He explained the latest innovations in Medical Equipment's products and how

the hospital would benefit by purchasing the solution from Medical Equipment rather than from Wilson's. As an example, Grover showed them the new software of the EEG with its improved speed and diagnosis capabilities. Grover ended his presentation by providing the cardiologists with a vision of where their Cardiology Department would stand in comparison to similar departments in other leading hospitals in Saudi Arabia if they purchased Medical Equipment's solution.

August 11, 2006

The next step was to make presentations to the entire staff of the Cardiology Department. These presentations took place in shifts over a period of three days in order to avoid affecting the department's functionality. Grover conducted a lot of research to ensure that his presentation addressed clinical details that were relevant to the staff.

August 15, 2006 to September 20, 2006

Following these presentations, Grover met with Dr. Saxman and his team approximately seven more times. Grover knew that building relationships was important for a large-scale order. It was also customary when conducting business in Saudi Arabia. Grover was always welcomed and everyone was very friendly to him.

Meetings With the Biomedical Engineering Department

August 17, 2006

Following these presentations and meetings with the Cardiology Department, Grover held meetings with Ashraf Walid, an Egyptian national and the head of Biomedical Engineering Department, and the other biomedical engineers. The Biomedical Engineering Department would be responsible for the maintenance of the equipment. Grover utilized his engineering background to explain how Medical Equipment's solution could easily be integrated into the hospital's system. Grover became aware that the biggest selling point for the engineers was the reduced need for maintenance of the equipment in comparison to the maintenance needs required by the equipment from Wilson's.

August 21, 2006 to September 21, 2006

During this period, Grover met Walid at least five more times, for the purpose of building a stronger relationship with him. However, Grover was aware that his many meetings had not yet produced tangible results.

Meetings With the Purchasing Department

August 25, 2006

The final step was to meet the purchasing director, Sulaiman Al Humaidi.

In the absence of the director, Grover met the purchasing manager, Asif Sultan. Grover felt he had developed good rapport with Sultan in their first meeting.

August 28, 2006 to September 15, 2006

Grover made multiple visits to the Purchasing Department during this time period, but he was not able to meet Al Humaidi. He was told by the receptionist that Al Humaidi was out of the hospital but not on vacation. During these visits, because Grover could not meet Al Humaidi, he settled with meeting Sultan approximately five times to continue building and strengthening the relationship with him. Grover was concerned whether building a relationship with Al Humaidi's subordinate would be as helpful as building a relationship with Al Humaidi himself.

September 21, 2006

Grover was finally able to meet Al Humaidi on September 21. Grover felt that their discussion was rather formal especially when compared to his past conversations with the cardiologists and the biomedical engineers. Grover told Al Humaidi about the positive results of the meetings he had with the cardiologists and the biomedical engineers. He also mentioned that both groups were supportive of the Medical Equipment solution, which would help the hospital in the long run. When prompted, Grover was able to offer a discount of 10 per cent based on the latitude given to him by the company.

Closing the Sale

September 25, 2006 to October 18, 2006

Grover continued to make frequent visits to the hospital to strengthen his relationships with all the departments and to facilitate not only the present order but also all future orders. He was confident that Dr. Saxman and Walid had strong preferences for Medical Equipment's solution over that of Wilson's. Despite making repeated attempts, Grover met Al Humaidi only one more time. The meeting lasted a few minutes because Al Humaidi was very busy. During the meeting, Al Humaidi stated that they were still deciding which order to pursue. It was taking a long time to get to a decision, and Grover did not know whether he was any closer to securing the order.

October 27, 2006

When Grover asked him about the status of the order, Dr. Saxman replied:

Ankur, it seems that Al Humaidi is about to give the order to Wilson's. Even though we cardiologists prefer Medical Equipment's solution, we do not have much say here. It seems to me that Al Humaidi has a strong relationship with Hamad Najjar. There is good reason to believe that Najjar is offering a bribe to Al Humaidi.

A Colleague's View

Grover had invested a great deal of time researching, analysing and building relationships to complete this sale. Dr. Saxman's statement made Grover wonder whether he needed to offer Al Humaidi something beyond what he had already offered. He was also aware of Medical Equipment's code of conduct (see Exhibit 4 for an excerpt) that did not support giving bribes to secure orders. Many multinational companies, including Wilson's, had such statements of ethics. Grover asked Samer, one of his colleagues at Medical Equipment, whether he had experienced or known of any similar situations and how they could be handled. Samer said:

No, I have not run into a similar situation. If you are going to offer some incentive, you should make sure that whatever you give is properly documented on paper and is shared with senior management. We cannot give cash, but we can discuss giving them certain software options free of charge and try to convince Al Humaidi with the selling point that the Prince Khalid Specialist Hospital will become much more innovative with Medical Equipment's solution compared to other hospitals in the country. Secondly, we can offer to send him to the United States or France for a visit to our showrooms where all the latest technology in the medical field is demonstrated provided that it is properly documented.

What Next?

Despite several months of work on this sales order, Grover felt discouraged and confused. If Saxman were right, then the order would be given to Najjar from Wilson's unless Grover would find another means of swaying Al Humaidi. One possible option was to offer to send Al Humaidi to the United States or France for a visit to Medical Equipment's showroom. The visit could be easily documented and it fit well with Medical Equipment's policies. But Grover wondered where the notion of unethical behavior started and where it ended. Had he failed to understand the concept of "building relationships" with Saudi nationals?

Exhibit 1   Saudi Arabia

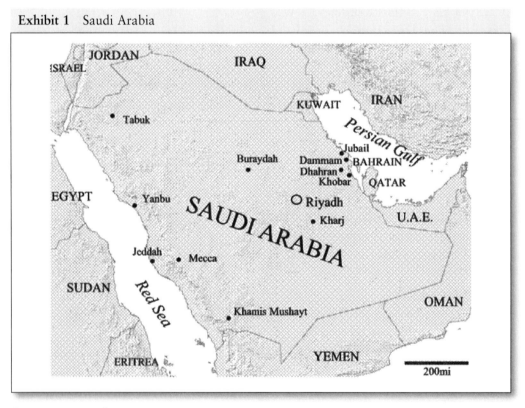

Source: www.google.ca

Exhibit 2   Cardiology Equipment in the Portfolio of Medical Equipment
Clinical Systems

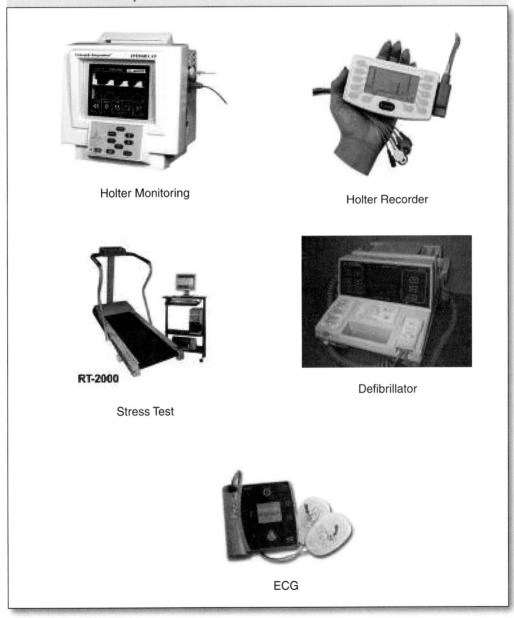

Holter Monitoring

Holter Recorder

RT-2000

Stress Test

Defibrillator

ECG

Source: Google.com

Exhibit 3   Medical Equipment Saudi Arabia: Organizational Chart

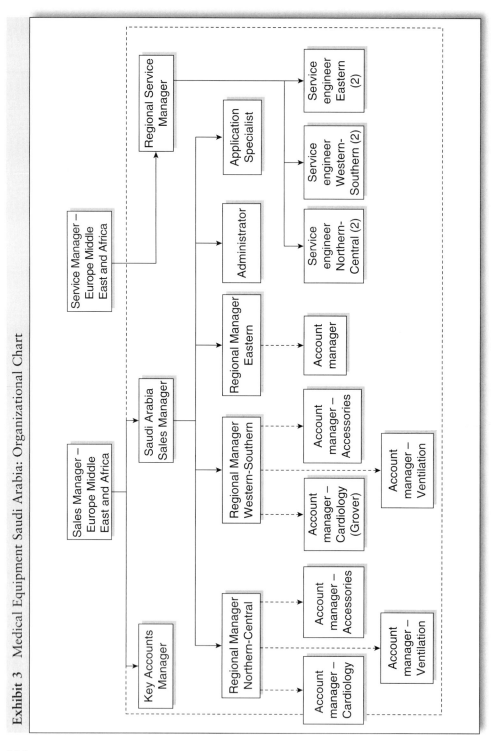

Note: The Key Accounts Manager handles major projects like catering to companies that build hospitals and equip them rather than hospitals that buy several pieces of equipment each year. The Regional managers have a mentor-like relationship with Account managers who often reported to the Country Sales Manager directly.

Exhibit 4   Medical Equipment's Code of Conduct

Purpose and Application of the Code of Conduct

We recognize that the key to enhancing the corporate value of Medical Equipment Inc. is fulfilling our corporate social responsibility in our day-to-day work. Therefore, we will faithfully observe the provisions of this Code of Conduct.

Basic Position

Comply with all applicable laws, rules, regulations, and in-house regulations, including this Code of Conduct, in every aspect of our corporate activities at all times. We will strive to ensure that all corporate activities are in compliance with normal business practices and social ethics.

Respect the fundamental human rights of all people in every aspect of our corporate activities. Do not act in such a way that may offend the dignity of any individual or be prejudicial on the grounds of race, beliefs, gender, age, social position, family origin, nationality, ethnicity, religion, or physical or mental handicap.

Maintain impartial, fair, and open relationships with all the stakeholders of our company and conduct business in a fair manner with them.

Do not take any action pursuing our personal or a third party's interests against our company's legitimate interests.

Do not take any action whatsoever that may damage Medical Equipment's social trust or honor.

Relations with Customers, Business Partners, and Competitors

Product and Service Safety

Always focus on customer satisfaction, observe all applicable laws, rules, and regulations, and be mindful of the quality and safety of our products and services.

Free Competition and Fair Commercial Transactions

Conduct fair commercial transactions with all business partners based on the principle of free competition and in compliance with anti-trust, competition, and fair trade laws and all other applicable laws, rules, and regulations.

Do not undertake any action that inhibits free and fair competition, including collusion and cartel formation. Do not participate in meetings or in exchanges of information that may limit free competition or engage in any activity that may be construed as doing so.

Always keep relations with customers, business partners, and competitors that are open and fair. In addition, carry out all commercial transactions with integrity.

Policies on Transactions with Suppliers of Materials and Services

Carry out commercial transactions with suppliers of materials and services in a fair and equal manner while being compliant with applicable laws, rules, regulations, and contracts.

Do not abuse any superior position that we may have as a customer to cause inappropriate disadvantage to suppliers.

(Continued)

Exhibit 4 (Continued)

Do not seek personal gain by accepting any benefits or special convenience in procurement or other purchasing operations.

Policies on Entertainment and Gifts

Engage in sound business practices and social norms when providing or receiving entertainment or exchanging gifts with business partners or others.

Do not, under any circumstances, offer bribes to heads of regional public organizations, members of prefectural or municipal assemblies, or officials of government agencies or regional public organizations (including personnel of public corporations and other government-affiliated organizations). In addition, do not provide any benefits to gain unfair business advantage, entertain in a way that could be construed as offering benefits, or offer gifts or any other treatment that lacks justifiable grounds.

Do not conduct any acts involving foreign officers such as officials of foreign governments or regional public organizations that could be construed as bribery or the provision of benefits to gain an unfair business advantage under any circumstances under applicable laws, rules, and regulations.

Be aware of the difference between improper payments and reasonable and limited expenditures for gifts, business entertainment and customer travel and living expenses directly related to the promotion of products or services or the execution of a contract. These payments are acceptable, subject to specific Medical Equipment corporate and business guidelines.

Do not give a gratuity or other payment to government officials or employees to expedite a routine administrative action without fully disclosing it to Medical Equipment's legal counsel. Some national laws that prohibit bribery outside that nation include an exception for "facilitating payments" to expedite a routine administrative action to which a person is otherwise entitled. These payments are often illegal under local anti-bribery laws, and Medical Equipment strongly discourages them. Make sure you understand the difference between a bribe—corruptly giving someone else a thing of value in exchange for exercising discretion in your favor—and a facilitating payment, which involves the payment of a small amount of money to expedite a routine action to which you are entitled.

Governance Failure at Satyam[1]

Ajai Gaur
Nisha Kohli

Satyam, a word in Sanskrit—an ancient Indian language—means truth. Ironically, a company by the same name was involved in one of the largest scandals in the history of the Indian corporate world. On January 7, 2009, B. Ramalinga Raju, chairman of Satyam Computer Services Ltd., wrote a letter to the company board in which he took responsibility for fraud of about 50 billion Indian rupees (INR) (see Exhibit 1).

The fraud took the corporate world by surprise, not only due to its size but also because Satyam had been touted as a pioneer of corporate governance practices. Satyam won the Golden Peacock Global Award for Excellence in Corporate Governance given by the World Council for Corporate Governance in 2008, just three months before the scandal. Satyam also won the Golden Peacock National Award for Excellence in Corporate Governance in 2002, and was rated as having the best corporate governance practices by the Investor Relations Global Rankings (IRGR) for 2006 and 2007. In his letter, Raju acknowledged that the fraud had been going on for several years. As analysts tried to understand how a company with strong corporate governance practices could keep such a huge fraud under wraps, about 115 independent directors on the boards of listed Indian companies resigned in the one-month period following the Satyam scandal. Following the scandal, the big question facing the corporate world and the regulators was how to ensure good corporate governance, moving beyond the ceremonial adoption of best practices by firms.

History of Satyam

Satyam Computers Limited (Satyam) was India's fourth-largest software development and information technology (IT) consulting company based on 2008 figures.[2] A private limited company incorporated by two brothers—B. Rama Raju and B. Ramalinga Raju—in 1987, Satyam's success became synonymous

---

[1]This case has been written on the basis of published sources only. Consequently, the interpretation and perspectives presented in this case are not necessarily those of Satyam Computer Services Ltd. or any of its employees.

[2]Prowess database, Centre for Monitoring of Indian Economy.

with the success of the Indian IT industry for the next 20 years. Satyam was converted from a private limited company to a public company in August 1991, issuing shares to the public in 1992. The money raised in the stock market was used to build a software technology park and a 100 per cent export-oriented unit. In the following year, Satyam made its first global foray by entering into a joint venture with the U.S. company Dun and Bradstreet. In 1996, Satyam set up its first foreign office in the United States, followed by another one in Japan. It developed new business partnerships in several other countries including Australia, Canada and some European countries. Meanwhile, Satyam continued its growth initiatives in the domestic market, opening new offices and facilities in different parts of India, promoting four subsidiaries—Satyam Spark Solutions, Satyam Renaissance Consulting Ltd., Satyam Enterprise Solutions Pvt. Ltd. and Satyam Infoway Pvt. Ltd.—and opening IT schools—the Indian Institutes of Information Technology (IIIT). The IIITs were a result of public-private partnership, with several of these schools being promoted by global corporations such as IBM, Microsoft and Oracle in different parts of India. In 1997, Satyam became the first Indian company to receive Information Technology Association of America (ITAA) certification for Y2K solutions.[3]

To capitalize on the IT boom in the late 1990s, Satyam made its first greenfield investment in the United States in 1998, opening a software development centre in New Jersey and subsequently opening several such centres all over the world in Singapore, the United Arab Emirates (UAE), Australia, Malaysia, China, Egypt and Brazil. In 1999, different subsidiaries of Satyam were merged with the parent firm, and Satyam was listed on the NASDAQ. The money raised by the NASDAQ listing was used for further growth initiatives including new ventures. Satyam entered into several alliances and long-term contracts with global bodies and corporations such as World Bank, Microsoft, Yahoo!, SEEC Inc, Healthaxis, Insur-Enroll Solution, Computer Associates, Saint-Gobain Abrasives, Venture Global Engineering, Vignette Corporation, Computer Associates, Emirates, SAS Institute Inc, i2 Technologies and Ford. As of 2008, Satyam had a revenue of more than US$2 billion, more than 51,000 associates of more than 60 nationalities, 654 customers which included one-third of the Fortune Global and US 500 companies, a presence in 63 countries and 31 global solution centres. It was listed on the New York Stock Exchange in the United States, Euronext in Amsterdam

---

[3]http://content.icicidirect.com/Research/HistoryCompany.asp?icicicode=SATCOM, accessed on January 7, 2009.

and Bombay Stock Exchange and the National Stock Exchange in India.[4]

Along with its phenomenal growth, Satyam and its employees also won several national and international awards and recognitions. In 2000, Satyam was named a Web Business 50/50 award winner for its corporate intranet. In the same year, Satyam won the national Human Resource Development (HRD) Award for its outstanding HRD efforts. Dataquest, a leading IT magazine, named Raju as IT Man of the Year for 2000. Hong Kong-based Far Eastern Economic Review ranked Satyam as one of the 10 most well-regarded companies in India, based on a survey conducted in 2000. Satyam also won the Frost & Sullivan market engineering award for competitive strategy in 2001, and the application service provider category IBM Lotus award for innovation in 2003. These awards and honours were clear reflections of Satyam's prestige and reputation amongst its clients, employees and society in general.[5]

Governance at Satyam

Satyam had a relatively small promoter holding for a traditional family-run firm in India (see Exhibit 2); in fact, the promoters' ownership share had steadily declined over the years. Foreign institutional investors had the maximum holding, varying between 40 and 50 per cent. Other important groups of investors included the Indian public, banks and financial institutions as well as mutual funds. With a relatively high level of ownership in the hands of domestic and foreign institutional investors, it was important for Satyam to have a "good" corporate board to gain legitimacy amongst its different stakeholders.

As of December 2008, Satyam had five independent and four internal members on its board (see Exhibit 3). Ramalinga Raju and Rama Raju, the two founding brothers, were the only relatives on the board. Ramalinga Raju was the chairman of the board; the other two internal directors included Ram Mynampati, an internal employee, and Krishna Palepu, a Harvard Business School professor who was listed as an internal director because he also worked as a consultant for Satyam. The audit and compensation committees had four members each who were all independent directors. The audit committee met eight times in the year preceding the scandal, while the compensation committee met three times.

The composition of the board and different committees was in total

---

[4]Satyam Annual Report, 2008.

[5]http://content.icicidirect.com/Research/HistoryCompany.asp?icicicode=SATCOM, accessed on January 7, 2009.

compliance with the prescribed rules and regulations in India; in addition, Satyam seemed to follow the governance standards beyond what was prescribed by law, as is evident from the company's philosophy on corporate governance, stated in the governance reports that Satyam submitted to regulatory authorities:

> Corporate Governance assumes a great deal of importance in the business life of Satyam ("the Company"). The driving forces of Corporate Governance at Satyam are its core values—Associate Delight, Investor Delight, Customer Delight and the Pursuit of Excellence. The Company's goal is to find creative and productive ways of delighting its stakeholders, i.e., Investors, Customers, Associates and Society, thereby fulfilling the role of a responsible corporate representative committed to best practices.

> Satyam believes that sound Corporate Governance practices provide an important framework to assist the Board in fulfilling its responsibilities. The Board of directors is elected by shareholders with a responsibility to set strategic objectives to the management and to ensure that the long term interests of all stakeholders are served by adhering to and enforcing the principles of sound Corporate Governance. Thus, the management is responsible to establish and implement policies, procedures and systems to enhance long-term value of the Company and

delight all its stakeholders (Associates, Investors, Customers and Society).[6]

Financial Health

Satyam's balance sheet showed all the signs of a healthy company (see Exhibits 4 through 6). In eight years from 2001 to 2008, Satyam's turnover increased from INR14.12 billion to INR84.73 billion. Profit after tax also showed a consistent gain, with the net profit margin increasing from 10 per cent to 20 per cent. Satyam expected revenue of about US$2.7 billion in the 2008/09 financial year (as stated in its 10k form for the 2007/08 financial year).[7] These figures meant an increase in growth rate from 24 per cent to 26 per cent between 2008 and 2009. Basic earnings per American Depository Receipts (ADS) for 2009 were expected to be between US$1.44 and US$1.47, implying a growth rate of 15.2 per cent—up 17.6 per cent from the previous year. The earnings per share (EPS) for 2009 were expected to be between INR29.54 and INR30.04, with a growth rate of 17 per cent to 19 per cent over the previous year.

Satyam's financial health was based on a robust profile of customers: its top 100 customers accounted for 85 per cent of the company's revenue. Satyam had two customers with annual run rates greater than US$100 million,

---

[6]Satyam Annual Report 2007.

[7]Satyam Annual Report 2008.

while 50 customers exceeded an annual run rate of US$10 million. There were 230 customers with annual run rates of US$1 million. Satyam was the first Indian company to post its audited results for the 2007/08 financial year in accordance with the International Financial Reporting Standards (IFRS).[8] The company's chief financial officer (CFO), Srinivas Vadlamani, commented on reporting results according to IFRS:

> We see considerable value in adopting IFRS. As a global standard, it enables comparison and comprehension of financials, regardless of a company's location. And, since Satyam has adopted the standards, our operational reporting can be understood, without reconciliation, by more than 100 countries that already permit or require IFRS reporting. Further, the move provides clarity and consistency to Satyam's investors in Europe, where our company is growing quickly.[9]

The Unfolding of the Crisis

On December 16, 2008, Satyam's board approved a 51 per cent stake acquisition of Maytas Infra, a listed company in the Bombay Stock Exchange for US$1.3 billion, and a 100 per cent stake in the unlisted firm Maytas Properties for US$300 million. Both of these firms were in the construction and real estate business and were promoted by the two sons of Satyam's chairman, Ramalinga Raju. Raju's immediate family and friends held a 36 per cent stake in Maytas Infra and 35 per cent stake in Maytas Properties. The successful completion of the acquisition required borrowing US$300 million to add to the US$1.2 billion of cash that Satyam claimed to possess. Satyam justified the diversification into the real estate and property business on the grounds that real estate was a sunrise industry in India, and that diversification was essential given the sluggish growth of IT business in key markets such as the United States and Europe.[10]

The investors reacted very negatively to this news, resulting in a 55 per cent decline in Satyam's ADRs. Following stiff resistance from investors in general and institutional investors in particular, Satyam called off the acquisition on December 17, 2008; however, this did not pacify the negative sentiments and share prices, which fell by 30 per cent on the Indian bourses. Given the significant related party transactions involved, investors and media also started raising doubts over the corporate governance practices at Satyam; to restore investor confidence, Satyam

---

[8]Satyam Annual Report, 2008.

[9]Ibid.

[10]Ravi Kant, "Satyam-Maytas deal: A mockery of corporate governance," Merinews, December 18, 2008, www.merinews.com/article/satyam-maytas-deal-a-mockery-of-corporate-governance/153334.shtml, accessed on March 13, 2009.

scheduled a board meeting to consider a share buyback on December 29, 2008. On December 23, the World Bank suspended Satyam for eight years from doing any business with itself, on the grounds that Satyam was offering bribes to World Bank staff for obtaining lucrative contracts. While Satyam vehemently denied the allegations, its share prices continued to fall. On December 26, Mangalam Srinivasan—who had been an independent director since 1991—resigned, taking the moral responsibility for not opposing the acquisition decision in writing. On December 28, Satyam postponed the board meeting scheduled for December 29; on the same day, Infrastructure Leasing and Financial Services (IL&FS) Trust sold 4.41 million Satyam shares at INR139.83 in the open market. Raju and his family had pledged these shares in lieu of the loans obtained from IL&FS Trust; as a result, Raju and his family's stake in Satyam diluted to 5.13 per cent by late December, from a high of 8.65 per cent in September 2008.[11] Satyam's market capitalization eroded by 40 per cent in just two weeks in the latter half of December 2008.[12]

In the midst of this disaster, someone claiming to be a former senior executive in Satyam wrote an anonymous email to one of the board members: the email had details about financial irregularities and fraud at Satyam. The letter also mentioned that Satyam did not have enough liquid assets that could be confirmed with its bankers. The email was forwarded to all the board members along with the chief executive officer (CEO), B. Ramalinga Raju. Some people speculated that this letter ultimately became the basis of the uncovering of the financial fraud. Facing heat from the market and criticism from the analysts, three more independent directors—Rammohan Rao, who headed the board meeting that approved the acquisition, Krishna Palepu and Vinod Dham—resigned from the board.

On January 7, 2009, B. Ramalinga Raju wrote a resignation letter to the Securities and Exchange Board of India (SEBI), which was the market regulator in India. In his resignation letter (see Exhibit 1), Raju admitted that he falsified the financial statements to the tune of INR71.36 billion: this falsified amount included INR50.46 billion in non-existing cash and bank balances. Raju confessed that he overstated the profits, as the profit margins were as low as three per cent; he also stated that the financial gap in actual and stated profits was known to senior officials including the chief operating officer and the CFO. Raju stated that he was forced to overstate the profits to maintain the share price level, which was important to make sure that Satyam was not

---

[11]Ibid.

[12]"Satyam promoters may have lost stakes," Livemint, Reuters, December 29, 2008, accessed on March 12, 2009.

subjected to a hostile takeover. Raju further stated that he never profited from the high market prices of Satyam shares because he never sold any of his shares, but only pledged them with family and others to raise loans to bridge the gap between fake and real assets. Raju described the situation in his letter: "It was like riding a tiger, not knowing how to get off without being eaten."

To meet Satyam's cash commitments, Raju had to take loans from his friends, family and others by pledging his shares: his ownership stake declined from 20.74 per cent in 2003 to 8.74 per cent in 2008. Justifying his actions, Raju stated in the letter that in his last attempt to save Satyam from a hostile takeover and to bridge the gap between actual and stated cash, he tried the Maytas deal that failed; consequently, he chose to resign.

This scandal had many consequences: Raju was arrested and imprisoned; shares of Satyam fell to INR39.95 on the Bombay Stock Exchange from a 52-week high of INR544; DSP Merrill Lynch terminated its engagement with the company; Raju's brother Rama was also arrested; a special team of auditors from SEBI began investigations into the fraud; several law suits were filed in different courts including in the United States; and the government of India disbanded the Satyam board and appointed new directors and an interim CEO.

Investigations

The Central Bureau of Investigation (CBI) was asked to initiate an inquiry into the financial fraud at Satyam. According to the CBI, the amount of manipulated profits was more than INR96 billion.[13] Other findings were also different from what Raju stated in his letter. The biggest puzzle for the shareholders, investigators and the general public was how Raju could have hidden the evidence of fake assets from various regulators such as the income tax authorities, SEBI and the Reserve Bank of India for seven years. Further, what was the role played by governance mechanisms such as the board and internal/external auditors, whose main job was to make sure that firms did not indulge in such irregularities? Raju's claim that Satyam was earning only three per cent net profits was hard to believe given that other competitors made 20–25 per cent net profits during the same years. Such a massive case of fraud without intention to make private gains was difficult to believe.[14]

According to a CBI charge sheet dated April 7, 2009, Raju and his family had a total of 327 companies registered

---

[13] "Satyam fraud could amount to Rs10,000 cr:CBI," Livemint, Press Trust of India, March 22, 2009.

[14] K. Venkatasubramanian, "Satyam Computer—Open Offer: Reject," Hindubusinessline, June 21, 2009.

in their names, with family members often being directors in these companies.[15] Since these firms were not registered in the stock markets, they were not required to follow standard governance practices or to publicize the details of their business dealings. It was surprising how these and other facts could be hidden from the multiple layers of audit that a firm goes through.

There were typically three levels of auditing that occurred in any company. Firstly, an internal audit by the team headed by the CFO. This was followed by an external audit, which was performed by PricewaterhouseCoopers (PwC) in Satyam's case. Finally, the board had the audit committee, headed by an independent board member. In Satyam's case, there was a failure at all the three levels.

Satyam contracted PwC as its statutory auditor since 2000. During the five-year period from 2003–2008, PwC's audit fee tripled to INR430 million. The audit fee that Satyam paid was about twice as much as what its peers in the IT industry paid to their auditors; for example, three other leading IT companies in India—Wipro, Infosys and Tata Consultancy Services—paid INR280 million, INR153 million and INR277 million, respectively.[16] All

these companies were listed in domestic and foreign stock exchanges and had to comply with international accounting regulations similar to Satyam. The auditors from PwC issued a brief statement:

> The audits were conducted by Price Waterhouse in accordance with applicable auditing standards and were supported by appropriate audit evidence. Given our obligations for client confidentiality, it is not possible for us to comment upon the alleged irregularities. Price Waterhouse will fully meet its obligations to cooperate with the regulators and others.[17]

Given the relatively higher fees that Satyam paid to PwC, it was suspected that the external auditors allowed various accounting irregularities such as improper verification of cash and bank balances.[18] Cash audit is one of the easiest forms of audit, as auditors only need to have a written confirmation from the bank that so much money exists. If the bank does not verify the cash, then an auditor cannot give an opinion of true and fair view. Initially, Satyam's bankers declined to comment on the company's accounts, citing client confidentiality. Later, however, the bankers were also pulled into the investigation to verify the huge amount of money shown as bank balance in the financial statements.

---

[15]CBI charge sheet, April 7, 2009, p. 41, signed by Chief Investigating Officer A.V. V. Krishna.

[16]Prowess Database, Centre for Monitoring of Indian Economy.

[17]www.indianexpress.com/news/satyam-auditing-based-on-evidence-says-pric/408575/, accessed on June 22, 2009.

[18]CBI charge sheet, April 7, 2009, p. 50.

Raju admitted that Satyam's fixed deposits, which supposedly grew from INR33.2 millions in 1998/99 to a massive INR33.20 billion in 2007/08, were all fake. The auditors were supposed to have an independent bank confirmation of such things in the form of a bank statement. Under Indian law, banks had to deduct tax at source for any interest income that exceeded US$200 per year: this money had to be paid directly to the government. Such a large amount of money could only be hidden by creating fake documents, which should have been checked by relevant authorities at different levels.[19]

There were other indications of potential financial irregularities at Satyam that were ignored by the internal and external auditors; for example, Satyam closed the 2007/08 financial year with a debt of INR2.36 billion, even after having an enormous INR44.62 billion lying unused in its accounts.[20] This amount was neither distributed among shareholders in the form of dividends, nor was it used to earn valuable interest, as is usually done; as such, the auditors could avoid responsibility only if he or she could demonstrate that there was no gross negligence in conducting the audit. Following the unearthing of the scandal, PwC's audit head in India resigned, and the two partners who signed on Satyam's balance sheet—S. Gopalakrishnan and Srinivas Talluri—were suspended and imprisoned.

The Aftermath of the Crisis

The fraud resulted in a decline of more than 78 per cent in Satyam's market capitalization. The immediate challenge for the government-appointed board was to protect the interests of shareholders and employees by making sure that the firm survived. In February 2008, the market regulator (SEBI) gave a green signal for sale of a 51 per cent stake of Satyam through a global bidding process. Investors with more than US$150 million in net assets were invited to bid. The bidding involved two steps: in the first step, the successful bidder had to acquire equity shares representing 31 per cent of Satyam's share capital; in the second phase, the bidding firm had to make a public offer to buy a minimum of 20 per cent more. In case the bidding firm failed to acquire 51 per cent even after the close of the open offer, it would be eligible to subscribe to additional equity shares. Tech Mahindra, a Mahindra and Mahindra group company, won the bid for Satyam at INR58 per share. It paid INR17.57 billion for a 31 per cent stake in Satyam. Tech Mahindra planned to run Satyam as an independent company with separate liabilities.[21]

---

[19]CBI charge sheet, April 7, 2009, p. 26.

[20]Satyam Annual Report, 2008.

[21]"Tech Mahindra completes 31 pc acquisition in Satyam," IBN Live, May 6, 2009, http://ibnlive.in.com/news/tech-mahindra-completes-31-pc-acquisition-in-satyam/91897-7.html, accessed on May 31, 2009.

Exhibit 1   Letter by Satyam CEO

January 7, 2009

To
The Board of Directors
Satyam Computers Services Ltd.
From B. Ramalinga Raju
Chairman, Satyam Computer Services Ltd.

Dear Board Members,
It is with deep regret and tremendous burden that I am carrying on my conscience, that I would like to bring the following facts to your notice:

1) The balance sheet carries as of September 30, 2008
   a. Inflated (non-existent) cash and bank balances of Rs.[22] 5,040 crore[23] (as against Rs. 5,361 crore reflected in the books).
   b. An accrued interest of Rs. 376 crore, which is non-existent.
   c. An understated liability of Rs. 1,230 crore on account of funds arranged by me.
   d. An overstated debtors position of Rs. 490 crore (as against Rs. 2,651 reflected in the books).

2) For the September quarter (Q2) we reported a revenue of Rs. 2,700 crore and an operating margin of Rs. 649 crore (24% of revenues) as against the actual revenues of Rs. 2,112 crore and an actual operating margin of Rs. 61 crore (3% of revenues). This has resulted in artificial cash and bank balances going up by Rs. 588 crores in Q2.

The gap in the balance sheet has arisen purely on account of inflated profits over a period of last several years (limited only to Satyam standalone, books of subsidiaries reflecting true performance). What started as a marginal gap between actual operating profit and the one reflected in the books of accounts continued to grow over the years. It has attained unmanageable proportions as the size of company operations grew significantly (annualized revenue run rate of Rs. 11,276 crore in the September quarter, 2008 and official reserves of Rs. 8,392 crore). The differential in the real profits and the one reflected in the books was further accentuated by the fact that the company had to carry additional resources and assets and justify higher level of operations—thereby significantly increasing the costs.

Every attempt made to eliminate the gap failed. As the promoters held a small percentage of equity, the concern was that poor performance would result in take-over thereby exposing the gap. It was like riding a tiger, not knowing how to get off without being eaten.

The aborted Maytas acquisition deal was the last attempt to fill the fictitious assets with real ones. Maytas' investors were convinced that this is a good divestment opportunity and a strategic fit. Once Satyam's problem was solved, it was hoped that Maytas' payments can be delayed. But that was not to be. What followed in the last several days is common knowledge.

---

[22]Rs. is an abbreviated form of the Indian rupee (INR).

[23]One crore equals 100 million.

I would like the Board to know:

1) That neither myself, nor the Managing Director (including our spouses) sold any shares in the last eight years - excepting for a small proportion declared and sold for philanthropic purposes.

2) That in the last two years a net amount of Rs. 1,230 crore was arranged to Satyam (not reflected in the books of Satyam) to keep the operations going by resorting to pledging all the promoter shares and raising funds from known sources by giving all kinds of assurances (Statement enclosed, only to the members of the Board). Significant dividend payments, acquisitions, capital expenditure to provide for growth did not help these matters. Every attempt was made to keep the wheel moving and to ensure prompt payment of salaries to the associates. The last straw was the selling of most of the pledged share by the lenders on account of margin triggers.

3) That neither me, nor the Managing Director took even one rupee/dollar from the company and have not benefited in financial terms on account of the inflated results.

4) None of the Board members, past or present, had any knowledge of the situation in which the company is placed. Even business leaders and senior executives in the company, such as, Ram Mynampati, Subu D., T. R. Anand, Keshab Panda, Virender Agarwal, A. S., Murthy, Hari T., S. V. Krishnan, Vijay Prasad, Manish Mehta, Murali V., Sriram Papani, Kiran Kavale, Joe Lagioia, Ravindra Penumetsa, Jayaraman and Prabhakar Gupta were unaware of the real situation as against the books of accounts. None of my or Managing Director's immediate or extended family members had any idea about these issues.

Having put these facts before you, I leave it to the wisdom of the Board to take the matters forward. However, I am also taking the liberty to recommend the following steps:

1) A task force has been formed in the last few days to address the situation arising out of the failed Maytas acquisition attempt. This consists of some of the most accomplished leaders of Satyam: Subu D., T. R. Anand, Keshab Panda, and A. S. Murthy, Hari T. and Murali V. representing support functions. I suggest that Ram Mynampati be made the Chairman of this task force to immediately address some of the operational matters on hand. Ram can also act as an interim CEO reporting to the board.

2) Merrill Lynch can be entrusted with the task of quickly exploring some merger opportunities.

3) You may have a "restatement of accounts" prepared by the auditors in light of the facts that I have placed before you.

I have promoted and have been associated with Satyam for well over twenty years now. I have seen it growing from few people to 53,000 people with 185 Fortune 500 companies as customers and operations in 66 countries. Satyam has established an excellent leadership and competency base at all levels. I sincerely apologize to all Satyamites and stakeholders who have made Satyam a special organization, for the current situation. I am confident they will stand by the company in this hour of crisis. In light of the above, I fervently appeal to the Board to hold together to take some important steps. Mr. T. R. Prasad is well placed to mobilize support from the government at this crucial time. With the hope that members of the Task Force and the

(Continued)

Exhibit 1 (Continued)

financial advisor, Merrill Lynch (now Bank of America) will stand by the company at this crucial hour, I am marking copies of this statement to them as well.

Under the circumstances, I am tendering my resignation as the Chairman of Satyam and shall continue in the position only till such time the current board is expanded. My continuance is just to ensure enhancement of the board over the next several days or as early as possible.

I am now prepared to subject myself to the laws of the land and face consequence thereof.

(B. Ramalinga Raju)

Copies marked to:

1) Chairman SEBI
2) Stock Exchanges

Source: www.hindu.com/nic/satyam-chairman-statement.pdf, accessed on January 15, 2009.

Exhibit 2   Ownership Details (Percent of Shareholding)

Category	2003	2004	2005	2006	2007	2008
Promoter's holding						
Indian promoters	20.74	17.35	15.67	14.02	8.79	8.74
Foreign promoters	0	0	0	0	0	0
Persons acting in concert	0	0	0	0	0	0
Subtotal	**20.74**	**17.35**	**15.67**	**14.02**	**8.79**	**8.74**
Non-promoters						
Institutional investors						
Mutual funds and UTI	8.88	7.39	7.58	5.70	6.00	4.88
Banks, financial inst., insurance company (central/ state govt. inst./non-govt. inst.)	4.37	4.33	3.32	1.74	5.63	8.13
Foreign inst. investors	43.02	51.27	56.06	52.48	47.22	48.09
Subtotal	**56.27**	**62.99**	**66.96**	**59.92**	**58.84**	**61.1**

Category	2003	2004	2005	2006	2007	2008
Others						
Private corporate bodies	2.34	1.58	1.00	0.95	0.94	0.33
Indian public	8.47	6.06	4.47	4.06	10.64	10.25
NRIs/OCBs	1.56	1.37	1.24	1.11	1.27	0.00
Any other	10.61	10.65	10.66	19.94	19.52	19.58
Subtotal	**22.99**	**19.66**	**17.37**	**26.06**	**32.37**	**30.16**
Grand Total	**100**	**100**	**100**	**100**	**100**	**100**

Source: Prowess Database, *Centre for Monitoring of Indian Economy.*

Exhibit 3   Board Composition

Pre-crisis Board Directors			
Name	**Affiliation**	**Qualification**	**Occupation**
Ramalinga Raju	Executive chairman, promoter-director	MBA	Promoter of Satyam Computers
Rama Raju	Managing director, promoter-director	MBA	Promoter of Satyam Computers
Ram Mynampati	Executive director, declared interim CEO	MCA	Employee and executive director on board of Satyam
Prof. Krishna G. Palepu	Non-executive director, consultant	Ph. D.	Professor at Harvard Business School
Dr. (Mrs.) Mangalam Srinivasan	Non-executive director, independent	Ph. D.	Management consultant and advisor to Kennedy School of Management
Mr. Vinod K. Dham	Non-executive director, independent	B.E./M.E. (Electrical)	Director of New Path Ventures LLC, NEA—Indo U.S. Ventures LLC
Prof. M. Rammohan Rao	Non-executive director, independent	Ph. D.	Former dean, Indian School of Business
Mr. T.R. Prasad	Non-executive director, independent	M.Sc.Physics/F.I.E. (Fellow Institution of Engineers - India)	Retired bureaucrat (cabinet secretary, Government of India)

(Continued)

Exhibit 3 (Continued)

Pre-crisis Board Directors			
Name	**Affiliation**	**Qualification**	**Occupation**
Prof. V. S. Raju	Non-executive director, independent	Ph. D.	Chairman of the Naval Research Board, Defense Research and Development Organization, Government of India
Post-crisis Board Directors			
Mr. Kiran Karnik (Chairman)	Non-executive chairman, independent	B.Sc., P.G.D.B.A, IIM	Member, Scientific Advisory Council to Prime Minister
Mr. Deepak Parekh	Non-executive director, independent	B.COM./Fellow Chartered Accountant (India, England and Wales)	Chairman of HDFC Bank
Dr. Tarun Das	Non-executive director	Ph. D.	Chief mentor, Confederation of Indian Industry
Mr. S. B. Mainak	Nominee director, independent	B. Com., Chartered Accountant	Head of treasury operations, Life Insurance Corporation India.
Mr. T. N. Manoharan	Non-executive director, independent	B. Com., Fellow Chartered Accountant (India)	Past president of ICAI and visiting professor, RBI
Mr. C. Achuthan	Non-executive director, independent	L.L.B./M.A., Economics	Former presiding officer, Securities Appellate Tribunal

Source: Prowess Database, *Centre for Monitoring Indian Economy.*

Exhibit 4 Financial Performance*

Year	2008	2007	2006	2005	2004	2003	2002	2001	2000
Equity paid-up	134.10	133.44	64.89	63.85	63.25	62.91	62.91	56.24	56.24
Net worth	7,357.60	5,789.36	4,333.64	3,217.02	2,580.80	2,134.88	1,930.40	812.91	350.06
Capital employed	7,381.30	5,803.15	4,346.21	3,226.89	2,588.10	2,153.24	1,936.20	984.89	641.39
Gross block	1,486.50	1,280.40	1,153.16	937.70	838.80	775.89	739.24	545.85	418.55
Sales	8,137.30	6,228.47	4,634.31	3,464.22	2,541.50	2,023.65	1,731.90	1,220.00	672.81
PBIT	1,947.80	1,580.84	1,448.61	867.76	662.69	369.75	494.11	540.37	176.65
PAT	1,715.70	1,423.23	1,239.75	750.26	555.79	307.42	449.38	486.29	129.98
Market capitalization	26,453.00	31,259.30	27,552.30	13,041.40	9,281.90	5,565.96	8,418.90	6,577.30	24,907.00
EPS (annualized) (unit curr.)	24.99	20.77	37.22	22.85	17.06	9.49	14.24	17.17	22.86
Payout (%)	13.99	16.77	18.91	21.89	23.49	31.61	8.32	4.66	9.93
Cash flow from operating activities	1,370.90	1,039.06	786.81	638.66	416.55	501.14	594.38	222.86	161.81
Cash flow from investing activities	−641.22	−1,678.60	−53.85	−341.17	−240.28	−1,256.90	−147.98	−2.71	−147.19
Cash flow from financing activities	−227.79	34.10	−43.94	−103.58	−94.18	−50.79	500.20	−174.84	52.79

(Continued)

Exhibit 4 (Continued)

Year	2008	2007	2006	2005	2004	2003	2002	2001	2000
Key ratios									
ROG-sales (%)	30.65	34.40	33.78	36.30	25.59	16.84	41.96	81.33	77.93
Debt-equity ratio	0.00	0.00	0.00	0.00	0.01	0.01	0.06	0.40	1.04
Long-term debt-equity ratio	0.00	0.00	0.00	0.00	0.00	0.00	0.05	0.28	0.72
Current ratio	5.41	5.91	6.50	7.12	6.42	6.15	5.30	2.81	2.02
Fixed assets ratio	5.88	5.12	4.43	3.90	3.15	2.67	2.70	2.53	1.89
Inventory ratio	0.00	0.00	0.00	0.00	0.00	0.00	0.00	0.00	0.00
Debtors ratio	4.20	4.49	4.91	5.10	4.74	4.62	4.49	4.13	4.20
Interest cover ratio	327.91	207.73	436.25	1,141.79	883.59	699.88	51.47	10.73	4.34
Return on capital employed (%)	29.55	31.15	31.34	29.85	27.95	24.64	33.83	45.55	33.44
Return on net worth (%)	26.10	28.12	26.85	25.88	23.57	20.55	32.76	55.46	50.28

Source: Prowess Database, *Centre for Monitoring Indian Economy.*

*Absolute values in INR100 million.

Note: PBIT = profit before interest and tax. PAT = profit after tax. EPS = earnings per share. ROG = rate of growth.

Exhibit 5 Financial Data for Major Competitors*

Year	Infosys Tech Ltd.			Wipro Ltd.			Tech Mahindra Ltd.		
	2008	2007	2006	2008	2007	2006	2008	2007	2006
Equity paid-up	286.00	286.00	138.00	292.30	291.80	285.15	121.40	121.20	20.80
Net worth	13,490.00	11,162.00	6,897.00	11,556.70	9,320.40	6,420.45	1,228.40	878.00	597.86
Capital employed	13,490.00	11,162.00	6,897.00	15,433.10	9,558.40	6,470.61	1,323.40	927.00	597.86
Gross block	4,508.00	3,889.00	2,837.00	2,282.20	1,645.90	2,364.52	550.50	442.80	306.96
Sales	15,648.00	13,149.00	9,028.00	17,658.10	13,758.50	10,264.09	3,604.70	2,757.70	1,197.14
PBIT	5,118.00	4,153.00	2,737.00	3,586.50	3,183.40	2,342.81	404.60	133.60	240.64
PAT	4,470.00	3,783.00	2,421.00	3,063.30	2,842.10	2,020.48	325.70	65.20	220.12
Market capitalization	81,804.60	112,641.00	81,830.30	62,155.40	80,740.20	79,649.20	8,578.33	17,289.00	0.00
EPS (annualized) (unit curr.)	72.50	64.35	81.41	19.94	18.61	13.47	25.90	5.07	19.76
Payout (%)	45.86	17.74	55.10	30.07	32.18	37.12	21.25	43.25	50.56
Cash flow from operating activities	3,834.00	3,263.00	2,316.00	715.90	2,669.60	1,911.08	209.70	3.20	133.47
Cash flow from investing activities	−978.00	−1,091.00	−392.00	−1,123.90	−1,881.90	−1,685.50	−198.30	−142.40	−205.45
Cash flow from financing activities	−777.00	−316.00	172.00	2,290.90	238.50	59.80	35.60	119.10	−0.72

(Continued)

Exhibit 5 (Continued)

Year	Infosys Tech Ltd.			Wipro Ltd.			Tech Mahindra Ltd.		
	2008	2007	2006	2008	2007	2006	2008	2007	2006
Key Ratios									
ROG-sales (%)	19.01	45.65	31.60	28.34	34.05	41.06	28.34	130.36	29.79
Debt-equity ratio	0.00	0.00	0.00	0.19	0.02	0.01	0.19	0.03	0.00
Long-term debt-equity ratio	0.00	0.00	0.00	0.19	0.02	0.00	0.19	0.00	0.00
Current ratio	3.85	3.75	2.77	2.15	1.57	1.46	2.15	1.38	1.55
Fixed assets ratio	3.73	3.91	3.60	8.99	6.86	4.97	8.99	7.36	4.05
Inventory ratio	0.00	0.00	0.00	51.29	70.73	74.37	51.29	0.00	0.00
Debtors ratio	5.81	6.90	6.52	5.70	6.10	6.12	5.70	4.58	3.80
Interest cover ratio	5,118.00	4,153.00	2,737.00	30.71	442.14	748.50	30.71	95.28	0.00
Return on capital employed (%)	41.52	45.99	45.09	28.70	39.72	41.01	28.70	86.22	44.53
Return on net worth (%)	36.26	41.90	39.89	29.35	36.11	35.72	29.35	72.05	40.74

Source: Prowess Database, *Centre for Monitoring Indian Economy.*

*Absolute values in INR100 million.

Exhibit 6 Share Market Data of Satyam From December 2008–February 2009*

Date	Opening Price	High Price	Low Price	Closing Price	Average Price	No. of Trades	Market Capitalization
Feb. 27, 2009	46.45	46.45	39.30	41.50	43.86	128,519	27.96
Feb. 20, 2009	48.00	50.90	44.50	45.45	47.90	266,951	30.62
Feb. 13, 2009	48.50	49.00	41.15	46.30	45.97	272,405	31.20
Feb. 6, 2009	53.10	61.00	45.35	47.40	51.02	520,114	31.94
Jan. 30, 2009	39.70	60.00	39.70	54.05	51.63	916,756	36.42
Jan. 23, 2009	24.90	39.30	23.05	38.85	29.70	632,440	26.17
Jan. 16, 2009	28.60	40.00	20.00	24.45	28.07	691,184	16.47
Jan. 9, 2009	180.00	188.70	11.50	23.85	102.45	1,114,151	16.07
Jan. 2, 2009	175.30	186.00	173.40	177.60	179.95	198,450	119.64
Dec. 31, 2008	133.00	176.40	129.60	170.20	159.67	546,502	114.65
Dec. 26, 2008	163.00	168.60	114.70	135.50	143.31	531,998	91.30
Dec. 19, 2008	225.00	231.90	153.80	162.80	188.42	461,004	109.70
Dec. 12, 2008	230.00	238.70	212.60	220.80	226.34	45,968	148.75
Dec. 5, 2008	246.00	251.00	222.00	224.40	231.19	41,595	151.21

Source: Prowess Database, *Centre for Monitoring Indian Economy.*

*Price values are in INR, market capitalization is in billions of INR.

Part IV

Appendixes

Excerpts from the UN Global Compact Website

Appendix A

The Corporate Commitment[1]

T he Global Compact is a leadership initiative, involving a commitment by a company's Chief Executive Officer (or equivalent), and supported by the highest-level Governance body of the organization (e.g., the Board).

Participation in the Global Compact is a widely visible commitment to the implementation, disclosure, and promotion of its ten universal principles. A company joining the initiative is expected to:

1. Make the Global Compact and its principles an integral part of business strategy, day-to-day operations and organizational culture;

2. Incorporate the Global Compact and its principles in the decision-making processes of the highest-level governance body (i.e. Board);

3. Contribute to broad development objectives (including the Millennium Development Goals) through partnerships;

4. Integrate in its annual report (or in a similar public document, such as a sustainability report) a description of the ways in which it implements the principles and supports broader development objectives (also known as the Communication on Progress); and

---

[1]In order to participate in the UN Global Compact, a Letter of Commitment must be submitted to the secretary-general of the United Nations and signed by the chief executive expressing commitment to (1) the UN Global Compact and its ten principles; (2) engagement in partnerships to advance broad UN goals; and (3) the annual submission of a Communication on Progress (COP). See http://www .unglobalcompact.org/docs/how_to_participate_doc/Online_Application_Guideline_Business.pdf.

5. Advance the Global Compact and the case for responsible business practices through advocacy and active outreach to peers, partners, clients, consumers and the public at large.

Source: http://www.unglobalcompact.org/HowToParticipate/Business_Participation/index.html.

Appendix B

The Communication on Progress

One of the explicit commitments that a company makes when it participates in the Global Compact is to produce an annual Communication on Progress (COP). A COP is a disclosure to stakeholders (e.g., consumers, employees, organized labour, shareholders, media, government) on the progress the company has made in implementing the ten principles in their business activities and, where appropriate, supporting UN goals through partnerships.

The purpose of the COP requirement is to ensure and deepen the commitment of Global Compact participants, safeguard the integrity of the initiative and to create a rich repository of corporate practices that serves as a basis for continual performance improvement. For companies, the COP is a tool to exercise leadership, facilitate learning, stimulate dialogue, and promote action.

Step One: Creating a COP

While there is no single structure for the creation of a COP, a COP must include:

- A statement of continued support for the Global Compact in the opening letter, statement or message from the Chief Executive Officer, Chairman or other senior executive.
- A description of practical actions that participants have taken to implement the Global Compact principles during the previous year.
- A measurement of outcomes or expected outcomes using, as much as possible, indicators or metrics such as those developed by the Global Reporting Initiative.

The first element underlines the importance of top management engagement for the successful implementation of corporate citizenship issues on a long-term basis. "If top management does not campaign relentlessly for the vision, set clear signals and priorities and behave as a role model, change will slow down and the organization will return to business as usual."[1]

The second element provides a description of practical actions taken, including the process of implementation used to integrate the Global Compact principles into companies' operations. As the Global Compact is a voluntary initiative based on multi-stakeholder dialogue, this component is essential in helping to build a repository of best practices.

The third element—measurement of outcomes and expected outcomes—refers to one of the core strengths of the Global Compact: its recognition of continuous incremental improvement. A crucial component of improvement is therefore the measurement of outcomes via indicators. The most well developed set of globally applicable indicators is the GRI G3 guidelines. While the GRI G3 Guidelines do not represent the only way of preparing a COP, they do offer globally-recognized reporting guidance that can help produce strong COPs and are recommended by the Global Compact. If the information provided in the Communication on Progress has been assured, it is suggested that the company also provides details on how this was accomplished.

Step Two: Sharing the COP With the Company's Stakeholders

It is important to note that the COP is not a communication with the United Nations Global Compact Office. Rather it is intended to provide a means for participants to communicate their progress on implementing the ten Global Compact principles directly with their stakeholders. Therefore, ideally, COPs should be integrated into a company's existing communication with stakeholders, such as an annual financial or sustainability report. A stand-alone COP should *not* be created, unless the company has no other vehicle to report on corporate citizenship issues.

Just as important as the medium chosen for conveying the COP is the method of distributing it to stakeholders. Submission to the Global Compact website is not sufficient and companies should use the established methods where stakeholders would expect to find sustainability information (e.g. websites, direct mailings, employee alerts, open houses) to share their COP.

Step Three: Submitting the COP to the Global Compact Website

In addition to sharing the COP with stakeholders, companies are expected to post an electronic version (and web link if available) of their COP on the Global Compact website. Participants are also expected to briefly describe how COPs are made available to stakeholders.

Note: For more information about this important document, see http://www.unglobalcompact.org/COP/COP_Guidance.html.

---

[1]Raising the Bar, Creating Value with the United Nations Global Compact, Fussler/Cramer/van der Vegt, 2004, p. 201.

Appendix C

Leadership Blueprint

*Blueprint for Corporate Sustainability
Leadership Within the Global Compact*

The Blueprint is a new model of leadership within the Global Compact which has been designed to inspire advanced performers to reach the next level of sustainability performance. It identifies criteria for leadership practice in three distinct but overlapping dimensions: (i) integrating the ten principles into strategies and operations; (ii) taking action in support of broader UN goals and issues; and (iii) engaging with the UN Global Compact as well as cross-cutting components.

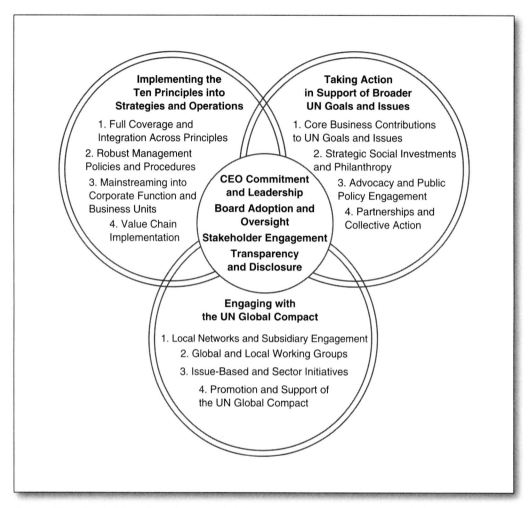

Appendix D

UN Global Compact Communication on Progress and the Global Reporting Initiative (GRI)

The GRI Reporting Framework in Brief[1]

The GRI Reporting Framework provides guidance on how organizations can disclose their sustainability performance.

The Framework is applicable to organizations of any size, type or location, and already has been used worldwide by more than a thousand companies, associations and organizations in all sectors as the basis for sustainability reporting. It is continuously improved and expanded as experience with sustainability reporting evolves, and the needs of report-makers and report-users change.

GRI uses an open process to develop new Framework components or update existing material through collaboration among businesses, civil society, labour and other professional institutions worldwide in a consensus-seeking approach. The core Sustainability Reporting Guidelines are in their third generation (G3) and were released in October 2006 following a three-year, innovative development period that engaged more than 3,000 individuals from diverse sectors worldwide.

The G3 Guidelines document is the foundation upon which all other GRI reporting components are based, and outlines core content for reporting that is broadly relevant to all organizations regardless of size, sector or location. The G3 Guidelines contain Reporting Principles for defining report content and ensuring the quality of reported information, as well as Reporting Guidance on how to set the report boundary. It also

---

[1]This appendix is drawn from "Making the Connection," a joint publication of the UN Global Compact and the Global Reporting Initiative. For the complete publication, visit http://www.unglobalcompact.org/docs/news_events/8.1/Making_the_Connection.pdf.

includes Standard Disclosures made up of Profile Disclosures, Disclosures on Management Approach, and Performance Indicators. Indicator Protocols provide detailed guidance on how to respond to indicators, and include definitions of key terms, compilation methodologies, and other technical references.[2]

Sector Supplements complement (not replace) use of the G3 Guidelines by capturing the unique set of sustainability issues faced by different sectors such as mining, automotive, financial, public agencies and others. National Annexes will soon be developed for use in conjunction with the G3 Guidelines, and will address country or regional sustainability issues.

The G3 Guidelines also include an Application Levels system which is intended to demonstrate a pathway for incrementally developing, expanding and deepening reporting over successive reporting cycles. The Levels provide a system for an organization to inform readers about which elements of the GRI Reporting Framework were applied in preparation of their report. For a description of the requirements for each level, please refer to the GRI website (http://www.globalreporting.org/Services/ReportServices/ApplicationLevelsCheck/ApplicationLevelsCriterion/).

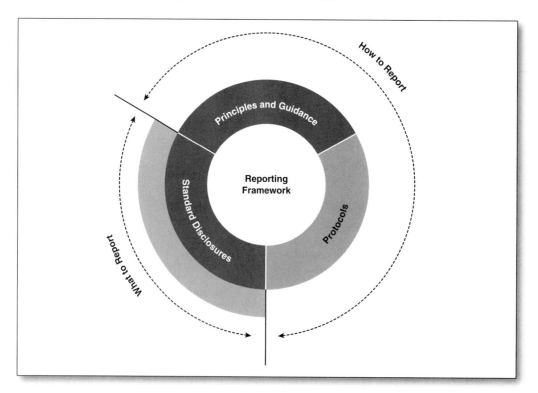

---

[2]Please visit the GRI website and refer to the G3 Sustainability Reporting Guidelines for further guidance on what to include in Profile Disclosures and Disclosures on Management Approach. Refer to the Indicator Protocols for definitions and compilation methods for each performance indicator.

Making the Global Compact–GRI Connection

Use of the GRI G3 Guidelines can enhance Global Compact participants' communication with their stakeholders in a number of key ways:

- The GRI G3 Guidelines address the status of implementation and performance for each Global Compact principle.
- GRI's indicators and disclosures ensure presentation of a company's performance and achievements in an appropriate and relevant context (strategy and vision, management systems and other context-setting information).
- Aside from content coverage, the GRI G3 Guidelines provide guidance on many relevant decisions related to reporting that enhance the quality of the COP.
- The GRI G3 Guidelines offer an incremental approach that allows companies to increase reporting at their own pace. This is consistent with the concept of continuous improvement on which the COP is based.
- Knowledge accumulated in the GRI Guidelines over the last ten years provides a global, multi-stakeholder view on how to assess performance around many of the same issues covered by the GC principles.

As both the Global Compact and the GRI are based on the concept of encouraging continuous improvement, there is significant alignment in approaches to quality and scope of reporting. Neither organization is in a position to judge the veracity of the reported information submitted under their respective frameworks. Therefore both organizations have developed systems—the GRI Application Levels and the Global Compact "Notable COP" program—that assess the degree to which the reporting frameworks have been applied. A list of Notable COPs can be found on the Global Compact website (http://www.unglobalcompact.org/COP/notables.html).

"Companies participating in both initiatives have long stressed the understanding that the GRI is a practical expression of the Global Compact."

Georg Kell,
Executive Director
United Nations
Global Compact Office

The table below summarizes how the G3 Guidelines cover the key COP elements. A more elaborate table that outlines how the ten principles can be directly addressed and woven throughout a GRI sustainability report is located on pages 7–14 of "Making the Connection." A table that summarizes the links between the GRI indicators and Global Compact principles can be found in Annex A. Additional resources for further understanding both initiatives can be found in Annex B.

Summary of Alignment Between COP Elements and G3 Guidelines	
UNGC COP Element	**G3 Guidelines Disclosures**
A statement of continued support for the Global Compact in a message from the Chief Executive Officer or other senior executive.	**Strategy and Analysis:** Support for the Global Compact and how the ten principles influence the company's strategy can be presented in a CEO letter.
A description of practical actions (commitments, policies, systems, and activities), including, if appropriate, partnerships created, that participants have taken to implement the Global Compact principles during the previous year	**Governance, Commitments, Engagement:** Descriptions of statements of mission or values, codes of conduct, principles, charters, or other initiatives the company endorses that assist the company in addressing sustainability issues, along with high level processes for setting strategies, defining risk and opportunities, can be used to demonstrate commitment to implementation of GC principles.
	Disclosure on Management Approach (DMA): Overview of the company's management approach in each category (e.g., human rights) can be used to describe how the GC principles are put into practice.
	Select Performance Indicators: Select performance indicators ask for descriptions of actions in addition to quantitative data.
Measurement of outcomes using, as much as possible, standard indicators or metrics.	**Performance Indicators:** Stating performance shows outcomes and results for economic, environmental and social categories. Performance on each of the GC principles is covered with one or more indicators.

Annex A: Global Compact Principles–GRI Indicators Cross Reference Table

The following table shows which GRI G3 performance indicators relate to each of the ten Global Compact principles. Including such a table in a COP, along with page numbers where the indicator/principle is covered, can prove useful to stakeholders seeking more information about how a company is implementing the Global Compact principles.

Issue Areas	GC Principles	Relevant GRI Indicators
Human Rights	Principle 1 – Businesses should support and respect the protection of internationally proclaimed human rights.	EC5, LA4, LA6 – 9; LA13 – 14, HR1 – 9, SO5, PR1 – 2, PR8
	Principle 2 – Businesses should make sure that they are not complicit in human rights abuses.	HR1 – 9, SO5
Labour	Principle 3 – Businesses should uphold the freedom of association and the effective recognition of the right to collective bargaining.	LA4 – 5, HR1 – 3, HR5, SO5
	Principle 4 – Businesses should uphold the elimination of all forms of forced and compulsory labour.	HR1 – 3, HR7, SO5
	Principle 5 – Businesses should uphold the effective abolition of child labour.	HR1 – 3, HR6, SO5
	Principle 6 – Businesses should uphold the elimination of discrimination in respect of employment and occupation.	EC7, LA2, LA13 – 14, HR1 – 4, SO5
Environment	Principle 7 – Businesses should support a precautionary approach to environmental challenges.	EC2, EN18, EN26, EN30, SO5
	Principle 8 – Businesses should undertake initiatives to promote greater environmental responsibility.	EN1 – 30, SO5, PR3 – 4
	Principle 9 – Businesses should encourage the development and diffusion of environmentally friendly technologies.	EN2, EN 5 – 7, EN 10, EN 18, EN 26 – 27, EN30, SO5
Anti-Corruption	Principle 10 – Businesses should work against corruption in all its forms, including extortion and bribery.	SO2 – 6

An online tool that cross-references the GRI G3 indicators to the Global Compact principles is available on the GRI website: http://www.globalreporting.org/griportal/GRI/G3Online/frmManagementNorms.aspx.

Annex B: Resources

Communicating Business Contributions to the Millennium Development Goals
http://www.globalreporting.org

Global Compact Communication on Progress Website
http://www.unglobalcompact.org/CommunicatingProgress/index.html

Global Compact Integrity Measures
http://www.unglobalcompact.org/AboutTheGC/integrity.html

GRI Sustainability Reporting Guidelines
http://www.globalreporting.org

The GRI Sustainability Reporting Cycle: A Handbook for Small and Not-So-Small Organizations
Global Reporting Initiative, 2007.
http://www.globalreporting.org/sme

Leading the Way on Communication on Progress
http://www.unglobalcompact.org/docs/communication_on_progress/4.3/leading_the_way.pdf

Making the Connection: The GRI Guidelines and the UNGC Communication of Progress
http://www.unglobalcompact.org/docs/news_events/8.1/Making_the_Connection.pdf

Practical Guide to Communication on Progress
http://www.unglobalcompact.org/docs/communication_on_progress/4.3/pock_guide.pdf

Raising the Bar—Creating Value With the United Nations Global Compact
Claude Fussler, Aron Cramer, and Sebastian van der Vegt, Greenleaf Publishing, 2004.
http://www.greenleaf-publishing.com/catalogue/rtbar.htm

Striking the Balance—Sustainable Development Reporting
Heemskerk, Pistorio, Scicluna, 2002.
Available at the World Business Council for Sustainable Development's sustainability reporting website (http://www.sdportal.org) at http://qpub.wbcsd.org/web/sdportal/publication/20030106_sdreport.pdf.

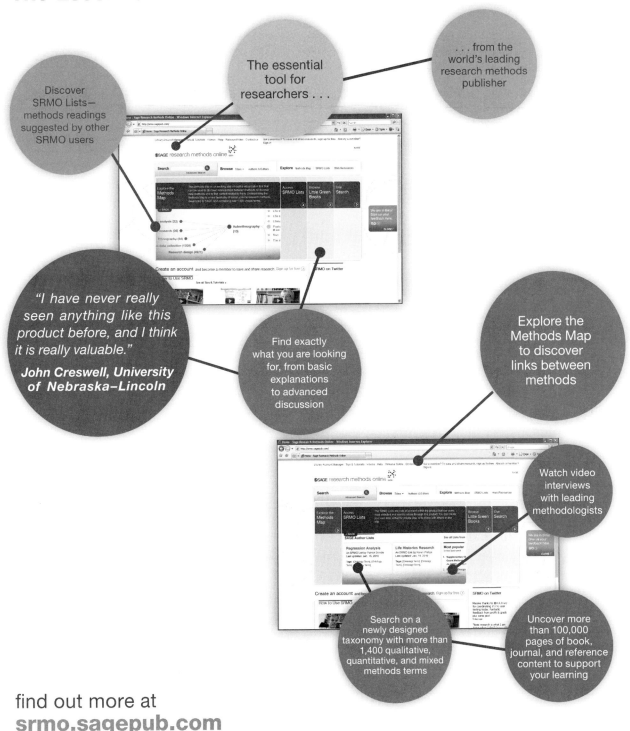